D1083291

DRINKING AND INTOXICATION

Distributed by
College and University Press
and
Publications Division, Rutgers Center of Alcohol Studies

DRINKING AND INTOXICATION

Selected Readings in
Social Attitudes and Controls

WITH SIXTEEN PLATES

19473

EDITED BY

RAYMOND G. McCARTHY

Professor of Education, Rutgers University

COLLEGE AND UNIVERSITY PRESS • New Haven, Conn.

IN ASSOCIATION WITH

RUTGERS CENTER OF ALCOHOL STUDIES
New Brunswick, N. J.

MANUFACTURED IN THE UNITED STATES OF AMERICA BY
UNITED PRINTING SERVICES, INC.
NEW HAVEN, CONN.

To
Dr. E. M. Jellinek

CONTENTS

List of Illustrations   xiii

Preface   xv

Contributors   xix

Introduction   1

PART I

Physiological and Psychological Effects of Alcohol

1. Physiological Effects   7
   Alcohol in the Body   7
       Leon A. Greenberg
   Other Effects of Alcohol   13
       Mark Keller

2. Psychological Effects   18
       Edith S. Lisansky

3. Alcohol Intoxication and Opiate Addiction   26
   Intoxication and Addiction   27
       Donald L. Gerard

Supplementary Readings   35

PART II

Drinking Practices, Ancient and Modern

Introduction   39

4. Our Drinking Heritage   42
       Andrew Poznanski

5. The Classical World   44
       Arthur P. McKinlay
   Attic Temperance   44
   Non-Attic Greek States   51
   Early Roman Sobriety   53
   Roman Sobriety in the Later Republic   54
   The Roman Attitude toward Women's Drinking   58

6. Non-Classical Peoples   62
   Arthur P. McKinlay

7. Central and South America   73
   Chichicastenango and Chamula   73
      Ruth Bunzel
   South American Indian Drinks   86
      John M. Cooper
   Andean Indians   91
      William Mangin
   The Working Class in Santiago de Chile   99
      Juan Marconi, Anibal Varela, Enrique Rosenblat,
      Guido Solari, Ines Marchesse, Rolando Alvarado
      and Walter Enriquez

8. The Far East   106
   India   106
      R. N. Chopra, G. S. Chopra and I. C. Chopra
   China   113
   Chinese Wine Drinking   114
      Merrill Moore
   Chinese Food and Drink   120
      Weston La Barre
   Drinking among New York City Cantonese   123
      Milton L. Barnett
   Japan   124
      Bufo Yamamuro

9. Russia   130
   Russia, Yesterday   130
      Vera Efron
   Russia, Today   141
      Mark G. Field

10. France   149
    Drinking and Its Control   149
       Gabriel Mouchot
    Public Opinion   158
       H. Bastide

11. England   160
       B. Seebohm Rowntree and G. R. Lavers

12. Canada   170
        Robert E. Popham

Supplementary Readings   175

PART III

Drinking Practices, U. S. A.

Introduction   179

13. Who, What, and How Often?   182
        John W. Riley, Jr. and Charles F. Marden

14. In One State   190
        Milton A. Maxwell

15. In High School   205
        High School Drinking Studies   205
            Raymond G. McCarthy
        The Kansas Study   210
        Summary of Essential Findings in the Kansas Study   211
            Marston M. McCluggage, E. Jackson Baur,
            Charles K. Warriner and Carroll D. Clark

16. In College   219
        To Drink or Not to Drink   220
            Robert Straus and Selden D. Bacon

17. The Motivational Pattern   231
        John W. Riley, Jr., Charles F. Marden
        and Marcia Lifshitz

18. Group Influences   239
        John L. Haer

Supplementary Readings   246

PART IV

Cultural, Religious, and Ethical Factors

Introduction   249

19. Primitive Societies   251
        Donald Horton

20. Cultural Differences in Rates of Alcoholism   263
        Robert F. Bales

21. Ethnography of Alcoholism 278
    Ruth Bunzel

22. A Psychocultural Analysis of the Alcoholic 287
    Harriet R. Mowrer

23. Personality and Social Factors in Intoxication and Addiction 298
    Donald L. Gerard

24. Alcoholism: The Role of Social Ambivalence 306
    Abraham Myerson

25. Skid Row 313
    The Skid Road Alcoholic 313
    Joan K. Jackson and Ralph Connor

26. Alcohol and Morality 324
    Attitudes of the Churches 325
    Olin T. Binkley
    The Ethics of Alcoholism 330
    Howard J. Clinebell, Jr.
    The Wets and Drys 338
    Howard W. Haggard

Supplementary Readings 342

PART V

Controls

Introduction 345

27. Sweden and Finland 347
    The Liquor Control System in Sweden 347
    M. Marcus
    Sweden: Sequel 355
    Arne Skutin
    Prohibition in Finland 356
    Sakari Sariola

28. The United States 368
    Prohibition and Repeal 369
    Raymond G. McCarthy and Edgar M. Douglass
    The Logic of Prohibition 383
    Byron C. Kirby
    Industrialists' Opinions on Prohibition 388
    Irving Fisher

29. The Woman's Christian Temperance Union   398
    Social Structure and Moral Reform: A Study of the WCTU   398
        Joseph R. Gusfield

30. The New Prohibition Drive   412
        Alfred McClung Lee

31. Patterns and Attitudes   429
    Systems of Legal Control   429
        Raymond G. McCarthy and Edgar M. Douglass
    The Present Situation   433

Supplementary Readings   435

32. Conclusion   436

Index   447

ILLUSTRATIONS

		Facing Page
Plate		
I.	Beer Brewing in Ancient Egypt	38
II.	Grape Harvesting and Wine Making in Ancient Egypt	39
III.	Assyrian Royalty Drinking Wine	68
IV.	A: An Indian Ruler Feasting and Drinking B: Hollanders Drinking Beer in Bali	69
V.	A: Sumerian Libation Ewer B: Chinese Ceremonial Wine Vessel	114
VI.	A: Swedish Drinking Horn B: Chinese Ceremonial Wine Ladle	115
VII.	Wine and Arms. From the Bayeux Cathedral Tapestry	160
VIII.	A: Wine Market, Early 16th Century B: Medieval Distillery	161
IX.	Wine in Religion. A: Dionysos B: The Mass	248
X.	Wine in Religion. A: The Seder B: Communion	249
XI.	Drink and Love	306
XII.	Drink and Music	307
XIII.	A: Kiddush Cup B: Greek Wine Cup C: Dutch Drinking Glass	342
XIV.	A: Punch Bowl B: Spirits Kegs	343
XV.	A "Speakeasy" in Colorado	404
XVI.	A: A Saloon in Montreal B: Women Against Liquor	405

PREFACE

Public awareness of alcoholism as an illness has been enormously stimulated during the last two decades and the establishment of treatment services in a majority of the states and Canadian provinces has culminated in a demand for a program of prevention. The inquiry into the cause of alcoholism has inevitably raised questions about the role of alcohol in our society—questions which have been argued vigorously for three generations.

Why has the custom of drinking persisted for thousands of years in spite of efforts to reduce or eliminate it? What are the attitudes of Americans in general toward drinking? Toward intoxication and alcoholism? How do the people of other countries regard these questions and how have they attempted to resolve them? Is alcohol the cause of alcoholism? Does social drinking contribute to alcoholism? How can public intoxication be controlled? Is the custom of social drinking increasing? What about the use of alcoholic drinks by women and young people? Do we need more legislative controls? What about prohibition? Has it worked effectively in other countries? Can a legislative act significantly change a social custom?

There is an extensive literature about alcohol but it resides chiefly in scientific journals. Temperance organizations release quantities of popular material but the emphasis is on individual total abstinence supported by stringent legal controls of the alcoholic-beverage industry as the solution to problems of intoxication. Many official and voluntary agencies issue newsletters and pamphlets to lay and professional groups but the focus is on alcoholism and its treatment. The student of alcohol problems will find all three groups of material interesting, but they usually explore one specific question in great detail and rarely offer a comprehensive approach to a series of interrelated issues.

This volume, it is hoped, will provide a comprehensive source of readings which will reflect *attitudes toward drinking and intoxication* among different peoples at different periods. The readings also contain an account of attempts to control the social excesses arising from intoxication—for example, by enactment of total or modified prohibition; by government monopoly of distribution with restrictions on retail purchases; and by social controls through the operation of group sanctions. Particular attention is given to historical and contemporary drinking customs and attitudes in the United States.

Although references to alcoholism appear frequently in this volume, no attempt is made here to analyze in detail the nature and extent of the illness and the efforts now being made to reduce the prevalence of the disorder. For example, the low rate of alcoholism among the Chinese or the Jews is discussed primarily in conjunction with the concept of social controls. However, the student who wishes detailed treatment of the public health aspects of alcoholism will find appropriate references in the supplementary reading lists.

This book will serve as a convenient compilation of background material for the adult reader and especially for the undergraduate student in the social sciences—particularly in sociology, social psychology, and anthropology. Although the collected readings deal almost exclusively with drinking customs, the significance of the Wet and Dry controversy is interpreted as a conflict over values more pertinent to cultural dynamics than to the social behavior of accepting or rejecting a drink or buying or selling a beverage containing alcohol. It is necessary to look beyond the charges and countercharges to the motivations, aspirations and ideals expressed in various societies of past and present times, and to examine the degree to which drinking or abstaining has been incorporated in the value systems of different groups and subgroups. This has been accomplished by reprinting selections from the works of specialists who have conducted research studies in the various areas.

The twenty-six figures in Plates I–XVI are not intended to illustrate the text but rather to supplement it by depicting man's multifarious engagement with alcoholic beverages from very early times. Thanks are due to Mark Keller and Vera Efron for their help in selecting and arranging these pictorial materials. The picture collection of the New York Public Library was especially useful for locating materials and the staff of that section were patiently helpful. Thanks are due also to the administrators, curators and photographers of the various museums and galleries who supplied prints for reproduction. Acknowledgment is made to the several sources directly on the plates.

For permission to reprint articles or abstracts of published works, grateful acknowledgment is made to the authors and to the following publishers:

Abingdon Press, Nashville, Tennessee.
American Institute of Public Opinion, Princeton, New Jersey.
American Journal of Sociology, Chicago.
American Sociological Review, New York.
The Classical Bulletin, Saint Louis, Missouri.
International Journal on Alcohol and Alcoholism, London.
Longmans, Green & Co., Inc., New York.
McGill Medical Journal, Montreal.
P. A. Norstedt & Söner, Stockholm.

North Carolina Alcoholic Rehabilitation Program, Raleigh.
Psychiatry, Journal for the Study of Interpersonal Processes,
    Washington, D. C.
Quarterly Journal of Studies on Alcohol, New Haven, Connecticut.
Scientific American, New York.
Scientific Temperance Journal, Westerville, Ohio.
The Mrs. John S. Sheppard Foundation, New York.
Smithsonian Institution, Washington, D. C.
The Standard Encyclopedia of the Alcohol Problem, Westerville, Ohio.
Social Problems, Waltham, Massachusetts.
Yale University Press, New Haven, Connecticut.

The source of each article is cited in the footnote attached to its author's name.

Grateful acknowledgment is made to Vera Efron, Assistant Editor of the Quarterly Journal of Studies on Alcohol, for her valuable assistance in searching the alcohol literature and suggesting materials for inclusion in this text. Acknowledgment is also made to Mrs. Marie Donchian for her assistance in preparing the manuscript for publication and to Gabriella H. Woese for editorial proofreading.

CONTRIBUTORS

Rolando Alvarado
Selden D. Bacon
Robert F. Bales
Milton L. Barnett
H. Bastide
E. Jackson Baur
Olin T. Binkley
Ruth Bunzel
G. S. Chopra
I . C. Chopra
R. N. Chopra
Carroll D. Clark
Howard J. Clinebell, Jr.
Ralph Connor
John M. Cooper
Edgar M. Douglass
Vera Efron
Walter Enriquez
Mark G. Field
Irving Fisher
Donald L. Gerard
Leon A. Greenberg
Joseph R. Gusfield
John L. Haer
Howard W. Haggard
Donald Horton
Joan K. Jackson
Mark Keller
Byron C. Kirby
Weston La Barre

G. R. Lavers
Alfred McClung Lee
Marcia Lifshitz
Edith S. Lisansky
William Mangin
Ines Marchesse
Juan Marconi
M. Marcus
Charles F. Marden
Milton A. Maxwell
Raymond G. McCarthy
Marston M. McCluggage
Arthur P. McKinlay
Merrill Moore
Gabriel Mouchot
Harriet R. Mowrer
Abraham Myerson
Robert E. Popham
Andrew Poznanski
John W. Riley, Jr.
Enrique Rosenblat
B. Seebohm Rowntree
Sakari Sariola
Arne Skutin
Guido Solari
Robert Straus
Anibal Varela
Charles K. Warriner
Bufo Yamamuro

INTRODUCTION

Alcohol is, among other things, a sedative and an anesthetic—like aspirin or ether. Its sedative action has been sought consistently in all ages, and its therapeutic value has been widely accepted. The earliest known book, the Ebers Papyrus, probably written about 1500 B.C., contains many references to beer and wine, including a medical prescription which advises eating castor berries and washing them down with beer. Hippocrates included wine in a list of therapeutics and used it as a wet dressing for ulcers.

In some ancient cultures, as well as in certain contemporary primitive cultures, both drinking and intoxication have been accepted as part of religious ritual or as customs carrying full social approval. Drinking to excess was considered a mark of virility in Rome.

Today millions of people continue to use alcohol for widely divergent purposes and in corresponding varying amounts. But today, perhaps more than ever before, we are faced with the problem of the "alcoholic" who as a result of his dependence on alcohol makes a pseudo adjustment to life which merely complicates existence for himself and for those associated with him.

Why has alcohol played so important a role in man's life for so long?

Horton points out that a custom does not long survive, or spread from its point of origin, unless it solves some human problem.[1] But conversely, a custom that does not really solve the problem nevertheless survives until a better way has been found to satisfy the same need. The beast of burden and the wheeled cart soon took the place of older modes of transportation; and men readily gave up the bow and arrow when firearms became available. But the custom of social drinking continues, and it must be suspected that even today it serves a need better than anything else so far discovered. It is this practice of social drinking that the present volume seeks to examine, in an effort to understand better its motivation and its results, to define the areas where control is needed to meet the problems associated with drinking, and to point the way toward methods of control which are likely to be successful.

The problem is complex. In the past, the time, place and occasion for drinking were ordinarily determined by custom as interpreted by

1. Donald Horton, "The Functions of Alcohol in Primitive Societies," in *Alcohol, Science and Society* (New Haven, Quarterly Journal of Studies on Alcohol, 1945), pp. 153–73.

1

the medicine man, the priest, or the leader. Individual drinking out-side of the sanctioned period was almost entirely unknown, and where it occurred, group punishment was immediate and conclusive. In early societies, at least, there appears to have been no relation between the act of drinking to the point of intoxication as a group member and the development of individual alcoholism as it is defined at the present time.

Projection to contemporary life of patterns of group behavior ob-served in simple societies is not entirely realistic. Modern society may include many subgroups each with its distinctive cultural beliefs, at-titudes, and sanctions regarding behavior. Different sets of values may operate, and this is particularly applicable in respect to the use of alcoholic beverages and to intoxicated behavior. Intoxication within the structure of the group which does not pose a threat to the group may be acceptable at one social level but condemned at another. Re-peated and persistent drunkenness which interferes with the ordinary responsibilities of living, however, is usually condemned at all levels.

Motivation for the use of alcohol today varies among different so-cieties. Where drinking has been an accompaniment to a meal or to a religious ritual, extreme intoxication has not been sought. Drinking as one aspect of family recreation and sociability has been a means of strengthening familial and social bonds. In such circumstances, drunkenness does not become an end in itself.

American drinking habits developed in a pattern which reflects the characteristics of a mobile and heterogeneous culture. According to Bloch, in European cultures drinking has been a phase of deeply rooted stable and integrated patterns: "To separate drinking from the well-established social and recreational procedures of which it has traditionally been a part, and focus attention upon it as an isolated element apart from the social amenities of group recreation, renders it a problem and not a spontaneous social art. With Europeans, for example, drinking has traditionally been a phase of the occasion of the group's coming together; with Americans, conversely, coming to-gether has all too frequently provided the occasion for drinking." [2]

Understanding and evaluation of the extent and significance of in-toxication in America (no less than in Europe) cannot be gained by isolating it from the social and recreational patterns, particularly those which involve drinking customs. Reduction and, if possible, elimina-tion of the excesses attributed to intoxication remain desirable objec-tives. But repressive measures sanctioned only by law are unlikely to be effective. They have not been workable in the past—for ex-ample, in Finland, Sweden, and the United States—and there is little

2. Herbert A. Bloch, "Alcohol and American Recreational Life," *The American Scholar, 18* (1948), 54–66.

likelihood that they will operate successfully in the immediate future. Drinking practices have their roots in group culture, and controls are likely to emerge only through consent of the group as a whole.

The selections in this volume suggest ways by which restrictions have been applied in the past, some with success, others futilely. There is no blueprint for the future, although as understanding and appreciation of the significance of drinking increase, new insights may lead to improved techniques of control.

PART I

PHYSIOLOGICAL AND PSYCHOLOGICAL
EFFECTS OF ALCOHOL

1. PHYSIOLOGICAL EFFECTS

Although alcohol has been used by man for centuries, the development of scientific methods for determining the action of alcohol in the body is comparatively recent. Previous to 1860, physiologists believed that alcohol was completely oxidized in the body. About 1860, animal experiments showed that alcohol could be recovered from the urine and expired air. Researchers then concluded that alcohol was not metabolized at all.

The modern study of alcohol metabolism began about 1870, when numerous researchers, investigating the amount of energy liberated by the oxidation of alcohol, concluded that alcohol can be utilized as a foodstuff by the organism. During the early years of the present century the rate of metabolism of alcohol in animals and in man was calculated. Widmark's micromethod for alcohol determination in 1922 was an important step forward.[1] During the next ten years, he and others cleared up the general facts about alcohol absorption, distribution, and elimination in the animal and human body. The following section is a summary of present knowledge of the action of alcohol in the body. For medicinal uses, see below, pp. 16–17.

ALCOHOL IN THE BODY

by Leon A. Greenberg *

Ethyl alcohol, the beverage kind, is only one of many alcohols. What mainly distinguishes it from the nonpotable alcohols is that the body destroys it (by oxidation) rapidly. A man who drinks a pint of whisky in a day has no alcohol left in his body the next day. But it would take him about a week to get rid of this amount of methyl (wood) alcohol. Moreover, the body oxidizes methyl alcohol into a poison that damages the nerves, often causing blindness by attacking the optic nerve.

Pure ethyl alcohol is a clear, colorless liquid with little odor but a powerful burning taste. No one drinks pure alcohol; it is always taken as an ingredient of wine, brewed beverages, or distilled spirits. Wine is as old as prehistoric man; primitive peoples knew that fruit juices exposed to the air in a warm place made a lively beverage. Brewing also is very old, but distillation is a fairly recent development.

* First published in *Scientific American, 189* (Dec. 1953), 86 ff.

1. Erik Jacobsen, "The Metabolism of Ethyl Alcohol," *Pharmacological Reviews,* 4 (1952), 109.

The fermentation of fruit juices is effected by tiny yeast plants which settle in the liquid from the dust in the air. In the presence of an abundance of sugar, fermentation can proceed to an alcohol content of about 14 per cent, at which point the alcohol inhibits the yeast. Some wines are fortified by addition of alcohol to a content of 20 per cent. The brewing of beer or ale also is a fermentation process, but in this case the raw material is a broth made from cereals, and malt is added to break down the starch to sugar so that the yeast can act on it. The process is stopped when the alcohol concentration of the brew has reached 3 to 6 per cent, and hops are usually added for flavor. Wines and brewed beverages retain the minerals and some of the vitamins of the fruit or cereal.

The stronger liquors are made by distillation of the fermented beverages —brandy from wine and whisky from a beerlike brew. In the distilling process all the solids, minerals, and vitamins are lost. The distilled beverages usually have an alcohol content of 40 to 50 per cent. The term "proof" as the measure of strength comes from the early distillers, who tested alcohol by wetting gunpowder with it; when the distillate was at least 50 per cent alcohol, the powder would burn. Since combustibility of the gunpowder was 100 per-cent proof of this alcohol content, "100 proof" came to mean 50 per cent alcohol.

So much for alcohol in the bottle; our chief subject is what happens to alcohol in the drinker. Unlike most foods, it is absorbed into the blood without digestion. A small part goes into the blood slowly from the stomach itself; the rest passes into the small intestine and there is absorbed by the blood rapidly and almost completely. The alcohol exercises no intoxicating effect until it reaches the brain in the circulating blood. How soon it will do so, and how much effect it will have, depends a great deal on how much food is in the stomach. A full stomach retards the passage of ingested alcohol into the small intestine and thus delays and minimizes the effect. This is why a single cocktail on an empty stomach has more "kick" than three or four drinks after a large meal. A "hollow leg" usually means that the drinker has eaten well. Fatty foods, such as olive oil, are commonly supposed to be most effective as a bulwark again intoxication, but actually some proteins are more effective. A few glasses of milk can provide fortification against a session of social drinking.

Some beverages, notably beer, contain food substances which in themselves slow absorption. A given amount of alcohol has less effect when consumed as beer than when taken as distilled spirits. On the other hand carbon dioxide hastens the passage of alcohol from the stomach into the intestine and thus speeds absorption. This explains the common observation that champagne and other effervescent wines "go to one's head." It also accounts for the fact that soda taken with whisky tends to minimize irritation of the stomach by the alcohol.

The alcohol absorbed from the digestive tract is held temporarily in the tissues until it is broken down and eliminated. More exactly, it is distributed evenly in the water of the body, and its concentration in any given tissue will depend on the water content of that tissue. Since blood is about 90 per cent water, as compared with about 70 per cent for the body as a whole, it will contain about one and a quarter times as much alcohol per unit as the rest of the body. Consequently it is possible to predict quite accurately from the concentration of alcohol in the blood how much has been absorbed in the tissues, and conversely, from the amount absorbed, the concentration that will occur in the blood. In a 160-pound man the alcohol in an ounce of whisky or a bottle of beer produces an alcohol concentration of about 0.02 per cent in the blood; a half pint of whisky raises the concentration to 0.15 per cent.

As soon as alcohol is absorbed by the tissues, it begins to break down by oxidation. Ordinarily the rate at which food is oxidized depends on the amount of energy the body is using for work, but this is not the case for alcohol. The rate of oxidation of alcohol is essentially constant. In a man of 160 pounds it amounts to the equivalent of about three-quarters of an ounce of whisky per hour. Thus he could sip whisky at this rate, consuming more than a pint in 24 hours, without accumulating alcohol in his body or becoming intoxicated. If he drank the same amount within a few hours, the effects would be disastrous.

The first stage in the oxidation of alcohol is its conversion to acetaldehyde. This conversion, it has recently been discovered, occurs only in the liver, with the help of a liver enzyme. Acetaldehyde is much more toxic than alcohol itself, but as fast as it forms it is carried to all the tissues of the body, where it is rapidly oxidized further to acetic acid, a harmless substance. Finally the acetic acid is broken down to carbon dioxide and water. An animal whose liver has been removed cannot oxidize alcohol. Ethyl alcohol then acts like wood alcohol, disappearing very slowly from the body. Antabuse, a drug sometimes used to control alcoholism, is effective because it inhibits the oxidation of acetaldehyde. The patient is given a dose of Antabuse daily. The drug has no apparent effect as long as he stays away from liquor, but if he takes a drink, even a small one, the acetaldehyde formed accumulates, with severe and extremely unpleasant symptoms. Antabuse thus acts as an automatic check on compulsive drinking.

Many attempts have been made to increase the rate of alcohol oxidation and thus to shorten the period of intoxication. As yet, none has been successful. Such drugs as thyroid extract, which raise the general metabolism, appear to have little or no effect on the rate at which the liver oxidizes alcohol. Inhalation of oxygen does not hasten the process, nor does increased work. There is no basis for the popular belief that intoxication can be "worked off" by exercise. Sobering up is essentially a matter of time.

The fact that certain drugs and black coffee appear to have a sobering effect does not mean that they hasten the disappearance of alcohol. These stimulants merely counteract some of the depressant action of alcohol on the brain and wake the person up. Awake or asleep, the man is still drunk.

Fifty years ago the question of what alcohol does to a drinker used to be disposed of with graphic simplicity. You broke an egg into a tumbler of alcohol. The albumen of the egg turned white, coagulated, and shriveled. This was supposed to show how drink affected the organs of the body: the gray matter of the brain clotted and shriveled; the liver dried up until it resembled the sole of an old boot. Research has now established a more accurate and detailed picture. Let us see what really happens.

First of all, the 40 to 50 per cent concentration of alcohol in whisky is strongly irritating to tissues, as anyone can find out by putting a drop in his eye. Straight whisky irritates the lining tissues of the mouth, throat, esophagus, and stomach as it goes down. Frequent and repeated drinking of strong liquor will inflame and may actually damage these tissues: this accounts for the "whisky tenor" voice and the chronic gastritis of habitual drinkers who take their whisky "neat." Alcohol also irritates the sensory nerves and thereby provides a momentary stimulation, in exactly the same way that smelling salts do. After passing into the blood, however, the alcohol no longer has an irritating effect, because even in an extremely intoxicated person the blood concentration never rises to the level of irritation (15 to 20 per cent). Thus the alcohol circulated to the body tissues by the blood cannot destroy cells, corrode them, dissolve them, or dry them out.

In moderate amounts alcohol stimulates the flow of gastric juice and promotes stomach motility. These effects produce the sensation of hunger and explain the popularity of cocktails and other alcoholic appetizers. There is no evidence that alcohol ever causes gastric ulcers, but doctors forbid their ulcer patients to drink because of the increased gastric flow. Moderate amounts of alcohol do not interfere with digestion; they may even promote it. Amounts leading to intoxication stop digestion.

Pure alcohol has a strong affinity for water, and this has led to the popular superstition that heavy drinking dehydrates the body. The fallacy gains support from the intense thirst that usually accompanies a hangover. This thirst arises, however, not from a loss of water, but from a shift in its distribution. Normally about two-thirds of the water in the body is held within the cells; the rest makes up the fluid in which the cells float. But when one has drunk enough alcohol to become severely intoxicated, water is drawn from the cells into the spaces between them. This shift of distribution explains the powerful morning-after thirst, and also the so-called "wet brain" of the acute alcoholic.

Like other foods, alcohol can be used by the body for energy. An ounce of whisky liberates 75 calories of energy—about as much as four and a half teaspoons of sugar, one and a half pats of butter, or a large slice of bread. Alcohol is fattening, provided the consumption of other foods is not reduced, because it curtails the oxidation of foods. A daily cocktail can be as threatening to a woman's figure as the nibbling of bonbons. On the other hand, a heavy drinker usually cuts down his food consumption severely. His appetite declines, and he gets into the habit of "drinking his meals." If he drinks a pint of whisky a day, its 1,200 calories will supply half of his daily energy requirements, but he fails to get the minerals, proteins, and vitamins that the equivalent amount of ordinary food would provide. Excessive drinkers often suffer deficiency diseases such as beriberi and pellagra and the degeneration of nerve fibers.

Heavy drinking may also produce in some people the condition called pylorospasm—a spastic closure of the valve between the stomach and the intestine. When the valve closes, much of the alcohol drunk may stay in the stomach for hours, and pylorospasm often causes nausea and vomiting. It may spring from an unusual sensitivity of the stomach or from psychological factors. Needless to say, people who are prone to develop pylorospasm from drinking do not become heavy drinkers.

The most pronounced physiological effect of alcohol is on the brain. The amount and the extent of the disturbance depend on the concentration of alcohol in the blood and brain tissues. A blood concentration of about 0.05 per cent of alcohol, which in a person of average size results from drinking two or three ounces of whisky, depresses the uppermost level of the brain—the center of inhibitions, restraint, and judgment. At this stage the drinker feels that he is sitting on top of the world; he is "a free human being"; many of his normal inhibitions vanish; he takes personal and social liberties as the impulse prompts; he is long-winded and can lick anybody in the country. Such a man has undergone an obvious blunting of self-criticism.

At a concentration of 0.1 per cent in the blood, from five or six ounces of whisky, alcohol depresses the somewhat lower motor area of the brain. The individual staggers slightly; he has difficulty in putting on his overcoat; he fumbles with his door key; his tongue trips over familiar words.

These first two states are commonly designated as slight or mild intoxication. Their important feature is depression of sensory and motor functions. Contrary to old and popular belief, alcohol does not stimulate the nervous system. The illusion of stimulation results from the removal of inhibitions and restraints. The effect may be compared to a releasing of the brakes, not a stepping on the accelerator. Even with a few drinks, digital dexterity is reduced; auditory and visual discrimination fall away; tactile perception is lowered; the speed of motor response drops. Despite these measurable losses, the drinker often asserts that his reactions, perception, and discrimination are better.

A concentration of 0.2 per cent of alcohol in the blood, resulting from drinking about 10 ounces of whisky, disturbs not only the entire motor area of the brain but also the midbrain, where emotional behavior is largely controlled. At this point the individual tends to assume a horizontal position; he needs help to walk or undress; he is easily moved to rage or tears.

At 0.3 per cent, from about a pint of whisky, alcohol attacks the still lower, more primitive area of the brain, concerned with sensory perception. The drinker becomes stuporous; although still conscious, he has little comprehension of what he sees or hears. When alcohol reaches the level of 0.4 or 0.5 per cent in the blood, it suppresses the whole perception area of the brain and the drinker falls into a coma. Finally, a concentration of 0.6 or 0.7 per cent affects the centers that control breathing and heartbeat, and death rapidly ensues.

Throughout this sequence the concentration of alcohol remains far too low to cause any organic damage. The disturbance is entirely one of nerve functions, and up to the last stage it is reversible; when the alcohol disappears the effect goes with it, as in anesthesia. Alcohol is in fact an anesthetic like ether or chloroform. In deep intoxication surgery could be carried out painlessly.

Besides its primary depressant effect on the central nervous system, alcohol has other secondary effects on various organs of the body. It apparently interferes with the liver's handling of fat, for after severe intoxication this organ is often swollen and yellow with fat. Very likely impairment of the liver's handling of fat is responsible for the development of cirrhosis of the liver, a serious disease which occurs with particularly high incidence among alcoholics.

Does tolerance to alcohol increase with prolonged use? The belief that it does is firmly entrenched, but the evidence is far from clear. It is true that different individuals, and the same individual at different times, vary widely in their responses to a given amount of alcohol. But it has already been pointed out that the amount of food in the stomach and the kind of beverage drunk have much to do with the effect; the body absorbs alcohol from beer, for instance, much more slowly than from whisky or champagne. Furthermore, the individual's temperament plays a large part in his behavior reactions. A few drinks may make a phlegmatic individual normal, a normal person the life of a party, and a vivacious person a nuisance. The end result depends on the starting point. As O. Henry once remarked, some people are "half drunk when they are sober."

The folklore of drinking also includes the idea that tolerance of alcohol is affected by mixing drinks: "When I take a drink of rye I'm fine, but if I follow it with a drink of scotch and then gin the effect is amazing." What the drinker overlooks is that in mixing his drinks he has taken more of them. Moreover, at the level of one or a few drinks, intoxication is profoundly influenced by suggestion. A person who thinks he will get drunk quickly usually finds that he does.

The experienced drinker's "habituation" to alcohol may be largely, if not entirely, psychological. He becomes practiced in controlling and compensating for his overt reactions. The Yale University Center of Alcohol Studies compared the effects of a moderate amount of alcohol on two groups, one consisting of habitual, heavy drinkers and the other of occasional, light drinkers. While the latter showed the usual signs of intoxication (unsteady gait, aggressiveness, noisiness, giggling) the heavy drinkers seemed almost completely sober! But they turned out to be fully as much below par as the inexperienced drinkers in tests of speed of motor response, auditory and visual discrimination, tactile perception, digital dexterity, and other faculties. They merely had their "sea legs."

True physiological tolerance to alcohol means resistance of the central nervous system to its depressive effects. By that test the differences detected among individuals have been relatively small.

The scientific evidence, then, can be summarized as follows: Habitual, heavy drinking produces—aside from its social, economic, and moral havoc —serious and permanent bodily damage, mainly through nutritional deficiencies and other metabolic disturbances. There is no evidence that small or moderate amounts of alcohol are harmful. By improving blood circulation to the body surface, a little alcohol can bring comfort to elderly patients. A small amount of alcohol increases the appetite and lessens tensions and irritations. It does not greatly affect normal blood pressure, but it does prevent the pressure from rising during anxiety. Alcohol certainly does not stimulate thought, but it may relieve worry. Undoubtedly it is because of this relief from environmental stresses and emotional tensions that the moderate use of alcohol has persisted for thousands of years.

The effect of alcohol on the brain, stomach, and liver has been noted. Questions about its action on other organs of the body and its effect on health are also frequently raised.

OTHER EFFECTS OF ALCOHOL

by Mark Keller *

The Kidneys. In spite of old notions, alcohol is not particularly damaging to the kidneys. It does increase their urinary activity. Recent studies indicate that this is caused not by direct action of alcohol on the kidneys but by its effect on the pituitary gland. This gland is a small extension of the lower part of the brain. One of the materials which it produces, and releases into the blood stream, controls the formation of urine by the kidney. As alcohol reduces the activity of this gland, the kidney forms more urine.

The Glands. The pituitary gland takes part in many important bodily activities. It influences the work of other very important glands—the

* From *How Alcohol Affects the Body,* Popular Pamphlets on Alcohol Problems, No. 3 (New Haven, Publications Division, Yale Center of Alcohol Studies, 1955), p. 8 ff.

thyroid and the adrenals. It influences growth and sex development. Does the temporary suppression of a part of this activity by alcohol have any permanent damaging effect? From all the evidence of research thus far it appears that occasional drinking, or even regular drinking of small amounts of alcohol, does not cause such damage. The frequent drinking of large amounts is another matter and may be harmful to these and other glands.

From experiments with animals it has been learned that a large dose of alcohol causes the adrenal glands to discharge their secretions. These little glands, located atop the kidneys, are very important in helping man to meet the stresses and strains of life. They are known to shoot off their chemicals into the blood stream in case of sudden fright or shock, for example. Thus the sudden intake of a large amount of alcohol may be a strain, causing the adrenal glands to discharge. Again, there is no evidence that the body is impaired if this happens once in a while, since it is organized to meet such emergencies. But it is suspected that repeated severe demands on this gland over many years may exhaust its ability to work.

The adrenal glands also take part in many other body activities—for instance, the distribution of minerals in the body. All or some of these activities may be altered while a man is drunk. As far as is known, the normal state is restored in hours to days after the intoxication wears off, depending on how severe it was.

It used to be thought that the sex glands were especially subject to damage by alcohol. Old superstitions blamed all sorts of defects in children on the supposed drunkenness of their parents. The children were thought to inherit weak or crippled minds or bodies because the seed of their parents had been injured by alcohol.

Actually, drinking alcoholic beverages cannot damage the sex glands or the seed cells. This can be understood if the manner in which alcohol reaches these tissues and cells is recalled. The alcohol first enters the blood stream and is vastly diluted. Even in severe drunkenness, the alcohol strength that reaches the glands or seed cells is not likely to be as much as one-half of one per cent. Yet if an alcohol solution of one per cent were applied directly to those tissues and cells, they would not be harmed. Thus the old notions about children of drunken parents being born defective can be cast aside, together with the idea that alcohol can directly irritate and injure the sex glands. Again, the result of years of heavy drinking, or the effects of the alcoholism of parents on the health and welfare of growing children, are other matters . . .

The seeming stimulation of sex activity by drinking is not caused by any effect of alcohol on the sex glands. It results from the action of alcohol in putting to sleep that part of the brain which controls certain kinds of behavior. Very large amounts of alcohol reduce sex activity in the same way that they lessen all activity—by making the drunken man unable to carry out planned actions, or by putting him to sleep . . .

*　　*　　*

The Heart and Circulation. A drink of whisky may make the heart beat faster and give a sensation of warmth to the skin. This is caused by the momentary irritation of the nerve endings in the mouth, throat, and gullet by the strong alcohol solution. The faster heartbeat increases the blood flow; the blood vessels near the surface of the skin become dilated, and this produces the feeling of warmth there. Actually this causes a slight loss of heat from the body.

These short effects of a drink or two cause no lasting changes in the heart. There is no evidence that moderate amounts of alcohol cause heart disease, high blood pressure, or hardening of the arteries. Getting drunk does tax the heart and would be dangerous for a man with heart disease.

Alcohol and Energy. At one time people thought that alcohol was especially helpful in doing hard work. They even supposed that heavy laborers could not work well without it. Perhaps in olden times this was true in an indirect way. Some men labored so hard and long each day that they might not have been able to bear the pain and fatigue without the sedation of alcohol. As their labor was not skilled, the amounts they drank did not interfere noticeably with their efficiency.

When the belief that alcohol improved muscular work was challenged, however, it was shown to be a fallacy. A farmhand, for example, could work just as well, or even better, if not plied with liquor during the day, provided he was well fed otherwise. Later, certain laboratory experiments with muscle work were thought by some to mean that the body could not use alcohol as a food or fuel at all.

The fact is that as alcohol is used up (oxidized) in the body it is changed to various substances, one of which is acetate. This compound is formed from the oxidation of many foods, and the body uses the acetate from any source for its energy needs, for work or heat. Thus alcohol can be a source of energy for the work of muscles, and in this sense at least, it is a food. But two important facts should be remembered in this connection:

First, the amount of alcohol that the body can burn is limited, as noted before, to about half an ounce per hour. Thus only a limited part of the energy needed for work can be supplied by alcohol.

Second, though alcohol supplies calories, it does not provide certain essential needs of the body which come in other foods—the vitamins, minerals, and proteins, for instance, which come along with the calories in bread, milk, meat, fish, eggs, cereals, fruits, and vegetables.

Anyone who relied on alcohol for any large part of his energy would end with some serious diseases. That, in fact, is what happens to many excessive drinkers.

Length of Life. One question that crops up in discussions of effects of alcohol is whether drinking has an influence on how long one may live. There is no question that those who drink to excess over many years have a shorter average life span than those who abstain or drink moderately. But what about the moderate drinkers compared to abstainers? This question is not so easy to answer as might be supposed. The best source of information on length of life is insurance company records. But these records do not definitely point out who is a "moderate drinker." Scientists who have carefully reviewed all the studies on this question are of the opinion that truly moderate drinkers are not different in length of life from abstainers.

Other Effects. Research in many laboratories has shown a great variety of changes in the body with the drinking of different amounts of alcohol. For the most part, these changes take place only with large amounts. For example, the body puts out an excess of potassium in the urine after a large amount of alcohol is drunk. It is important to bear in mind that by no means all effects of alcohol on the body have been dealt with here. But what has been said about those which were described applies generally. The changes are temporary. The body returns to its usual state soon after it has disposed of the alcohol. Some of the changes cause temporary impairment of the work of one or another organ. Some of these changes may be the body's way of defending itself from being hurt by the sudden presence of a large amount of alcohol.

As far as the over-all health of the body is concerned, none of these changes is important if not repeated often or allowed to go to an extreme degree. The main physical danger in drinking more than the body can oxidize within a short time is in becoming intoxicated, getting drunk. The body of the drunken man is always in danger, for its director, its brain, its safety guard, is working under a handicap—it is under an anesthetic.

Alcohol as Medicine. Thus far we have considered alcoholic beverages taken by healthy people for certain effects which they find agreeable, or because they want to go along with social customs. Some people, however, use these drinks as medicines for different ailments. Some believe a drink of one sort or another is good for their health—or even necessary for good health. Alcoholic beverages are prescribed by physicians for certain disorders, and some physicians inject alcohol directly into the blood stream of certain patients. What are the effects of these uses on the body? Do alcoholic beverages contribute directly to health?

The use of alcoholic beverages in the treatment of many disorders has a long history. No doubt they must have been of benefit to patients who were in pain and distress with all sorts of scarcely understood diseases. For alcohol acts on the brain as a sedative and thus suppresses the sensation of pain. Men noticed that the sick "felt better" after taking some wine, for example, and so they assumed that the beverage had the quality of a medicine for the particular illness. Thus there grew up a tradition of the medicinal properties of alcoholic beverages, and even ideas of the special fitness of this or that wine for this or that disease.

When distilling became popular in Europe, in the 16th century, brandy and other spirits gained attention as useful in medicine, and no wonder. A strong distillate was much more efficient in relieving pain than a wine with only a fifth as much alcohol in it. At times alcohol was the only anesthetic for the performance of surgery. Soon special kinds of distilled spirits were recommended for particular ailments. One example was gin for the kidneys, because gin seemed to promote urination. Actually, experiments have shown that ordinary alcohol has the same effect on the flow of urine as gin.

In more recent times the real causes of many illnesses came to be understood, and medications which act directly on the cause of the symptoms could be prepared. Thus 50 years ago alcohol was prescribed for diabetes —with little benefit. Nowadays the diabetic is treated successfully by control of diet and injections of insulin. Serums, sulfa drugs, and antibiotics replaced alcohol in the treatment of pneumonia. The prescription of alcohol thus declined sharply.

In popular usage, however, and especially for common ailments for which there are as yet no specific medicines, the taking of alcohol persists. Rum is taken for a cold. It does not cure a cold. It may, however, relieve the aches and pains, as would other analgesic drugs. Whisky is still given for snakebite. It does not counteract the venom, but it may relax the victim a bit and thus ease his pain and terror. Brandy is given to someone who has fainted. It does not work on the cause of the fainting but helps revive the victim by its irritant action in the mouth and throat. Smelling salts do the same thing and are safer than pouring a liquid down the throat of an unconscious person. Wine is said to build blood. It may dampen the pain that goes with anemia, but the physician today has really effective treatment for that disorder.

There are certain conditions, however, for which physicians find alcohol a valuable drug, making use of its special properties. One action of alcohol is to dilate some blood vessels. A drink is therefore sometimes prescribed for elderly patients suffering from hardening of the arteries. Alcohol also acts as a sedative. For the old, therefore, a drink may be prescribed as a means of getting several effects at once: dilating their blood vessels; relieving their aches, pains, and feeling of chilliness; reducing their tenseness and irritability; and rousing their appetite.

Alcohol also provides calories. This quality is used to advantage by surgeons in the cases of patients who cannot be fed after an operation. The alcohol is injected slowly into a vein so that the patient receives at the same time a certain amount of nourishment and a sedative for his pain. This use of alcohol by physicians has nothing to do with the ordinary drinking of beverages by healthy people, but it illustrates the variety of effects that alcohol exerts on the human body.

2. PSYCHOLOGICAL EFFECTS

by Edith S. Lisansky *

It is apparent that drinking an alcoholic beverage in moderate or large amounts does affect one's behavior and feeling. But much of what we know of the effects of alcohol is based on popular observation and not on controlled laboratory experimentation. Although the behavioral sciences have advanced rapidly over the last half century, there has been a disappointing lack of research interest in the effects of alcohol.

What is meant by the "psychological effects of alcohol?" Alcohol may mean small or medium amounts, that is, quantities consumed in normal social usage. Alcohol may also be consumed in large quantities, sufficient to produce intoxication. The present discussion refers only to *small amounts,* defined as approximately two highballs or a quart of beer taken on an empty stomach, and producing a blood alcohol concentration of 0.05 per cent or less. There are no experimental data regarding the effects of large amounts.

What do we mean by *psychological effects?* For the sake of clarity, we will divide human behavior into two classes: non-emotional and emotional behavior. Under the *non-emotional behaviors,* we include sensation, perception, reaction time, the performance of motor tasks and skills, and the processes of learning, remembering, thinking, reasoning, and solving problems. Under the *emotional behaviors,* we can distinguish (1) the more or less stable patterns of emotional response which lead us to characterize an individual as a fearful man, a tense woman, a hostile person, and (2) the more temporary and transient states of emotion or feeling such as being momentarily angry or depressed or on edge. This distinction between non-emotional and emotional behaviors is, of course, arbitrary, and the overlap is obvious. The way we perceive and learn and solve problems influences and determines the patterns of emotional behavior we acquire. Conversely, we bring our emotional patterns with us to shape any task of learning or reasoning or motor reaction. This distinction, between emotional and non-emotional behavior, is merely a convenient way of classifying the experimental work which has been done.

Non-emotional Behaviors

In a classic review of studies on alcohol by experimental psychologists up to 1940, Jellinek and McFarland discuss research done in many areas:

* Prepared especially for this volume. Doctor Lisansky is a Lecturer in Psychology, Yale Center of Alcohol Studies.

reflexes and sensations, attention, simple reaction time, muscular response to tasks involving heavy manipulation of tools, tests of dexterity and skill, learning simple material and learning more complex material, memory, reasoning, judgment, intelligence, volition, and so on. The trend of these research findings must, however, be interpreted with caution. Most of the work reported in this review belongs to an earlier stage of experimental psychology. Of the 200 experiments reported, 50 involved only one subject and, in half these instances, the experimenter himself was the subject. In current experimental work we are careful to control certain variables which were not often controlled in the early studies. For example, alcohol dosage is not equal if two subjects, one weighing 125 pounds and the other 225 pounds, are given the same amount of alcohol. In current experiments, dosage is varied according to body weight. The time interval which elapses between a subject's drinking and his test performance is a variable which must be kept equal throughout an experiment but was not always constant in the early experiments.

Keeping these limitations in mind, however, what were some of the experimental observations made?

Auditory Discrimination.[1] A test of auditory discrimination involves dropping a metal ball on a metal plate from different heights and determining the smallest sound which can be heard by the individual without alcohol, and then the smallest difference between sounds. In other words if *A* is the smallest sound and *B* is the next smallest sound, how many people can determine the difference between *A* and *B*? Hundreds of trials have been made in order to establish a series of norms. The subjects are given alcohol in relatively small amounts so that the concentration at no time is more than 0.04 or 0.05 per cent. The test is usually administered an hour after the alcohol has been consumed. With these small amounts of alcohol in the blood, softer sounds are heard: there is actually an increase of acuity. But there is also a loss in discrimination.

Something similar has happened in vision tests. Again, various techniques are used to arrive at norms according to which different degrees of light are distinguished. The subjects are given small amounts of alcohol. After a period of about an hour the individual can detect finer light reflections, but discrimination is reduced to some extent. These two generalizations (and they are rather weak ones) perhaps account for the fact that music seems more appealing to some people with 0.05 per cent of alcohol in the blood. But their discrimination may not be so fine. Without alcohol some of the music might be displeasing.

Tactile Sensation. So far as tactile sensation is concerned, the sensation

1. The following has been condensed and edited from Raymond G. McCarthy, *Alcoholism: A Personal and Community Problem,* Papers Presented at the First Annual Summer Studies on Facts about Alcohol, North Carolina Alcoholic Rehabilitation Program, 1952.

of touch neither increases nor decreases. The sensation of pain is diminished and the ability to localize points of stimulation is slightly diminished. We do not know exactly how alcohol affects sensory functions. There may be some interference with the transfer of oxygen from the blood stream to the nerve cells. There are other theories, including the one that there are blockings of the electrical impulses in the nervous system. When the brain gets a stimulus which calls for movement, there may be some interference so far as muscular performance is concerned.

Muscular Strength. This question comes up not only in the laboratory, but in practical experience. It used to be assumed that men who did hard physical work, men in the shipyards and foundries, men in the fields during harvest time, needed alcohol to maintain physical vigor. In certain industries provision for a quota of liquor in some form was written into the agreement entered into by the workers.

What do laboratory tests reveal about muscular strength, the capacity to do heavy work of a coarse nature? One-half to one small glass of whisky may increase the output of work for a short time; with one and one-half to two glasses there is only negligible increase; on three glasses there is either no change or a decrease. Apparently small amounts have no effect on coarse muscle performance.

There is a decrease in effectiveness in fine muscle coordination. The response to a flashing light or the sound of a bell by pressing a button or key is less efficient. Other variables are involved.

Every report on psychological changes due to small amounts of alcohol refers to the rifle-shooting experiments. Jellinek summarized the data in a story: "John has made target shooting a hobby. In practice he can score nine out of ten bull's-eyes. In competition he gets jittery, nervous, and upset and is lucky to hit only five out of ten. After two drinks he can score seven or eight out of ten shots." [2] Does this prove that there is improvement in his marksmanship as a result of the alcohol? Actually there was an improvement in his competitive score. What happened was a mild reduction in anxiety, a reduction in tension, so that he became competitively normal. But his skill was lowered too, so that he could not score at his best.

Two and one-half glasses of whisky (50 per cent alcohol was taken as a standard) showed 0.6 per cent decrease in efficiency in skilled marksmanship; 45 minutes later, without any more drinking—there was a decrease of 1.5 per cent. These are not significant changes unless one is dealing with very small relationships.

Further Experiments. Student typists suffered an increase in errors of 40 per cent and a reduction in speed of 3 per cent. However, when professional linotype operators were tested there was no increase in errors but there was a reduction in speed of 15 per cent. In other words, this skilled

2. *How Alcohol Affects Psychological Behavior,* Lay Supplement No. 11. New Haven, *Quarterly Journal of Studies on Alcohol,* 1944.

performance was affected to a degree of making the individual more careful. His speed was reduced but his effectiveness, so far as errors are concerned, was not. The student typists, who had not developed skilled patterns of performance, ran into difficulties.

Jellinek summarizes these data as follows: "It would seem that on the whole the effect of small amounts of alcohol on skilled performances increases as the tasks become more complex, but that the effect on a complex but familiar task may be less than on a simpler but unfamiliar one, and that the effect may be less on persons accustomed than on persons not accustomed to drinking. Furthermore, the so-called simple laboratory tasks do not seem quite appropriate for drawing conclusions concerning the effect of alcohol on skill. There remains, however, no doubt that the properties of alcohol that are conducive to sedation or relaxation are by no means conducive to task efficiency." [3] In other words, small amounts which may produce relaxation, which may have a mild sedative effect, usually interfere to some degree with efficiency, with such exceptions and such limitations as we have discussed.

Word Association. It has been found that under the effects of alcohol there is an increased flow of ideas but they are less effectively organized and less integrated, and there is less discrimination in reporting words. A recent study [4] indicates that alcohol generally reduces verbal fluency although in one of the fluency tests used in this experiment, the alcohol resulted in improved performance.

Impairment of Judgment. This is a vague term and has been used by different experimenters to mean various things. It is clear that the judgment of time is impaired under alcohol. Judgment of one's own performance is also affected and this is the most significant danger in using alcohol even in relatively small amounts while driving. Individuals sometimes have inflated estimates of their driving skill; when the estimate is enhanced by small amounts of alcohol, the setting has been prepared for an accident.[5]

Jellinek believes that on the whole the fact of impairment of judgment under alcohol cannot be questioned, even though no meaningful estimate can be made of the degree of impairment.

Higher-order Intellectual Functioning. Jellinek and McFarland conclude that even though ". . . there is no material on tests of general intelligence . . . the cumulative evidence of tests on memory, association, judgment, reasoning, etc. definitely establishes the impairment of intelligence in alcoholic intoxication." [6] No inference, however, can be drawn about the

---

3. *Ibid.,* p. 12.

4. P. Hartocollis and D. M. Johnson, "Differential Effects of Alcohol on Verbal Fluency," *Quarterly Journal of Studies on Alcohol, 17* (1956), 183–9.

5. K. Bjerver and L. Goldberg, "Effect of Alcohol Ingestion on Driving Ability," *Quarterly Journal of Studies on Alcohol, 11* (1950), 1–30.

6. E. M. Jellinek and R. A. McFarland, "Analysis of Psychological Experiments on the Effects of Alcohol," *Quarterly Journal of Studies on Alcohol, 1* (1940), 361.

permanent effects of alcohol or the effects in chronic alcoholism; the small amount of evidence available suggests very little effect on intelligence test performance of chronic alcoholic subjects.[7]

One may raise the question whether alcohol has the invariable effect ascribed, that is, impairment, and under what conditions, if any, alcohol has different effects. Research in progress at present at Yale University is exploring the question of the effects of alcohol on higher-order problem solving.

The relationship of alcohol to creative work needs more exploration. There have been painters, poets, authors and other creative artists for whom drinking was a problem, yet for whom the creative process went on in spite of alcohol. The most recent example is the tragic Welsh poet, Dylan Thomas. Roe's study of 20 leading American painters indicates that such a situation may be exceptional; only one of the artists found it easier to paint when drinking.[8] Study of the facilitating and inhibiting function of alcohol in the artistic, creative process is needed.

Emotional Behaviors

Balanced against more than 200 studies in the review discussed above is a very small number of experiments in the area of emotional behavior.

Masserman [9] presented the results of experiments in which cats were placed inside a box and learned to press a switch in order to be fed. After learning this, the animals were exposed to a series of air blasts or electric shocks which resulted in the cats' refusing to press the switch. The animals showed fear reactions to the switch; the refusal to eat and the fear behavior is described by Masserman as a ". . . highly complex neurotic reaction." When the cats were fed an alcohol solution in milk, they then responded by working the switch and by feeding. In another experiment, the alcohol and milk solution was given *before* the air blast or electric shock and Masserman's results suggested that the effect of the air blast or shock may thus be lessened or "mitigated."

Conger's [10] experiments are essentially similar although done more rigorously within the framework of modern psychological theory about conflict. Rats were trained to approach the end of a runway and to eat

7. G. A. Peters, "Emotional and Intellectual Concomitants of Advanced Chronic Alcoholism," *Journal of Consulting Psychology, 20* (1956), 390.

8. Anne Roe, "Alcohol and Creative Work, Pt. I. Painters," *Quarterly Journal of Studies on Alcohol, 6* (1946), 415–67.

9. J. H. Masserman and K. S. Yum, "An Analysis of the Influence of Alcohol on Experimental Neuroses in Cats," *Psychosomatic Medicine, 8* (1946), 36–52. Also J. H. Masserman, M. G. Jacques, and M. R. Nicholson, "Alcohol as a Preventive of Experimental Neuroses," *Quarterly Journal of Studies on Alcohol, 6* (1945), 281–99.

10. J. J. Conger, "The Effects of Alcohol on Conflict Behavior in the Albino Rat," *Quarterly Journal of Studies on Alcohol, 12* (1951), 1–29.

there. They were then given electric shock in this feeding area. Placed at the beginning of the runway again, they refused to run or eat, a ". . . delicately balanced approach-avoidance conflict" having been set up. At this point, one group of rats was injected with water, the other group with alcohol. On the first trial following this, the water-injected group continued their refusal to eat but the alcohol-injected group did eat. In a second experiment, Conger demonstrated that it is primarily a decrease in fear (avoidance) behavior rather than any increase in hunger (approach) which produced the change in the alcohol-injected group.

Although there are unanswered questions, these reports demonstrate that we can approach the study of the effects of alcohol on complex emotional behavior in an experimental way. And although done in a laboratory situation and with temporary, experimentally induced conflicts, they suggest that this line of investigation into the role of alcohol as diminisher of fear is a promising one and merits further research.

Recent experiments by Carpenter [11] indicate that a complexity of relationships exists between alcohol and emotion in human subjects. These studies are based on the assumption of a relationship of autonomic nervous system activity and emotion on the one hand, and a relationship between autonomic nervous system activity and the electrical conductance of some skin areas on the other hand. This electrical conductance may be precisely measured and offers an index of a person's emotional state.

In the Carpenter experiment, electrodes were fastened to the subjects' feet and skin conductance was measured under five different conditions. These conditions included (1) total sobriety; (2) two ounces of wine; (3) twelve ounces of wine; (4) two ounces of an alcohol solution; and (5) twelve ounces of an alcohol solution. Both the alcohol solution and the wine contained 12 per cent alcohol.

The drinks were consumed over a fixed period of time during which the subjects were kept busy, although not under pressure, by alphabetizing a set of filing cards. About thirty minutes after the subjects had finished drinking, an extremely loud, unpleasant and unexpected noise was sounded on an electric horn. Changes in skin conductance, that is, changes in emotional level, were measured.

In general it was observed that two ounces of wine affected skin conductance very little. With 12 ounces of wine, there was a marked drop. Stated in a different way, two ounces of wine hardly affected the emotional response to the sudden stress; after 12 ounces the emotional responses were markedly diminished. It may be observed from these data that rela-

11. J. A. Carpenter, "Effects of Alcoholic Beverages on Skin Conductance," *Quarterly Journal of Studies on Alcohol, 18* (1957), 1-18. Also J. A. Carpenter and L. A. Greenberg, "The Effect of Alcoholic Beverages on Skin Conductance and Emotional Tension. *I.* Wine, Whisky and Alcohol," *Quarterly Journal of Studies on Alcohol, 18* (1957), 190-204.

tively moderate amounts (12 ounces) of a beverage containing 12 per cent alcohol, less than the amounts which produce intoxication, do reduce emotional tensions. This was the first time a relationship between emotional tension and alcohol was demonstrated experimentally in human subjects.

The demonstration of a relationship between alcohol and fear reduction in animal subjects and between alcohol and emotional responsiveness in human subjects may be taken as a beginning. More study and experimentation are needed.

Speculations

There are several ideas that should be considered in thinking through the effects of alcohol on human behavior.

First, alcohol obviously affects different people differently and it may affect the same person quite differently at different times. Under some circumstances, taking a drink wards off and banishes mild feelings of depression and anger; under other circumstances, it may augment such feelings. We know virtually nothing about the effects of alcohol and the stable patterns of emotional behavior or the personality traits to which such effects are related.

Second, people carry to a drinking experience a set, an attitude toward alcohol, an expectation of how it will affect them. There is the individual who boasts of his capacity, of his "hollow leg," and there are also those who report they feel intoxicated at the smell of the cork. This set is a complex thing, based partly on past experience with alcohol but also based on motivation, class status, occupation, ethnic group and religious membership. How does expectation of effects influence the observable effects of alcohol?

Third, drinking for most people who drink is a social act. Whether one drinks with family, business associates, friends, the casual acquaintances at a cocktail party or people standing around a bar, drinking for most people means social drinking. To study the individual isolated under laboratory conditions and to generalize to the social situations in which drinking occurs raises problems. But these are not major obstacles to research. One may study the effects of alcohol on individuals in groups. Social psychology offers new techniques of investigation and the techniques of marketing motivation research, public opinion surveys and anthropological investigation could be used.

Fourth, it would seem that for many people alcohol serves as a social lubricant and that it facilitates much of American party life because it serves to diminish those inhibitions which keep some individuals reserved and cautious when meeting people. In a sense, such drinking is a form of regressive behavior. We are able to be a little freer in speech, less cautious, more friendly or, at other times, less friendly; in other words, we can behave a little more as we did when we were children, before the processes of socialization taught us to control and to mask feelings to a greater or lesser extent. It is an adaptive sort of regressive behavior when practiced within limits, because such return-to-more-childish-behavior is more or less acceptable under social drinking conditions in our society. Apparently many people need and seek such releases occasionally.

However one approaches the issues, more research is needed. The vistas of our ignorance about the psychological effects of alcohol are such that the investigator may profitably start almost anywhere in the field of alcohol studies.

3. ALCOHOL INTOXICATION AND OPIATE ADDICTION

Some people in all periods of history have sought intoxication by taking either alcohol or opiates. Drug addiction [1] has been less common in countries of the West than in the Orient because of limited supply, rigidly imposed legal controls, and social sanctions against nonmedical opiate use.

The popular belief that the physiological and psychological effects of alcohol and opiates can be fully equated has circulated widely. Temperance publications designed to discourage drinking have associated alcohol with drugs in the hope that the social stigma and fear attached to drug addiction would also become identified with the use of alcohol. Legislation requiring schools to provide instruction about alcohol frequently incorporates the phrase "alcohol and other narcotic drugs."

Alcohol is classified pharmacologically as an anesthetic. The predominant characteristic of an anesthetic is a progressive descending depression of the central nervous system. In varying dosages, alcohol may act as an analgesic, a soporific, an anesthetic, a narcotic, or a hypnotic. An Expert Committee of the World Health Organization has stated:

"Alcohol must be considered a drug whose pharmacological action is intermediate in kind and degree between addiction-producing and habit-forming drugs, so that compulsive craving and dependence can develop in those individuals whose make-up leads them to seek and find an escape in alcohol. With this substance the personal make-up is the determining factor but the pharmacological action plays a significant role. Damage to the individual may develop, but does so in only a minority of users. The social damage that arises extends, however, beyond these individuals themselves." [2]

There are significant similarities and differences in the gratification achieved by uncontrolled drinkers and opiate addicts. These differences, involving physiological action, psychological response, and motivation both in the "high" and the "withdrawal" stages are analyzed by Donald Gerard in the following pages.

1. There are an estimated 60,000 drug addicts in this country who have been in contact with law enforcement officers. The total number of addicts is probably somewhat higher. This figure compares with 4,500,000 alcoholics.

2. WHO, Technical Report Series No. 84, Expert Committee on Alcohol, *First Report* (March 1954), pp. 10–1.

26

INTOXICATION AND ADDICTION

by Donald L. Gerard *

Alcoholic beverages and opiate drugs have been used for millennia in many different cultures and societies. All have been used to facilitate or improve the quality of living for the individual or the group. Generally speaking, alcoholic beverages and opiate drugs were and are used because their effects are experienced as helpful and pleasurable. However, both alcoholic beverages and the opiates can be harmful to the individual. Of particular interest to the psychiatrist is the fact that alcoholic beverages and opiate drugs can be used in a compulsive fashion, motivated by goals and desires which are outside the user's awareness. The present paper will discuss some of the general features of the compulsive use of alcohol and opiate drugs from a psychiatric perspective.

The generalizations to be offered here will be focused upon the drinking and opiate using patterns of the "essential" type of alcoholic, as defined by Knight,[3] and opiate addicts; they are not intended to be applied to users of alcoholic beverages or of opiate drugs in general. Excluded also is the reactive excessive drinker who began to use alcoholic beverages in the context of an overtaxing adult situation, as well as the individuals whose alcohol problem is one facet of a neurotic or psychotic syndrome. Furthermore, these generalizations pertain to men, although they may also be applicable to women; the greater predominance of male alcoholics and opiate addicts as well as accidents of training and experience have brought the writer into contact with far more male than female alcoholics and opiate addicts.

Acute Intoxication

There is a general sequence of events which commonly occurs when a sober person begins to drink alcoholic beverages.[4] These events are expressions of the degree to which the person has lost control over his speech, emotional expression, and motor behavior. The rate at which this effect takes place is related to the quantity of alcohol ingested, to the rapidity of absorption, and to the body weight of the drinker. With the first few "social" drinks, the individual's judgment and inhibitions are affected. He talks and otherwise participates more freely in social interaction. In the

* From *Quarterly Journal of Studies on Alcohol*, 16 (1955), 681–9.

3. R. P. Knight, "The Dynamics and Treatment of Chronic Alcohol Addiction," *Bulletin of the Menninger Clinic, 1* (1937), 233–50.

4. Cf. *Alcohol, Science, and Society. Twenty-nine Lectures with Discussions as Given at the Yale Summer School of Alcohol Studies* (New Haven, Quarterly Journal of Studies on Alcohol, 1945), Lectures 3–5.

early stages of intoxication the individual's cultural expectations about the effects which alcoholic beverages should have on behavior or mood may lead to the expression of such effects long before sufficient alcohol is ingested and absorbed to "account" for these effects in neurophysiological terms. As intake continues and the blood alcohol level rises, motor coordination becomes progressively poorer. The drinker's insight into his level of coordination may also become poorer, so that he may endanger himself and others by driving a car, attempting feats of strength or skill, and so forth. As drinking continues, motor uncoordination is accentuated and social behavior deviates even more from the individual's usual social and personal roles and norms. Finally, with continued drinking, stumbling, slovenliness, loss of bladder control, anesthesia, stupor, and even coma ensue.

Acute intoxication with opiates is very different. In part, but not entirely, effects for the novice are different from those for the habituated user. The common sequence of events after administration of a dose of opiates is as follows:

First, there is a transitory nausea which may, particularly in the novice, be followed by effortless and emotionally nondistressing vomiting.

Second, there is a period of maximal appreciation of the subtle effects of the drug for the individual. Some of these are: (a) body sensations— for example, a feeling of impact in the stomach, bodily warmth, pins and needles, itching sensations of a rather pleasant and eroticized nature; (b) a feeling of lethargy, somnolence, relaxation, relief from tension or anxiety; (c) the experience of the "high." This experience, as reconstructed from the reports of addicts and some normal subjects, is a feeling of comfortable detachment from and lack of involvement in current experiences. The opiate user feels "out of this world," all his demands have been fulfilled, everything is taken care of. Perhaps the most instructive of a variety of phrases used by addicts to describe this experience is "being in the junky's paradise."

Third, following the period of maximal appreciation of the effects of the drug, there will be a gradual return to a "normal" state. The user returns to his normal activities but continues to maintain, although to a lessened degree, the comfort, detachment, and loss of tension which he had experienced most intensely in the first hour or two after taking the individually proper amount of drug.

In general, acute opiate intoxication is an achievement of an inward-turned, separated, detached condition in which "loss of control" plays no part. Some writers have hypothesized that opiate intoxication causes a damping down of all impulses from within. They have suggested that opiate intoxication does not free a person from his controls but rather makes control unnecessary by diminishing the impulses over which control ordinarily needs to be exercised.[5]

5. As I shall point out later, there is actually a paradoxical "loss of control" in

The alcoholic commonly recognizes that if he drinks too much, he will become unkempt, slovenly, stuporous, and so on. Despite this knowledge, most alcoholics drink to the point of drunkenness. Thus the expressed wish of the alcoholic is usually disparate with what he achieves. Indeed, this is one way of differentiating the alcoholic from the social drinker. The alcoholic states, for example, that he wants to become convivial, to enjoy the taste of the alcohol, to feel more relaxed in a difficult situation, to relieve himself of the tensions of a particular day, task, or experience. His expressed aim may be to socialize with his peers or with members of the opposite sex, or to have a quiet, relaxing drink by himself. He interprets his drinking as means to a specific end, often of a casual, insignificant nature. He states that he does not wish to become intoxicated. In Rado's terms,[6] he wishes to use alcohol in aid of the ego; however, because of the effects of alcohol on his inhibitory processes (repressions and weak sublimations), he becomes overwhelmed by his primitive regressive urges for an infantile, euphoric, oblivious state. Instead of using alcohol in aid of the ego he dissolves the ego along with the superego; he becomes drunk.

The picture of what the opiate user achieves in his acute intoxication corresponds closely to what he says he wants to get. The addict rarely desires and rarely achieves the unconsciousness or oblivion of the alcoholic in the late stages of intoxication. The opiate user's intoxication is of such a nature that he can be aroused at any time to participate in normal activities in a manner which would not distinguish him, except to the skilled observer, from a sober individual. Thus the opiate addict, while intoxicated, can work at his usual job, which may require average motor skill, without apparent disturbance. He may function more slowly than ordinarily, but his efficiency need not otherwise be impaired. An addict can cut hair, work a drill press, or do other motor tasks while intoxicated. According to some addicts, they have been able to carry out some of their daily tasks better while intoxicated with opiates than they can otherwise. This is not to suggest that the opiates generally improve motor performance. These addicts were individuals unable to function in their life tasks because of anxiousness, tension, ambivalence, or other disturbances. The fact that they are able to function better under the influence of opiates is consistent with recent studies which suggest that heroin or morphine, at least for individuals who have been addicts, effectively dissipates or quells profound anxieties.[7]

The alcoholic, on the contrary, is rarely able to carry out his usual work while intoxicated. Many studies have indicated that ingestion of

opiate addicts which differs in its timing, rather than in the type of behavior elicited, from the "loss of control" in alcoholism.

6. S. Rado, "The Psychical Effects of Intoxication," *Psychoanalytical Review, 18* (1931), 69–84.

7. C. Kornetsky, "Effects of Anxiety and Morphine on the Anticipation and Perception of Painful Radiant Thermal Stimuli," *Journal of Comparative Physiology and Psychology, 47* (1954), 130–2.

relatively small quantities of alcohol not only affects the rate at which tasks are done but also diminishes efficiency and accuracy. Thus, in contrast to the expressed aim and the common achievement at least of certain types of "better" function for the opiate addict, the alcoholic commonly experiences that his intoxication disrupts and disorganizes him in his work and in his social relationships.

Chronic Intoxication

Chronic intoxication with alcohol may be defined as a state in which an individual maintains an intake of alcohol sufficient to keep him in a condition of severely or progressively reduced control over motor behavior, coordination, and emotional expression. The semantic questions which a stricter definition might entail are here purposely avoided. We are dealing with individuals who, colloquially, can be said to be "drunk" for a prolonged period, and who describe themselves as having been on a binge. The binge, of course, can last days, weeks or even months. While it lasts, alcohol intake keeps up with and at times gets slightly ahead of the rate at which alcohol can be metabolized. The effects of chronic intoxication with alcohol must be considered in two aspects: there are the effects which would be observed in the controlled laboratory situation, and there are the effects which take place in the community.

The first and most evident effect of chronic intoxication is a persistent disturbance in motor coordination, i.e., a disorder of equilibrium and balance. Next, there is a progressive inability to care for body needs in a neat and socially acceptable manner. In the laboratory the individual can be protected from falls or from bumping into hard or sharp objects, and he will be kept clean by attendants or nurses. In the community, on the other hand, the individual will not be hindered from falling and is likely to suffer injury. His appearance may and frequently does become unkempt and slovenly. These first and second aspects of chronic intoxication are, of course, related. The inability to care for body needs is in part an expression of malcoordination as well as of "acting out," bravado, and regressive behavior.

Thirdly, there are the variable consequences of loss of normal inhibitions, leading to inappropriate and usually aggressive social behavior. In the laboratory, because of the limited number of social interactions along with protection by attendants, the individual is not likely to suffer much for his improper behavior. In the community, on the other hand, the alcoholic is often involved in fights which he loses or wins in accord with his subtle needs and the state of his motor coordination. He may have property stolen from him. He becomes involved in inappropriate social relations, including sexual approaches to individuals of his own and the opposite sex, which are provocative, impulsive, and generally regressive. In the community he must take the consequences of this behavior, i.e., he experiences the counterhostility of the partners to his interactions.

Fourthly, the maintenance of caloric needs through alcohol affects the total body economy. There is a striking difference between the situation in the laboratory and in the community. In the laboratory, the individual can be protected against the effects of vitamin deficiency, protein depletion, and dehydration. In the community, in the natural setting in which chronic intoxication with alcohol takes place, the individual commonly takes little or no food other than alcohol itself. Consequently, he does become dehydrated; he suffers progressive protein depletion and vitamin deficiency.

Fifthly, in the laboratory but especially in the community, the chronically intoxicated alcoholic becomes progressively more restless, tense, depressed, guilty, and anxious. In the laboratory, these moods, states of body activity or tension are at least not malignantly influenced by the benign, supportive, interpersonally neutral atmosphere. In the community, on the other hand, these moods and states of body tension are often accentuated by solitude in unfamiliar surroundings and by the hostile or retaliatory behavior of individuals willing to take advantage of his disturbed condition. Continuing to drink may take the edge off some of these feelings, but it will in no sense lead to any improvement of a genuine if even transitory nature.

The effects of interruption of chronic intoxication with alcohol in the community depend on the duration of the intoxication and on what has happened to the drinker while he was intoxicated. In general, the individual who remains chronically intoxicated until, through arrest, medical emergency, accident, or intervention of the family, he is brought to a hospital will often be found to suffer from a variety of symptoms. Tremors, restlessness, and anorexia are commonly observed, as are the accidental and variable symptoms which are a consequence not of his intoxication but of the events experienced while chronically intoxicated, such as head injuries, infection, pneumonia, loss of blood, dehydration, and so forth. A common sequel is a delirium tremens syndrome, with disorientation, hallucinations, and extreme tremulousness. Less common psychiatric conditions associated with chronic intoxication, or more accurately with a life in which chronic intoxication is a frequent event, are Korsakoff's syndrome and Wernicke's syndrome. In the laboratory, recent evidence suggests that withdrawal of alcohol from a subject who has been protected from dehydration, avitaminosis, and protein depletion can precipitate delirium tremens in which convulsions and hallucinations may occur.[8]

The term "chronic intoxication" can be applied only with some difficulty to the compulsive use of opiate drugs. The person who makes prolonged use of opiates is not intoxicated in the same way as the one who maintains

8. H. Isbell, H. F. Fraser, A. Wikler, A. J. Eisenman, R. E. Belleville, and T. L. Nash, "Experimental Chronic Alcoholic Intoxication" (motion picture), described in *Federation Proceedings, 13,* Pt. I (1954), 370. See also H. Isbell, H. F. Fraser, A. Wikler, M. A. Belleville, and A. J. Eisenman, "An Experimental Study of the Etiology of 'Rum Fits' and Delirium Tremens," *Quarterly Journal of Studies on Alcohol, 16* (1955), 1–33.

a chronically impairing intake of alcohol. The chronic regular user of opiates has a different set of drug-connected problems than has his alcoholic "cousin." In place of the overt (relatively) easily recognized disturbances in function which accompany prolonged heavy use of alcohol, the prolonged daily use of opiates produces subtle effects which are quite different.[9]

The first and one of the most important effects of chronic opiate use is the phenomenon of tolerance. Instead of, as is the case with alcohol, responding to the cumulative or increasing effects, the regular user of opiates becomes tolerant to an extraordinarily high level of dosage. The regular compulsive user of opiates can take single doses of morphine which would be fatal to the nonhabituated or to the nonuser. This tolerance is more evident in some body systems than in others.[10] The regular user of opiates acquires tolerance to the pupillary constriction, analgesic effect, and smooth muscle and sphincter contracting effects of morphine at different rates and degrees.

From the psychiatric standpoint the most important aspect of the regular nonmedical opiate user's tolerance lies in the area of the psychic effects. It is of interest that patients who use morphine for analgesia—for example, those patients with cancer—do not usually request progressively larger doses. But those who use opiates for subtle psychological effects on mood, ideation, and motor function, and particularly for getting "high," almost always need to increase their dosage in order to continue to get these effects. However, they reach a point at which they will level off, no longer increasing the dose but maintaining it at a fairly high level. Though I know of no laboratory evidence which directly supports the following interpretation, I believe this leveling off occurs because the user has "adapted out" entirely to the psychic effects of the drug. In Rado's term, they require a "free period" before they can again experience the psychic effects they desire.[11] There are a few regular users, interestingly, who do not develop tolerance. These are individuals who time their doses so that no cumulative effect occurs. Heroin users, for example, who take a dose at 24-hour or longer intervals, usually at the beginning or end of their work day, can continue for months or years without increasing the level of dosage, and are able to get the subtle psychic effects they find desirable indefinitely. The prevalence of this practice is not known. However, the relative rarity of this type of heroin use, i.e., without the development of tolerance, suggests the question, Why do most opiate users in our society become twice or more-frequent daily users, thus establishing tolerance and increased need, and finally "adapt out," so that they require a free period away from the

9. Although it is true that opiate users can look "drunk," e.g., become stuporous or malcoordinated, this is the exception rather than the rule, an event associated with an overdose rather than with an intended dose.

10. L. Goodman and A. Gilman, *The Pharmacological Basis of Therapeutics,* New York, Macmillan, 1941.

11. S. Rado, "Psychoanalysis of Pharmacothymia," *Psychoanalytical Quarterly,* 2 (1933), 1–23.

drug? This question leads to the second aspect of regular opiate use, craving, and its converse, dependence.

In the early stages of the frequent taking of an opiate drug for its effects on mood, ideation, and motor activity, the drug provides far more satisfaction than work, recreation, or relationships. The user craves acute opiate intoxication more frequently. This craving is like the craving for sweets, for alcohol, or for excitement and impulsive action. In satisfying this craving the individual progresses from sporadic to regular use, and from intervals sufficient to prevent cumulative doses and the acquisition of tolerance to a frequency which leads to cumulative doses and tolerance. He feels that he "needs" the drugs in order to live comfortably. This need does not differ psychologically from the "need" of the alcoholic. But a new element enters the picture with the opiate drugs which radically differentiates their compulsive use from the compulsive use of alcoholic beverages. While the opiate user is still taking relatively small doses of opiates on a daily or twice daily basis,[12] his body becomes dependent upon the drug to maintain relatively normal function. This is something quite apart from consciously experienced craving.[13]

Not only does the regular user require drugs to satisfy his craving, but if he attempts to cease using them, his dependent body releases highly distressing symptomatology. Some of these symptoms are sweating, lacrimation, muscular cramps, restlessness, insomnia, fever, diarrhea, vomiting, and gooseflesh. The intensity of this discomfort is related to the duration of regular use and to the level of tolerance which he has established. The longer he has been using drugs and the higher the level of tolerance, the greater the dependency and the more intense the withdrawal syndrome. The final feature in chronic regular use of opiates is the fact that the symptomatology of the withdrawal syndrome is alleviated by the opiate drug upon which the individual has become dependent, or by other related opiates.

In the phenomena of tolerance, craving, dependence, and an abstinence syndrome relieved by the drug (or an analogous drug) upon which the individual is dependent, we see one of the crucial differences between chronic alcohol intoxication and chronic opiate use. The addict is comfortable and functions well as long as he receives large enough quantities of drugs to stave off his abstinence syndrome.[14] The chronically intoxicated

12. In the case of morphine one dose daily is sufficient; in the case of heroin, two doses daily are required.

13. Parenthetically, decorticated dogs can become dependent on opiates (A. Wikler, *Opiate Addiction. Psychological and Neurophysiological Aspects in Relation to Clinical Problems,* Springfield, Ill., Thomas, 1953) even though there is no reason to believe that they are experiencing anything analogous to craving. Monkeys, interestingly, may experience something analogous to craving in humans (*Conferences on Drug Addiction among Adolescents,* New York, Blakiston, 1953).

14. The term "large enough" may be misleading. At retail pharmaceutical prices a dollar or two a day will be more than ample for his habitual daily dosage.

alcoholic, on the other hand, cannot function normally as long as he maintains his intoxicating intake of alcohol. In subjective terms, the chronically intoxicated alcoholic becomes tense, depressed, irritable, restless, guilty, and anxious while he is consuming large quantities of alcoholic beverages. He can drive off some of these symptoms by becoming stuporous or comatose, and he may perhaps delay the onset of delirium tremens, with its hallucinations, disorientations and tremors, by a maintenance dose of alcohol; but he cannot improve his general level of functioning until he is detoxified and the secondary aspects of his intoxication have been treated. The opiate addict, on the other hand, has the same subjective experiences but his tension, depression, restlessness, anxiousness, and guilt occur when he cannot get his drug. And he can improve his general functioning immediately upon incorporating a sufficient quantity of an opiate drug. Thus the chronic alcoholic can be said to suffer during intoxication, while the opiate addict suffers primarily during abstinence.[15]

15. For discussion by Doctor Gerard of personality and cultural factors in opiate addiction, see below, pp. 298–305.

Supplementary Readings for Part I

There is an extensive literature dealing with the physiology of alcohol. Many of the references suggested are general in treatment and readily available.

1. *Alcohol, Science and Society,* Twenty-Nine Lectures with Discussions as Given at the Yale Summer School of Alcohol Studies. New Haven, Quarterly Journal of Studies on Alcohol, 1945; 6th printing, with a new preface, 1954. Lectures 3–6, pp. 31–82. Lecture 7 is the "Effects of Small Amounts of Alcohol on Psychological Functions."
2. R. G. McCarthy and E. M. Douglass, *Alcohol and Social Responsibility.* New York, Thomas Y. Crowell Co. and Yale Plan Clinic, 1949. Chapter 6: "The Individual and Alcohol: Physiological Factors." Chapter 7: "The Individual and Alcohol: Psychological Factors."
3. H. W. Haggard and E. M. Jellinek, *Alcohol Explored.* New York, Doubleday, 1942.
4. E. M. Jellinek and R. H. McFarland, "Analysis of Psychological Experiments on the Effects of Alcohol," *Quarterly Journal of Studies on Alcohol, 1* (1940), 272–371.
5. E. Jacobsen, "The Metabolism of Ethyl Alcohol," *Pharmacological Reviews, 4* (1952), 109, is an analysis in technical language of current research data on the metabolism of alcohol.
6. Popular Pamphlets on Alcohol Problems. New Haven, Publications Division, Yale Center of Alcohol Studies. No. 3: *How Alcohol Affects the Body.* No. 4: *What the Body Does with Alcohol.*
7. *Drug Addiction among Adolescents.* New York, Blakiston, 1953.
8. *Law and Contemporary Problems,* Vol. 22, No. 1: *Narcotics.* School of Law, Duke University, 1957.
9. D. Maurer and V. Vogel, *Narcotics and Narcotic Addiction.* Springfield, Ill., Thomas, 1954.
10. World Health Organization, Technical Report Series, No. 21, Expert Committee on Drugs Liable to Produce Addiction, *Second Report,* March 1950.
11. World Health Organization, Technical Report Series, No. 57, Expert Committee on Drugs Liable to Produce Addiction, *Third Report,* March 1952.
12. World Health Organization, Technical Report Series, No. 84, Expert Committee on Alcohol, *First Report,* March 1954.
13. The *Quarterly Journal of Studies on Alcohol,* issued at 52 Hillhouse Avenue, New Haven, is the outstanding publication in the field of alcohol studies. Original reports of research on the physiological and psychological effects of alcohol appear frequently.

PART II

DRINKING PRACTICES, ANCIENT AND MODERN

PLATE I

Beer brewing in ancient Egypt. Painted limestone from Saqquara, ca. 2500 B.C. Archaeological Museum, Florence. Courtesy of the Soprintendenza Antichità, Firenze.

PLATE II

Grape harvesting and wine making in ancient Egypt. Wall painting from the tomb of Nakht, ca. 1500 B.C. Courtesy of the Metropolitan Museum of Art, New York.

INTRODUCTION

Although alcoholic beverages have been used in nearly every culture since ancient times, only recently have systematic attempts been made to evaluate the extent and effects of drinking on the individual and the community. The collection of taxes imposed upon brewers and tavern keepers has provided some indication of the amounts of beverage legally produced, but in most early civilizations this represented only a small proportion of the beers and wines actually manufactured and consumed.

In modern times, a few studies have been made in selected population groups which suggest who drinks what and why. For information regarding drinking practices in early cultures, the student must turn to the writings of the essayists, poets, playwrights, geographers, travelers, and philosophers. Some of the data are derived indirectly, for example from dramatic incidents arising in connection with the "symposia" or drinking parties of the Greeks, or with the limited wine ration allowed Spartan soldiers. More direct evidence is available in specific attempts to control drinking. Plato recommended that wine be prohibited to children under eighteen, to slaves, male and female, to magistrates in office, to pilots and judges, and to councilors on duty. He further urged that drinking parties be regulated and that a drinking captain or supervisor be appointed for each affair.

Socrates, Aristotle, Plato, Cicero, and others inveighed against intoxication as debasing the dignity of man. The Spartans and Carthaginians limited drinking among soldiers on active duty for reasons of efficiency. The Ethiopians, who were water drinkers, boasted of their long life and vigor in contrast to the shorter life span of their wine-using neighbors, the Persians.

The barbarian Gauls invading Roman territories reacted violently when they discovered the effects of wine. This was noticed by Roman leaders and by the Greeks, who avoided giving battle until the invaders were stuporous from drinking, then slaughtered them easily. But it should be noted that although Egyptian civilization attained a remarkably high level, both men and women gorged themselves with wine to the point of deep intoxication. The Spanish and Portuguese people, on the other hand, appear to have been remarkably abstemious.

Various attempts at regulatory controls of drinking appear in the ancient literature. In China during the Chou Dynasty (1134–256 B.C.) and the reign of the fourth emperor of the Yuan Dynasty, about 1312 A.D., laws against the manufacture, sale, and consumption of wine were established and repealed no less than forty-one times. Penalties for violation of the decrees were extremely severe.

Because the people of India made a fermented drink called *tari* from the sap of a palm tree, the government at one time ordered the trees to be cut down in an effort to reduce drunkenness. Restrictions on planting vineyards in Gaul were imposed by the Romans. Governmental controls aimed at eliminating a source of raw materials have been usually short-lived and ineffective, in both ancient and modern times.

No attempt has been made in Part II to cover completely the role of wine and other alcoholic beverages in early and modern cultures.[1] Materials have been reproduced which provide a broad perspective on the drinking customs of various peoples at different times, together with varying attitudes toward drunkenness. The attitudes are sometimes explicit, sometimes only implicit in a chance remark or deduction from evidence of lack of control, from the social status of the drinkers, or from the circumstances in which drinking is carried on.

Very roughly, the material starts with the Athenians and proceeds to the Greek culture of Southern Greece and Italy and the settlements of the eastern shores of the Aegean Sea. Customs and attitudes toward drinking of the Romans and of the non-Grecian peoples of the areas around the entire Mediterranean and the Near East are reviewed. Brief investigations of ancient and modern India, China, and Japan are reported, as are four studies of the peoples of Central and South America.

The change in attitudes and practices toward alcoholic beverages in Russia from the 10th to the 19th century is examined, along with a report derived from newspaper accounts of contemporary drinking practices in the Soviet state. There will be found a detailed account of existing social and economic problems of alcohol in France as seen by the physician Gabriel Mouchot, who, although a teetotaler by choice, is not a propagandist for prohibition. A descriptive analysis of drinking practices in present-day England as reported by social scientists is included. The final paper presents findings of a study of alcoholism and alcohol consumption in the provinces of Canada contrasted with rates in the United States and several European countries.

Although the papers are arranged roughly in a chronological time sequence, they may be read separately by students seeking data concerning a particular period or nation. These materials are presented as the observations of various researchers. The reader will draw his own conclusions regarding the effectiveness of different attempts to

1. For a recent comprehensive analysis of the ritualistic symbolism of wine in classical antiquity, see Erwin R. Goodenough, *Jewish Symbols in the Greco-Roman Period* (New York, Bollingen Foundation, 1956), Vols. 5 and 6.

achieve regulation of intoxication by authoritarian fiat or social controls. The significance of drinking as a social act will be considered in greater detail in Part III.

Students who wish to learn the original sources on which the following scholarly articles are based should consult the footnotes of the first publication of these articles. Limitations of space have made it necessary to omit most of the notes here.

4. OUR DRINKING HERITAGE

by Andrew Poznanski *

The word "alcohol" is derived from the Arabic *al kohl,* originally designating a fine powder of antimony used for staining the eyes. When we call our liquor "eyewash" we little realize how closely this expression corresponds with the etymology of the word.

Alcoholic beverages have been known to almost all people from before the dawn of history. The discovery of late Stone Age beer jugs has established the fact that some use of fermented beverages existed in the Neolithic period. Records of ancient civilizations refer to the use of alcoholic beverages. The origin of these "necessities" of existence was ascribed to the gods. The Egyptians attributed to Osiris the cultivation of the vine, the manufacture of the wine, as well as the manufacture of a type of beer from grain. In fact, barley beer and not wine is probably the oldest drink in the world. To the Greeks and Romans the giving of it was one of the beneficent acts of Bacchus. Hebrew tradition ascribed to Noah both viniculture and the discovery of how to manufacture wine. Noah is also related as having indulged too freely in this beverage.

The ancients had a large number of wines. It seems unlikely, however, that these would appeal to our modern palates. The Greeks added seawater to their wines. They also added resin (which apparently is still used in modern Greece), pitch, myrrh, aloes, poppies, wormwood (as in the modern vermouth), chalk, and many other substances. Moreover, the wine was exposed for some years in the fumarium to the smoke and warmth of a fire, and in many cases became so inspissated as to be quite thick when poured out.

Alcoholic beverages were produced from grains such as barley and wheat; the northern countries, where the grape was not available, produced mead from the honey of wild bees. In other areas various sap plants such as the toddy palm were used. The Tartars used the sugar of milk, fermenting it to form koumiss. Even primitive people like the Tasmanian aborigines have devised a method of making fermented liquor. They tap a species of gum and let the sap accumulate in a hole in the ground, where it undergoes natural fermentation.

*   *   *

Medicinal Uses

Numerous medical writers, including Galen, used wines in medicine and gave recipes for their production. Arnold of Villanova (1235–1311),

* From "Our Drinking Heritage," *McGill Medical Journal* (1956), 35–41.

physician, surgeon, botanist, alchemist, and philosopher, is perhaps the first to have written a book about wines. In his *Treatise on Wine* he discusses how the various wines should be prepared, and discusses their medicinal attributes. Wormwood wine, for instance, appears as a general panacea. He claims it is good for the intestines and for intestinal worms; it has power to strengthen; it is good for the stomach, the spleen, and the liver; it relieves jaundice, purifies vision, and is useful when someone loses his wit. It drives out the urine, purges the "woman's ailment," resists poisonings. If vapor of the wine is let into the ear, it helps deafness; when a wound is washed with it, no fistula or bad flesh grows in it; it cures scabious skin; if it is drunk before a sea voyage, it prevents nausea and vomiting. It prevents poisoned air from harming the patient; it induces sleep. It cures pains and swellings; if it is poured into the throat in gargling it is good for tumor of the tongue. This writer also states, "No physician blames healthy people for the use of wine, unless he censures them for the quantity or for mixing it with water. If wine is taken in the right measure, it suits every age, every time, and every region. It is good for the old and for young children."

Distilled spirits are a relatively late development. The Arabian physician Rhazes is credited with the discovery of distillation in the 10th century. Inebriety existed long before brandy was invented, but distillation gave to wide circles a convenient and concentrated source of inebriety. The first distilled liquors were used not as beverages but as medicine; only later when they became plentiful and cheaper did they begin to be used widely as beverages.

The European alchemists believed that in distilled liquors they had discovered the long sought antidote to senility; consequently they called it aqua vitae, the water of life, which is also the meaning of the Gaelic *usquebaugh* (Webster: usquebaugh, from Gaelic *uisge beatha*) from which the word whisky is derived. These liquors began to be regarded as cures for almost all ailments of the human body.

Thus brandy, or *spiritus vini vitis,* and whisky, or *spiritus frumenti,* became an important part of the pharmacopoeia. It is only recently that their use in medicine has decreased. This has occurred mainly because of careful scientific work on the pharmacological action of alcohol.

Much interesting work was done on this subject in the 19th century, and quaint theories persisted even then. Robert McNish, a member of the College of Physicians and Surgeons of Glasgow, in 1835 in a book *Anatomy of Drunkenness,* discussed the peculiar phenomenon of spontaneous combustion of drunkards, a condition which, he claims, is well documented and in which the whole body, starting with the viscera, is burned in a few hours by a combustive process which for some reason does not even singe the surrounding furniture. The same writer also suggested the use of opium in the cure of drunkenness, dismissing the risk of addiction as the lesser of two evils.

5. THE CLASSICAL WORLD

Grecian civilization represents one of the highest cultural levels of ancient times. Grecian architecture, sculpture, and philosophy have been the wonder of every succeeding generation. The concern of Greek scholars with the nature of man and his relations with his fellows and to the gods reveals insights important to modern man.

Many classical scholars attribute to the Athenians a degree of moderation in wine as well as in the pursuit of life's goodness. According to McKinlay, Gudeman assumed that Southern people generally were temperate; [1] Seymour speaks of the temperate Greeks; [2] and Robinson, emphatic in his praise of Greek temperance, holds that the studious avoidance of both luxury and excess was the most marked feature of Athenian life. [3]

McKinlay disagrees with these and other classical scholars in their belief that the Greeks were temperate. He considers men to be temperate when they do not drink enough to interfere with affairs personal or public, and he establishes from critical analysis of classical literature that, with the exception of the Spartans, the Greeks were not a temperate people.

ATTIC TEMPERANCE

by Arthur P. McKinlay *

* * *

In the attempt to appraise Attic judgments pertinent to this study, one may first assemble evidence bearing on Attic temperance in general. Data that seem to question whether the Greeks were significantly temperate are plentiful. There is Theopompus' comparison of the Athenians to the loose-living Chares (35 B.C.), for they "lived his kind of life, consorting with loose women and engaging in drinking bouts in their youth." There is the judgment expressed by Plutarch and his many authorities when they blame Pericles (fl. 469) for making the people wanton instead of temperate.

* From *Quarterly Journal of Studies on Alcohol, 12* (1951), 61–102.

1. In a note on Tacitus, *Germania* 22, in his *Tacitus, Agricola, and Germania,* Boston, Allyn and Bacon, 1899.

2. T. D. Seymour in a note on *Iliad* 1:225. *Homer's Iliad,* Books 1–3, Boston, Ginn, 1887.

3. C. E. Robinson, *A History of Greece* (New York, Crowell, 1929), p. 366.

There is more than suggestion in Critias' (d. 403) description of an Attic drinking party. He says: "They have bowls and toasts, too. Then after their drinking they loose their tongues to tell scandalous stories and they weaken their bodies; upon their eyes a dark mist settles; memory melts away into oblivion; reason is lost completely." Surely this is a description of no isolated phenomenon, especially when interpreted along with the two passages in which Critias compares the Athenians with the Spartans, much to the discredit of the former. Critias seems to have based his prophecy on personal observation when he said that Anacreon would be popular as long as lads served wine and dealt bumpers around. The pertinency of this passage, of course, depends on whether one can toss off bumpers of wine and still be labeled "temperate." When Plato categorizes revelers into drunk and sober, he shows that there was enough loose drinking at Athens to furnish a category in an argument.

Wine drinking must have been the occasion of much at Athens that would afford observers food for thought. We note one such observer in Plutarch who had never been sorry for having drunk water instead of wine. His testimony that he had been sorry for the opposite shows that there was at least one Greek who sometimes drank too much. Thence came Socrates' (b. 469) advice to beware of habit-inducing drinks, to refrain from drinks that tempt one to drink even when one is not thirsty, and to feel that one should not expect to find good friends in men addicted to the wine cup. There is Plutarch's suggestion that Cimon (fl. 466) might have become a first-rate general if it had not been for his drunken ways. One may well note Polemon's (fl. 315) advice to drink with an eye on the morrow. That Themistocles (fl. 480) should replace carousals with fasting as a preparation for a public career is here a case in point. That Zeno the Stoic's (fl. 330) hale old age should be ascribed to his abstemiousness necessitates the visualization of many who failed to live so long and so well by reason of drinking too much. The Aristotelian Economist's (ca. 300) remark on the tendency of wine to make even freemen insolent may have had a basis in the experience of Athens. In fact, the writer may in this passage be following Xenophon (b. 434) or Aristotle (b. 384), for the first book of the treatise from which this citation is derived largely goes back to these economists. The story that Alexander did not see much in a play of Antiphanes (b. 408) ilustrates what went on in Attic drinking circles. The playwright suggested to his critic that, to appreciate the play, one must have engaged in many a bout over loose women. It would seem that there were enough folk of that sort in Athens in the 4th century B.C. to warrant Antiphanes in thinking he would have an appreciative audience. Theophrastus (fl. ca. 320), Chamaeleon and Aristotle (b. 384), too, evidently had seen enough heavy drinking among the Athenians to give occasion for their essays on drunkenness.

That the Greeks had a word for the headache that follows a debauch certainly is significant of what must have frequently happened in Athenian drinking circles. It is also significant that "to drink wine" may mean "get drunk," and a "drunken uproar" meant "misbehave at the wine." The same may be said of the case made out for heavy drinking. Hard drinking, according to Plato (b. 428), reveals the goodness of the good man and the rascality of the wicked; it teaches moderation by experience with excess and by purging the soul may make it more sure of itself and more modest. One may judge the attitude of Athenians toward wine drinking from their reaction to the advisability of replacing some portion of their wine ration with water. Of such, Athenaeus says: "But if any of us find this irksome . . ." (Gulick's translation).

*   *   *

When Aristotle cites Nestor and Phoenix for their vigorous old age and attributes this to the fact that they had not had too much to do with drinking, wenching, and eating in their youth, he gives by way of contrast a pretty good idea of what was going on among the young men of his day. That older Athenians, too, drank intemperately is evidenced by Diogenes' complaint that people injured their health feasting at the very sacrifices they performed to insure their health. One may possibly judge the attitude of Attic society in the main toward self-restraint in the use of wine when Xenophon (b. 434) makes Simonides say to Hiero: "I notice that many respected men deliberately restrict themselves in the matter of meat and drink." It would seem from this passage that there were men who, observing the possibilities latent in wine drinking, acted accordingly; Xenophon in his citation of such persons singled them out from the crowd in general. Plato's (b. 428) use of "as now" in his assumption that it was a common thing for "unsober" (Shorey's translation) drinkers to quarrel over their wine must be explained away by those who would put the Athenians in the category of the temperate. The same thing must be said of Aristotle's (b. 384) assumption that when children have grown up they will be drinking deeply (Rackham's translation of the *Symposium*). That the same author should note the tendency of wine drinkers to fall on their faces when drunk, and beer drinkers on their backs, would indicate a considerable manifestation of such phenomena. The way drinkers carried on at drinking parties makes Mnesimachus (375 B.C.) think of them as being minded to excess.

*   *   *

The attitude of Athenians toward the regulation of drinking practices is a commentary on Attic temperance. Such attempts included a provision for selling wine diluted; [4] another provision that dinners by the magistrates

4. There are numerous references to the wine being watered. This apparently has influenced some writers to accept the concept of temperate drinking. Natural

be held at the Prytaneum, where things might go on decently; the appointment of wine inspectors to supervise the drinking at these dinners; and elaborate sets of rules for drinking parties. It throws some light on the attitude of drinkers toward being regulated to learn that the wine inspectors were held in low esteem. The unpopularity of these officials is indicative of conditions at Athens, for man is likely to rebel at interference with his wishes. The provisions for watering the wine seem to have irked drinkers. Thus Achaeus playfully makes Satyrs indignant at the thought of watery wine. Antiphanes plans for a stronger mixture. Diphilus (ca. 300) says, "Make it stronger; everything watery is an evil to the soul." Pherecrates (fl. 438) even makes a character rate a mixture of two parts water to four of wine as fit only for frogs.

Though one may not infer too much from the fact that the Athenians needed drinking rules, which included fines for starting rows and insulting guests, there may be some significance in the fact that members persisted in their offenses, that masters of the feast sometimes overlooked such recalcitrance, and that drinkers even rebelled at the good offices of the wine god. Accordingly, though the seeming need for drinking regulations at Athens may not warrant deductions as to their efficacy, yet their reception by Attic drinkers would seem to have fallen short of the ideal.

Plato's stress on the regulation of drinking parties makes the student shake his head at the notion that the Athenians were significantly temperate. Plato (b. 428) bases his proposals for the regulation of drinking parties on the fact that banquets regularly became drunken bouts. He qualifies his willingness to allow drinking parties only if rightly regulated. Among the provisions that he had in mind was to put someone in charge of the feast. The lawgiver specifies that this "master of the feast" should be a "sober" man. Now, if Athenian drinkers were in the main sober enough to warrant such "characterisms" as "in the eyes of the temperate Greeks," why should Plato have had to worry about drinking captains that could stay sober? Again, Plato would not allow young men under forty to attend symposia, thus corroborating Mantitheus' picture of what was going on in the younger circles of the day. Plato would punish any drinker who refused to obey the

fermented wines rarely attain an alcohol content of 15–16 per cent. When watered, the concentration would be considerably reduced. Greek wines were strong and the amounts consumed at a session were tremendous; for example, Alexander tossed off a six-quart measure and then undertook to repeat the feat. In such quantities even diluted wine could produce intoxication. Seneca discourses on drunkenness in *Epistolae morales* 83 to the effect, "What glory is there in carrying much liquor? When you have won the prize, and the other banqueters, sprawling asleep or vomiting, have declined your challenge to still other toasts; when you are the last survivor of the revels; when you have vanquished every one by your magnificent show of prowess and there is no man who has proved himself of so great capacity as you,—you are vanquished by the cask." The evidence is strong that the practice of watering the drinks was extremely unpopular.

captain more severely than for an infraction of military rules. The implication of such a drastic provision hardly consoles one who would believe in the constitutional bent of the Athenians for temperance. In fact, Plato avows himself ready to become a thoroughgoing prohibitionist "unless the state shall make an orderly use of the institution (of drinking bouts), taking it seriously and practicing it with a view to temperance. But," he continues, "if on the other hand, this institution is regarded in the way of sport and if anyone whatsoever is allowed to drink whenever he likes and with anyone he likes and that, too, in conjunction with all sorts of other practices, then I would vote against allowing such a state or individual ever to drink at all, going further than the Cretans and Spartans and even beyond the Carthaginian law which prescribes water only as the drink for soldiers on the march."

A summing up of Plato's demand for liquor regulation may be seen in the speaker of the Platonic Corpus who praises Minos' liquor laws, which made the Cretans and their followers, the Spartans, blessed throughout the ages. Along with Plato's contemplation of prohibition and censorship in giving a line on the drinking conditions of his time is his final statement on the problem, his wish that no city will need many vineyards and that the citizens will devote less time to the cultivation of the vine than to any other of their occupations. In addition to laws for drinking parties, Plato proposes restrictions for society in general, complete prohibition for children under eighteen, for slaves, male and female, in the city, for magistrates in office, and for pilots, judges, and councilors on duty. Plato discourages the drinking of wine in the daytime, and by parents at the time of procreation. He forbids the guardians to get drunk. Some of the possibilities for intemperance latent in Attic life appear when Plato would censor the Poet's praise of drunkenness, saying: "Is it fit or conducive to temperance for a young man to hear such words?"

*   *   *

In the attempt to find an answer to the question of the place of wine in Athenian life, one should note that Athenian social affairs were called symposia, "drinkings together." This stress in choice of name on drinking rather than on eating or fellowship is indicative of the part drinking played in Greek consciousness. That drinking counted heavily with the Greeks is corroborated by Athenaeus, who says that the Greeks (including Athenians, no doubt) went to a feast to drink even more than to eat, be merry, dance, or engage in a love affair. Confirmation of this point of view appears in Plutarch (b. A.D. 80), who in referring to a banquet speaks of the company's being at their wine, not at their food; or again in Lucian (b. ca. A.D. 125), who makes his bereaved father lament that his dead son will no more get drunk with his fellows, saying nothing about eating.

As to eating at Athenian dinners, in contrast to drinking, the authorities have little to say. Though very elaborate menus of Macedonian and Thracian feasts have come down, the cuisine of an Athenian banquet seems to have been of so little moment that Plato and Xenophon say nothing about what their diners had to eat. To get a social slant on Athenian dinners, one may go to Cicero, who contrasts the Greek and Roman points of view by noting the etymological difference between symposium and convivium. Just how much weight will be given to the literal meaning of the Greek word will depend on how one accepts the testimony of the preceding pages in judging Athenian temperance.

The tendency of ancient writers to play up the abstemiousness of Sparta seems to set off by contrast the state of affairs elsewhere. A word about the situation in Sparta will help to clarify the discussion. According to Gulick, the Spartans were pre-eminent for frugality. They were extremely moderate in the use of wine. Lycurgus allowed wine drinking only for the relief of thirst. The Spartans, alone of the Greeks, had no drinking parties. Drunkenness was practically unknown and in social disfavor. A drunken reveler might come in for a beating. The ration of wine may have been a pint a day, or possibly about a pint and a half if one is to judge from Lycurgus' provision that each Spartan should furnish eight choes (46 pints) of wine each month to the general mess.

*   *   *

In writing of conditions at Sparta, the ancients leave the reader to infer that they were different from those prevailing in their home town. Thus Xenophon, praising the Spartan mess system, asks what opportunity did such a practice give a man to ruin himself or his estate by gluttony or wine-bibbing? The same author says of Spartan dinners that they afforded little room for drunken uproar. Plutarch notes that the Spartan bridegroom went in to his bride not drunk but sober. Xenophon remarks on Lycurgus' doing away with compulsory drinking, characterizing the custom as ruinous to body and mind. The same writer infers that Spartan diners had to be careful about drinking enough to interfere with their going home. The same certainty of contrast lurking in all these items comes out in a story as laconic as it is Spartan. Someone asked Leotychides why the Spartans drank so little wine. He replied: "That we may consult about others rather than that others should consult about us." There is Plutarch, who contrasts Spartan diners at the common mess with others who ruin their characters and their bodies by giving themselves over to every desire and all sorts of surfeiting. Again, the Athenian Critias, when he said that it was not the custom of the Spartans to practice the drinking of toasts at banquets, nor pledge loving cups to one another, compels the inference that such was the practice at Athens and that Critias praises the one at the expense of the other. The same writer says of the Spartans that they set aside no day to intoxicate the body with immoderate potations.

The Platonic tradition confirms these other authorities in setting off the moderation of the Spartans in comparison with what seems by a necessary inference to have been a significantly less degree of temperance elsewhere. There is the speaker in the Minos who lauds Sparta for her drinking laws and congratulates her upon having been made happy by them. Plato himself points the contrast between Sparta and his own land. Drinking conditions in Athens were so bad that he would devise a stringent set of drinking regulations. But the Athenian point of view on this matter was so hopeless that Plato, singling out Sparta and Crete as places that had worked out a satisfactory solution of the drinking problem, still was willing to pass them up as models and to contemplate the possibility of total prohibition. In view of this very considerable body of material that stresses the moderation of the Spartans as something unusual, it seems strange to find the Athenians linked with them as pre-eminently frugal.

Physicians, too, leave the impression that there was much hard drinking, at least from the 5th century on. The Hippocratean tradition knew of enough wine being drunk in excess to make everybody familiar with the baneful effect of such excess. Enough heavy drinking was going on to account for the prescription of an emetic in such cases. From the Corpus we may infer that wine had had a part in cases of epidemic fever.

*   *   *

This review of what the ancient Athenians thought about their drinking practices suggests a sort of hierarchy in the realm of ancient temperance. First came the Spartans, who were confessedly temperate on their daily ration of a pint; second, the Athenians, who are linked with the Spartans by Gulick but considered by the Athenians themselves as having solved the drinking problem far less satisfactorily than did their Peloponnesian rivals; third, the other Greeks in general, who, though excluded from Gulick's category of the "pre-eminently frugal," still are called temperate by him, by Seymour and by other scholars; and last, the Barbarians, who rated men for their manliness by their ability to drink the most. There will be, no doubt, little objection to putting the Spartans at the top of the list. But when it comes to the experiences of Byzantium, Thessaly, Mytilene, Miletus, Boeotia, Megara, Tarentum, Syracuse, Chalcedon, Methymna, Erythrae, Cardia, Naxos, and Samos, as well as Teos and Sybaris, to cite at random from the Greek states where intemperate drinking went on, one may not be so sure that the Greeks generally did not allow drinking to interfere with business. An unbiased interpretation of the data of this study in the light of ancient deliverances on the subject, may well lead one to wonder where modern scholars got their notion that the Athenians were decidedly temperate.

A glance over the résumé of what Greek writers have thought about the "temperance" of the Athenians will produce various reactions. There will be a disposition in some quarters to discount the authorities adduced; to dismiss Isocrates as a crabbed schoolteacher, Xenophon as spoiled by his admiration for the ascetic Spartans, Plato as a theorist, Aristotle as a pedant, and Critias as an aristocrat trying to discredit the democracy. Elsewhere there will be a feeling that where there is much smoke, there must be some fire . . .

NON-ATTIC GREEK STATES

by Arthur P. McKinlay *

* * *

Menander, in his *Flute Girl,* says that Byzantium makes all the traders tipsy. A speaker in the play tells how he drank there all night long and got up with a head on him big enough for four. This is the Byzantium where, during a siege, the soldiers grew weary of manning the walls and kept leaving their posts. They had a resourceful captain who ordered booths for wine sellers to be set up on the wall; whereupon the desertions ceased. Aelian tells how the Byzantines financed their drink bill. They did so by renting out their houses and wives to foreigners while they themselves put up at the taverns.[5]

* * *

Macedonian drinkers served ancient writers right well in their search for spectacular tales. There is Archelaus, who succeeded in usurping the throne of Macedon by getting his rivals drunk, inveigling them into a carriage at night, taking them for a ride, and murdering them. Philip, father of Alexander the Great, was a notorious toper, reputed to have gotten drunk daily. Philip would often sally forth into battle drunk. He had a fondness for vulgar companions in drink and would elevate them to positions of power. Admirers of ready wit have this tippling of Philip to thank for one of the most brilliant retorts of ancient times. The king, in a state of intoxication, condemned a woman unjustly. She cried out: "I appeal." Astonished, he said: "To whom?" She replied: "To Philip, but to Philip sober." Startled out of his drunken state by this reply, he came to his senses,

---

* From "Ancient Experience with Intoxicating Drinks: Non-Attic Greek States," *Quarterly Journal of Studies on Alcohol, 10* (1949), 289–93.
    5. According to McKinlay, an inscription circa 5 B.C. is to be seen near the stadium at Delphi which forbids the carrying of wine into the stadium or thereabouts on pain of 5 drachmas fine. A present-day visitor to the football stadium of Southern Methodist University in Dallas will observe a similar sign bearing a prohibition against carrying alcoholic beverages of any variety into the grounds. A comparable regulation is in effect at Harvard University Stadium.—Ed.

and going into the case more carefully, rendered a fairer decision. Another story of Philip's drinking came down. The king and the tippling son of Dionysius the Elder were drinking. Philip asked his companion how his father, in the pressure of his duties, could find time for writing poetry. The young man replied (in effect): "Father devotes to such pursuits the time you and I put in drinking." On the occasion of his taking unto himself a new wife, Philip even tried to kill his own son Alexander, whom the father of the bride had grossly insulted. But Philip was so drunk that he tripped and fell; whereupon Alexander maliciously said: "Behold! He who is making ready to cross over into Asia is upset in crossing from couch to couch."

Alexander did not take this narrow escape of his enough to heart to prevent him from becoming the most talked about drinker of ancient times. There have been, it is true, various attempts to clear Alexander of the charge of drunkenness. Justin admits some drinking, but holds that it was really poison that took him off and that the drinking stories were spread by the perpetrators of the deed so as to deflect suspicion from themselves.

In early years Alexander seems to have been on his guard against drunkenness. According to Plutarch, pleasures of the body had little hold on him when young; he would sit long and talk rather than drink; he had the most complete mastery over his appetite. He was encouraged in this attitude, no doubt, by such advice as that of Androcydes, who said to him: "O King, when you are about to drink wine, remember that it is the blood of the earth you will be drinking." Pliny the Elder, after quoting this item, goes on to say that if Alexander had only obeyed his adviser, he would not have had to answer for slaying his friends in a drunken fit. However, drink got the upper hand of the fine young man. After a spree he would sleep for two days and nights together. At a dinner in Thessaly he drank twenty separate toasts and replied to them. He then went off to sleep. Polyclitus of Larissa says that Alexander used to drink until daylight.

Later, Alexander's heavy drinking made him quarrelsome and, to quote Justin, he "often left a banquet, stained with the blood of his companions." In particular, he killed his bosom friend Clitus in such a quarrel. Arrian pities him for this mishap. In time, life with Alexander became one unending revel culminating in his death from a long debauch. Ephippus' account of this circumstance runs as follows: Alexander, challenging Proteas, drank a six quart draught. The latter matched the feat and shortly afterward, tossing off six quarts more, challenged the king to do the same. Alexander accepted the dare but failed in the midst of the attempt; he sank back on the cushion and let the cup drop from his hands. As a result he fell ill and died. Aside from the mere fact of their rehearsal, such implied criticisms of wine drinking on the part of Alexander are reinforced by direct denunciations. Alexander's namesake, Severus, is reckoned among such critics. Of Alexander, Quintus Curtius Rufus says: "Whom Persian arms had not taken, his vices conquered; to wit, unseasonable carousals and the insane allurements of drinking and staying up all night long." Curtius thinks that these lusts of Alexander's younger days might have quieted down with the advent of old age.

EARLY ROMAN SOBRIETY

by Arthur P. McKinlay *

Early Rome is here taken to include the period of the kings and the republic down to the time that the educative power of the Comedies and associations with more sophisticated people began to have effect.

Early Rome is to be placed among the nations of simple living, if one may take the ancients themselves as authority. The evidence for a relatively abstemious way of living among the early Romans largely derives from a tradition widely prevalent in later times that Bacchic ways at Rome had sadly degenerated with the centuries. There is Tiberius who contrasts what went on at dinner parties of his day with times when frugality prevailed. Plutarch points the laxity of later times with the discipline of earlier days. Dio and Polybius, Seneca and Pliny, by stressing the corrupt ways of later days, compel the inference that in earlier times the Romans were significantly less corrupt. Sallust even more virulently compares the new with the old, to the great disparagement of the former. Diodorus vouches for the simplicity of earlier times in comparison with the extravagance of succeeding ages. In early times heavy drinking in Rome was under the social ban. In fact, the cultivation of the vine came in at a comparatively late date. If anyone engaged in drinking bouts, he was called crassator (thick-headed). An exception to the prevailing practice of abstemiousness was so rare as to occasion comment. Horace's half-pint of wine included in a simple diet is probably indicative of the wine portion of early days. The one-eighth pint of wine rationed among the Romans beset on the Capitoline Hill by the Gauls ca. 390 B.C., though a siege ration, when compared with the allowance of grain, one-half pint, probably indicates a scanty though regular use of wine at least among soldiers in early days. Children, young men under the age of thirty, and servants were forbidden to drink at all.

The authorities gave few instances of heavy drinking in these early times. Among these is the drinking party that wound up with the Lucretia Episode. Then there is the story that Romulus once when dining out drank little because he had business on hand for the next day. One would infer from this citation of restraint that there were others who drank more.

* From *Classical Bulletin, 24* (1948), 52.

At least a companion is reported to have said: "Romulus, if everybody did as you do, wine would be cheaper." "Nay, rather," he replied, "it would be dearer if each one drank as much as he wished; I have, in fact, drunk as much as I wish." This tale may be a bit apocryphal; the investigator, however, will be on firmer ground historically when he comes to Papirius Cursor and the stories of his heavy drinking. Papirius' apostasy from ancestral decorum seems to have made quite a sensation. Or at least there came under the eyes of Dio Cassius the report that Papirius' countrymen remonstrated with him for his bibulous practices. Besides, Livy notes a tradition in regard to this Papirius that, owing either to his robustness of body or to much practice, he could digest large quantities of food and wine. Aside from these instances and the carousing on feast days there is little historical evidence of heavy drinking at Rome until the time of Scipio the younger, 165 B.C. Pacuvius' going through a mock funeral daily after dinner with the attendant wake is hardly an exception, since the poet was of Greek extraction from Southern Italy.

*   *   *

In this appraisal of drinking conditions in early Rome one must note, however, that on feast days there was a noticeable relaxation of social ways. At the festival of Hercules wine would flow copiously. Statius speaks of a tipsy December at the Saturnalia. At this festival the slaves reveled. On the Parilia drunken farmers sang a chant to Bacchus. Tibullus speaks of tipsiness as quite in good form at another country festival. The feast of Anna Perenna was much in vogue with the commonalty that matched the number of cups they drank with the years they hoped to live.

By way of conclusion, it would seem that in its vigorous control of wine drinking early Rome lines up with Sparta. Ammianus Marcellinus says that the sumptuary laws of the Romans were brought in from the edicts of Lycurgus, and that for a long time they were strictly observed, and that, having fallen into abeyance, they were re-established by Sulla. The brevity of this paper is a sort of mute witness of the situation in early Rome. The paucity of Bacchic data for almost six hundred years assembled in so few pages may be indicative of the place of the wine god and his wares during those centuries.

ROMAN SOBRIETY IN THE LATER REPUBLIC

by Arthur P. McKinlay *

According to the authorities wine drinking in the later Republic shows a marked change from earlier times and for the worse. Plutarch and Dio-

* From *Classical Bulletin*, 25 (1949), 27–8.

dorus note how the old Roman discipline gave way to a laxity of morals. Of this change Dio says that the Roman conquerors of Asia, corrupted by the provincials, took to luxurious living. This deterioration spread to the city (Rome) as well. As evidence of this falling away from the ancient ways Mommsen cites a passage from Macrobius describing how jurymen of 161 B.C. acted. Coming to the place of judgment drunk, they put in their time shaking dice with crowds of harlots looking on. Late in the afternoon they send a messenger to bring back word of what is going on in the assembly. Then, afraid of being served with a summons, they follow. On their way *nulla est in angiporto amphora quam non inpleant quippe qui vesicam plenam vini habeant.* Arriving, they bid the accused speak and call for witnesses. A juryman leaves. When he comes back, he claims to have heard everything. Then he looks over the records, but can hardly see for the wine he has drunk. The jurymen retire. One of them says: "What have I to do with these tiresome folk? Why don't we have a drink and follow it with a fat thrush and a good fish?"

At least one young spendthrift drank up a goodly estate. A Roman consul, a brother of the impeccable Flaminius, disgraced his country and his family by killing a suppliant to please a favorite. Even by the time of Cato, the vineyard, if it yielded well in either quality or quantity, was the most important activity of the farm. A little earlier yet, the women scandalized the puritan Romans by their Bacchanalian revels. These ceremonies came into Italy from the East after the First Punic War along with the influx of other sophisticated ideas, being first imported into Etruria by a Greek of lowly origin. After they were established there, they spread to Rome. "The pleasures of wine and feasting were added to allure a greater number of proselytes. When wine, lascivious discourse, night, and the intercourse of the sexes had extinguished every sentiment of modesty, then debaucheries of every kind began to be practiced since every person found at hand that sort of enjoyment to which he was disposed by the passions predominant in his nature. About the middle of the Second Century B.C. one of the Catos is even found married to a woman who was fond of wine. A little later the Younger Scipio was having to choose between the old way and the new. Polybius goes at length into the decadence of the Romans after their contact with Greek degeneracy. He uses such expressions as: "vicious tendencies, tendency to extravagance, infected by Greek laxity." He points his diatribe with the Younger Scipio, who set before himself the opposite way of life and became a marked man for his temperance. That by this time high society was going in for late carousals is indicated by the story concerning the father of the Gracchi. Tiberius, it seems, was so known for his puritanical ways that during his censorship, when he was returning home after supper, the citizens put out their lights for fear they would be thought to be holding a drinking party. Some idea of conditions at Rome at this time may be had from Plutarch's contrasting others with the temperate and austere Gaius. At this time a Roman general felt the need of banning the sale of wine in camp. An ex-consul, famous for his military exploits, fell to drinking with a band of retainers and made an unseemly spectacle of himself. A dictator shamed his patrician lineage by drinking in the company of lewd stage folk. Gabinius, however, preserved his country's tradition for abstemiousness by being the only person at Mithridates' drinking contest in 81 B.C. that didn't take part. That a drinking bout was a regular part of a feast in at least one Italic town around 100 B.C. is clear from the clause, "While the drinking bout was at its height," found in Appian's account of Vidacilius' suicide.

Romans began to forget their ancient discipline. In the First Punic War a Roman general laid the blame for a military reverse upon his soldiers being drunk. In the Jugurthine War they roamed over the countryside and sold their loot for wine. In the same war some Roman officers were caught off their guard at a feast and massacred. Roman society of the decades following Sulla called forth the bitter gibes of Sallust at its degeneration in contrast with the self-restraint of earlier times. He charges the Romans with being given up to their bellies and delighting more in harlots and banquets than in the military pursuits of their ancestors. He notes that the Roman military, contrary to the custom of the ancestors, had become devoted to love and drink, a change brought in by Sulla in the early part of the first century B.C. In Spain at Castulo some Roman soldiers under Sertorius took to drinking and would have fallen an easy prey to the natives if it had not been for their resourceful commander. A Roman official, the notorious Verres, started one of the most villainous episodes in the history of imperialism at a dinner described by Cicero with such phrases as "drinking in the Greek fashion," "calling for larger cups," "when things warmed up." Even Caesar's men drank so much at the looting of Gomphi that they might easily have fallen before a watchful enemy. A prefect of the city after drinking at a banquet fell into a drunken slumber in the Senate and had to be carried home. A custodian of the city (Rome) would drink most of the night and sleep until noon. During the age of Cicero or of the authorities he uses, drunkenness must have been a familiar phenomenon or he would not have repeatedly linked the hallucinations of inebriety with those of dreams and insanity.

From this time on things moved fast. Diodorus notices a marked swing away from the discipline of earlier days, documenting along with other extravagances the price of seventeen dollars for a jar of wine. Tavern keepers had become numerous enough to be cited with other lowly classes. The Catilinarian conspirators were inopportunely drinking and wenching. Even a winebibber became corrector of public morals. A woman was acting as *magistra bibendi* and was proving recreant to her duty by being more drunk than the tipsy grape. The authorities brand Sulla as soiling himself with wine, lust and living the life of stage players. They record the

sot Cimber as saying of himself: "I cannot carry my liquor." They parade
the bibulous Antony along with their temperate heroes. They represent
him as impersonating Bacchus, and ordering himself to be proclaimed as
Dionysus throughout the cities. They recount a prank of Antony's at
Athens, where he set up a booth in plain sight of the theater and furnished
it in Dionysiac style. There he and his suite drank all day while Italian
artists staged shows and Greeks looked on. He got drunk at a wedding
feast and next day smeared the public tribunal with his vomit. He and his
drunken followers looted Pompey's wine cellars in an orgy of drinking.
Cicero accuses Antony of hanging around a tavern and drinking. According
to Dio, Antony allowed his passion for Cleopatra and for getting drunk
to interfere completely with affairs of state. At the close of his career,
Antony, driven to desperation, gave himself a mortal wound, and possibly
to hasten the end, called for a drink, drank it, and soon breathed his last.
During this time lived the younger Cicero, whose main ambition was to
outdo Antony in drinking and whose chief claim to fame was that he could
drink down twelve pints of wine, one after the other. Once young Cicero,
when drinking, so far lost control over himself that he threw a wine cup at
Agrippa.

All brands of wine became fashionable. Gladiatorial combats were being
staged at which Romans, when glutted with food and drink, were ap-
plauding the contestants when they got their throats cut. Lucullus, a bon
vivant of Rome, who as a boy saw Greek wine, served it to the people in
large quantities. Caesar served several brands of wine to the populace
both at his triumph and at his grand banquet in 46 B.C. The young men of
good families were being introduced to the night life of Athens. Some of
the men proscribed by Antony and Octavius were surprised and slain at
banquets. One, Salvius, gave a sort of farewell dinner. Soldiers broke in
on the drinking, and cut off the head of the host. It was at one of a series
of banquets that Octavius and Antony might have been cut off if Sextus
Pompey's captain had had nerve enough to act upon his own initiative and
cut out his master's galley when Sextus' turn came to entertain. The laxity
shown by these items is confirmed by the proposal of Cicero to deny women
the privilege of taking part in nocturnal feasts; "for," as he says, "the clear
light of day should guard the reputation of women."

It is noticeable that in the records of early Rome there is no considerable
roster of men cited for their temperance or intemperance. The Later
Republic shows a marked change in this respect. The authorities note the
abstemiousness of many prominent men, such as Cato the Elder, Scipio
the Younger, Tiberius Gracchus the Elder, Tiberius and Gaius Gracchus,
Marius, Pompey, Sertorius, Crassus, Cassius, and Julius Caesar in contrast
to the general run of things. The plenitude of items in this period in contrast with the poverty of such data in the first six hundred years (almost)
of Rome reinforces the charges of Roman degeneracy made by Plutarch,

Diodorus, Dio Cassius, Sallust, and Polybius. Aristotle, Cicero, Mommsen, and others seem vindicated in their belief in the conditioning power of comedies, unless we are to hold that business interests of today are mainly actuated by their love of art when they spend hundreds of millions of dollars depicting the efficacy of their wares in helping the user to take his place in society.

THE ROMAN ATTITUDE TOWARD WOMEN'S DRINKING

by Arthur P. McKinlay *

In these latter days when women crowd the cocktail parlors so that returned soldiers have to take a back seat, the long-range thinker is inclined to wonder how things went on in ancient times, to ask: how was it with wine and women in Ancient Rome?

Beginning with early Rome, one notes there a stringent prohibition of women's drinking. Plutarch says that women were not to touch wine at all. Athenaeus says that no freeborn woman at Rome was allowed to drink wine. Pliny corroborates this statement; so also do Polybius, Isidore, Valerius Maximus, Cicero, and Aelian.

The reason given for this prohibition is that drinking leads to sex irregularities. Valerius Maximus says in accounting for the practice, "lest thereby they slip into some disgrace." Isidore justifies the prohibition because wine is an incentive to lust. A law of Romulus, noted by Dionysius of Halicarnassus, provides the death penalty for women who drink as well as for those caught in adultery. Note that these two penalties are found in one and the same sentence. Dionysius explains this association of crimes by the fact that wine leads to debauchery. Cato notes the same collocation of penalties.

These regulations against women's drinking at Rome were stringently executed. There is a note from Polybius on this point worth quoting entire: "It is almost impossible for them [women] to drink wine without being found out. For the woman does not have charge of the wine; moreover, she is bound to kiss all of her male relatives and those of her husband down to her second cousins every day on seeing them for the first time; and as she cannot tell which of them she will meet, she has to be on her guard. For if she has but tasted wine there is no occasion for any formal accusation." A passage from Pliny corroborates this statement from Polybius.

Severe penalties inflicted on women for violation of the prohibition law are found in the records. One Egnatius Mecenius beat his wife to death with a stick because she had drunk from the wine vat. He was absolved by

* From *Classical Bulletin*, 22 (1945), 14–5.

Romulus. Valerius Maximus says: "He (the husband) was freed by the consent of all." Fabius Pictor tells of a Roman lady who was caught opening the purse in which the keys of the wine cellar were kept. The family met to consider her case. They affirmed the death penalty and starved her to death. Lactantius tells of Fatua (Fauna), the wife of the mythical king of early Italy, Faunus. She was ordinarily quite impeccable in her ways; but once she fell from grace, drank up a whole jar of wine, and got disgracefully drunk, contrary to ancient customs and royal decorum. Her husband, Faunus, beat her to death with myrtle switches. After she was gone, he missed her greatly, and by way of atonement decreed divine honors for her.

There is evidence that throughout Italy these stringent restrictions on women's drinking prevailed. Athenaeus tells a story confirming this statement. One day in his travels Heracles got thirsty and stopped at a house by the wayside near Croton. He asked for a drink. The master went to get some wine; the wife had secretly broached the cask herself and in fear of detection remonstrated at opening it for a mere stranger and suggested water instead. Though Heracles heard what she said, he saved her from being found out by turning the cask, wine and all, to stone. In gratitude, women of that region took this for a sign and drank no wine. Even as late as Cicero this prohibition of women's drinking seems still to have remained on the books. Even in the time of Augustus women seem to have been under restrictions against drinking. Horace's *Neobule* complains that she may not drown her lovelonging in wine, and Ovid's *Hero* feels that she could while the time away waiting for Leander better if only she were not denied the use of wine. But with the ameliorating course of time the death penalty seems to have fallen into abeyance, for instance, being replaced by loss of dowry in the case of one lady that drank more than what was requisite for her health and that drank without the knowledge of her husband. About the middle of the second century B.C. a man of good family had a wife noted for her love of wine.

In later Rome, when the plain-living Romans had been inoculated with the sophistication of older societies, Roman women would be as free as their brothers. The poet Propertius visualizes one of these new women in his *Cynthia,* who on one occasion finds her lover carousing with some boon companions and frail beauties, and breaking in upon them, proceeds to break up the party. Again, Propertius is drinking with his sweetheart when she falls into a mad rage, pushes away the table with angry hands, and throws goblets of wine at him. Seneca writes of women going to the extreme in imitating men's drinking practices. Ausonius pays his respects to Meroe, a drunken hag, and says that she got her name, not from the Egyptian Meroe, but from her drinking of undiluted wine (*merum*).

Even highborn ladies in Rome stooped to reveling and thereby gained immortality. A daughter of Augustus reveled and caroused in scandalous fashion and went into exile with the added penalty of having to give up the use of wine. Many other women were also brought before Augustus on the charge of reveling. When Claudius' queen Messalina was staging her mock marriage with her lover Silius, she accompanied the ceremony with Bacchanalian revels. The mother of Nero was glutted with strong drink at the time of her shipwreck.

Other authorities pay their respects to tippling old ladies. The Roman writer Ovid, in his *Fasti,* pictures an old woman reveling like a Bacchant. Someone asks why one of her age should carouse so. Ovid replies: "Hers is the bibulous time of life that loves the bounty of the vine." In his *Amores* Ovid describes one such dame called Dipsas (Thirst). He catches her coaching his lady-love to be a gold-digger (silver-puller, as Plautus in his *Menaechmi* puts it). He felt like tearing out the old hag's wine-shot eyes but let her off with a curse of "everlasting thirst."

Nurses in ancient times, like Sairey Gamp, liked to tipple. In the prologue to the *Poenulus* of Plautus, the speaker tells nurses to stay at home lest they become thirsty. In the *Truchlentus* provisions made for the comfort of the nurse include a leathern bottle of old wine that she may "tipple day and night." Servingmaids, too, in the *Pseudolus,* are scolded for drinking. In the *Mother-in-Law* of Terence a speaker warns a nurse to see to it that she feeds her ward after she has filled herself up on food and drink. Ovid's *Hero* pictures an old nurse as helping to pass the time away pending the arrival of Leander. Finally the lamp sputters, a good omen. The nurse, to confirm the omen, drops wine on the wick and then—takes a pull at the bottle herself. A speaker in Terrence's *Lady of Andros* berates a prospective midwife for being a drunken hag.

The Christian writers from St. Paul to the later Fathers have left evidence that women of the Empire drank enough to cause the church authorities much worry. Thus Paul urges old women not to be enslaved with too much wine that they may train the young women to be sober. Pope Clement warns of the deadly association of wine and women; he criticizes women for reveling in luxurious riot, gulping down wine so as to make a show of themselves, and hiccuping ostentatiously like men; he advises boys and girls to keep away from wine as an arouser of the passions. The author of the *Constitution of the Holy Apostles* urges widows to be sober. Tertullian speaks of winebibbing being common among women. Arnobius insinuates that pagan women did not refrain from winebibbing. St. Basil pictures tipsy girls performing a wanton dance in a church.

Chrysostom would have a husband not be too hard upon a drunken wife. The same writer knows of women given to the vice of drunkenness and of handsome women disfigured by being drunk. According to Jerome girls of good family could be found at questionable resorts. Augustine writes of a maid that got into the habit of tippling. Chrysostom addresses women thus: "How many free women are such (addicted to drink)?" evidently expecting the answer, "Many." Again, he says to women: "Hear this, ye that pass your time in drunken revels."

There will be critics who will characterize the data just adduced from the Christian Fathers as exaggerations. In reply one may say that Christian readers knew their pagan associates and would laugh their leaders to scorn if their charges were much overdrawn. Modern scholars accept such characterizations in the main. Thus Dr. Broadhus says of Chrysostom that he consistently saw what was going on about him, and Dr. Browne takes Chrysostom as good authority for what went on in his times.

This brief survey of wine and women in ancient Rome seems to indicate that women are much like men. If it is the fashion to be abstemious, women will be quite simple livers; when social ways loosen up and go in for alcoholic titillation, the women will follow suit.

6. NON-CLASSICAL PEOPLES

by Arthur P. McKinlay *

Beginning with Gaul in the search for data bearing on these topics, it will be noted first of all that this country was not always the land of champagne. Evidence of this statement is found in Caesar's mention of the special bravery of the Belgae, which he ascribed to their being uncorrupted by foreign luxuries. Later, when accounting for the warlike qualities of the Nervii, a Belgian tribe, who were to give him a great scare, Caesar specifically cited wine as among these luxuries and stated that its importation was under the ban. Even as late as the first century B.C. the poorer sort of Gauls drank a beer (*corma*) made from wheat and honey. A century earlier Rome entered into a compact with Marseilles designed to head off the planting of vineyards in Gaul and thereby to protect the wine trade of Italy. This embargo, though probably more honored in the breach than in the observance, was not lifted till the time of Probus (A.D. 280).

How the Gauls, in early days no producers of wine, were initiated into the delights of Bacchus is told graphically by the authorities. The prime agent in this initiation was one Aruns, an Etruscan of Clusium. His wife, it seems, had been debauched by a young ward of his, an Etruscan too powerful to be held to account. With a deep-laid scheme of revenge Aruns went off to Gaul and, ostensibly to earn his living, began to import wine. Greatly taken with the novel commodity, the Gauls wanted to know what land produced such delicious fruit. Upon learning that Italy was the place, forthwith they started, with their belongings, women and all—in great numbers—and guided by Aruns over the Alps, they laid siege to Clusium. This invasion of the Gauls wrecked the Etruscans as a power, avenged Aruns, and eventually led to the capture of Rome in 390 B.C. by the Gauls.

Pliny the Elder gives a variant of this story. He says that it was Helico, a Swiss, who inoculated the Gauls with the idea of going to Italy. Helico had gone down to Rome to work. Upon his return he took back samples of figs, grapes, and wine. When the word got around, there was a rush for the place that produced such delights. These stories corroborate the statement that the vine came late into France; and the prohibitory acts of the Belgae and Nervii show that by 57 B.C. northeastern Gaul was still a vinous desert.

Belgian legislators seem to have had some sound basis of experience for their ban on wine. The Gauls never could carry their liquor. Ammianus Marcellinus, the great historian of the later empire, states that the Gauls

* From "Ancient Experience with Intoxicating Drinks: Non-Classical Peoples," *Quarterly Journal of Studies on Alcohol, 9* (1948), 388–414.

were fond of wine and other liquors, and that many of the humbler sort went crazy from much drinking and ran about aimlessly in all directions. Polybius, writing about 150 B.C. charges the Gauls with such brutal drunkenness that after a victory they would fall to fighting and destroy themselves and their loot. Appian corroborates his predecessors. He pictures the Gauls as being intemperate by nature, flabby in flesh, and simple in diet. Then, as opportunity offered for eating and drinking to excess, they became heavy and corpulent, short of breath, and easily exhausted by running. The Celts found wealthy men to indulge them in their desires. Thus, Ariamnes feasted his people for a whole year on food and desires. According to Diodorus, the inhabitants of Gaul used a beer (*zythos*) made of barley and drank the washings of honey, probably mead. Being exceedingly disposed toward wine, they bought imported wine; and drinking it greedily and getting drunk, fell to sleep or became mad. They were so eager for wine that they would trade off a boy for a jar of it.

The very Gauls who took Rome were no exception to the rule, for after the capture of the city they spent the ensuing night in debauch and drunkenness. Thereupon Camillus rallied the townsmen and dispatched the besiegers, "heavy with wine and sleep." Thirteen years after the evacuation of Rome, an enormous horde of Gauls again moved upon the city. They did nothing while in camp except drink and revel all day and all night. They, too, like their kinsmen of the previous episode, fell a prey to Camillus.

Wandering still farther afield, in 278 B.C., a numberless army of Gauls overran the Balkans and threatened Delphi. At their approach the Oracle forbade the farmers to carry off their wine while retiring before the invaders. This order puzzled the folk until the Gauls, running true to form, got drunk and attacked the temple. The priests, as related by Justin, a late Latin epitomizer, staged some kind of theophany in which a handsome young man, dressed up like Apollo, seems to have taken a part. The befuddled brains of the attackers were deceived by the trick. A panic ensued, resulting in the destruction of the Gauls and the saving of the temple. Their leader, Brennus, severely wounded as he was, committed suicide by drinking heavily of neat wine. About the middle of the 3d century B.C. some Celts, operating with the Carthaginians in Sicily, got drunk and fell a prey to the Romans. In view of these experiences the liquor legislation of the Belgae was very much to the point, and the Gauls might well have adopted the resolution cited in a fragment of Cicero's *Pro fonteio* to the effect that they would drink their wine less strong than formerly "because there seems to be some poison in it."

Beyond Gaul to the north lay Ultima Thule, variously identified as Iceland, Mainland, and Norway. Its people had for a beverage a drink made from grain and honey. Such a beer was in use in Spain and Portugal, and in Liguria. Although beer as a beverage is noted occasionally in ancient annals, its use was hardly *en règle* socially. Ammianus Marcellinus says that it was a drink used by the poor people, and that sport was made of Valens, the emperor, because he drank beer (*sabaia*). At about the same time, the Emperor Julian wrote an epigram on beer: "I know Bacchus the god of wine, for he smells of nectar; but all I know of the god of beer is that he smells of the billy goat." Had Julian read widely enough he would not have been at a loss for a patron of beer, for he could have found out from Diodorus that Osiris, in the lands where the vine did not grow, taught the people to make beer. Julian need not have depended on the bouquet of his drinks in order to distinguish between them, for Aristotle hands down the information that a man will go to sleep lying on his face if he is drunk on wine; but he will lie on his back if he has had beer (*krithinon*) to drink.

Taken as a whole, however, these Westerners had a reputation for being abstemious. Thus among all the Spaniards a strict abstinence prevailed. The same restraint is noted in the case of the Iberians, who were water drinkers in spite of their great wealth. The Lusitanians, an Iberian tribe, drank mostly water. The inhabitants of the Balearic Islands were abstainers also; not from choice, however, but because they had no wine. The early inhabitants of Italy were rated among the temperate. The Ligurians in northwestern Italy had but little wine, having instead a drink (*krithinon poma*) made of barley. The early Lucanians of southern Italy brought their children up on milk and water for drink. Posidonius (50 B.C.) extends this custom to the early inhabitants of Italy as a whole.

The temperance of these early Westerners, accordingly, seems fairly well attested; yet there is evidence to the contrary. Thus Plato knows nothing of the water drinking of the Iberians and classes them with the intemperate Thracians. The Balearic Islanders deserved little credit for their self-control; for, having no wine, they desired it all the more. The Tyrrhenians had been vigorous enough to establish themselves among the militant settlers of northern Italy, but by spending their lives in drinking and unmanly ease lost their ancestral glory.

To the south beyond the Mediterranean Sea lies Africa; its peoples supply some data for this study. Most of the Africans, like the Westerners, were reputed to be temperate. There were the Numidians who were said by Appian to be the most robust of all the African races and to be the longest-lived of all those long-lived nations. The reasons assigned for this superiority were climate, simple food, and a very sparing use of wine. No less abstemious were the Moors, who lived a severe life without any bread, wine, or, in the words of Procopius, any other good thing. Neighbors of these tribes were the Carthaginians. Unlike the Moors and the Numidians, they were great drinkers, though not entirely wedded to their cups, for they had a law that denied wine absolutely to soldiers on the march.

The ancient geographers show some interest in the drinking practices of scattered tribes. Among these were the Sardoi Libyans, who had no utensils except drinking cups and swords. Beyond the desert of Sahara, according to Mela, was a race of men whose lips were grown together except for a passage under the nose. Through this, by means of straws, they were wont to drink.

East of Sahara was Ethiopia, where a king, though greatly taken with a present of wine from some Persian envoys, is represented by Herodotus as poking fun at the Persians for their diet of bread and wine and consequent short life; whereas the Ethiopians, with a regimen of meat, fish, and milk, lived six score of years and beyond. Over on the Red Sea were the Fish-Eaters, who drank nothing at all. In northern Arabia lived the Saracens. Like the Ethiopians, they ate meat and drank milk for the most part. Ammianus Marcellinus says that he had seen many Saracens who were entirely unacquainted with the use of wine.

Many of the peoples already mentioned have furnished but scanty data for this study; but from Egypt there have come down more items on which to base conclusions. Lutz has already collected the significant material bearing on drinking in ancient Egypt. Although he devoted most of his efforts to the technique of the subject, yet he did not neglect the social side of the liquor question. He has treated the topic far more adequately than the scope of the present study permits, dealing, as it does, largely with the monuments of Greece and Rome. Lutz found that the Egyptians had developed no general feeling against excessive drinking.

He noted that drunkenness was common among women, at social affairs, and throughout life in general. Women got disgracefully drunk in old Egypt. On a Theban wall-painting a woman is represented as becoming so drunk at a party that she vomits on the floor. In another view of the same painting a slave is holding a dish for the relief of her nauseated mistress. In an elaborate scene from the tomb of Paheri servants urge women to drink, saying: "Drink to drunkenness! Drink! Do not spoil the entertainment." One lady needs no urging but calls to the porter: "Give me eighteen cups of wine; don't you see I want to get drunk! My insides are as dry as straw." Egyptian women did not overlook the chance to cajole men in their cups. Lutz describes a monument on which girls are represented as embracing a drunken man and putting a wreath around his neck. Feminine aptitude for drinking is symbolized in the story of Hathor, the wine goddess whose temple was known as the place of drunkenness. This is one of the early "flood" tales. Men had become so wicked that the god Re determined to punish them for their wickedness. Taking out his eye, he sent it under the form of Hathor with instructions to punish the people. She executed her orders so vindictively and killed so many of the folk that for several nights she waded in human blood. Fearing that mankind would be utterly exterminated, Re flooded the earth with blood-red beer. The goddess took to drinking of the beer and returned home in an intoxicated condition, having overlooked some of the intended victims. Therefore Hathor came to be called the "mistress of drunkenness."

Egyptian men at their parties were no more abstemious than their consorts. Lutz shows a representation of three slaves carrying their drunken master on their heads; and again of two slaves supporting a man by his head and feet. At these social gatherings, drinking songs were in vogue. If one may judge from the specimens that have come down, they give more warrant for the artistic power of the Bacchic emotion than do their so-called counterparts in Greece and Rome. The monuments contain a satire on a minstrel who lost his art from overmuch drinking.

The inhabitants of Egypt need not have been heavy drinkers. Wine among them was less of a necessity than it was in Greece; for the water of the Nile, being cool and sweet, needed no flavoring to make it palatable in comparison with the hard waters of the North. Yet they drank enough wine to earn them the epithet "lovers of wine." Much of their drinking took place at social and religious functions. To encourage drinking at rich men's banquets after dinner it was the custom for a man to carry around the image of a corpse in a coffin. Showing it, he would say to each guest: "Drink and make merry; but look on this; for such thou shalt be when thou art dead." Herodotus, who is responsible for this story, also tells of a pilgrimage to Bubastis. This was one long carouse, ending with a great feast at which more wine was drunk than in all the rest of the year. Besides wine, the Egyptians had a beer made of barley.

There is plenty of evidence that the Egyptians did not restrict their drinking to social gatherings. There was carousing among students, if one may rely on a letter written by a teacher to his pupil.

> I am told that thou forsakest books
> (and) dost abandon thyself to pleasure.
> Thou dost wander from tavern to tavern.
> Every evening, the smell of beer,
> the smell of beer frightens men away (from thee).
> It corrupts thy soul,
> (and) thou art like a broken oar.
> O, that thou wouldst comprehend that wine is an abomination
> and that thou wouldst abjure the pomegranate-drink;
> that thou wouldst not set thy heart on fig-wine,
> and that thou wouldst forget the carob-wine.

On the contrary, a fond mother encouraged her schoolboy son in drinking by taking to him two jars of beer daily.

Among other classes of the population that drank alcoholic beverages were the soldiers, who were given as a daily ration enough wine to make them drunk. The priests were not overlooked either, receiving and—presumably—drinking 722,763 jars of wine and jugs of beer during the thirty-one years of the reign of Rameses III.

*   *   *

Of the early Mesopotamian peoples, Lutz says: "The frequent mention of wine and beer in the Sumero-Akkadian documents makes it quite certain that the quantities of intoxicating liquors consumed by the ancient Babylonians and Assyrians were enormous." Lutz's discussion of the liquor problem in these lands is not less satisfactory than was his corresponding treatment of Egypt. The Gilgamesh epic tells how Enkidu became initiated in the ways of polite living. He had not been taught to drink beer but his feminine mentor says to him: "Eat food, O Enkidu, the provender of life! Drink beer, the custom of the land." So "Enkidu ate food until he was satisfied. Beer he drank, seven goblets. His spirit was loosened, he became hilarious. His heart became glad and his face shone."

Even more is known of the Semites. Prominent among these were the Chaldeans whose chief city was Babylon. Here as early as 2225 B.C. man's experience with liquor drinking was registered in the laws of the land. Khammurabi's code has several provisions relative to the selling of liquor. In one it was forbidden to take silver in pay for wine. Corn was the medium of exchange. It was also forbidden to cut prices. For a merchant who violated any of these provisions, there was a penalty phrased as follows: "One shall give her a ducking." Again, "If a wine merchant has collected a riotous assembly in *her* place and has not seized those rioters and driven them to the palace, that wine merchant shall be put to death." "If a nun, not living in a convent, shall open a wine shop or has entered a wine shop for drink, that woman [in the phraseology of C. H. W. Johns' translation], one shall burn her." "If a wine merchant has given sixty measures of best beer at harvest time for thirst, she shall take fifty measures of corn." It is interesting to note that in every case the dealer is a woman.

The same Babylon was the city of Belshazzar and his famous story. The tale, as given in the Book of Daniel, is corroborated with variations by Herodotus, who has Cyrus catch the Babylonians unawares making merry at a festival.

West of these Mesopotamian cities the peoples took to drinking wine and beer in very early days. In northern Syria lived the Hittites, who as early as the 13th century B.C. sipped beer through reeds. The attitude of the Hittites toward wine drinking may be judged from a very handsome adoration of a wine god found on the rock sculpture at Ibriz.

To the south lived the Arabs of the desert, whose wine poetry throws considerable light on the question whether the Bacchic emotion may be held to be an inspirer of significant poetry. The writer finds less evidence in the poetry of Horace, for example, for the affirmative of this proposition than has been ordinarily supposed; but as in the case of Egyptian poetry, so also in pre-Islamic literature there is verse that Bacchus might claim as his without trespassing on the preserves of Venus and other accredited sponsors of the poetic afflatus. This judgment seems warranted from the selections presented by Lutz, e.g., "The wine-skin is a kingdom to him who possesses it, and the kingdom therein, though small, how great it is!" Lutz is in error, however, when he says that our sources for forming an idea of the use of wine among the pre-Islamic Arabs are exclusively old Arabic poems; for Strabo has left an item about the Nabataeans, an Arab tribe, to the effect that their kings held many drinking bouts in magnificent style; no one, however, might drink more than eleven cupfuls. Diodorus, however, makes the Nabataeans water drinkers, noting that they drank honey mixed with water, and cites one of them as trying to dissuade Demetrius from invading their land by saying that it had no wine. A band of marauders from northern Arabia once got caught carousing and was all but exterminated by David.

*　　*　　*

Not only has the Bible contributed much, but the philosopher Philo and the historian Josephus have added their lore. All remember Noah and his lapse from decorum, the feast of Belshazzar with the handwriting on the wall; the parable of the rich fool with his more and bigger barns; the golden calf the people set up for themselves; the drugging of Lot by his daughters; Jacob's finding Leah on his hands; the law allowing capital punishment for gluttonous and drunken sons who persist in their rebelliousness; . . . the parable of the drunken steward; the drunkards of Ephraim who got trodden under foot; and the mother who cautioned King Lemuel not to drink wine lest he forgot the law and render perverse decisions. Wine figures in all these reminiscences. In addition, there are old friends noted for their abstinence: Samson, Hannah, Samuel, Daniel, and John the Baptist, the Nazarites, and the Rechabites.

Jewish experience with wine crystallized itself into the memorable sayings of the moralists: the famous recitative beginning, "Wine is a mocker, strong drink is raging, and whosoever is deceived thereby, is not wise." The fearsome warning of the Teacher, "Who hath woe? Who hath sorrow? They that tarry long at the wine; they that go to seek mixed wine. Look not thou upon the wine when it is red, when it giveth his color in the cup, when it moveth itself aright. At the last it biteth like a serpent and stingeth like an adder." The warnings of Isaiah, "Woe unto them that rise up early in the morning, that they may follow strong drink, that continue until night, till wine inflame them"; the same prophet's excoriation of the priest and the prophet who had stumbled and erred through strong drink. And the curse of Habakkuk on him "that giveth his neighbour drink."

Amid all this warning on the dangers of drink, there is now and then encouragement for the use of wine: the turning of the water into wine at Cana, and St. Paul's advice to Timothy to drink water no longer but to use a little wine for his stomach's sake. The Hebrew poets, too, occasionally have a good word to say for wine which "maketh glad the heart"; or

PLATE III

Assyrian royalty (King Assur-bani-pal, 668–626 B.C., and his queen) drinking wine in the palace garden. Bas relief from Nineveh. Courtesy of the British Museum, London.

PLATE IV

A. An Indian ruler feasting and drinking. Adjantâ cave painting, 6th century A.D. Courtesy of the Musée Guimet, Paris.

B. Hollanders drinking beer in Bali. Bas relief from a North Balinese temple, 19th century. (Photograph by Rose Covarrubias.) From *Island of Bali,* by Miguel Covarrubias. (Copyright by Alfred A. Knopf, Inc.) Reproduced by permission of the publisher.

"causeth the poor man to forget his misery." That the liberals prevailed over the puritans by the time of Christ appears from Peter's refutation of the charge that the "speaking of tongues" at the Pentacost was but drunken babble. His statement that men could not be drunk in the morning proves by the converse that heavy drinking was common in the evening.

* * *

More evidence comes from the Persians and neighboring peoples. These Easterners prided themselves on their high living. One of their spokesmen, in the *Acharnians* of Aristophanes, is made to say:

> For the Barbarians consider those men only
> Who drink and eat the most.

The reply is:

> But we the most debauched and dissolute.

The Persians, before they conquered Lydia, were water drinkers, not using wine. Authority for this statement is Herodotus, who represents Croesus as contemplating his expedition against Persia when a certain Lydian cautioned him thus: "O king, the men against whom you are making ready to go wear leathern breeches and other raiment of that sort. They eat not what they want but what they can get. They make no use of wine but drink water." Persian boys drank only water. Duris, the Greek historian, says that their king was allowed to get drunk only on the day they sacrificed to Mithra. Cambyses seems to have extended this privilege to other days, thereby bringing upon himself much criticism from his people. His reaction to such objections was to drink all the harder. Then, to prove that his drinking had no effect on him, he proposed a test. He emptied still larger cups, drinking more recklessly than ever, and when quite heavy and drunk with wine he stood the son of his dearest friend and most persistent critic up at a distance and taking aim at the lad's heart made a dead center hit. Retribution overtook the bibulous king, however; for mad with drink and debauchery he got himself assassinated by reason of his stupidity.

The Persians, having become a world power, soon forgot their abstemious habits and become greatly given over to wine. By the time of Xenophon's *Cyropaedia* they drank to such excess that after a meal they had to be carried out. . . . Herodotus reports a custom of the Persians that turns up again in Germany: "They deliberate and decide while drunk and reconsider their decision next morning when sober." The Persians seem to have reformed by the time of Ammianus, who says of them that they avoided hard drinking as they would the plague. Compare also an item from the newly enacted penal code of Persia. This law provides that drinkers, upon being found guilty of the habit, shall have a heavy cord strung through the dividing membrane of the nose and then be led through the main streets of the village. Persistent offenders are bound hand and foot and tied with a cord through the nose to a post in a public square fcr several hours.

*   *   *

To the north of Persia, in what is now Russia, was Scythia. Among the eastern tribes of that country were the Sacae and the Massagetae. It may be noted here, however, that the drink of the latter was milk. The ancients had much to say about the Scythians. A reason for this interest was the trip of Anacharsis, a Scythian philosopher, to Athens about 600 B.C. The wine drinking of the Greeks seems to have made a great impression on him. At least several bons mots imputed to him have come down through the ages, being preserved for us in Diogenes Laertius' *Lives of Eminent Philosophers.* Being asked one day how one could avoid becoming a drunkard, Anacharsis replied: "By keeping before your eyes the unseemly actions of drunkards." When insulted by a boy over the wine, he said: "If you cannot carry your liquor when you are young, boy, you will be a water-carrier (the last job of a derelict) when you are old." Being asked if there were flutes in Scythia, he replied: "No, nor yet vines." Anacharsis also declared that the vine bore three kinds of grapes: "The first of pleasure, the next of intoxication, and the third of disgust."

*   *   *

The skepticism shown by the Scythians toward the claims of Bacchus found a counterpart in Dacia where dwelt the Getae, a crushed and drunken horde. About the middle of the first century B.C. they had a king by the name of Boeribistas. He wished to do something for his people, and so he associated his god with himself in the business of state, using Decaeneus, a priest, as intermediary in the new theocracy. The partnership was evidently successful, for shortly there was an organization that in later years worried the Roman legions considerably. Boeribistas' constructive policy embraced the liquor problem, which he solved by persuading the people to cut down their vines and live without wine.

In their fondness for alcoholic drinks the Dacians were not unlike their Teutonic neighbors to the north and west. These Germans, on the whole, were hard drinkers. They lived simply, it is true, yet they drank heavily. A doubtful passage from Tacitus suggests that a good way to conquer Germans is to give them all they want to drink. The authorities, besides characterizing the Germans as intemperate in general, specify more particularly in a few instances. Thus Procopius says of the Vandals that they were the most luxurious of all peoples. The same historian speaks of the Erulians and their drunken ways, complimenting an Erulian officer of Belisarius for his steadiness by saying that it is not easy for an Erulian not to give himself over to drunkenness. When the Goths heard the cry of "meat and drink" they did not take kindly to such refinements as poetical recitations. Professor Johannes Grüss, from his studies in dregs from ancient drinking vessels, would ascribe to prehistoric Germans familiarity with beers of high alcohol content. Grüss holds this fact as indicative of heavy drinking among prehistoric Germans.

*   *   *

Although in general the Germans were greatly addicted to drink, there were German tribes who objected to wine at least. Among these were the Suevi, who had a strict law against the importation of wine, as had the Nervii, and for the same reasons. The Cimbri, too, were unused to wine and strong drinks. . . .

Germanic records dating from the collapse of classical culture contain much that throws light on the attitude of early Germanic peoples toward drink. If with Gronbech one may suppose that a later custom hangs over from earlier times, there is plentiful corroboration of Tacitus' charging the Germans with being a drink-conscious folk.

*   *   *

The propensity of the Central Europeans to carousing seems to have infected one of their visitors, Attila the Hun, of whom this gruesome story is told. One day he took unto himself a new wife. The occasion demanded some fitting recognition, and so he became intoxicated and fell into a drunken stupor. He was subject, it seems, to severe attacks of bleeding at the nose. One of these attacks came on while he was lying asleep on his back. The blood, not being able to escape from his nostrils, settled down into his throat and choked him to death. The comment of Priscus, the historian of the Hunnish Wars, on this circumstance is: "Thus drunkenness brought a king renowned for his wars to a shameful end. . . ."

This survey of the peoples living around the outskirts of the Mediterranean Basin may warrant the drawing of some conclusions. In general, the inhabitants of the west and south are rated by most writers as somewhat restrained in the use of alcoholic beverages; whereas the peoples of the Near East, of central Europe, and of the Balkans were contrariwise-minded. An occasional exception to this general rule appears. The more simple the state of society among a given people, and the farther away it was from well-developed centers of population, the more likely it was to have a reputation for sobriety. The romanticizing principle of distance lending enchantment to the view may have had something to do with some of these roseate characterizations. On the contrary, when a folk of primitive culture came in contact with wine, drunkenness usually followed and repeatedly did such indulgence end in catastrophe. So well aware of these possibilities were the peoples of the so-called Nordic extraction in particular, and so bitter was their experience with wine drinking, that they often inveighed against the use of wine and occasionally tried to protect themselves by prohibitory edicts. It is also quite evident that ancient records show a widespread interest in the data of drinking, and that the writers lost no opportunity to play up startling phenomena connected with the practice.

7. CENTRAL AND SOUTH AMERICA

CHICHICASTENANGO AND CHAMULA

by Ruth Bunzel *

In the course of ethnographic work among Indian populations in Mexico and Guatemala, the writer was forced to take cognizance of the role that intoxication plays in these cultures and to consider the sociological and psychological factors involved in what has sometimes been called Mexico's greatest problem.

The places from which the material to be presented was drawn were the Indian villages of Santo Tomas Chichicastenango in Guatemala, and Chamula in the State of Chiapas, Mexico. These are two large and culturally important villages in inaccessible regions of the Central American highlands. Except for the fifty mestizo families of Chichicastenango, the inhabitants are Indians of pure racial stock, who speak related dialects of the Maya language. In these villages both men and women wear home woven regional costumes, and in all ways maintain their distinctive cultures. These cultures are an amalgam of aboriginal and 16th century Spanish elements.

* * *

Alcoholism [1] in Central America can be understood only if we bear in mind its special historic background. Among the ancient Aztecs and the people who came under their influence, intoxicating beverages were consumed as part of their religious worship. Las Casas, who alone among the early missionaries espoused the cause of the Indians against the Spanish invaders, reports as follows concerning drinking at fiestas among the Indians of the area in which the present studies were made:

. . . On the days (of the fiesta) they held great banquets in which they ate many birds and much game, and drank different wines; and those who did this were chiefly the chief lord and the high priest, and other great lords, one day in the house of one, and another day in the house of another. They danced and leapt before the idols, and gave them to drink of the best wine that they had, drenching their lips and faces

* Reprinted by permission of The William Alanson White Foundation, from "The Role of Alcoholism in Two Central American Cultures," *Psychiatry*, 3 (1940), 361–87. Copyright by The William Alanson White Foundation, Inc.
 1. Alcoholism as discussed in this paper refers to a variety of patterns of drinking and intoxicated behavior.—Ed.

with it. And those who held themselves most devout brought vessels and bladders of wine and drank copiously of it, and this they did for no other reason than religious zeal, believing this kind of sacrifice was more pleasing to their gods than any other common act of devotion; and for this reason the chief one who became intoxicated was the lord or reigning king, and other important lords, and among them were some who did not drink enough to become intoxicated, so that they might rule the town and country while the monarch was drunk in his devotions.

Drinking as a form of worship still persists; it is a part of the ritual, and the more venerable participants show their devotion by the quantities of *aguardiente,* a strong, raw distillate of sugar, that they consume. There is drinking in the houses of the mayordomos before the saints, and this is an essential part of the worship; it is the obligation of the mayordomos to provide aguardiente and serve it to all who come. In personal ritual libations of aguardiente are poured out on the altar, and the participants also drink —it would be an offense and insult to the gods not to partake after having invited them. Even in the church, when the priest is looking the other way, aguardiente is poured out among the candles and rose petals, and the bottle is passed around. All this is the honoring of an ancient tradition.

But secular drinking is largely a product of modern conditions. The Codex Mendoza, which describes in native hieroglyphic writing the daily life of the Aztecs, depicts the heavy penalties for drunkenness, which, in accordance with the severity of Aztec laws, was a capital offense. From this punishment only men and women over seventy years of age were exempt. Drinking, except in the worship of the gods, was the prerogative of age.

The introduction of stronger alcoholic drinks by the Spaniards, and the breaking down of the ancient tribal rule were completely demoralizing. Moreover, the Spaniards quickly recognized and took advantage of the use of alcohol as a tool of imperialism. For most of the material possessions of the invaders the Indians had no use and no desire. Alcohol was one thing the Spaniards had which the Indians craved, and for which they would contract debts and sell themselves and their children into slavery. Until very recently, the alcoholism of the Indians was an essential part of the whole economic structure of Latin American countries.

Many of the areas of intensive cultivation and large scale production, especially those producing coffee, sugar, cotton, and tropical fruits, are situated in the unhealthy coastal plains at a considerable distance from the large centers of indigenous population which are all on the plateau; therefore the plantations must constantly recruit their labor supply among the inhabitants of the free mountain villages. Many of these villages are self sustaining or industrially so specialized that they can satisfy their basic needs through the ancient system of intervillage barter. Frequently aguardiente is the largest, sometimes the only considerable need which cannot be satisfied through the normal channels of aboriginal trade. Intoxicating drinks form the bulk of the expense for all social ceremonies, such as baptisms, marriages, house warmings, funerals, and saints' days. It is largely to finance these ceremonies, rather than to feed and clothe themselves, that men contract for labor on the plantations. The other great expense which Indians in free villages must meet is fines. Until the whole contract labor system was abolished in its entirety in 1934 in Guatemala, and in 1936 in Mexico, it was customary at fiestas to imprison great numbers of Indians, on the charge of drunkenness, impose heavy fines, which the agent of the plantation paid, and which the victim had to work off on the plantation. The local authorities who made the arrests received a bonus for each Indian so "trapped." To prevent the peon from working off his debt, the consumption of alcoholic drinks on the plantations was encouraged by the owner and overseer. Alcoholism, therefore, entered at two points into the economic shackling of native populations. In spite of enlightened attitudes in the Government, the forces that introduced alcohol into native economy are still potent. As a coffee planter remarked, "Take aguardiente away from the Indian and what will become of coffee? Coffee plantations run on aguardiente as an automobile runs on gasoline." Any attempt on the part of the Federal Government to combat alcoholism meets with the united opposition of local groups, not only the distillers and tradespeople who profit directly, but also the planters, the local officials, and the Church. Prohibition of the sale of intoxicants in Indian villages, far from improving the situation, has simply opened the door to political occupation more crass than that of the prohibition era in the United States. But even with full cooperation of Federal and local authorities, the problem cannot be solved by any system of legislation and law enforcement, for alcohol plays so important a role in Indian life that any attack on the problem from outside is futile.

However, although alcohol everywhere is such an essential part of Indian culture that the Indians feel that their whole social life would be dislocated by its removal, this role is not everywhere the same. There are different patterns of drinking, different typical pictures of drunken behavior, and, so far as the individual is concerned, different significance and, undoubtedly, different etiology.

* * *

Chichicastenango

Consumption of alcohol at Chichicastenango, a Guatemalan Indian community of 26,000, is confined to market days and the many festivals, large and small, of which it forms one of the most conspicuous features. Quiche Indians say that life in the mountains—at home—is "sad," only the town is "gay."

The daily routine of sowing and reaping and grinding and weaving in the isolation of mountain farms is punctuated by the weekly market and the yearly cycle of fiestas, when thousands of people gather in the town for concentrated social life. There is a market each Sunday that draws crowds from all the neighboring towns. It is one of the great markets of Guatemala. On this day the resident priest performs baptisms—about twenty-five each week—and responses for the dead. The native soothsayers and medicine men come on this day to leave their offerings of candles in the church. The litigants in domestic and property disputes come to be heard before the judges. The Indian houses, closed all week, are open for the day, and crowded with men, women, and children. The bars do a thriving business. The baptisms are performed at noon. The market breaks up soon after, and the greater part of the afternoon is given over to drinking by those who are so inclined and can afford it.

The fiestas have all the features of the Sunday market on a larger scale. There is a large market and a great gathering of people. The actual fiesta is in the hands of the *mayordomías,* groups selected by the municipal officers to carry on the traditional ceremonies in the cult of the saint. These include in addition to the masses and processions common to all Catholic communities, a series of preparatory rituals of which the central features are the preparation and consumption of sacramental meals of *atole* and *cacao,* two of the ritualistic foods of the aboriginal culture. At these ceremonies aguardiente is consumed in large quantities, especially by the older and more responsible members—the mayordomos, musicians, and municipal officers, who are usually so drunk as to need assistance in moving about.

To defray the expenses of fiestas, each set of mayordomos holds several times a year *zarabandas,* dancing parties at which *chicha*—fermented drink of fruit juice and brown sugar—and aguardiente . . . are sold to those who come to dance. Zarabandas are held on Sundays after the market. They begin about 4 o'clock in the afternoon and continue all night and all day Monday, and if well attended, throughout Monday night ending at dawn on Tuesday. Each mayordomía holds a zarabanda at its fiesta after the mass and procession of the Saint. As an Indian explained to me: "Now we have finished in the church and are celebrating the Saint according to our own customs."

For these occasions the rooms where the images of the saints are kept, and which serve as chapels for votaries of the cult, are cleared and decorated with pine, a marimba is installed in one corner, and in another an improvised bar is set up. One of the mayordomos is in charge of the sale of drinks and is supposed to keep accounts by chalking them up on the wall. Actually everyone is too drunk to make such accounting feasible. The marimba plays continuously, candles burn on the altar, men and women buy drinks and dance before the altar. They become very intoxicated; dancing is sometimes interrupted for weeping and praying. Prayers on these occasions are frequently self-accusatory. During the zarabandas there is a great deal of erotic behavior that contrasts sharply with the extreme decorum observed at other times. Men and women dance together and embrace; often a man with two women, or a woman with two men. Often men and women retire to copulate in the sweat bath or in the little cornfield behind the yard. Such promiscuity is counter to all the avowed sexual morality, and leaves behind a great residue of guilt. Also quarrels break out at zarabandas. More men than women attend zarabandas, but the women drink as freely as the men. At any time after it is well under way there will be a few persons dancing and numbers of men and women sleeping in drunken stupor in the room and in the yard.

In addition to zarabandas and the formal drinking of participants at ceremonies, all the bars sell large amounts of alcohol on Sundays and feast days. As the market place empties, the bars fill up. Often a returning merchant spends all his earnings in one of the bars that guard the exits from the town, and much merchandise is lost, stolen, or damaged, while its owner is drinking or stumbling home at night in the rain over slippery trails. Although this drinking is quite secular, it is nevertheless a characteristic feature of the corporate life of the market place as opposed to the family life of the farm. Also it always occurs at the end of the day, following the fiesta or the market, as a part of the dissolution of corporate life into its individual units. The colossal sprees in which men stay drunk for days on end, as long as their money and their credit last, invariably occur in the days immediately following fiestas.

The ceremonial pattern of Chichicastenango is cumulative. A fiesta begins when a single mayordomo gathers together the members of his group. One by one other groups are drawn in, the market builds up slowly, dance groups are added. The entrance of each new element is announced by rockets, bells and music. The climax is the procession which takes place at the peak of the market, and which is accompanied by the greatest number of bands, drummers, rockets, and the continuous ringing of bells. For the procession the groups which for days have been pursuing independent courses coalesce for a brief half hour. With the procession formal ritual ends, the corporate life disintegrates, the crowd rapidly disperses. Then tension built up over days is discharged in the zarabandas of the public bars. The only fiesta which does not end in general drunkenness is Holy Week, which terminates with the procession of the Penitentes, in which the masked penitents are tormented by the crowd, and the burning of Judas in which a dummy representing Judas is torn limb from limb, hurled down the church steps and burned in a great bonfire. Any mestizo boy who approaches the church or the bonfire is lashed by minor officers of the municipality, who stand about, armed with long horsewhips.

The old men drinking in the plaza or in the houses of the saints accept their drinks ceremoniously from young cup bearers. The boys kneel as they present the cup, offering it on a folded hand woven cloth, as ritual drinks are always offered. The old men accept their drinks with thanks, saying grace over them and blessing the boy. Men drinking ceremonially retain their dignity. They may have to be assisted when their ceremonial duties take them from place to place. But they continue to discharge their duties apparently unimpaired.

Secular drinking in the zarabandas and the *estancias* is apt to be more abandoned and disruptive.

For drunkenness itself the Indians have no feelings of censure or disgust. The "drunk" is always treated with kindness and consideration. When he experiences difficulties of locomotion some helpful bystander lends a hand. When he falls into drunken stupor someone puts a bundle of rags under his head. When a man is on a spree his wife follows him around, waiting to pick him up and take him home when his violence has spent itself and yielded to exhaustion. It sometimes takes several days.

But, on the other hand, drunkenness is feared for what it may lead to: waste, sexual transgressions, and quarrels.

As we read through the texts of penitential rituals we find among the confessions of sin, the following sins committed when drunk:

> I, his father, know certain things which he has done and perhaps I remember them when I am drunk. . . .
> When my father took aguardiente sometimes he lost track of his money and I did not give it all back to him, but I spent it and ate bread which I bought. I also took aguardiente with my father and sometimes alone outside; and after I had taken aguardiente I would speak to women and give them aguardiente and then I would lie down with them in the fields or sometimes I went with them to prison. This I did with the money (of my father's) which I spent. . . .
> With my family and relatives we held land in common among us. So it happened then that what they gave to me was not equal to their portion. So it happened that I reproached them, I quarreled with them. Perhaps I beat them when I drank. . . .
> There is a certain gentleman whom I beat in the streets a long time ago. We were drunk, and I did not know what I was doing, and afterward when I was well they told me, those who had seen us. Yes it is true, I beat him, this gentleman, but I did not know anything, I was very drunk. . . .

In all these cases the ancestors have punished the wrongdoer, or else the injured man himself has retaliated with sorcery. For this reason a man chooses his drinking companions carefully. There is no drinking in the *cantones*—country hamlets—or in private houses; except at family fiestas conviviality is discouraged within the family or among neighbors because of the dread of quarrels, and of activating old grudges between individuals who already have experienced a conflict of interest. In the colossal sprees that follow when resistance to alcohol once breaks down, a man will spend his whole capital, or lose it through carelessness, and then try to borrow more to stave off, as long as possible, the painful process of sobering up and facing the havoc. Frequently they stay drunk for a week. On such protracted sprees, the craving for alcohol seems to increase, and there is a progressive loss of control; outbursts of undirected violence alternating with depression. I had little direct personal experience with men in this condition, although it was a common enough sight in the streets, the zarabandas, and the *cantinas* during fiestas and on any Sunday.

The only Indians who ever tried to borrow money from me were drunken Indians. Some of my special friends, all men of standing and authority in the community, and individuals of great personal dignity, who when sober would not dream of borrowing, would when drunk come to me at the Convent or track me down in the houses of informants to try to extract money to continue the spree. On one occasion a friend to whom I had refused to lend money returned in a few minutes with a magnificent kerchief which he offered to me for a ridiculously low price. Although I pointed out to him that the price was absurd, he and his thirsty companions insisted that I buy it. Next day he wanted to get it back; his wife, who had woven it, was incensed at his having sold at such terms. Next week he was back trying to sell me a blouse under similar conditions. The man was a mayordomo, the "treasurer" of the religious hierarchy, a man of great dignity and authority, with a commanding presence, and most cultivated manners. The tendency to contract debts when drunk in order to postpone the painful process of sobering up makes Indians easy prey to the tactics of the plantation agents.

But the most serious results are the quarrels that break out under the influence of alcohol. A quarrel of this sort took place among my informants while I was in Chichicastenango at the fiesta of All Saints. The central figure in this quarrel was Miguel, the leader and organizer of one of the dance groups. Miguel was one of the leaders of the community, an ex-mayordomo, the contact man for one of the plantations, and the owner of a "factory" for the manufacture of dance costumes. He had been married several times and had many children ranging in age from a son of about thirty-five to an infant. The eldest son, Diego, lived with his father in accordance with the Quiche pattern. He was married and had a number of children, the oldest of whom was a girl of fourteen. In this rather disorderly household I never succeeded in sorting out the younger children. During the week of the fiesta Miguel followed the dance group he directed from house to house; everywhere he was offered many drinks. The cumulative effect of such continuous imbibing began to be apparent the third day of the fiesta; he was staggering around, roaring and unruly, followed everywhere by his patient wife and several cowed children. That night at a zarabanda a quarrel broke out between Miguel and his son Diego. No one could say how it started, but presently Diego seized a stick of firewood and attacked his father. They beat each other up badly before they were separated, and resumed the quarrel again later. After this Miguel drank more heavily than before; next day he was wandering through the streets and roads, roaring and raging. In this state he sought me out at the house of another man, to borrow money from me. One of his children came to warn us that his father was on his way and that he was drunk. Soon Miguel came, staggering across the fields in which the unharvested corn was still standing. His head was still bloody from the night's encounter. He had several scalp wounds, one eye was closed, and his jaw and lips were cut and bruised. His clothing was disordered and covered with filth from his many falls in the gutter. His son-in-law and the women managed to get rid of him after a violent scene. The son-in-law, a sober, industrious man, said Miguel's spree would probably last a week, if he could get sufficient credit. It continued another day, and then he was violently sick for three or four days. Diego meanwhile stayed at home, sullen and depressed, ashamed to appear in the village while he bore traces of the quarrel. For a son to turn against his father is the worst sin in the Quiche code. Between these two there was continuous tension, under apparent cooperation. Miguel recommended Diego, an unintelligent and uninformed man, as informant, and Diego then tried to supplant his father. Miguel on the other hand demanded that he, as head of the family, should be paid for the blouse that Diego's wife was weaving for me. Diego was considered a bad son, but Miguel was not approved of either.

Tomas, the sober son-in-law, was a teetotaller. He was a man of about thirty, married to an inept and unattractive woman for whom he had little love. They had three young children. He had been educated in the capital, and could read and write in Spanish and Quiche. He was secretary and official interpreter of the town, a notary, and also a wealthy merchant and a sorcerer and diviner. Later he became one of the leaders of the stiffening Indian resistance to White encroachments. He told me that as a younger man he had liked to get drunk in the plaza, and that he had lost much money that way. He had given money to women with whom he had sexual relations, and when he was drunk he had quarreled with his wife and beaten her. For these sins and for his hostile feelings toward his wife, he had been punished by a mysterious sickness of which he had been cured only by being initiated as a sorcerer. Since then he had not drunk any hard liquor. But his old sins lay heavily on his conscience. During the latter part of my stay he was beset with anxiety because of the sacred knowledge which he had given me. To this he attributed a loss of money which he sustained at that time, and various minor ailments of his children. He was worried that I might lose my life on the return trip which seemed to him extraordinarily hazardous. For this reason he wished to perform ceremonies for my safe homecoming. The divinations preceding this ceremony came out unfavorably and increased his anxiety. Several ceremonies were required, and one of the objects that I had to furnish along with candles for the sacrifice, was a sworn statement, signed and sealed on official paper, that I would never endanger him, my teacher, by using rituals of sorcery to harm an innocent person. This document lay on the altar during the sacrifice. After a period of great stress he overcame his anxieties, but he became the leader of the anti-White faction of the village.

These two case histories of the drinker and the abstainer illustrate the disruptive effects of alcohol in Chichicastenango, the way in which it activates latent hostilities and leaves behind it an enduring aftermath of guilt and anxiety.

*   *   *

Chamula

The second community to be considered is the *municipio* of Chamula, in the mountains of Chiapas, near the colonial city of Las Casas. Although alcoholism on a large scale is general among all Indian communities in Mexico, the town of Chamula is recognized as one of the worst from this point of view. The Chamulas are regarded by Whites in the State of Chiapas as "bad Indians," the most depraved of the region, the most violent and hostile, but also the most enterprising and intelligent.

*   *   *

A fiesta means that the guardian of the saint decorates his house, makes atole, a nourishing drink of slightly fermented corn mash, buys a five gallon jug of aguardiente, and entertains all who come. There are a few musicians to play the guitar and harp. There are two tunes. The Chamulas do not tell myths or folk tales, they have no songs, no graphic art, and dancing at fiestas is minimal. They have no sports. Their knowledge of the outside world is limited, and they display little curiosity about it. . . . Their lives are uneventful, they have only moderate interest in gossip, and their only pastime is getting drunk.

In Chamula everyone from the youngest child to the oldest woman drinks. Men, as a group, drink more than women, but all women drink and some of them imbibe truly enormous quantities. Children are habituated to aguardiente from early infancy. At drinking feasts I saw women remove their infants from their breasts to pour aguardiente between their lips. Children in general do not like aguardiente and try to avoid drinking it. One little boy of nine threatened to run away from home if I gave a party at his house, because he did not want to be forced to drink, and another boy of fourteen who was being drafted by the elders for the post of secretary asked me to hide him in the school closet, because public office meant that he would have to drink great quantities of alcohol. The boy was found and, after a violent scuffle, was dragged off and inducted into office. He later described how he always carried a flask concealed under his blanket, and contrived to pour his drinks into it unobserved. On the other hand, I knew one boy of ten who was a confirmed drunkard; the son of a thoroughly depraved father, who included assault and incest among his misdeeds, he had been "sold" to the plantations by his father. There he learned to drink, and at the age of ten, spent all his earnings for aguardiente and would beg, borrow, or steal additional money.

At fiestas the whole town is in varying degrees of intoxication for a day or a week. During one fiesta the writer counted eighty individuals lying in a stuporous condition in the yard of the church and the market place. This was at two o'clock in the afternoon. At a fiesta given by the writer eighteen persons finished a *garafon*—five gallons—in twenty-four hours, and demanded more so that the fiesta could continue. Although it was Sunday two men walked the ten miles to town to get another half garafon. There were certain individuals who in several months of daily contact were never seen sober, others who were raving drunk several times a week, and no one at all who was not seen highly intoxicated on a number of occasions. The average daily consumption is said to be ⅓ liter—13 ounces—per day per person. The amount is so variable that I could not check this. Officers of the municipality who must drink continuously in the course of their duties drink a great deal more, but the average mountain-dwelling Chamula probably consumes no such amount, but gets drunk about once a week when he goes to town to market. The chief alcoholic drink is aguardiente. . . . I did not analyze it, or make any tests of its physiological effects. Of secondary importance is chicha . . . milder and cheaper than aguardiente and drunk only when one can no longer afford aguardiente.

In Chamula drinking is a social act. The solitary drinker, or the man who drinks while others abstain is as unknown as the total abstainer. Not only is drinking always social, it is always ceremonial. Drinking forms a part of every ceremony, religious or social—the worship of the saints, the curing of the sick, the celebration of marriage or baptism, the closing of a contract, whether it be a betrothal or the sale of sheep, the termination of a journey, or any other occasion when men and women come together. Even the casual drinking of the road or the market place is ceremonious. No one drinks alone, no one buys or pours his own drink, and, even in the cantinas, drinks are never bought over the counter. The full social import of drinking is best seen if we consider the casual drinking on the road or in Las Casas. If several Indians meet in town on market day, if they have any money at all, they go to a cantina to drink together. One man buys a bottle—a *litro,* a *botella,* or a *media,* depending on how much money he may have. Even when several men contribute to the cost of a bottle, one man buys it. The liquor is drawn off from large barrels. If no one in the group has an empty bottle, a bottle and glass are borrowed from the bar keeper. The group does not drink in the cantina but withdraws to the patio, or in the country in good weather, anywhere along the roadside. The man who has bought the bottle presents it to someone whom he wishes to honor—an official from whom he wishes a favor or whom he wishes to thank, a mayordomo of one of the saints, or anyone to whom he feels an obligation. This man accepts the bottle with a speech of thanks and calls some boy or young man to pour out the drinks. He bows in turn before each man and woman who touches his head in blessing, the usual greeting between individuals of different age or status. With those of his own age he shakes hands. Then he pours the drinks; the first is offered to the man who "owns" the bottle, the second to the man who bought it, and then to the other men in order of age or rank, and afterward to the women in order, and after the women have drunk, to the children. Children are not given full glasses. At some point, usually after the first two men have drunk, the "owner" of the bottle interrupts to pour a drink for the young cup bearer. The drinks are poured in one- or two-ounce glasses. Each person on receiving his drink, holds it in his hand while he says, "May I drink, Mayordomo?"—asking each man or woman in turn, calling each by the appropriate title or relationship term. Parenthetically, in accordance with their classificatory relationship system anyone with whom a person has social contacts is either a "brother," "brother-in-law," or "uncle." The person so addressed says, "Yes, drink." If he is already asleep, he is roused to make the proper answer. If all attempts to rouse him are unavailing, the older men say, "Never mind. Go ahead and drink." No one is permitted to refuse a drink. If, after several rounds, a man does not wish to drink he takes one sip from the glass and pours the rest into a flask which he carries under his blanket, or else hands it over to his wife to pour into her bottle—women drink less, and have steadier hands. This is done over the protests of the rest of the group. Women more often than men put their drinks aside. If anything is left in the bottle after the first round, a second is poured. The men are all very expert in gauging the amount left in a bottle and measuring out the drinks so that all get an equal share. After the bottle is empty the cup bearer bows again before all his seniors, the bottle and cup are returned to their owner, everyone shakes hands with everyone else saying, "We have drunk together." Thereafter the party breaks up unless, having met for some purpose, they proceed to the business in hand. All of these formalities are observed in drinking in the home where none but members of the family are present.

The usual drink is crude and strong, and is rapidly absorbed. The effects of intoxication are apparent almost immediately. The Indians describe their first reaction as a feeling of pleasant warmth. The village lies more than 8,000 feet above sea level and experiences damp penetrating cold for the greater part of the year; so important is the feeling of warmth that the usual phrase in going for a drink is, "Come, let us warm ourselves." After from two to four drinks the optimum is reached. This is the stage of "feeling high." At this stage men are in complete control of their faculties. They may have slight difficulty in walking or standing, but they can play the guitar or handle a machete with perfect safety. The Indians have no firearms. Some of them have rusty old rifles, but they cannot afford ammunition. The machete is the all purpose tool and weapon. Men do not usually have machetes with them when they drink, or else they lay them aside. There is no erotic behavior at this or later stages of intoxication. The complete absence of sexual interest was one of the most striking aspects of Chamula alcoholism in contrast to that of Chichicastenango. The general feeling tone of this stage of intoxication is warm, good-natured irresponsibility. Lack of judgment is displayed by the irresistible impulse to continue drinking after the optimum is passed. Although women drink less than men, their tolerance seems greater. Even after prolonged drinking, they manifested none of the more extreme types of behavior. It is usually after the fourth drink that individual behavior patterns manifest themselves. It is not easy to say, however, at what point the more extreme types of behavior appear, because many individuals drink fairly continuously, and one may be observing the cumulative effects of many potations.

The usual course of intoxication is a progressive numbing of mental faculties terminating in stupor. There may be violent retching before the stuporous sleep, but this is by no means usual. Continued retching and cold sweat are interpreted as signs of other illness. The motor disturbances are familiar, but there seems to be less interference with speech than among inebriates in our culture. In this state men frequently go through familiar routines, apparently in full control of their faculties, and even transact complicated business of which they later have no memory. One day I went to town accompanied by one of my informants and his little boy. I planned to return the following day. After leaving me at my hotel Diego went to the market place to attend to his purchases and met some companions with whom he went to a cantina on the edge of town. He had what for an Indian was a goodish sum of money with him, which he spent in drink. In the late afternoon he insisted on returning to Las Hollas. The little boy made no attempt to dissuade him and went along, in view of the fact that no one ever tries to cross or argue with a drunk. After they had gone about five miles it began to rain and they took shelter under some trees, where Diego went to sleep. When he woke up it was getting dark. The child was then able to persuade him to return to town to sleep, since no Indian feels safe on the roads at night. Next day Diego had no memory of any of this.

* * *

There is no condemnation of drinking per se. Alcohol forms a necessary part of every social contact. It is, indeed, the medium of contact. A betrothal is validated when the girl's father accepts a drink from the spokesman of the suitor; a contract is sealed when the seller accepts a drink from the purchaser; the plaintiff in litigation offers a bottle of aguardiente to the judges to hear his case—they all drink together, and the litigant who wins a case is ordered to treat everyone to several rounds of drinks, so that everyone may go away feeling happy at the settlement. When two friends meet, they go at once "to warm themselves." What else would they do? It is the copious applications of alcohol that keeps the social mechanisms in operation. Alcohol is considered a necessity, and as such has no critics. Nor does anyone feel any guilt or shame over having been drunk. A man has no hesitation in explaining an absence, or failure to complete any required task by saying he was drunk. Nor is there any shame at the loss of control. A man enjoys the story of his own silly behavior as much as anyone else. A person who is drunk is not responsible and his offenses are condoned. It has already been pointed out that it is far worse to beat a woman when one is sober than when one is drunk. But the waste, the quarrels, and disruptions of life for which alcohol is responsible are all deplored. They reckon that the economic cost of alcohol is not only the actual outlay for drink which in itself is sufficient to absorb any surplus and keep standards of living at a very low level and drive them into debt when money is needed for any unusual expense. Aguardiente represents the largest item in the expense of getting married, curing a sick child, or burying a dead relative. It is to meet these expenses that men must borrow. To the actual cost of alcohol must be added the loss of working time and reduced efficiency, and the expense of sickness—more alcohol for the medicine man who cures the alcoholic. Thus Indians reckon in the cost of aguardiente the losses sustained while drunk. This may be damage to clothing, loss or theft of property. It is not unusual for an Indian drunk on the road to be robbed of everything he has with him. On the reservation and in the town of Las Casas the drinking habits of the Chamulas protect them from the worst types of abuse. There is no solitary drinking, the drinker always has companions whom he has chosen; frequently there are women among them who remain relatively sober; treachery between relatives and neighbors is rare. The absence of erotic stimulation protects the Indians from being robbed by prostitutes. But in the plantations and on the roads it is a different story. It is not unusual for a returning worker to be beaten while drunk and robbed of his pay and all his possessions.

The other great havoc wrought by drinking is the unleashed violence. However, between Chamulas all fighting is done with the hands—anyone who carried a weapon would be disarmed by his companions—and so the injuries inflicted in drunken brawls are not usually very serious. There are a great many bloody noses and cut lips and minor lacerations, but very few injuries are not well by the time the hangover is gone. Nor do drunken quarrels have further repercussions. Toward a drunken man everyone assumes a protective and conciliatory attitude. He is not considered responsible. If he is belligerent no one tries to cross him or argue with him. No one, unless he too were drunk, would assume a belligerent or condemnatory attitude. Therefore the man whose head is cracked knows that he himself is to blame. If he tried to air his grievance he would get no support. "He was drunk, why did you fight with him?" This is quite different from the resentment felt at Chichicastenango over a drunken quarrel, which will rankle for years and drive men to take the most extreme forms of revenge. The one exception to the general rule that drunken quarrels are trivial and pass off with no aftermath is the case of quarrels when a man beats his wife. In such cases, the belief is that sickness may result. If the latter becomes sick, it is because "her heart was hurt when her husband struck her." But most frequently it is the children who become sick through the psychic hurt of their mothers. But there is a simple ritual for setting this right. If the child dies in spite of curing ceremonies, the death is attributed to other causes— "the spirit called him"—and the guilt is not fastened upon the father.[2]

SOUTH AMERICAN INDIAN DRINKS

by John M. Cooper *

Fermented alcoholic beverages—*chicha, massato, kashiri, paiwari, kawin, kawim*—were reported in use in the West Indies, Middle America, the Andean cultural region from Colombia to southern Middle Chile, and most of the Silval region by the earliest White explorers, colonists, and missionaries, and undoubtedly had long been part of the pre-Contact aboriginal culture. Distilling is practiced at present by certain Indian groups, as a rule largely Europeanized in culture, here and there from Honduras and Nicaragua to Colombia, Ecuador, and Peru, but is of post-Contact introduction from Hispano-American culture. Nearly all South American Indians in close touch with Whites have taken readily to our distilled liquors; the Ona of Tierra del Fuego are one of the rare exceptions.

While the use of home-made or bartered alcoholic beverages is today widespread in South America, it is not universal. . . .

The Fuegians had no alcoholic drinks until relatively recent times; the Tehuelche none until about the middle of the 18th century, and even in Musters' day (1869) made none of their own, although the Poyas, of the Lake Nahuelhuapi region adjacent to Araucanian territory, who may have

* From *The Comparative Ethnology of South American Indians,* Vol. 5 of Julian H. Steward, ed., *Handbook of South American Indians,* Bureau of American Ethnology, Bulletin 143 (Washington, 1946), pp. 539–46.

2. For discussion by Dr. Bunzel of cultural and psychological factors contributing to differences in behavior under alcohol of the people of Chichicastenango and those of Chamula, see Part IV, pp. 278–86.

spoken a Tehuelche dialect, were brewing a beverage from fruits in the early 18th century. Whether the "Puelche" of the western Argentine Pampa had intoxicants prior to the middle 18th century is uncertain. Of the Chaco tribes, the Mbayá-Guaicurú were using fermented drinks from algaroba beans when first observed in the second quarter of the 16th century.

In recent decades, alcoholic beverages are reported absent from considerable sections of three areas in the tropical and subtropical forests, viz., sections of: (1) eastern and southern Brazil and Paraguay; (2) Bolivia; (3) the Montaña. Occasional isolated tribes, such as the Arhuaco-Cagaba of Colombia and Carimé of Brazilian Amazonas, also lack alcoholic beverages of their own.

Among the alcoholic beverages of aboriginal South America, those made from maize are used by the greatest number of people and have the widest geographical distribution. They are chiefly found in the great fairly continuous area from Honduras to the Isthmus in Middle America, and along the Andean cultural belt from the Isthmus and northern and western Colombia through Ecuador and Peru to western Bolivia, the Atacama, the Diaguita country, Middle Chile, Chiloé, and, by later introduction from Chiloé, to the southern limit of maize-growing on the Guaitecas Islands; the Antilles; Venezuela and the Guianas; the Tupí-Guaraní regions of the Amazon, the Paraguay-Paraná, and the Brazilian coast and hinterland. They are also common in much of the Montaña, the Orinoco, and upper and middle Amazon and their tributaries, eastern Bolivia and the Chaco, Mato Grosso, and non-Tupí Eastern Brazil.

Alcoholic beverages from manioc rank second to those from maize, and have approximately the same distribution as the latter except for two chief areas in which they are lacking, viz., the Andean cultural belt from northern Colombia all the way south to Chiloé; and most of the Chaco. In the major regions where both maize and manioc beverages occur, there are numerous tribes or small subregions, where only one or the other is recorded. In some of these major regions, as in the Guianas and the Amazon lowlands, premier rank is held by manioc beverages; in others, as in most of the Tupí-Guaraní territory, by maize beverages.

Ranking next to maize and manioc beverages are those from palms, algaroba, and honey; and next to these, those from bananas and plantains, pineapples, sweet potatoes, and sugarcane.

Palm wine, from the sap or fruit of various palms, occurs in two main areas; a larger one to the north, embracing much of the Antilles, Middle America, northern and eastern Colombia, the Montaña and upper Amazon, the Rio Negro, Venezuela, and the Guianas; a smaller one, in the Mato Grosso, middle Paraguay, and middle Paraná regions.

Algaroba beer from the seeds of the carob tree holds first place among the Chaco tribes and is made by the Chiriguano to the west and by the

"Pampa Indians" and the Argentine Araucanians to the south. It is also recorded in early Colonial times from the Diaguita region. It is brewed mostly during the season from about November to February or later when the seeds are ripe.

Mead, of fermented honey, occurs in two main areas: in parts of Middle America; and widespread though far from universal in a great crescent belt, more or less marginal to the southern Amazonian watershed, extending from the southeastern Brazilian coast to Southern Brazil, Paraguay, and Uruguay, through the Chaco, to the Siriono of eastern Bolivia. In this area it is or was brewed by a number of the Tupí-Guaraní and southern Ge, by the Botocudo and Charrua, and by most of the Chaco peoples. . . . That mead is not more widely brewed in South America is probably due to the fact that in most areas other materials for alcoholic beverages are so much more readily procurable than honey in quantities sufficient for large numbers of drinkers.

Fermented drinks from bananas, pineapples, sweet potatoes, and sugar-cane occur fairly commonly in and are mostly confined to the tropical and subtropical forest and savanna regions of Middle America, Venezuela, the Guianas, and the Orinoco and Amazonian watersheds. There are occasional occurrences outside this area, such as brews from sweet potatoes among the Island Carib, Camacan, and Caingang; bananas among the Abipón.

Among the more localized alcoholic drinks, with some records of occurrences of each, are those from quinoa, oca, pine nuts, cashew, agave, mistol, mamey, white potatoes, apples, wheat, barley, pears, quinces, strawberries, molle berries, pumpkins, melons or watermelons, papaya. Numerous other fruits and berries are also used here and there sporadically.

As regards three of the most important South American alcoholic beverages, those from maize, manioc, and algaroba, the general rule seems to hold that in any given tribe or area the favorite beverage is made from the food that bulks largest in the dietary. There are, however, exceptions to the rule, as among some of the tribes of Costa Rica, whose staple food is plantain but whose favorite drink is from maize.

The fermented beverages are made in two main ways: without or with mastication.

Beverages from palm sap, honey, sugarcane, pineapple, and fruits or berries rich in sugar are made without mastication. By way of exception, the Abipón chewed honeycomb in their mead making. Beverages from palm fruits, bananas or plantains, and sweet potatoes are very commonly reported as made with mastication. Beverages from manioc, and from maize, algaroba, and other seeds rich in starch are usually made with mastication, although there are exceptions as regards maize and manioc and algaroba, and in a great many cases our records are silent as regards presence or absence of mastication. In general, however, the custom of mastication is found very commonly and very widely diffused over practically our whole area in which aboriginal alcoholic beverages occur: Middle America (from Honduras south), the West Indies, and continental South America down to and including the Chaco and southern Middle Chile.

With ingredients rich in sugar, the brew material is left to be acted upon directly by wild yeasts. With those rich in starch, sprouting without mastication is here and there relied on to promote conversion of starch into the simpler carbohydrates or sugar upon which the yeasts can feed; but far more commonly resort is had to mastication through which the ptyalin in the saliva changes part of the starch into sugar and so hastens fermentation by giving the yeast a quicker start.

Details of the process of preparation of alcoholic beverages differ somewhat according to tribe or area, to material fermented and to use or nonuse of mastication. Grains are dried and crushed or ground to flour, in some areas after being steeped in water until they sprout. They are then usually boiled or heated. The masticated grain may be added to the non-masticated before or after this boiling, or between a first and second boiling. The liquid is then allowed to ferment, commonly about two to four days. Manioc beer preparation follows the same general lines; it may be ready to drink within 24 hours. The sap from palm wine is more commonly collected from incisions in the upper trunk, with or without felling of the tree. For some areas—parts of the Chaco and of the Montaña—concepts of plant spirits and animistic rites to promote fermentation and to strengthen the brew are specifically reported and, to judge from scattered hints in our sources, are probably much more widespread.

The liquor is very commonly prepared and stored in large troughs made of hollowed tree trunks; sometimes, in earthen jars. Preparation of fermented beverages is predominantly the woman's task. The women, too—though in some cases only the old or the young women—ordinarily do the masticating, although here and there the men, or the men and the children, do all or part of it.

To promote fermentation, the Guaraní and the Guaratägaja add certain leaves to their brew; the Caingang, the woody stem of a fern. To promote fermentation or to give flavor or greater strength, or to do both, leaves, palm stems, sugarcane juice, goat or sheep excrement, and other ingredients are or were added by tribes here and there. Brews of mixed maize and cassava are also reported occasionally.

In some regions, particularly the Andean and parts of the forested low-lands, fermented beverages are drunk as a common everyday beverage. Most of the drinking, however, throughout the great brewing area of the West Indies, Middle America, and continental South America is in con-nection with drinking sprees, of a social and/or magicoreligious nature in which groups participate. These drinking bouts are main or attendant features of gatherings of all kinds, especially in connection with hunting, fishing, harvesting, and other food-getting activities, with visiting and hospitality to guests, with war, victory, and peacetime councils, with births, naming, initiations, weddings, and funerals, and with magicoreligious festivals, rites, and celebrations—the specific occasions differing from tribe to tribe and from area to area. The sprees may last from a few hours up to many days, usually until all the available liquid is exhausted. The participants imbibe until they reach various stages of intoxication, from mild tipsiness to complete alcoholic coma. Among nearly all people on whom we have information, the bouts are accompanied by and end in the airing of grudges and hurling of insults, which lead to quarrels and fighting more or less violent and not uncommonly fatal. Sex intrigues and orgies are equally common accompaniments. Only here and there, as among the lower Xingú tribes, and the Ashluslay and Chorotí, is quarreling specifically reported absent. In both the Guiana and Chaco-Pampa area, to prevent grave or fatal results, the women hide all weapons before intoxication has reached an advanced stage. In a good many regions, as in the Chaco, the women (at least the younger and middle-aged ones) do not take part in the drinking, or at most drink quite moderately. In others, as in the Panamá region, and parts of the Montaña and Andean Highlands, they as well as the men get drunk.

Some medicinal use is made of alcoholic beverages, as among the Aymara, but the usual purposes of drinking and of drinking sprees are hedonic, social, magicoreligious, or, as more commonly, combinations of all three. That the hedonic bulks large is obvious from our sources. The sprees are eagerly anticipated, and are joyous and hilarious affairs, at least until the fighting starts. Some of the social purposes, such as symbolizing hospitality and so forth, are clear from the above-given list of occasions on which drinking is indulged in. Dobrizhoffer adds particularly the desire of the Abipón through drinking to acquire acuteness in counsel and bravery in fight. Guests and hosts among the early Peruvians customarily exchanged and drank together maize chicha.

Alcoholic beverages were common offerings or sacrifices to supernatural beings and/or the dead in the Andean cultural belt and such sacrifices were early reported by the Carvajal expedition of 1542 far down the Amazon east of the mouth of the Río Negro. They play an important part in girls' rites in parts of the Panamá and Montaña regions, and in many other feasts among the Jívaro and Canelo. In the Montaña, Mato Grosso, and elsewhere they are important accompaniments of shamanistic training and practice.

We have no published intensive field study of the functions of alcoholic beverages in contributing to the stability or instability of society or of the individual in any South American tribe or community.[3] Such field studies

3. See, however, the detailed study of the functions of alcohol in two Central American Indian communities by Bunzel, above pp. 73–86; and see also Mangin's article, below, pp. 91–99.

are an urgent desideratum. A short paper by Rodrigues Sandoval (1945) reviews the motives for and rationalizations under which the Indians of the Ecuadorean Sierra drink, viz., to "warm the blood" and impart physical energy; to prolong life; to "rejoice the heart"; to give courage and peace of spirit; to manifest friendship, hospitality, and solidarity; to ask favors, to maintain status by thus evidencing wealth; to conform to festival requirements; and so forth.

Habitual addicts proper, driven to daily or periodic alcoholic excess by psychosomatic impulsion, appear to be rare, even, at least in most regions, nonexistent. To judge from the continuous distribution of intoxication over the whole range of alcoholic beverages, and from the fact that getting drunk or being made drunk is customary or obligatory indiscriminately for participants in the rites, festivals, and socio-civic observances, such impulsion as exists looks more social and magicoreligious—and in this sense more cultural—than psychosomatic. The degree to and manner in which in individual cases physiological and psychological or psychopathic factors, such as physical craving, anxiety, frustration, escape, and so forth, may enter into the picture awaits intensive field investigation, investigation which should yield some rich returns.

Nonfermented drinks made from maize, manioc, palm sap and fruits, honey, pineapples, and various berries and other fruits are reported from most areas of the continent. Often our later as well as earlier sources are not clear as to whether the drinks they record are fermented or not, this being particularly the case as regards beverages made from palm and from honey.

ANDEAN INDIANS

by *William Mangin* *

The present paper deals primarily with the drinking of alcoholic beverages by the residents of an Indian hacienda, Vicos, in an intermontane valley in the Peruvian Andes. Peru is a country of some 7½ million people most of whom live in the mountains. Lima, the capital city on the coast, has a probable population of close to a million, and there are several other urban centers in the country, but the bulk of the population lives in settlements of less than 5,000 people and most of these are farmers. Peru is predominantly rural. There is, as in many Latin American countries, a vast difference in way of life between the average rural Peruvian and the few wealthy upper and middle class citizens.

* From "Drinking among Andean Indians," *Quarterly Journal of Studies on Alcohol, 18* (1957), 55–66.

Without going deeply into a discussion of social class in Peru, it is necessary at least briefly to mention the major differences between the groups called Indian and Mestizo in the following pages.

Peru has been subject to Spanish and other foreign influences for over 450 years and the Indian and Spanish traits have become so interwoven that it is no longer possible to speak of pure Indian or pure Spanish elements in Peruvian culture. After three centuries of interbreeding it is also impossible to think of Indian and Mestizo as racial classifications. Indians and Mestizos are best thought of as two cultural groups, with some overlap and lack of definition between them. The term Indian as used here refers to people who speak Quechua or Aymara as their primary or only language, do agricultural labor on their own farms or as tenants on other lands or on haciendas, participate almost exclusively in the activities of their own communities and hardly participate in the "national culture" of Peru. This does not mean that Indians do not contribute to the national economy, since they constitute the bulk of the rural working force of the country; but they do not generally consider themselves to be citizens of Peru. Their primary identifications are with local communities and regions. They seldom celebrate national patriotic festivals, as such. They do not vote, play national lotteries, follow horse racing and soccer, and so forth. Essentially Indians are a rural, culturally isolated peasantry.

The group referred to as Mestizo might also be called, for our purposes, non-Indian. This refers to a class-stratified group ranging from second-generation Indian farmers to millionaire sophisticates of Lima. This group makes up from half to two-thirds of the Peruvian population and their drinking habits will not be described here. The general patterns and problems of drinking of Peruvian Mestizos would not sound strange to one familiar with drinking in the United States. The same types of situations seem to arise with somewhat different frequency and intensity.

The 1,800 residents of Vicos are Indians and Vicos is, in many ways, a very conservative community compared to other communities in Peru. Each family is obligated to send one of its members to work for the hacienda 3 days a week as payment for the lands they hold in usufruct and work themselves. Although Vicosinos are subject to Peruvian national laws, Vicos is primarily a self-contained community. They participate in what Beals has called an "internal prestige system." As a result of this, a child in Vicos has a reasonable assurance that he or she can, by acting in a prescribed and feasible manner, achieve many of the goals set as desirable by the society's norms.

The "internal prestige system" is largely centered around an interrelated complex of political-religious offices and religious fiestas. A very important adjunct of political office and fiesta participation is the drinking of alcoholic beverages. These fiestas encompass national and religious holiday celebrations, plant curing and harvest ceremonies, and the festive aspects of formal and informal visiting.

Fiestas perform the obvious function of marking life crises. Inter- and intrafamilial bonds are strengthened by the small private fiestas which mark baptisms, haircuttings, weddings and funerals; placing the ceremonial recognition of these life crises in religious and recreational settings serves to make them maximally pleasant and reassuring. The character of the funeral ceremony is somewhat different from that of the others, but the same function is served. In all private fiestas, the individual or individuals in whose name the fiesta is being held seldom holds the center of the stage for long. The main activity concerns the relationships between the parents and the godparents, the kinsmen, the survivors—in short, all those members of the interacting personnel of the ceremonial.

Fiestas afford an opportunity for some release of tension to many individuals. Occasionally, this is disturbing to a community. In such towns as Chichicastenango in Guatemala and Tajin in Mexico, and among the Tarahumara in Mexico, fiestas often serve as the stage for the acting out of severely aggressive, violent and socially disruptive scenes involving large numbers of individuals. In a book on the Andean Indian issued by a Protestant missionary organization, several authors refer to scenes of degradation and brutality which they witnessed during Indian fiestas in Peru and Ecuador. In Vicos, during the field study, only two cases of wife-beating were reported, and neither was in connection with a fiesta, although both involved drunkenness. Fighting on the part of a few individuals is not uncommon during Vicos fiestas, but serious injury is rare and the great majority of the population is quite orderly.

Fiestas also serve to provide a formal structure for the release, exhilaration and pleasure afforded by the drinking of alcoholic beverages, while yet keeping the drinking in a context where it does not interfere with other important segments of behavior. Drinking is such an integral part of the fiesta complex and such an important aspect of Vicos life that it needs to be discussed in some detail. Practically every published study of Andean life contains reference to the drinking of alcoholic beverages, yet no one has described it in any detail.

Many observers of the Peruvian scene have commented on the excessive drinking of alcoholic beverages by the people they describe as "Indians" or "Cholos." The popular view in Mestizo and Creole Peru is that coca-chewing and alcoholism among Indians are social evils, "vices," which must be eliminated as the first step in bringing the Indian into the national culture as a citizen of Peru.

Drinking is practically universal among Indians in Peru. In Vicos, small children are given corn beer and everyone over 16 years of age drinks. Drinking by most adults, particularly adult males, is usually followed by drunkenness, and in many instances a man or woman may be drunk for several days in succession. The incidence and frequency of drinking and the amounts consumed, seem to be very high. Drinking is a social activity, however, and drinking customs are integrated with the most basic and powerful institutions in the community. Drinking and drunkenness do not seem to lead to any breakdown in interpersonal relations, nor do they seem to interfere with the performance of social roles by individuals. The incidence of extreme pathologies related to drinking seems to be low.

In Vicos, this dearth of alcohol-related pathology seems to be associated with a long tradition of ceremonial drinking which existed long before the European invasion; with a strong sense of social solidarity which is enhanced by ritual and convivial drinking; with a lack of conflict, guilt or ambivalence connected with the overt act of drinking itself; with the fact that drunkenness not only does not interfere with the performance of social roles but is a prerequisite to the successful performance of the most important social roles in the society; and with an irrational defense of tradition which says: to become intoxicated frequently is our custom, so it must be good.

Like most cultural explanations, this is not a causal explanation. The items mentioned are interdependent, and exist in a state of equilibrium which is also dependent on the peculiar place of the highland hacienda in the larger social structure of Peru. They are not inherently important in all individual cases of alcohol-related pathology, but they are suggestive of some of the reasons for group differences in rates of alcohol pathologies— for instance, between Vicosinos and Mestizos.

There is a long tradition of drinking and drunkenness in Peru which goes back well beyond the Conquest. Drinking and drunkenness had long been associated with ceremonial activity in the Inca tradition and probably before, and continue to be so associated in most parts of Indian Peru today. Among Indians, the primary association of drinking is with ceremonial and festival.

Distilled liquors were introduced from Spain following the Conquest, and distilled liquors and wines of national manufacture appeared early in the history of post-Conquest Peru. Previously there had been no distilled beverage in Peru, the only alcoholic drink having been a corn beer, *chicha,* which had a wide distribution throughout the American continent. Some believe that chicha may have been a stronger drink in the pre-Conquest period; in any case, it was quite capable of producing drunkenness and was simple to manufacture. Vicosinos make no temporal distinction between chicha and *aguardiente,* the distilled sugarcane liquor so popular in the sierra, in spite of the fact that chicha is locally made and aguardiente is purchased. That is, they are not aware that chicha is an aboriginal drink and that distilled alcohol is imported. Both are integrated completely into the ceremonial customs and each is enjoyed for its own effects. The fact that aguardiente is much more potent in terms of producing drunkenness is well known, and the general feeling is that it is very difficult to get drunk on chicha. The latter, however, is enjoyed for its taste, its mildly intoxicating properties, and its refreshing qualities. The Indians rarely mix it with alcohol, the common practice of Mestizos. Chicha is often given in small amounts to children and is very popular for quenching thirst after work. It is also considered to have healthful, strength-giving characteristics.

Chicha is primarily a fiesta drink. It is rarely purchased, but women do bring it from Marcara to the plaza during fiestas, and Vicosinos do buy it. Chicha is freely shared, and is, in a sense, a family drink.

Aguardiente, distilled sugarcane alcohol, is always purchased. There are at least 40 persons who sell aguardiente in Vicos and it is sold in almost every Mestizo home in Marcara. Aguardiente is served in bars, and always accompanies chicha at fiestas. Often, in the case of a sudden death, there will not be time to prepare chicha; then aguardiente will be the only beverage offered. Chicha is considered a "cold," or "fresca" food in Vicos, while aguardiente is "hot." In spite of this, there is no hesitation about drinking both on the same occasion. Some few people claim that aguardiente has made them sick. The writer never heard sickness attributed to the drinking of chicha. In terms of actual volume consumed, chicha probably leads aguardiente; but in terms of alcohol absorbed, the largest amount would be from aguardiente. Except for the thirst-quenching and assumed strength-giving value of chicha, there seems to be little difference between chicha and aguardiente in terms of use, meaning or function.

Commercial wines, beers and liquors are familiar to most Vicosino men, and to some women, and are consumed with apparent satisfaction. In response to questioning, most express a preference for chicha and aguardiente. On several occasions, when the author offered to provide wine, beer, pisco, rum or aguardiente as a gift for services rendered, the choice was invariably the latter.

Drinking is occasional and any time of the day or night and any place except church is considered appropriate for drinking if the context of the situation warrants it. Drinking is done in the context of patron saint and other religious festivals, at family festivals, political meetings, harvest and agricultural celebrations, cooperative work projects, and at funerals. It accompanies formal visiting, and any meeting outside of regular daily contact with a *compadre* carries with it a strong obligation for the individuals involved to drink together.

Probably two statements about Vicos drinking which come as close to being absolute as statements about social customs can be, are:

1. Everyone over 16 years of age drinks alcoholic beverages.

2. There are almost no solitary drunkards.

Since most drinking is done in the context of fiesta situations, those who attend the same host's parties customarily drink together. And, since most persons who attend the same fiestas together are relatives and neighbors, most drinking is done with such persons. Young men, usually the unmarried ones, often attend fiestas together, or meet in the plaza if they are attending separate mayordomo affairs. Young women often do the same. Older men also tend to form temporary drinking groups during a fiesta. Marriage and motherhood rather than age seem to be an important basis for making up women's groups, and married women seem to stay with female relatives and neighbors. Friendship among men is usually age-graded, but in fairly loose groupings of 5- to 10-year periods. Men and women tend to separate into conversational groups during a fiesta, but as the party progresses, these groups become less distinct.

To the author's knowledge there are no formal restrictions regarding those who may drink together. Age, sex, kinship, *compadrazgo*, and so forth, do enter into the informal structure of drinking groups but, in theory and in practice, anyone can drink with anyone (e.g., men with their wives, compadres with their godchildren, young boys with their grandfathers).

Vicosino drinking in bars, when it does occur, is almost exclusively done in groups. The members of the group contribute to the purchase of a bottle and the use of a glass (often only one) and then retire to a corner of the bar—or, if the weather is clear, outside—to drink. In Marcara there are bars that serve Indians and bars that do not, and few attempts are made to cross these lines.

On the average, women drink less than men do. Certain people in both groups never refuse a drink; others drink lightly. In Vicos, musicians, dancers, hosts, and other functionaries occasionally develop avoidance behavior in some fiesta drinking situations; in contrast to Mestizo fiesta behavior, few others feel called upon to seek them out to force the issue. In both cultures a certain deference is accorded to old men and women by younger people, and although the different age groups drink together, young people rarely apply pressure to elderly persons to drink.

Drunken behavior in Vicos is an exaggeration of sober behavior. The popular United States idea, also present among Peruvian Mestizos, of the meek man who becomes a tiger when drunk, is not known. Alcohol is not necessary for, nor is it conceived of as, oil for the wheels of social intercourse. People interact rather easily, drunk or sober. There is no insecurity about getting drunk faster than others because no one fears what "they" or "my friends" will "do to me," nor is there any fear of performing some act which will arouse guilt feelings afterward. There is some maudlin behavior in Vicos, but it occurs mainly among individuals who tend to be maudlin when sober. Vicosinos tell the same kinds of jokes, the same kinds of stories, and indulge in the same sort of boisterous, ribald humor when drunk as they do when sober. Perhaps this behavior is increased, and the laughter is louder and easier when drunk, but otherwise there is no difference. As people learn to drink, so do they learn how to act while drunk.

Alcohol has its physiological effects on the body, but within limits, these appear to be modifiable. Even "passing out" (losing consciousness) can be culturally conditioned. In Vicos, passing out is not uncommon at fiestas, and it is characteristic behavior for the chief male mourner at a funeral. Passing out, however, is not equivalent in Vicos to retiring from the situation, as among the Mohave. On the contrary, the unconscious person usually remains at the affair until he awakens and begins again. The phenomenon of "blacking out"—that is, of having partial or total amnesia for parts of drunken episodes—which is diagnostic of problem drinking, is not known in Vicos. Vomiting is infrequent but taken matter-of-factly when it does occur during drinking bouts. The author observed one such case in all the occasions of drinking witnessed. The hangover also is not an important factor in Vicos drinking. A few older men will admit to "pains in the body" after 4 or 5 days of drinking, but it does not seem to impair their behavior; most men will say they feel fine after drinking and they at least act as though they do. It is difficult to draw conclusions about this. The demands made on a Vicosino are not too great, but there is no reason to assume that hangover symptoms would be concealed. No instance was noted of a person in Vicos incapacitated by a hangover. The morning-after pick-me-up is the subject of much joking in Mestizo culture. The same saying is known to many Vicosinos—"a drink to cure your head"—but a drink is seldom taken in Vicos for that purpose after a fiesta is over. Some say that on the day after the *octava* of a fiesta, one drinks to cure one's head, but this is not the morning-after drinking to avoid withdrawal symptoms. There is no feeling against morning drinking as such, as long as it is done in the proper context. On a few occasions the author offered alcohol to Vicosinos on work mornings, and no one ever refused if he were joined by the author. This was drinking in the context of a social obligation, however.

Violence seems to increase in frequency when people are drunk; but drunk or sober, there is actually very little violence in Vicos. Few fights were noted during the field investigation, and of those noted, the same two men seemed to be involved most of the time.

Sexual activity of a premarital variety appears to increase during fiestas, but this may not be a function of drinking. Several male informants told the author that they purposely stayed sober at times during fiestas so that they could "escape" with a girl. Extramarital sexual activity, which is a disruptive force in Vicos culture, seems to occur mostly when individuals are quite sober (e.g. while a woman or a man is pasturing animals near the house or field of the other, or while the woman's husband is away on a hacienda work assignment).

Most of the crimes committed by Vicosinos during the field study were carried out while sober. In only two cases (one of which occurred before the field study and one during it) could it be documented that drunkenness was associated with criminality. Several years ago, H.C., one of the most violent men in Vicos and a cultural deviant, poured alcohol over a customer in his bar who had complained about its purity, lit the alcohol with a match, and thrashed the customer with a heavy stick. He was jailed for 6 months. Observers said he was drunk at the time. The other instance involved a psychotic individual who, while drunk, kicked his pregnant wife in the stomach, causing her to abort. He also was jailed. In the vast majority of cases (e.g. stealing, accomplice in stealing, military violations, breach of contract), drunkenness was not involved. In most cases of stealing, drinking seemed to be studiously avoided.

Drinking and drunkenness have a good cultural "fit" in Vicos. As has been pointed out above, there is little ambivalence or guilt connected with drunken behavior; there is, in fact, an extremely permissive attitude toward it.

It might be said that the conditions of cultural learning necessary for the development of an addict do not exist in Vicos. Bales has said:

> . . . there are three general ways in which culture and social organization can influence rates of alcoholism. The first is the degree to which the culture operates to bring about acute needs for adjustment, or inner tensions, in its members. The second way is the sort of attitudes toward drinking which the culture produces in its members. The crucial factor seems to be whether a given attitude toward drinking positively suggests drinking to the individual as a means of relieving his inner tensions, or whether such a thought arouses a strong counter-anxiety. The third general way is the degree to which the culture provides substitute means of satisfaction.

Riley has suggested, from a survey of public attitudes toward drunkenness in the United States, that inconsistency of group attitudes toward drinking is a factor in problem drinking within the group; such inconsistency is prevalent in the United States. In Vicos, there is a consistent attitude toward drunkenness which is effective because, although there is no consistency in the larger Peruvian culture, outside attitudes rarely impinge on Vicos attitudes. Mishkin noted that alcoholic beverages are considered sacred in themselves in Kauri. No evidence of this was seen in Vicos. But alcoholic drinks are used as an integral part of religious rituals and ceremonials as much as convivial accompaniments to these ceremonials. There is no abstinence feeling and a minimum of utilitarian manipulative drinking. Drinking is seldom used as a means of personal social adjustment, as a persuasive in business dealings or sexual advances, or to combat hangover symptoms. A few Vicosinos seemed to use drinking at one time or another as a means of solving personal problems, and two apparently mentally disturbed individuals seemed to experience an intensification of their problems when drunk. Generally, however, the drinking of alcoholic beverages in Vicos does not seem to be primarily associated with the sort of anxiety that Horton found to be associated with drinking in his study of preliterate societies.

Vicosinos are, of course, not without anxieties. Other oral activities, however, such as eating and coca-chewing, do not seem to be foci of this anxiety. Sorcery and gossip seem to be the most common outlets for aggression and for tension release. Many deaths are thought to be caused by sorcery, specifically by poisoning, and fellow Vicosinos, generally not neighbors or kinsmen, are usually thought to be the agents. Any description which emphasizes integration without consideration of its logical opposite —whether it be called "dysfunction" or "nonintegration" or "disorganization"—is likely to give an unrealistic and static quality to the cultural system. In matter of fact, the Vicos community exhibits features of nonintegration or dysfunction operating internally. The fiesta complex and associated drinking behavior, however, provide little opportunity for the expression of these dysfunctional features. Other aspects of the culture, such as sorcery, do provide such opportunities. The contention of this paper is that Vicosino drinking behavior is prevailingly integrative, as is the total fiesta system. There is consensus about drinking. There is little ambivalence or guilt associated with drunkenness. Drinking and drunkenness seem to create few social strains and they do not interfere with an individual's performance of his various social roles.

THE WORKING CLASS IN SANTIAGO DE CHILE

*by Juan Marconi, Anibal Varela, Enrique Rosenblat, Guido Solari, Ines Marchesse, Rolando Alvarado, and Walter Enriquez ***

. . . The present communication reports the results of a direct survey of a sample of the population of a suburb of Santiago, selected as representative of the working class. The inquiry was intended to determine the prevalence of alcoholism and some other forms of abnormal use of alcohol. It is obvious that the identification of alcoholism in the so-called healthy population must be based on symptoms easy to detect. We selected, as characteristic symptoms, (a) the frequency of drunkenness, (b) the habitual ingestion of alcoholic beverages before breakfast, and (c) the frequency and duration of bouts of drinking (sprees).

* From "A Survey on the Prevalence of Alcoholism among the Adult Population of a Suburb of Santiago," *Quarterly Journal of Studies on Alcohol, 16* (1955), 438–46.

There is no doubt that the frequency of drunkenness is a good index of behavior in relation to alcohol, allowing itself to be classified as normal or abnormal within a population. The habitual ingestion of alcohol before breakfast and drinking bouts are considered as characteristic of definite stages in the evolution of alcoholism.

Other symptoms, such as loss of control over drinking and alcoholic amnesia, are difficult to assess in a survey. To establish their presence, deeper analysis and prolonged observation of individuals are needed, and these are incompatible with the conditions of a survey.

Procedure. The survey was carried out between January and May 1954 on a sample of the population dwelling in a suburb of Santiago, called Comuna Quinta Normal. This population can be considered as typical of the working class in urban areas. Like the general population of Chile, the sample is ethnically homogeneous.

The selected area is one that has been employed for more than 10 years as a pilot zone for field work by the National Public Health Service. This situation has resulted in the establishment of a close relationship between each family and the members of the staff of the Public Health Center. The families continually receive medical and social care and are accustomed to give true information to the nurses and other members of the staff who, in turn, are well aware of the medical and social problems in each family. This condition guarantees a high degree of accuracy in the results of the survey.

The total population of the selected zone is 33,450, grouped in 7,597 families. To make the sample representative of the universe investigated, a list of families was elaborated by the geographic location of homes, and from this list the families numbered 1, 11, 21, etc., were selected. For this survey we chose only subjects who were 15 years of age or above, of whom there were a total of 19,850 (9,683 males and 10,167 females). Our sample contained 1,976 persons (905 males and 1,071 females), comprising 787 families.

A blank schedule was filled with the data obtained in the interview of each individual. For the purpose of the survey, any alcohol intoxication of such degree as to produce overt motor incoordination was considered as "drunkenness." The frequency of drunkenness was classified as follows: (1) absence of drunkenness, (2) less than once a month, (3) once a month, (4) twice a month, (5) each week-end, (6) more than 1 working day during each week, and (7) every day. Each individual was included in any of the preceding classes according to the general pattern of his behavior as observed during the year 1953.

The habitual drinking of alcoholic beverages before breakfast was divided into two categories: (1) those who drank in the morning after an episode of drunkenness, and (2) those who drank on any morning independently of preceding drunkenness.

A "bout of drinking" was defined as any state of continuous drunkenness, maintained by repeated ingestion of alcoholic beverages, which lasted 2 days or more. The frequency of bouts was classified as follows: (*1*) less than four times a year, (*2*) once every 3 months, (*3*) once every 2 months, (*4*) once a month, (*5*) twice a month, and (*6*) weekly. For this classification, too, only the general pattern exhibited during 1953 was considered.

The data obtained in each interview were checked with information given by other members of the family.

Frequency of Habitual Drunkenness. The frequency of habitual drunkenness in the surveyed population is reported in Table 1. A low proportion of the men (28.5 per cent) and a very high proportion of the women (94.3 per cent) had not experienced an episode of drunkenness during 1953. On the other hand, 36.6 per cent of the men, but only 1.2 per cent of the women, became drunk at least once a month.

If, for reasons to be discussed later, we classify as an alcoholic any person who exhibits daily drunkenness or becomes drunk 2 or more working days each week, then 69 of the men (7.7 per cent) and 7 of the women (0.6 per cent) can be considered as alcoholics.

Frequency and Duration of Bouts. Experiences of bouts of drinking during the survey year were found in 66 men (7.3 per cent) and 2 women (0.2 per cent) in the surveyed population. Their frequency as well as their maximal duration among the men are summarized in Table 2.

TABLE 1.—*Frequency of Drunkenness*

	Males		Females	
	No.	*%*	*No.*	*%*
Never	258	28.5	1,011	94.3
Less than once a month	316	34.9	47	4.5
Once a month	92	10.1	4	0.4
Twice a month	81	9.0	1	0.1
Each weekend	89	9.8	1	0.1
Two or more working days each week	26	2.9	5	0.4
Every day	43	4.8	2	0.2
Totals	*905*	*100.0*	*1,071*	*100.0*

TABLE 2.—*Frequency and Duration of Bouts of Drinking among Males*

	Number of Cases	Maximal Duration (Days)			
		2	*3*	*4–6*	*7+*
Less than 4 a year	21	10	5	4	2
Once every 3 months	11	5	4	1	1
Once every 2 months	7	1	1	4	1
Once a month	12	0	6	2	4
Twice a month	7	1	0	3	3
Weekly	8	1	3	4	0
Totals	*66*	*18*	*19*	*18*	*11*

In order to interpret the significance of bouts of drinking as a symptom of alcoholism, it is necessary to bear in mind that in Chile the excessive use of alcohol for social celebrations is so prevalent that it is not unusual to observe persons who cannot be considered as alcoholics indulging in a bout of drinking during family or popular festivities. Half of the persons in the surveyed population who exhibited bouts of drinking did so relatively infrequently—that is, not more than four times a year—and these may have been occasioned by festivities. It seems necessary, therefore, to differentiate the bouts of drinking according to a criterion of severity. Obviously this criterion cannot be based only on the duration of the bouts but their frequency also must be considered. We have classified as significant bouts of drinking those with a frequency higher than four times a year and producing absenteeism from work of more than a sixth of the working days during the year.

The preceding criterion points to 18 men (and no women) as exhibiting significant bouts of drinking. Of these 18, 12 had shown drunkenness either every day or during 2 or more working days each week. Of the remaining 48 men whose bouts of drinking were classified as not significant, 37 exhibited drunkenness only once a week or less frequently, 9 of them only occasionally, as shown in Table 3.

We think it justified, for reasons to be discussed later, to consider as alcoholics the 18 men suffering from significant bouts of drinking, but not all these cases are to be added to the 69 already classified as alcoholics according to their frequency of drunkenness, because there is an overlapping of the conditions. In fact, 12 of them are classified as alcoholics for both reasons.

Drinking before Breakfast. The analysis of the meaning of the use of alcoholic beverages before breakfast, or as a part of the breakfast, is rather difficult. The habitual use of beer mixed with a kind of toasted whole wheat flour (*harina tostada*) is very prevalent not only among men but also among women, and especially among nursing mothers.

TABLE 3.—*Bouts of Drinking in Males in Relation to Frequency of Drunkenness*

| | Number of Cases | Number Exhibiting Bouts | | |
		Nonsevere	Significant	Totals
Never	258	0	0	0
Less than once a month	316	9	0	9
Once a month	92	3	1	4
Twice a month	81	10	1	11
Each weekend	89	15	4	19
Two or more working days each week	26	4	2	6
Every day	43	7	10	17
Totals	*905*	*48*	*18*	*66*

The results of the survey showed that 46 per cent of the men and 40 per cent of the women used alcoholic beverages before breakfast or as a part of it. Since drunkenness is very infrequent among women, it is justified to think that this habit is not related to alcoholism. But among the men, too, drinking before or at breakfast time was observed in many of those who never became drunk.

The use of alcoholic beverages before breakfast but only on the morning after an episode of drunkenness was observed in 94 men (10.4 per cent). These cases are distributed more or less regularly in all the classes of frequency of drunkenness. Altogether 105 men (11.6 per cent) customarily drank before or at breakfast either after an episode of drunkenness or independently of it.

There is no doubt that this habit could be the expression of a physical dependence on alcohol, and in some cultures "morning drinking" is regarded as pathognomonic of alcoholism, but in Chile individual analysis would be necessary to determine whether or not this is symptomatic of alcoholism. Such individual study could not readily be done in a survey.

Summarizing, the use of alcoholic beverages before breakfast or as a part of it does not constitute a fact that in the present survey can be used as an aid in the identification of alcoholics.

*   *   *

TABLE 4.—*Distribution of the Surveyed Population*

	Males		Females	
	No.	%	No.	%
Never drunk	258	28.5	1,011	94.3
Drunk less than 12 times a year	316	34.9	47	4.6
Periodic excessive drinkers	256	28.3	6	0.5
Alcoholics	75	8.3	7	0.6
Total sample	*905*	*100.0*	*1,071*	*100.0*

Discussion. The prevalence of alcoholism among the surveyed adult population was higher than Jellinek's estimate for Chile obtained according to his estimation formula. There are two possible explanations for this difference. The first is that the diagnostic criteria employed in our survey may include people who would not be considered as alcoholics according to other standards. The second is that it may not be warranted to generalize to the whole country the results obtained in our sample.

As to the first possibility, there is no doubt that a clear boundary cannot be established between some excessive drinkers and alcoholics. The borderline zone could be so broad that the proportion of alcoholics can be varied only by changing the boundary. In the present instance we do not have the impression that our diagnostic criteria pushed the boundary into the nonalcoholic zone but, on the contrary, it seems to us not impossible that it leaves outside the group of alcoholics some persons who should actually be considered as alcoholics.

The first element of the identifying criteria for alcoholism—the presence of drunkenness every day or during 2 or more working days each week—implies, it seems to us, a strong suggestion that these people are clearly dependent on alcohol. The second element—the presence of significant bouts of drinking, of such frequency and duration that they cannot be attributed to sociocultural behavior—is, in our opinion, a clear expression of loss of control in the drinking situation as defined by Jellinek.

Concerning the possibility of generalizing the results of the survey to the whole Chilean population, we may point out that though our sample is characteristic of the working class of big cities, we do not know whether similar conditions prevail in the working class of the small cities and of the rural areas. According to the last census, the working class of large cities represents about a third of the total population of the country. Thus, it seems reasonable to assume that our sample may be considered as representative at least of this portion. We do not know whether our findings apply to other social classes or to workers in less urban areas. This can only be determined by corresponding surveys.

Finally, it is not impossible that the coefficients used in Jellinek's formula should need a correction for Chile.

An outstanding finding in our survey is the amazing frequency of episodes of drunkenness in men who, we believe, should not be considered as alcoholics. We must emphasize that we have classified as drunkenness only such alcohol intoxication as induces overt motor incoordination, which, obviously, goes much further than euphoria.

About 30 per cent of the adult men have episodes of drunkenness every weekend, twice a month, or monthly. These episodes are seen during holidays and probably on paydays. It is possible that some of these individuals are actually dependent on alcohol and, therefore, could be classified as alcoholics, but we believe that in the majority of cases of drunkenness which occur exclusively on holidays the behavior is a manifestation of a cultural pattern of drinking rather than a sign of alcoholism.

It is important, furthermore, to point out that in some cases occasional drunkenness could be prolonged into a bout of drinking. Such bouts have not been classified as significant according to the criterion employed, because they are infrequent and last only for a short time. We believe that although nonsevere drinking bouts cannot be differentiated from those observed in alcoholics, they are rather the consequence of culturally determined habits of drinking. In support of this opinion we may mention that it is not uncommon for persons who become drunk only occasionally (less than four times a year) to indulge on those occasions in a bout of drinking.

Finally, our results show that there is a sharp difference between the sexes in the frequency of drunkenness and alcoholism. In fact, the male–female ratio for alcoholism was 13.2 and for drunkenness of any frequency, 12.5. The alcoholism rate among men is more than double that reported by Jellinek and Keller in the United States. We do not know whether this difference has its roots in cultural, psychological or physiological bases.

8. THE FAR EAST

INDIA

by R. N. Chopra, G. S. Chopra and I. C. Chopra *

In India the earliest reference to the use of alcoholic drinks is traceable to 2,000 B.C. The ancient Aryan invaders of India, who appear to have been well versed in the art of brewing, used a beverage called soma. The exact nature of the soma of the Vedic period is still wrapped in mystery and the juice of about a dozen different plants has been regarded as the soma of Sanskrit literature. Hemp and ephedra figure in this list. According to Professor Max Muller, soma was probably a kind of fermented liquor. Soma was made from the homa plant (Sarcostemma) and was imported into India by the Mongolian Tartar races. When properly squeezed, the plant yields a juice, which after fermentation and mixing with honey produces an exhilarating and intoxicating drink. Three kinds of drinks were known in the time of Manu, viz., gouri, prepared from molasses, madur, from the sweet flowers of *Bassia latifolia,* and paishti, from rice and barley cakes. Of these, paishti was reckoned as the most common. The suras were included under the generic term, madya, which included every kind of alcoholic drink. Jagla, a kind of rice beer, is mentioned in the Susruta—a Sanskrit medical treatise written in the 5th century A.D. Khola, another beverage, mentioned in the later editions of the same treatise, was prepared from powdered barley. It would appear that the art of fermenting starchy and saccharoid substances was understood and practiced in India from very early times. In all probability the aboriginal races of India learned the art of brewing from the Aryan invaders, since from immemorial times they have been preparing and using such beverages.

Certain drinks and beverages commonly used in many parts of the Himalayas appear to be similar to those commonly used by the Mongolian races. Some of these preparations resemble shamshu and sake used in China and Japan. The reason for this is not far to seek. The Mongolian stock invaded India from the northeast by degrees, and the evidence of this invasion still exists in the Mongolian characteristics of the Himalayan races at the present day.

Ethnological Factors. The question of race is a very important factor. To quote the majority conclusions of the Research Committee appointed by the Society for the Study of Inebriety, races that have long been exposed

---

* From "Alcoholic Beverages in India," *Indian Medical Gazette, 77* (1942), 225 ff., 230, 293, 296, 363.

to the action of alcohol have grown more and more temperate. For example, Greeks, Italians, people of southern France, Spaniards, Portuguese, and the Jews, who have been most exposed to the action of alcohol, have grown more temperate. The nations of northern Europe, on the other hand, who have been comparatively less exposed to the action of alcohol, for example, the British, the Scandinavians, and the Russians, are more prone to drink; whereas most uncivilized races, such as the Eskimos, the Red Indians, the aboriginal inhabitants of Australia, and others who have had little or no racial experience of alcohol, are more prone to excessive drinking. West Africans are an exception to this rule; they are comparatively temperate, even though they consume a lot of palm wine. This rule also holds in India. In this country the habit of drinking and drunkenness is much commoner among the aboriginal races, when an opportunity is offered to them, than among those that are more cultured. The Aryans and the white races, who introduced the use of alcohol from their original home in central Asia, have grown more temperate, while the races such as the Sonthals, Bhils, Gonds, Nagas, and other hill tribes belonging to the aboriginal stock, who have been less exposed to the use of alcohol, are more prone to excesses, when an opportunity is offered. It was observed that these races, although they are ordinarily given to the use of country beers, always drink to excess if they can get stronger distilled liquors. Drunkenness is always common when economic conditions allow primitive peoples to buy strong alcoholic drinks. Fortunately, their means usually do not allow them to go beyond the cheap beers.

Climatic Factor. Taking the influence of climate, and treating India as a whole, it has been observed that the consumption of fermented and weak distilled liquors generally prevails in areas of heavy rainfall, e.g., in the mountainous and submountainous tracts of the Himalayas, Chota Nagpur, and along the Western Ghats. Weak alcoholic beverages, such as country beers, are commonly believed to be a necessity of life for dwellers in malarious tracts. In drier climates, such as those of the Punjab, Sindh and the United Provinces, and parts of the Bengal and Bombay Presidencies, where greater extremes of heat and cold prevail, strong spirits are more commonly used.

Religious and Social Factors. Religious and caste factors also determine to a large extent the use of liquor in this country. The use of alcoholic drinks is prohibited among the Mohammedans and certain classes of Hindus, such as Jains and Vaishnavites, and prohibition is strictly observed by the last two named. Generally speaking, among the upper and middle strata of society of India drinking is uncommon except in moderation; this is especially the case among those who take to European habits and customs, such as the Mohammedans and most of the high caste Hindus. In the Tantric sect of "Saktas," on the other hand, drinking is not only permissible but even enjoined, for both personal use and worship. A similar practice prevails among many of the most backward castes, notably on the east coast of Madras and in the forest tracts between Chota Nagpur and Godaveri. Among the Dhobis of the Punjab and the United Provinces an offender is required, as a caste punishment, to provide drink for the *panchayet* of the caste. This custom also prevails in certain other parts of India among the lower working classes, such as Charmars, on religious grounds. Recently there have been big demonstrations in Bombay over prohibition brought in by the Congress Government of that province and also by the Parsees, for similar reasons. The use of pachwai is considered necessary at religious and social festivals by Sonthals, Garros, Koch, Dhangars, Mandais, Tipperas, and other aboriginal tribes. The Sonthals, especially the women, object to the use of pachwai that is bought from a shop.

There is a general belief among the hill tribes that fermented liquors are less injurious than distilled spirits. The use of these fermented liquors is not only permitted but encouraged by custom. On the occasions of religious worship, among many of the backward races inhabiting the western Ghats and in the hilly tracts between Chota Nagpur and Godaveri, the use of these liquors is considered essential. Men, women, and children all indulge, there being no restriction as to caste or creed. Among the Sonthals and Bhumji tribes of Chota Nagpur fermented liquors are considered to be indispensable at funerals, marriages, and other ceremonial occasions. Mohammedans are forbidden by their religion to take alcohol, and for that reason in the western Himalayas, where the population is predominantly Mohammedan, these liquors are not much used.

Occupation. This is perhaps a more important factor than caste and religion in influencing the consumption of alcoholic drinks. A departure from the pursuit of agriculture has commonly the effect of weakening the traditional restrictions against indulgence in alcohol, an effect which is enhanced by the difficulty of maintaining the old customs under the more complex town life. The conditions of employment in Indian factories and industries, such as jute, cotton, coal and mining, cause the workers to feel the need of a stimulant after the day's work is done, and the high wages enable them to satisfy this desire. The mill hands in Calcutta, Bombay, and other industrial towns, such as Cawnpore, are a good example. It is for this reason that about a dozen of the large cities in India with the bulk of the industrial population account for approximately one-fourth of the total alcoholic drinks consumed in India.

There are other factors, such as the presence of a floating population at the time of certain fairs or gatherings, which lead to a heavy consumption of alcohol. We have observed that during festivals the consumption goes up by 40 to 80 per cent in certain localities.

Belief in Medicinal Value. When a relative or friend is feeling "out of sorts" or "seedy," a man habituated to liquor often suggests a dose as a prophylactic or curative. There is a belief among certain sections of the population in this country that the use of alcoholic beverages is a necessity, as it keeps out damp and cold and is a prophylactic against malaria, coughs, and colds.

As a Source of Vitamins and Digestive Adjuncts. Beers generally are regarded as stimulating, refreshing, and thirst-quenching beverages that have a definite food value. According to analysis done in our laboratory, most of them contained 1.4 gm. of sugar and 0.6 gm. of albuminoids per 100 cc.; there is no doubt, therefore, regarding their food value. In fact they have the combined value of a food and a stimulant. The quantities of carbon dioxide and other substances present may even promote digestion by stimulating various digestive juices, and thus they may act as adjuncts in facilitating the digestion of other foods. They also supply quantities of salts of potassium and sodium, calcium phosphate, etc., which are among the more important of minerals required for the repair of the tissues after the wear and tear of hard physical exertion.

It is well known that plants of all kinds, including lower forms of vegetable growth, contain water-soluble substances which promote growth and nutrition. Brewer's yeast is a recognized source of vitamins. The crude beers which contain both molds and yeasts should therefore form very rich sources of water-soluble vitamins belonging to the groups B_1 and B_2, and probably also vitamin C. Most of the people who habitually take country beer are very poor and cannot always secure for themselves a varied diet containing all the principles required for proper nutrition. Our inquiries have convinced us that the majority of such tribes are subsisting on a monotonous, restricted, and sometimes unbalanced diet. It is remarkable, however, that these primitive people are particularly free from any of the diet deficiency diseases which have wrought havoc in some parts of the world. It is not unlikely that the supply of vitamins gained through beer drinking is responsible for the absence of deficiency diseases in these communities. Yeasts, which also occur in these beers, contain hematopoietic principles, and they have been used successfully in the treatment of anemia.

As Food. Most of the common alcoholic beverages used in India have considerable food value. During the process of fermentation many undigestible carbohydrates are converted into more readily assimilable sugars. The nutritive value of rice beers, such as pachwai and zu, is undoubtedly substantial. The Nagas never drink milk or use milk as a food; they always drink zu prepared in their own homes. In the mountainous regions of India, where economic conditions are poor and the natural craving for a stimulant is greater on account of climatic conditions, the use of country beers and spirits, offered at prices commensurate with the means of the people, are to the poor what the different varieties of expensive alcoholic liquors are to the well-to-do.

As a Euphoric. For the most part people resort to alcoholic drinks in order to tide over the feeling of exhaustion after a day's hard labor in the fields, in the tea gardens, or during the trying winter season. Pachwai is used by practically all the male and female workers in the coal mine areas of Bengal and Bihar, and is usually indulged in after the day's labor is done. The work is so hard, uninteresting, and monotonous that it would be difficult for them to get through it every day without prospect of their beer. The quantities taken are often moderate, just sufficient to relieve the feeling of fatigue and ensure sound sleep.

Economic Conditions. All circumstances which affect the prosperity of the people in general have a direct influence on the consumption of alcohol. Consumption rises in good years and falls in bad years; it falls to the minimum during famine years. The present authors observed that the consumption rises after the harvest season in the Punjab, when people have plenty to eat. Furthermore, consumption in the shops in the mill areas rises higher on pay days than on other work days.

Epidemics. Outbreaks of epidemics such as cholera and plague may also be accompanied by a large increase in the consumption of liquors, owing to the people taking liquor partly in the belief that it is a prophylactic and partly to overcome the fear of the disease. This tendency was clearly observed in the last great plague epidemic in the Punjab during 1902, and it has been observed in other epidemics since.

Relation to Other Intoxicants. It is of interest to discuss here the comparative consumption of other forms of intoxicants used in India along with alcohol and how their consumption affects that of liquor. An attempt has been made to compare the consumption per annum in different provinces of spirits, country beer, opium, bhang, ganja, and charas. The popularity of alcoholic beverages in the same area may vary from time to time according to the fluctuations in prices of different intoxicants. The people sometimes take to toddy instead of spirit when the prices of spirits are high. This is a common occurrence in the South Kanara, Surat, and Konkan districts in the south.

A very remarkable instance of a change of stimulants following an increase of taxation is that of people resorting to country beer in Bombay and Madras Presidencies, where the taxation on distilled spirits has been raised to a high level.

Exciting Causes. Ease of access to alcoholic beverages must be considered as an important causative factor in leading to their regular use. It has been found that the drinking habit is easily picked up and is quite common among the aboriginal tribes and in families where some other members of the family take alcohol. The use of alcohol is universal among the tribes who are allowed to manufacture their own drinks or who have easy access to it.

Drunkenness and Addiction

The important precipitating or immediate causes of habitual use of alcohol are related to the previous uses of such beverages in medical treatment, to self-treatment for the relief of pain, and to recourse during emotional stress. In an investigation carried out by the present authors, over 50 per cent of the habitués attributed their addiction to contact or association with other habitués, to a desire for experience, to satisfy curiosity, to obtain a thrill, or to alleviate emotional distress.

The persons below 30 years all attributed their addiction to contact and association with other habitués. Ten per cent of cases attributed it to the previous use of drugs in medical treatment and to self-administration for the relief of pain.

The underlying causes of habitual use of alcohol are related to the inherent constitutional make-up of the individual. Individuals with unstable nervous systems are more prone to the habitual use of alcohol and other drug habits than those with a stable constitution. This is one way of saying that those with mild psychic disorders are more prone to alcoholic excess. An approach to the partial solution of alcohol addiction must therefore take into account the mental and hygienic factors involved.

Tari. The harmful effects of the abuse of alcoholic beverages were realized from very early days. Tipu Sultan found drunkenness from tari so prevalent that he ordered all tari trees to be cut down. Sir Brown Ellis gave similar orders, for the same reason, with regard to date palm trees growing on the government waste lands in Bombay Presidency. The Excise Commissioner in Bengal in 1884 found that much of the drunkenness attributed to outstills was really due to tari. Our own inquiries in parts of Bombay and Madras Presidencies, from old alcoholics, show that before the introduction of control it was not uncommon to find the entire village, including men, women, and children, drunk with tari. This state of affairs is sometimes met with even in these days in remote areas, in forests where Government control is not efficient, for instance, in the Agency Tracts of Madras, the Panch Mahals of Bombay, and the areas inhabited by the Maria Gonds in the Chanda district of the Central Provinces. In certain parts of Bihar, populated by aborigines, and in the mining areas of Bengal there is a certain amount of difficulty in keeping women or servants sober.

Pachwai. Drunkenness due to drinking pachwai, which is a mild drink, also exists in certain parts of India. Some of the aboriginal races drink this beverage to a state of intoxication, when they get an opportunity. Among the hill tribes in Chota Nagpur, Bengal, and Assam there is a tendency to take large quantities of pachwai if it can be had ready made in shops, but on account of the paucity of the supply of rice they do not manufacture it in their own homes. Drunkenness due to pachwai is not uncommon in the mining areas in Bengal and Bihar. The evidence in favor of pachwai being taken mostly for its nutritive effects is also not so strong as in the case of such beers as zu and laopani, since the rice in the former becomes unpalatable and bitter after fermentation, and is not consumed but thrown away.

Among the hill tribes in Assam the beers ordinarily consumed are weaker and the manner of their consumption is also different, the beverage being taken in the form of a thick gruel and rice eaten with it. It is a part of the diet of the inhabitants of the whole range of hills right up to Tibet and Burma. These tribes, who have a fine physique and are hardy, use as much as 25 per cent of their rice crop for this purpose. This in itself would seem to be proof that the beer cannot be very harmful and probably is not abused. Convivial drunkenness, however, does occur among these tribes, and many individuals may become incapacitated for days together after drinking bouts. Among the tea-garden coolies the state of affairs is much worse, and there is considerable drunkenness from this source. The coolies get so accustomed to the use of beers that they will starve themselves in order to get rice for brewing laopani or zu. In the United Provinces the evidence we have collected goes to show that excessive use of beer and drunkenness is confined chiefly to festive occasions. In Jaunsar, taluk, pachwai, and rabra are chiefly used on such occasions as New Year's Day, Dewali, and certain other festivals. In the Punjab, although evidence of drunkenness and even of debauchery was produced before the Excise Committee, lugri drinking usually is only conducive to merry-making of a harmless type. In South India beers are used to a much smaller extent, there being only one or two small areas where they are still consumed.

It has sometimes been urged that the use of such beverages should be totally stopped. On the other hand, there are authorities who think that any attempt to restrict their production would do more harm than good and would encourage drinking of stronger liquors or the resort to narcotics such as opium or hemp. The use of beer to the extent of producing uncontrollable intoxication is rare. Repeated doses of these beverages in excess may produce a state of intoxication similar to that commonly produced by stronger forms of alcoholic drinks. The accompanying heedlessness of danger and the feeling of bravery induced in such cases is partly the result of the temperament of these more or less primitive races, though also in many cases it is due to a state of mental confusion induced by poisons such as dhatura, aconite, and nux vomica, with which the beers are not infrequently adulterated.

There is no doubt, however, that in a few instances drinkers of country beer intoxicate themselves simply for the purpose of inducing a state of intoxication. These gross instances of producing drunkenness from country beer correspond to actions of excessive drinkers of alcohol in the West;

they are fortunately not common. Very large quantities have to be taken before such a condition can be produced, and this is often beyond the means of the drinkers.

CHINA *

Although the use of intoxicants seems to have been known to the Chinese at a very early time, they seem never to have been given to excessive indulgence in alcoholic beverages. In ceremonials, especially weddings and burials, and in libations to the gods, alcohol has been well-nigh omnipresent, and it has invariably been an important factor in the numerous popular feasts. At these feasts drunkenness has always been common; but as these celebrations occur most frequently among the official and wealthy classes, intoxication has been more general in these ranks of society than among the middle and lower classes. China is, however, a country of most perplexing contradictions, and this rule is subject to exceptions. Taking the nation as a whole, the Chinese are remarkably abstemious in the use of alcoholic beverages. Considerable difference of opinion exists among Sinologs concerning the nature of the beverages in use among the ancient Chinese, this difference being mainly due to the several translations of the Chinese character *tsieu*.

From the earliest times rice, millet, and other substances have been used in the making of alcoholic beverages in China. The grape is not indigenous to that country. It is supposed to have been brought from the region of the Caspian Sea in the First Han dynasty (206 B.C.–A.D. 23). The Chinese name for it is *p'u-t'ao*, and according to the *Pen Ts'ao*, the Chinese "Herbal" (completed in 1578), it is derived from *p'u*, "to drink deeply," and *t'ao*, "drunk," or "tipsy," in allusion to the use and abuse of the wine made therefrom.

Dr. Joseph Edkins, in the *Chinese Recorder* for 1885 (p. 307), states that the Chinese "Herbal" enumerates 66 kinds of fermented liquors, devotes three pages to distilled liquors, and divides wine into two classes—distilled and nondistilled. Edouard Biot, in the *Journal Asiatique* (2, 1843), gives a brief account of the ancient Chinese method of making tsieu. The following translation of it is from the Appendix to the Prolegomena of Vol. *4*, Pt. I, of Legge's *Chinese Classics:*

> In all the descriptions of solemn feasts mention is made of wine [*tsieu*] as the habitual drink. Men who became unruly in their behavior are reproached for their love of spirits. As at the present day, this wine was a fermented drink extracted from rice. . . . They allowed the fer-

* From *Standard Encyclopedia of the Alcohol Problem*, Ernest H. Cherrington, editor (Westerville, Ohio, 1924), 2, 581–2, 588.

mentation to proceed during the winter, and the wine [*tsieu*] was drunk in the spring of the following year. They separated it from the lees by straining it through herbs, or through a basket with a rough bottom, after which it was fit to be served at feasts. They mixed spirits with Chinese pepper and meat, to render them aromatic. The wine was kept in vases or bottles of baked earth. The baked earth could not be porcelain which was not common in China till a much later period. Common people drank from horns, either unpolished or carved. . . . In the times of the Chou Dynasty, the princes used cups formed of a precious stone. At solemn feasts the wine was served in large vases.

In Scarborough's *Collections of Chinese Proverbs* there is a chapter entitled "The Pleasures of Wine," many of the sentences being commendatory and others condemnatory as, for example:

Excessive joy leads to sorrow; excess of wine, to disorder.
Over the wine-cup the conversation is trifling.
No wine, no company; no company, no conversation.
When drinking, remember the property of your family.
Wine can both help business and hinder it.
Wine is a discoverer of secrets.
Men drink the wine and hogs eat the refuse of the grain.
Do not drink more wine than you are able to carry.
Do not begin to drink at daylight or you will be very drunk before dark.
Three glasses of wine can set everything to rights.
Medicine may heal imaginary sickness; wine can never dispel real sorrow.

CHINESE WINE DRINKING

by Merrill Moore *

Wine was primarily invented to drown worries, according to Chinese legends concerning its origin. Wine is said to have been invented by a woman who wished to stop her beloved emperor from worrying himself to death.

She was Yi Tieh, a maid in the palace of Emperor Yu, the ruler who coped with a disastrous flood some 4,000 years ago. Emperor Yu is famous for having devoted eight years to fighting the flood without going into his own home, although in carrying out his labors he is said to have passed by the doorway of his home three times. His name is a synonym for conscientiousness.

Modestly believing that the country was not doing well under his rule, Emperor Yu worried so much that he could hardly eat or sleep. He was an elderly man and his health soon showed the effects of this strain. His conviction concerning his inferiority preyed on his mind and tortured him so

* From "Chinese Wine. Some Notes on Its Social Use," *Quarterly Journal of Studies on Alcohol, 9* (1948), 270–9.

PLATE V

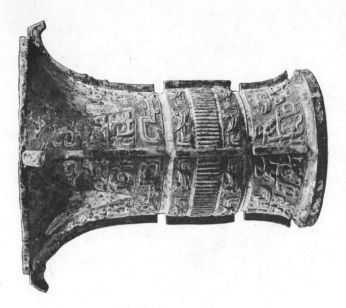

B. Chinese ceremonial wine vessel (tsun), bronze, Early Chou Dynasty, ca. 1000 B.C. Courtesy of the Cleveland Museum of Art, J. H. Wade Fund.

A. Sumerian libation ewer, bronze, ca. 3000 B.C., found at Kafaje, Iraq. Courtesy of the Oriental Institute, University of Chicago.

PLATE VI

A. Swedish drinking horn, wood with bronze mountings, 13th century. (Photograph by Antiquarisk-Topografiska Arkivet.) Courtesy of the Statens Historiska Museum, Stockholm.

B. Chinese ceremonial wine ladle, bronze, ca. 1000 B.C. Courtesy of the Metropolitan Museum of Art, New York, Munsey Bequest Fund.

much that it became obvious he was ruining his health. Everyone in the palace was worried.

One day, while sitting at his table, Emperor Yu again pushed aside his chopsticks and rice bowl and shook his head desperately. "I feel terrible," he said, "I can't eat! I have no appetite. I just don't care for food!" Suddenly he smelled something sweet and fragrant, something that was entirely unfamiliar. It was wine. Yi Tieh had prepared some for him in an earthenware jar which she was opening in the next room to stimulate the appetite of the worried emperor.

The Emperor decided to try it. He ordered a cup served. He liked it and felt better. His appetite returned. He ate his meal and with it drank the wine. Cupful followed cupful and for the first time in many months his thousand cares were dissipated and his worries drowned.

After that, wine became an important item in the palace provisions. The recipe for making wine gradually become known to the outside world and since that time the people in China have used the wines called *Samshu, Kaoliang, Shaoshing,* and others.

The Chinese never let a legend stop. There is always a legend behind the legend, and one behind that. For example: How did this girl in the Forbidden City learn to make wine?

Here enters another legendary figure, known as the Jade Girl, who before her marriage to Emperor Yu as an imperial concubine was a servant to a goddess in the distant Western Paradise. It is said that she had brought the formula from Paradise and taught Yi Tieh to make wine. The story does not stop there. The Jade Girl, also called The Jade Concubine (an honorific title, like the modern play titled "The Respectful Prostitute") is said to reappear, even today, especially after banquets on or near the premises where she lived. Her legend has spread. She is credited with having lived at one time near Peking where, as late as 1946, she was reported to have been seen by a former attendant of the last Manchu Empress, Tzu Hsi. On beholding the Jade Concubine drifting through the palace hallway carrying a wine jar, the symbol of her identity, the attendant swooned and could not be revived for two days. This account is credited by some savants with being as good an alibi for a hangover as any.

Why "Shaoshing" Means Wine. Emperor Yu spent much time in a place now known as Shaoshing, in the province of Chekiang. This region, incidentally, is today one of the best producing centers of the so-called "Samshu," which should properly be known as "Shaochiu" or Shaoshing wine.

They say that people in Shaoshing always make many jars of wine when a daughter is born. This wine is kept for many years and is opened only when the daughter is married. The older it is the better its taste. Because of this custom, one kind of Shaoshing wine is known as "The Dainty Red Maiden" and used especially at weddings.

Chinese Drys and Wets. Many Chinese are of the "not-a-single-drop" type as far as wine drinking is concerned. Some, on the other hand, drink heavily and habitually.

"A dry Chinese is as dry as a rock and a wet one can drink more than any other people on the globe," is another well-known proverb.

"Bury me near the kilns," a wine-lover in the old days earnestly instructed his relatives and friends when he was breathing his last. "Years later they may use the soil which my body has fertilized to make the wine pots. Then I may never be parted from wine!"

In many respects Chinese and foreigners are different in the way they drink today. It is generally said that the Chinese sip while the foreigners gulp. Chinese prefer to be seated when they drink. Rarely can Chinese drinkers be found standing near brass rails and emptying the glasses hastily. They drink slowly but not necessarily less wine. Like the tortoise in the race with the hare, they get there.

It would be doing the Chinese wine-lovers a gross injustice, however, to assume that they cannot take wine in big mouthfuls. The evidence of their ability to gulp wine is that Chinese toasts are always drunk with three cups, one after the other. In the old days when a high official said farewell to the Emperor before departing on an important mission, he would usually be granted three cups of wine from the imperial cellar—to be emptied right in front of the throne. When a warrior brought in the head of an enemy, his chief would confer a similar honor on him.

Other occasions when they drink fast are when they concede defeat in their finger games, sometimes when they wish to show appreciation of good music or a good poem, or when they simply feel "alcoholically" thirsty. This action of emptying a cup of wine is known as *kam pei,* pronounced "gom bay," i.e. "Bottoms up," or "Drink it down." If one does not wish to accept this challenge to kam pei he may say *sue bien,* pronounced "sway be yen," which means, "As I please and not as you insist." This type of drinking takes up a lot of time at public banquets and entertainments.

Wine Served with Food. When a Chinese drinks, he must have a dish or two, whatever it may be. The dishes may be the cheap stewed beans or fried peanuts. They may be stewed prawns or steamed crabs. True drinkers sometimes drink more and eat less, while the "green hands" eat more and drink less.

Some Chinese drink regularly at every meal. When the dishes are placed on the table and the rice bowls filled, all the other members of the family may proceed with the rice but the head of the family may drink. He is customarily the first to start and the last to finish, and he may take as much time as he likes over his regular half or whole *catty* of Shaoshing. The catty is the unit of wine measure in China.

The Chinese often declare that their way of drinking is more "civilized" than the foreign way. They believe that foreigners do not have a chance to appreciate the full taste of the beverage because they pour large quantities into their mouths each time and gulp them down to quench their thirst. When Chinese drink, it is not to quench thirst but to appreciate every drop of the wine. They even have a saying to this effect: "Do not waste one drop of this wine; remember the labor the farmer put into growing the rice they made it from."

But one legendary wine-lover broke this rule: Having for years enjoyed every drop of the wine with his tongue, mouth, and throat, he decided one day to give his entire body a treat. He ordered a large tub filled with wine and after drinking several potfuls he stripped and stepped into the tub. "Now for the first time I have given all parts of my body an equal chance to taste and enjoy this wine," he exclaimed, and stayed in it for hours.

Although Chinese youths are not encouraged to drink much these days, students of the old days were more or less required to cultivate the ability to drink. To be able to drink at least a half catty (about half a pint) was considered the minimum requirement for entree into certain select literary circles. The ability to drink was thought to be as important as the ability to compose verses.

Wine at Ceremonies. In offering sacrifices to gods and to ancestors, wine is always set on the table. If friends are being entertained wine must be served and must be offered first to the guest. This is one of the strictest requirements of Chinese etiquette.

If an after-dinner speech must be made, the speaker must wait until the third round of wine is served, preferably after the sharks-fin soup or the main dish is put on the table.

The Temperance Idea. The famous Chinese doctrine of moderation and temperance is applied also to wine drinking. Very few Chinese are found so drunk outside the bars or so intoxicated on the street as to create disturbances. To be drunk to such a degree, according to Chinese reasoning, is not only detrimental to health and "immoral" but also a disgrace in that it shows one cannot "stand" the liquor. It is tantamount to confessing that one is not a "he-man" so far as drinking is concerned.

But Chinese do get drunk, once in a while, although rarely to such a degree as to be classified "drunk and disorderly." Whenever they find themselves drunk, they promptly resort to their pet methods to "awaken" themselves, and there are thousands of these just as there are many private hangover "cures" in the United States. One of these pet methods is to drink a bowl of soya bean sauce diluted in water. Another is simply to drink a quantity of hot tea.

In the ancient days the methods of "awakening" a drinker were more elaborate. It is said that the famous poet Li Po, for instance, was served with a fish soup prepared by the imperial chef when he was summoned from a bar to the palace to read a message from a barbarous tribe whose dialect no one but he understood. After taking the fish soup the poet immediately felt sound and hale and received imperial favors not only for being the sole scholar able to read the strange language but also for his ability to write a reply in that tongue.

In the homes of Chinese nobility of ancient days, according to historical records, there was a certain kind of precious stone which, it is said, had the miraculous power to remove the influence of liquor as soon as it was put under the tongue of a drunken man. The name of the stone, as well as the recipe for the remarkable fish soup that so quickly sobered the poet Li Po, has now been lost, sad to say.

The poet Li Po is immortal not only for his literary talent but also for his ability to drink. In many a Chinese wine shop may be found tablets inscribed: "The fashion inherited from Li Po."

"Dry" Laws. Despite the doctrine of moderation and temperance, dry laws more strict and rigid than those in force in parts of the United States are no novelty in China. But in most instances prohibition was enforced in China not for moral and social reasons but to reduce the consumption of grains, chiefly rice, with which most beverages in China are brewed.

Within a period of about 2000 years, between the middle of the Chou Dynasty (1134–256 B.C.) and the reign of the fourth emperor of the Yuan Dynasty (about A.D. 1312) laws against the manufacture, sale and consumption of wine were established and repealed no less than forty-one times!

Not all of the prohibition orders were enforced on a nationwide scale. Most were local.

The penalties varied in those prohibition days. Some of the decrees were extremely punitive, providing death for those who manufactured wine. In some periods the manufacturers faced confiscation of their estates, and in certain periods members of their families were made slaves.

When restrictions were enforced in the early days of the Han Dynasty, wine was not entirely prohibited. Only "drinking parties" were banned. Thus if more than three persons gathered to drink for "no purpose," each was to be fined 4 taels of silver. In those days this was a heavy fine.

On two or three occasions the prohibition order was applied to the capital city alone—as a means of preventing overindulgence by public functionaries.

Perhaps the most unique action to restrict wine consumption was the order issued by Emperor Tai Tsung of the Tan Dynasty, in A.D. 632 to be exact. This emperor, alarmed at the people's indulgence in "reddening their faces" (a Chinese phrase for getting drunk), ordered a pamphlet printed and had his ministers see to it that copies were circulated among the populace to teach them the ethics of wine drinking!

Government monopoly in wine making was another step taken by some of the emperors. One way in which Chinese wines differ from American and European wines is that they are usually made locally. Thus there is not such uniformity in Chinese wines. It is usually one kind, just wine (yellow rice wine), and not a particular brand. In some of the large cities special brands are known, but generally wines are not manufactured, bottled, branded, and distributed the way they are in America. They are made locally by anyone (usually a wine merchant) and are largely consumed locally, without much aging or transport. Consequently they are sometimes a little raw.

Wine and Relaxation. Chinese restaurants would be even more noisy if every guest joined in some of the varied "wine games" handed down during many centuries. In all of these wine games the losers have to drink, as if wine drinking were a punishment. When a loser drinks, it is a rule that the minimum he pours into his stomach at one time is a cupful. Sometimes 10 or more cups are at stake. Shaoshing wine, also known as "yellow wine," is always favored in wine games as it is milder than Kaoliang or the Peikan, which are the favorites of the northerners. "Finger-guessing" undoubtedly is the most popular wine game today. Some foreigners become expert at it although not a few confuse that game with the "Paper-scissors-stone" game which is very popular among Chinese children. Finger-guessing is a game simple to learn but hard to master. One must be a quick thinker and a good mind reader before he can succeed as a "finger-guesser." The game is played in pairs. Each player holds out from one to five fingers (or none) and each, in turn, at the same time guesses a number which he believes will be the total of the outstretched fingers. If one guesses the right number of fingers, he wins, and the loser is given the "punishment" of drinking. When a Chinese plays the game he does not call the figures simply one, two, three, and so on. For each number there is a sentence or a phrase meaning some good omen to himself and to the opponent as well as the host and hostess. For "one," for instance, the player says "Yih ping," meaning "The first rank in officialdom." The other "good omen" terms for the respective numbers follow:

Two: "Liang hsiang hou" or "Good to both of us."
Three: "San yuan" or "Pass three grades of imperial examinations."
Four: "Sze shi" or "Happiness (satisfaction) of four kinds—longevity, officialdom, wealth, and plenty of children."
Five: "On ching kwei" or "Five pieces of gold."
Six: "Loh loh shun" or "Good luck wherever and whenever."
Seven: "Chih chao" or "Everything clicks."
Eight: "Pah sien" or "Eight immortals."
Nine: "Chiu chiu chiu" or "Wine, wine to you."
Ten: "Chuan foh" or "Complete happiness."

Another game, more popular among scholars, is to assign subjects by lot for the writing of poems. The writer of the best poem will be congratulated with toasts.

Still another game is popular among the fair sex. A maid servant plays a drum outside the parlor while the guests pass a flower around. When the drum stops the guest then holding the flower is required to sing, to tell a joke or to do something which is her specialty. If she fails to do something, a fine in the form of one or more cups of wine is imposed.

These wine games were played in China at least two centuries before the birth of Christ.

Legend has it that a nobleman in the province of Shantung started this custom by staging wine games as part of the entertainment during an official dinner he was giving. Exactly what the games were that he played is not recorded, but in all probability they were much the same as those played today whenever friends in China get together to eat, relax, and enjoy good wine.

The Wine Goblin's Temple. In large cities there are sizable groups of wine merchants. In Hangchow, for example, where every year immense quantities of wines of various kinds are consumed, the city's wine merchants are numbered by the thousands. According to an ancient custom these wine dealers must assemble once every year in the Wine Goblin's Temple (*Chiu Hsien Tien*). There they offer up incense and prayers, and then agree upon the prices at which they will retail their wines during the ensuing year. These prices, with their corresponding grades of wine, must then be written upon large placards to be hung in a conspicuous place in their respective shops for the information of the public.

It is said that any wine dealer who fails to attend this gathering and perform his obeisance to the god of wine will soon find his wines all turning back to water and his business failing. But as for those who faithfully observe the ancient custom, not only will they have a prosperous year but they may even take pure water (from West Lake) and by adding a little wine to it they will immediately have wine as good as of the oldest vintage!

These meetings and trade agreements may be compared in general to our conventions of wine dealers. In China, however, they are held under religious auspices. Several cities have temples or shrines dedicated to the Wine Goblin, but the one in Hangchow is particularly remarkable.

CHINESE FOOD AND DRINK

by Weston La Barre *

The impression I got when visiting Chinese homes was that the children were fed constantly and incessantly. There was never an obsession with

---

* This brief statement on orality among the Chinese is quoted from a much larger study, "Some Observations on Character Structure in the Orient. The Chinese, Part II." Reprinted by permission of The William Alanson White Foundation from *Psychiatry, 9* (1946), 375–80. Copyright by The William Alanson White Foundation, Inc.

time or any suggestion of prohibition of "eating between meals"; nor was
there any moralization of food or dichotomy into what was "good for" the
child and what was forbidden candy or "dessert." The Chinese seem to
identify with the child's pleasure in eating, and to obtain a real pleasure
from this identification which was quite without anxiety or preoccupation
with oral "right" and "wrong."

After a stay in China one feels that the average American parent is a
violent psychotic in need of restraint with regard to children and food.
The Chinese have no incessant anxious nagging of their children to eat.
Chinese mothers breast-feed their children without any question at all,
and there is no suggestion of false shame in feeding them in public at any
time whatsoever. The first and most complete of interpersonal relationships,
that of mother and child, is accomplished in China with the untroubled
smoothness of biological perfection. The Chinese have a superb oral hold
on life. Even the ordinary peasant has an indestructible cheerfulness, an
inexpugnable dignity and self-identity. The Chinese are oral optimists
whom no calamity can threaten. The Chinese are superbly matter-of-fact
in their thinking, material-minded in their judgments, sane, sensible, and
oriented to reality. Profound satisfaction of the earliest of the great human
appetites has bought a willing and unquestioned love of their parents and
an easy and loyal acceptance of their traditional cultural values. The
Chinese are traditionalists partly because they really love their parents.

It is striking how food remains in later life a vehicle in Chinese interpersonal relations. No social or business transaction, not even a simple
visit to the bank, is complete without the offering of tea; and what would
otherwise be the briefest of military conversations is also made gracious by
the offering of food. In social situations the Chinese talk about food as
readily as the Englishman does about the weather, and the avid discussion
of food at past banquets is the staple of conversation while awaiting another. The chief way to honor a friend is to spread a sumptuous feast for
him, with the most delicious and recondite dishes possible. Indeed, the
most delicate courtesy of the host or expression of affection for a friend is
to transfer a particularly succulent and flavorsome morsel from one's own
plate to another's.

* * *

As for drinking, the Chinese indulge in it on all occasions of eating, and
without the slightest discernible ambivalence, lacking the really very
intricate attitudes that have been built up toward it in the West. But the
Chinese are not so violently addicted to excessive use of alcohol as have
been some North European peoples. They seem not to seek either the
frenzy or the escape of intoxication, though they will drink to a point of
overflowing benevolence in social contexts. But the solitary Chinese drinker
is unthinkable and the problem alcoholic an evident rarity. This is true
despite the fact that at parties the Chinese will merrily, even half-mali-

ciously, urge drinking upon their guests with an obligatory *gam bei* or "down the hatch," as well as the more lenient *sui bien,* or "as much as you like." The fact seems to be that in spite of ample and even copious consumption of alcohol on defined occasions, its use appears never to become an emotional problem.[1]

*   *   *

On the whole, a summary picture of the character structure of the average Chinese would be that they lack any strong visceral disciplines, such as are so insistent and strong in the Protestant ethic. In the Chinese, "sphincter moraiity" is poorly developed, with regard to all body products. The internalization of the superego is weak, the sense of sin nearly absent. The id-demands almost uniformly secure undeterred physiological gratification, and libidinal tensions are low. The ego, as the result of a strong and mutually gratifying oral relationship to the mother, as well as a characteristically untraumatic cleanliness training, is sturdy and reality oriented in the direction of the physical world; but in the patriarchal family it is relatively thin-skinned in its responses to the human world. The average Chinese is cheerful, dignified, discreet, poised, un-anxious, proud, secure, realistic, and kindly. Hypertension, stomach ulcers, compulsion neuroses, alcoholism, hysteria, and schizophrenia, one would believe, must be uncommon among them, though perhaps with a relatively higher incidence of the manic-depressive psychoses and paranoia.

1. The differing cultural contexts in China and America may not be ignored. The Chinese is caught up in a entirely different framework of values with regard to dependence and passivity; their virtues are of filial obedience and paternal responsibility. Not for them are the fierce virilities of nomad individuality and independence of a frontier-nurtured America. Drinking in China celebrates interpersonal relationships and cements the bonds of social communion which are indices of mutual dependence; drinking in the West relaxes the inhibitions which hold both aggressiveness and passivity in check. Since the alcoholic personality and the drug addict are psychiatrically related it may be well to mention that even the use of opium is not the same in China and in the West. The moderate use of opium, and even its abuse, has been widely prevalent in modern centuries in China; but at least part of this has been due to European economic pressures, which burst forth in the Opium Wars, and to a studied fomentation of the habit, as by the Japanese. But more than this the cultural judgments both of the pleasures and the passivities of alcohol and of drugs are different in China and in the West. Passivity and dependence are sometimes a necessity in familial Chinese society, aggressiveness and independence in individualistic America.

DRINKING AMONG NEW YORK CITY CANTONESE

by Milton L. Barnett *

M. L. Barnett investigated attitudes and practices of New York's Chinatown in relation to alcoholic beverages. He noted the persistence of patterns of drinking acquired in China where wine is early introduced to the male child. Drinking is sanctioned; one learns to drink early and to know one's capacity. Drunkenness is not condoned or considered humorous.

In Chinatown, parents are less permissive. Chinese women drink only after marriage and are excluded from ritual drinking; but some of the young women are adopting Western attitudes.

Chinese wines are popular but the widest use is made of Cognac and Scotch and Canadian whiskies. Drinking with meals is basic; about three ounces of whisky per meal is consumed by the head of the household. At banquets or feasts, drinking games are played which aim at getting the other player drunk. Wine is served in tiny Chinese cups, but if the dinner takes place in a restaurant American cups and often whisky will be used, leading to consumption of large amounts. Drinking games usually involve men of the same generation. They are accompanied by various stratagems in order not to lose face, or to get drunk.

Ceremonial use of wine on occasions of births, weddings and funerals is general. Wine is included among the offerings brought for the dead. Alcohol is used medicinally and prophylactically—e.g., for old people, to provide warmth. Beer is not considered healthful. In some Christian homes, total abstinence may be practiced.

Drinking is regarded as a social function. As long as it serves to cement social relations, it is approved. When it threatens group harmony, it is disapproved. Public drunkenness does occur but it is rare. The community keeps a check on its members and the intoxicated individual is often shielded and protected until he recovers. Alcohol addiction occurs very infrequently and only a handful of individuals in this community of some 13,000 were identified in the study as alcoholics. Police and hospital records substantiate this fact.

In general, traditional Chinese values dominate the community. Much drinking is done at celebrations and for conviviality but internalized norms and external forces inhibit extreme behavior. The intoxicated Chinese is usually quiet; some release of aggression may be manifest in expansive behavior and speech but rarely in violence. The second generation exhibits

* Summarized from "Alcoholism in the Cantonese of New York City: An Anthropological Study" in *Etiology of Chronic Alcoholism*, O. Diethelm, ed., Springfield, Ill., Thomas, 1955.

considerable acculturation but social controls are still stronger than disorganization.

JAPAN

by Bufo Yamamuro *

Confucius (550–479 B.C.) said, "Drinking knows no limit, but never be boisterous with drinking." Confucianism encourages moderation but not abstinence. Primarily, this teaching is moral and political philosophy but not religion. Its classical literature was early introduced into Japan through Korea when, during the reign of Emperor Ohjin (270–313 B.C.), Prince Ujinowakiiratsuko studied Confucianism under the Korean scholars Ichiki and Wani. Confucian teachings later exerted profound influences on Japanese thought and culture.

Buddha (565–478 B.C.) stressed total abstinence. The last of his Five Commandments forbade drinking.

1. Never kill living beings.
2. Never steal.
3. Never be lewd.
4. Never tell a lie.
5. Never take strong drink.

These were daily rules for every follower of Buddha. One of the sutras of primitive Buddhism enumerates six sequels of drinking: (1) loss of property, (2) disease, (3) discord and strife, (4) loss of reputation, (5) disturbance of temper, and (6) daily loss in wisdom. Other sutras mention ten disadvantages and thirty-six faults of drinking. Not only personal abstinence but refraining from the sale of strong drink is an essential qualification for Bodhisattva (Buddha elects) of Mahāyāna (the Greater Vehicle). Except on rare occasions for medication, Buddha emphatically advocated the strictest principle of total abstinence. Buddhist scriptures, naturally, are full of teachings on the matter. Buddhism was introduced into Japan in A.D. 552 and became the national religion before long.

The native religion of Japan is Shintoism, with a shamanistic background, which later developed into monolatry. Japanese history dates back to 660 B.C., when the Emperor Jimmu, the first emperor of the present dynasty of the Imperial Family, was enthroned. The prehistoric myths contain many references to *sake,* taken from fermented rice, but this was originally sweet sake without alcohol content. Divine sake is inseparably entwined with Shinto worship. However, the Miyake Shrine dedicated to Prince Ninigi (grandson and legal successor of the Goddess Amaterasu), the national ancestor, and the Tsuma Shrine dedicated to Princess Kono-

* From "Notes on Drinking in Japan," *Quarterly Journal of Studies on Alcohol,* 15 (1954), 491–8.

hanasakuya, the national mother, are situated in the Province of Hyuga (Miyazaki Prefecture), the southern island of Kyushu, and both exclusively use *amazake* (sweet sake without any alcohol content) from time immemorial. This ancient custom was followed by the Grand Shrine of Ise and many others. Moreover sake was used only at the time of festivals.

Sake was etymologically an abbreviation of *"sakae"* (prosperity) because the merry feeling associated with intoxication reminded drinkers of prosperity. The original form of the Chinese character representing strong drink symbolizes the shape of a pot for strong drink.

The origin of alcoholic beverages was *yashiori no sake,* fermented by Prince Susanoono, younger brother of the Goddess Amaterasu. He made the eight-headed monster serpent drunk with it, and killed him. Prince Yamatotakeru, son of the Emperor Keiko (A.D. 71–131), again intoxicated Kumaso, the vicious Ainu lord, and killed him.

There are a number of Shinto sake gods, the most conspicuous among them being Okuninushi-no-Mikoto (Ohmiwa Shrine), his son Ohyamakui-no-Mikoto (Matsuo Shrine), and Sukunahikona-no-Kami. These gods belonged to the Izumo race, original inhabitants of southern Japan, which was conquered by the Tenson race, forefathers of the more temperate present Imperial Household and their followers.

The most primitive method of fermentation was to chew the grains to initiate natural fermentation. Another method was to lead sprouting and saccharifying grains to fermentation. During the reign of the Emperor Ohjin a Chinese named Susuyari became a naturalized subject and taught an excellent method of fermentation. In this way refined sake (a transparent liquid) gradually became popular, taking the place of amazake and raw (unrefined) sake. Rice, leaven, and water were used to produce refined sake. Even in Shinto festivities or ceremonies, refined alcoholic sake became predominant.

After Buddhism became the national religion, prohibition was decreed from time to time. The following dates are on record:

Under Emperor Kohtoku, March, A.D. 646.
Under Empress Kensho, July, A.D. 722.
Under Emperor Shomu, July, A.D. 732.
Under Emperor Shomu, May, A.D. 737.
Under Empress Koken, February, A.D. 758.
Under Empress Shotoku, July, A.D. 770.

These Imperial decrees were usually intended to counteract menaces, due to famines or epidemics, by religious and moral effects rather than economically.

Lord Tabito Ohtomo, an outspoken and reactionary decadent, contributed thirteen poems in praise of sake to the noted *Manyo Shu,* a collection of 4,500 31-syllabled Japanese poems published about 1250 years ago, of which the following are examples:

Far better to get drunk and weep
Than sagaciously speak like a wizard.

Rather be a pot of sake than a human being
To be saturated with sake.

If only merry in this present world
Never mind being insect or bird in the next.

During the Heian Era (A.D. 794–1184) with the capital in Kyoto, prohibition or temperance was often decreed to guard against luxury, riotous festivities, and extravagant banquets. Denkyo and Kohboh, two outstanding Buddhist leaders, were both staunch advocates of total abstinence.

The Kamakura Era (A.D. 1184–1333), with the seat of authority in Kamakura, marked the start of the feudal age, and Bushido, or knighthood, came into power. Under the influence of Myoe, noted Buddhist saint, the Hohjohs, the feudal rulers, exemplified temperance and thrift, laying foundations for Bushido. The Mongolian invasion was a great national calamity, and Tokiyori Hohjoh prohibited the sale of sake (dated Sept. 30, 1252). It is recorded that 37,274 pots of sake were destroyed in Kamakura alone. After this manner was the spirit of loyalty and patriotism fostered in those days. Eison and Ryokan were distinguished Buddhist social workers and courageously upheld national prohibition. Eisai was the great pioneer of Zen Buddhism. He brought tea seeds from China and universally encouraged tea drinking instead of sake drinking. He composed a volume on the "Tea-Drinking Regimen." Throughout Japan, a stone pillar stands at the entrance of every Zen Buddhist temple with the inscription: *Garlic and wine never to be admitted into the gate.*

The popular Buddhism of Shinran, founder of the Shin Sect intended for the salvation of the masses, tended to "only-believism" and antinomianism. Together with the new Nichiren Sect, it loosened the principle of total abstinence.

During the Edo Era (1603–1867), laws to diminish sake production drastically were enforced from time to time to meet floods, famines and other emergencies. A considerable number of feudal lords established prohibition or encouraged temperance on their estates. Some leading scholars advocated or required total abstinence among their followers.

The Restoration of Meiji (1867) was the dawn of a new international civilization and culture. The new temperance movement prospered among early-day Protestants. On the other hand, Western liquors were imported with the introduction of new drinking customs. Around 1886 the Yokohama Temperance Society, Hokkaido Temperance Society, a Japanese branch of the Woman's Christian Temperance Union, and other temperance groups were organized, together with the Hanseikai of the awakened

Buddhists. A national organization, the Japan Temperance Alliance, was formed in 1897. A Prohibition Law for Minors was instituted on April 1, 1922. Ever since then the temperance organizations have fought to raise the obligatory abstinence age to 25. The W.C.T.U. has supplied teaching materials to all schools regularly for many years and the Salvation Army has endeavored to promote the cause of total abstinence among the masses. The Emperor Hirohito is not only a distinguished biologist but is also internationally known as a staunch total abstainer and nonsmoker.

In the present section some of the drinking customs peculiar to Japan will be described briefly.

Toso. The toso custom was originally introduced from China over a thousand years ago. On New Year's Eve a number of medicines were presented to each native village. These were put in a sack and hung in the wells. On New Year's Day they were brought out and mixed with sake, to be taken for the prevention of disease. If a family member had it, the family should be free from disease. If one family had it, the entire community should be free from disease. The youngest in the family drank the toso cups first, then the elders in ascending order of age. At the Imperial Palace an unmarried lady offered the Toso cups to the Emperor. When people make New Year's calls nowadays they are offered cups of toso. At present, toso is ordinary sake drunk at the New Year season.

Shirozake. White sake is specially prepared and used particularly for the Doll's Festival on March 3. The Festival is observed by girls with dolls of the Emperor, the Empress, Ministers of the Left and the Right, three court ladies, five musicians, a number of footmen, left-hand cherry tree, right-hand mandarin orange, and so forth. Rhombic rice cakes and pellet rice dumplings are offered to the dolls. The celebration of the Festival has a history of over a thousand years. It was originally an aristocratic event but gradually became popularized among the common people. Family members and guests take cups of white sake in its celebration.

Moonlight Party. In autumn, when the sky is clear, the moonlight party is held to view the full moon. August 15 and September 13 (lunar calendar) are the dates for moon-viewing banquets for poets and persons of a romantic turn. Autumnal plants, such as pampas grass, Partinia scabiosaefolia, Chinese bell-flowers, etc., are put in a vase on one side. Boiled potatoes are offered to the moon on the other side. On a wooden stand at the veranda a big liquid measure of sake and white dumplings of boiled flour are placed. Enjoying cups of sake, poems are composed by every participant.

Sansankudo (literally, three-three-nine cups). At the Shinto wedding rite in particular, cups of sake are taken by both the bride and the bridegroom to solemnize the ceremony. Three cupfuls are offered to each of the new couple thrice. Usually, three cinnabar-varnished, round, and shallow cups are piled up for the purpose.

Sakazuki (cup). Originally small, round, and shallow unglazed earthenware cups were used. Even today they are used in Shinto ceremonies and offerings, though more usual now are lacquered wooden cups of the same shape.

Sakana (relishes taken with sake). As accompaniments of sake, various fishes and vegetables are taken. In banquets they precede the serving of the proper meal or rice. Slices of raw fish, sea breams broiled with salt, vinegared dishes (particularly fish), dried cuttlefish, peanuts, bean custard, mashed sweet-potato sweetened and mixed with chestnuts, sweet white kidney beans and black peas, vinegared herring roe, boiled and cooked vegetables, and the like are most frequently provided.

Sakazuki-goto (events of cups). Promises between two parties, marriages and so forth, are represented by this term.

Kan. Sake is poured into an earthen bottle and heated by putting it into a kettle of warm water over a fire. Sometimes it is directly boiled in a pot. The most appropriate temperature for drinking is said to be 50° C.

Niiname-sai (harvest festival). On November 23, offerings of the new crop of rice and new rice wine, sake, are made to the Emperor and Shinto deities who are Imperial ancestors. In the year of enthronement of every emperor, this festival is called Daijoh-e and is held on a far larger scale.

Japanese attitudes on drinking are characterized in the following proverbial expressions:

What is the cherry-blossom (national flower) without wine?
Wine is the panacea for all ills.
Good wine makes good blood.
When the wine goes in, the wit goes out.
Firstly man drinks wine, then wine drinks wine, and finally wine drinks man.
Bag of liquor and sack of food (referring to those who eat the bread of idleness).

The Contemporary Scene. The war brought about radical changes in various aspects of Japanese life. In consequence of wartime scarcity, strong drink and tobacco were rationed. Though a dry and tobacco-free day was observed throughout Japan each month, on the other hand many weak abstainers yielded to drinking as one of the few consolations available in those weary and fearful days. With the gradual postwar return to normal life, the production of alcoholic beverages has been restored almost to the prewar level.

Things Oriental and Occidental now coexist and mingle in Japan. Modern big cities like Tokyo and Osaka have many bars, cafés, cabarets, night clubs, etc., where strong drink is provided, besides the traditional pot-houses and restaurants. Beer halls are prospering. Cocktail parties are often held for the reception of Western residents and visitors.

Before the war there were 17 dry villages, 106 partially dry villages, about 200 dry factories, mines, railroad temperance unions, and the like, 15 dry steamers, and about 3,800 temperance organizations affiliated with the Japan Temperance Union (formerly the Japan National Temperance League), with a combined membership of well above 3,000,000. The war drastically undermined and diminished the temperance forces. The American and British occupation brought with them a series of alcohol-related problems. Beer halls, cabarets, night clubs, etc., encircling the bases; violence and crimes by drunken servicemen; the smuggling of Western liquors following the reopening of international traffic; and illicit manufacture by Korean residents—all these aroused public concern.

As the number of motor vehicles increases, so do traffic accidents. The Tokyo Metropolitan Police Board operates a number of Japanese-made machines for determining blood alcohol by the breath test, but the test is not yet universally adopted in Japan.

Despite recommendations by the World Health Organization, alcoholism is not yet taken up as a public health problem by the authorities and the general public, as is the problem of narcotic addicts. Japanese-made disulfiram is on sale now and is prescribed for the treatment of alcoholism in rehabilitation centers affiliated with the Japan Temperance Union. American films, like "Something to Live for," have introduced and popularized the ideas of the Alcoholics Anonymous. To meet the urgent need of those who seek advice or help from the Consultation Section of the Japan Temperance Union, a Japanese equivalent of Alcoholics Anonymous was started in September 1953. Close touch is maintained between this Japanese group and the A.A. group of American servicemen in Tokyo.

Temperance education has been neglected hitherto. As a new move, lantern lectures on alcohol questions have been initiated at high schools, civic centers, churches, factories, women's and young people's groups, etc., by the executive director of the Japan Temperance Union. New pamphlets and handbooks on alcohol problems are also in preparation.

The Japanese National W.C.T.U. is endeavoring to have references to alcohol, tobacco, etc., inserted in various secondary-school textbooks. All the temperance forces are striving to have the prohibition age raised from 20 to 25. A majority in Parliament appear to favor the bill personally, and it has passed one of the two Houses from time to time, but it faces persistent blocking by opposing forces.

The Japanese people have been traditionally tolerant of and lenient toward misdemeanors of drunkards. However, the temperance forces are planning to submit a new bill to the Parliament for severer handling of drunkards. Another effort under way is to make the financial support of rehabilitation centers for alcoholics a national or public responsibility through new legislation.

9. RUSSIA

RUSSIA, YESTERDAY

by Vera Efron *

A passionate denunciation of the pernicious practices connected with drinking in Russia was published in Moscow in 1868 under the title *The History of Saloons in Russia in Relation to the History of the Russian People*. The author of this book, Ivan Gavrilovich Pryzhov, was a man of considerable talent whose life was marred by poverty, misfortune, and tragedy. . . . In his foreword to the first edition, Pryzhov states:

The first volume of the *History of Saloons,* the first study of the drink trade in Russia, was finished in 1863. Since then it has steadily diminished in size. After the first, the so-called official history of saloons, materials for the two subsequent volumes were prepared, namely a historical survey of saloon life, (and) the origin and life of saloonkeepers, of the drunkards . . . and the innumerable frequenters of the saloons—beggars, runaways, thieves (rebels), and robbers.

Our aim was to study the drink trade from the viewpoint of that fertile life upon which grew saloons, booze, saloonkeepers—to look upon it with the eyes of the millions of people who, without understanding political economy, saw in drunkenness a punishment from God and who, at the same time, by drinking their *death cup* registered their protest against all the social boons—in other words, who *drank from misery*.

The book starts with the glorification of the easy, free and pleasant life led by Russians of old and attributed in the folk epos to the time of Prince Vladimir (end of 10th century). There were no peasants, no *muzhiks,* only people. A man was able to work his land in peace, he could proudly shake hands with the Prince in a brotherly fashion, and all affairs were decided together in the people's *duma* (parliament, council). The whole people, together with the non-Slavic tribes of the border lands, led in the main one type of life. Community life, brotherly life, was the core of the social structure. One of the manifestations of this ideal state of affairs was the common practice of brotherly drinking. Every discussion, every community affair, began with drinking or a festivity (*pir,* from *pit',* to drink). Hence beverages were of tremendous cultural importance in the social life of the people. Those were ancient drinks made of barley or honey: beer, small beer, mead, ale and *kvas,* the latter a purely Slavic

* From "The Tavern and the Saloon in Old Russia," *Quarterly Journal of Studies on Alcohol, 16* (1955), 484–503.

130

beverage which could be made of any fermentable material, including bread. Even grape wine was known in the old Slavic lands and even the plain people could afford it. Pryzhov cites old chronicles showing how much was drunk and of what kinds of beverages. Each family brewed its own beer and mead to the extent that they were needed for everyday life. In some cases the beverages were brewed by several families together, or communally. The wealthy had cellars for the storage of mead, beer and imported wines. Any public occasion whatsoever was hailed with a drink and apparently copious drinking was done by all.

In this kind of life, in pre-Moscow Russia [prior to 1450], there was no drunkenness. It did not exist as a vice gnawing at the people's organism. Drinking was gladness, pleasure, as is seen in the words attributed by an old-Russian scribe to Prince Vladimir: 'Drinking is a joy to Russia, we cannot do without it.' . . . Around drinking man met man in brotherly fashion, man met woman; and, held together by joy and love, the social life of the people progressed, brotherhoods (German, *Gilden*) sprang up, and the drinking house (*Korchma*) [Tavern] became the center of the community life of each district.

At the opening of Russian history (10th century) the Russian land was covered by woods which lent themselves to abundant beekeeping. Many Russian localities were famous for the excellence of their honey, the production of which was of major importance in the economy of the land. Pryzhov gives many details on the organization of apiculture in those times and on the extent of the trade in wax and honey and the profits from it. Western travelers who noted in their journals the great wealth of Russia in honey and wax are quoted. After citing old Russian laws pertaining to beekeeping and describing the mode and extent of taxes on honey and hops, Pryzhov concludes that in the 14th and 15th centuries the people lived in good circumstances, growing hops, brewing beer and mead, and paying taxes on these goods.

Having paid the taxes for malt and hops, the people peacefully brewed their beverages and peacefully drank them at home in the family circle, or at brotherhoods, or at fraternal drinking parties in the taverns. Among the main signs of an established, mature society are the imprints of its social structure which manifest themselves in the organization of its drinking communities . . . and in the institution of community drinking houses. For a person who has emerged from savagery, it is unthinkable to drink alone, at home or in a drinking house, so as to get drunk. . . . On the basis of simple physiological law—that pleasurable exhilaration enhances digestion, that it is easier to eat and drink while among people, with others—people gathered to drink together; and in the friendly talk around wine, in the brotherly getting together of person with person, social life got its start among them.

Pryzhov points out the parallel existence of drinking houses serving similar functions in ancient Athens (*kapeleia*), in Rome (*taberna*), and later in Germany (*Herberge*). He spends an interesting page or two following up the derivation of the words for "drinking house" in several languages, including the French *cabaret*, the Roman *caupa, popina*, the German *Herberge*, and the old-Russian word *korchma*.

The old-Slavic community drinking house was called korchma. The derivation of the word is ancient, and the root, as traced by Pryzhov, is from the Persian *chorden*, to eat. The "korchma was the place to which people came to eat and drink, to talk and to celebrate with songs and with music. . . . Among the western Slavs officials proclaimed orders of the Government in the korchma, judges held court, affairs with travelers were threshed out, and for a long time the taverns served as council chambers and guest houses."

Among the western Slavs in Bohemia and Poland, beginning in the 11th century, there was always a tavern on the market place. Some cities had more than one. "These western taverns were at first, as everywhere, free institutions where people gathered peacefully on market days." Later they came to be owned by the Government, by princes, or by the clergy or monasteries, or by those who ran them. "Then the people began to organize their secret korchmas, the *taberna occulta* known since the 12th century." A similar development took place in other parts of the Slavic world, except that in some regions the free tavern was still in existence in the middle of the 19th century in scattered communities. Thus in southern Russia in some sections of the Ukraine the tavern was still in Pryzhov's time the meeting place for men and women, young fellows and unmarried girls, where they ate, drank, and made merry. The different evolution of the ownership of the taverns in various parts of Russia is then traced in the *History*.

Interesting are Pryzhov's remarks on the northern democratic cities of Novgorod and Pskov. There the taverns were the property of the municipality; the Prince, who came to office by election, was specifically barred from operating or owning a tavern. Foreign merchants were sometimes allowed to sell beer within their own "courts" but only on payment of a tax to the city. In Novgorod the Prince was head of the Army and the executor of decisions handed down by elected judges, receiving for his services one half of the court taxes. He was not allowed to acquire land in Novgorod and could trade only through its citizens. These rules prevailed until Novgorod lost its independence when subjugated by Moscow at the end of the 15th century. At that time Novgorod merchants were exiled and Moscow merchants were imported. Along with other restrictions the right to have free taverns was prohibited to the once free people of Great Novgorod. In 1543 Tsar Ivan IV (the Great, the Terrible) caused eight "Tsar taverns"—owned by the Tsar and operated by his appointees—to be opened in this city. Much drunkenness was the immediate result and the head of the Church in Novgorod was moved to write to the Tsar of the rising inebriety and crime which followed on the institution of the tavern "from above." An illicit drink trade also made its appearance.

The beginning of bootlegging, of secret taverns and of the resulting drunkenness, in this case, Pryzhov ascribes to the imposition of a tavern "from above" on a people who had been used to a democratic way of life since time immemorial. They had run their own "free" taverns in accordance with their own wishes and they had elected their tavern keepers from among themselves. Now the newcomer "bossed" it over them, and they did not wish to drink and eat in "his" place. Hence the secret taverns, the bootlegging.

All evil emanated from Moscow, according to Pryzhov. Before that city ever came into being, Kiev and Novgorod were rich towns with a high civilization and wonderful, genuinely Russian folkways. Though founded by Slavic tribes, the new settlement received a foreign (Finnish) name— "muddy river." Here, amidst physical hardships, the Muscovite tribe began to assert itself, gaining in material strength at the cost of all the culture that should have been its heritage. By the middle of the 16th century all was lost. Here serfdom originated around 1600. Tartar influence played an important role in this evolution of Russian cultural history and Pryzhov takes great pains to trace familiar Russian words with unpleasant connotations to Tartar roots. Among these is *kabak,* the name of the hateful saloon where one drank but did not eat. This word replaced the Slavic noun korchma, the tavern, where one drank and ate as well.

Actually kabak among the Tartars meant an inn where food and drink could be bought. After his return from Kazan (1552), Ivan IV introduced a kabak in Moscow exclusively for the use of his guard and courtiers, a place where they could congregate to eat and drink. The rest of the population was barred from it. Nor, for that matter, were others at first allowed to drink distilled spirits, which became known throughout Russia during the 16th century. The idea of the kabak and of control over the drinking of his subjects seemed to please the Tsar exceedingly. Directives went out to subjugated cities, vassal princes, and Government officials to close the existing taverns, where drink and food were served, and to open up "Tsar kabaks." In these houses only drink was sold, no food. "The monstrous appearance of such 'drinking houses' left its imprint upon the whole history of the Russian people thenceforth."

Pryzhov stresses the significance of the pernicious new custom—drink sold without food. Lacking food, the kabak, the new saloon, could not function as the socially important meeting place to which the people were accustomed. To make matters worse, the common folk were not allowed any longer to brew their own drinks. Distilled spirits—vodka—was introduced and gradually displaced other beverages. The saloon replaced the tavern.

The kabaks spread fast. In 1552 there was but one of these saloons—in Moscow. In 1588 Giles Fletcher, ambassador from Queen Elizabeth to the court of Ivan, wrote: "In every great towne he hath a Caback, where is sold aqua vitae which they call Russe wine, mead, beere."

Among the "goods" which the boyars, the landed aristocracy, received from the Tsar in return for services was the right to brew, distill, sell or tax alcoholic beverages. The extent of the privilege came to depend on the hierarchic rank of the boyar. Generally a boyar did not have to buy Government beverages. If he traveled to Moscow from his country place, he prepared enough for himself and his people and took it along. Since he could produce his own beverages, the boyar could easily own a saloon; the right to operate it was often granted by the Tsar as "food" to the vassal.

This is how Pryzhov describes the change which suddenly took place in towns and villages over most of the northern parts of Russia—a change originating in that first kabak instituted by Tsar Ivan for his henchmen.

In the old days, when people prepared for a celebration, a *pir* (feast) or a *pominki* (funeral repast), they brewed the necessary amount of beverage, usually mead and beer. Now, suddenly, the people were told that brewing and distilling were forbidden, though the "better" class could still brew their beer and mead. Vodka could be bought only in the kabak.

Not only were the peasants not allowed to make their own brew, but they were supposed to set up the saloon, be responsible for running it, and pay taxes on it. Vodka was distilled in Government plants situated near the saloons or was supplied them by Government contractors or by the concessioners. The saloon could be run according to one of two systems: as a concession, or "on faith"—that is, by someone elected by the people. As originally planned, the saloon managers were to be elected by turns: everyone in rotation would do his duty in running the local place. This, however, was abandoned very quickly, being quite impractical. The "elected" citizen was forced to quit his regular occupation and put to collect the state's profits in the saloon, without provision for his own livelihood. Thus, naturally, only the rich could afford election, or those who had nothing to lose anyway and hoped to make a living by cheating in the running of the saloon. The plain folk always endeavored to avoid this duty.

Circumstances invariably forced the saloonkeeper to rob his customers. In order to earn a livelihood he was obliged to overcharge or to reduce the quality (in the case of vodka, the alcohol strength) of the beverages he sold. When first elected, a saloonkeeper was expected to pay for the vodka supplied by the Government; he thus began by getting into debt. He had to be tough and to exact every kopek his customers owned. In becoming the keeper of the local saloon the elected man became entwined in a system of duties, obligations and supervisions. Among other things he had to swear to his good faith and just dealings by kissing the cross; hence the Russian name for the saloonkeeper, which in time became a word of opprobrium, *tseloval'nik:* one who kisses. Needless to say, the cross-kissing was nothing but sham, for the tseloval'nik cheated both the Government and the people. In 1679 the Patriarch requested that the tseloval'niks be exempted from swearing on the cross, so as to avoid "taking false oaths and spoiling of the soul." Often the people and the clergy petitioned for the abolition of the saloon, for "next to the Tsar's kabak life is impossible." This was sometimes granted. In some cities the people succeeded in establishing, alongside the saloons, their own "kvas kabaks," but by 1705 all mash, kvas, and vinegar production was given over to concessioners.

A tax rate was fixed for each individual saloon, based on the income realized the previous year, the size of the concession, and other circumstances. The main and constant rule in determining the quota was that the profits should exceed those of the previous year. To accomplish this the tseloval'nik was allowed to act "without fear." For the delivery of the profits he was to expect thanks from the Tsar and not be afraid of the people. Chiefly, "he was not to send away the drunkards." No excuses were accepted for the non-payment of the expected income: neither that the people did not want to drink nor that they had no money to drink with. The Government demanded its share. A saloonkeeper who wrote to the Tsar, "In your Tsar kabak, Sire, there are too few drunkards," was answered: "You should be looking for more profits, compared to the previous ones. Instead you want to abandon the kabaks—which never happened before!" When profits declined because of crop failure or other disaster the Government sent out inspectors to make sure the saloonkeepers did not take advantage of this circumstance to rob the treasury. People were interrogated together and separately, "and whoever can say anything against the saloonkeeper . . . will be recompensed by the Government . . . and, besides, will get the saloonkeeper's livelihood." The tseloval'nik had to despoil his customers or perish.

As noted previously, no private person might distill vodka, nor were the peasants allowed to brew the milder beverages. There were occasions, however—weddings, christenings, funerals, memorials and holidays—for which a peasant, on payment of a tax, could obtain a permit to make his own beer. He had to declare how much he would brew and how much would be drunk. The production of vodka, however, was prohibited without exception.

Again Pryzhov stresses that the Government saloon run by the concessioner or the elected tseloval'nik was an innovation. The rule that they must declare how much they brewed or how much they drank was also new and foreign to a people

> which had been accustomed for long centuries to the free use of beverages that constituted a daily need, as much as bread. The people could not acquiesce in this new rule and took all possible means to continue their old "tavern" life, although this way of life was now pronounced illegal,

a crime not to be condoned. Thus suddenly all of Russia became guilty of *"korchemstvo"* [taverning], and paid for it during almost 300 years. In the 17th century "taverning" spread like an infection. Among the common people it was completely natural and understandable, caused by necessity, while among the higher ups it became a means of profiteering and robbery.

The tseloval'niks were expected to see to it that there was no bootlegging which could undermine the profits of the saloon. Thus the saloonkeepers and later, in the 17th century, special saloon spies, were allowed to supervise the social and home life of the people, to enter houses and make searches, "with force, causing shame and insulting the moral dignity of man."

Every market day the town criers reiterated the decree that no one should keep any beverages nor distill alcohol. The people paid no heed. They continued to brew beer, make vodka, and keep up their secret taverns. They would not go to the kabaks: there only drunkards gathered. Bootlegging was engaged in by everybody.

The whole burden of the liquor regulations fell upon the peasant. When a peasant needed vodka for a celebration and did not want to go to the saloon for fear of being made drunk there, or robbed, or even because it was far away, he might buy a supply elsewhere. Once he did that, however, he was at the mercy of the lawless elements, who could rob him without fear; at the same time he could be severely punished by law. If caught, or denounced, the peasant was beaten and the vodka taken from him. In addition, he would be fined, and if unable to pay, had to endure a special form of punishment for defaulters taken over from the Tartars. This consisted of being kept under guard barefoot in front of the court house daily, except on holidays, from sunrise until after the departure of the judges. For about an hour each day the executioners mercilessly beat the naked legs of the debtor with a stick. Usually there were several executioners who shared the current victims among themselves, beating them seriatim by pacing from one to the next. The term of punishment was one month or until the fine was paid.

In spite of ever more severe sanctions—in 1711 the penalty for bootlegging became exile to Siberia at hard labor, and for failure to denounce it, fines—bootlegging spread steadily through the Moscow lands and all the regions neighboring upon it: the Ukraine and White Russia to the south and west, and the territories of the non-Slavic tribes to the east.

A special chapter is reserved for the introduction of distilled spirits among these Siberian tribes, subjugated by the Russians during the 16th and 17th centuries. Pryzhov starts his account with these words: "In reading . . . descriptions of the life of the natives, one statement is met constantly, that they are all inordinately devoted to strong spirits. But if we look into the course of their history their fateful passion for drunkenness will assume an entirely different significance."

Extensive commerce with the natives living to the northeast (Perm, Pechora and Ugra) could have brought civilization to them, Pryzhov goes on. These peoples had used alcoholic beverages from time immemorial. They had their own beer and *kumys* (fermented mare's milk). However, they knew only fermented beverages and their first contact with vodka was disastrous for them. When the subjugated Samoyed (living along the Arctic coast of the Ural area and in eastern Siberia, comprising the tribes of the Yurak, the Tawgi and the Ostiak) would bring their annual taxes to the frontier trading center, the Moscow official (*voyevoda*) of the center or city would meet the arriving natives and treat them to drinks, making them drunk. The inexperienced Samoyed would drink up the goods they had brought as taxes, their dog teams, all their possessions. Officials appointed to Siberian outposts went supplied with ample quantities of vodka. The Yakutsk voyevoda in 1638, for instance, was directed to take with him 100 vedro of vodka (equivalent to 325 U. S. gallons) for "native tax expenses." Gradually the brewing of the native drinks was prohibited to all the tribes and, as the kabaks were planted in the Siberian cities or about the native settlements, the tribesmen were required to buy their beverages in these saloons. In 1627 the Cheremiss were still paying taxes on honey and mead but later they too, like the Samoyed, the Yakut and others, were ordered to buy their drinks in the saloons of the cities to which they officially belonged. Thus, by the end of the 17th century, the kabak was established in all the main centers of Siberia. With it came the persecution of home brewing and of the trade in native beverages.

In Great Russia concessions to run a kabak were granted not only to the boyars but also to churches and monasteries. In 1651 Tsar Alexei abolished all concessions and tried to regulate sales. The kabak (even then an opprobrious word) was rechristened *kruzhechnyi dvor* (literally a "cup yard"); the management of the dvor was to be "on faith," as in earlier days. Around that time it was estimated that the total number of the renamed saloons in the whole country was one thousand. They brought the Government a tremendous revenue. In this connection Pryzhov cites a remarkable document, an order from Tsar Alexei to the Uglich authorities, dated 1652. The Tsar decreed that there should be not more than one kruzhechnyi dvor in every large village, and that smaller villages should have none. Only one cup of vodka should be sold to a customer, while known drunkards were not to be allowed about the place, nor might anyone give them vodka. Beer and mead were prohibited henceforth; whatever stocks of these beverages were on hand must be sold out before September 19, 1653. In other words, Pryzhov remarks, there was to be left in the saloon only vodka for sale. Moreover, all the benefits of the high-sounding reforms were nullified by the final sentence of the ukase which, as if left over by accident from the language of former decrees, ordered that the saloonkeepers were to deliver profits above those of the previous year. Pryzhov adds that this seeming forgetfulness was logical: by that time it was no longer possible to reform the Moscow kabak merely by changing its name. Nor could drunkenness be eradicated by such a simple rule as selling only one cup to a customer.

The suppression of the concessions lasted eleven years. In 1663 they were introduced again. And so it continued: rules were changed from time to time; the saloons were renamed; once they were even prohibited (in 1676, by the 14-year-old Tsar Fyodor Alexeyevich). But much revenue was lost and the old practices were reinstated.

Russia did not surrender to the saloon without a fight, Pryzhov declares. The people everywhere fought back with bootlegging. But there were also statesmen who tried to stem the tide of drunkenness. One such was A. Ordyn-Nashchokin, appointed voyevoda in the city of Pskov in 1665. Inasmuch as the Tsar kabak showed very little profit in Pskov, Ordyn-Nashchokin was able to establish free trade in the city, whereby local beverages became taxable. The system was hailed as very sound. Conditions became much more bearable. The "shameless goings on" in and around the saloon were stopped. In spite of this, some of the "better people" complained that free trade was not profitable to them and the Tsar decided on a plebiscite: a Government monopoly saloon or free trade. Of the peasants, some voted for free trade. But 670 peasants, together with others—in all 2,115 persons—said they "did not know." Moscow decided to let the concessions take over.

From a 17th century book written by a Serbian Catholic priest, Urii Krizhanich, who came to Moscow in 1659 but was shortly after exiled to Siberia, Pryzhov quotes the following description of conditions:

"You can travel over the whole wide world and nowhere will you find such horrible, disgusting, filthy drunkenness as here in Russia. The reason for this is the tavern monopoly, or the kabaks. Owing to that monopoly people may not brew beverages without an official permission, and in the latter it is written that they must drink up everything they prepare within three or four days and may not keep any of it at home longer. In order to consume faster what they have brewed, people drink perforce and get drunk. . . . Further, people of small means are not able to make vodka or beer at home, and there is no korchma where they could go occasionally to drink except the Tsar's korchma, where both place and vessels are worse than any pigsty and the beverage is most revolting . . . and costs a devilish high price. Besides, even these hellish kabaks are not close by the people but each city has only one or two. Therefore, I say, little people are deprived of drinks almost all the time and therefore become greedy for drink, shameless and almost possessed, so that no matter how large a vessel of vodka is offered them they consider it a duty before God and Tsar to down it in one draft. And when they gather a little money and go to the kabak hell, they become completely possessed and drink up all the belongings they have at home and the clothing off their backs. Thus all evil, unseemliness, sinfulness, vanity and shame of the whole people come from this damned korchma monopoly."

Thus Krizhanich, writing between 1660 and 1675 in Siberia. Pryzhov ventures the guess that his exile was caused by his outspokenness.

Pryzhov concludes his sorry tale of Muscovite Russia with a pathetic paragraph:

The 17th century closed the history of ancient Russia which had started with such largesse and abundance but later could not cope with itself and was shaken. The people's *veche* [democratic council] fell silent, the brotherhoods disappeared, the commune was dead, and there was neither popular nor social action. The Moscow kabak, having displaced the free korchma in the Novgorod and Pskov lands, now was spreading to the Ukraine. . . .

The unhealthy evolution of the Government kabak in southwestern Russia is the theme of the next part of the *History*. Separate chapters are devoted to developments in Kiev and in Poland. While these furnish additional details and some documentation, essentially the material repeats what was described in the first 126 pages. Pryzhov then narrates the further developments in the 18th century, but far less colorfully than in the preceding part of the work. Perhaps he had tired of his task or perhaps, in his estimation, the decisive point had been passed: "Moscow" had subjugated all free elements, destroyed all "true" social life. The rest of history represented only variations on the old theme and progressive deterioration of conditions. A few of the more interesting items are worth citing.

Pryzhov attributed the extensive development of infusions and liqueurs in Russia to the prohibition on home brewing of beer and mead. He took the trouble to trace the names of some of these "medicinal" concoctions to their originators.

Considerable space is given to a description of the concessions in the time of Catherine the Great. During 1765–69 the liquor revenues in the Great-Russian and Siberian Gouvernements amounted to as much as 17 million rubles a year. It was in this reign that, after many local changes and adjustments, a uniform system of concessions was instituted throughout the Empire (1795).

In the development in the popular mind of the image of Yarilo as the God of Vodka, a Great-Russian Bacchus, Pryzhov saw an interesting reflection of the ever growing inebriety. In the middle of the 18th century the hitherto obscure Yarilo holiday suddenly became popular in seven Great-Russian Gouvernements, that of Voronezh among them. In 1765 on

May 30—the last day of the Yarilo celebration—drinking was furious and drunken people were lying about in the streets of Voronezh. Bishop Tikhon came out to talk to his beloved people. They listened to him and smashed the barrels. The Yarilo celebration became taboo in Voronezh. The concessioners complained that the Bishop influenced the people not to drink vodka and thus diminished the country's revenue. Tikhon was forced to retire in 1767. This is one example of many cited to show that any decline in the Government's liquor income was followed by punishment of anyone thought to be responsible.

Strewn over the land were special officers for the prosecution of bootleggers. The concessioners had complete freedom of action and their profits were incalculable. New rules were often introduced and abolished. Thus in the beginning of the 19th century food could be sold in the saloons. Their number began to increase enormously and had to be limited by regulation. In 1807 peasants were allowed to brew beer; soldiers were not allowed to sell vodka in the barracks; and so on and on: different rules, changed regulations, but always the concessioners were taken care of and drunkenness increased.

Pryzhov cites Russian proverbs illustrating the conditions. Thus, "Not to drink—might as well not live" had gradually become a rule of life. And even though vodka did not always help, people went on drinking their sorrowful cup. And so tippling, a man gradually began to drink "without letting up"—a never ending cup to his very grave, says Pryzhov (in our terminology, became an alcoholic).

And through the village there sounded the desperate howl of the wife: "The man drinks!" And there rose up a tremendous, monstrous drinking seen nowhere else on God's earth, and it moved all across the Russian land, provoking drunkenness in all—in some, quiet, broken, sad; in others, wild and spirited. The kabaks caused drunkenness, drunkenness caused *zapoi* (the drinking without letting up, alcoholism), and for zapoi treatment was needed.

The book could well have ended at this point. Yet Pryzhov found enough material to fill 30 more pages. Facts are piled upon facts, without discrimination, all pointing to the main theme: how concessioners exploited the people, got rich, and caused inebriety. Rather interesting is the bit of information on the decrease of beer production in the middle of the 19th century as a result of high taxation. Revenue from beer in 1863 in Russia contributed only 1 per cent of the total from alcoholic beverages. In England at the same time this source accounted for 38 per cent of the corresponding total. In most civilized countries, Pryzhov thought, beer was the main alcoholic beverage. In the United States, for example, all the inhabitants drank mostly beer. "If they drink distilled liquor, they immediately take water after it. No one knows what it means to get drunk on distilled spirits and only Negroes and the impoverished Irish drink it."

Pryzhov also described temperance organizations started around 1858–59 in several places, independently of each other. He insisted that the idea originated with the people, quite simply: they got together and took the pledge not to drink. "On rare occasions when they could not do without drink, they bought grape wine." Concessioners lowered their prices; concessioners offered free spirits—people did not drink; the idea of sobriety spread. Pryzhov here becomes even more undisciplined. Facts, statistics, quotations from newspapers are presented without much apparent organization. The book does not end. It just stops, as if in mid-sentence.

In spite of this breakdown in organization as well as in the selection of data, the *History* remains an important document. The first part of the book, particularly, dealing with the early development of the saloons, provides unique materials and constitutes a source of lasting interest. As Al'tman pointed out, not only did Pryzhov gather all the available first-hand sources of information, his book itself became a first-hand source. Finally, the surprising parallels with Western patterns in this relatively inaccessible work add facets of interest for students of comparative culture.

RUSSIA, TODAY

by Mark G. Field *

Juvenile and Adolescent Delinquency. Juvenile delinquency, which appears to be a problem of major proportions, is characterized primarily by considerable drinking among adolescents and sometimes by the formation of gangs for criminal purposes. Although Soviet law prohibits the sale of alcoholic beverages to minors, the latter do not as a rule appear to experience any difficulties in purchasing drinks either from package stores or from drinkshops.

Soviet sources place a great deal of the responsibility for this delinquency directly at the doorstep of the Young Communist League (Komsomols) and its affiliated children's organizations (Pioneers, Oktobrists) for their failure to curb drinking among their members and among youths in general, for their tolerance of rowdyism, and for their inability to provide and devise programs that will hold children's interests and channel their energies into useful and more constructive activities. Parallel to the problem caused by the Komsomols' inability to cope with juvenile delinquency, is the concern caused by the emergence of a *jeunesse dorée,* consisting primarily of the sons of powerful officials and successful intellectuals, whose life, according to the press, is an almost continuous round of pleasure, dissipation, debauchery, and sometimes crime. Particularly revealing as

* From "Alcoholism, Crime, and Delinquency in Soviet Society," *Social Problems, 3* (1955), 100–8.

an illustration is an article in *Komsomolskaya Pravda,* the Komsomol central organ, which describes the life of some of these young men. Their night life revolved around the "Cocktail Hall" on fashionable Gorki Street in Moscow, where they spent most of their evenings drinking and carousing. Leaving the Hall almost at dawn they would get into a car, "round up some girls," and then go to a summer cottage belonging to the family of one of the gang, and here the party would resume.

One of the suggested answers is that the parents are to blame. For example, a cartoon in *Krokodil,* the Soviet satirical magazine, entitled "Mama's One and Only" shows a wife berating her husband for giving their son "only a measly one hundred roubles," to go out. She adds that children of "good" (*Solidnyi,* solid) parents go to restaurants, whereas her son "like an orphan" will have to go "drink beer," obviously a sign of lower-class activity.

Drinking and "White-collar Criminality" among the Cultured Classes. One of the giants of Soviet literature, Fyodor Gladkov, the author of *Cement,* in an article published in the *Literaturnaya Gazeta,* the organ of the Union of Soviet Writers, maintains that writers should set an example, in their personal behavior, of the "new Soviet man's morality." Yet there are certain Soviet writers who drink to excess and who generally deport themselves so as to bring discredit and disrepute upon the writing profession. Furthermore, writers who occupy administrative positions in the Union (of writers) have been known to embezzle large sums of money and to have remained unpunished. What is even worse, Gladkov maintains, is that other writers view this either with indifference or with tolerance or even some kind of benign amusement. He calls for a campaign against "violators of socialist ethics," against drunkenness and debauchery, because "everything tolerated today becomes tomorrow's encouragement to further drunken hoodlumism." There are, according to him, in the healthy circle of Soviet writers some who, having closeted themselves in their cozy apartments, have lost touch with the "masses":

> Soviet writers should not be judged by these bohemian rakes and nouveauriches with their bourgeois ways. They are alien . . . unworthy of bearing the title of Soviet writer. . . . The Union of Writers and (its) Party Organization should genuinely rouse public opinion against petty bourgeois egotism, dissoluteness, drunkenness and brawling. A complacent . . . attitude is politically shortsighted. . . . Strict measures must be taken promptly to make unthinkable any outrage and amoral acts which are alien to our community life.

In a follow-up Gladkov points out that not only writers drink to excess, but also artists and composers "whose names have become synonymous with tavern boozers and hoodlums." He reports having received letters indicating that people in all walks of Soviet cultural life drink to excess. For example, at a teachers' district conference, a "respected man of letters" from Moscow was to deliver a lecture: "There appeared on the platform a man drunk as a lord, who talked rubbish and mixed up Euclid with Eucalyptus."

One further complaint is that not only too many artists and writers drink but that too many artistic productions embody, in one form or another, a glorification or at least a very passive attitude toward the problem of drinking. There is hardly a play, a movie, a radio program, or a popular music record that does not encourage the listener or the reader to raise his glass and drink up. And the effect of such encouragement upon younger manual workers can readily be imagined. This cannot leave the regime unconcerned, because this affects industrial production, an area of vital importance in the Soviet scheme.

Drinking and Crime among Soviet Workers. Hard drinking seems to be widespread among Soviet manual workers. Apparently it is considered, in some workers' circles, a sign of manliness and serves as a badge of acceptance. The worker who can blow one hundred roubles on drinks in one evening becomes something of a hero. On the other hand, those who refuse to join in are accused of being "weak sisters." There have been reported cases when foremen discriminated against workers or refused to hire them if they did not pay them a tribute in vodka. Furthermore, it is far easier for a worker to obtain vodka and drinks than reading material. Workers who drink turn out shoddy goods, their production falls, they are often absent, and are downgraded to menial jobs or worse. While drinking appears to be more prevalent among those engaged in hazardous occupations, such as coal mining, it generally affects most manual workers, including fishermen and even railroad workers. In the first five months of 1954 there were not less than nineteen cases of workers appearing drunk for work at the Moscow-Kursk railroad depot. In addition, workers who drink often join criminal elements. For example, *Trud,* the central organ of the trade unions, published an article early in 1954 describing the sentencing of three young unmarried workers to long terms of imprisonment for burglary and robbery. They had gone to work in a large enterprise and lived in a dormitory. While things at work went well, life outside working hours and particularly in the dormitory was boring. Newspapers and books were unavailable; they did not know what to do with themselves. One evening an unfamiliar young man walked into the room. . . . He smelled of vodka. . . . The boys told the stranger about themselves and complained of boredom. The stranger said: "Bored, eh? You babies. All you need is two hundred grams of vodka apiece and things will be lively enough. Give me ten roubles." Later, vodka . . . appeared on the table. The young man accompanied each glass with a comment. "You have to know how to live! Get it? Working is for fools. We'll get along without work. Get it?"

After that, evening life seemed more interesting, but in the morning heads ached and hands shook. The boys had no desire to go to work, they came late, or did not come to work at all. They would disappear in the evening, no one knew where. Soon they appeared at work every other day. The foreman decided to turn in their names to the manager for court action, as is the procedure in Soviet labor law, but before the court got to the case they were arrested for burglaries, one of which ended in a murder attempt. With crime and particularly alcoholism on the increase, industrial production is bound to suffer. "Even a single case of absenteeism," says an article in *Trud,* "thwarts the efforts of conscientious workers in conditions of complex machinery and mass production." And by the same token, the regime is also concerned with the phenomena as they apply to the collective farmers and to agricultural production, a sensitive area in the Soviet Union.

The Situation on the Farms. Drinking among collective farmers appears to be prevalent, and is often sparked by festivals of all conceivable types, some celebrating local saints, others regional or national figures. Writing in *Literaturnaya Gazeta,* V. Sapozhnikova describes, for example, the celebrating of St. Tikhon Day, typical of many such a holiday:

> Visitors flooded the village of Polubabino from morning. They came from every direction to drink. . . . By all accounts a notable drinking spree was in the offing. A month previous, people had begun to make home brew and to prepare refreshments. Three days before the "holiday" fifty collective farmers, more than one-fourth of the entire working force, had gone to the nearest workers' settlement to make purchases . . . glasses clinked in every house. A strong intoxicating odor of home brew pervaded the air, and discordant songs issued from the windows. . . . "Who is this Tikhon, grandmother?" I asked an old woman. "What did he do to the people to be so honored?" "Tikhon?" she replied, "Who cares? It's not for us to bother. He is home brew, that's all." . . . Those who collapsed were dragged over a fence, doused with water, and left to lie until they came to and resumed drinking. Zaitsev, Chairman of the Rural Consumers' Cooperative (he is also secretary of the Party organization at a neighborhood collective farm), did a brisk trade in vodka.

Apparently, the regime here is caught on the horns of a dilemma of its own making. In line with its post-Stalin policy of conciliating the population, it has toned down its antireligious policy. In the countryside, the stronghold of religious beliefs, Party officials attempt not to antagonize the population and give permission for holidays to be celebrated. These holidays, the meaning of which, apparently, has been lost to most, often turn into drunken brawls during which, of course, none or very little of the field work gets done, and for which Party officials will later carry the responsibility.

In the Moslem parts of the Soviet Union, where drinking is less of a problem, Moslem pilgrimages and holidays are also said to interfere with collective farm work. In the Vologda Province, for example, 10,000 work-days were reportedly lost to religious festivals at the height of the 1954 harvest. The persistence of religious beliefs is blamed on poor "ideological" work among collective farmers on the part of Party organizations. Party and Komsomol members are accused of compromising with "alien in-fluences" and sometimes of participating in the religious celebrations them-selves. If it is remembered that agricultural production is still very much of a critical problem in the Soviet Union, one can understand the regime's concern with the countless religious festivals celebrated in the countryside because of the drinking and the loss of time which accompany them. There appears to be less criminality among collective farmers than among in-dustrial workers, although there are numerous reports of collective farm chairmen abusing their authority and terrorizing the farmers. "The root of evil" writes a reader in a letter to the editor of *Izvestiya*, "is the con-stant drinking of collective farm officials. . . . Ivanov, the collective farm chairman, drinks ceaselessly. He has surrounded himself with drunkards, flatterers, and thieves, just like himself." There are also reports of the production of home brew (often abetted by collective farm chairmen them-selves and sometimes with fatal results) and of petty thefts of collective farm property and produce.

The Official Explanation. Social problems, and alcoholism in particular, according to official Soviet ideology are the products of a diseased and disorganized economy and society, i.e. of capitalism. This view originally derives from Engels' work in the *Condition of the Working Classes in England,* in which he maintained that under capitalistic conditions the over-worked, exploited, underfed, ill-housed, and ill-clothed worker seeks temporary solace and oblivion in alcohol. The exploiting classes, in ad-dition, encourage the use and sale of alcoholic beverages not only because these bring in huge profits but also because alcohol, just like religion, dulls the worker's social consciousness and revolutionary ardor; alcohol is thus another tool in the capitalist arsenal. Therefore, a successful fight against alcoholism is possible only where the capitalist system has been eliminated. This means that "In USSR where class exploitation has been ended forever, where the welfare of the population increases all the time, the social roots of alcoholism have been extirpated." Yet, the incontrovertible fact remains, and the Soviet press confirms it, that alcoholism and its attendant evils, rather than disappearing from the Soviet scene may, on the contrary, be on the increase. What, then, accounts for its existence? The theoretical explanation is one that has been used time and again to explain away cer-tain embarrassing features of Soviet society: it is that of the famous "remnants of capitalist consciousness" still existing in the minds of some Soviet citizens. It is part of the accursed heritage of the past, a legacy from a blighted period, a "lag" between changes in the "social structure" and the "consciousness of the people." Thus the Communists place the responsibility for social disorganization not on conditions existing under the Soviet system, but squarely on a political and social structure that was eliminated more than thirty-five years ago. The explanation as to how these remnants manage to exist, persist, and grow in the conditions of a socialist society is as follows:

> The Party proceeds from the viewpoints that life worthy of socialism does not come about by itself . . . automatically, but demands a struggle, a constant uprooting of the heritage of the capitalist society. The Party always considers that survivals of capitalism are still alive, that they will not disappear in the course of one generation, but may even be strengthened if a fight is not carried against them constantly. . . . There is evidence that quite often there is indifference . . . to some of the most harmful survivals of capitalism. . . . Quite often . . . at Party meetings devoted to drunkenness at work, this problem is greeted with smiles. With such an attitude somehow we legalize drunkenness. . . . There is a lot of drunkenness on the collective farms. Where there is no campaign conducted against drunkenness, there are cases of drinking among adolescents, school children. . . . But we must be careful that (in this struggle) some lecturers and authors do not exaggerate. . . . One predicted the most terrible diseases if lumbermen drank as much as eighty to one hundred grams of vodka. . . . This can only cause an ironic attitude. It only weakens the struggle against alcoholism.

This, then, is the manner in which, officially speaking, there is a rationalization of the fact that the elimination of capitalism did not lead to the automatic elimination of alcoholism and related forms of social disorganization. What, then, are some of the factors which, according to the Soviets and at a practical everyday level, facilitate, indeed even encourage, drinking and crime in contemporary Soviet society?

Factors Facilitating Alcoholism and Crime. The first factor is, of course, that of availability. Soviet citizens of all ages find it easy to purchase alcoholic drinks, and particularly vodka (its price has recently gone down). These are sold everywhere, particularly in the streets, in booths, bars, and drink stands called "green sentry boxes," which are dotting, in increasing and alarming numbers, Soviet cities and workers' settlements. The sale of alcoholic beverages is a state monopoly and its financial contribution to the state budget is far from negligible. In addition, this serves to drain off excessive purchasing power and has a salutary effect on inflationary trends. Yet Soviet authorities are obviously and genuinely disturbed about the abuse of alcohol and the increasing ease with which it has become available to the population: there are, for instance, many street stands originally designed to sell ice cream, mineral water, and tea, which now dispense vodka. Booths and drink shops are not, of course, operated by private individuals or entrepreneurs. They belong to state food-handling trusts. These organizations, in turn, are run commercially and must show a profit at the end of their financial year. Managers have found out that it was much easier to fulfill or overfulfill their financial plans by dispensing alcoholic beverages than any other item. But perhaps more important, as a contributory cause, is the boredom and drabness that seem to characterize the leisure hours of the Soviet citizenry, particularly the industrial workers and the youths. One article recently published in *Izvestiya* describes the almost unbelievable dreariness of a Sunday in a workers' settlement: the same movie is shown time and again, there is no entertainment.

Sunday is boring in Khokhol; everyone passes the time as best he can, and the only place where there is any life is in the tearooms and the snack bars. . . . The district Soviet passed a resolution banning the sale of vodka on the premises but the strong-drink addicts have managed to circumvent the resolution. People drink at home too, and not just vodka but bootleg alcohol as well. There are always a lot of drunks on the streets on Sunday. Drunken orgies and brawls have become common at the Culture Center.

What is true of industrial workers is also true of the youths and adolescents, who often turn to drinking, to the forming of gangs, and to criminal activities, sometimes only for the thrill and excitement. These children's predilection for the "Western" type of amusement, their imitation of "American bourgeois-gangster mannerisms" is, as noted before, a source of amazement and concern for Soviet authorities. Finally, as a contributory factor to the rise in crime, the Amnesty Decree of 1953 should be mentioned. Many of those who had been amnestied were not, for many reasons, able or willing to live as law-abiding citizens, and returned to a life of criminality. Some of these have been caught and sent back to prison or camps.

Proposed Remedies. If drinking is such a problem, and given the totalitarian nature of the Soviet system, why then does the government not pass a dry law or at least severely restrict the production of alcohol? The Soviets are not unmindful of the failure of Prohibition in the United States, and seem to have resigned themselves to the idea that people will drink, prohibition or no prohibition. Indeed, they realize that such a move would raise more problems than it would solve. They describe a dry law as something hypocritical, "a puritanical measure alien to the Soviet people." They thus prefer to control drinking as much as possible and to prevent abuses. The measures advocated are: intensifying propaganda against the consumption of alcoholic beverages, particularly hard liquor (vodka), encouraging the population to drink beer and wines, a stiffening of public opinion toward habitual drunkards, increase in recreational activities, bolstering the authority of the police (*militsia*), and a demonstration of the harmful consequences of alcohol for the human organism. While the Ministry of Health is expected to carry this last part of the program, the full weight of the regime's means of mass communication has been enlisted in that direction. Indeed, the picture of alcoholism and crime as it emerges from the Soviet press and on which this paper is based would not be available if such a campaign had not been launched. In its campaign against crime, the death penalty has recently been reintroduced in cases of premeditated murder, and steps are being taken to reinforce the law forbidding the sale of liquor to minors. It still remains to be seen whether the regime will be successful in this, particularly in view of other factors not mentioned in the press.

Some Further Hypotheses. Drinking and other related social problems, particularly among the younger members of the population, may well be linked to the erosion of family functions that accompanies industrialization and the removal from the home, during working hours, of the father and, in Soviet society, quite often the mother. Since 1936 the regime has taken drastic measures to increase family stability and to reverse the "light-minded attitude" toward family obligations which had resulted from earlier policies of easy divorces and legalized abortions.

There is as yet little evidence that such measures have been successful. Furthermore, the youths of today are part of the "war generation," brought up without close parental supervision, under conditions of severe deprivations, often forced to fend for themselves without knowledge of a peaceful, normal life. These youths may find it difficult to adapt themselves to a more orderly way of life and may prefer to keep on dodging work and living on the fringes of Soviet society.

At the same time, alcoholism and crime may well be linked to a general weariness on the part of the population with both the tempo and the drabness of Soviet life, with unfulfilled promises, with excessive demands put on human beings and lack of commensurate rewards. This certainly is the burden of much of the criticism made by refugees who left the Soviet Union immediately before and during the war; and from all evidence available, this applies equally to the postwar period. Furthermore, it may be presumed that the hardening of the stratification lines that has been in progress since the middle thirties has made social mobility difficult to achieve for the lower classes, so that there is less incentive on the part of the members of these classes to "be sober" and apply themselves in order to rise in the social structure. The presence of a "gilded youth" of adolescents who can ride on their parents' coat-tails and enjoy the life of leisure of "young aristocrats" is another index of the decrease in mobility and of careers open to those who work hard.

And finally, as anyone acquainted with the prerevolutionary literature well knows, alcoholism and its attendant evils are not a new phenomenon in Russian life. To say the least, the inability of the Soviet regime to break away from this pattern makes its claim of having changed "society" and the "nature of man" subject to certain qualifications.

10. FRANCE

DRINKING AND ITS CONTROL

by Gabriel Mouchot *

Wine, Cider, and Beer. Since the beginning of the 20th century too much wine has been produced in France; 60 million hectoliters were produced in 1950. This fact is sometimes denied by producers who claim that people could, would, and even should drink more if only they could afford it. Like car manufacturers and other industrialists their attitude is that the capacity of the market to absorb their goods is limited only by financial considerations; if only people were paid more and could afford it, they would buy more wine and there would be no overproduction. This is not true. In 1934, when the bottom fell out of the wine market and prices crumbled to half of what they had been previously, one would have expected a great increase in consumption. In fact, only a 5 per cent increase took place. The truth is that Frenchmen already drink too much, and with the best will in the world could hardly drink more.

Algeria is in theory at least part and parcel of France as much as the Isle of Wight is part of England. Algerian wines (well over 14 million hectoliters per year) must be added to French wines. Indeed when as much wine as possible has been exported there still remain about 10 million hectoliters to make the despair of wine producers.

In the 18th century a hectare (2.47 acres) produced from 15 to 20 hectoliters of wine; today it produces over 50.

Formerly when there was overproduction of a product, its producers turned to something else. Nowadays it is up to the government to prevent prices from falling; even before the war the French Parliament had generously decided that wine which had found no thirsty throat to quench would in future be bought by a special agency which would transform it into alcohol. Since nobody knows what to do with it, as much as possible is put into the petrol sold to motorists. Economists have remarked that financially speaking the operation is very costly and means a loss of millions of pounds sterling; motorists whose cars have been made to burn petrol and not alcohol complain that the mixture sold to them damages their motors, and nobody is pleased.

The wine problem is already complicated enough but it is not the whole story. In Normandy and a few other places people drink cider containing 5

* From "Letter from France," *International Journal on Alcohol and Alcoholism,* *1* (1955), 75–84.

per cent alcohol, and it is estimated that 17 million hectoliters of it are produced and drunk every year. To be honest it must be said that nobody knows exactly how much, for the simple reason that in Normandy everybody has apple trees and makes his own cider. Norman peasants simply do not know what to do with their apples; the result is too much cider and apple brandy. . . .

Beer is not a problem in France. Only 8 million hectoliters are produced, and its alcohol content is low. . . .

Spirits. There is hardly a French province without its brandy: in Normandy they make Calvados out of cider; in Carentes, Cognac out of white wine; in Lot et Garonne, Armagnac; in Alsace, Kirsch out of cherries; etc.

There are two different kinds of producers: industrial producers and private individuals. The activities of the first can be controlled and could easily be curbed. The main difficulty is represented by the second category, and we must go into some detail. If you are an agriculturalist, you are allowed to make brandy for your own use without paying any duty; this is called the privilege of the "bouilleur de cru." The idea is that you make brandy with your own apples, wine, cherries, or whatever it is. It would be an unwarrantable intrusion into the privacy of your home and a breach of individual freedom to prevent you from doing what you like with your own property so long as it is for your own use.

Naturally you make brandy for yourself and your family but you cannot very well refuse to sell a gallon or more to friends. Indeed in Normandy one of the recognized ways of making a fortune is to buy brandy from local farmers (at approximately 15 shillings [1] a gallon) and take it to Paris, where you can sell it at a good profit. However respectable this trade may be, it is not legal and there are drawbacks. If caught by the police heavy fines and the confiscation of the lorry will be the consequences. That is why this trade is left to youngsters; if you have not a penny of your own you will lose nothing, and the lorry will be old and decrepit and possibly not even your own. If you are lucky, you will make a fortune; if you are not, you will do a few months in jail and try to find another profession.

A garage man was caught carrying Calvados in petrol cans. He did six months and had to sell his garage. Of course he was a fool. Far more clever was the ne'er-do-well son of a doctor who borrowed a lorry and took a cartload of brandy to Belgium. He was caught by the police, but barring sending the man to jail nothing could be done; it was not his lorry.

The main point is that socially speaking there is no stigma of dishonor either in smuggling brandy or in being convicted for having done it. Lots of perfectly honest people will just smile at it, and they may even go and buy a bottle of Calvados for 3 shillings and so encourage people to defraud the excise.

1. The English monetary system is followed in this report.

Considering the amount of brandy made on farms and private dwellings, then, it is well-nigh impossible to give accurate figures as to the amount consumed in France; one can merely guess at the importance of this alcohol torrent going down French gullets. . . .

In lower Normandy it is customary to offer a cup of coffee to any friend you meet or who calls upon you. Now, a cup of coffee is only partly filled with coffee, generally a very bad one: a copious helping of apple brandy is added. Indeed the etiquette is that the brandy must overflow into the saucer. Not to do so would be a sign of stinginess, of which I have seen few examples. You drink a third of the mixture and fill up again with more brandy. Naturally if you have been invited by a friend to have a "cup" at the local pub you cannot refuse, and having drunk his cup you must at once call for another. And if there are three or four men together, each of them will stand the company a drink. . . .

Apart from such social occasions, nobody would think of ending a meal without a cup of brandy, and there are at least three meals a day. I should say that an average Norman peasant takes five cups of brandy a day, and on market days and social occasions it may be two or three times as much. In every Norman farm there is a bottle of brandy on the table; if it is not, it is produced at once, as soon as anyone enters the house. Not to do so would be a terrible breach of etiquette.

To drink a liter of Calvados (alcohol content 60 per cent) a week is moderate, and an acquaintance of mine who looks upon himself as almost abstemious is of the opinion that one cannot well drink less. A woman patient of eighty-three whose blood pressure was 290/160 expressed her astonishment at this high pressure: "I eat very sparingly and a liter of Calvados lasts me a month now"; what more she could do she was unable to say. To drink only a liter of brandy a month is almost to drink nothing at all.

The other liqueurs are made industrially and present no special problem; besides, the alcohol they are made with is bought by the makers from the Government Alcohol Agency. We must also mention the rum which is imported from Martinique, Guadeloupe, and Réunion. The quantities which may be imported into France are limited not because the government is very desirous to reduce the incidence of alcoholism but because it does not want to increase the difficulties of the wine producers, whose electoral importance is far greater than that of the inhabitants of these far-away islands.

The Government Alcohol Agency. This agency buys alcohol from beetroot and wine producers. During the first war the government, which needed alcohol to make explosives, decided to buy up all the alcohol that could be produced, and for a mixture of economic, social, and electoral reasons—the latter being the most powerful—the practice was continued. The result is that it pays people to grow beetroot to make alcohol instead of sugar and that there is no inducement for wine growers to reduce their production, the government being sure to buy their unsold alcohol. The net financial loss amounts to 18 million pounds. Politicians have never been known for their electoral courage, and to put an end to this would be tantamount to political suicide. Nonetheless they are forced to do something, and the government is trying to reduce the amount of alcohol it is willing to buy.

Alcohol Consumption. In 1951, the amount of pure alcohol consumed in France in the form of wine, cider, beer, and distilled spirits was close to 820 million liters, of which 70 per cent came from wine.

How much alcohol can be drunk safely is a disputed question, but it cannot be denied that 28 liters of pure alcohol a year is too much for anyone. This latter amount, which was the per capita consumption for the adult population in 1951, was the highest consumed by any nation and was double that of the next highest consumer, Italy, and three times greater than the consumption of Great Britain.

If we compare the amount of alcohol drunk in various countries with the national income, we will see that the Frenchman spends proportionately more money on liquor than anybody else in the world. The amount of pure alcohol (in liters) per $100 of national income is as follows: France 4.1, Italy 4.0, Belgium 1.1, Switzerland 1.0, Great Britain 0.7, Denmark 0.5, Sweden 0.4, and the United States of America 0.4.[2]

It has been estimated that 675 million pounds are spent each year on alcoholic drink, which represents 10 per cent of all private expenses or 7.3 per cent of the national income. One must point out that health expenses amount to only 6 or 7 per cent of the national income, so that the French spend more on drink than on doctors, chemists, and hospitals. And this is very likely an underestimate, because, as already noted, the wine, cider, and brandy that is drunk by farmers who consume what they produce can hardly be reckoned. Most agriculturalists think that brandy costs them nothing because they make it themselves; it is very difficult to convince them that if they were to produce something else and sell it, they would be better off at the end of the year. These figures show conclusively that if the French insist on drinking as they do, it can only be at the cost of doing without other important things. But although the French spend enormous sums on drink, alcohol remains a very cheap commodity; wine indeed is in the reach of the poorest man's purse. Taxes on drink are low and are often evaded. The result is that it is cheaper to buy a glass of brandy than a glass of Vichy water or fruit juice. In my part of the world apple brandy costs 3 shillings a liter, but a meal costs 10 shillings. The consequence of such a state of affairs is easy to foresee.

Public Houses. The number of sales outlets for alcoholic beverages in France is enormous. It is estimated that there is one for every forty-five

2. From G. Malignac and R. Colin, *L'Alcoolisme*, Paris, Presses Universitaires de France, 1954.

people, and the French piously hope that no country can do so well. And in a country where one can get a drink in every form this means that nobody need remain thirsty for very long. It has been estimated that there are ten pubs for every bakery and this proportion shows the importance of drink in the social and economic life of the country.

Alcoholism and the Law. In February 1955, after a decision to do something about alcoholism, all the laws and regulations concerning drink, pubs, and cognate subjects were codified. As far as can be seen, the only advantage is that for 2 shillings one can buy a nice red booklet of fifty pages wherein the attitude of the law concerning alcohol is clearly stated in a hundred paragraphs. One puts this Codex of the liquor trade aside with a feeling of despair and boredom. It is evidently the child of a politician whose main aim was to give the impression that he was doing something but who was not fool enough to come to grips with the real problems. To attack alcoholism in France is dangerous. Naturally one finds good things in the Codex, but they are few and far between. Besides, the point is not so much what the wording of the law is but how far it is put into practice. It is very well to say that in places where there are 450 people per pub no new one may be opened. The trouble is that France is already remarkably well provided with pubs, and merely to prevent new ones from being opened will achieve nothing. I live in a village where there are seven pubs per thousand inhabitants, where every farmer will sell brandy. This is normal in France, but the law will do nothing about it.

It is stated that prefects may prevent pubs from operating in the neighborhood of churches, hospitals, schools, and the like. But I have never heard of any prefect brave or foolhardy enough to take such a step. He would certainly not be backed by his home secretary, and he would lose his job in no time.

One can read in the Codex that anybody found drunk in the street will be fined up to 1,200 francs. A second conviction may land him in jail for a month, and the fine may be up to 72,000 francs. My impression is that police are not very zealous on this matter, and if they were the public outcry would be too much for them.

The Codex decides that a publican who has sold drink to a man obviously drunk may be fined up to 1,200 francs, and a second conviction may be punishable by a month in jail and the fine may be 72,000 francs. A few may have been so punished but I have never heard of it, and my own experience is that it would be impossible to make a case against a publican. He would be a brave man who would come up before a judge and give the evidence required; besides, how does one recognize that a man is drunk?

The long and short of it is that one could drive a coach and four through this act of parliament and that so far all French governments have been unable to do anything or have been too cowardly to try. . . . The law cannot do much when it is not backed by public opinion. . . . French law, however lax we may consider it, is rather in advance of public opinion and cannot even be put into practice. We must admit that it is of no use to enact hard laws and to threaten to inflict severe penalties on people who are looked upon by almost everybody as doing something perfectly normal.

Alcoholism and Public Opinion. Almost everyone in France thinks that wine or brandy or whatever he drinks is good for him. No French worker can be convinced that it is possible to work without alcohol in some form or other. You cannot meet a friend without being offered a glass of liqueur, you cannot have the plumber or the electrician doing an odd job in your house without giving him something to drink. In every walk of life, in every social class, alcohol is there to help one celebrate a success, drown a sorrow, cheer one up, put one in the proper frame of mind to work—or to stop working and pass the time. All my patients would offer me brandy and it took me years to establish the privilege that I could walk into a house without drinking anything.

Public opinion polls on the subject were conducted in 1948 and 1953. An enormous majority (85 per cent the first and 80 the second) were of the opinion that wine was good for the health.

Curiously enough, most people will admit that excessive drinking is bad. Public opinion accepts the idea that accidents at work or on the road are often the result of drunkenness. But I have hardly ever met a man who recognized that he drinks too much. Drunkenness—like sin—is always something others should be ashamed of. More often than excessive drinking, "sophisticated" beverages are blamed, but everybody is convinced that his special potation—whether wine, brandy, cider, or whatever—is wholesome and strength-giving.

Some people still hold the belief that wine has almost magical virtues and lots of people used to say that the first war had been won owing to it. The collapse of the second war rather damped the ardor of these protagonists of liquor.

In 1939 a Minister of Education had propagated the slogan that wine was the healthiest drink. Indeed Pasteur had actually said it, though taken out of its context it was made to mean something Pasteur never meant.

Alcohol producers are numerous, rich and powerful. Their advertisements are in every paper and over the radio. They have prevented papers from publishing articles attacking alcoholism merely by threatening no longer to buy space. They have made a film to defend their interests.

Public opinion is very favorably disposed toward alcohol, and people wax lyrical and patriotic when they broach the subject of wine and brandy. Every pleasant trait of character is ascribed to wine; if people are happy, carefree, or humorous, it is because they drink this or that wine; if they are brave, it is due to some alcoholic potation. Almost everyone in France

believes that alcohol will cure "La Grippe" which makes one wonder how
most people can ever get it to begin with. It is well understood that one must
have an "apéritif" to give an edge to one's appetite before a meal. Then,
having eaten and drunk well, one needs a "digestif"; and if one feels weak,
he has a whole gamut of "fortifiants." . . . If your digestion is bad, you
will naturally think of improving it by drinking something called "digestif"
—with a name like that it will naturally do you good. Besides, winebibbers
have a score of great men they summon to defend their cause. French
literature is full of kind remarks on drink.

Social life, history, folklore, all are an encouragement to drinking
against which no man is proof. Unconsciously people are processed in a
thousand ways into accepting an attitude of mind according to which one
must drink. Not to do so is to cut oneself off from his friends. . . . In
every walk of life, drink smooths social relations. You are invited not
to have a friendly chat but to drink. . . . Of course nobody is obliged to
drink, but you cannot very well go to a cocktail party and ask for a glass
of milk. I am a water drinker by taste, not out of principle, and I upset
every party I go to: "Won't you really have a glass of champagne, oh,
well, let me offer you brandy?" It takes me a long time to explain that I
prefer water, and it casts a gloom on the company. Of course it is the same
in most countries, but public opinion is particularly strong in France. Besides, soft drinks are not popular. Fruit juices and lemonade can be found
if asked for, but so far have met with little success. Coca-Cola started a
wide publicity campaign a few years ago with no marked result. I understand that some people are currently engaged in trying to find a soft drink
which would appeal to French palates and would have a French label, because the American label of Coca-Cola has hampered sales. Communists—
superpatriots for that occasion—came out very strongly against a foreign
and filthy potation.

I would not like to give the impression that the situation is absolutely
hopeless; indeed there is a glimmer of hope. Anti-alcoholic propaganda is
beginning to tell, and young people drink less than their elders—in certain regions at least. Confirmed drunkards are naturally past redemption
and most of them will never be cured; but one can point out to their sons
that drink is a danger, and a boy whose father has died with delirium
tremens can easily be convinced.

Alcoholism and Politicians. Too many people convinced of the dangers
of alcoholism declare that something must be done and expect Parliament
to do it. French politicians as a body are not respected or highly thought
of, but I am sure they are not wicked or as silly as they are often supposed
to be; they merely cannot lead their electors where they refuse to be led.

Indeed those who expect Parliament to "do something" are generally
those who show the same lack of courage as politicians. It is up to doctors,

indeed to everybody who has the courage to call a man a drunkard. . . . Public opinion must first be reformed; and only when people have been re-educated will the government be able to take steps.

Besides, it must be admitted that even if electors were to take an enlightened and intelligent attitude toward alcoholism, important difficulties would remain. Several million French people depend on liquor for their daily bread. Millions of acres are covered by vineyards; to decide that half of them should be used to grow wheat is easy enough, but it would spell ruin to countless peasants. And would wheat sell better than—or even as well as—wine? Who would decide which vineyards would be uprooted and what to grow instead, and who will pay the costs? . . .

So long as we have no precise ideas as to how and where to resettle the wine producers, publicans, still-owners, and others who would be declared redundant, it is childish to expect politicians to do anything. Members of Parliament are supposed to defend the interests of their electors, and the interests of too many of them are connected with liquor. Somebody once wrote that one Frenchman in seven depends on drink for his living in one way or another. Even if public opinion were educated and the people concerned were desirous to help, the excessive production of wine, brandy, etc. would still be a baffling problem.

We must first educate public opinion, but we must also study far more seriously than has been done the economic consequences of the necessary reforms and not expect a category of people to carry the burden alone. Alcoholism is a national problem; it must be tackled on a national basis, and the load must be spread evenly.

Not only are politicians expected to do more than they have the courage to undertake but they are very susceptible to the arguments brought forward by wine producers and others. They tell us that there is no scientific basis to our opposition to alcohol and point to a few dozen old drunkards who apparently enjoy the best of health. Statistical arguments rarely carry conviction. How many doctors have given up smoking now that it has been statistically proved there is a connection between lung carcinoma and tobacco? Too many of our arguments fail to convince those who have a personal interest in not being convinced, and politicians are among them.

Though the point is moot, I have heard it argued that since more people suffer through alcohol than benefit from it, a brave and uncompromising attitude might pay, even electorally. I am not a politician and cannot express an opinion, but M. Mendès-France, who tried to attack the liquor barons, wine producers, beetroot producers, and others was speedily turned out of office. The measures he devised were never put into practice.

Some people think that the importance of wine and liquor in the political life of the country has been overrated and that politicians are victims of an optical illusion. They say that the wives of all drunkards would back any government courageous enough to tackle the problem. That may be, but those with a vested interest in alcohol are organized and vocal while their opponents are not. Anyhow, we are back to where we started. One must first win over public opinion and not expect much from politicians. . . .

Governments, being always short of money, are not likely to leave drink untaxed, even in France. Indeed, with some smugness, smokers and drinkers like to consider that they are the financial prop of the state. In 1952, wine, brandy, etc. contributed 54 million pounds to the French exchequer. This argument is never forgotten by all those who deal in liquor: their trade is profitable to the state and must be protected.

Unfortunately quite a lot of people never pay a farthing. When it is remembered that there are 3 million "bouilleurs de cru" who are entitled to make their own brandy without paying any tax and who carry on a brisk and profitable trade by selling their untaxed brandy, one is forced to the conclusion that liquor should be an even more profitable source of revenue.

But this is not all; the main objection to this line of argument is that alcohol costs the community at least three times what it brings the state. Economists and statisticians have examined the problem thoroughly, and the figures are there for everybody to see. Every year millions of pounds sterling are spent to give medical care to drunkards, to keep them alive while they convalesce. Alcoholics are more prone than others to have accidents, and it costs the community 17 million pounds a year to treat workers who have been injured while under the influence of drink.

Drunkards make also an excessive—though quite involuntary—use of judicial services, tribunals, and jails provided by the state. In fact, were it not for alcoholism many judges would be on the dole. The net result of all that is that alcoholism costs France 152 million pounds a year.

One might think that it would be easy to increase the taxes sharply and collect them more zealously. I once tackled a member of Parliament on this very subject; his answer was that mild as were present taxes, they were already evaded on a large scale, and to increase them would merely be to encourage fraud. I must say the man was right. In a small village not far from where I live something happened a few years ago which is typical of the present state of affairs. Excise men, having good reason to believe that brandy was being illegally distilled, turned up in force. The local peasantry ran to the nearby church, rang the bell, and called for help; very soon the excise men were faced by a crowd of angry-looking farmers who evidently meant business. Discretion being the better part of valor, they prudently retired. This incident was not considered as in any way out of the normal, and we must admit that increasing taxes is out of the question when levying them is already difficult.

It is of course impossible to say how far alcoholism is responsible for the appalling state of housing in France. Alcohol has always been an easy solution for present difficulties and the man who lives in a shack can always exchange the ugliness of reality against the dreams and torpor cheaply provided by alcohol. Indeed, most Frenchmen spend less on rent than they do on either drink or tobacco. It is a vicious circle: People cannot afford decent houses because they drink, and they drink because they live in slummy dwellings. To solve (?) the problem, the government controls rents, and landlords cannot afford to repair houses. It is difficult to levy taxes on drink, so foodstuffs are heavily taxed, and to keep wine producers contented and quiet, prices are artificially sustained and drink is subsidized. In short, the problem of alcoholism in France is a good example of democracy gone mad: it shows to what silly extremes a country will go that has no political courage.

PUBLIC OPINION

by H. Bastide *

A survey of public opinion concerning the use of alcoholic drinks in France was carried out in 1948 and repeated in 1953. A sample of 1,070 men and 1,078 women was drawn and similar techniques were employed in each year. The significance of French attitudes toward wine is revealed in the responses to some of the questions.

TABLE 1.—*Importance of Wine (by Per Cent of Respondents)*

	1948			1953		
	Male	Female	Total	Male	Female	Total
For a man doing physical work:						
Wine is indispensable	51	37	44	32	18	25
Wine is useful	45	57	51	58	67	63
Wine is good for the health			80			80
Wine is nourishing			79			70

Actual consumption of absolute alcohol per capita of adult population in liters in 1951 was: France 30.5, Italy 14.2, United States 9.4, and Great Britain 9.3. French opinion is shown in Table 2.

Of the sample questioned, 47 per cent thought a child of ten should have no wine; 46 per cent thought up to 0.25 liter daily. A woman might have 0.5 liter; 41 per cent believed a man of moderate activity could have

* Abstracted from "Une enquête sur l'opinion publique à l'égard de l'alcoolisme," *Population, 9* (1954), 13–42.

TABLE 2.—*Do the People of France Drink More than Others?*
(*by Per Cent of Respondents*)

French drink:	England	Italy	America
More than	47	35	27
As much as	19	26	19
Less than	12	9	28
No answer	22	30	26

1 liter; 25 per cent consider 2 liters daily appropriate for a man doing physical work.

Distilled spirits were thought to be responsible for most of the drunkenness and two-thirds of the respondents considered aperitifs bad for health if taken daily. Almost all thought drinking a factor in accidents at work and in traffic. There was agreement that drinking aggravated some diseases, for example, liver disorders and mental disease.

Three-fourths of the replies indicated belief that there are many alcoholics in France and that alcoholism causes harm to the country as a whole. Measures to control alcoholism were favored as follows: education, 86 per cent; reduce number of drinking places, 76 per cent; curtail advertising, 70 per cent; eliminate private distilling, 54 per cent; and deny right to drink, 49 per cent. Opinions on the last two items varied greatly according to occupation and place of residence. Women generally favored reform measures. There were no significant differences by region of the country but urban–rural and sex differences were great.

11. ENGLAND

by B. Seebohm Rowntree
and G. R. Lavers *

Before embarking on our examination of the problem of drink as a factor affecting contemporary English life, we should perhaps make our position clear. We are neither of us teetotalers, although one of us is by inclination and practice virtually so. It follows that we are neither of us prohibitionists. We feel, therefore, that we can claim with some confidence that we approach the matter with objective and undistorted minds.

Drunkenness

A common error in considering the drink problem is to imagine that it is synonymous with that of drunkenness. If that were so, there would indeed be grounds for substantial satisfaction, for the number of convictions for drunkenness in England and Wales fell from 183,514 in 1913, and 44,954 in 1938, to 28,600 in 1948. Although the figures for 1948 were considerably above the lowest previously recorded (16,901 in 1945), a nation in which the convictions for drunkenness are equivalent to approximately 0.7 per cent of the population must be considered tolerably sober. Allowance has of course to be made for the fact that neither convictions nor even prosecutions for drunkenness truly represent the incidence of that condition. It is safe to say that only quite a small proportion of persons obviously drunk in public are prosecuted. However, we do not intend to deal with drunkenness in this chapter, because even after multiplying the figures of known cases several times to allow for the unrecorded cases, it is still happily a rare condition.

The problem of drink arises, in fact, from the behavior of the regular but moderate drinker, whether he takes his whisky and soda in his drawing room or his pint of mild at the "local."

*   *   *

Drinking Habits

Detailed information about drinking habits was obtained by Research Services Ltd., in the course of the Hulton Readership Survey, from which we have permission to quote. The survey was confined to persons over the age of 16, and was conducted on a statistical basis which expert statisticians

* From *English Life and Leisure* (New York, Longmans, Green, 1951), pp. 159–98.

PLATE VII

Wine and Arms. From the Bayeux Cathedral Tapestry, 11th century, representing part of the preparations of William the Conqueror for the Battle of Hastings. The legend reads: *Isti portant armas ad naves et hic trahunt carrum cum vino et armis.* ("These are carrying arms to the ships and here they are dragging a cart with wine and arms.") Reproduced by permission of Phaidon Press, Ltd., London.

PLATE VIII

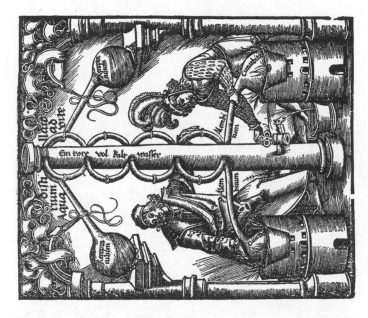

B. Medieval distillery. From woodcut on title page of *Das Buch zu Distillieren* . . . , by Hieron Brunschwig. Strassburg, 1532.

A. Wine market, early 16th century. From a Latin prayerbook of Bruges, now in the Bavarian State Library, Munich.

regard as affording information which is representative of the population as a whole. The proportion of these who drink alcoholic beverages are: beer only 19.3 per cent; spirits only 1.9 per cent; wine only 4.6 per cent; beer and spirits 6.2 per cent; beer and wine 3.1 per cent; spirits and wine 8.0 per cent; beer, spirits and wine 25.3 per cent; no alcoholic liquor 31.6 per cent.

TABLE 1.—Frequency of Drinking (by Per Cent of Respondents)

	Beer	Spirits	Wine
Every day	8.7	1.5	0.7
More than once a week but not daily	12.1	3.3	1.7
Once a week	11.5	4.8	2.8
Less than once a week	21.9	31.9	36.0
Never	45.8	58.5	58.8

These statistics show the drinking pattern of the community as a whole fairly clearly. Nearly one-third (31.6 per cent) of persons over 16 never take alcoholic drink at all, and if the numbers of "occasional" drinkers (i.e., those who drink less often than once a week) is added to those who do not drink at all, we can see what proportion of the community are "regulars," [1] namely:

32.3 per cent are regular beer drinkers.
9.6 per cent are regular spirit drinkers.
5.2 per cent are regular wine drinkers.

The real core of the drinking community are, however, those who drink every day, namely:

8.7 per cent who drink beer every day.
1.5 per cent who drink spirits every day.
0.7 per cent who drink wine every day.[2]

If the drinking habits of the two sexes are considered separately, the fact emerges that, as might be expected, the percentage of women who never drink alcoholic liquors (40.1 per cent) is almost twice as high as the corresponding figure for men (21.5 per cent). Again, as might be expected, the largest percentages of men who never take alcohol is found in the youngest age group (16-24) [3] but, rather unexpectedly, more women in

1. "Regular" here means once a week or more often.
2. There will be some overlapping here, particularly in beer and spirit drinking, as the habit of drinking neat spirits washed down with beer is fairly common in some parts of the country, and, at any rate in the north, this habit is given the descriptive name of "chasers."
3. It is illegal to serve a person under 18 with alcoholic liquor on licensed premises, or to buy alcoholic liquor for such a person, but in practice it is often impossible to judge a young person's age (particularly a girl's) to a year or two, and most

the age group 45 and over (46.4 per cent) say that they do not drink alcoholic beverages than is the case in the age group 16–24 (44.0 per cent). The largest percentage of both men and women who drink are in the age group 25–34.

Where Do People Drink?

We turn now to consider the question, "Where do people drink?" The answer is threefold. First, in their own homes or in the homes of others. Second, in registered clubs. Third, in licensed premises, including hotels.

Liquor for drinking at home is purchased at an establishment holding an "off" license,[4] that is to say either at a licensed hotel or public house (for every "on" license automatically includes an "off" license), a grocer, or a chemist. Registered clubs, with which we deal below, are also authorized to make "off" sales to members. Although the fact is not widely realized, it is not unusual for chemists to hold an "off" license, although in many cases their sales are restricted to medicated wines. . . . The sales of intoxicants by grocers under an "off" license undoubtedly leads to home drinking by many persons who would not think it "respectable" to visit even the off-sale counter of a public house. It is virtually impossible to estimate how much liquor is sold for consumption at home—the very fact that an "on" license includes an "off" license prevents any calculation at all. One can only say that the total amount is obviously large, or there would not be so many shops, and departments of grocers' shops, maintained expressly for the purpose of "off" sales.

Registered Clubs. Registered clubs, the second of the three sets of places where people drink, present considerable difficulties in describing the drink problem, because the law that regulates them is itself unsatisfactory. As stated above, in 1948 (the latest year for which figures are available) there were 18,370 registered clubs in England and Wales, and they varied from eminently respectable social and political clubs, including the most famous clubs in the country, to places existing solely as drinking establishments, sometimes in sordid surroundings. It is impossible to say how many persons were active members of the 18,370 registered clubs, but it is probably safe to say that they totalled more than a million.

For the establishment of a registered club, it is only necessary for the Clerk of the Justices of the Petty Sessions to be notified of the club's existence, and registration is then automatic on payment of a fee of 5s.

young people of 17, and perhaps even 16, can get beer and other drinks easily enough if they wish.

4. Licenses for the sale of liquor are of two kinds—those for the sale of alcoholic beverages to be consumed on or off the premises. They are commonly referred to as "on" and "off" licenses. "On" licenses are further divided into "full" licenses (i.e., for sale of all alcoholic beverages) and "beer" licenses, and still further into "six-day" and "seven-day" licenses. A "six-day" house cannot open on Sunday.

and the supply of information as to the title, address, rules and membership of the club. Membership must not be less than 25. A Court of Summary Jurisdiction can strike a club off the register for various forms of misconduct, but the same proprietor can register another club in premises adjoining those of the first club, with another name but the same membership, immediately after having been struck off.

It would be wrong to give the impression that the majority of clubs are anything except desirable institutions, performing a thoroughly useful function, but some are little more than drinking houses that contrive to be exempt from the regulations applied by statute to licensed premises.

* * *

Licensed Premises

We come now to the question of premises licensed for the sale of liquor for consumption on the premises. They are of four kinds—hotels, public houses, restaurants and bars, the last being a comparatively new type of drinking place. We do not intend to deal with the sale of alcoholic liquor in restaurants for consumption with meals, nor in hotels for sale to residents. Our interest is in places where people "go in for a drink," and in the people themselves who visit them. Before discussing these, however, we want to make a rough estimate of the number of people who enter public houses in the course of a week. As the basis for our calculation we take the estimate arrived at for the city of York in 1935. It was estimated then (on the basis of an actual count of the number of persons entering a proportion of the public houses during a given week) that in that city of 100,000 persons there were about 180,000 visits to public houses every week. If the drinking habits of the citizens of York are approximately those of the nation as a whole, and there seems to be no reason why they should not be, this would represent nearly 80,000,000 visits a week, with the population of England and Wales at its 1949 level, if its drinking habits were still those of 1935. We know, however, that since 1935 the consumption of beer has increased by more than one-quarter, and we therefore conclude that many more than 80,000,000 visits are now paid to public houses in England and Wales every week. We have no means of knowing how many individual persons pay these visits, but it must be a high proportion, quite possibly a majority, of the 33,500,000 persons who are over the age of 16.

Bars and Public Houses as Centres of Social Life. We turn now to a consideration of bars and public houses, and the part they play in the lives of those who frequent them. As they undoubtedly have an important influence on the characters and opinions of a considerable proportion of the population, we thought it necessary to obtain first-hand information on an adequate scale. To obtain this information one of us (G.R.L.) visited a substantial number of bars and public houses in different parts of the country, in both urban and rural areas. Our views are based on what he observed and on conversations that he had with customers, licensees and employees in the various premises visited.

*   *   *

Bars. We deal first with American bars, often known simply as "bars" or "lounge bars." These exist for the most part only in towns of some importance, where at least a section of the local inhabitants are leisured and well-to-do. Bars of this kind are often run in conjunction with hotels or restaurants. In American bars catering for the "best class" of trade, it is usual for only wines and spirits (including cocktails) to be sold. Beer is not served, but soft drinks are available although very seldom asked for, except to mix with alcoholic drinks as, for instance, gin and ginger beer. In bars in industrial areas, however, bottled beer is quite frequently served, and everywhere in bars that seek to attract a less exclusive clientele bottled and sometimes draught beers are served.

A good deal of attention is usually paid to the decoration of bars, both as regards the fittings and furniture, which tend in the most exclusive bars to be expensive, and in the cheaper to be flashy.

It is generally held that bars are more respectable, and socially more select, than public houses. They are therefore frequented, for the most part, by people who would not normally go into a public house, except perhaps their own rural or suburban "local," and, in the case of the cheaper bars, by young people anxious "to see life and have a good time." The better bars are patronized almost exclusively by the upper middle-class and, in the provinces, by some of the local businessmen. Each bar normally has its core of regular customers, and it is by no means unusual for a few of the "regulars" to visit their favorite bar twice a day on five days a week. Other customers, who might be considered "regulars," pay two or three visits a fortnight, year after year.

Both men and women are to be found in nearly all bars, although usually there is a preponderance of men. Nevertheless, in the more sophisticated parts of the country it is quite common to find women in pairs or threes "dropping in for a drink" in exactly the same way as men do. It is unusual for a woman—except for a small minority who are definitely hoping to be "picked up"—to enter a bar alone, unless she has arranged to meet somebody there.

The function of a bar is to provide for those who like to "drop in" somewhere for a drink. It exists solely to sell alcohol and there is no question of any social contacts between its customers unless they already know each other. It is as completely impersonal as a chemist's shop. That is not to say that one cannot strike up an acquaintance with a stranger in a bar; it is often possible to do so, but with no greater ease than would be experienced in making the same person's acquaintance in, say, a queue or railway carriage.

Since most of the conversation in bars is between persons who are already acquainted, it follows that it ranges over a wide variety of subjects, and that much of it is purely personal.

* * *

Perhaps the only surprising fact about the subjects of conversation in bars is the number of times business matters are discussed. The head barman of one of the best-known bars in London told G.R.L. that a great deal of business is done in the best bars, especially by the regular customers.

It is only rarely that any customer in a bar shows by his behavior that he has drunk too much. The barman in one bar in London said, "The only trouble we have is when young fellows in the twenties spend the afternoons drinking in the clubs and then come in here at 5:30 when we open for the evening." [5]

Some bars, including a few that cater for a "good-class trade," are occasionally used by prostitutes as places to seek customers, but this is not often the case.

The prices charged in bars are high, for example a large whisky and soda seldom costs less than 5s., and often costs 7s. or even 8s., and in addition to these high prices the barmen expect tips, though tipping is noticeably less frequent and less generous in industrial areas than in London. As a result the personal expenditure of individuals in bars is often extravagant.

* * *

Public Houses. The diversity of public houses is so great that to give a comprehensive picture of them and of their customers would need a book to itself. We hope, however, to give a general impression within reasonable compass. The nature of any public house is largely determined by the locality in which it is situated, for that determines the type of customers, and the customers in turn determine the atmosphere of the house. Thus, in the centre of a large city, where there are practically no residents but only a heterogeneous crowd of passers-by, some of whom want a drink, public houses tend to be impersonal, "cold," and often rather sordid. At the other extreme, in rural areas, and in some small towns and suburbs, public houses are not infrequently social institutions of considerable importance to the communal life of the neighborhood. In between the two extremes there is an immense number of variations—"tough" pubs in the docks; palatial houses complete with dining-rooms, usually in middle-class residential

5. The clubs referred to are registered clubs run for profit. They should observe the same hours for sale of drink as licensed premises, but in some of them drink is sold illegally out of the permitted hours.

areas; public houses outside stations, catering mainly for travelers; public houses catering for factory workers or for white collar workers, or for both in separate rooms of the same establishment; and so on. Broadly speaking there is somewhere a public house for almost every male taste.

Taking public houses as a whole, their customers thus tend to be a cross-section of the male population. In the case of women, however, the situation is rather different. A large proportion, probably a majority, of women of all classes of society never enter public houses. Indeed, in some parts of Britain, particularly in the north, there is strong feeling against women entering them at all, unless there is a special room set apart for them.

A fair proportion of young people of both sexes visit public houses, usually in pairs or groups. Oddly enough, the young women tend to take more alcohol than the young men, for the latter often drink a bottle of light ale, while the girls frequently drink gin or rum, with either orange or lime juice. A publican is required by law to refuse to serve any person under 18, but it is extremely difficult to judge the exact age of a young stranger, and in the course of our investigations many young people, almost certainly under 18, were seen to be served in public houses of different types. Indeed, in one rural house the publican was seen to serve three young men with whom he was acquainted, although he knew they were barely 17.

Most public houses have a proportion of regular customers, varying from a small number in houses that cater mainly for passers-by to a high proportion in those houses that cater specifically for the requirements of one special locality, such as a village or a housing estate. Although the etiquette of town and country public houses varies a good deal, regular customers have much the same characteristics in both. They tend always to occupy the same seat or corner, and are annoyed if some other customer occupies it. They expect extra consideration, and minor privileges. For example, one public house, visited during the beer shortage in 1947, had a printed notice in the saloon bar, "Half-pints of beer only. If the chap next to you has a pint—don't grumble. He's a regular."

Conversation in public houses is as diverse as the personal backgrounds of the customers. The majority of customers in public houses belong to the working or lower-middle classes and the most popular subject of conversation is undoubtedly horse racing. Greyhound racing is not discussed much, except in public houses in the vicinity of dog tracks, and in some of the poorer working-class districts. Football pools are discussed surprisingly little, except on Saturday evenings and Sundays. Politics are scarcely ever mentioned, and are discouraged by most publicans since an exchange of political opinions is thought to lead to some customers becoming offended. Items from the newspapers are often talked about, particularly those of a sensational nature, and there is exchange of rather doubtful stories among a certain type of customers, although the majority hold themselves aloof from this. Sport of every kind is discussed, quite apart from any question of betting, and items of personal scandal about mutual acquaintances seem to be much appreciated both by men and women. In public houses with a particular neighborhood connection, such as a village "local," there is always plenty of talk about purely local matters, such, for instance, as whether it is too early to plant the potatoes, or whether So-and-so is not getting so feeble that he will soon have to go to the workhouse, or whether one man or another is the better wicket-keeper for the village cricket team. The subjects of conversation in public houses do nevertheless have one thing in common. They are almost invariably trivial, although for the most part harmlessly so.

As was stated before, the atmosphere of a public house is principally determined by its location and the type of persons from among whom, in consequence, it draws its customers, but whether a public house is a happy or a friendly place, or the reverse, depends also largely on the publican and his assistants. It is strange that there should be so many morose publicans—only a minority, of course, but an appreciable minority. This state of affairs may merely be a result of the "seller's market" that existed for some nine years in the retailing of liquor, and which came to an end in 1949. The happiest public house is often where the publican's family assist him, in place of a paid bar staff.

*   *   *

Besides being places of relaxation and sociability, a proportion of public houses provide facilities for groups of people to meet for specific purposes. As Lord Beveridge pointed out in *Voluntary Action and the State,* some of the great Friendly Societies originated in groups of persons meeting in public houses. It is still quite usual for public houses to run slate clubs which share out at Christmas, and in some there are small provident clubs, although this is unusual since the introduction of comprehensive legislation for social security. In rural areas the village pub often shares with the village hall the position of social centre for the community, and it is the meeting place of such bodies as the committee of the village cricket team.

There is thus a good deal that is useful and even admirable in the best type of public house, but the fact remains that they exist for the sole purpose of retailing alcoholic liquor, and scarcely anybody enters them who does not wish to take alcohol in small or large quantities.

*   *   *

Places of Licensed Premises in National Life

Our next task is to try to assess what place each of the various kinds of licensed premises that we have described above fills in our national life. The two extreme views are first that of the most fervid temperance reformers, to whom all licensed premises are anathema, and second that of persons (often themselves financially interested parties) who advance the view that public houses are "poor men's clubs," and are indeed almost community centres. We believe that neither of these views is true of licensed houses as a whole.

We conclude that on the whole bars are undesirable places, particularly those where only the strongest forms of alcoholic liquors are sold. Although the practice of drinking an aperitif before a meal (even a strong cocktail) is probably held by most people to be comparatively harmless, bars certainly encourage the "aperitif" to take the form of several highly concentrated drinks. Bars also offer a strong inducement to people to form the habit of "dropping in" for the sole purpose of taking alcohol in considerable quantity.

As far as public houses are concerned, we feel that we cannot state our conclusions about their desirability or otherwise better than by quoting from an earlier work written by one of us.[6]

Public houses provide facilities for people to meet for recreation and social intercourse under conditions chosen and created by themselves. They are enjoyed and taken advantage of by many thousands of people, young and old, of both sexes, every week and would be greatly missed if they were closed.

The "atmosphere" or "tone" of public houses, where people mix together so freely, tends to be that of the majority, and any young fellow or girl who makes a habit of frequenting them comes under its influence. If, previously, their ideals were higher than those generally held in the public house, its influence upon them will probably be bad. On the other hand, if a misanthrope frequented a public house, he might be persuaded by what he saw and heard around him that the world was a kindlier place than he imagined. On the whole, however, I cannot but think that thoughtful parents, even if they are not teetotalers, and place no teetotal embargo on their elder children, would not like to see them making a habit of spending their evenings in the public house. How often, too, one has heard the expression, when men's names were being considered for responsible posts, "I am not very keen on that fellow —he spends too much time in the public house!"

In giving this view we do not, however, overlook the fact that some public houses are genuine centres of communal life in the areas that they serve. But they are only a minority of the whole, and are found mainly in rural areas.

*   *   *

Education about Alcohol

A striking fact about the drink problem in England today is the ignorance of the ordinary citizen, not only about the problem in its national

6. B. S. Rowntree, *Poverty and Progress* (New York, Longmans, Green, 1942), p. 366.

aspect, but also in its purely personal application. The trade, through its propaganda, and the cinema, by so often representing drinking as part of the kind of life many of the audiences would like to live, have a virtual monopoly in educating the public about drink. There is little objective teaching, and instruction about the nature and effects of alcohol is only given in a small proportion of schools. An enquiry made by the British Temperance League in 1945–46 suggested that frequent instruction was given in less than one-sixth of all day schools, while in more than two-thirds instruction about this matter was not given at all. Without vouching for the accuracy of the figures, which we have not personally checked, we imagine that they give a pretty fair indication of the situation. That this should be so seems to us to be clearly a failure of the education system. We believe that factual education about the whole alcohol problem should be given in every school. Temperance workers, particularly those connected with churches, should also be more active in making their special appeal in Sunday schools, youth clubs, and in centres of adult education.

Although later in this book we deal at length with the cinema, and briefly with broadcasting, we feel that we must say here that the British Board of Film Censors and the British Broadcasting Corporation could help a good deal more than they do in educating young people to understand the true nature of alcoholic liquor. Without suggesting that either films or radio should undertake positive measures of education, it would be a considerable gain if films were prohibited from giving their present prominence to drink and drinking places, and if joking references to the subject were forbidden on the radio.

12. CANADA

by Robert E. Popham *

As more is learned about the drinking habits of Canadians and the prevalence of problem drinking and alcoholism in this country it becomes increasingly apparent that the pattern here is peculiarly Canadian and not merely the reflection of what is done in the United States or elsewhere. It is also clear that the Canadian pattern has been developing and changing over the years from pioneer days, past the turn of the century, through two world wars, prohibition, boom years, and depression. A vast complex of factors has been at work forming and reforming the picture revealed in this report.

Chart I.—Drinking Tastes in Canada in Three Periods and Current Patterns in Three Countries. Based on imperial gallons of spirits, beer and wine converted to absolute alcohol for direct comparison.

HOW DRINKING TASTES HAVE CHANGED IN CANADA

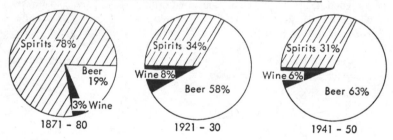

THE CANADIAN PATTERN IS DIFFERENT

* From "A Statistical Report Relating to Alcoholism and the Use of Alcoholic Beverages in Canada," *International Journal on Alcohol and Alcoholism, 1* (1955), 5–22.

Take the question of how much alcohol has been consumed by Canadians down through the years, and what varying proportions of it were in the form of spirits, beer, and wine. Table 1 gives as many facts as are available on this point; and the accompanying Chart I tells the story in brief.

Consumption of Alcoholic Beverages in Canada

The information contained in Table 1 indicates a gradual decrease in the consumption of spirits during the early period from 1871 to 1890. A decrease in the consumption of wine is evident in the same period. The consumption of beer, however, shows a small but steady increase over this period. From the end of the period of general prohibition in 1921 down

TABLE 1.—*Apparent Consumption of Alcoholic Beverages (in Imperial Gallons per Capita Aged 15 Years and Over), Convictions for Drunkenness (per 100,000 Aged 15 Years and Over), and Estimated Number of Alcoholics (per 100,000 Aged 20 Years and Over) in Canada, 1871–1952*

| | SPIRITS | | BEER | | WINE | | TOTAL | RATE OF | |
| | Abs. | | Abs. | | Abs. | | ABSOLUTE | CON- | RATE OF |
	Bev.	Alc.	Bev.	Alc.	Bev.	Alc.	ALCOHOL	VICTIONS	ALCOHOLISM
1871–75	2.18	0.94	3.84	0.19	0.31	0.04	1.17	—	—
1876–80	1.56	0.67	3.56	0.18	0.17	0.02	0.87	—	—
1881–85	1.66	0.71	4.36	0.22	0.19	0.03	0.96	396	—
1886–90	1.25	0.54	5.25	0.26	0.16	0.02	0.82	426	—
1891–1900	—	—	—	—	—	—	—	—	—
1901–05	—	—	—	—	—	—	—	440	—
1906–10	—	—	—	—	—	—	—	742	—
1911–15	—	—	—	—	—	—	—	1020	—
1916–20	—	—	—	—	—	—	—	534	—
1921–25 *	0.43	0.18	6.54	0.33	0.19	0.03	0.54	460	732
1926–30	0.59	0.25	8.35	0.42	0.49	0.07	0.74	506	1337
1931–35	0.38	0.16	6.69	0.33	0.51	0.09	0.58	320	1353
1936–40	0.55	0.24	7.91	0.40	0.44	0.07	0.71	436	1508
1941–45	0.65	0.26	10.91	0.55	0.49	0.08	0.89	500	1566
1946–50	1.04	0.42	17.26	0.86	0.54	0.09	1.37	772	1810
1951	1.18	0.47	18.30	0.92	0.53	0.09	1.48	861	1581
1952	1.09	0.44	18.90	0.95	0.52	0.09	1.48	858	1629

* Four-year average for consumption figures only: 1922–25.

to and including 1952 there is a definite trend toward increased consumption of all forms of alcoholic beverages, particularly beer. Although an increase in the consumption of spirits is indicated since 1921, the actual consumption for any given period is much less than for the period prior to prohibition for which data are available. The period 1946–50 shows the greatest increase in the consumption of all beverages. The figures for 1951 and 1952, on the other hand, may indicate a leveling off. This tendency is confirmed to some extent by the consistency of similar results in the tables containing the records for individual provinces.

The number of convictions for drunkenness achieves a peak during the period 1911–15 which may reflect the rise of attitudes leading to general prohibition. This is followed by a sharp reduction, beginning in the period 1916–20, and leveling off until 1946–50, when a rather marked increase is evident. Rates of alcoholism show a rather consistent rise since 1921. The increase is probably due, at least in part, to an increase in the number of users of alcoholic beverages in the population. Indeed, in the evaluation of trends based upon these data, it is well to have in mind the following historical information regarding prohibition in Canada:

> During the years 1916 and 1917, as a war policy, legislation prohibiting the sale of alcoholic beverages . . . was passed in all provinces except Quebec where similar legislation was passed in 1919 . . . After the war the provinces continued under prohibition for varying periods . . . During 1921 Quebec and British Columbia discarded the existing prohibition laws . . . The same course was followed by Manitoba in 1923, Alberta in 1924, Saskatchewan in 1925, Ontario and New Brunswick in 1927 and Nova Scotia in 1930.[1]

National Beverage Preferences

Table 2 illustrates some significant differences in the drinking habits of thirteen countries, including Canada. Finland, Sweden, and Norway rank first, second, and third in the contribution of spirits to the total consump-

TABLE 2.—*Percentage Contribution of Spirits, Beer, and Wine to Total Consumption (per Capita Aged 15 Years and Over, in Imperial Gallons of Absolute Alcohol), and Numbers of Alcoholics (per 100,000 Aged 20 Years and Over) in Canada and Certain Other Countries* *

	Spirits % Cont.	Beer % Cont.	Wine % Cont.	TOTAL CONSUMPTION Rate	TOTAL CONSUMPTION Rank	ALCOHOLISM Rate	ALCOHOLISM Rank
France	24	8	68	2.95	1	5200	1
United States	37	52	11	1.66	3	3952	2
Sweden	68	28	4	1.06	7	2580	3
Switzerland	21	28	51	1.60	4	2385	4
Denmark	16	73	11	1.29	6	1950	5
Canada	30	64	6	1.48	5	1804	6
Norway	56	37	7	0.62	8	1560	7
Finland	77	17	6	0.55	9	1430	8
Italy	10	2	88	2.05	2	500	9
Belgium	10	89	1	1.65	—	—	—
Netherlands	49	48	3	0.94	—	—	—
United Kingdom	11	85	4	1.28	—	—	—
Ireland	27	70	3	0.98	—	—	—

* Most of the consumption figures apply to years between 1949 and 1952 (Canada 1952). Rates of alcoholism apply chiefly to years between 1946 and 1948; the 1948 rate for Canada was employed to make the data as comparable as possible.

1. Ottawa, Dominion Bureau of Statistics, *The Control and Sale of Liquor in Canada* (1936), p. 4.

tion; Belgium, the United Kingdom, and Denmark lead in that order in the proportion of beer consumed; Italy, France, and Switzerland lead in proportionate contribution of wine. No apparent relationship between type of beverage most frequently consumed and rate of alcoholism is indicated. On the other hand, there would appear to be a slight positive cor-

Chart II.—Consumption of Alcohol Compared to Rate of Alcoholism in Six Countries.

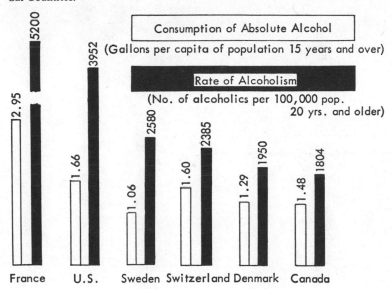

relation between total consumption and rate of alcoholism (Chart II); countries with the highest rates of alcoholism tend also to have the highest rates of consumption.

U.S.–Canadian Drinking Habits

The contents of Table 3 provide some comparative data for the United States and Canada concerning social differences in proportion of users and abstainers. Comparison of the total population reveals that relatively more Canadians than Americans admit to the use of alcoholic beverages. Perhaps the most striking difference, however, is the fact that 64 per cent of the Canadian female population are users of alcoholic beverages, as compared with 46 per cent of the American female population. This difference in the number of female users in the two countries accounts, in large measure, for the difference in the total population of users. In both countries a decrease in the proportion of users with age and an increase in proportion of users with education, socio-economic status, and size of community are indicated.

TABLE 3.—*Social Differences in Proportion of Users and Abstainers in Canada and the United States (Expressed as Percentages of the Population 21 Years of Age and Over)*

	CANADA		UNITED STATES	
	Users	Abstainers	Users	Abstainers
By Sex:				
Men	76	24	70	30
Women	64	36	46	54
By Age:				
21–29	75	25	64	36
30–49	72	28	65	35
50 and over	59	41	48	52
By Religion:				
Jewish	—	—	87	13
Catholic	71	29	79	21
Protestant	70	30	59	41
By Education:				
Less than high school	65	35	62	38
High school or more	73	27	70	30
By Socio-economic Group:				
Poor	66	34	62	38
Average	72	28	66	34
Prosperous	76	24	70	30
By Size of Community:				
Farm	62	38	46	54
Under 10,000	67	33	—	—
10,000–100,000	72	28	—	—
Over 100,000	76	24	—	—

It is also of interest that, in the United States, 79 per cent of the Catholic population are users as compared with 59 per cent of the Protestant population. In Canada there is little difference between these two groups in this respect.

SUPPLEMENTARY READINGS FOR PART II

1. *Standard Encyclopedia of the Alcohol Problem,* Ernest H. Cherrington, editor-in-chief, 6 vols., Westerville, Ohio. This general reference work offers extensive historical background material on drinking customs in various periods and on the development of the temperance movement in the United States and other countries to 1930.
2. J. D. Rolleston, "The Folklore of Alcoholism," *British Journal of Inebriety, 39* (1941), 30–36.
3. J. D. Rolleston, "Some Aspects of the Alcohol Problem," *British Journal of Inebriety, 39* (1942), 45–59.
4. J. D. Rolleston, "Alcoholism in Classical Antiquity," *British Journal of Inebriety, 24* (1927), 101–20.
5. T. D. Crothers, "Inebriety in Ancient Egypt and Chaldea," *Quarterly Journal of Inebriety, 25* (1903), 142–50.
6. E. E. Cornwall, "Notes on Use of Alcohol in Ancient Times," *Medical Times* (New York), *67* (1939), 379–80.
7. D. Dorchester, *The Liquor Problem in All Ages.* New York, Phillips and Hunt, 1884. A classic 19th-century treatment of the effects of alcohol and the necessity for total abstinence.
8. S. Morewood, *History of Inebriating Liquors.* Dublin, 1838.
9. Arthur P. McKinlay, University of California, has published a series of detailed studies of the ancient use of wine. Students particularly interested in the Early and Classical Periods of Greece and Rome should consult, in addition to the material included in the present volume: "The Indulgent Dionysius," *Transactions of the American Philosophical Association, 70* (1939), 51–61; "How the Athenians Handled the Drink Problem among Their Slaves," *Classical Weekly, 37* (1944), 127–8; "The Wine Element in Horace," *Classical Journal, 42* (1946–47), 161–8, 229–36; "Christian Appraisal of Pagan Temperance," *Anglican Theological Review, 30* (1948), 44–54; "Temperate Romans," *Classical Weekly, 41* (1948), 52, 146–9; "Roman Sobriety in the Early Empire," *Classical Bulletin, 26* (1950), 31–6; "Roman Sobriety in the Comedies," *Classical Outlook, 27,* No. 5 (1950), 56–7.
10. *Soviet Medical Encyclopedia,* 2d ed. (1956), Vol. 1, pp. 726–62.

PART III

DRINKING PRACTICES, U.S.A.

INTRODUCTION

Statistics on drinking practices in the United States reveal a mixed public reaction to the question of drinking or personal abstinence. Approximately 60 per cent of the adult population are users and the remaining 40 per cent abstain from alcohol in any form. The consumers vary from minimal and moderate users to excessive drinkers and alcoholics.

Estimates of the proportion of drinkers suggest a leveling-off since World War II. Field interviewers of the American Institute of Public Opinion have asked a cross-section of adults 21 years of age and over: "Do you ever have occasion to use alcoholic beverages—such as liquor, wine, or beer—or are you a total abstainer?" The replies show that the following percentages of those asked indicated that they were users of alcoholic beverages: in 1945, 67 per cent; 1946, 67 per cent; 1949, 58 per cent; 1950, 60 per cent; 1951, 59 per cent; 1952, 60 per cent; 1956, 60 per cent; 1957, 58 per cent; and 1958, 55 per cent.

More women than men are abstainers; 50 per cent of the women and 33 per cent of the men report that they do not use alcohol in any form.[1] The largest number of nondrinkers is found in the South, and the smallest number in the New England and Middle Atlantic region.

A survey by Riley and Marden indicated that 65 per cent of adults were drinkers in 1946, and Maxwell reported 63.3 per cent in the State of Washington in 1951. (Both studies are reprinted in this section.) Rates vary according to sex, being substantially higher for men, who also drink more frequently. The highest rate of use noted in all studies appears in the age range 20–29. There are significant differences in rates between urban and rural populations and according to church affiliation.

Statistics on the consumption of different beverages have been available since 1850. Table 1 shows the per capita consumption computed on the basis of the "drinking age population" (15 years of age and over) in the period 1850–1957. A marked decline in the average consumption of distilled spirits took place, from 4.2 gallons in 1850 to 1.7 in 1957. Wine consumption increased from 0.5 gallons in 1850 to 1.2 in 1957. The most dramatic change occurred in the consumption of beer, which rose from 2.7 gallons per capita of drinking age in 1850 to 20.6 gallons in 1957.

1. News release of March 4, 1958, American Institute of Public Opinion, Princeton, New Jersey.

The numbers of total gallons are not particularly revealing. By reducing total gallonage to absolute alcohol, as in Table 1, more realistic values are reached. In 1850 the total absolute alcohol consumed (per capita of drinking age population) was 2.1 gallons. This increased to

TABLE 1.—*Apparent Consumption of Alcoholic Beverages, per Capita of Drinking Age Population (Persons Aged over 14 Years), U.S.A. 1850–1957, in U.S. Gallons* *

| | SPIRITS | | WINE | | BEER | | TOTAL |
	Beverage	Absolute Alcohol	Beverage	Absolute Alcohol	Beverage	Absolute Alcohol	Absolute Alcohol
1850	4.17	1.89	0.46	0.08	2.70	0.14	2.11
1860	4.79	2.16	0.57	0.10	5.39	0.27	2.53
1870	3.40	1.53	0.53	0.10	8.73	0.44	2.07
1871–80	2.27	1.02	0.77	0.14	11.26	0.56	1.72
1881–90	2.12	0.95	0.76	0.14	17.94	0.90	1.99
1891–95	2.12	0.95	0.60	0.11	23.42	1.17	2.23
1896–1900	1.72	0.77	0.55	0.10	23.72	1.19	2.06
1901–05	2.11	0.95	0.71	0.13	26.20	1.31	2.39
1906–10	2.14	0.96	0.92	0.17	29.27	1.47	2.60
1911–15	2.09	0.94	0.79	0.14	29.53	1.48	2.56
1916–19	1.68	0.76	0.69	0.12	21.63	1.08	1.96
—	—	—	—	—	—	—	—
1934	0.64	0.29	0.36	0.07	13.58	0.61	0.97
1935	0.96	0.43	0.50	0.09	15.13	0.68	1.20
1936	1.30	0.59	0.64	0.12	17.53	0.79	1.50
1937	1.43	0.64	0.71	0.13	18.21	0.82	1.59
1938	1.32	0.59	0.70	0.13	16.58	0.75	1.47
1939	1.38	0.62	0.79	0.14	16.77	0.75	1.51
1940	1.48	0.67	0.91	0.16	16.29	0.73	1.56
1941	1.58	0.71	1.02	0.18	17.97	0.81	1.70
1942	1.89	0.85	1.11	0.20	20.00	0.90	1.95
1943	1.46	0.66	0.94	0.17	22.26	1.00	1.83
1944	1.69	0.76	0.92	0.17	25.22	1.13	2.06
1945	1.95	0.88	1.13	0.20	25.97	1.17	2.25
1946	2.20	0.99	1.34	0.24	23.75	1.07	2.30
1947	1.69	0.76	0.90	0.16	24.56	1.11	2.03
1948	1.56	0.70	1.11	0.20	23.77	1.07	1.97
1949	1.55	0.70	1.21	0.22	23.48	1.06	1.98
1950	1.72	0.77	1.27	0.23	23.21	1.04	2.04
1951	1.73	0.78	1.13	0.20	22.92	1.03	2.01
1952	1.61	0.72	1.21	0.21	22.97	1.03	1.96
1953	1.68	0.76	1.18	0.20	22.81	1.03	1.99
1954	1.61	0.72	1.18	0.20	21.73	0.98	1.90
1955	1.66	0.75	1.18	0.20	21.74	0.98	1.94
1956	1.76	0.79	1.23	0.21	21.53	0.97	1.97
1957	1.70	0.77	1.21	0.21	20.62	0.93	1.91

* From Mark Keller and Vera Efron, *Selected Statistics on Alcoholic Beverages (1850–1957) and on Alcoholism (1910–1956)*, New Haven, Journal of Studies on Alcohol, 1958.

2.6 gallons during the 10-year interval of 1906–15, which includes the years before World War I, when legal prohibition was in effect in many states and counties. At no time since 1915 have we reached the consumption of that period. Wartime conditions during the period 1941–45, followed by release of supplies in 1946, brought the level to 2.3. Since 1947, a plateau has developed with consumption stabilized at approximately 2 gallons of absolute alcohol annually per capita of drinking age.

Gross consumption figures reveal little regarding the adults who drink, the amount and frequency of their drinking, the factors which facilitate drinking practices, and the attitudes of users toward the social custom of drinking. Until recently, relatively few such data were available. Any study of complex behavior patterns in a large sample of the population constitutes a major undertaking which requires adequate financing. Financial support for such projects has until recently been almost entirely lacking. However, studies completed at Rutgers and Yale Universities and Washington State College are available and are reprinted in this section.

Surveys of drinking by young people of high-school age in separate counties in three different states are reported. There is an extract from a study of drinking in college in which 17,000 students in 27 public, private and sectarian institutions participated. Statistics concerning the number of users and abstainers among students in different types of institutions, frequency of drinking, and the socioeconomic background of drinkers are illuminating. Of particular significance are the expressed motivations for social drinking, the reported effect of advice regarding drinking received from various sources, and the absence of any basic information and considered judgments concerning drinking as a factor in our society.

13. WHO, WHAT, AND HOW OFTEN?

by John W. Riley, Jr.
and Charles F. Marden *

What is the pattern of alcohol drinking in the United States? Considerable effort has been made to estimate the over-all prevalence of drinking in our society, but there has been little systematic analysis of the relative prevalence of drinking among the various social components of the total population. In the course of a national survey of public attitudes toward alcohol and alcoholism, data were acquired which throw light on this question. The survey itself was based on a scientifically prepared sample of the total adult population of the United States. These data yield a new over-all estimate of the incidence of drinking in 1946, and delineate for the first time, we believe, the social pattern of drinking in the United States. In short, they offer substantial answers to the questions: (*a*) How many people drink? (*b*) What are their social characteristics? (*c*) Where do they live? and (*d*) What do they drink?

Since answers to such questions as these are of importance to students of the problems of alcohol and alcoholism, this segment of the findings is published in advance of the results of the larger study. While the main contribution of this report consists of factual data delineating the current pattern of drinking, in some instances the findings have been compared with earlier studies in order to ascertain clues to the trend of change. Finally, certain portions of the data have specific bearing on particular problems of interest, and the implications of these for related hypotheses are pointed out.

How Many People Drink. Almost two out of every three adults in postwar America report that they drink some kind of alcoholic beverage. Although a recent estimate on the extent of drinking in the United States places the figure at 50 per cent of the population 15 years of age and over, in this survey, based on a representative sample 21 years of age and over, 65 per cent of the respondents said they sometimes drank alcoholic beverages and only 35 per cent said they did not.

Allowing for the fact that this survey eliminated the age group 15–20, which would tend to overstate the percentage of the drinking population, the results nevertheless point to some basic changes in the pattern of American drinking.[1]

* From "The Social Pattern of Alcoholic Drinking," *Quarterly Journal of Studies on Alcohol, 8* (1947), 265–73.

1. Our data are borne out in a survey by the American Institute of Public Opinion

Frequency of Drinking. The investigation probed further into current drinking habits in order to obtain some measure of the frequency and type of drinking. The data indicate how often people drink but not the quantities drunk. Therefore no attempt can be made, on the basis of these findings, to distinguish between the moderate and excessive drinker. The distinction made throughout this report is between abstainers, occasional drinkers, and regular drinkers. "Regular" drinkers are defined as those who drink at least three times a week. All other drinkers are designated "occasional" drinkers. The data show that a sizable portion, 17 per cent of the total population or better than one out of every four drinkers, consume some alcoholic beverage at least three times a week, while 48 per cent are occasional drinkers and 35 per cent are abstainers.

What People Drink. According to this survey, the following percentages of the total population reported that they drank the kinds and combinations of alcoholic beverages listed: Wine only, 4%; beer only, 15%; wine and beer only, 6%; liquor only, 7%; wine and liquor, 3%; beer and liquor, 11%; wine and beer and liquor, 16%; and other (cordials, liqueurs, etc.), 3%; making a total of 65% of the population reporting themselves as drinkers of alcoholic beverages.

From this it is apparent that 37% of the population drink distilled spirits either exclusively or intermittently with wine or beer. Put in another way, more than half of all those who drink at all use distilled spirits. But these data explode the myth that any sizable proportion of the American population are exclusive drinkers of "hard liquor." Nearly two-fifths of the drinking population report using no distilled spirits.

Drinking is apparently part of the accepted behavior pattern within all segments of the population—whether male or female, rural or urban, rich or poor, educated or uneducated, Protestant, Catholic, or Jew—but the degrees of acceptance present some significant variations.

Sex. Among the more interesting of the differences in drinking habits is that between men and women. Of the male population 75 per cent are drinkers, as against 56 per cent of the women. While exactly the same proportions (48 per cent) of both sexes drink occasionally, over three times as many men (27 per cent) as women (8 per cent) are regular drinkers.

For the purpose of making a trend analysis of drinking habits according to sex, the only study available was one made by Ley in 1940 on a sample of 10,000 life insurance policyholders. As Figure 1 shows, the comparison is striking even when one makes allowances for the fact that Ley's sample was based exclusively on policyholders.

Although the data are not exactly comparable, since the age intervals

reported in September 1946, in which 67 per cent of the total population said that they drank. Furthermore, in studies of this type there is no reason to suppose that people would report that they drink alcoholic beverages if, in fact, they do not.

are not the same, certain observations can be made from free inspection of the two parts of Figure 1. The increase in drinking among women stands out. Not only is the incidence of drinking among both men and women,

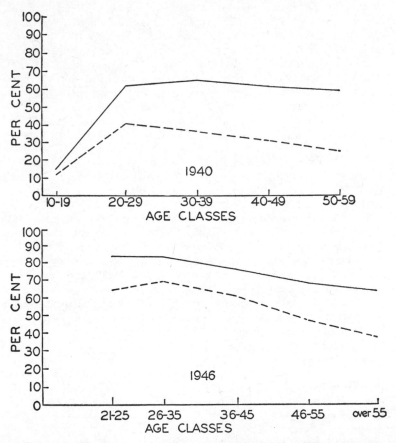

Figure 1.—Incidence of drinking among men (solid lines) and women (broken lines) in 1940 and 1946. Data for 1940 from H. A. Ley, Jr., "The Incidence of Smoking and Drinking among 10,000 Examinees," *Proceedings of Life Extension Examiners, 2* (1940), pp. 57–63.

particularly in the 20's and 30's, characterized by a sharp rise from 1940 to 1946, but the gap between men and women, particularly in the age brackets under 50, is smaller than it was six years ago. This narrowing of the gap between the sexes in respect to drinking would appear to be in line with the general trend in our society toward less and less differentiation in the social behavior of men and women.

Urban-Rural. Clear-cut urban-rural differences are also observable between drinkers and nondrinkers, the proportions decreasing systematically from as high as 77 per cent drinkers in large metropolitan centers to 46 per cent in farm communities. This pattern is clearly illustrated in Table 1, as are the steadily decreasing proportions of "regular" drinkers from city to farm. Only one slight deviation was noted, and that is in the proportion of regular drinkers in the rural nonfarm classification.

TABLE 1.—*Incidence and Frequency of Drinking, by Size of Place*

Population	Abstainers, %	Occasional Drinkers, %	Regular Drinkers, %
Over 1,000,000	23	52	25
Under 1,000,000	28	53	19
2,500 to 50,000	39	46	15
Rural nonfarm	43	41	16
Farm	54	39	7

An interesting hypothesis presents itself on the basis of the observations thus far noted in terms of a change in drinking mores. In the discussion of sex differences in drinking habits it was suggested that women are apparently moving away from a widely established pattern of abstinence and, in this respect, assuming the mores and relative freedoms formerly reserved for men. Similarly, in the case of urban-rural differences, although there are no statistical materials available for comparison, the number of drinkers, even in small communities, and the definiteness and consistency of the data, suggest a similar breaking down of primary-group mores. The clear-cut, systematic decrease in drinking from the largest to the smallest communities suggests that the characteristically more lenient urban attitude toward drinking is sifting down through the smaller cities, towns, and villages to the farms. If this does, indeed, turn out to be the case, further increases in the extent of drinking, particularly in the smaller places, may be expected in the future.

Economic and Educational. This hypothesis is also strengthened when respondents of different economic and educational levels are compared with respect to their drinking habits, although here, too, a definite interpretation is hampered by the paucity of material for comparative purposes. The data in Table 2, however, repeat the pattern of Table 1. The same directional increase in the over-all incidence and in the frequency of drinking that was noted from farm to city is clearly seen within the range of economic status as one moves from the "poor" to the "prosperous" level.

Educational breakdowns yield corresponding results: 70 per cent of respondents who had at least a high-school education and 62 per cent of those who had not graduated from high school said they sometimes drank alcoholic beverages; 18 per cent of the more educated respondents, however, and almost as many (17 per cent) of the less educated were classified as regular drinkers.

TABLE 2.—*Incidence and Frequency of Drinking, by Economic Level*

	Abstainers, %	Occasional Drinkers, %	Regular Drinkers, %
Prosperous	30	49	21
Average	34	49	17
Poor	38	46	16

Although many inferences might be drawn relative to these apparent socioeconomic shifts in the pattern of drinking, Dollard has suggested one of the more interesting in which he explains the history of our Prohibition legislation in terms of the failure to recognize the tendency of "behavior patterns to sift downward in our society . . . for the highest people socially did not [at the time] taboo drinking and their social customs are stronger than legislative controls." [2]

Race, Nationality, Religion. While racial differences were discovered to be relatively insignificant, a comparison based on place of birth of respondents' parents and grandparents points up ethnic differences in drinking customs. Thus 75 per cent of respondents with foreign-born parents and grandparents, 73 per cent of those with mixed backgrounds, and only 55 per cent of those with native backgrounds were classified as drinkers. The difference is intensified when frequency of drinking is taken into account. One out of every four respondents with foreign parentage, but only 12 per cent of those having native backgrounds, were classified as regular drinkers.

Since organized religion has traditionally been more or less concerned with the problems of alcohol, it is also interesting to note that the proportions of drinkers and abstainers according to broad religious groupings appear to reflect the differences in outlook or emphasis on this question. Only 59 per cent of the Protestant respondents, but 79 per cent of the Catholics and as high as 87 per cent of the Jewish respondents said they drank alcoholic beverages (Table 3).

TABLE 3.—*Incidence and Frequency of Drinking, by Religious Affiliation*

	Abstainers, %	Occasional Drinkers, %	Regular Drinkers, %
Protestant	41	46	13
Catholic	21	52	27
Jewish	13	64	23

2. John Dollard, "Drinking Mores of Social Classes," in *Alcohol Science and Society* (New Haven, Quarterly Journal of Studies on Alcohol, 1945), Lecture 8.

The high percentage of drinkers among Jews is of especial interest in connection with the question of the relationship of the prevalence of drinking to the incidence of alcoholism, a subject deserving of intensive research. Numerous studies agree that Jews as a group have a lower rate of alcoholism than any other ethnic group. The majority of explanations which have been offered for this phenomenon have stressed either the realization of danger and the necessity of avoiding social scandal of all kinds, or the religious and ritualistic factors connected with the use of wine among Jews.

Whatever the reason for this particular drinking pattern coupled with conspicuous lack of excess, it tends to support the hypothesis that the incidence of alcoholism within any specific cultural group is not necessarily related to the proportion of the group which drinks. Stated in another way, it suggests that moderation can become a central and powerful force within the mores of drinking. As Myerson puts it: "The synthesis of temperance, of the wise use of alcoholic beverages, is a necessary part, I think, of the battle against alcoholism. Against unwise hedonism, against extravagant asceticism, we need to build up the code of temperate hedonism and successful self-control." [3]

These detailed findings suggest that the complex of folkways, mores and social rules governing the drinking habits of the American people is far from crystallized. It is, in fact, far from homogeneous, and subject to rapid changes. The force of basic social trends is apparently reducing the proportion of total abstainers. On the other hand, the marked variations among the various social segments of the population suggest that drinking in the United States has not yet become a national custom. While it does have a well-established status within particular ethnic groups in this country, and within larger populations elsewhere, it is, in those instances, traditionally and logically consistent with other cultural values.

What the ultimate cultural definition of alcoholic beverages in the United States will be, no one can tell. At the moment, drinking has an uncertain and changing status. While fewer people perhaps now regard it as a sin, it has not yet achieved the universal respectability of well-established patterns of social behavior. Such an ultimate crystallization will depend upon the extent to which our culture finds a basis for the logical integration of alcoholic drinking together with prevailing attitudes, actions, anxieties, and traditions. Certain of our data, not reported here, will serve to throw some light upon this general question.

Summary and Conclusions

The factual conclusions and interpretation of our findings may be briefly summarized as follows:

3. A. Myerson, "Alcohol: A Study of Social Ambivalence," *Quarterly Journal of Studies on Alcohol, 1* (1940), 13–20.

Sixty-five per cent of the adult population of the United States drink alcoholic beverages.

More than half of those who drink use distilled spirits, although not exclusively.

In terms of the frequency of drinking, 17 per cent are "regular" drinkers and 48 per cent are "occasional" drinkers.

Three-fourths of the male population drink as against 56 per cent of the female population, and three times as many men as women are "regular" drinkers.

The proportion of drinkers varies positively with increasing size of community, from 46 per cent in farm areas to 77 per cent in cities with more than 1,000,000 population.

The percentage of drinkers increases from low to higher economic levels.

By educational classification, those who have had high-school education or better show a higher percentage of drinkers than those with less than high-school education.

The percentage of drinkers decreases positively in terms of longer native background. A two-to-one difference in "regular" and "occasional" drinkers is found between those of foreign as distinct from native background.

A striking difference is noted according to broad religious groupings. The proportion of Protestant abstainers (41 per cent) is twice that of Catholics (21 per cent), and three times that of Jews (13 per cent).

In terms of changing trends, a comparison of these findings with earlier estimates indicates (a) an increase during the war period in the proportion of people who drink, and (b) a greater proportional increase in the number of drinkers among women than among men.

An analysis of the influence of social and cultural trends upon the incidence of drinking suggests the following interpretations:

The rise in the relative proportion of female drinkers apparently reflects the increasing trend toward the emancipation of women which has been operative in American society throughout this century. Since this trend has not reached its peak, it should operate to increase still further the total proportion of drinkers.

It is seen that the more urbanized the community the greater is the prevalence of drinking. The United States has become increasingly urbanized throughout this century. The influence of urbanization has been to attenuate the strength of primary social controls upon the behavior of individuals. Since the trend toward urbanization has not yet spent itself, the positive relationship between size of place and the incidence of drinking should operate to increase the proportion of drinkers in our society.

Closely related to the previous point is the fact that the farm-village and small-town culture of America has been predominantly Protestant. While drinking has occurred, it has not had the definite social acceptance or moral approval which is to be found in certain Catholic and Jewish cultures; for example, wine drinking in Italian culture. The changed religious composition of our population throughout the century has operated, together with urbanization, to increase the proportion of people who drink.

Since all these general social trends point to a further increase in the number of people who drink, approaches to the problems of alcohol through sumptuary legislation will apparently have increasingly harder sledding.

Finally, it is important to emphasize again that the particular data presented in this article do not deal directly with the problem of alcoholism as such. The frequency of drinking among Jews, however, a group with a low rate of alcoholism, adds support to the hypothesis that the incidence of alcoholism is not necessarily correlated with the prevalence of drinking within any cultural group.

14. IN ONE STATE

by Milton A. Maxwell *

Greatly needed by students of alcohol problems in the United States is a reliable picture of the drinking behavior to be found in the population as a whole and in its various segments. Such a picture, to be complete, would include the attitudes, motives, and knowledge upon which the drinking behavior rests.

One of the instruments for obtaining some of this information is the sampling technique employed by public opinion polls. Its usefulness was demonstrated by the survey of drinking behavior and related attitudes conducted by the National Opinion Research Center in 1946, and reported by Riley and Marden (see above, pp. 182–89). Illuminating data were thus provided for the answering of such questions as: How many people drink? What do they drink? In what categories of the population are they to be found?

In view of the limitations of the polling technique, however, the answers supplied by the above study (and by occasional questions put by the American Institute of Public Opinion) can scarcely be presumed to be final. Only as other and more intensive studies, using polling and other techniques, are added—only as many studies check, modify, and corroborate each other—can scientists become confident that their pooled efforts have yielded reliable findings on actual attitudes and behavior with regard to alcoholic beverages.

These considerations made it desirable to take advantage of the facilities of the Washington Public Opinion Laboratory (WPOL) of the State College of Washington for the more intensive study of one state. The present writer, with the help of the WPOL staff, designed a schedule for the poll which was conducted in May 1951.

The purpose of the present article is to report on most of the more obvious findings of this "alcohol poll." Further analysis will probably justify additional reports. Here the main over-all findings with regard to the actual drinking behavior of the adults of the state, as well as the reasons they cite for drinking or abstaining, and their knowledge about alcohol, alcoholics, and the rehabilitation of alcoholics, will be detailed. As a cross-sectional picture of the State of Washington, this study should take its place alongside national studies and more intensive studies of other states or selected segments of the population.

* From "Drinking Behavior in the State of Washington," *Quarterly Journal of Studies on Alcohol, 13* (1952), 219–39.

Drinking Behavior: Statewide Findings

How Many Drink? Our tabulations show that 63.3 per cent of the sample population (all 21 years of age or older) reported drinking alcoholic beverages—some only five or fewer times a year, some daily. The remainder, 36.7 per cent, stated that they do not drink at all. The percentage of drinkers is slightly less than that reported in the Riley and Marden study of 1946 (65 per cent) and in the Gallup studies of 1945 and 1946 (67 per cent). It is not certain that there are relatively fewer drinkers in the State of Washington than in the United States as a whole, but the likelihood exists. The state has the national percentage of urban dwellers, but it has no cities of 1,000,000 or more—in which population category Riley and Marden found the highest proportion of drinkers (77 per cent).

The difference between the number of men and women who drink is marked: 76.2 per cent of the men, and 51.4 per cent of the women. This compares to 75 per cent of the men and 56 per cent of the women in the Riley and Marden study.

*   *   *

How Often Do They Drink? To state that 63.3 per cent of the people drink gives no indication, however, of how frequently they drink. Table 1 presents a breakdown of drinking frequency. For one thing, it shows that relatively infrequent drinking predominates: 18.2 per cent drink only between one and five times a year; and another 11.9 per cent, only once a month. This means that 54.9 per cent of the respondents drink not at all or not more than five times a year; and that 66.8 per cent abstain or drink not more than once a month.

TABLE 1.—*Drinking Frequency, by Percentage of Drinkers*

	Total, %	Men, %	Women, %
Each day	3.6	7.5	0.0
4–6 times a week	2.5	4.0	1.2
3 times a week	4.9	7.9	2.0
1–2 times a week	8.0	10.1	6.1
2–3 times a month	14.2	15.9	12.7
Once a month	11.9	14.5	9.4
1–5 times a year	18.2	16.3	20.0
Total	*63.3*	*76.2*	*51.4*

Chi squared = 17.404; $P < .01$

The difference between men and women, in frequency of drinking, is also significant. Abstainers and those who drink not more than five times a year include 40.1 per cent of the men and 68.6 per cent of the women. Nondrinkers and those who drink not more than once a month comprise 54.6 per cent of the men and 78.0 per cent of the women. Stated in terms of the most frequent drinking, 19.4 per cent of the men drink three times a week or more, but only 3.2 per cent of the women drink that often. In the Riley and Marden study, 27 per cent of the men and 8 per cent of the women drank three times a week or more.

Because the frequency categories used in Table 1 constitute too fine a breakdown for significant comparisons in a sample of this size, all who drink three times a week or more will, throughout the remainder of this report, be called *regular* drinkers; all other drinkers will be called *occasional* drinkers; and the remainder of the sample will be called *abstainers*.

Two Generations Compared. A comparison of the respondents and their parents of the same sex, shown in Table 2, reveals a definitely higher proportion in the present generation who drink. Of the male respondents, 76.2 per cent drink, compared to only 49.1 per cent of their fathers; of the female respondents, 51.2 per cent drink, compared to only 18.7 per cent of their mothers. Information on the drinking of the parents is based on report by the children.

Most of the change is a shift from no drinking to occasional drinking, however. The increase in the percentage who drink regularly is greater in

TABLE 2.—*Drinking Frequency of Respondents and Their Parents of the Same Sex*

	% Regular Drinkers	% Occasional Drinkers	% Abstainers
Male respondents	19.4	56.8	23.8
Fathers of male respondents	13.9	35.2	50.9
Female respondents	3.2	48.2	48.6
Mothers of female respondents	2.8	15.9	81.3

Men and their fathers: Chi squared = 35.344; $P<.01$
Women and their mothers: Chi squared = 57.96; $P<.01$

TABLE 3.—*Beverages Most Frequently Used*

	% of Respondents
Beer as first choice	*54.2*
Beer only	19.7
Beer and liquor *	32.8
Beer and wine	1.7
Liquor as first choice	*42.8*
Liquor only	25.2
Liquor and beer	13.9
Liquor and wine	3.7
Wine as first choice	*3.0*
Wine only	1.7
Wine and beer	1.0
Wine and liquor	0.3

* "Liquor" was the term used in the schedule to distinguish distilled spirits from beer and wine.

the case of the men than of the women, but in neither case is the difference statistically significant. Comparing the two generations as a whole shows that 33.4 per cent of the parents drank whereas 63.3 per cent of the respondents drink. This is an almost exact reversal of the proportions of drinkers and abstainers.

What Do People Drink? Beer is the first choice of over half (54.2 per cent) of the drinking respondents, as shown in Table 3.

Liquor is the first choice of 42.8 per cent, and wine the first choice of only 3.0 per cent of the respondents. If the most often used and the next most often used beverages are lumped together, there are more (74.9 per cent) who drink liquor than beer (69.1 per cent), although only 25.2 per cent drink liquor only. Beer drinkers give liquor as second choice more often than liquor drinkers give beer as second choice.

Striking is the small percentage of persons who prefer wine (3.0 per cent) or place it among the two most used beverages (8.4 per cent). The latter percentage compares to 19 per cent in the Riley and Marden study, and this may represent a regional, nationality background, or other social difference.

TABLE 4.—*Quantity of Most-Used Beverage Usually Consumed at a Sitting, by Percentages of Respondents*

	Total, %	Beer, %	Liquor, %	Wine, %
Small amount *	81.9	81.8	80.3	100.0
Medium amount †	14.2	16.9	12.0	0.0
Large amount ‡	3.9	1.3	7.7	0.0

Chi squared = 116.39; $P<.01$

* *Small:* 1–2 bottles of beer; 1–2 drinks of liquor; 1–2 glasses of wine.
† *Medium:* 3–6 bottles of beer; 3–4 drinks of liquor; 3–6 glasses of wine.
‡ *Large:* 7+ bottles of beer; 5+ drinks of liquor; 7+ glasses of wine.

TABLE 5.—*Quantity Consumed at a Sitting, by Frequency of Drinking*

	Regular Drinkers, %	Occasional Drinkers, %
Small amount	68.0	84.9
Medium amount	24.0	12.1
Large amount	8.0	3.0

Chi squared = 8.104; $P<.02$

How Much Do They Drink? An analysis of the quantity of the "most-used beverage usually consumed at a sitting" is summarized in Table 4. All wine users drink only small amounts (as defined at the bottom of Table 4) at a sitting. The same may be said of four out of five users of beer and liquor. Most of those who consume large amounts prefer liquor to beer.

When the amounts usually consumed at a sitting are correlated with frequency of drinking (Table 5), it will be seen that while two-thirds of regular drinkers confine themselves to small amounts, 85 per cent of the occasional drinkers do. Medium and large amounts, on the other hand, are reported more than twice as frequently by regular than by occasional drinkers. In other words, there is a significant correlation between regular drinking and the consuming of larger amounts. Occasional drinkers are more likely to drink only small amounts (although 3 per cent report drinking large amounts when they do drink).

Where Most Drinking is Done. Most drinking is done at home. In fact, three out of four do most of their drinking in private homes, either their own or those of friends. More women (83.3 per cent) do their drinking in homes than men (70.6 per cent). Almost as many women (7.9 per cent) drink in clubs or at cocktail bars as men (9.1 per cent).[1] The tavern contrast is the greatest. Only 2.4 per cent of the women do most of their drinking in taverns, whereas 14.1 per cent of the men do.

*   *   *

When Most Drinking is Done. More persons (55.5 per cent) drink on weekends and holidays than at any other time; but 40.5 per cent stated that they have no regular time of the week. Only 4.0 per cent listed specific weekdays. A significantly greater proportion of women (67.5 per cent) usually do their drinking on weekends and holidays than is true of the men (46.9 per cent). On the other hand more men (48.0 per cent) drink on any day of the week than women (30.1 per cent).

*   *   *

As for the time of the day, four out of five usually drink in the evening (after 5 P.M.), the percentage being slightly higher for women (85.7 per cent) than for men (78.9 per cent). Just as men report drinking any day of the week more often than women, so more men (14.3 per cent) report drinking any time of the day than women (4.0 per cent). Differences between men and women are not significant with regard to morning drinking, afternoon drinking, or drinking during meals.

One striking fact, especially when contrasted with European practice, is the extremely small proportion (1.0 per cent) of respondents who say they do most of their drinking with their meals. Drinking with meals is not typical of the American pattern, but it is to be wondered whether drinking with meals is as uncommon throughout the United States as it seems to be in the State of Washington.

*   *   *

Drinking by Selected Population Categories. In the present section, the findings on the incidence and frequency of drinking in selected population

1. The State of Washington has been essentially a "monopoly state" with package sales through state outlets. Beer was available in taverns, and wine in restaurants. But liquor by the drink was available only in licensed private clubs until 1949. At that time, liquor by the drink was legalized for bars associated with bona fide restaurants.

segments will be taken up in the reverse order of their statistical significance —that is, beginning with the categories in which the least difference in drinking was found and proceeding to those with greater and greater difference.

Native and Foreign-born. The fact that no significant differences in the frequency of drinking were found between the native and the foreign-born is itself noteworthy. Table 6 shows, as might be expected, that more of the foreign-born drink regularly, but the percentage is small (13.3 per cent) and the difference is not significant. Contrary to expectation, a smaller proportion of the foreign-born drink (58.3 per cent), but again the difference is not statistically significant. To be truly meaningful, foreign-born–native comparisons need to be made by specific countries. The present sample, however, was too small for such a detailed examination.

TABLE 6.—*Native and Foreign-born Status and Drinking Frequency*

	Regular Drinkers, %	Occasional Drinkers, %	Abstainers, %
Native, 3d generation	9.8	52.4	37.8
Native, 1st and 2d generation	11.2	54.2	34.6
Foreign-born	13.3	45.0	41.7

Chi squared $= 2.83$; $P < .60$

Occupations. The fact that no significant correlation between drinking frequency and occupational level was found may in itself be a valuable finding. The possibility remains, of course, that the occupational breakdowns in Table 7 are not well scaled from a social-status point of view. Differences between certain categories do show up, although none of them is statistically significant. Regular drinking is most infrequent (3.3 per cent) among persons in the agriculture-fishing-forestry category, but the proportion of abstainers (36.1 per cent) in this category differs little. It may also be found in the professional-managerial, unskilled, and skilled classifications, but there is scarcely a difference between these three categories. This study does not point to occupational differences as a clue to variations in drinking frequency.

TABLE 7.—*Occupation * of Breadwinner and Frequency of Drinking*

	Regular Drinkers, %	Occasional Drinkers, %	Abstainers, %
Professional–managerial	15.0	51.7	33.3
Clerical, sales	7.8	66.7	25.5
Skilled	14.0	61.4	24.6
Service and semiskilled	10.6	53.0	36.4
Agriculture, fishing, forestry	3.3	60.6	36.1
Unskilled	14.3	53.6	32.1

Chi squared $= 14.704$; $P < .20$

* Retired persons and members of armed forces not included.

Size of Community. Riley and Marden found that drinking and drinking frequency increased with the size of the community. No such significant correlation was found in the State of Washington (Table 8, upper half). The table shows that fewer rural persons drink regularly but that more of them drink than is true in communities of 2,500 up to 100,000. It may be that the general rural–urban contrasts simply are not so sharp in this state as in some other parts of the United States.

There is, however, a significant correlation between drinking frequency and the size of the community in which respondents were reared, as shown in the lower half of Table 8. Among those reared on farms or in communities under 2,500, significantly fewer are regular drinkers (6.4 per cent) and significantly more are abstainers (42.6 per cent). The percentage of drinkers and regular drinkers goes up with the size of the community of rearing until the category of 100,000 and over is reached. In this last category, the percentage of drinkers and regular drinkers falls to a point approximately midway between the rural and the small city communities. In the State of Washington, at least, the most drinking and the most regular drinking is to be found among persons reared in cities between 10,000 and 100,000 in size.

TABLE 8.—*Size of Community and Frequency of Drinking*

Population	Regular Drinkers, %	Occasional Drinkers, %	Abstainers, %
COMMUNITY OF PRESENT RESIDENCE			
100,000 and over	14.6	51.0	34.4
10,000 to 99,999	13.1	47.4	39.5
2,500 to 9,999	19.0	42.9	38.1
Under 2,500 and farm	6.9	55.8	37.3
Chi squared = 7.536; P<.30			
COMMUNITY IN WHICH RESPONDENTS WERE REARED			
100,000 and over	12.8	53.9	33.3
10,000 to 99,999	18.2	59.7	22.1
2,500 to 9,999	15.9	52.4	31.7
Under 2,500 and farm	6.4	51.0	42.6
Chi squared = 12.606; P<.01			

TABLE 9.—*Religious Affiliation * and Frequency of Drinking*

	Regular Drinkers, %	Occasional Drinkers, %	Abstainers, %
Protestant	8.8	52.2	39.0
Catholic	14.8	53.7	31.5
No affiliation	23.3	58.1	18.6
Chi squared = 13.999; P<.01			

* Respondents with Jewish or other affiliation were not represented in sufficient numbers for meaningful correlation.

The most important finding in this comparison may well be the suggestion that drinking behavior correlates more with the size of the community in which individuals were reared than with the size of the community in which they now live.

Religious Affiliation. The frequency of drinking definitely correlates with religious affiliation (Table 9). This study supports the Riley and Marden findings that a greater percentage of abstainers is to be found among Protestants than among Catholics, and that fewer Protestants than Catholics drink regularly. The Protestant–Catholic difference is not so great in Washington, however, as was shown in the Riley and Marden study, which reported 41 per cent Protestant abstainers and 21 per cent Catholic abstainers. In the present study, 39.0 per cent of the Protestants are abstainers and 31.5 per cent of the Catholics. This suggests that in an individual Protestant's or Catholic's case, other social factors, such as urban residence or ethnic affiliation, also play a significant role.

A new and striking finding in Table 9 is the much higher proportion of drinkers (81.4 per cent) and regular drinkers (23.3 per cent) among those who say they have no religious affiliation whatever (9.0 per cent of total respondents).

Sex. When the sexes are compared, a significant difference in drinking and drinking frequency is found. It has already been noted that more men (76.2 per cent) drink than women (51.4 per cent); and that men drink more frequently (19.4 per cent regularly, 56.8 per cent occasionally) than women (3.2 per cent regularly, 48.2 per cent occasionally).

It has also been pointed out, however, that the differences between men and women in the above comparisons are not so great as they were among the parents of the respondents. The trend seems to be toward more equal behavior.

TABLE 10.—*Education and Frequency of Drinking*

	Regular Drinkers, %	Occasional Drinkers, %	Abstainers, %
1 year college or more	6.0	57.8	36.2
1–4 years high school	11.7	53.8	34.5
1–8 years grade school	11.5	49.0	39.5

Chi squared $= 15.048; P<.01$

Education. Insofar as educational level is reflected by the number of years of schooling completed, a significant correlation exists between education and drinking frequency, as shown in Table 10. The only continuous correlation to be noted, however, is the increase in the percentage of occasional drinkers as one goes up the scale (grade school, 49.0 per cent; high school, 53.8 per cent; college, 57.8 per cent). It may also be noted that relatively fewer (6.0 per cent) of those with some college education drink regularly than in the other two categories (11.5 and 11.7 per cent), although this difference is not statistically significant. The total percentage of drinkers and abstainers does not vary in one direction, however; there are more abstainers at the top and at the bottom of the educational scale, and fewest in the group who have one to four years of high school. But again, this difference could be due to chance.

Veterans and Nonveterans. It is widely believed that a stint in the armed services increases the likelihood of drinking. This belief is not upheld by the data obtained in the study. Actually, a smaller proportion of veterans drink at all (74.1 per cent, compared to 78.3 per cent of the nonveterans), and a smaller proportion drink regularly (17.3 compared to 21.0 per cent of the nonveterans), but the difference is not statistically significant.

*   *   *

TABLE 11.—*Age and Frequency of Drinking*

	Regular Drinkers, %	Occasional Drinkers, %	Abstainers, %
70 and over	9.1	22.7	68.2
60–69	12.8	38.6	48.6
50–59	5.5	46.6	47.9
40–49	14.7	56.9	28.4
30–39	14.2	62.6	23.2
20–29	7.2	67.5	25.3

Chi squared = 49.0; $P < .01$

Age. A highly significant correlation is found to exist, in this study, between drinking and age. As shown in Table 11, fewer and fewer persons drink as the age class rises. In the 20's and 30's, three out of four drink. In the 50's and 60's, the proportion of one in two is approached. In the 70's, less than one in three drinks.

It may be that the older respondents are reflecting the pattern of their youth, and the younger respondents the trend toward an increased proportion of drinkers. It was noted previously that only one-third of the parents of the respondents drank, compared to two-thirds of the respondents. We may, therefore, be moving toward a still higher percentage of drinkers for the adult population as a whole—about 75 per cent, judging by the lower age classes in the present sample.

On the other hand, it is possible that in the course of growing older, a significant number of persons give up drinking altogether. It will be seen later that 30.5 per cent of the abstaining respondents did drink earlier in their lives. It may be, as Table 11 suggests, that occasional drinking tends to give way, with increasing age, either to heavier drinking or to abstention—and chiefly to abstention. Only longitudinal rather than cross-sectional studies can throw light on this question.

Income. The most significant and consistent correlation of all is to be found between income and drinking frequency. As shown in Table 12, the percentage of drinkers definitely increases with income; and the largest

TABLE 12.—*Annual Family Income and Frequency of Drinking*

	Regular Drinkers, %	Occasional Drinkers, %	Abstainers, %
$5,000 and over	27.0	54.1	18.9
$4,000–4,999	12.0	68.0	20.0
$3,000–3,999	8.0	58.9	33.1
$2,000–2,999	10.6	45.5	43.9
$1,000–1,999	3.7	34.0	62.3
Under $1,000	14.0	26.0	60.0

Chi squared $= 134.68; P < .01$

proportion of regular drinkers (27.0 per cent) is to be found in the highest income category. Conversely, the highest proportions of abstainers are found in the two lowest income categories.

Attitudes toward Drinking

To what extent does drinking behavior coincide with expressed attitudes toward drinking? In general, the correlation found in this study is high. When asked, "In general, do you approve or disapprove of moderate social drinking?" 62.8 per cent said they approved (63.3 per cent drink) and 32.6 per cent said they disapprove (36.7 per cent do not drink). Yet analysis reveals that 15.9 per cent of those who approve are abstainers; and that 23.4 per cent of those who disapprove, drink. A comparison of men and women, on this point, shows that 76.2 per cent of the men drink but only 52.8 per cent approve; 51.5 per cent of the women drink while only 47.2 per cent approve. Apparently there is more drinking than expressed approval of moderate social drinking; and apparently the drinking behavior of women is more consistent with their expressed attitudes than is the case with men.

*   *   *

Attitudes toward Drunkenness

Table 13 presents the expressed attitudes (strongest reaction) toward drunkenness in men and in women. Disgust leads the list, pity and loss of respect being the other two chief reactions. The differences are not significant at any point, although it may be noted that loss of respect is more often a reaction to drunkenness in women than in men; and that there is less pity for women than men—and less indifference. Not shown in the table is the fact that men and women share these differences in reaction to drunkenness on the part of men and women—with one exception:

TABLE 13.—*Strongest Reaction toward Drunkenness, by Percentage of Respondents*

	Drunken Men	Drunken Women
Disgust	41.0	46.1
Pity	20.4	16.6
Loss of respect	14.4	17.9
Indifference	7.3	3.5
Desire to help	4.6	4.8
Tolerance	3.3	2.3
Amusement	2.3	2.3
Intolerance	2.1	2.1
Scorn	1.9	2.3
Fear	1.9	0.8
Other	0.8	1.3

women more often have pity for the drunken person whether he be male or female.

Reasons for Drinking

Of all the information sought in this study, the reasons for drinking were held in advance to be the most difficult to obtain and the most likely to be unreliable. Yet there seemed to be no hesitancy on the part of respondents, in the pretests and in the actual poll, to state whether they would or would not take a drink for each of 13 reasons, read one at a time. For whatever they are worth, the replies are summarized in Table 14, where the reasons

TABLE 14.—*Reasons for Drinking*

Reasons	% Would Drink	% Would Not Drink	% Don't Know
1. At some formal gathering because it seems the thing to do	68.1	26.9	5.0
2. On certain holidays	66.0	23.3	10.7
3. To relax after a hard day	65.8	30.5	3.7
4. On some social occasions because it would help me to fit in better with the others	63.9	31.5	4.6
5. Sometimes just because it tastes good	57.3	39.1	3.6
6. If a person I liked offered it to me	54.5	34.9	10.6
7. At some social occasions because it would help me to have a more enjoyable evening	52.5	41.5	6.0
8. At some social gatherings because I wouldn't want to be different	48.3	46.4	5.3
9. To relieve some illness or physical discomfort	46.6	46.3	7.1
10. Sometimes just for the devil of it	40.3	51.7	8.0
11. Just to get a little high	21.7	74.3	4.0
12. To get along better with people I didn't know so well	21.0	71.3	7.7
13. To get away from my worries	17.7	78.6	3.7

are listed in the apparent order of importance. As for any differences between the replies of men and women (not shown), more men (71.8 per cent) than women (63.2 per cent) say they would take a drink to relax after a hard day; and more men (67.6 per cent) than women (58.7 per cent) say they would take a drink to fit in better socially. Except for these two items, the replies of men and women differed little.

Reasons for Abstaining

More reliable, perhaps, are the reasons why abstainers do not drink. The leading reason (44.1 per cent) is the belief that drinking is wrong (contrary to religious beliefs; "it's just wrong"). Other reasons given were: Don't like taste (19.3 per cent); health or efficiency (17.9 per cent); bad experience of someone else (15.9 per cent); past loss of control (1.4 per cent); and once pledged not to drink (1.4 per cent). There was no significant difference between the replies of men and women.

It is interesting that 30.5 per cent of the present abstainers stated that they did drink earlier in life. The majority (57.4 per cent) stopped drinking during their 20's and 30's. The distribution of the ages at which once-drinking abstainers stopped drinking is as follows: 10–19 years, 10.7 per cent; 20–29; 23.4 per cent; 30–39, 34.0 per cent; 40–49, 12.8 per cent; 50–59, 17.0 per cent; 60–69, none; and 70–79, 2.1 per cent.

Also of interest is the finding that a significantly greater proportion of once-drinking abstainers drank four times a week or more (25.5 per cent) than is true of present drinkers (9.7 per cent). Even though only a few of the abstainers who once drank admitted that they had once lost control, it is possible that a larger number had found abstention to be the solution to what they may have conceived as their drinking problem.

* * *

Knowledge about Alcohol

In the following two sections, findings are reported that will be of particular interest to the persons concerned with education about alcohol and alcoholism. The findings give some clue as to the effects of educational efforts in recent years.

Effect on Judgment, Memory, and Speed. Three questions were asked regarding the effect of two drinks of whisky, in the case of an average-sized man, upon (*1*) his judgment, (*2*) his memory, and (*3*) the speed with which he could get things done.

The answers to the three questions were quite uniform. About half answered all three items in the correct direction. This may be a larger proportion of correct answers than would have been found 10 or 15 years ago (there are no comparative data), but it does show that half of the adult population still needs education in this area. The proportion who believe that two drinks will not make any difference is highest in the case of judgment and lowest in the case of speed. This may be a reflection of more educational emphasis, in connection with driver education, upon the slowing down of reaction time.

Alcohol as a Stimulant. The illusion that alcohol is a stimulant is still strong. Seven out of ten persons believe that two drinks of whisky will have a stimulating effect, and only 12.5 per cent state that the effect will be the opposite (the words "depressant," "sedative," and "narcotic" were not used). Apparently people *feel* stimulated, and their own experience impresses them more than the statements of the physiologists. The others answering the question said either that the two drinks would have no effect, that the effect would depend upon other factors, or that they did not know what the effect would be.

The influence of formal education on this point is equivocal. Thus more persons with college training thought that two drinks would act as a stimulant than did persons with high-school or grammar-school education. But more college persons (18.8 per cent) seem to know that alcohol is a depressant than persons with only high-school (12.3 per cent) or grammar-school (10.3 per cent) education.

*   *   *

Knowledge about Alcoholism

Can the Alcoholic Stop Drinking? More than half (54.6 per cent) of the respondents believe that the alcoholic is unable to stop drinking by himself. But one-fifth attribute this inability to "weak will." In other words, about two in five think the alcoholic can stop drinking by himself; and another one in five attributes the alcoholic's inability to stop drinking to his being weak-willed. Apparently, three in five see the problem of the alcoholic in terms of will power. Only one in five states that the alcoholic cannot stop drinking because he is sick. There is no doubt that education concerning the nature of alcoholism is still widely needed.

That the level of schooling makes a difference in this respect is demonstrated by the finding that fewer persons with college education attribute the alcoholic's plight to being weak-willed (12.3 per cent) and more of them think he is sick (34.6 per cent).

*   *   *

Heredity and Environment. The idea that environmental factors play a much greater role than heredity has, however, taken hold. Asked, "If the child of an alcoholic parent becomes an alcoholic himself, is this mainly because he has inherited it, or is it because of his surroundings?" 81.3 per cent said it is because of his surroundings; 7.0 per cent, heredity; 3.4 per cent, both heredity and surroundings. The remainder did not know or gave other replies.

Alcoholics Known. Almost three out of four (72.0 per cent) claimed to know or to have known at least one alcoholic. Slightly over 23 per cent knew only one alcoholic, 17 per cent two, 9 per cent three or four, 6.9 per cent five or six, 7.6 per cent seven or more, and the balance did not specify the number.

More often than not, the alcoholic was an acquaintance (41.6 per cent) or fellow worker (17.9 per cent), but in 40.5 per cent of the cases the alcoholic was very close to the respondent—a close friend (17.0 per cent), a relative (16.7 per cent), or a member of the family (6.8 per cent).

Recovered Alcoholics Known. Over half (53.3 per cent) of the respondents had never known an alcoholic who had recovered; 46.7 per cent had.

When those who had never known a recovered alcoholic were asked about the possibility of recovering from alcoholism, 78.6 per cent stated their belief that recovery was possible; 13.6 per cent believed that recovery was impossible; and 7.8 per cent did not know. When those who believed that recovery was possible were asked their opinion on the means by which alcoholics can stop drinking, again will power leads the list, with 39.0 per cent of the replies. The other replies were: take the cure, 13.1 per cent; doctor or medical treatment, 11.6 per cent; religion, 8.4 per cent; outside help, 7.9 per cent; join Alcoholics Anonymous, 6.3 per cent; not associate with drinkers, 5.8 per cent; new interests, 2.6 per cent; get rid of reason for wanting to escape, 0.5 per cent; and don't know, 4.8 per cent.

When those who did not believe that recovery from alcoholism was possible were asked for their reasons, the replies were: "Just can't do it" (30.3 per cent); no will power (21.1 per cent); don't want to (15.2 per cent); bad disease or sick (15.2 per cent); no interest in life (3.0 per cent). The others did not know.

When those who had known a recovered alcoholic were asked by what means this alcoholic had gained sobriety, the replies ran somewhat the same gamut as described above. Will power is given the credit in one-third of the cases (33.8 per cent). Taking the cure is credited in 24.3 per cent, and Alcoholics Anonymous comes third with 14.9 per cent of the cases. After that come religion, (8.6 per cent), doctor's orders (5.9 per cent), help of family and friends (5.4 per cent), medical help (2.2 per cent), and left old friends (1.3 per cent). The others did not know.

Knowledge about Alcoholics Anonymous. In view of the success and growth of Alcoholics Anonymous, it is surprising that one-third of the respondents (33.6 per cent) said they did not know its purpose. Another 6.1 per cent thought that the purpose of A.A. was the prevention of alcoholism. Almost half (46.9 per cent) were vaguely right in their replies, but only 13.4 per cent had a clear enough concept of A.A. to state that it is a group of alcoholics who help each other. Lack of knowledge about A.A.

is significantly greater among abstainers (40 per cent) than among drinkers (30 per cent). It is possible that A.A. and its program were less well known in the State of Washington than in parts of the United States where A.A. has been established longer.

*   *   *

Sources of Information about Alcoholism. The final set of findings to be reported herein are the responses to the question: "If you have read or heard anything about the problem of alcoholism in the last 3 years, where did you learn most about it?" Over one-fifth (22.4 per cent) could not recall having read or heard anything about alcoholism during this time. Magazines were the chief source of information on alcoholism, reported by 30.1 per cent of the total sample; newspapers came second (18.0 per cent). Together, magazines and newspapers were the primary sources of information for over two-thirds (69.6 per cent) of those who had read or heard something about alcoholism during this period of time.

The meaning of these findings is uncertain. Are magazines and newspapers the best channels or simply the most used channels for adult education on alcoholism? Are radio, television, and movies not so effective as media, or have they not yet been used to a great extent? Perhaps those most concerned with the problem of education on alcoholism can answer these questions, or pursue investigations that will provide the answers.

*   *   *

Presented in this article have been the general results of a poll on drinking behavior and attitudes, knowledge about alcohol, and knowledge about alcoholism and its treatment, in a carefully selected sample of the population of the State of Washington. The findings have greatest value when placed in a modifying or corroborating position alongside other studies— all designed to build up a reliable picture of drinking behavior in the United States as a whole and in its various population segments.

The findings also have value in pointing up possible regional and other social differences obscured in national samples—suggestions which deserve further exploration.

Finally, the findings provide some measure of the results which have been obtained by educational activities in recent years, and some indication of the educational task still ahead.

15. IN HIGH SCHOOL

HIGH SCHOOL DRINKING STUDIES

by Raymond G. McCarthy *

Reliable information to indicate the extent to which students of high school and college age drink and their attitudes toward drinking practices has been almost entirely lacking. Statements concerning the use of alcohol by adolescents are frequently founded upon isolated escapades which receive publicity. Reports of arrests for sales to minors, accidents resulting from driving under the influence, and disorderly conduct in public places which involves intoxication provide little or no valid data except that which relates to the individuals directly concerned. Scientifically designed and conducted studies are needed before an adequate picture of the extent of use by young people can be projected. Such studies are presently in process in communities in Kansas, Michigan, and Wisconsin, but they need to be extended to include other representative sections of the country.

Information available at this time suggests that a considerable proportion of young people 14–18 years of age have had some experience with drinking. This has frequently been done with parental consent. However, drinking practices of young people can only be understood in terms of their social class, economic status, religious affiliation, and the drinking customs of their parents. Generalizations applicable solely to high school and college students as a group are likely to be misleading.

McCarthy and Douglass reported on the frequency of drinking by the students of a small suburban high school near Washington, D.C., in 1941, 1945, and 1947, as in Table 1.

TABLE 1.—*Frequency of Drinking by High School Students* †

		Never, %	Occasionally, %	Frequently, %
1941	Girls (332)	82.8	16.3	0.9
	Boys (250)	71.2	26.0	2.8
1945	Girls (351)	75.8	23.1	1.1
	Boys (248)	64.5	32.2	4.6
1947	Girls (343)	77.0	21.0	2.0
	Boys (315)	54.6	40.3	5.1

* From *Teen-Agers and Alcohol: A Handbook for the Educator* (New Haven, Publications Division, Yale Center of Alcohol Studies, 1956), pp. 20 ff.

† R. G. McCarthy and E. M. Douglass, *Alcohol and Social Responsibility* (New York, Thomas Y. Crowell and Yale Plan Clinic, 1949), pp. 155–62.

Analysis of the data reveals an increase over time in the percentage of occasional and frequent users, particularly among boys. The investigators concluded that the incidence of drinking increased among upper grade students; most of the drinking was done at home or at parties at the homes of friends; and most of the drinking was done with the consent of parents.

In 1948, a question about drinking was included in the Purdue Opinion Poll, which sampled 3,000 high school students in all parts of the country. Among the 28 questions to which students responded, two related to drinking.[1]

How do you personally feel about drinking intoxicants, such as beer, wine, or liquor?

I approve, 11%   I am neutral, 30%   I disapprove, 55%

Do you or do you not sometimes drink beer, wine, or liquor?
Do, 35%   Do not, 65%

The investigators stated:

According to our figures, boys approve of drinking to a slightly greater extent than do girls. A much higher proportion of boys than girls admit that they "sometimes drink." The double standard again is evident.

	Boys	Girls
% Approve of drinking	14	8
% Sometimes drink	45	27

The number of students who are willing to say that they approve of drinking goes up only slightly from the 9th through the 12th grade. The proportion of those who say they disapprove of drinking decreases steadily from 65% in the 9th grade to 48% in the 12th grade. There is a corresponding increase in the proportion of students who say that they are neutral. As we might expect from the foregoing, we find in question 17 that the proportion of students who sometimes drink beer, wine or liquor increases from 28% in the 9th grade and 10th grade to 47% in the 12th grade.

Grade:	9th	10th	11th	12th
% Disapprove of drinking	65	64	57	48
% Sometimes drink	28	28	37	47

While we find no important regional differences on the question of smoking, we do find such differences when it comes to drinking intoxicants. The strongest disapproval of drinking is voiced by students in the South, while the least amount of disapproval is voiced by students from the Mountain-Pacific region. In admitted actual drinking, wide differences appear. Midwesterners apparently drink the most, while students from the South drink the least.

	East	Midwest	South	Mt.–Pacific
% Disapprove of drinking	58	57	66	50
% Sometimes drink	34	41	28	38

1. Division of Educational Research, Purdue University, Lafayette, Ind., *The Purdue Opinion Poll for Young People, 8,* No. 2 (1949), 17–8.

When students are grouped according to their religion, we find in the results striking evidence of the role which culture plays in shaping both attitude and behavior. We know that Protestants, Catholics, and Jews have widely divergent views on the question of drinking. The Jewish religion contains no injunction against drinking; in fact wine is frequently used in religious ritual and in family religious observance. Neither does Catholicism take an official stand against drinking. The various Protestant denominations, on the other hand, are more inclined to oppose the use of alcohol than to approve it. There is little doubt that the Protestant churches were instrumental in securing the passage of the 18th Amendment and have been the mainstay of the temperance movement in America.

When we look at the figures, we find that Protestants and those with "some other" religious preference (other than Catholic or Jewish) most strongly disapprove of drinking. Catholics and those with no religious preference take a stand somewhere between that of the Jews and Protestants. Slightly more than half of the Catholics, Jews, and those students with no religious preference state that they sometimes drink intoxicating beverages. Only 28 per cent of the Protestants and those students with "some other" religious preference acknowledge doing so.

	Protestant	Catholic	Jewish	Some Other	None
% Disapprove of drinking	65	45	34	67	43
% Sometimes drink	28	52	52	28	51

A higher proportion of students from low-income homes than from high-income homes say that they disapprove of drinking, but both groups have about the same proportion of students who admit they sometimes drink.

	Low Income	High Income
% Disapprove of drinking	62	52
% Sometimes drink	34	37

Arthur D. Slater administered a questionnaire in 1951 to 1,177 students in Grades 10 and 12 in five high schools in different parts of Utah. Returns (Table 2) indicated that 20 per cent of the girls and 44 per cent of the boys sometimes drank alcoholic beverages.[2]

TABLE 2.—*Frequency of Drinking Reported by High School Students in Utah, 1951*

	Total	Never, %	Occasional, %	Frequent, %
Girls	614	79	19	1
Boys	563	56	42	2
Total students	1,177	68	30	1
Parents drinking				
Mothers	1,145	79	19	3
Fathers	1,151	56	33	9

2. Arthur D. Slater, "A Study of the Use of Alcoholic Beverages among High School Students in Utah," *Quarterly Journal of Studies on Alcohol, 13* (1952), 78–86.

Lumping the grades together, Slater estimated the mean age at which male students took their first drink as 14.4 years; and female students, 14.5 years. The data revealed that 28 per cent of the 134 Grade 10 students started drinking at age 12 or younger, as against 12 per cent in Grade 12. These observations as to beginning age are not borne out consistently by other studies. For instance, Straus and Bacon in their systematic investigation of drinking in college reported that of the drinking group, 36 per cent of the men and 47 per cent of the women had their first drink between the ages of 16 and 17; 53 per cent of the men and 44 per cent of the women began drinking at 18 years or older. Only 11 per cent of the men and 9 per cent of the women reported the onset of drinking between the ages of 11 and 15.[3]

Comparative Studies in Three Counties, 1951–55

Results of a well designed research study of teen-age drinking in selected high schools in Nassau County were released September 1953 by the Research Bureau of Hofstra College. The project was financed by a grant from the Mrs. John S. Sheppard Foundation of New York City.

Nassau County is a highly urbanized and industrialized area of 15 square miles on Long Island near metropolitan New York. Although there is a sizable farming area, industrial expansion and easy commuting distance to New York City have produced a population increase of 100 per cent in the decade 1940–1950, the present number being approximately 1 million.

Dr. Matthew Chappell, director of the study, sampled 29 of Nassau's 31 public and private high schools, selecting every tenth student 14 to 18 years of age among the 29,000 pupils in schools. The study was conducted with a group of 1,000 students, 483 boys and 517 girls.[4]

A similar project in Racine County, Wisconsin, in cooperation with the University of Wisconsin,[5] and a study in Sedgwick County, Kansas, conducted by the University of Kansas,[6] were both completed in 1956. Both surveys received financial support from the Sheppard Foundation. The Wisconsin and Kansas counties have metropolitan industrialized areas as well as a substantial farm section. Sedgwick County experienced a 55 per cent population increase from 1940 to 1950, to the present figure of 280,-000 people. The population of Racine County, which has remained relatively stable, is 110,000.

3. Robert Straus and Selden D. Bacon, *Drinking in College* (New Haven, Yale University Press, 1953), p. 121.
4. *Use of Alcoholic Beverages among High School Students,* a study made by Hofstra Research Bureau, Psychological Division, Hofstra College, Hempstead, New York, for the Mrs. John S. Sheppard Foundation, Inc., New York, 1954. Multilithed.
5. *Attitudes of High School Students toward Alcoholic Beverages,* a study made by the Bureau of Economics, Sociology and Anthropology, University of Wisconsin, for the Mrs. John S. Sheppard Foundation, Inc., New York, 1956. Multilithed.
6. See pp. 210–11 for a summary of conclusions drawn from the Kansas study.

The complete reports of the investigations in each of these studies should be read carefully.

TABLE 3.—*High School Students Who Sometimes Use Alcoholic Beverages*

	PERCENTAGE USING	Beer	Wine	Whisky
		PERCENTAGE USING		
Nassau	86	62	72	46
Wisconsin	64	60	64	44

TABLE 4.—*Percentage of Students Who Sometimes Drink, by Age*

Age:	14	15	16	17	18
Nassau	79	82	90	89	89
Wisconsin	51	59	65	71	78

TABLE 5.—*Percentage of Students Who Consumed Some Alcoholic Beverage in the Week Preceding Study, by Age*

Age:	14	15	16	17	18
Nassau	28	36	45	56	55
Wisconsin	12	18	31	32	48

In Nassau County 74 per cent of the students who drank stated they had parental permission to drink at home and 48 per cent had permission to drink away from home. In Wisconsin, 65 per cent of the 1,000 students had permission to drink at home. However, of this group 7 per cent were nondrinkers, 36 per cent drank only with permission at home, and 22 per cent both at home and away.

TABLE 6.—*Percentage of Students with Parental Permission to Drink at Home, by Age*

Age:	14	15	16	17	18
Nassau	68	70	77	85	95
Wisconsin	77	79	83	89	89

TABLE 7.—*Percentage of Students with Parental Permission to Drink Away from Home Sometimes, by Age*

Age:	14	15	16	17	18
Nassau	29	42	54	68	84
Wisconsin	26	42	60	71	–

The data from two of the three studies suggest a wide range of variability in use of alcohol by teen-agers. The Nassau figures are surprisingly high, i.e., 90 per cent for 16-year-olds. The percentage of use by girls is larger than by boys. In Wisconsin and Nassau the figures regarding the use with parental permission are significant, particularly in planning a program of instruction.

The extent to which Nassau County is typical of the country at large is open to question. Among this highly urban population 95 per cent of the parents drink. Fifty-two per cent of the children of the 5 per cent of abstaining parents in the study are users of alcohol. The investigators state that students did not report evidence of peer group pressure to drink in order to maintain status. This is not entirely consistent with reports from students in other areas of the country. It is probable that Nassau represents a socially mobile population reflecting stratified, segmental attitudes in support of drinking. For example, of the student sample, one-half were Catholic, one-third Protestant, and one-sixth Jewish.

A study of drinking practices of high school students in Nova Scotia (Table 8) was carried out in 1955 by Donald R. Gilchrist, Director of Temperance Education, Department of Education, Province of Nova Scotia.[7] Questionnaires were administered to pupils in Grades 9 to 12. Situations in which drinking occurred and extent of consumption were analyzed under several categories, e.g., religious ceremony, wedding only, family custom, one drink, occasional but not tight, occasional and tight, moderate, and frequent use. Of 5,409 students in the age range 14–19 in 43 high schools, 2,581 (48 per cent) never drank and 2,828 (52 per cent) had tasted an alcoholic beverage under some circumstance. Excluding those who drank for reasons of ritual or family custom, 1,636 (30 per cent) occasional, moderate, and frequent users were designated as the drinking group.

TABLE 8.—*Distribution by Age, Nova Scotia High School Students*

	Never Drank		Drank at Some Time		Total
	N	%	N	%	N
Under 14	95	55	77	45	172
14	400	55	343	45	743
15	763	51	732	49	1,495
16	726	47	832	53	1,558
17	421	43	548	57	969
18	151	39	232	61	383
19 and over	25	28	64	72	89
Total	*2,581*	*48*	*2,828*	*52*	*5,409*

THE KANSAS STUDY

Interest aroused by the reports of the experiences with alcoholic beverages of high school students in Nassau County, Long Island, and

7. D. R. Gilchrist, *A Survey of Drinking Habits of High School Students in Certain High Schools of Nova Scotia*, 1955. Mimeographed.

Racine County, Wisconsin, described above, resulted in a research project among 10th, 11th, and 12th grade students in Kansas. The study was carried out by a research team of the Department of Sociology and Anthropology of the University of Kansas.[8]

Because it was impossible to select one county representative of the varied rural population of Kansas, a sample of 1,207 students was drawn from the metropolitan area of Wichita and another one of 1,119 students from 23 non-metropolitan counties of eastern Kansas. According to the investigators, the 1954 population of Sedgwick County, which includes Wichita, was 280,199, a 26 per cent increase over the county population in 1950, which in turn represented a 55 per cent increase over 1940. This growth is attributed to the development of a manufacturing, particularly defense, industry. Wichita is a marketing and distribution center for a rich agricultural region.

The procedures followed in the research were in general comparable to those used in the Nassau and Wisconsin investigations. Comparisons may be drawn between the data derived from Nassau County students, representing a highly urbanized section adjacent to New York City, the relatively stable population of Racine County, and Kansas, reflecting somewhat different nationality and ethnic origins, degree of urbanization, and other social and cultural factors. It became possible also to compare the behavior of metropolitan and non-metropolitan students in the Kansas region and to evaluate the effects of urbanization on drinking behavior.

SUMMARY OF ESSENTIAL FINDINGS IN THE KANSAS STUDY

by Marston M. McCluggage,
E. Jackson Baur, Charles K. Warriner,
and Carroll D. Clark *

The basic finding of this study is that relatively few public high school students in the areas of Kansas which we surveyed drink alcoholic beverages. Only about half of them had ever had a drink of anything alcoholic as compared with about two-thirds of the high school students in Racine County, Wisconsin and 86 per cent of the high school students in Nassau County, New York. Although half the Kansas youth had at some time taken

* From *Attitudes of High School Students toward Alcoholic Beverages,* a study made by the Department of Sociology and Anthropology, University of Kansas, for the Mrs. John S. Sheppard Foundation, Inc., New York (1956), pp. 95–108.

8. *Attitudes of High School Students toward Alcoholic Beverages,* a study made by the Department of Sociology and Anthropology, University of Kansas, for the Mrs. John S. Sheppard Foundation, Inc., New York, 1956. Multilithed.

a drink of an alcoholic beverage there are significant differences within the state between the Wichita metropolitan area where 56 per cent say they have used alcoholic beverages and the non-metropolitan area of eastern Kansas where 44 per cent are users. In both of these areas the boys who are users exceed the girls by about 20 per cent. As students advance through high school an increasing proportion have experience with alcoholic beverages reaching a maximum of about two-thirds of the seniors in metropolitan high schools and half the seniors in non-metropolitan schools.

An indicator of the prevalence of drinking that is less affected by memory lapse than the question on past experience is the information on the number of drinks consumed during the week preceding the interview. In the Wichita area 17 per cent and in the non-metropolitan area 11 per cent reported having had one or more drinks during the past seven days. These percentages compare with 26 per cent in Racine County and 43 per cent in Nassau County.

The beverage most frequently experienced by high school students was 3.2 (per cent) beer, which has the lowest alcohol content. Half or more of the boys are users of 3.2 beer. But two-thirds of the users of 3.2 beer drink it less often than once a month. The boys who say they regularly drink 3.2 beer once a week or more comprise 8 per cent of the metropolitan and 5 per cent of the non-metropolitan sample.

Regular drinking of beverages other than 3.2 beer by boys is reported by no more than one in fifty students of either sex. Hard liquor of all kinds is consumed regularly by no more than one in a hundred students.

The incidence of heavy drinking appears to be very small. Three per cent of the metropolitan boys said they had more than twenty drinks during the preceding week and the other categories by sex and area reported lesser frequencies. Even the consumption of more than four drinks during the preceding week is reported by but 9 per cent of the metropolitan students and half that proportion of the non-metropolitan youth. In Racine County the percentage having this amount to drink is identical with the rate for the Wichita area.

The proportion of students who had ever experienced an intoxicating effect from drinking are one-third of those in the Wichita area and about one-fifth of those in the non-metropolitan area. They said they had been "high," "gay," or "buzzed" at some time in the past. However, boys who say they have had this experience outnumber the girls by two to one. The more extreme effects, characterized as "tight" or "drunk," are half as frequent as the milder states. The frequency of intoxicating effects during the four weeks preceding the day of the interview are reported by about one-fourth the proportion of students who say they have ever had these effects. The proportions experiencing intoxicating effects in the Wichita area are very similar to those of Racine County.

The irregularity of much of the drinking by Kansas youth is implied by the fact that the circumstance which is reported by more students than any other is "special occasions." The least frequent occasions are when alone and before going to parties. These different occasions have the same rank in Racine County.

Data on the conditions under which students are introduced to alcoholic beverages indicate that most of those who use alcoholic beverages have their first experience after they have passed their sixteenth birthdays. More of them have their first drink at home or at the home of a relative than with friends or in public places. The motives for early drinking are varied. For beer and hard liquor, curiosity is most common, followed closely by "holiday or special celebration" and social pressures and expectations. Wine is more often tasted first on holidays or special celebrations.

One-fourth of the parents of Kansas teen-age children permit them to drink 3.2 beer at home and about one-fifth extend this freedom to other alcoholic beverages. Parental permission is more restricted than in Racine and Nassau counties where one-third and three-fourths of the parents permitted their high-school-age children to drink at home. About one-fifth of the boys and one-tenth of the girls who have home parties report serving alcoholic beverages when their parents are home. Among those who have parties when their parents are not at home the proportions serving alcoholic beverages are about doubled.

The percentage of students in Kansas who drink more away from home than their parents know about, ranges from 6 per cent for girls in the non-metropolitan area to 25 per cent for boys in the Wichita area. For the sexes combined the percentages are 18 in the metropolitan and 14 in the non-metropolitan area. These proportions are slightly greater than the 10 per cent reported for Racine County but much below the 31 per cent for Nassau County.

A close relationship was found between the use of alcoholic beverages by parents and children. A majority of the students who use alcoholic beverages come from homes in which the parents keep alcoholic beverages and a majority of the abstainers come from homes in which alcoholic beverages are absent. The frequency with which children drink alcoholic beverages is correlated with the frequencies with which their parents drink. The children of parents who drink occasionally or regularly are more often occasional or regular drinkers than the children of parents who never drink.

The influence of the parents on drinking by youth is also apparent in the data on broken homes and the absence of one or both parents. In the Wichita area these abnormalities in family life are associated with decreases in the rate of abstinence and increases in the rates of occasional and regular drinking. However, these family influences do not affect the drinking of youth in non-metropolitan areas to any significant degree.

Drinking by high school students is related to the size of the community. In the Wichita metropolitan area with a population in excess of a quarter of a million, 56 per cent of the high school students are users of alcoholic beverages. In the communities of eastern Kansas having populations from 1,000 to 25,000 about half of the students are users. In places of less than a thousand and in rural districts about 40 per cent of the high school students are users.

In the Wichita area drinking is more prevalent among children from families of higher economic and educational levels. The proportion of users increases from about half in the lowest to about two-thirds in the highest level. In the non-metropolitan area this relationship is less apparent.

There is no clear general relationship between student drinking and the indicators of social adjustment used in the survey which are school grades, school activities, interscholastic athletics, participation in organizations, and offices held in organizations. Analysis by sex shows that for girls there is no association between these factors and drinking except among those who take part in interscholastic athletics among whom drinking is more prevalent than among those who do not take part in interscholastic athletics. For boys there is significantly less drinking among those who hold office in two or more organizations, and in the non-metropolitan area the boys who make higher grades include a smaller proportion of users of alcoholic beverages than is found among the boys whose grades are lower.

Religion and drinking are connected. Roman Catholics—both the children and their parents—use alcoholic beverages more often than Protestants. Those high school students who are active participants in church affairs drink less than those who attend infrequently.

Students who recalled receiving formal instruction in school or at home on the subject of alcoholic beverages were no different in their drinking behavior from those who had not received instruction. But those who had received instruction in church included a larger proportion of abstainers than those who had not received instruction in church.

A small proportion of the students attempt to buy alcoholic beverages while under the legal age. The largest such category is about one-third of the boys who have attempted to buy 3.2 beer in a restaurant, bar, or tavern. One girl for every three or four boys tries to buy illegally under the same circumstances. Attempts to buy illegally from package liquor stores are almost nonexistent among the girls, but are reported by 17 per cent of the metropolitan and 11 per cent of non-metropolitan boys. The use of false evidence of legal age is confined to the boys and, among them, to only 13 per cent of the metropolitan boys and to about half that percentage in the non-metropolitan area. Of the boys who attempted to purchase while under legal age about one-third were never refused at the package stores, two-fifths were never refused at bars or taverns, and two-thirds were always successful in grocery stores.

The students who do not drink at teen-age parties do not thereby suffer any loss of popularity. A majority of students among both users and abstainers have a favorable opinion of other students who do not drink at parties. Those who do drink at parties gain the approval of only about half of the users and about one-fourth of the abstainers.

Among the statements on which students were asked to express agreement or disagreement, the users and abstainers were sharply divided on only two. "There is nothing wrong with drinking on certain special occasions" was acceptable to three-fourths or more of the users, but to only a third or less of the abstainers. "Moderate drinking is fun and harmless" was assented to by about half the users, but by only about 10 per cent of the abstainers.

The overwhelming majority of students agree that people don't need alcoholic beverages for good social relations and reject the statements that drinking at a party makes people get along better and that alcoholic beverages make a party a success. In this respect the Kansas and Racine County students are similar.

Interpretation of the Findings

To explain why some high school students drink alcoholic beverages and others do not depends, as does an explanation for any other kind of human behavior, on knowledge of many different factors. No single influence alone is sufficient to explain why students use or abstain from drinking alcoholic beverages. The causes operate in combination and interdependence with one another.

Implicit in this research has been the hypothesis that environmental influences are crucial for understanding why people do or do not drink. Many questions in the schedule were designed to collect data on social, cultural, and economic factors in the environment of high school students which may have a bearing on their drinking behavior.

The data collected in the questionnaires were analyzed by relating these factors to differences in the use of alcoholic beverages. Differences in drinking took several forms: Greatest use was made of the simple distinction between users and abstainers. For each of the four kinds of beverage (3.2 beer, strong beer, wine, and hard liquor) the frequency of drinking was classified as never, seldom, occasionally, and regularly. Each of these terms is objectively defined in terms of number of drinks per week or month.

* * *

Many of the findings are understandable in the light of sociological and psychological knowledge. Three broad scientific ideas are useful for understanding drinking and non-drinking among high school students—cultural differences, socialization, and social control.

By cultural differences in drinking behavior we refer to the fact that among some groups of people drinking is customary on many different occasions including its daily consumption as a beverage with ordinary meals. On the other hand in some groups the consumption of alcoholic beverages of any kind is completely taboo. Every social group tends to develop a distinctive culture and drinking is one of the kinds of human activity which may differ from one group to another. For each group its own customs are the "right" ways of doing things.

This survey of high school drinking behavior uncovered many differences among high school students which can be satisfactorily explained by cultural differences between groups. Much of the contrast between students in the metropolitan and non-metropolitan areas may be explained by the existence of urban and rural cultures with divergent drinking customs. Urban people appear to define drinking as appropriate on more occasions and to permit wider participation by children in these activities. Further support for this explanation is the association between use of alcoholic beverages and size of community. The extent of use increases as one moves from the rural communities to towns, cities, and metropolitan centers.

There are cultural differences between religious groups that influence the amount of drinking. There are relatively more users among Roman Catholics as compared with Protestants. Furthermore a greater proportion of the drinking by Catholic youth takes place within the context of the family. There also seem to be differences among Protestants between those who are active members of denominations and those who attend irregularly or not at all.

There is also evidence of social class differences in drinking customs. At least in the metropolitan area there is more drinking among students from families of higher socio-economic levels. There is also an indication of ethnic differences in the fact of greater use among those whose grandparents were born in foreign countries.

The patterns of behavior which we call the culture of a group of people are acquired by the individual member as he grows to maturity. He learns the conduct which is considered appropriate by the members of his group. This is the process of socialization through which the growing child acquires the culture of his group. It provides us with a second explanatory principle. That the amount of drinking is associated with increasing maturity is evident from the increasing proportion of users in the sophomore, junior, and senior classes.

The most pervasive and enduring patterns of conduct are learned from persons with whom the child has close ties of intimacy and identification. The family and peer group are most influential in this process. Family influences were strikingly apparent in the high correspondence between the frequency of drinking by parents and their children. More direct evidence is the fact that as students grew older greater proportions of them drank with the permission of their parents. Almost all of the students reported that they were introduced to alcoholic beverages by parents, relatives, or friends. Very few began alone or in the company of strangers.

The behavior patterns learned from the peer group sometimes conflict with those inculcated by the family. There is some evidence from our research that this is the case with drinking alcoholic beverages. The milder beverages, 3.2 beer and wine, as contrasted with strong beer and distilled liquors, are more frequently introduced to the student by members of the family rather than by friends, while hard liquor is introduced much more frequently through friends than by relatives. These divergent patterns that are presented to some of our youth and the pressures to conform to conflicting expectations by family and peer group cause tensions in family relationships and precipitate problems of personal adjustment.

The kind of drinking which conforms to group culture and is learned in primary groups might be thought of as normal drinking. It takes place on occasions and in amounts which conform to the expectations of others in the group. The third kind of interpretation explains abnormal drinking which violates customs of the group. It is conceived of as arising when the effectiveness of group controls breaks down. The individual finds himself without clear guides to conduct. Group norms of conduct are conflicting or nonexistent. He lacks stable and intimate relations with persons after whom he can model his own way of living. In this condition of anomie or normlessness the person may make an abnormal adjustment through pathological behavior. Excessive drinking is one of the possible kinds of deviant behavior which may result. However, deviant behavior does not develop in a social vacuum. Very often deviant patterns arise which are developed by and learned from others who are in a similar plight and together they form a deviant group or gang in conflict with conventional society.

The statistical evidence from this survey indicates that abnormal drinking among Kansas high school students is rare. Those who drink excessively and those who have experienced the extreme forms of intoxication are a small fraction of the student population. Although there arc few individuals who are problem drinkers among high school students there is some evidence that drinking increases when social controls are weakened. In the metropolitan area there is a greater proportion of users among the students who come from broken homes as compared with those from complete families. There is a larger incidence of drinking at home parties when parents arc not at home than when the parents are home.

Social controls are more effective for certain people and in certain situations. There is evidence from this study that girls were more effectively controlled than boys and that controls are generally more potent in small than in large communities. This is inferred from the lesser amount of drinking in these categories and especially the virtual absence of excessive drinking. The low incidence of drinking among non-metropolitan girls may be an instance where two factors reinforce one another. The cultural traditions prescribe greater restraint and moderation for the female role than for the male, and the consequences for violating the mores may be more punishing for the girls than for the boys. In the smaller communities drinking may not only be frowned on by more groups and informal control by means of gossip be more effective, but the community may be more completely integrated so that breakdown in some one institution like the family may impose less of a strain on the individual child. Other groups and institutions may provide the needs which in the metropolis might go unsatisfied or be filled by a delinquent gang.

The effectiveness of social controls in the smaller communities and for girls is evident in the lack of any significant increase in the amount of drinking in these categories after passing their eighteenth birthdays. Under Kansas law 3.2 beer may be purchased by persons who are eighteen years of age, though other alcoholic beverages may not be bought until age twenty-one.

Since some of the Kansas high school students questioned in this survey were 18 or more years old, it is possible to test the influence of the law as it applies to 3.2 beer. Although there is no significant increase in the proportion of users of alcoholic beverages at age 18 there is a significantly larger proportion of eighteen year olds than seventeen year olds who say that they drank an alcoholic beverage during the preceding week. At age 18 there is a striking increase in the proportion of occasional and regular drinkers of 3.2 beer among boys in the Wichita area. No such increase occurs in the drinking of hard liquor which may not be legally purchased until age 21. This difference between 3.2 beer and hard liquor suggests that the law does affect the amount of drinking, especially for boys in the metropolitan area among whom extra-legal social controls are not as effective as they are in the non-metropolitan area and for girls in both areas.

These conclusions are in the nature of hypotheses which are plausible but not verified. To convert them into tested theories will require further research which might take the form of intensive case studies of certain types of groups and situations, time-span studies of children in different cultures, and experiments to measure the effect of specific temperance programs.

16. IN COLLEGE

The Straus and Bacon study [1] is the most comprehensive analysis of the use of alcohol by young people available in the literature at present. However, it is concerned only with a college-age group. Questionnaires were administered to 17,000 students in 27 public, private, and sectarian colleges. Men's, women's and coeducational colleges participated, white and Negro, urban and rural, with large and small enrollments, in various parts of the country. Of the students who completed the questionnaires, 74 per cent reported having used alcoholic beverages to some extent, while 26 per cent were abstainers. The investigators urge caution in interpreting these data, stating: "Furthermore, 74 per cent is not the incidence of drinking by students in a particular college; and it does not take into account observed differences between the sexes. There were twice as many abstainers among the women (39 per cent) as among men (20 per cent) who took part in the survey."

Wide differences were found among colleges, as is indicated in Table 1.

TABLE 1.—*Incidence of Drinking, by Type of College*

	Men, %	Women, %
Private, men or women, nonsectarian	92	89
Private, coed vocational, nonsectarian	92	84
Private, coed vocational, "dry"	65	39
Private, coed vocational, general	83	74
Public, coed vocational, teachers	79	44
Public, coed vocational, southern Negro	81	40

The study indicated a relationship between family income and use of alcohol.

Economic factors are important in determining the nature of many aspects of behavior. Just as a person's wealth affects his choice of a house, the clothes he wears, the people he associates with, the food he eats, and may determine the college to which he sends his son or daughter, so it also influences his use of alcoholic beverages. . . . Among those students whose family income is $10,000 or more, 86 per cent of the men and 79 per cent of the women drink. The incidence of use varies directly with income down to 66 per cent of the men and 30 per cent of the women for those with family incomes below $2,500.[2]

1. Robert Straus and Selden D. Bacon, *Drinking in College.* New Haven, Yale University Press, 1953.
2. *Ibid.*, p. 49.

Religious affiliation was another factor which apparently influenced drinking.

TABLE 2.—*Incidence of Drinking, by Religious Affiliation*

	Men, %	Women, %
Jewish	94	94
Catholic	90	78
Protestant	77	60
Mormon	54	23

The Jews have no sanctions against moderate drinking. The Catholic church, while encouraging abstinence for young people, particularly by a pledge at confirmation, does not prohibit drinking among adults. Protestant denominations are divided on the issue, some opposing vigorously any association with drinking, others being less stringent.

The incidence of drinking increases with each college year, which presumably reflects progression to adult status and privileges. However, four out of five of the men and two-thirds of the women who had ever used alcoholic beverages had their first drink before coming to college. College students constitute a selected population and the data derived from this study are not applicable to the adult population or even to the college population in general. They do provide the first comprehensive picture of drinking practices and attitudes in a large sample of young people 17 to 23 years of age, particularly the influence of social, economic, and religious factors in the total situation.

To Drink or Not to Drink

by *Robert Straus*
and *Selden D. Bacon* *

This chapter surveys the phenomena of drinking from the viewpoint of the individual whose behavior was being studied. As he or she remembered and interpreted the memory, what messages were received bearing upon the drinking of alcoholic beverages? Who gave advice, command, or suggestion? Were the messages consistent or inconsistent? Parents, teachers, ministers, athletic coaches, physicians, friends, and college authorities are the major sources considered. In addition to the opinions, warnings, or suggestions received from others, there is the matter of the individual's own explanation of why he behaves as he does.

The way information, advice, or orders are received and personal opinion is formulated may differ significantly according to the age of the individual.

* From *Drinking in College*, (New Haven, Yale University Press, 1953), Chapter 5.

Certain young people in the age group 17 to 23 are faced with many difficult problems and decisions. This is the time when the strength and extent of ties of dependence on the parental family are reduced and responsibilities of independent living and independent thinking are increasingly assumed. It is the crucial period of transition from adolescence into adulthood as it is conceived in our society. One of the many questions which young people face during this period is whether or not to drink alcoholic beverages.

For many, this is by no means an easy matter to decide. While there are specific drinking customs in some cultural groups in America which form an integral part of various social functions, the use of alcoholic beverages is also associated with many abuses and has created numerous problems for our society. So young people are faced with conflicting pressures, sanctions, and even conflicting motivations with respect to drinking.

Some of them may have grown up in homes where they have watched their parents drink but have themselves been forbidden to do so. Explanations have often been inconsistent and inadequate in the face of parental example. Others, with parental example and even parental approval for drinking, may have met with strong conflicting advice from church or school. Still others may have grown up in homes where abstinence is both practiced and urged but later find themselves associated with groups where drinking is expected and where the abstainer is subjected to ridicule or ostracism or at least made to feel different and uncomfortable.

Students in the survey were asked whether they had ever received "specific advice concerning the use of alcoholic beverages." More than 90 per cent reported yes (men, 91 per cent; women, 92 per cent). Furthermore, nearly half indicated that this advice had been designed to make them abstainers (men, 47 per cent; women, 45 per cent). Less than a fourth of the students who were Jewish or Catholic by religion reported having received specific advice to abstain, as compared with about half the Protestants and more than three-fourths of the Mormons.

At first glance there seems to be no doubt that advice to abstain is associated with effective negative sanctions as far as drinking is concerned. Of the men who had received such advice, 30 per cent were abstainers as compared with only 18 per cent of those who had not been so advised (for women, 56 per cent and 35 per cent respectively).

However, for those advised to abstain, rather startling differences were found in the incidence of drinking according to the source of the advice. As shown in Table 1, where it came from family members, only 60 per cent of the men drank, as compared with 82 per cent of those who reported that they had never been advised to abstain. But of those whose advice came from the church (but not from parents) 84 per cent were users; and of those advised to abstain by schoolteachers (but not by parents or church) 90 per cent drank. So it appears that while sanctions against drinking are definitely effective (as compared with no negative sanctions) when they come from parents, advice not to drink which originates with the church or school may be actually less effective than no advice.

Among women somewhat similar findings occur. Only a third of those whose families advised abstention were drinkers, as compared with two-thirds of those receiving no such advice. However, half the women advised against drinking by the church (and not by parents) were drinkers, as were 77 per cent of those advised by school (and not church or family). As with

TABLE 1.—*Incidence of Drinking, by Source of Specific Advice to Abstain (in Per Cent)*

Source of Advice to Abstain	Men, %	Women, %
From parents	60	33
From church (not parents)	84	50
From teachers (not parents or church)	90	77
No advice to abstain	82	65

the men, negative sanctions originating in the family are associated with an impressively high incidence of abstinence. Church sanctions appear more effective than no advice, while sanctions coming from the school are actually associated with a greater incidence of drinking than no advice at all. A comparison of the four religious groups by incidence of drinking in relation to advice from the church to abstain shows no difference for Protestants, Jews, Mormons, and Catholics.

Reasons for Abstaining

While sanctions against drinking which originated in the church or with religious leaders do not appear to be directly associated with abstention by college youth, religious sanctions nevertheless appear to play a major role in the decision to abstain. All nondrinkers (including former drinkers) were provided with a check list of possible reasons for abstaining and asked to check a most important and a second most important reason. Factors of religion ("contrary to religious training," "immoral," or "pledged not to drink") were listed as most important by 34 per cent of the male abstainers and as second most important by an additional 18 per cent; as most important by 37 per cent of the female abstainers and as second most important by an additional 20 per cent. Thus, of the students who abstain, over half list factors of religion as major reasons for not drinking. In contrast just a third of the students listed disapproval by parents or friends as reasons for abstaining. These findings are not consistent with the relationship between incidence of drinking and the source of advice to abstain.

For purpose of comparison, reasons for abstaining have been ranked by a score which assigns a double value for listings as "most important" and a single value for listings as "second most important" reason. The large majority of these reasons are seen in Table 2 to fall into three groups: (*1*) dislike for the taste or ill effects of alcohol or a feeling that it is detrimental to health; (2) religious training, morality, or a pledge not to drink; (3) disapproval of family or friends. The concept of personal problem drinking does not assume great importance for young people who abstain. Very few abstain because they have lost control of their drinking in the past or because they cannot afford to drink. While a majority of the abstainers report that their close friends also abstain, practically none list that fact as a reason for doing so themselves. It is obvious that students' perceptions of their reasons for abstaining are not always consistent with certain measurable sanctions.

Comparatively few report that they abstain because of participation in sports. College athletes report a relatively high incidence of drinking when compared with students who do not take part in sports. On the other hand,

TABLE 2.—*Value Rating of Reasons for Abstaining, Based on Most Important and Second Most Important Reasons*

Reasons for Abstaining	Men, %	Women, %
Don't like taste, makes ill, or detrimental to general health	35	35
Contrary to religious training, immoral, or pledged not to drink	27	32
Parents or friends disapprove	12	16
Bad experience of someone else	7	4
Can't afford it	4	1
Interferes with participation in sports	4	1
Friends never use	1	2
Have lost control of drinking in the past	1	0
Other	9	9
Total	*100*	*100*

participation in sports was the major reason cited by those students who report that they have at some time or other "gone on the wagon." Of those who did report going on the wagon (males only) and attributed this to some outside pressure, 47 per cent listed participation in sports, 14 per cent credited advice from parents, 15 per cent the advice of a steady date, 9 per cent the advice of a religious leader, 6 per cent the advice of a doctor, 5 per cent the advice of other friends, 4 per cent cited school or college rules.

When reasons for abstaining are compared for students at different types of colleges, the only noteworthy difference which appears is that reasons of a religious and moral nature play a more prominent role for both men and women students from religious "dry" colleges than from other types of schools.

Comparisons according to religious affiliation reveal several notable differences. Reasons of religion or morality receive more than a 50 per cent value rating from Mormons, as compared with about a 25 per cent rating for Protestants, 15 per cent for Catholics, and zero for the few Jewish abstainers. For Jewish students nearly all reasons cited are those of taste, ill effect, and health. The "bad experience of someone else," which was rarely noted as important by Jewish, Mormon, or Protestant students, received ratings of 15 and 12 per cent respectively from Catholic men and women.

No significant differences in reasons for abstention were found when abstainers were compared according to family income, although oddly enough "can't afford it" was given most frequently by students in the highest ($10,000 or more) family income brackets.

College Policy and Student Drinking

College students are not alone in facing difficult decisions about their drinking behavior. The problem has long bothered college administrators and continues to haunt them. The many letters of inquiry that have come from college officials in the course of preparing this study bear impressive witness to the deep concern and uncertainty of those responsible for molding college policy.

While giving questionnaires to students, members of the survey staff also discussed college policy toward student drinking with officials of most of the 27 colleges which participated in the study. They found no instance of a clear-cut policy with which deans and other administrative personnel were generally satisfied. Where there were stringent regulations forbidding drinking by students, administrators were aware of deep resentment and rather violent reaction on the part of some students. Where liberal policies were followed, administrators were sensitive to criticism from town residents and parents whenever incidents involving drinking by students occurred. As a result some college administrations have avoided formalizing any policy and have fitted regulations and official statements to the particular circumstances.

A measure of the uncertainty and vacillation in this area can be found in the students' own perception of the policy of their particular college. The question was asked: "In your opinion, what is the attitude of your college officials toward drinking on the part of students?" Space was provided for the students to formulate their own reply. Answers were classified, first independently and then jointly, by two members of the survey staff. Responses were grouped under "unqualified disapproval," "liberality or indifference," and several categories of conditional approval. Just over half of all the students (both men and women) felt that their college's attitude toward student drinking was one of unqualified disapproval, while 21 per cent of the men and 15 per cent of the women felt that college officials were liberal or indifferent to drinking. A complete classification appears in Table 3.

These responses represent the students' perception of an attitude or policy. Like all reports on attitude perception they are subjective interpretations of manifest actions. Although not specifically identified as sanctions, these perceptions define the college sanctions of drinking in the most meaningful way possible, not necessarily as they are perceived by those from whom they derive but as they are perceived by those toward whom they are directed. Let us now relate this perception to student drinking behavior.

TABLE 3.—*Students' Ratings of Official College Attitude toward Student Drinking*

	STUDENTS' RATINGS	
Classifications of College Attitude	Men, %	Women, %
Unqualified disapproval	52	54
Conditional (disapproval but tolerance)	7	10
Conditional (on amount and frequency)	16	16
Conditional (on age, place, behavior)	4	5
Liberality or indifference	21	15
Total	*100*	*100*

First it is of interest to consider to what extent individual colleges have clear-cut attitudes, as perceived by their own students, toward drinking. That is, to what extent is there student agreement on the policy of their own school? Of the 27 colleges surveyed, there were five at which at least 75 per cent of the students (men and women) perceived the college attitude as one of unconditional disapproval. At three the vast majority of students perceived either a liberal-indifferent or a conditional attitude (two of these were colleges for men only, the other for women only). At the other 19 schools substantial numbers of students assigned the college attitude to each of the extremes, indicating no general agreement as to the official attitude.

The students' perception of college policy is not likely to be objective. A college having what an objective observer would term a middle-of-the-road attitude might seem liberal to some abstainers because it tolerates drinking at all, yet disapproving to some heavy drinkers because it opposes heavy drinking. In a majority of the schools where the attitude was not clearly defined, it was found that abstainers were more likely to perceive a liberal attitude while students who were frequent users were more likely to perceive an attitude of disapproval.

It was also found that perception of an extreme attitude on the part of the college (either unqualified disapproval or liberality) was correlated with extreme personal views about drinking. Of the male students who in other questions expressed themselves either as positively disapproving or positively approving of drinking by others, 89 per cent indicated a perception of extreme views on the part of college officials. On the other hand only 67 per cent of those whose personal attitudes were conditional saw the college position as extreme.

To examine the relationship between perception of the college attitude toward drinking and actual student drinking behavior, colleges were ranked according to a liberality score determined by taking the percentage of student responses in each school which indicated a conditional attitude on the part of the college plus twice the percentage of responses which indicated liberality or indifference. When liberality scores are correlated with the per cent of users at each school it becomes clear that the more liberal the college attitude as perceived by the students, the more users in the college population.

In a similar manner, the liberality score was correlated with the percentage of the users in each school who had ever reached the level of intoxication defined as "tight." Findings here indicated no significant correlation, positive or negative. Thus although college sanctions against drinking seem to be definitely associated with a lower incidence of drinkers at a particular school, they have no effect on the extent of drinking among users as measured by the criterion of having been tight. There is some suggestion, illustrated by a few selected schools, that, among male students, drinkers at "dry" schools are more apt to have been tight than those at schools with liberal sanctions.

A definite relationship appeared between the incidence of drinking or abstaining at particular schools and the extent to which male students who drink have experienced intoxication. The five schools having the lowest percentage of users ranked in the highest ten by percentage of users who have been tight. Exactly the same relationship was found at the next level of intoxication defined as drunk. There is certainly a suggestion here that male students who drink in violation of generally accepted practice are apt to go further in their drinking than students for whom the use of alcoholic beverages is more or less accepted behavior. This reaction is illustrated by the comment of a student in a southern "dry" college: "When you go to the trouble of driving 50 miles to drink, you don't have just two drinks."

In summary, it can be noted that the uncertainty and indecisiveness expressed by many college officials in personal conversations with members of the survey staff are reflected in the students' perception of college drinking attitudes and sanctions. While college sanctions may be correlated with the number of students who drink, they appear to have no effect on the extent of drinking among drinkers in any particular college.

Students' Explanations for Their Drinking

Having examined the various pressures and sanctions which students perceive being exerted to keep them from drinking, and having reviewed the reasons for abstaining given by the nondrinkers, let us consider the explanations of the users for their drinking.

A check list of 13 reasons for drinking (Table 4) was provided. Students were asked to indicate for each of the items listed whether it was of considerable importance, some importance, or no importance in his or her own use of alcoholic beverages. . . .

TABLE 4.—*Perception of Drinking Motivations: Relative Importance Attached to 13 Selected Reasons for Drinking (in Per Cent of Drinkers)*

Reason for Drinking	DEGREE OF IMPORTANCE FOR MEN				
	Considerable	Some	(Total)	None	Total
Because of enjoyment of taste	29	43	(72)	28	100
To comply with custom	13	51	(64)	36	100
To be gay	16	46	(62)	38	100
To relieve fatigue or tension	13	41	(54)	46	100
To get high	12	35	(47)	53	100
To get along better on dates	4	30	(34)	66	100
As an aid in forgetting disappointments	5	21	(26)	74	100
In order not to be shy	4	21	(25)	75	100
To relieve illness or physical discomfort	3	22	(25)	75	100
For a sense of well-being	1	19	(20)	80	100
To get drunk	7	9	(16)	84	100
As an aid in meeting crises	1	8	(9)	91	100
To facilitate study	1	2	(3)	97	100

Reason for Drinking	DEGREE OF IMPORTANCE FOR WOMEN				
	Considerable	Some	(Total)	None	Total
Because of enjoyment of taste	22	47	(69)	31	100
To comply with custom	15	50	(65)	35	100
To be gay	8	44	(52)	48	100
To relieve fatigue or tension	7	36	(43)	57	100
To get high	3	14	(17)	83	100
To get along better on dates	4	35	(39)	61	100
As an aid in forgetting disappointments	2	10	(12)	88	100
In order not to be shy	3	15	(18)	82	100
To relieve illness or physical discomfort	6	26	(32)	68	100
For a sense of well-being	2	13	(15)	85	100
To get drunk	*	1	(1)	99	100
As an aid in meeting crises	1	5	(6)	94	100
To facilitate study	*	1	(1)	99	100

* Less than 0.5 per cent.

It is not easy to explain why the reason "because of enjoyment of taste" leads the list of motivations for drinking as reported by both male and female students. Without imposing personal value judgments it can be said that we did not consider that most beverages containing alcohol were noted for a pleasing taste by a majority of drinkers. Different types of beverages have quite different tastes. If taste is such an important reason for drinking it might be expected that the ratings of taste would vary according to the particular types of beverage reported by the students as well as according to the type of beverage most frequently used. It was found that ratings of the importance of taste as a reason for drinking showed no significant differences whether the type of beverage preferred or most frequently used was beer, wine, or distilled spirits.

Remembering that these motivation ratings represent merely the students' perceptions of the reasons why they drink, we offer as a possible explanation of the relative importance assigned to factors of taste the theory of the "rational man." The rational man seeks a sensible, logical explanation for all behavior and phenomena. The most logical explanations for ingesting foods and liquids are first that they are nutritious and beneficial to us and second that they have a pleasing taste. There being few arguments which hold alcoholic beverages nutritious or beneficial to the body, the factor of taste is the logical reason left for the rational man to use in explaining his drinking.

In a sense, all the reasons cited as of importance in drinking may reflect to some extent a groping for rational explanations. However, the reasons other than taste have a greater basis of reality in known physiological or social functional value.

It is apparent in Table 4 that reasons having primarily a social connotation, e.g., "to comply with custom," "to be gay," "to get along better on dates," are generally considered of greater importance than those suggesting primarily a psychological motivation, e.g. "as an aid in meeting crises," "to get drunk," "for a sense of well-being," and "in order not to be shy."

There is a high degree of agreement between men and women in the relative importance which they assign to each reason for drinking. In only two instances did the ratio of women ascribing importance to an item exceed that of men by even as much as 5 per cent. Women to a greater extent than men think that they drink in order to get along better on dates and in order to relieve illness or physical discomfort. Both of these items deserve further comment.

At most of the colleges which participated in the survey, members of the survey staff were available for discussions with the students following the questions; some dealing with physical or psychological reactions to alcohol; some with the questionnaire itself; some with problems of alcoholism, usually in reference to a particular alcoholic known to them; and some with personal confusion regarding their own drinking in the face of conflicting social pressures. College girls occasionally brought up the problem of feeling that they have to drink in order to be acceptable to their male dates. It is in this connection that we believe many of the girls have attached importance to the item "get along better on dates." That is, they drink because they feel it is expected of them in mixed company among certain social groups. They fear that if they don't drink they will not be invited again. This type of explanation is quite different from that referring to the relief from personal anxiety which alcohol may afford in boy-girl situations.

There is no doubt that alcohol, since it is a mild anesthetic, can provide genuine if temporary relief for certain types of physical discomfort. Its efficacy in physical illness is a matter on which physicians do not agree. Certainly it is prescribed in a medicinal sense less frequently today than formerly. To a considerable degree the use of alcoholic beverages for medicinal purposes is associated with survivalistic folk beliefs, and continues to be prescribed as a home remedy rather than by doctors' orders. There is one medicinal use for alcohol which is restricted to women—in connection with menstruation. Two questions on this use were included in questionnaire forms for women. Although about a third of the girls failed to answer one or both of these questions, approximately 7 per cent of those who did reply reported using alcohol in connection with menstrual pain. In response to the other question 7 per cent reported that alcohol has a greater appeal for them either just before, during, or just after the menstrual period than at other times. The girls who used alcohol for relief from menstrual pain were not necessarily the same ones who reported a heightening of alcohol appeal in connection with menstruation. This association of alcohol use with the menstrual cycle is sufficient to account for the sex difference in designating relief of illness or physical discomfort as a motivation for drinking.

The greatest discrepancy between the sexes was in items associated with the effect from drinking, such as "to get high," which was noted as of importance by 47 per cent of the men and only 17 per cent of the women, and "to get drunk," which was important for 16 per cent of the men and for only 1 per cent of the women. Only 12 per cent of the women, as compared with 26 per cent of the men, noted drinking "as an aid in forgetting disappointments."

A few interesting differences in perception of drinking motivations were noted among the religious groups. Jewish men and women ran ahead of all other religious groups in attaching importance to drinking to comply with custom. This was of some or considerable importance for more than 80 per cent of the Jewish students, as compared with about 60 per cent of the Protestants, Catholics, and Mormons. Catholic men ran considerably ahead of those of other faiths in ascribing importance to taste, as did Catholic women in the case of "relief of illness or physical discomfort." Mormon men, who when they drink do so mostly in the face of strong negative sanctions, attached greater importance than other men to drinking "to be gay," "as an aid in forgetting disappointments," "to get high," and "to get drunk." Mormon women put particular emphasis on "to be gay" and "in order not to be shy."

No significant differences in perception of drinking motivations were found among men or women of different family income levels.

Summary

Two approaches to a more effective understanding of drinking behavior have now been presented. The first indicated patterns of drinking or abstinence according to group membership or according to such characteristics as income of parents. The second concerned ideas or advice or commands given the individual by those in particular roles, and the individual's own explanation for his drinking or abstinence. Although the two approaches are quite distinct, both are essential for understanding the facts of drinking behavior. They are also interrelated: the types of advice received and of individual explanation both vary in accord with the category or group. The Jewish group, for example, showed few instances of commands to abstain and a greater tendency than those of other faiths to explain one's own drinking behavior on the basis of group custom.

The discrepancy between actual behavior and the message or norm presented by individuals or organizations attempting to initiate, maintain, or change behavior is of significance for teachers, ministers, parents, legislators, or others concerned with drinking or any other behavior. Often enough, perception of the discrepancy leads merely to condemnation of those not following the prescription, or to more intensive and extensive repetitions of command or advice. The two methods of approach just indicated permit of more effective response. They suggest that persons in different sociological categories present different degrees of susceptibility to techniques for changing, modifying, initiating, or blocking behavior. It is plain that advice for complete abstinence given uniformly to children of poor and wealthy parents, to southern Negroes and to Jews, to those of Mediterranean and English backgrounds, is going to be received variously and to be effective in extremely different degrees.

It is also clear that the agency or source of opinion or command is an important factor. A command issued by a father to his son may prove effective, whereas issued by a clergyman to the same boy it may have little effect. Social scientists are interested in developing generalizations about behavior, about the consistency or variability of various forms of behavior, and about the relative strength of different types of sanctioning agency for maintaining or changing behavior in a variety of situations by various techniques. The educator, minister, or parent wishes to make practical use of specific facts in particular situations. As patterns of behavior, rules, and opinions emerge from the data on student drinking, certain suggestions will be posed and more cogent questions will be asked aimed at providing new insights on both a theoretical and a practical level.

17. THE MOTIVATIONAL PATTERN

by John W. Riley, Jr.,
Charles F. Marden,
and Marcia Lifshitz ＊

The question of motivation is clearly one of the most important theoretical and practical problems in the study of drinking behavior. Perhaps its most crucial aspect is to determine whether the motivation of those who become alcoholics differs from the so-called "normal" drinkers. There seems to be little doubt that the drinking motivation of the true alcoholic, when he has reached that stage, is in the nature of an irresistible compulsion. In fact, it may be said that the compulsive desire to drink has become the main motivation in his life. It is generally agreed, however, that the stage of true alcoholism is preceded by many years of drinking. Are the motivations of the prealcoholic different in the first place? If so, what are the potentially dangerous motivations? If not, do the motivations change during the course of the drinking history from those which are not potentially dangerous to those which are? Or do individual differences in physiological reaction to alcohol, regardless of motivation, predispose some to follow a nondisorganizing path in their drinking, while others became alcoholics?

As a result of a nation-wide survey of public attitudes and knowledge concerning the drinking of alcoholic beverages, certain data were acquired which constitute material pertinent to this problem. The purpose of the present communication is to present this material and to indicate its implications with reference to the larger basic problem stated above. The data are the verbalized responses of consumers of alcoholic beverages to the question, "What would you say is your main reason for drinking?" It is recognized at the outset that such data have limitations. Verbal responses to questions of motivation may be rationalizations—due either to the desire of the respondent to provide a reply which is morally approved or to the well-known fact that often we honestly do not know why we do certain things. On the other hand, the data here presented have the virtue of being based upon a cross-section sample of the entire American public, sufficiently large to permit comparison breakdowns of the responses within significant categories of the population.

A survey of this sort, however, obviously does not permit comparison of alcoholics with nonalcoholics. The direct value of the data from the

＊ From "The Motivational Pattern of Drinking," *Quarterly Journal of Studies on Alcohol, 9* (1948), 353–62.

viewpoint of the central problem stated at the outset is, consequently, limited. Why Americans drink and the variations in motivation among different population groupings based on age, sex, and frequency of drinking can only hint at a relationship between motivation and tendencies toward alcoholism. Since, however, there is increasing emphasis on drinking histories as a continuum, any and all further material on the motivations of drinking are grist to the mill. Insofar as our results tend to confirm researches into the motivations of drinking by other approaches and techniques, they contribute to scientific agreement. Insofar as they differ, they challenge resolution of the differences by the application of more exacting methods.

Of the entire sample (2,677), 65 per cent (1,744) indicated that they sometimes drank alcoholic beverages. The reasons they gave for drinking are presented in terms of main classifications in Table 1. The replies pointed to a major division into reasons which are called social, where the respondents attribute their drinking mainly to the stimulus of the social situations in which their drinking takes place; and to reasons called individual, where the respondents attribute the main reason to the pleasurable effects or consequences of their drinking. The total replies divide approximately equally into these main divisions. The very fact that they fell easily into this twofold division suggests the basic significance of these categories of motivation.

TABLE 1.—*Reported Reasons for Drinking*

	Per Cent of Drinkers
Social reasons	43
Sociability	38
To keep husband company	2
On festive occasions	2
Brought up with it	2
As business courtesy	1
Subtotal	*45* *
Individual reasons	41
Makes me feel good	16
I like it	12
Quenches thirst	6
Stimulates appetite	4
Other health reasons	4
Subtotal	*42* *
Both social and individual reasons	6
Other reasons	2
No reason given	8
Total	*100*

* These apparent discrepancies are due to the fact that more than one answer was possible within the major categories.

Much more frequently than any other single reason, people say they drink "to be sociable." While some few respondents reserve drinking for festive occasions such as weddings and christenings, and others consider drinking a necessary adjunct in business contacts, the bulk of social reasons for drinking were stated in general terms—"just to be sociable," or "because all our friends drink," or "to be a good sport."

Within this general grouping, however, were included persons who drink because otherwise the social situation threatens mild ostracism, and others who are apparently merely following the dictates of fashion. While these distinctions are not clear-cut enough to be handled statistically, they suggest possible clues for approaches to the larger question. The following are some of the answers of those who seem most influenced by the fear of group pressures:

A young New Yorker, recently discharged from the armed forces: "Liquor is always sold in the places I frequent. You can't have a soda in a night club. It's just not done." A Pennsylvania housewife: "People think you're dead if you don't drink." A well-to-do professional woman, wife of an architect, New York City: "I hate to make a fuss about refusing. I don't like to be a poor sport." A poor, elderly, west-coast farmer: "Just to be a good fellow. You make people mad if you don't."

The following are typical replies of those for whom the normative pressure of the group, be it custom or fashion, describes the main reasons given:

The wife of a Kansas City service-station attendant: "Sometimes when we have company I drink it to be sociable." A young rural Wisconsin schoolteacher: "I guess just to be sociable. I don't care for it at all. I just choke it down." A linesman for the telephone company in a southern town: "All of our friends drink, so we drink too." A young nurse: "I go to the dance hall and everybody else is drinking, so I just drink too."

Students of family life will be interested in the special class of answers which are headed "keep husband company." While the percentage of such replies is small, it seems significant that, of all of the various and special reasons which are given for drinking, as many as 2 per cent of the drinkers —which of course means a much larger percentage of wives—offered this as a main reason for their drinking. This may well reflect the tendency for a common sharing of recreational interests in the emerging companionship marriage and indicates an active effort of wives in this direction.

Half of the drinkers, however, report that they drink for other than social reasons, such as to feel better, to quench thirst, to stimulate appetite or digestion, or to keep in good health. Some simply say they like to drink. While most of the categories under this second major classification are sufficiently specific to be self-explanatory, the general heading "makes me feel good," ascribed to one drinker out of every six, covers a variety of responses. Typical answers range from drinking for relaxation or for euphoric effect to drinking as an escape from worries, responsibilities, or frustration:

A domestic employee in an Oklahoma town: "A bottle of beer makes me feel rested after a hard day's work. Then I can get up and clean my house." A building contractor in Charlotte, N.C.: "When I drink I feel important." A young man, unemployed, in Peoria, Ill.: "I drink because of disappointments in life. I don't want to face reality." A Georgia farmer: "Drinking takes me right on up. Then I just forget this world." A salesman of electrical appliances in New York City: "Why do I drink? To keep alive."

Of still greater significance to the basic problem of why people drink is the comparison of the relative weights of social and individual reasons when various population groupings are examined. In interpreting the following comparisons it should be recalled that the population as a whole—that is, adults 21 years of age or older—was divided approximately equally between these two main reasons.

TABLE 2.—*Reported Reasons for Drinking, by Sex*

	Males, %	Females, %
Social reasons	33	55
Individual reasons	49	31
Both	7	6
Other reasons	2	1
No reason given	9	7

Women give social reasons far more frequently than men, as Table 2 shows. Similarly, comparisons based on age (Table 3) show the individual reasons becoming consistently more frequent with each successive age group, while the younger the respondents the more common is the emphasis on social reasons. The newest additions to the drinking population—women and young people—tend to be social drinkers.

TABLE 3.—*Reported Reasons for Drinking, by Age* *

	21–25	26–35	36–45	46–55	56+
	(PER CENT IN EACH AGE CLASS)				
Social reasons	51	46	44	39	38
Individual reasons	36	37	40	43	47
Both	3	7	8	6	5
Other reasons	2	1	1	3	1
No reason given	8	9	7	9	9

* This table omits six respondents whose age was not ascertained.

Since the differences in motivation between the sexes were so striking, and particularly in view of a recent finding that in recent years there has been a much "greater proportional increase in the number of drinkers among women than among men," the data of Table 3 were further refined.

When sex is held constant within each age group, it becomes readily apparent that the consistent relationship between age and motivation for drinking is largely contributed by women, although even among men there is a slight tendency to assign "individual" reasons for drinking with increasing age. Table 4 thus shows the distribution of men and women of various age groups who drink for "individual" reasons. Among men, almost as many in the youngest group drink for physical effect as in the oldest group. On the other hand, only 25 per cent of the youngest women drinkers, but as many as 41 per cent of the oldest, give individual reasons for drinking. Obviously, then, if drinking customs are changing more rapidly among women than among men, this occurs mainly through the influence of social pressures, particularly among the women. Sixty-one per cent of the women drinkers in the 21–25 age group say they drink only for social reasons.

TABLE 4.—*Individual Reasons for Drinking, by Age and Sex*

Age Class	Males, %	Females, %
21–25	45	25
26–35	47	28
36–45	50	30
46–55	49	33
Over 55	50	41

Another profile of the data, leading to a similar general interpretation, is noted when the reasons given for drinking are related to frequency of drinking. Table 5 shows clearly that the greater the frequency of drinking, the greater is the proportion of individual as distinct from social reasons for drinking. The trends are not only consistent but the range of variability is wide: 67 per cent of those who claim to drink very occasionally give social reasons for their drinking, whereas only 20 per cent of the daily drinkers claim to be socially motivated.

The relationship between frequency of drinking and motivation was examined separately for men and for women in order to determine more accurately the source of the sharp differences noted in Table 5.

TABLE 5.—*Reasons Reported for Drinking Compared with Frequency of Drinking* *

	Daily Drinker	3–5 Times a Week	1–2 Times a Week	2–3 Times a Month	Once a Month	Less than Once a Month
		(PER CENT IN EACH CATEGORY OF FREQUENCY)				
Social reasons	20	26	36	50	52	67
Individual reasons	59	55	46	36	32	23
Both	8	8	9	4	6	3
Other reasons	3	—	1	1	3	2
No reason given	10	11	8	9	7	5

* This table omits 13 respondents whose frequency of drinking was not ascertained.

Apparently, as Table 6 shows, among both men and women, the more frequently one drinks the greater is the tendency to drink for individual reasons or physical effect rather than for sociability. Again, however, consistent with the observation that recent changes in drinking customs are more strongly influencing women, the relationship between frequency of drinking and motivation is more pronounced among female respondents than among males.

TABLE 6.—*Reasons Reported for Drinking Compared with Frequency of Drinking, by Sex* *

	Daily Drinker	3–5 Times a Week	1–2 Times a Week	2–3 Times a Month	Once a Month	Less than Once a Month
			(PER CENT IN EACH CATEGORY OF FREQUENCY)			
Males						
Social reasons	21	25	31	39	43	54
Individ. reasons	56	56	51	46	41	35
Both	8	7	10	5	4	2
Other reasons	3	1	1	1	3	2
No reason	12	11	7	9	9	7
Females						
Social reasons	18	27	45	60	61	73
Individ. reasons	70	51	38	27	23	18
Both	6	10	7	4	9	3
Other reasons	0	0	0	0	3	2
No reason	6	12	10	9	4	4

* This table omits 13 respondents whose frequency of drinking was not ascertained. Note also the small bases for some of these percentages. They are presented for comparative purposes only. Individual figures should be interpreted cautiously.

Finally, although sociability is fully as important a reason for drinking as is physical effect, in terms of proportional distribution of responses by the population, nevertheless the tendency for more seasoned drinkers to assign individual reasons for drinking suggests a difference in the strengths of the two motivational patterns. To test this hypothesis, the reasons people gave for drinking in legally dry areas were compared with those expressed in the rest of the country (the wet areas). The results (Table 7) clearly support the hypothesis. Where alcoholic beverages are hard to get, a much larger proportion of people drink for individual than for social reasons. Conversely, where alcoholic beverages are easily available, sociability is the more frequently reported reason for drinking. Even in dry areas, however, 29 per cent of the drinkers are willing to go to the trouble to secure liquor, although they drink just to be sociable.

Despite the theoretical limitations of these data as indices of "true" motivation, the impression grows, after qualitative and internal consistency analysis, that the respondents, on the whole, stated quite frankly and without reservation their main reason for drinking, within the limits of conscious awareness. Furthermore, the statistical stability of the data, particularly in comparisons among various population segments, as noted above, is in itself impressive evidence of the meaningfulness of individual responses at the level of everyday articulation.

TABLE 7.—*Reported Reasons for Drinking in Wet and Dry Areas*

	Wet, % N = 1,531	Dry, % N = 213
Social reasons	46	29
Individual reasons	39	48
Both	6	6
Other reasons	1	4
No reason given	8	13

Implications and Significance of the Findings

Within this framework of interpretation the data support three hypotheses related to motivation for drinking. In the first place, they suggest the feasibility of applying standard analytical procedures to this aspect of the problem of consumption of alcoholic beverages. While further research is obviously needed, particularly in the direction of deeper probing into the mechanisms of motivation, the conceptual value of this twofold classification as a starting point is clearly indicated. Secondly, the data lend powerful support to the hypothesis that drinking is as directly motivated by the influence of social pressures as it is by acquired inner drives. (The modifying word "directly" has been used because there can be little argument that all drinking is affected indirectly by social factors.) Of all the people who state that they sometimes drink, more than two out of five assign main motivation to group pressure. Thirdly, the relative weight of external social pressures versus inner acquired drives varied widely between different classes of drinkers. Direct social pressure is much more influential in motivating the drinking of women compared with men, the young compared with the old, and the occasional or infrequent compared with regular drinkers. On the other hand, seasoned and regular drinkers tend to state that their reasons for drinking lie more within themselves than in the direct pressures from the group situation.

While neither the data themselves nor the hypotheses they support relate directly to the problem of the compulsive drinker, they do, however, pertain to the question of prevention. If it be assumed that drinking in general cannot be eliminated from our society, the search becomes one for effective controls directed at the clearly demonstrable problem aspects of drinking—drunkenness and alcoholism. Since the above findings document in statistical terms the proposition that social pressures play a large part in motivating drinking, they also by indirection indicate that social pressure can be brought to bear to limit drinking. But what type of social pressure is here involved? It is probably not custom—except in the case of those who descend from particular ethnic backgrounds. It is something too short-lived for that. It is certainly not institutional pressure, since with few exceptions the basic institutions of our times denounce drinking, however much the individual members may not practice what the mores admonish. It is rather the kind of transitory social pressure which characterizes so much of the personal behavior of people in a rapidly changing social order when the old mores are outmoded and new mores, or authoritatively sanctioned rules of behavior, have not replaced them. From this point of view the effective control of the problem aspects of drinking requires the establishment of new authoritative group sanctions, founded on science and supported by the basic institutions. In the meantime anything which can be done to alter the one-way influence on drinking patterns of these temporary normative pressures will point in the same direction.

The possibility of introducing such changes may be illustrated by the admonition in a pamphlet issued by the National Committee for Education on Alcoholism, a suggestion perhaps not so trivial as it may at first sound: "Never insist on anyone taking a drink. Following this simple rule of etiquette may have greater consequences than you know. If all hosts and hostesses heeded it, the problem of alcoholism might be greatly reduced."

The effect of instituting such a small change in fashion, for example, as the serving of both alcoholic and nonalcoholic beverages at gatherings, and in such a manner that either choice seems appropriate, might be, in the long run, far reaching. Certainly for the "dry" alcoholic (the alcoholic who has regained his sobriety) it would have immediate significance, for he knows, as his host and friends frequently do not, that he must not take one drink. In addition, there are those adults who do not like to drink, or have been ordered not to drink for physical reasons, but "choke it down just to be sociable." Finally, and probably of greatest significance, are the younger people who have not become regular consumers of alcoholic beverages or have not yet accepted the proposition that drinking always goes with sociability. Science has not discovered how to distinguish the potential alcoholic from those who may drink within controllable limits all their lives. Until it does, the trend toward the automatic association of drinking with sociability must take its place in the complex of factors contributing to the problem of alcoholism.

18. GROUP INFLUENCES

by John L. Haer *

Social norms and behavior concerning drinking, and attitudes toward alcoholic beverages, have long been subjects for argument and study. Re-cently, the interest of some research workers has shifted from the inebriate and his problems, and the physiological effects of alcohol, to study of the drinking patterns of "normal" drinkers. The lack of facts in this area has led several investigators to undertake surveys of large population segments in order to discover possible uniformities in behavior and attitudes regarding alcohol.

Questions concerning individual motivation and group influences in the establishment of drinking patterns have been approached by ascertain-ing the personal and social characteristics that distinguish types of drinkers or attitude holders. Thus, for example, differences in social class, nation-ality, and religious background, as well as differences in age, sex, and education, have been shown to be significantly related to variations in drinking patterns. These findings seem to suggest that drinking behavior, and influences on drinking behavior, are not the products of random choices by individuals but vary according to cleavages in the social norms peculiar to various population segments and social groups.

The present study seeks to throw additional light on the problem of motivation and group influence on drinking by determining (1) the manner in which the drinking patterns (i.e., frequency of drinking) of individuals are associated with those of certain family members and friends, and (2) the manner in which this association varies with selected personal and social characteristics (e.g., sex, age, education). Findings related to the correspondence of the drinking patterns of individuals and certain associates may provide hints as to the most relevant sources of influence on the normal drinker. And findings pertaining to the manner in which such associations vary by personal and social characteristics may suggest some of the factors underlying the drinking behavior of groups. The present study, then, seeks to detect an association or correspondence between the drinking patterns of certain individuals; from these findings conclusions may be drawn regarding influence and drinking norms which may form a basis for testable hypotheses in future research.

* From "Drinking Patterns and the Influence of Friends and Family," *Quarterly Journal of Studies on Alcohol*, 16 (1955), 178–85.

The Data and Method of Research

The data to be analyzed were gathered in a survey conducted by the Washington Public Opinion Laboratory of the State College of Washington, in May 1951. In this survey a sample of 478 adults in the state of Washington was interviewed. This sample was selected in a manner designed to represent all segments of the state's white population 21 years of age and older.

Information concerning drinking behavior was obtained by asking each individual in the sample to estimate how often he (or she) drank an alcoholic beverage. The informants also estimated how often their spouses, mother and father, and most friends, drank. Then, in order to ascertain

TABLE 1.—*Drinking Patterns of Sample, Friends, Spouse, Father, and Mother*

ENTIRE SAMPLE (*N* = 478) *

	3 or More Times a Week		Once a Month to 3 a Week		5 Times a Year or Less		Abstainers	
Most Friends	No.	%	No.	%	No.	%	No.	%
3 or more times a week	35	71.4	11	22.4	1	2.0	2	4.1
Once a month to 3 a week	20	12.7	128	81.0	4	2.5	6	3.8
5 times a year or less	5	6.0	32	38.1	41	48.8	96	7.1
Abstainers	8	4.9	34	20.7	26	15.9	96	58.5

Chi squared = 404.95; $P = .001$; $T = .94$

Spouse								
3 or more times a week	17	38.6	10	22.7	3	6.8	14	31.8
Once a month to 3 a week	17	11.9	78	54.5	16	11.2	32	22.4
5 times a year or less	5	6.6	12	15.8	40	52.6	19	25.0
Abstainers	5	3.2	15	9.7	18	11.7	116	75.3

Chi squared = 246; $P = .001$; $T = .76$

Father								
3 or more times a week	18	35.3	8	15.7	7	13.7	18	35.3
Once a month to 3 a week	20	12.9	56	36.1	17	11.0	62	40.0
5 times a year or less	9	11.4	12	15.2	20	25.3	38	48.1
Abstainers	11	6.5	13	7.7	13	7.7	131	78.0

Chi squared = 99.66; $P = .001$; $T = .47$

Mother								
3 or more times a week	5	10.0	5	10.0	6	12.0	34	68.0
Once a month to 3 a week	4	2.5	22	14.0	19	12.1	112	71.3
5 times a year or less	1	1.2			12	14.6	69	84.1
Abstainers	2	1.2	5	2.9	5	2.9	159	93.0

Chi squared = 52.89; $P = .001$; $T = .34$

* In the following tables, sample sizes do not equal 478. In one comparison, only married persons were included; in the others, information on drinking was lacking for one or both individuals being compared.

the extent to which the behavior of each subject corresponded with the estimated behavior of these other individuals, the findings on each were related and a chi-squared test of independence was applied. Where significant relationships were revealed, an index of the degree of relationship, a T coefficient, was obtained. On this basis it was possible to decide whether the drinking behavior of individuals was significantly associated with that of spouse, parents, and friends, and whose behavior was most closely associated with that of the individuals studied.

Results

Drinking Patterns of the Sample as a Whole. Table 1 shows the distribution in the relationship between the drinking pattern of the sample and spouse (unmarried subjects omitted in this comparison), father, mother, and friends. The probability values indicate that in each instance the association in drinking behavior is statistically significant, and it therefore may be assumed that such an association exists in the state's population. The index of degree of association, T, shows that the drinking patterns of subjects are most closely related to those of friends, then spouse, then father, and finally, mother.

The T values in Table 1, for the association between friends and spouse, compared to that of parents, bears out the widespread impression that drinking norms have changed greatly in the last few decades. The data strongly suggest that the behavior of contemporaries—friends and spouse —are much more potent in establishing drinking practices than the behavior of the previous generation.

TABLE 2.—*Statistical Values Derived from Analysis of the Relationships between Drinking Patterns of Males and Females and Those of Their Friends, Spouses, Fathers, and Mothers*

	Chi Squared	Probability Level	Degree of Relationship (T)
Males ($N = 233$)			
Friends	83.12	.001	.62
Spouse	86.86	.001	.66
Father	93.66	.01	.64
Mother	6.66	.001	.17
Females ($N = 245$)			
Friends	83.60	.001	.62
Spouse	154.80	.001	.85
Father	27.84	.001	.35
Mother	38.08	.001	.40

Drinking Patterns of Selected Groups

Sex. Table 2 shows the relationship between the drinking patterns of subjects divided according to sex and those of friends, spouse, and parents.

In order to conserve space, in this and the tables that follow only the values for chi squared, probability level, and T will be presented. In all cases the data from which these values were derived were arranged in the same pattern as in Table 1.

The four relationships studied concerning each sex were statistically significant. In the case of males the degree of relationship between their drinking patterns and those of friends, spouse, and father were about the same. However, the relationship between the behavior of male subjects and their mothers was slight.

The findings on female subjects seem to suggest a great dependence on the norms of spouse, somewhat less on friends, and much less on those of parents. This may imply that the husband plays the role of leader in establishing drinking norms for married couples, with friends next in importance. The differences in the degree of association between the drinking patterns of males and females and their parents may suggest also that males are most influenced by the father, and females by both parents to about the same degree.

Age. In Table 3 the same relationships are arrayed for subjects divided according to two age groups: 40 years and over, and under 40. In the group under 40 the degree of relationship between drinking patterns is largest for subject and spouse, and smaller for friends and parents. For subjects aged 40 and over the closest relationship is between friends, then

TABLE 3.—*Statistical Values Derived from Analysis of the Relationships between Drinking Patterns of Age Groups and Those of Their Friends, Spouses, Fathers, and Mothers*

	Chi Squared	Probability Level	Degree of Relationship (T)
Age under 40 ($N = 183$)			
Friends	28.48	.001	.40
Spouse	68.08	.001	.62
Father	26.25	.001	.39
Mother	26.55	.001	.39
Age 40 and over ($N = 295$)			
Friends	165.60	.001	.77
Spouse	83.30	.001	.58
Father	50.22	.001	.42
Mother	11.68	.01	.06

spouse, father, and mother. These findings for the two age groups appear to bear out the suggestion made above that drinking norms vary significantly in the generations. For in the younger group, drinking behavior accords with that of parents as much as friends; while in the older group the greater "distance" between generations seems reflected in the finding that contemporaries, especially friends, appear most like the sample in drinking patterns.

Education. Variations in the relationships between drinking patterns are shown for subjects divided according to educational attainment in Table 4. In the group having a year or more of college, drinking behavior conforms to a high degree with that of friends, spouse, and father, and to a lesser extent with the mother. In the group with one to four years of high school, behavior accords most with that of spouse, then father, but little with

TABLE 4.—*Statistical Values Derived from Analysis of the Relationships between Drinking Patterns of Educational Groups and Those of Their Friends, Spouses, Fathers, and Mothers*

	Chi Squared	Probability Level	Degree of Relationship (T)
College ($N = 85$)			
Friends	50.84	.001	.79
Spouse	31.50	.001	.67
Father	42.90	.001	.73
Mother	10.79	.01	.36
High School ($N = 225$)			
Friends	10.75	.01	.22
Spouse	126.48	.001	.79
Father	44.73	.001	.46
Mother	10.85	.001	.22
Grade School ($N = 158$)			
Friends	32.78	.001	.47
Spouse	8.04	.01	.24
Father	12.08	.01	.28
Mother	4.56	.05	.17

friends or mother. The grade-school group reveals the highest association in behavior with that of friends, and less with father, spouse, and mother.

Assuming that educational attainment may serve as an index of socio-economic status, the above findings may be explicable in terms of social class or status differences. Relationships found in the college group may bear out the opinion that on the upper status levels drinking seems to be conventional and widely accepted. On the other hand, the middle levels, consisting of persons having but one to four years of high school, may drink mostly in the home and with the family. The relationships obtained in the grade-school group may indicate that on this level drinking occurs mostly in the company of friends. Moreover, the small magnitude of the relationships in the latter group may suggest that no clear-cut drinking norms exist among these people, or that conflicting norms typify various segments of this group.

TABLE 5.—*Statistical Values Derived from Analysis of the Relationships between Drinking Patterns of Residential Background Groups and Those of Their Friends, Spouses, Fathers, and Mothers*

	Chi Squared	Probability Level	Degree of Relationship (*T*)
Urban (N = 252)			
Friends	143.38	.001	.82
Spouse	106.96	.001	.75
Father	170.91	.001	.90
Mother	237.30	.001	.36
Rural (N = 219)			
Friends	141.01	.001	.77
Spouse	75.14	.001	.58
Father	30.68	.001	.36
Mother	16.87	.01	.27

Rural–Urban Background. Table 5 shows the relationships in drinking patterns for individuals divided according to rural and urban background. Persons who lived on farms or in places of less than 2,500 population for most of the first 20 years of life were classified as rural in background, the remainder as urban. In the urban group a high degree of relationship exists between the drinking patterns of the sample and father, friends, and spouse. In the rural group the closest relationship is found in the association between the sample and friends, then spouse, and finally parents. Differences in these two groups may again reveal significant variations in the way drinking norms have changed in different sections of the country in the past few generations. The data seem to imply that in the urban setting such norms have remained relatively stable except as they pertain to the behavior of women; whereas in rural areas the drinking norms of both sexes have shifted.

Summary and Conclusions

The present study has presented data concerning the relationship between the drinking patterns of individuals and those of their friends, spouses, fathers, and mothers. These patterns were observed to vary in significant ways both in the sample representing the total population of the State of Washington and in selected segments of this population. Insofar as inferences regarding sources of influence may be drawn from statistical relationships, a number of hypotheses have been suggested which may account for motivations in drinking patterns.

One general conclusion which may be drawn from this analysis is that the drinking patterns of individuals conform more closely to those of their contemporaries, friends, or spouses, than to those of members of the previous generation. This finding, which certainly is not unexpected in a dynamic society, seems to imply that friendship cliques and the primary family constitute reference groups of great significance in regard to drinking norms and behavior.

The analyses pertaining to the .four characteristics studied—sex, age, education, and rural–urban background—seem to suggest, however, that the degree of influence exerted by friends, spouse, father, or mother varies significantly in different population segments. This finding is probably a consequence of rapid and widespread social change. In a large and heterogeneous population the emergence of new values, or the degree to which older customs and behavior patterns are retained, might be expected to vary according to the social characteristics and group affiliations of individuals.

SUPPLEMENTARY READINGS FOR PART III

1. *Use of Alcoholic Beverages among High School Students,* a study made by Hofstra Research Bureau, Psychological Division, Hofstra College, Hempstead, N.Y., for the Mrs. John S. Sheppard Foundation, Inc., New York, 1954. Multilithed.
2. *Attitudes of High School Students toward Alcoholic Beverages,* a study made by the Bureau of Economics, Sociology, and Anthropology, University Extension Division, University of Wisconsin, for the Mrs. John S. Sheppard Foundation, Inc., New York, 1956. Multilithed.
3. *Attitudes of High School Students toward Alcoholic Beverages,* a study made by the Department of Sociology and Anthropology, University of Kansas, for the Mrs. John S. Sheppard Foundation, Inc., New York, 1956. Multilithed.
4. R. Straus and S. D. Bacon, *Drinking in College.* New Haven, Yale University Press, 1953.
5. *Facts about the Licensed Beverage Industries. A Comprehensive Survey of the Licensed Beverage Industry, Its Role in the American Economy and Its Contributions to the Social Welfare.* New York, Licensed Beverage Industries, Inc., 1956.
6. Survey Reports of the American Institute of Public Opinion, Princeton, New Jersey. Polls of attitudes toward drinking and prohibition have been released in many years since 1934.
7. C. Sower, B. McCall and G. L. Maddox, *Teenage Drinking: A Sociocultural Analysis. A Preliminary Report.* East Lansing, Michigan State University, 1958. [In press.]

PART IV

CULTURAL, RELIGIOUS,
AND ETHICAL FACTORS

PLATE IX. Wine in Religion.

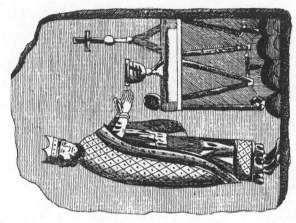

B The Mass. Anglo-Saxon priest, Middle Ages. From *Tableau Historique des Costumes, de Moeurs, et des Usages des Principaux Peuples de l'Antiquité et du Moyen Age,* by Robert de Spalart. Metz, 1810.

A. Dionysos, Greek god of wine, is served by his son, Oinopion. Shown on an Attic black-figure amphora, signed by Exekias, ca. 540 B.C.

PLATE X. Wine in Religion.

A. The Seder (Passover feast). Redrawn by Anne Marie Jauss, from an illustration in the 14th-century *Darmstädter Pessach Haggadah*. Reproduced from *Holidays Around the World,* by Joseph Gaer (copyright by Little, Brown & Company, Boston), by permission of the publishers.

B. Communion. Early Protestants, Bohemia. From a painting by Brozik.

INTRODUCTION

The persistence of drinking customs from earliest times and the prevalence of alcoholism in some societies and not in others present a challenge to researchers in a number of disciplines.

Anthropologists have noted the effects of alcohol intoxication in producing a kind of hysterical ecstasy among certain tribes in connection with group ritual observances. They noted also that social controls were so effective that individual drinking culminating in alcoholism was nonexistent. Life among primitive peoples was rarely uncomplicated. There were persistent dangers—threats of severe punishment of one kind or another sufficient to produce an accumulation of anxiety and defensive aggression. Where a society through accepted substitute channels provided for release of aggression, behavior under intoxication rarely became extremely violent. Conversely, as Bunzel reported in her study in Chichicastenango,[1] when a group imposes rigid sanctions against aggressive acts in customary social relations, inhibitions diminish rapidly under alcohol, with a release of violent and uncontrolled aggression.

A century ago, psychiatrists discovered that persons suffering from mental disease offered valuable sources of information about the psychological development of the normal individual. A somewhat parallel situation has arisen in the treatment of alcoholics. Many clinicians consider alcoholism an expression of neurosis, of the failure of the individual to achieve a mature emotional development. The depressant action of alcohol produces a mild regression in all drinkers. For the average social user of alcohol, regression takes place within a narrow range which is both pleasurable and sanctioned by the drinking group. The alcoholic, however, regresses to relatively early levels of psychosexual development and experiences gratification at these levels which is repugnant to the ordinary user of alcoholic beverages.

The psychoanalytic interpretation of uncontrolled drinking, while it offers a formulation for individual treatment, is not entirely adequate to explain the absence of alcoholism among some cultural groups. Tension, anxiety and counteranxiety in varying degrees are characteristics of most individuals in modern complex society. Alcohol even in small amounts relieves tension. But tension (which is not explicitly defined by most writers) is a result of many forces, some within the individual, others in the social milieu. Many neurotics use alcohol without becoming alcoholics. A similar situation prevails among many

1. Cf. pp. 75–81.

tense, anxious people whose lives are uncomfortable but who experience only limited relief from alcohol.

The sociologist is interested in the behavior patterns of a cross-section of society. He observes that individuals and groups of individuals respond differently to varying amounts of alcohol. He is aware of individual and social disorganization in connection with alcohol but also notes that a majority of drinkers do not exhibit the extreme behavior of intoxication which contributes to social pathology.

The pharmacological properties of alcohol in the body cannot be disregarded in interpreting the social significance of drinking and alcoholism. But existing knowledge of biochemical differences in individuals is not sufficiently definitive to explain the evidence of control or lack of control over alcohol which is apparent among a large number of drinkers.

Alcohol has a definite appeal which in effect is both physiological and psychological. To the degree that tension exists in a group and the use of alcohol is sanctioned, social drinking is likely to occur. Where there are strong social sanctions against drunkenness, drinkers who seek intoxication must either conform or find another group holding less rigid sanctions. In our society, with its numerous subgroups and subcultures, the availability of alcohol combined with the range of sanctions on drinking behavior makes possible a wide variety of drinking practices.

The selections reprinted in Part IV represent attempts to reconcile theoretical analyses of the bases of drinking customs and alcoholism with field studies and clinical experience. They suggest the direction in which further analysis of these complex questions may be profitably undertaken.

19. PRIMITIVE SOCIETIES

by Donald Horton *

The antiquity of the use of alcohol, and its nearly universal occurrence as an item of human behavior, tell us that this custom is a very strong one as measured by its power to survive in the face of competing customs. This surmise or generalization is based on the anthropological doctrine, which is, after all, very easily confirmed by common sense, that a custom, a traditional way of thinking and acting, does not survive and spread from its point of origin unless it gives men some satisfaction, unless it solves some human problem.

Survival of Customs

Think back over the long history of the use of alcoholic beverages. Then compare the changes that have occurred during the same period in other aspects of culture, other aspects of primitive customs—the ease with which many forms of behavior which seemed to be an essential part of primitive life have changed and disappeared under the impacts of higher civilization. That should give you an idea of what I mean when I say that alcohol appears to be a strong and successful custom in the face of competition with other customs. Think of how men, faced with the problem of obtaining game, invented the bow and arrow and various kinds of traps. Give them an opportunity to trade the bow and arrow for a firearm, or their native log-trap for a steel trap, and the native inventions disappear.

The primitive man, at the time of the invention of alcoholic beverages, undoubtedly carried his burdens on his back or on a rough sledge dragged along the ground. Somewhere along the way these customs disappeared and were replaced by others that fitted his needs in a more successful way. The beast of burden, the wheelcart, took the place of the old modes of transportation. But the use of alcoholic beverages has continued and spread, and every year penetrates into areas where it did not exist before.

Not only has this custom been successful in terms of sheer survival, but it has been successful in the face of very severe opposition. We know, for instance, that a good many of the higher civilizations of the past have fought against alcoholic beverages and tried to control and prohibit them. We know that in China at various times, in India, in Mesopotamia, and among the Incas and the Aztecs—the high civilizations of the Americas— attempts were made either to prohibit alcoholic beverages entirely or to

* From "The Functions of Alcohol in Primitive Societies," in *Alcohol, Science and Society* (New Haven, Quarterly Journal of Studies on Alcohol, 1945), Lecture 13.

control their use, and these attempts invariably failed. In other words, the use of alcoholic beverages as a custom prevailed in the face of definite, organized, and consciously directed opposition. At one period the Hindus went probably further than any others in attempting to make the manufacture, transportation, sale, barter, or use of alcoholic beverages a capital offense. But this severe law apparently had as little success in stopping the development or continuation of this custom as any of the others. We have to conclude from this, then, that some important human value is involved here that makes alcohol hard to abolish. This observation, in turn, leads to another generalization, namely, that despite this value, the use of alcoholic beverages is frequently regarded as a dangerous custom, and attempts are made to control or abolish it.

Restriction of Customs

Sometimes the controls or the restraints are of a relatively limited sort. For instance, in a great many primitive societies men are permitted to drink as much as they choose, but women are severely restricted as to the amount they may drink. In a few instances, women are prohibited entirely from drinking the alcoholic beverage even though they may be the ones who make it in the course of their preparation of food. In some societies, permission to drink is only obtained after one has reached the age of maturity, however maturity may be defined.

There are also many kinds of limitations with regard to the proper time or the proper circumstances under which one can drink. These limiting conditions do not go nearly so far as the attempt at prohibition in higher civilizations. But it seems quite clear, even from these examples, that there is definitely an ambivalent attitude, an attitude which is contradictory, an attitude which, on the one hand, approves drinking and permits it to exist and has given it a long life, as the life of a custom goes; and, on the other hand, an attitude of some anxiety, of fear, of suspicion which leads to attempts to restrict the use of alcohol in various ways.

*   *   *

Alcohol for Relief of Anxiety

This would seem to imply that the appeal to tradition, the religious validation, the food value, are, in a sense, rationalizations. They may have some subsidiary function, but there is something more important than that. Intoxication is the thing. In the state of intoxication, and in what it means to men, apparently lies the answer to the positive value of alcohol. By positive value I mean that this is the thing for which the alcoholic beverage is treasured, honored, preserved as a custom through the ages. The best possible explanation that I can offer you, based on a review of the use of alcohol in a good many primitive societies, is that the value is primarily in its anxiety-reducing function. This is apparently the only explanation which will serve as a key that has universal validity, with which you can begin to understand the use of alcoholic beverages, the customs surrounding their use, the attitudes that people have toward them in any society anywhere in the world, whether it is a highly sophisticated and civilized society or a very simple society of hunters and gatherers of seeds and berries.

Alcohol is an effective sedative. Among its sedative effects is that of reducing the activity of those physiological mechanisms that produce anxiety. Anxiety, or fear, a state of tension, is a painful condition. Any man who is anxious, who is in a state of anxiety, is actually faced with a problem. In anthropology we frequently find that it is very useful to try to analyze a custom in terms of problems and the solution of problems. If we say to ourselves, "Now, to what problem could this custom be a solution?—how could it be solving a difficulty?—how could it be resolving some kind of conflict for the primitive society in which we find it?"—then we begin to get further insight into the meaning of the custom which, on the surface, might be quite mysterious to us. I suggest that when you have a state of anxiety existing in any individual, or in all the members of the population, you have a problem, an unresolved situation, a tension, which seeks to be reduced. You have a need which has to be met, even though at times it may be unconscious—the people who have this state of tension may not be aware of it. We know that anxiety is a universal phenomenon because it is a very simple thing in its functions. It is merely the anticipation of danger, as when a man has experienced pain or has been exposed to a danger. Thereafter, whenever he comes into the presence of the same danger, whenever it is suggested to him, he will have a slight rise in tension, he will have this anxiety, which warns him that the danger is close and prepares him to evade or avoid or counteract it in some way.

Human life is full of dangers of all kinds. Among primitive peoples there is the danger of external enemies, the enemies who surround the tribe. Remember that in many societies, especially prior to the coming of the European government, when one man kills another it is incumbent on the family—the father, brothers, and near relatives of the murdered man— to exact vengeance, to kill the killer. Sometimes these feuds would become automatic and reciprocal, so that once a feud started it would never end, because when the killer was killed his family would, in turn, avenge his death, and so on. In many societies there is a constant state of tension due to the operation of this mechanism, because all people are potential enemies to everyone except close kinsmen.

This method of law and order involves a certain anxiety toward everybody, because it means that each individual is a potential victim of somebody else's crime, the potential victim of the thing that his brother or father does, and so on. Of course, there were peculiar customs which were not universal by any means. Thus, in many societies in many places in the world, head-hunting was a custom. That meant that if there was a tribe of head-hunters, then all other tribes in the surrounding region had to be constantly on guard against the raids of these head-hunters, and there was constant anxiety in that respect. These are not universal things, but much more universal is the fact that being a primitive man, a member of a society on a very primitive level, means being subject to instability of food supply, to famine, and to the dangers of an undeveloped productive technique. The primitive man is always very close to the margin of existence. There is never a very great supply of food ahead. He is rather helpless in the face of such dangers as, say, a grasshopper plague which may eat the garden crop, insects of various kinds, floods and droughts. There is no secure water supply, there are only limited facilities for meeting a drought. The primitive man is helpless in the face of unpredictable seasonal variations in the yield of his crops; or, if he is a hunter, he is faced with the danger that wild life may suddenly disappear, the game animals on which he depends may be decimated by one of the mysterious epidemic diseases that sweep among game animals.

*   *   *

Alcohol is only one of the substances capable of fulfilling the anxiety-reducing function. Among the Asiatic people, for instance, many prefer opium. It is characteristic of some parts of the Asiatic world that where alcohol is not used, opium is used, and where opium is not used, alcohol is. Among the American Indians there are many who seem to prefer certain drugs such as peyote, the fruit of a certain cactus from which they get a trancelike effect with visual hallucinations, color visions, and so forth. It is characteristic of these Indians, too, that those who use peyote do not use alcohol, and vice versa. Others use various other drugs. The Jimson weed, for example, is very common throughout California and Mexico.

Alcohol as a Sedative

Alcohol has a special virtue for primitive peoples as a sedative inasmuch as it has relatively few or no harmful physiological effects and thus there is no necessary interference with productive activities. It does not put the drinker in a semicoma, so to speak, for an indefinite period, and recovery is not accompanied by a long period of illness, as in the case of some drugs. It can be indulged·in for an evening, one can obtain a sedation which reduces anxiety, and yet the next day the drinker can perform his daily tasks without any serious hangover effect. Another factor is that the materials for the production of alcohol are universal. All this great variety of fruits and berries and tubers and cereals which I have already mentioned makes it possible for practically every people in the world to produce an alcoholic beverage. In the case of the drugs, they are limited by the fact that they occur only in certain places and that in many places such drugs are not available. Furthermore, not only are the materials abundant and the technique for the production of alcohol simple and easily mastered, but the process itself is cheap. It does not take a great deal of labor to produce fairly large quantities of an alcoholic beverage.

Another important consideration, it seems to me, is the fact that its effects can be enjoyed along with other gratifications. I have never particularly studied the use of opium, but my impression is that to use it, one has to withdraw somewhat from society. It is a kind of private practice, and you cannot very well conceive of smoking or eating it in an ordinary social gathering as you can use alcohol in the course of a normal social event. Alcohol has the advantage of reducing those tensions that arise among the members of a society when they get together. Inasmuch as people always stand in a slightly competitive relationship with one another in regard to their functions in life, the goods they need, and so on, their relationships are always fairly complicated and subject to the possibility of getting out of kilter. A slight tension can and frequently does arise when certain people get together in a social situation. It is not the kind of thing that makes them enemies by any means, but it is there, and the alcoholic beverage, because it can be used in a social situation, can reduce these tensions and thus actually facilitate the social intercourse which is a part of and the desirable end of the occasion.

*   *   *

Alcohol and Aggression

We have said that alcohol reduces anxiety and that anxiety is a signal of danger, that it is a response to danger of some kind. But some of the dangers to which men learn to respond with anxiety are internal dangers, dangers within themselves. That is to say, over and above the dangers involved in the threats from external enemies or failure of the food supply, there are also dangers which take the form of antisocial impulses within the individual himself. On frequent occasions he may be in a situation in which he has the momentary impulse to harm someone, to be aggressive, to strike a blow, to damage, even to kill. Everywhere, to some extent, the aggressive impulse is forbidden and punished when it occurs within the cooperating social group, particularly within the family group, within the clan, within the village, or even within the tribe.

This group—the family, the clan or village group—must work together, must have a harmonious system of social relations, must have a minimum of conflicts, in order to survive, for all the people in the group are dependent upon one another for their survival. Impulses of aggression toward the members of one's own group must therefore be inhibited. They must be inhibited during childhood. The child must learn that when he has such impulses they must be stifled. This is a part of the process of making a child into a social human being.

A child starts out as a mere organism without social character, without culture, without habits to fit him for human life. To this child must be imparted all the behavior that will be required of him as an adult member of the particular society into which he was born. As part of this process of becoming a human being capable of carrying on joint social activities which will enable him and the other members of the community to survive in the face of dangers in nature, the child must learn, among other things, to suppress all his constant impulses to respond with aggression, with hostility, to those who temporarily frustrate him, forbid him to do what he wants to do. Especially will he be punished for aggression toward his parents, because his relations with them must be maintained in a certain form, otherwise the parents may fail in making the child into a productive member of society. The parents must have absolute authority. Parents who have the wisdom of their culture, inherited in turn from their parents, must have control over the child's life. No hostility on the part of the child may be tolerated for long.

From the very beginning every individual in any society learns to control his aggressive impulses, and eventually he forces them down to the point where he is no longer aware of the fact that these impulses are being generated and being repressed. To be sure, some forms of aggression are permitted him. He may be given an opportunity to release all the stored-up aggressive impulses which he has felt toward his parents, neighbors and close associates, against some permitted objects, against enemies in warfare, in head-hunting, and against evildoers and criminals. He may be permitted to take part in their punishment. He is always permitted to exercise his aggression against those who are regarded as public enemies. Or he may take it out against those individuals who merely turn out to be queer, who turn out to be not like others; against these he may express his aggression in the form of ridicule. Or there may be some very special forms of physical contests, sports, games of a warlike variety, gladiatorial in character, and he may release some of his aggression in this way. But these various exceptional ways in which aggression may be relieved in a socially accepted form merely emphasize the fact that the taboo on aggression within the society is absolutely universal.

Now the strength of the aggressive impulses arising out of social experience depends largely on how much frustration and thwarting of hopes and ambitions occurs within the group. Some societies produce a human character which is highly aggressive, in which you find an aggressive response occurring in all members of the society very frequently in day-to-day situations. This is especially present in those societies in which the whole nature of the society is solely competitive, in which people are accustomed to striving to get the best of one another, to be superior to one another. There are some societies in which the highest social achievement is to be able to shame your rival by showing that you can accumulate a greater mass of property than he, and then destroying it in front of his eyes. The rival is challenged to accumulate as much property as you were able to get and destroy it. Greatness is manifested by the ability to achieve great things and then to destroy them. In other societies we find that a man's advancement along the road of life and his achievement of distinction and power depend entirely on the good will of certain older people who stand in a particular relationship to him. If these older people choose, they can forever thwart his hopes of attaining the highest status to which he might aspire. In a situation such as that, a tremendous amount of aggression may be accumulated. On the other hand, there are societies in which there is no ruthlessness toward weaker members, in which there is very little competition, in which there are very slight inequalities in wealth, in which opportunity is a matter of no importance between men, where corporate activities are the order of the day, and where anybody who chooses to be too self-seeking is frowned upon. In such societies there is very little evidence of the hidden aggression which has been repressed.

The expectation of punishment for the aggressive impulse arouses anxiety. The psychological mechanism is fairly simple. Punishment is a danger; whether it is direct corporal punishment or a matter of being excluded from some special occasion which is valued very highly, it is a punishment. This punishment, when first perceived, gives rise to anxiety. To escape the anxiety the aggressive impulse is inhibited or repressed. If alcohol has been consumed, this mechanism fails, because it depends upon anxiety. The anxiety is reduced and the aggression is aroused. There is nothing to prevent it, nothing to inhibit it, nothing to repress the aggressive thought, and it then manifests itself in action. In point of fact, aggressive behavior under the influence of intoxication is almost universal. Among primitive societies it ranges from its very mildest form, which is simply the exchange of insults and harsh words, to its extreme form in which assault and murder occur.

Release of Aggression

As an example of the first case we may take the Lepcha, a people of about 25,000, who live on the slopes of Mt. Kinchinjunga in the Himalayas in northeastern India. These are among the most peaceful people ever reported in the anthropological literature. Their life is almost without conflicts. It does not run to ostentation, display or the accumulation of wealth. It is a life that involves a year-round series of operations in the fields, growing rice and millet, and religious rituals. These go on year after year in their accustomed way—everybody has enough, nobody has too little and nobody has too much. There are no sharp distinctions with respect to class or wealth. These people, who have a calm and even temperament, have a beer called *chi,* which is made from millet. They have it in abundance because they have enough millet to supply their food needs and to make as much beer as they want. They customarily drink until they are pretty well intoxicated, but this intoxication takes the form of increased jollification and loquacity. Some of them will show slightly heightened sexual behavior, but nothing serious, and in the end the men will gradually go to sleep under the effects of the beverage.

For a contrast, we may take the Indians of the northeastern part of North America—the Indians of eastern Canada. These were a people—they have now been destroyed—who, at the time the Europeans first came here, were living what we would call a marginal existence. They were exclusively hunters, with no other source of food than the game they were able to kill, the berries and seeds that they were able to gather, and the fish that they caught in the rivers and along the Atlantic shore. These people were constantly subject to the dangers of their existence. Game would frequently fail, the fish would fail to run up a certain river and the berry crop would not be abundant. There were many small tribes and they were constantly at war with one another over the hunting grounds, because game frequently became too scarce to support their populations. There was also great competition among the tribes to see who could reach and hold the best hunting grounds, who could surround the largest herd of caribou and fight off all comers. These people were very simple and they had a formal social organization that involved no real government. They had learned for their own good to keep under control all the aggression that arose among them as a result of the thwarting conditions of their natural life. They took out their aggression on their enemies and on their captives. This was one way they had of releasing the terrific aggressions that were built up in them as a result of the frustrations of their daily life. It is interesting, too, that this was accepted by all of the Indians, so that each man knew what to expect if he were captured by another tribe. It was accepted and regarded as a duty to show fortitude and stoicism and not to give one's enemies the gratification of hearing him scream. A man would, if possible, go to his death, perhaps eventually torn into shreds, without letting out a whimper. This was the accepted way of things and it had a deep psychological meaning for these people which was probably important to them. It is hard for us to evaluate, now that we have only the historical records about them, but, at any rate, this was the case. These people had managed, in one way or another, to keep their aggression under control, to give it outlet in warfare and in various ceremonies and rituals.

There was another form that their aggression took and that was that they practised sorcery against one another or believed that sorcery was being practised. This was a kind of projection of their own aggressive impulses. When alcohol was brought into the situation, these people were overcome by it because the aggression that was released was something they could not cope with. They had no institution for handling this effect; they had no police, they had no government, the Chief had only nominal power. When a warrior was given his first bottle of gin by a trader, and then became a maniac and went about killing people, who was to stop him, who would organize the people to stop him? They were not accustomed to dealing with this type of situation. When the whole community got gin and all the able-bodied men began to fight, to kill one another as well as their wives and children, there was just no power available to bring the situation under control. Thus some of these tribes actually were destroyed more by their own behavior as a result of the alcohol than by the direct assault of the Europeans. Of course this situation was complicated by the fact that when the Europeans came, the game became even more scarce, and the Europeans gave firearms to some tribes so that they were able to behave much more arrogantly and successfully in their own interests against others. The whole situation became much more tense.

*　　*　　*

Of course, primitive peoples do not know that there is alcohol in their drinks. All they know is that they have certain beverages which they regard as God-given, remarkable, and very valuable, which have the effect of producing a certain degree of happiness, and occasionally this happiness somehow mysteriously becomes transformed into fighting and somebody perhaps gets hurt a little, but you cannot help that. That is an inherent quality of this particular beverage, so that no grudge is held for it afterward.

They control the aggression problem by limiting it, not trying to prevent it entirely, but giving it a certain permission and always steering it along certain channels. Very frequently the sexual impulse is treated in the same way. It becomes recognized by the society that you can do things in the drinking situation which you may not do at any other time without being punished, so that this again becomes a permitted form of activity as long as it is kept within certain limits. Or it may be prohibited entirely, and in that case the problem is to punish the offender so severely that the next time he will not be able to reduce his anxiety to the point where this behavior will emerge. Another method, very nearly universal, is to exclude women from the drinking situation. If they are not permitted to drink, they are not permitted to be present, and this naturally reduces the instigation to sexual activity.

How successful these measures are will depend on local conditions. Absolute punishment for such behavior can only be successful where there is a fairly strong government with police powers. Many primitive societies lack these institutions, so that their forms of punishment are more like ostracism and other social penalties for bad behavior. In a very few instances, the only solution that the people have found for the problems of aggression and sex is to do without alcohol. This is quite remarkable, because very few primitive societies have been able to do this. Among the few are some of the Pueblo societies of the southwestern United States—the Hopi and the Zuni. They had their chance at alcohol. When the Spaniards came in, both of these tribes learned to drink distilled liquor and wine. Although their historical record has never been carefully analyzed from this point of view, I know that there are indications that the effect of drinking was to release these tensions, to produce aggression and sex behavior which was dangerous to them. But in their case they had something special at stake. They had a society which had lived in a desert situation for hundreds of years, and they had been able to maintain themselves in that desert environment only by demanding a degree of social cohesiveness and solidarity and cooperation which is remarkable even for a primitive society. These people were so closely bound together, and their whole culture depended so much on this question of cooperation, that they had made the nonaggressive, cooperative man their ideal, and they could not tolerate any deviation from this ideal. For them, it was a sheer matter of survival. Not only that, but they did not have to depend on the slow process of trial and error in applying social controls. They had a very highly cultivated system of governmental and priestly authority which included men of no mean philosophical achievement, men who were real thinkers, who actually perceived the problem. This again is a rare occurrence among a primitive people—they generally do not have the techniques of thinking which would enable them to see their social problems in a clear light. The Hopi and Zuni, however, saw their problems, and therefore passed a decree that thenceforward no member of their community could drink. This rule is breaking down somewhat. It is still forbidden to drink in the pueblos, but the young people who go out into American society—to boarding schools in American cities or to work on the railways or in the factories in the surrounding region—do occasionally become drinkers. Usually they give it up when they go back to their homes, because they know that it will not be tolerated there. I mention this last to show that the anxiety which would motivate drinking is present.

*   *   *

Alcohol and Culture

In primitive societies the culture is fairly uniform. The society is little, the population is usually small, and individuals are much more alike in their behavior than in our society. There are, in primitive societies, relatively few differentiated groups and there is no great differentiation of labor skill. You do not have the teacher on the one hand and the ditch digger on the other. Each man is something of a teacher to his son. Each is able to take what measures are necessary. Each labors in the same industry. Where there is a division of labor, it is usually in certain minor specialties. There will be the priest, the medicine man; there will be the few expert craftsmen who have a peculiar natural talent for making carved wooden objects or dugout canoes, or something like that. But, in general, there will be relatively few differences in culture. There will be no class differences, no great economic differences, so that there is no opportunity for the development of divergent personality types. That is why we are accustomed to say in anthropology that in primitive society the personality, the psychology of individuals, is likely to be fairly uniform for all members of the same sex. There will be differences between sexes, and slight differences due to age, but, in general, all the mature men will be very much alike in their inner psychological development and structure because they have all experienced the same things, they have had the same teachers, they have grown up under the force of the same tradition.

In our society, obviously, things are very different. We have a tremendous diversification of functions, roles and activities. We have the basic differences of occupations. We have differences in wealth, all kinds of diversities of opportunity, differences in national background, and racial differences. All of these make our society infinitely more complex than the primitive society. There is more opportunity for individuals to deviate from the norm because there are certain conflicting norms. Even a criminal, who in a primitive society would be immediately exposed and punished for his crime, may, in our society, seek out a society of criminals in which it is normal to be abnormal, in which one can flout the standards of society and yet be among people who approve the flouting attempt. Of course, such a thing is unheard of among primitive societies. In our society, if one has sexual abnormalities, it is possible to join a society of perverts in our big cities, consisting of a small group of people who agree that because they are perverted they will allow their practices, they will not take the attitude toward their abnormalities that society at large does. And as long as they act within their protected precincts, and do not go so far as to come into conflict with the other members of society, they can manage. In other words, the possibility of deviation is much greater, and the conflicts which give rise to tension within the individual are much greater and much more diverse, and can express themselves in more varied kinds of actual deviation from the norm.

In our society it is much more difficult, merely by an examination, to relate the behavior of an individual to his social context. It is much more difficult to study an insane man and state the social conditions which produced his insanity, yet we know that they must exist unless the insanity is due to an organic disturbance. In the case of psychiatric disorders for which there is no organic basis, however, we know of only one possibility— those disorders came out of the individual's experiences with society. But the society is so complex in this individual's experience, it has carried him through so many different competing situations, situations in which there were conflicting standards of behavior and conflicting attitudes, that it becomes a major job of the psychoanalyst to try to reconstruct the life experience of this individual and to see at what points his contacts with society have produced in him the reactions which now express themselves in a symptom that requires psychiatric treatment.

For us, then, this problem of personality in relation to culture is a far more complicated matter than it might be in a primitive society in which there is much greater uniformity and in which the experiences of all individuals are seen to be very similar if their effects are studied. But some of the larger issues are the same, even though we cannot take, say, the alcohol addict and immediately refer, merely by an examination of the society, to the specific conditions which would give rise to alcohol addiction. We would need a special technique of psychiatry to analyze the character structure in relation to experience, and then experience in relation to mode of life. Nevertheless, it seems to me that we can recognize certain relationships, again speaking of the social philosophy of alcohol addiction. . . .

There are general psychological conditions arising out of the conditions created and transmitted by our culture which it is now the task of the psychiatrist and the social psychologist to analyze for us. If we carry over what we have learned about primitive societies to our own society, we certainly cannot regard our problem as specifically the problem of alcohol —because alcohol is merely the agent. The problem is first seen as the use of alcohol, but from there we are led back directly to the anxiety, tension, unhappiness and frustration which led to the use of alcohol and which make it rewarding to the individual. The reduction of excessive anxiety may be tackled as a problem of individual therapy, and that is the standard way of doing it. But if I were asked to give one over-all statement, on the basis of my survey of primitive societies and the reference of this survey to our own society, it would be that the fundamental problem is one of social engineering rather than of individual therapy.

20. CULTURAL DIFFERENCES IN RATES OF ALCOHOLISM

by Robert F. Bales *

There are three general ways in which culture and social organization can influence rates of alcoholism. The first is *the degree to which the culture operates to bring about acute needs for adjustment, or inner tensions, in its members.* There are many of these; culturally induced anxiety, guilt, conflict, suppressed aggression, and sexual tensions of various sorts may be taken as examples. The second way is *the sort of attitudes toward drinking which the culture produces in its members.* Four different types of attitudes will be suggested later. The crucial factor seems to be whether a given attitude toward drinking positively suggests drinking to the individual as a means of relieving his inner tensions, or whether such a thought arouses a strong counteranxiety. The third general way is *the degree to which the culture provides suitable substitute means of satisfaction.* In other words, there is reason to believe that if the inner tensions are sufficiently acute certain individuals will become compulsively habituated in spite of opposed social attitudes unless substitute ways of satisfaction are provided.

These three factors may be used as the outline for the rest of this discussion. Under each heading one or more cultural groups will be discussed whose particular rates seem to reflect the factor in question. It is taken for granted that the three factors work together, and that any given rate depends upon their particular combination. If this is not mentioned explicitly in each case the omission is only a means of simplifying and saving time. It should also be noted that biological or physiological differences may play a part in some of these differences in rates; but if they do, what they may be or how they may operate is still unknown. Various theories to this effect have been offered in the past but they are hardly accepted by biologists and physiologists now. The three factors mentioned seem to make sense, both theoretically and practically. However, scientists are still very much in the process of interpreting cultural differences in rates, and in some ways the rates offer more problems than answers.

There is fairly good evidence that inebriety tends to be pronounced where the inner tensions or needs for adjustment of many individuals are high, other things being equal. In a careful statistical study of all the primitive societies for which data were available, Horton[1] found that

* From *Quarterly Journal of Studies on Alcohol, 6* (1946), 482–98.

1. D. Horton, "The Functions of Alcohol in Primitive Societies: A Cross-Cultural Study," *Quarterly Journal of Studies on Alcohol, 4* (1943), 199–320.

societies with inadequate techniques or resources for maintaining their physical existence also tended to have "strong degrees of insobriety." This does not necessarily mean that the members become compulsive drinkers, but that on the occasions when they drink they do so to the point of unconsciousness and their bouts of drunkenness are likely to last for days. Their drinking, in other words, shows a semi-compulsive character when once started, although it starts only on socially sanctioned occasions. The direct factor seems to be the anxiety induced by the basic insecurities of their lives, such as the constant danger of drought, insect plagues, floods, crop failures or other threats to the food supply. Those societies which were being broken up by contact with other more powerful groups invariably had high degrees of insobriety. In most of the societies with high subsistence anxiety there was also a great deal of pent-up aggression which emerged in the periods of drunkenness, sometimes in very extreme form.

Repressed aggression seems to be a very common maladjustment. It can be created by the way the social organization is set up, as well as by other sorts of deprivation or frustration. The data gathered by Hallowell [2] on the Northeastern Woodlands Indians relating to the time of their contact with the whites indicate a high degree of inhibition of aggressive impulses. They were forced by their culture to be restrained, stoic, amiable and mild under all provocations, and had to suppress all open criticism of one another. It is assumed that they had a great deal of pent-up aggression, because they had a highly developed system of witchcraft directed against one another. When they were introduced to alcohol the consequences were disastrous. In their bouts of drunkenness they strangled and beat themselves —a form of aggression directed against the self. They broke up everything in their wigwams and quarreled for hours together. Brothers cut the throats of sisters, husbands attacked their wives, mothers threw their children into the fire or into the river, fathers choked their children and children attacked their parents. Many others of the Indian tribes of the Eastern United States showed similar reactions. Their culture was broken up by the whites. They were crowded off their lands, beaten and cheated in their economic dealings, kidnapped and sent into slavery, and exposed to the ravages of strange diseases. In short, they were subject to the strongest sort of subsistence anxiety. This laid a part of the groundwork for the devastation alcohol worked among them. There was another factor, however, tied up with the fact that they had not known alcohol previously, which will be discussed shortly.

To illustrate more definitely the way in which the social organization can induce inner tensions in its members, the Irish peasantry may be taken

2. A. I. Hallowell, "Some Psychological Characteristics of the Northeastern Indians," in *Culture and Experience* (Philadelphia, University of Pennsylvania Press, 1955), pp. 141–2.

as an example.[3] The Irish have been noted for their inebriety during the past several centuries. In statistics of admissions for alcoholic disorders to various hospitals in this country the Irish have consistently had rates two to three times as high as any other ethnic group. In 1840 an Irish priest wrote:

> In truth, not only were our countrymen remarkable for the intemperate use of intoxicating liquors, but intemperance had already entered into, and formed a part of the national character. An Irishman and a drunkard had become synonymous terms. Whenever he was to be introduced in character, either in the theatre or on the pages of the novelist, he should be represented habited in rags, bleeding at the nose, and waving a shillelah. Whiskey was everywhere regarded as our idol.[4]

The English at this time wished to keep the Irish an agricultural people, so that the Irish would raise the sort of farm produce needed in England. As a part of this program they hampered the development of adequate means of transportation in order to prevent industrialization in Ireland. They had control of the land, with a complicated system of absentee landlords, and squeezed every last penny they could out of the Irish farmers. The farmers, for the most part, lived on the bare edge of existence. They raised so few different kinds of food that the potato blight resulted in severe periodic famines. Many people died during these famines because food could not be transported to them in time.

The small farms were crowded to capacity. There was no room on them for more than one extended family. The grandparents, who had retired, lived in the West Room of the cottage. The farmer and his wife with their children made up the rest of the family. They all had to work hard for their existence, the girls helping their mother around the cottage and farmyard, the boys helping their father in the fields. There was a strict separation of the sexes which they managed to maintain in spite of the fact that the whole family usually slept in the same room. The training of the children was apparently a very contradictory affair. The elders teased the little boys unmercifully—"codding" it was called—and sometimes prodded them into "scuffing" with one another. It was not unusual for a child to receive extravagant love and affection at one moment, and the next moment to be cuffed about or even beaten in a fit of anger. There was also a marked tendency to attempt to control children through an exaggerated fear of

3. The material on Irish social structure has been drawn chiefly from C. M. Arensberg, *The Irish Countryman*, New York, Macmillan, 1937; C. M. Arensberg and S. T. Kimball, *Family and Community in Ireland*, Cambridge, Mass., Harvard University Press, 1940; and M. J. F. McCarthy, *Irish Land and Irish Liberty*, London, Scott, 1911.

4. J. Birmingham, *A Memoir of the Very Rev. Theobald Mathew*, Dublin, Milliken & Son, 1840.

the "bogey man," "spooks," and "fairies." Conflict between family members was likely to be frequent and severe. Many children must have grown up in an atmosphere of fear and insecurity, both in the family and outside.

Because the farms were so small, they could not be divided. The boys could not marry until the "old fellow" was ready to give up the farm and retire. Then only one of the boys would get the farm. The other brothers and sisters would have to leave. Some of the brothers went into the priesthood. Others were apprenticed to tradesmen in town, or emigrated. One or two of the girls received a dowry and married. The others became nuns, were apprenticed, or emigrated. Very often the "old fellow" was not willing to give up the farm until his physical powers were spent, and this caused a great deal of resentment. So long as his sons stayed on the farm they had to work for him as "boys" and were treated as boys, even though they might be 45 or 50 years old. By the same token they had to stay away from girls. There were very severe sanctions on premarital sexual activity which were enforced both by the church and the peasantry. Thus there were many physically mature men, ready for a life of their own, who were kept under the father's thumb as "boys," dependent upon him even for their spending money, and deprived of sexual contacts.

Even social contacts between the two sexes were at a minimum. It was apparently not considered a good idea to encourage love affairs when the land would not support more families. When the "boys" were not working as laborers for their father, they were expected to spend their time with the other boys. Small male groups of every age met at various farmhouses or taverns to pass the time. Drinking and aggressive "horseplay" were major activities. The "teetotaler," as a matter of fact, was regarded as a suspicious character, since this implied he was not likely to be with the other boys and might be wandering around with the idea of molesting innocent girls. In short, the culture was such as to create and maintain an immense amount of suppressed aggression and sexuality. Both of these suppressed tensions found their outlet in drinking.

It is not entirely clear just what happened to this family system in urban America, but it seems to have broken down in various ways and created still other conflicts.[5] The males came in at the bottom of our occupational ladder, and no longer had the ownership of a farm as the mainstay of their self-respect and prestige. The tenement was not a place where aged parents could easily be kept after their working days were over. It was not easy to provide the money for their support out of small day-wages. There was uncertainty and inner conflict as to whether one was obligated to keep them at all. There was usually nothing a father could pass on to his son, or if he died and left a little property there was likely to be conflict over how it should be divided, since equal inheritance was not the rule in Ireland as

5. These interpretations are based on a study by the present author of some 80 detailed hospital case records of Irish alcoholic patients.

it is here. The father in many cases seems to have dropped into a role of impotence and insignificance, and the mother became the dominant member of the family. She tended to bind her sons to her in the way which was usual and natural in Ireland. In this country, however, a strong attachment between a son and his mother made it very difficult, and in some cases impossible, for the son to make a successful transition to independent adult status. In a survey of some 80 cases of alcoholic patients of Irish descent I found this mother–son dependence and conflict in some 60 per cent. Whether this is a higher percentage than would be found in other ethnic groups it is impossible to say at present, but the mother–son dependence pattern was certainly a prominent factor causing maladjustment in these Irish cases.

*　　*　　*

Although severe inner tensions or needs for adjustment are nearly always found as a background for compulsive drinking, this factor always works in conjunction with the particular attitudes toward drinking which are structured in the culture. Where these attitudes arouse strong counter-anxiety there may be little compulsive drinking in spite of severe maladjustment. Other outlets will be sought. On the other hand, where the attitudes are such as to permit or positively suggest drinking as a means of satisfying minor tensions, the effects of the drinking itself may generate acute maladjustments which result in its perpetuation. It is possible to distinguish four different types of attitudes which are represented in various cultural groups and which seem to have different effects on the rates of alcoholism.

The first is an attitude which calls for complete abstinence. For one reason or another, usually religious in nature, the use of alcohol as a beverage is not permitted for any purpose. The second might be called a ritual attitude toward drinking. This is also religious in nature, but it requires that alcoholic beverages, sometimes a particular one, should be used in the performance of religious ceremonies. Typically the beverage is regarded as sacred, it is consecrated to that end, and the partaking of it is a ritual act of communion with the sacred. This is a characteristic attitude toward drinking among many aboriginal peoples. The third can be called a convivial attitude toward drinking. Drinking is a "social" rather than a religious ritual, performed both because it symbolizes social unity or solidarity and because it actually loosens up emotions which make for social ease and good will. This is what is often called "social drinking." The fourth type seems best described as a utilitarian attitude toward drinking. This includes medicinal drinking and other types calculated to further self-interest or exclusively personal satisfaction. It is often "solitary" drinking, but not necessarily so. It is possible to drink for utilitarian purposes in a group and with group approval. The distinction is that the purpose is personal and self-interested rather than social and expressive.

One of the outstanding instances of the adoption of the attitude of complete abstinence, total prohibition on a large scale, is that of the Moslems. The taboo rests on a religious basis, the command given by Mohammed. According to one of the translators of the Koran, during the fourth year of the Hegira, or flight from Mecca, Mohammed and his men were engaged in expeditions against neighboring tribes. In the midst of this some of his leaders quarreled while gambling and drinking, and upset the plans of warfare. Mohammed then forbade the use of wine and games of chance forever. He supported his decree by a fable of two angels who were sent to Babylon to teach men righteousness. They disobeyed God's commandment not to drink, got into trouble with a woman, and were severely punished by God, who then forbade the use of wine to His servants forever after. It is evident here how the usual dangers to social order, excess aggression and sexuality, played a part in the prohibition. Another factor, perhaps operating in the beginning and certainly afterward in maintaining the taboo, was the danger that intoxication would profane the performance of religious duties. These duties were very strict and exact. A man might soil himself while intoxicated and say a prayer while in an unclean condition.

There do not seem to be any statistical data which might be used as an index to the actual extent of drinking among the Moslems but there is a great deal of evidence to show that the taboo has been very unevenly observed in the course of history, and in some cases flagrantly violated. All sorts of expedients and rationalizations have been employed to evade the spirit of the law if not the letter of it. One of these was to mislabel the contents of wine containers. Some Moslems assumed that all other alcoholic beverages except wine were permitted. Some protested that the law referred only to excessive drinking. Smuggling and private use have been common. All in all, the Moslem can hardly be regarded as a model of successful total prohibition. One of the chief defects of total prohibition seems to be the extreme difficulty of getting a genuine acceptance of the attitude. The breaking of this taboo becomes an ideal way of expressing dissent and aggression, especially where the original solidarity of the group is weak and aggression is strong. Thus total prohibition sometimes overshoots the mark and encourages the very thing it is designed to prevent. This situation is frequently found among individual alcoholics whose parents were firm teetotalers and absolutely forbade their sons to drink.

A similar situation arose among many of our East Coast Indian tribes when they were first introduced to alcohol. They made repeated attempts to enforce total prohibition when they saw the effects of the alcoholic beverages brought by the traders and colonists. They produced some famous temperance reformers, but they were unable to stem the tide. The old men were usually the most concerned, but the young men could not be controlled. The Hopi and Zuni Indians in Western New Mexico form an interesting exception. Although information about them is somewhat confused and contradictory, it appears that in their aboriginal state they used alcoholic beverages in a ritual manner, and often ended up with some rioting and sexual expression. When liquor was brought in by the Spaniards it was used for a period and then rejected entirely. It is not known just how this came about. It may be that the objectionable effects were accentuated by the new insecurity and stronger beverages. These people now put great emphasis on a quiet, calm, orderly existence. Everybody is expected to cooperate peacefully with his neighbors, and nobody tries to be outstanding. Insanity is greatly feared, and they seem to have identified drunkenness with insanity. Their life is highly and meticulously ritualized. It may be that their ritualism adequately took care of their insecurities and fears. It may be surmised, however, that if they had not previously used alcoholic beverages in a ritual manner, thus accepting its prohibition for all other purposes, they would not have been able to make total prohibition effective. The fact that they drank ritually before contact with the whites is one factor which distinctly sets them off from the East Coast Indians who had had no alcoholic beverages before and hence had not been able to build up any stable attitudes toward drinking, ritually or otherwise. An attitude capable of restraining strong impulses in all the members of a group cannot be created by fiat or even by rational decision of all the members. It has to be a natural part of the emotional training of the child, repeated and actively practiced throughout the life cycle, in order to be firmly built into the personality.

It would be hard to find a better test of the hypothesis of the significance of the ritual attitude than the case of the orthodox Jews. They are not total abstainers, as some people suppose. They drink regularly, mostly in a ritual manner, although to some extent in a social way. Yet they are very seldom apprehended for drunkenness, and their rate of admission with alcoholic psychoses to mental hospitals is remarkably low. In almost any table showing rates of this sort for different ethnic groups in this country the Jews are at the bottom, just as the Irish are at the top. There have been many attempts to explain this. Immanuel Kant, who was one of the first to offer an explanation, believed that since the Jews' civic position was weak they had to be very rigidly self-controlled and cautious. They had to avoid the scandal and perhaps persecution which might result from drunkenness. Fishberg emphasizes that the Jews have had to live under persecution, and says that the Jew knows it does not pay to be drunk. Myerson emphasized the Jewish tradition itself and the hatred the Jews have developed for the drunkard, along with the factors of danger. These hypotheses are not necessarily contradictory—they simply emphasize different aspects of a ramified pattern. Yet it may be seriously questioned whether any of these factors could have remained truly effective without the ritual use of alcohol. In my opinion it is the ritual activity, repeated and participated in from childhood up, which positively stamps into the personality the sentiments or emotions to back up the rational realization of the dangers. Our East Coast Indians certainly saw the dangers rationally, and repeatedly decided to avoid alcohol, but had no success. They simply did not have the time nor the ritual technique for building into the personality the necessary emotional support for their rational decision. Hence the rational decision could not hold up in a crisis.

If it should be supposed that the Jews simply do not have acute needs for adjustment, or inner tensions, strong evidence may be advanced to the contrary. Besides all of the reasons for maladjustment to be expected from their position and historic role, it can be shown that with one or two minor exceptions they are quite as frequently represented in the major mental disorders as other groups. It is the impression of most psychiatrists that the Jews have higher rates of neuroses, that is, the milder mental disturbances, than most other ethnic groups. If it should be imagined that the Jews have some kind of mysterious immunity to compulsive habits in general, no supporting evidence can be found. Jews are known to have high rates of drug addiction, at least in certain areas. In a study made in this country of all draftees rejected in World War I for psychiatric reasons, the Jews were found to have a higher rate of drug addiction than any other ethnic group. This emphasizes the fact that their immunity to alcoholism can hardly be explained in terms of either a general immunity to addiction or a lack of acute inner tensions.

The essential ideas and sentiments which may come to be embodied in the attitude toward drinking as a result of ritual drinking, and which seem to operate as a counterinfluence to the formation of the habit of excessive drinking, may be clearly seen in the Jewish culture. In the Jewish family at least one male child is greatly desired, so that he may say prayers for his parents after their death. The continuity of the family is through the male line. Eight days after the birth of the male child a ceremony is held for his circumcision. There should be at least 10 adult males present to make up the "minyan," or legal and ritually sufficient quorum, to represent the community and carry on worship in the synagogue. The circumcision is performed because of God's commandment, and signifies the entry of the son into the covenant between Jehovah and the Jewish people. The people say, "Even as he has entered into the Covenant, so may he enter into the Law, the nuptial canopy, and into good deeds." A benediction is then offered over a cup of wine, with the following words: "Blessed art Thou, O Lord our God, king of the universe, creator of the fruit of the vine." The drinking of the cup of wine is a visible symbol and seal of the completed act of union.

In the Jewish culture wine stands for a whole complex of sacred things. Wine is variously alluded to as "the work of God" and "the commandment of the Lord." Similarly, the Torah (the sacred body of the Law), Jerusalem (the sacred place), Israel (the sacred community), and "the Messiah" (the righteous) are all compared to wine. The wine must be ritually pure, untouched by an idolater, and any vessel in which it is put must be "kosher," or ritually clean. Drinking, like eating, has a sacrificial character and is vested with an element of holiness. The dietary laws are symbolic of the separateness of the Jewish people. They constitute a discipline of all appetites to the end of attaining the all-inclusive state of holiness which is so much desired in the Jewish religion. Undisciplined appetites are a defilement of the self.

The first religious education of the child is directed to the teaching of the proper benedictions for bread, fruit, milk and other foods. He is told very early, "Thou shalt not eat any abominable thing." He also learns to observe the prohibition against touching that which is "holy unto the Lord." The "fruit of the vine" in the form of grapes falls in this class of sacred things. They must not be eaten before the fifth year of the life of the vine. In the first three years they are "uncircumcised," and in the fourth year they are "holy, to praise the Lord withal." Jewish parents impress their children with a great awe and reverence for things sacred and divine. Both grapes and wine are referred to as the "fruit of the vine," as in the customary benediction over wine.

There are four rituals each Sabbath in which the drinking of wine is the central act of communion. The first is on Friday evening and is called "Kiddush," that is, the ritual which "sanctifies" the holy day. After a thanksgiving prayer by the master of the house, a cup of wine is blessed. The master first partakes, and the cup is then passed from member to member, in the order of their precedence, down to and including the domestics if they are also Jewish. The males wear their hats, as in the synagogue, for this is a religious as well as a familistic ceremony. Then one of the two special Sabbath loaves is broken and each person is given a portion. After the meal, grace is recited and another cup of wine is blessed and passed around as before. This is called the "cup of benediction." A similar ritual, ironically called "Great Kiddush," because of its lesser importance, precedes the benediction over bread before breakfast on the morning of the Sabbath and other festival days. The ritual called the "Habdalah," on the Sabbath evening, marks the separation of the holy day from the rest of the week. The father chants a prayer of separation, the winecup is poured to overflowing to symbolize the overflowing of blessing which is hoped for, is blessed in the regular way, and partaken of first by the master of the house and then by the other males. The females do not partake on this occasion. The wine is again blessed and this time the father drinks alone. He moistens his eyes with the wine, saying, "The commandment of the Lord is pure, enlightening the eyes." The remaining wine is finally poured upon a plate and the burning candle is extinguished by dipping it into the wine. It is interesting and important to note that the order in which the family members partake of the wine, first the father, then the lesser males, then the females, and then the domestics, emphasizes their relative status and also their relative closeness to the sacred. The same order in reverse is observed in the Habdalah, where first the females abstain and then the lesser males, so that finally only the father drinks. The various members are separated from the sacred in the order of the lesser first, and finally the most important.

The drinking of wine, or the specific abstention from drinking, figures in the various feasts and fasts of the yearly cycle. In general, where food is forbidden as a sign of mourning or as a sign of guilt and expiation, that is, where the ritual state is one of estrangement from the sacred, wine is forbidden. This is true of the "Black Fast" and of "Yom Kippur"—the Day of Atonement. After the season of estrangement, comes the season of reunion and restored favor with God in the Festival of the Booths. This reunion and restored favor is indicated by the taking of food and wine. On Purim, a more secular holiday, the Talmud says that the Jew should drink until he can no longer distinguish between "cursed be Haman" (the ancient persecutor of the Jews) and "blessed be Mordecai" (their ancient savior). Sometimes the old men pretend to become drunk to amuse the youngsters. Actually, however, this appears to be another one of those ironic inversions, like "Great Kiddush," and only emphasizes the extreme foolishness and danger of drunkenness by linking it with the memory of old persecutions. At the celebration of the Passover there are four ritual partakings of wine, each with a blessing. After this no more wine may be tasted that night. A cup of wine, which one of the boys tastes, is left for Elijah, who may come during the night. Finally, in the Rejoicing of the Law, a festival celebrating the time when the Law was given, wine is partaken of in the usual ritual manner.

At the time of marriage, the social union par excellence, the bridal couple and their nearest relatives partake of a consecrated cup of wine, and the glass is broken, apparently with the connotation of the finality and exclusiveness of the union. At the time of death, the final separation, the deep mourning is indicated by abstention from all food and wine. In all of these rituals, in which the child participates from the time he is able to understand, the partaking of the consecrated wine indicates a union with the sacred and the solidarity of the Jewish people in their covenant with God, while abstention from the wine indicates a temporary estrangement from Divine favor, a state of guilt, and the sad dispersion of the Jewish people.

In the Jewish culture the wine is sacred and drinking is an act of communion. The act is repeated again and again and the attitudes toward drinking are all bound up with attitudes toward the sacred in the mind and emotions of the individual. In my opinion this is the central reason why drunkenness is regarded as so "indecent"—so unthinkable—for a Jew. Rational precaution also probably plays a part, but the ritual use is the main mechanism which builds in the necessary emotional support for the attitudes. Drunkenness is a profanity, an abomination, a perversion of the sacred use of wine. Hence the idea of drinking "to become drunk" for some individualistic or selfish reason arouses a counteranxiety so strong that very few Jews ever become compulsive drinkers.[6]

We have other evidence that the counteranxiety connected with drinking can act as a factor to prevent drunkenness. Among the Balinese alcoholic beverages are distilled and used ceremonially by the people, but they very seldom become intoxicated. The anxiety here, however, seems not to have been created through specific ceremonial use but because it is so extremely important to these people to maintain their exact spatial and geographic orientation. If a Balinese is put into a car and taken suddenly by a winding way to a place where he loses his directions he becomes extremely anxious and actually sick. Eastward, inland toward their sacred mountain, and upward toward its summit are sacred directions. Westward, outward to the sea, and downward are profane. Each member is very careful to keep other members of higher status than himself to the eastward, inland, or on a higher seat. Drunkenness is likely to make one lose his directions and become confused in these relations. In the weaving and confusion of drunkenness one is likely to trespass on the sacred, put sacred things in profane places, or wander off into the dangerous jungle which they fear greatly. Hence the anxiety connected with drunkenness is so strong and immediate that the Balinese avoid it almost entirely. This is true in spite of the fact that they have extremely strong suppressed emotions, as is known from other facts about their culture.

Convivial drinking is a mixed type, tending toward the ritual in its symbolism of solidarity, and toward the utilitarian in the "good feeling" expected. Wherever it is found highly developed it seems to be in danger of breaking down toward purely utilitarian drinking. This breakdown is to

---

6. S. Rosenman ("Pacts, Possessions, and the Alcoholic," *American Imago, 12* [1955], 241–74) has advanced a theory to account for the relative absence of alcoholism among Jews. In his opinion the particular sin committed by the alcoholic is his symbolic alliance with Satan, a pact with or possession by the Bad Father. He seeks power, protection, and pleasure beyond other people; he fights against the restrictive Good Father, he must renounce the Lord and turn to Satan. After his ordeal with Satan the alcoholic is left helpless, an inferior sinner with Satan's mark on him. This is why the alcoholics form associations, why they think that a virtuous person, i.e. a nonalcoholic, cannot understand their weakness. To society the alcoholic is the Devil's agent and must be punished.

The idea of the contest between Satan and God as it pertains to alcoholism may offer an explanation of the low rate of alcoholism among Jews. The Hebrews succeeded in integrating all gods and divinities into a single image of God. Satan emerged as his Satanic majesty only with Christianity. The Jew deals only with his one God; alcohol, like everything else, remains a gift of God. "It is to be used to eliminate that hostile self-centeredness which prevents one from integrating solidary relations with God's creatures" as well as to make, seal, and consecrate a covenant with God.—Ed.

be found in marked form in the Irish culture. A drinking party is in order at all of the principal occasions in the life cycle, in the meeting of friends, in business dealings, political affairs, pilgrimages, and every other occasion when people come together. One writer in the last century says, "Hallow-E'en, St. Patrick's Day, Easter, and all extra-ordinary days are made apologies for a drinking bout; a week's excess is taken at Christmas." He continues:

> Baptisms are generally debauches; launching a ship; making men pay their footing (on board a crowded ship where the men had to stand on the deck), births, wakes, funerals, marriages, churns in the country, are all jovial and vehement occasions of universal revelry. Pledging, toasting, and offering spirits in courtesy is much in vogue; and if a visitor do not taste at any time a day, he gives offence, as in Scotland. Washer-women, wet nurses, coach drivers, carmen, porters, and others are all treated by their employers with whiskey. There are no dry bargains; and in provision stores and other places, allowances of whiskey are bound to the workmen in their articles of service. An Irishman is in the last stage when he begins to drink alone; which is the case also with the Scotsman; and numbers treat for the mere purpose of obtaining pleasant company.[7]

It is important to note that although drinking is a part of gatherings for occasions such as marriages, which have a ritual or ceremonial core, the people never drink as a part of the ritual itself. In the Mass the priest partakes of the wine but not the laity. On the sort of occasions where there is a ritual core, drinking is a purely secular, convivial celebration, before or after. Whisky is always liberally provided. No "good fellow" would be niggardly in providing whisky for a celebration. It is thought to be only "decent" to treat a friend. One shows that he regards the other as "a good fellow" by drinking with him. When relatives, or "friends" as they are called in Ireland, or acquaintances of the same social standing meet in a public house, it is a matter of strict obligation for one to "stand" for all the others. He must order drinks all around and pay for them himself. Each man is then obligated to "stand" in his turn, and so on until all have bought at least one drink around. If there are more than three or four in the party, they are necessarily fairly well intoxicated by the time each has done his duty. It is an unforgivable insult to refuse to take a drink with a man without a long involved explanation and a profuse apology.

The breakdown into a utilitarian attitude can be observed in the use of drinking in economic transactions. At the fairs, where the livestock is sold, there is usually a long, heated argument about the price. When an agreement is finally reached, the bargain is sealed with one or more drinks. Sometimes the seller takes his customer to the public house before the

---

7. From "Testimony of John Dunlop," in *Evidence on Drunkenness Presented to the House of Commons*, J. S. Buckingham, Esq. in the Chair. London; S. Bagster, Jun., Printer [ca. 1834].

agreement is reached and treats him a few times to "soften him up." In making the bargain for a marriage it is necessary to reach extensive economic agreements in the evaluation of the farm and livestock, since this determines the amount of the dowry the young lady's father will give. In one of these matchmakings the bargainers treat back and forth until all are well fuddled. One writer says, "To one who has lived for some time in England, the mixture of tippling and business seems like some incredible dream. Little bits of business get in, as if by stealth, between the drinks during the day!" The farmer typically comes home from a day at the fair in a very intoxicated condition indeed. His wife does not usually complain. In fact, if she is a very good wife, she may treat her husband the next morning with "a hair of the dog that bit him." Drunken men are usually treated with care and affection in Ireland. To the mother the drunken man is "the poor boy." Laborers seeing an intoxicated man coming home from the fair are prone to regard him with envy, rather than pity, since he is in a much better state than they.

Drinking to get over a hangover, "a hair of the dog that bit you," is a pure example of individualistic, utilitarian drinking. Here the alcohol is regarded as a medicine. According to Morewood, an Irish historian, whisky, or aqua vitae, as it was called, "was first used in Ireland only as a medicine, considered a panacea for all disorders, and the physicians recommended it to patients indiscriminately for preserving health, dissipating humours, strengthening the heart, curing colic, dropsy, palsy, quartan fever, stone, and even prolonging existence itself beyond the common limits." Aqua vitae was sold only in apothecaries' shops until sometime in the sixteenth or seventeenth century, and it has retained its medicinal virtues in the mind of the people to this day. It was the universal folk remedy, to "keep the cold out of the stomach," to produce a feeling of warmth after exposure, to restore consciousness in case of fainting, to cure the stomach ache, to cure insomnia, to reduce fatigue, to whet the appetite, to feel stronger, and to get rid of hangovers. In the cholera plagues of 1831 and 1849, which struck a mortal fear into the hearts of the people, brandy was firmly believed to be a preventive. People even sold their beds in their anxiety to get it. The country doctors prescribed it widely and used it themselves. In fact legends grew up about some of these old topers to the effect that the divine inspiration to cure did not possess them unless they were more or less "under the influence." In many cases a glass of whisky was all the poor peasant had to offer the doctor by way of payment. Whisky was given to children as a reward for good behavior. Drinking was the recommended cure-all for young men in low spirits, for whatever reason, just as prayer was recommended to women and old people.

There is little reason to doubt that the utilitarian attitude toward drinking, if commonly held, is the one of the four types which is most likely to lead to widespread compulsive drinking. There is no counteranxiety attached to the process of drinking in this case, and there is every suggestion for the individual to adopt drinking as the means of dealing with his particular maladjustment. The prevalence of this attitude in the culture of the Irish, along with widespread inner tensions, seems adequately to explain their high rate of alcoholism.

There are certain occupational groups with high rates that seem to trace mainly to an occupationally induced utilitarian attitude toward drinking. It is well known, for example, that rates are particularly high among individuals connected with the manufacture and sale of alcoholic beverages, such as brewery employees, public-house, hotel and innkeepers, barmen, waiters, and traveling salesmen. Certain manual laborers, who do heavy exhausting work, such as longshoremen, drink to reduce their fatigue or to escape chronic unpleasant conditions of work. They are likely to have high rates. Sullivan, in a statistical study of England made in 1905, drew a distinction between "convivial drinking," much as it is defined here, and "industrial drinking," which is one type of utilitarian drinking. He found that the highest rates of alcoholic disorders were associated with "industrial drinking, and not with convivial drunkenness." It is a well-known fact that a very high percentage of prostitutes become inebriates. The use of alcohol, both for themselves and as an attraction to their customers, is an indispensable part of their trade.

Finally ... :h seems to have a bearing
on rates ... ie culture provides suitable
substitute ... ıdjustment which it creates.
One of th ...)f other narcotic drugs. The
high rate ... ıas been mentioned. Many
Moslems ... ≥m to be habituated to very
strong te; ... o have a severe prohibition
against a ... a considerable degree, and
this patte ... : peoples in the East Indies.
The Japa ... ɔw rate of alcoholism, are
frequently users of opium.

Among the Balinese, who avoid drunkenness because of their anxiety about orientation, there is a peculiar trancelike state which seems to act as an outlet for their tensions. Their childhood training is one of constant stimulation to emotional response, followed by frustration. The mother fondles the child, but as soon as he notices and begins to respond emotionally, she "cuts him dead." Under this treatment the children finally withdraw into themselves and refuse to respond. But in their ceremonial dances, which symbolically recall the childhood situation, they go into trances and express extreme self-aggression with mingled emotions of "agony and ecstasy." Thus the trances seem to provide a way of restoring the balance, and to give the emotional purging which, in another culture, alcohol might provide. The complicated ritualism of the Hopi and Zuni

Indians, who were successful in total prohibition, may provide a somewhat similar substitute for reducing anxiety.

It is impossible to name all the sorts of things which might possibly serve as substitute means of adjustment, since this would depend upon the maladjustments which are acute in particular cultures, and these are very numerous and complicated. The three general factors discussed, the acute inner tensions or needs for adjustment, the attitudes toward drinking, and the provision of substitutes, seem to be fairly adequate in an over-all logical way, and give some insight into a few of the outstanding cultural differences in rates of alcoholism. There are many rates, however, which are not yet understood. It is still not possible to formulate precisely all the different types of maladjustment or tension which can be involved in compulsive drinking, to say nothing of our inability to measure just how acute they are in specific cultural settings. As to the types of attitude toward drinking, very little is known concerning just how they come about, what makes them endure or break down, or just how widespread particular attitudes are in particular places and cultures. These problems still require an immense amount of careful theoretical and research work.

It can safely be said, however, that all three factors are important. They all work together, and the rates are complicated end-results. With regard to the problem of reducing the rates of alcoholism in a particular place, there is no doubt that it must be attacked from all three angles. Anything which can be done to relieve the acute tensions of people, or steer them away from utilitarian attitudes toward drinking, or provide them with suitable and effective substitutes for the rewards which drinking brings them, may have a preventive effect in the long run. It seems clear, however, that no very conspicuous success can be expected unless all three factors can be modified together, and modified considerably for the whole group.

21. ETHNOGRAPHY OF ALCOHOLISM

by Ruth Bunzel *

Etiology

The propensity for drinking is developed in Chamula in very early child-hood, not only by the external fact of habituation of very young children to alcohol, but by the cultural conditions that affect personality structure. Too much importance should not be given to the purely physiological fact of early habituation. Even after years of this sort of habituation children do not crave alcohol. Children of nine or ten ordinarily do not like aguardiente, and if a glass is passed to them they usually merely sip it and hand it back. That alcohol has more than purely physiological significance is evident from the fact that however great the craving for alcohol may be, there is no solitary drinking. Since drinking is a social activity, we must look for its sources in the child's earliest social patterns. The outstanding facts of in-fancy are the unusually prolonged period of nursing, and the extreme intimacy of mother and child. This has already been suggested by their theories of sickness, and can be amply documented from case histories and by observation. In order to understand these facts, we must go back a little.

*   *   *

During childbirth men are excluded from the hut. The mother is assisted by a midwife who bathes the baby, wraps it in blankets, and lays it on the platform bed beside the mother. The child is covered with blan-kets, and for twenty days no one but the mother may see it. During the first four days the mother does no work. Relatives and neighbors come in to grind for her, but no one sees or mentions the new child. It is be-lieved that if anyone were to see the baby during this period it would die. At the end of twenty days it is shown to the father and after that may be seen by anyone.

During infancy the child is never separated from his mother. She carries him on her back in a carrying cloth even when she is at work. The infant sleeps contentedly in the carrying cloth, his head bobbing around, while his mother bends over the loom or the grinding-stone. He is removed from this position only to be suckled and to be cleaned, and at night he sleeps in the bed between his parents.

* Reprinted by permission of The William Alanson White Foundation, from "The Role of Alcoholism in Two Central American Cultures," *Psychiatry, 3* (1940), 361–87. (See also above, pp. 73–86.) Copyright by The William Alanson White Foundation, Inc.

The nursing period is exceptionally long. If no younger child is born children may continue to be suckled until they are six or seven. Children who are completely self sufficient during the day, even going off with older children to tend the sheep, will demand the breast at night or whenever they wish to go to sleep. Women describe nursing as a pleasurable activity. I have frequently seen women fall asleep with an expression of complete contentment, while suckling their babies. If another pregnancy intervenes, the first child may be weaned suddenly by smearing the nipples with lime. A child is never weaned before the eighteenth month, and usually not until well into the third year. Sometimes the mother continues to nurse the older child, even after the second child is born. By this time the older child is eating other food, and the breast feeding is largely considered as a consolation. In any case, the older child shows great resentment toward the mother "because he cannot suckle well." A little girl of two whose mother had just given birth to a baby, attacked me in frantic rage "because" my informant volunteered, "she is angry with her mother." This is considered the normal reaction of a child to a new baby.

* * *

Boys are believed to be more sensitive than girls. The importance given to the bond between mother and child in the native theory of disease has already been mentioned. Children are treated with the greatest tenderness by all adults. They are never punished and rarely scolded; the mildest reproof is considered sufficient. No one ever becomes angry at a child, or threatens him. Children are never excluded from any festivity. They are not excluded from serious affairs either; they learn early all there is to know about birth and death, sickness and misfortune. When fathers return from work, they give their attention to children, especially boys, playing rough and tumble games with them, or teaching them the one art they know—to strum the guitar. Parents in Chamula enjoy their children and spend their free time with them rather than seeking their adult friends.

* * *

Children sleep with their parents until they are weaned. Then they sleep in another bed or on the floor, boys and girls together under the same blanket. All people sleep without clothing. As they grow older girls accept a maternal attitude toward their brothers, making up their beds, looking after their clothing, and taking care of them when they are sick. It is considered proper for boys and girls to sleep apart after puberty, but this is rarely enforced. The nights are always cold and people sleep close together for warmth. All informants said that although brothers and sisters might sleep together after puberty, sexual intercourse never took place between them. . . .

In later life siblings support each other in all concerns of life. Brothers—

or brothers-in-law, when families are matrilocal—occupy contiguous plots of land and live in adjoining houses. The men co-operate in agricultural work, and their wives herd each others' sheep and mind each others' babies. Between related families there is constant visiting back and forth, borrowing and lending of all kinds of articles, and sharing of any special delicacies. If I contributed meat or fruit to the family meals, Diego, my host, would send a portion to his brother. If I brought back from town a bottle of aguardiente—an occasional treat was the only compensation that Diego would accept for my occupation of his house—a child would be sent to invite his brothers before the bottle was opened. On the other hand, any of Diego's brothers could be called upon to perform slight services for me without pay. "Brothers always help each other out." There are no quarrels between brothers over land or other matters, and Chamula could not understand a society in which such quarrels occur. In the four months in which I lived in the Government building and kept records of all litigation that came to the authorities for settlement there was only one case of a dispute between brothers. Most of the cases concerned difficulties between husband and wife or between father-in-law and son-in-law over marriage payments. The primacy of the blood grouping is uncomplicated by the presence of social groups that cut across the blood group and draw men together on the basis of age, likeness of occupation, military or religious achievements. Except for the superimposed political organization which affects but a small portion of the population, there are no mechanisms for effective social integrations. There is no basis on which men can come together except as "relatives" or casual companions of the road. The term "brother" is used to all males of one's own generation, related through either line. Applied to distant relatives from other hamlets it does not carry the implication of mutual cooperation that exists between true blood brothers and first cousins. It is significant, however, that it is the elder brother–younger brother reciprocals that are used most frequently when two men drink together. What has been said about brothers applies equally to brothers and sisters.

Unless there is a grown girl in the family the mother goes out nearly every day herding sheep, and takes the young children with her. Even very small children are useful in sheep-herding. A girl of ten is considered old enough to assume full responsibility for the sheep of the family. Herding is women's work, and boys over five will not go out with sheep unless it is necessary. A boy without sisters considers himself very unfortunate, since then he must be the shepherd. Nowadays the boys in the hamlet where I lived go to school; the school is only two years old, and most hamlets are unaffected. Formerly boys of school age began to go with their fathers to the cornfields, and even went to the plantations to work.

By the age of fifteen or sixteen every lad has been to the plantations. Either his father has bound him for plantation labor, or else having no father, he must go to the plantation to earn money to support his family.

We have already spoken of the short life span of men, which leaves many women widowed with young children. On these boys financial responsibility falls early. They must earn money for their "salt and chile," the phrase that is used to cover all non-local necessities, and must finance their own marriages. Most men report that they "learned to drink on the plantations." They had been introduced to alcohol in infancy and in the warm and cherishing family environment had rejected it; it is only when plunged into the hostile environment of the plantations that they acquire the taste for and addiction to strong drink. Everything is done to foster alcoholism: the boys are on their own, they have money for the first time in their lives, alcohol is cheap and accessible, when they are out of money they can get credit, they have brought with them no patterns of social life that do not involve alcohol. For in Chamula all social contact outside of the warm circle of the immediate family takes place in a medium of aguardiente. Until the recent restrictions on debt slavery were enforced unscrupulous plantation owners did what they could to encourage alcoholism, since through it Indians remained continuously in debt and in the power of the employers. In the past the Church, too, by encouraging fiestas and refraining from preaching sobriety or using its influence on the side of the angels, has added its bit to the debauching of the Indians. Under these conditions all form habits of drinking that persist throughout their lives, with the consequent impoverishment of social life.

Most Chamulas go to the plantations for a few months each year. Some remain away for several years, working alternately on the plantations and in adjacent towns. Some few, perhaps 5 per cent of the total, abandon their ancestral lands, marry mestizo women and settle permanently in the plantation country. But even these eventually desert their alien wives and drift back to their homes, reclaim their lands and marry women of their own tribe. I knew many such men, who after years of living on the plantations and in the ports, grew homesick for the places to which they "belonged." Often they said they came back "to take care of their mothers." They felt no such binding obligations to their mestizo wives and children. Nor did they feel any wish to bring these foreign women back. Genealogies failed to reveal any foreign women living in Chamula. "What could she do here? Could she weave my blankets?" Or perhaps the women do not care to leave the protection of their families for the hard life of the mountains among "wild" Indians.

When a man returns to assume adult responsibilities in his village, the habit of drinking learned on the plantations fits comfortably and honorably into the social scene. The society is essentially atomistic. Alcohol provides, so to speak, the fluid medium through which atoms communicate, one with the other.

In the preceding pages I have tried to show the sociological factors which tend to build up the drinking habits in the individual which form so conspicuous a part of Chamula life and determine not only the fact of alcoholism, but its typical form. Without deep individual analysis, suggestions concerning the role of alcohol in psychic economy must remain highly tentative. The typical drunkard of Chamula suggests the familiar clinical picture of the "essential alcoholic." We note especially at Chamula the absence of vomiting—a form of resistance to alcohol?—and erotic behavior, the rapidity with which sleep supervenes, the typical absence of hangover, the very small role of aggressive behavior, whether fighting or boasting, and the complete absence of guilt or shame. In describing their sensations all informants stress physiological sensations, such as "warmth" and "comfort," rather than psychological states such as "forgetting worries," or "feeling important," and the like. They show the reactions of the undeveloped rather than the inhibited personality.

The life histories of "essential alcoholics" in our culture are usually characterized by some form of maternal overprotection in infancy, difficulties of weaning and similar phenomena which produce overemphasis of oral satisfactions and a tendency to regress to early infantile levels. It is therefore relevant that analogous phenomena are conspicuously present in the system of child rearing typical of Chamula society. We have repeatedly emphasized the intimacy of the relationship between mother and child so extreme that it is given conscious recognition in the native theory that disease is frequently caused by physical or mental injury to the mother while the child is young. The psychic trauma of weaning or of the birth of a sibling after a child is already weaned is sometimes so drastic as to rob the child of all will to live. The culture furnishes the child with no adequate substitute for these lost satisfactions, and as an adult he tends always to regress to the one meaningful experience. This is borne out by the lack of elaboration of sex in the culture, and the great emphasis on food and the sharing of food and on drink and the sharing of drink. The marriage relationship also is cast into the mother–child pattern. It is the woman who takes care of and feeds the man. Her primary role in marriage is to make the tortillas, and her husband feels completely dependent on her. It is perhaps significant of the basic symbolism of alcohol that no one pours his own drink or buys drinks over the counter of a bar. Even when two men drink together they pour each other's drinks and offer them ceremoniously. It would seem that the mother–infant relationship is the only one that has any reality in the culture and all other relationships must be cast symbolically into this form. Two men drinking together at a bar must alternately assume the mother and infant roles in order to enter into any social relationship. Alcoholism, in this culture, is typically a pursuit of the pleasure principle on the most primitive level, the only one which they can recognize.

Conclusions

Even a completely factual and superficial description of behavior that makes no attempt at analysis or interpretation reveals that "alcoholism" at Chichicastenango is a very different phenomenon from "alcoholism" at

Chamula. Especially significant is the observable absence of vomiting, erotic behavior, and serious quarreling at Chamula, the prevalence of drinking within the family circle when there is no ceremonial occasion, and the etiquette that surrounds the sharing of drinks—all of them points of contrast with Chichicastenango. When we push our analysis further into the attitudes surrounding drinking and the character of the emotions that are released under the influence of alcohol, we find that these striking differences in behavior are symptomatic of very real and deeply rooted differences in the role which alcohol plays in the total economy of each of these cultures.

Alcoholism is not only an individual reaction, it is a social phenomenon. It is more prevalent in some societies than in others and, as we have seen, it assumes different forms under different cultural conditions. These predisposing conditions are not necessarily or exclusively the ones that are emphasized in popular literature dealing with sociological factors in alcoholism. The two communities studied are not conspicuously poor, oppressed, or uprooted. They are communities of landowning peasants and merchants, with great social solidarity and racial pride, who have maintained their cultural integrity in the face of four centuries of White aggression. Extreme manifestations of alcoholism are distributed among all strata of the population, among both sexes and all ages, and are especially prominent among the older, richer and most highly respected groups. Alcoholism as a social phenomenon is not simply a reaction to manifest frustrations in the environment.

Both groups have an ancient and honored tradition of the ritual use of intoxicants. Limited use of alcohol under prescribed conditions has the highest cultural sanction and is, in fact, a necessary part of all public acts. It is notable that in both groups studied, drinking under the prescribed conditions has no apparent emotional effects. It does not noticeably impair mental functioning or banish inhibitions. It is not under these conditions that "the superego is dissolved."

However, in addition to this ritual drinking, there are social factors which, in both groups, predispose individuals to avail themselves of excessive and unrestricted use of alcohol to satisfy individual psychic needs.

The typical picture for Chichicastenango is one familiar in our own culture—a picture of frustration and hostility, with repression and guilt as corollaries. The conflict-producing situation is the patriarchal system with extreme parental authority embodied in the property institutions and supernaturally sanctioned by the ancestor cult and the private use of death sorcery. The hostility between father and son produces great anxiety, with castration ideas conspicuous. To the patriarchal complex we must add as etiological factors the repressive sexual mores. In this culture puritanism falls with equal weight upon men and women, and provides a second source of hostility and anxiety.

Away from home and among trusted companions, the Quiche releases his aggressions in drinking, and his behavior while drunk and his subsequent guilt are just what one would expect in view of this etiology. Drunkenness not only reduces inhibition and releases aggression, but it is also a substitute for direct aggression. The one fiesta that does not end in drunkenness ends in open violence. . . .

In Chamula, however, no comparable conflict-producing situation exists. The Chamulas drink for pleasure—direct somatic pleasure of warmth, relaxation, and deep untroubled sleep. They find no social evil in alcohol; it is good to be drunk, except for the fact that aguardiente is expensive. In connection with this view of drunkenness as pure pleasure, it is significant that Chamulas do not normally vomit when drunk or suffer from hangovers. Undoubtedly the physiological reactions and emotional attitudes interact as cause and effect. Since they have no experience with abstinence, they are unaware that excessive indulgence shortens their lives—and perhaps would not care. In Chamula alcohol has displaced all forms of aesthetic expression, games, intellectual pursuits, conversation, and companionship, and has reduced sex to a role of minor importance as a source of pleasure. The prolonged breast feeding and the erotically tinged relationship between mother and child are probably the most important social conditions determining this particular choice of gratification. Prolonged breast feeding is common in primitive and peasant communities, but the interpretation of the mother–child relationship seems peculiar to this group.

Psychiatrists will undoubtedly recognize in these descriptions of typical forms of drunkenness analogues to individual cases which they have encountered in clinical experience. In cross-cultural studies these clinical types appear with a regularity that helps to isolate the social causes. The attitudes, emotions, defenses which these "symptoms" represent exist, not in "culture," but in the minds of individuals who have passed through certain life experiences. Since primitive societies are relatively homogeneous and the experiences of individuals are fairly similar, the same syndromes appear with a regularity that is not observable in our more heterogeneous society. In the foregoing pages I have tried to point out what the social forces are that mold individuals into certain stereotypes. However, there is another aspect to the problem: the regular appearance of certain syndromes in large numbers of a population reacts in turn upon the culture. This kind of sequence is especially marked in the impoverishment of Chamula culture because people are too engrossed in drinking to develop the arts of life. Commitment to one form of gratification has blotted out every other possibility.

*   *   *

It is obviously impossible to approach the solution of the problem of alcoholism in communities such as Chamula and Chichicastenango from the standpoint of individual therapy. As a social problem it must be dealt with in a social program that takes account of the etiological factors and the social and psychological role it plays in the culture.

The first part of such a program would have to deal with external causes. So long as there are those who profit from the debauching of the Indians, any anti-alcoholic legislation will be unavailing and will merely increase opportunities for corruption. The attack on the liquor traffic must be directed to its source, that is, it must be waged against all those who profit directly or indirectly from the degradation of the Indian population. The new labor laws now in effect in both Mexico and Guatemala go a long way toward dealing with this aspect of the economic problem. It is to be hoped that this part of the program will be carried through to a successful conclusion.

The removal of external economic stimuli is, however, only the beginning of a program to control alcoholism. Even if it were possible to stop the sale of alcohol to Indians, the Indians would themselves manufacture it. If, by vigilance, it were possible to stop this also, without offering adequate substitutes, it would, in a community such as Chamula, completely disrupt the society, since alcohol, despite its ill effects, plays a role in social integration. I am not considering at the moment what disastrous forms the inevitable hostility of the Indians to any such drastic interference with their established customs might conceivably take.

It should be borne in mind that each group presents a different problem; it is necessary in each case to find out what role alcohol plays *in that culture,* and to devise suitable substitutes or, where alcoholism is the result of frustration, to deal directly with the conflict-producing situation. For instance, the lessening of intrafamilial hostility at Chichicastenango would have more effect than the most rigidly enforced prohibitory statutes. In any successful program of directed social change, for every cultural trait that is taken away, something better must be offered—that is, something better *for that purpose.* Such programs require social insight and imagination. It is not within the scope of this paper to outline the details of such a program, but simply to indicate how it must be adapted to the specific needs of the group.

The problem would be simpler in Chichicastenango. Here the disruptive consequences of drinking are clearly recognized. The Indians made some attempt to control this evil by restricting their drinking to public places and indifferent companions. There are some abstainers. Some support would be found among the Indians themselves for stricter enforcement of the licensing laws, and for the substitution of milder drinks where ritual requires drinking. The problem is that of dealing with delinquency on a large scale. Effective control would mean social changes that mitigate the conflict-producing situation—complete overhauling of the land and labor laws in order to give greater independence and security to young men; education against supernatural fears and fears of sorcery, and an easing of sexual mores—anything that would make the individual feel less frustrated and frightened. But such a program would have to be conceived as a unit; it would be disastrous to wage a successful campaign against the supernatural sanctions against aggression while leaving untouched the economic causes of hostility.

The problem at Chamula is far more complicated. The Chamulas are not delinquent; alcohol is not socially disruptive among them, but a mechanism of social integration. They see no evil in it, only pleasure—the only pleasure immediately available to them. Therefore the desirability of disturbing a workable adjustment by "reform" is debatable. But assuming that one is presumptuous enough to think it both desirable and possible, the program would have to be adjusted to the peculiar circumstances, with full recognition of the fact that one is attacking the heart of the culture, with all the unforeseen dangers that that implies. All the effort would have to be on the positive side—providing other gratifications. Cultural missions that provided entertainment and encouraged social activities, the introduction of a new and pleasantly harmless drink, with its own elaborate ritual, with a build-up of prestige as being "from the capital," would be of some help. These, like economic laws, leave untouched the core of the problem, which is the character of the mother–child relationship. I see no way at the present time of dealing with this as a social phenomenon. The only hope would be that a richer social life might make certain individuals less dependent on the present form of gratification.

These programs are, as I have said, simply suggestions concerning direction of social therapy adapted to the specific cases described. When we come to recognize the extent to which the prevalence and forms of alcoholic indulgence are culturally determined, it may become possible to deal with it as a social problem more intelligently than we did in our last "noble experiment."

22. A PSYCHOCULTURAL ANALYSIS
OF THE ALCOHOLIC

by Harriet R. Mowrer *

Psychological studies of the alcoholic have been primarily from the psychiatric and psychoanalytic points of view. These studies have been clinical in nature and, except in a few instances, have represented merely the reflections of physicians or psychiatrists upon their cases, rather than any systematic analysis of case records. Among the few exceptions are the studies of Wall of one hundred male and fifty female alcoholics, Wittman's study of one hundred alcoholics and Knight's study of thirty cases. This is not to deny, however, the value of other studies characterized more as reflections upon clinical experience than as research, the most recent of which is that of Strecker and Chambers.

As to the etiology of alcoholism there is a wide divergence of opinion among psychiatrists themselves. In fact, theories applied to chronic alcoholism seem to have run the gamut of psychoanalytic theories and most of these have been worked out clinically in the field of the neuroses and the psychoses. Thus chronic alcoholism, like drug addiction, has long been associated with the neuroses and psychoses and each development or shift in emphasis in analytic theory has been followed by its application to the problem of the alcoholic.

Thus Abraham, in 1908, developed the psychological relations between sexuality and alcoholism and stated that drinking is the alcoholic's sexual activity. He concluded that sexuality, alcoholism, and neuroses are all interrelated. Juliusburger in 1913 stressed unconscious homosexuality as the cause of alcoholism. In 1919, L. Pierce Clark elaborated upon the conclusions of both Abraham and Juliusburger. Alcoholism, he concluded, is a substitute for neurosis and psychosis. In 1925, Sachs characterized drug and alcoholic craving as a compromise between a perversion and a compulsion neurosis. Weiss in 1926 and Kielholz in 1931 showed the relationship between the taking of toxic drugs and paranoid psychoses in which occurred delusions of being poisoned. In 1928, Weijl showed the importance of the Oedipus complex in the analysis of alcoholism and asserted that in drinking there is identification with the father orally (cannibalistic destruction) and attainment of the mother. Chambers in 1937 noted an underlying neurotic condition that makes alcoholism possible in certain individuals—an alcoholic compulsion neurosis.

* From the *American Sociological Review,* 5 (1940), 546–57.

It was not until recently that there has been any systematic attempt to study the personality characteristics of alcoholics. Since alcoholism was thought to be related to the neuroses and psychoses, then it would logically follow that the alcoholic has some or all of the characteristics of the neurotic and psychotic individual. What these characteristics are, however, is not specifically revealed. In these earlier studies, there are little or no research findings which would give support to the hypothesis that the alcoholic is psychopathic, since no attempt was made to study his personality and background.

Wall's study marks the transition from theorizing about alcoholism as a phase of psychopathic behavior to an attempted analysis of the alcoholic's personality. He found in the family background a doting, oversolicitous mother and a comparatively stern, forbidding father. This produced in the child a feeling of insecurity and helpless dependence, combined with a high percentage of alcoholic excess among the preceding generations. Emotional immaturity or instability, infantilism, passivity and dependence, pathological jealousy, oral eroticism, and latent homosexuality, were characteristic personality traits. Dr. Walter Miles gave greater emphasis to the hypothesis of homosexuality, pointing out that the traits described by Wall resemble in several respects the homosexuals described by L. M. Terman and C. C. Miles.

Generalizations in terms of such extensive traits as have been said to characterize the alcoholic, however, do not seem warranted. In the present writer's research with domestic discord cases, it may be said that many persons with domestic discord display some of these same traits but they cannot be classified either as psychopaths or homosexuals. However, the significance of Wall's study lies not so much in its content as in representing one of the first systematic attempts to study the personality of the alcoholic.

The studies of the alcoholic thus have tended to oversimplify the problem. Causes have been either in the form of data on isolated factors or so general as to apply to other groups of persons including the nonalcoholic. Furthermore, studies have not been comparable. It is impossible to compare analyses of data because of differences in fundamental background and premises, as well as differences in technique and scope. This has been complicated further by the fact that in some instances there have been no specific statements of techniques.

The purposes of this study were: (*1*) to make an analysis of the personalities of alcoholics in such a way as to reveal the basic reaction patterns which determine their adjustment to the social milieu; (*2*) to get at the genesis of the attitudes which constitute the personality; (*3*) to compare the personality patterns of the alcoholic with another group studied and classified as the escape-response type; [1] (*4*) to compare the alcoholic with a second group studied and classified as showing no personality disorganization.

1. This type is characterized by the habitual use of illness as a substitute adjust-

Case studies of all three groups were made in a comparable way as to frame of reference, interviewing technique, elements of personality genesis and development, social interaction, and later family adjustment. Each group consisted of twenty-five married individuals and their marriage partners; comprising, therefore, seventy-five cases, or one hundred and fifty individuals. None of the marriage partners in either of the three groups showed any personality disorganization. The basis of distinction between the alcoholic and the nonalcoholic was the fact that chronic drinking of the alcoholic constituted a part of his pattern of social maladjustment. Contacts were maintained with each case for an average period of three years, affording ample opportunity for checking upon the reliability of the analysis. Each analysis was made upon the basis of an extensive body of materials obtained through a series of firsthand interviews in response to the desire upon the part of the patient to have the assistance of the writer in the understanding and solution of some problem of personality or of domestic discord.

This analysis has been restricted to twenty-five case studies in each group in order to make it possible to study and compare three groups of cases.[2] The purpose of this comparison is to bring out more sharply the factors in early familial interaction which differentiate the alcoholic personality pattern from other types of personalties. Without such comparisons, as past experience has demonstrated, there is a tendency to look upon common factors as definitive of a particular type. Methodologically, the following procedure is equivalent to the use of a control group in statistical analysis without the attendant loss of the organic unity which characterizes the relationship between etiological factors.

Since this is a case-study analysis, quantitative results wherever utilized have been expressed in qualitative terms and introduced only as they are related to and consistent with the larger organic pattern which can only be portrayed in qualitative language. Quantitative statements, however, may be found in footnotes, but the reader is cautioned against interpreting these data too exactly since the number of cases involved is too small to insure statistical reliability.

In the analysis of the personality pattern, the following factors were assumed to be significant: (1) psychogenetic characteristics, including attach-

ment device in the hope of reclaiming and reinstating a social relationship developed in early family interaction and emotionally satisfying to the individual. More detailed descriptions of this type may be found in Harriet R. Mowrer, *Personality Adjustment and Domestic Discord*, New York, 1935.

2. There is no magical significance to the number twenty-five, but earlier experience of the writer has shown that where extensively developed case studies are utilized, the addition of ten or twenty more to a comparatively sizable group such as this does not essentially change the pattern. The number of additional cases is bound of course to be limited by the enormous expenditure of time required for making them complete and accurate. Thus the writer has found that the minimum time required for a study of seventy-five such cases is a period of three years. Cf. Harriet R. Mowrer, "Clinical Treatment of Marital Conflicts," *American Sociological Review*, 2 (1937), 277–8.

tachment to parents, rank and role in the family, relationship to siblings, marital adjustment of parents, etc.; (2) the physical pattern; (3) the cultural background, including education and early work history, vocational adjustment, intellectual, and artistic interests, etc.; (4) social and economic adjustment; (5) the sexual and response pattern, including early attitudes toward sex, sex education, sexual experiences prior to marriage, marital adjustments, nature of close attachments carried over from early family group, and the like; (6) cultural setting and circumstances surrounding the first appearance of the behavior which became the basic pattern of response, such as drink, gambling, "illness," attempts at suicide, etc.; (7) later family adjustment, including type of marriage partner, conflict and accord, history of role in the home, attitude of children, and so on; (8) rationalizations.

Psychogenetic Factors. What effect ordinal position has upon familial interaction is not entirely clear. Nevertheless, research has shown that the earliest role of the child in the family has a far-reaching effect upon his life organization and type of adjustment pattern. It is generally accepted that it is usually to a peculiar set of family circumstances that one has to look for an understanding of these reaction patterns.

Several writers have portrayed the alcoholic as more likely to be the only or youngest child. Another has attached no significance to ordinal position. It would seem that ordinal position is of no significance except to the degree to which it may be a factor in determining role. Thus in our culture, the youngest child is more likely to be the favorite and his infantilism is more likely to be prolonged. Witness the number of youngest children still referred to as "Baby," Junior," "Angel," and so on, by their parents! However, any child in the family, because of various peculiar circumstances, may have the role of the "youngest."

In the cases in this study, the alcoholics in ordinal position clustered around next to the oldest, youngest, and next to youngest.[3] As to role, it is significant that none of the youngest had the role one usually thinks of as typical of this group. The most significant factors in familial interaction, however, were a dislike or hatred for the father, a marked dislike or jealousy toward a brother thought to be favored by the father, a strong attachment for the mother or a sister who in turn favored them. If one can draw any conclusion here, it would seem ambiguity in role is what characterizes the alcoholic—a role in which his status is superior and assured in relation to some members of his family and uncertain and challenged in relation to others.

Comparing the group of alcoholics with those characterized by escape-response through illness, one finds a clearcut distinction. In the latter group, all are either youngest children or have the role of the "youngest." Here the typical family configuration is: favorite of both parents, close

3. Of the 25 alcoholics, 9 were next to the oldest; 1, middle; 7, next to the youngest; 6, youngest; and 2, only children.

attachment of siblings, protection from early responsibility, and no challenge to "favorite" role. Since women constitute the larger number of this group, one may question the validity of comparing all men with a predominantly feminine group. Perhaps the sex of the child is an important factor in the determination of role. With this hypothesis in mind, the escape-response-through-illness group (predominantly women) were compared with the wives of the alcoholics as to ordinal position and role. Here there was a striking difference, the wives of the alcoholics showing a preponderance of oldest and "middle" children.[4] In comparing the alcoholics with the group showing no personal disorganization, this same striking difference was borne out with both the men and the women although the men in this latter group showed a larger proportion of oldest children than did the women.[5]

With the overwhelming preponderance of oldest children in the group showing no personality disorganization and the presence of no "oldest" in the disorganized group under observation, it would seem that one can logically conclude that there must be a definite relationship between adjustment and ordinal position or role in regard to the oldest child.[6] The oldest child usually has the role of one who is taken for granted as conforming to the traditional role of the child, whatever that may be for the particular cultural group. For example, in one cultural group this may mean carrying on the profession or trade of the father even though it may not carry with it a great deal of prestige. Thus in general the American farmer has wanted his oldest son to be a farmer. In another group, it may not mean carrying on the trade of the father, but that glorified by the particular cultural group. The Jewish tailor, for example, does not wish his son to carry on his trade, but dreams of his being a learned man, a lawyer, or a doctor. Many an Italian immigrant laborer, likewise, dreams of producing a Caruso.

The relationship between adjustment and the middle child, while not as striking, is significant. Here he, like the oldest, is more likely to take his position for granted and to demand less recognition for himself than do persons in other ordinal positions.

Of undoubtedly more significance than ordinal position, but closely related to role, is the pattern of family relationships in the so-called organized group, which is characterized by a lesser degree of attachment toward either parent, in some instances, even by extreme detachment, fewer instances of preferential treatment by either parents or siblings, and little or no marked jealousies. In other words, the members of the organized group

4. Of the 25 wives of alcoholics, 17 were oldest and middle children.
5. The ordinal positions of the men were: 16 oldest, 5 middle, 1 in-between, 2 youngest, and 1 only; of the women, 10 oldest, 1 next to the oldest, 6 middle, 1 in-between, 3 next to the youngest, 1 youngest, and 3 only.
6. Combining both sexes in the cases in which there was no personality disorganization, out of 50 individuals, 26 were oldest children.

(predominantly "oldest" and "middle" children) seem on the whole to have accepted the roles assigned to them without conflict and those roles seem not to have conflicted with the rights of others. The result was that theirs were roles which could be maintained without conflict in later interpersonal relationships outside the family.

As to marital adjustment of the parents of the alcoholic group as compared with the group showing no disorganization, there is little significant difference, domestic discord occurred slightly less frequently in the alcoholic group. The parents of the escape-response group, however, show a higher degree of marital adjustment. It is interesting to note that the fathers of the alcoholic group are less often alcoholic than those of the non-alcoholic "organized" group.[7] This would be contrary to the belief that an alcoholic nervous system is transmitted from one generation to the other, about which there is little known.[8] It would more nearly agree with the conclusions of Knight of the Menninger Clinic who did not find alcoholism in the family background as a constant factor and is doubtful that there is an inherited predisposition. The most significant factor suggested, however, by the finding of more alcoholic fathers in the nonalcoholic group is a cultural one. Alcoholism may have a different meaning to the individual reared in a home where a parent is alcoholic. It may be to him a symbol of erratic behavior, shiftlessness, unhappy home life, etc. To the others, the symbol may be the traditional one of masculinity, virility, and strength.

Cultural Background and Economic Adjustment. The alcoholics show a wide range in cultural background from the clergyman's son to the son of the laborer. In this regard, there is no significant difference as compared with the "organized" group. As to economic status, the "escape-response" group is significantly higher than either of the other groups. Educational background is not essentially different except for a few instances of expulsion from school in the alcoholic group. The alcoholic group is characterized by considerable shifting in occupation, restlessness, dissatisfaction with occupation, and lack of definite drive. The "organized" group shows greater occupational stability and less ambitious aspirations. The alcoholic's background, like that of the "escape-response" type, shows more evidence of reading of an intellectual nature. More of the alcoholic group have artistic interests and when asked what they would most like to have been, the typical reply was, an artist, a musician, or an inventor. This might be said to bear out or throw more light upon Strecker and Chambers' hypothesis that the alcoholic's standards are higher than the average.

The Sexual and Response Factor. As has already been pointed out, the association of the sexual factor and alcoholism has long been accepted.

7. Three fathers of 25 alcoholics were alcoholic; 7 fathers of the 25 "organized" males.

8. The experimental work on animals as to the physiological effect of alcoholization of parents upon the progeny is not conclusive when applied to human beings.

This has for the most part taken the form of indicating the relationship between homosexuality and alcoholism. Theories have been read into fragmentary factual data on certain behavior reactions of the alcoholic, in an unwarranted fashion. For instance, it has been pointed out that men drink exclusively with men and that this is indicative of a latent homosexual trend. Men, of course, did drink almost exclusively with their own sex during the saloon and prohibition era because of the cultural taboo against women consuming hard liquor. Since repeal this is no longer true. Thus the more plausible explanation of the practice of males drinking with each other is the cultural pattern, rather than organic homosexuality, and this is further borne out by the heterosexual relationships of the alcoholic with the prostitute.

Another evidence of latent homosexuality is said to be that men become affectionate with men friends and swear undying friendship while under the influence of alcohol; but they also become quarrelsome and pugnacious with their best male friends as well as affectionate toward their female drinking companions. There is no behavior reaction here which may be said to be typical. Again it has been observed that most alcoholics have been married and divorced or have had domestic discord which illustrates their characteristic maladjustment with women. That separations and domestic discord are prevalent among the alcoholics there is no doubt, but it is rather ridiculous to contend that this is in itself evidence of homosexuality.

In the writer's study, it was found that an overwhelming proportion of the alcoholics had sexual experience prior to marriage. In the "organized" nonalcoholic group, less than half had such sexual experiences.[9] What can be the meaning of this difference? Since alcohol and brothels have long been associated, and since in several instances the sexual experience had been with prostitutes, one may raise the question as to whether this relationship might not have furnished the social situation for the onset of the drinking. Such a connection was not borne out, however, as none of the subjects either directly or indirectly linked the two together. Furthermore, the age of first sexual experience was invariably given as several years earlier than the onset of drinking. Both, it is true, are symbols in our culture of masculinity and strength. Perhaps the only conclusion that one is justified in making here is that there is significant evidence that the alcoholic group showed to a much greater degree the urge or necessity for trying to establish through overt expression their strength and masculinity than did the other groups.

The question then may be raised as to how consistent is this behavior with the personality pattern, the genesis of which, as has already been shown, is in familial interaction. Here the alcoholic's status was ambiguous— superior to some, challenged by others. It is only logical to believe that it would be the more favored role the individual would endeavor to maintain

9. Of the 25 alcoholic men, all but two had had sexual experience prior to marriage, whereas only 12 of the 25 "organized" men had had such experience.

and therefore be more demanding than could ever be realized in adult interpersonal relations. Thus his status continues to be threatened, and as the needs for defense expand, he becomes more dependent upon those transitory symbols by which the desired status is achieved.

The transitory character of these symbols of status toward which the alcoholic tends to gravitate is illustrated by the fact that in many instances the individual has made other attempts at maintaining status, and as one has failed hè has tried another. Thus one may cite the behavior of Mr. A. who had the typical familial background which has already been presented. He took up boxing, was successful, happy, and adjusted for the period that he was known as "Riley the Fighting Irishman." When he was no longer able to maintain this role, he began drinking and later became a chronic alcoholic. Other cases show a sequence of sexual exploits, gambling, and then alcoholism.

Marital Adjustment. That marital discord is not the result of alcoholism but that both are the result of the same etiological factors, research has demonstrated. This is not to say, however, that the domestic discord does not take on a characteristic pattern which is closely intertwined with the behavior of the alcoholic personality. The alcoholic tends to enter marriage handicapped by some economic insecurity, dissatisfaction with occupational choice, restlessness, and a tendency to resort to substitute adjustment devices. As a husband, his position in the family becomes an inferior one. His feelings of inferiority are reflected in the sexual relationship and his husband role becomes further complicated through chronic alcoholism by actual physical or psychological impotency. Intense jealousy of the husband, excessive sexual demands (which cannot be realized), with frequent sexual practices at variance with the normal, are found to be characteristic of this type of case.

Comparing the groups studied, it is found that the alcoholics seem to have placed more of a premium upon sexual potency than do the men of other groups and this was borne out by statements of wives as well. While various types of sexual maladjustments characterized both groups, there were more instances of extremely sexually inhibited wives in the alcoholic group than in the "organized" group. These findings might lead to much speculation as to the use of alcohol as a substitute for sexual relations. However, the women in the escape-response-through-illness group show a characteristic pattern of sexual inhibitions, yet no cases of chronic alcoholism were found among their husbands. This would suggest accordingly, that the factor in itself is not significant but may be of considerable importance when viewed in relationship to the many other factors which go to make up the total pattern. That is to say, the alcoholic husband seems to feel keenly that his difficulty at sexual adjustment with his wife is a challenge to his ego, role in the family, or the like.

Drinking and the Cultural Milieu. In any analysis of the personality of the alcoholic, one must keep in mind the cultural milieu. Accordingly, the reasons men give for drinking and the circumstances surrounding it are in themselves of little scientific value. The alcoholic no more than the person experiencing domestic discord can give unaided the real causes of his difficulty. What he gives is the cultural definition of the situation, that is, those causes approved by the culture of his group. In our culture, such happy occasions as weddings, births, sudden good fortune, etc., call for and furnish excuses for drinking. Likewise, sorrows occasioned by death, financial reverses, disappointments in love and marriage, etc., are crisis situations which can be met and conquered by alcohol, the magic medicine. It keeps those happy who are already happy and makes the sad happy again. Wine is often the symbol of fruitfulness, and drinking to one's health is interpreted as expressing the wish that the life principle in wine may do him good. Alcohol, likewise, is supposed to make the shy become bold and the weak strong. It has long been associated with masculinity and sexual prowess. Quite consistent, then, are the reasons given by the alcoholics: "I drink to make me happy"; "I drink to forget my troubles"; "When I drink I feel like a man"; "Drinking helps me to make a sale"; "Drinking helps me forget that I have no wife"; and so on.

Here, of course, the alcoholic does not distinguish between normal drinking and chronic alcoholism. The average individual probably experiences a satisfying glow and a feeling of contentment and happiness as the result of an occasional drink. But does this average person experience the same reaction in solitude as in the company of friends? This suggests a more general question: How much of the effect attributed to alcohol is due to the physiological response of the organism and how much to the social-psychological setting? This is not to deny that alcohol, particularly the chronic use of it, does not have any effect upon the physiological processes and psychological functions, but this paper is not concerned with this aspect.

It is doubtful, however, whether the chronic alcoholic experiences the oral satisfaction of the occasional drinker because he is inclined to drink hurriedly; in fact, his drinking often takes on the appearance of the performance of a ritual. While it is generally conceded that inhibitions are released through liquor, there is a wide variance as to how people behave under its influence. Not all shy persons become bold nor do all persons become happy. Many become sad and despondent; others, taciturn and unsociable; still others remain unchanged while under the influence of liquor. While the chronic alcoholic may say drinking enables him to meet his business associates and put across a deal, the clinical history may show this not to be the case. Alcohol, while it may increase sexual desire, decreases ability at performance, so in reality it can hardly be said to increase sexual prowess. Thus it would seem that the chronic alcoholic is in a paradoxical situation. Rather than having been betrayed by his mother through the nursing experience, as some psychoanalysts have contended, he has instead been betrayed by his culture which has held out to him a false panacea for his problems.

The Alcoholic Personality Pattern. It seems apparent that the behavior of the individual under the influence of liquor is not as significant for an understanding of the alcoholic as has been believed in the past. What is more important are the attitudes of the members of his family toward him as a consequence of his alcoholism. The importance of these subsequent attitudes is suggested by the fact that, like the "neurotic" woman, he does not want to be cured of his social handicap.

Instead of slowly ruining his life, as the portrayals of the influence of alcohol would have one believe, the alcoholic, through his drinking, achieves satisfactions which he can realize in no other way. As an aftermath to his drinking, his role becomes equivalent to that played in earlier familial interaction. While some members of his family are disgusted with him, strict in their attitude, consider him an "inferior," a problem, etc., there are others who pamper him all the more, give him unlimited attention, always believe in and fasten hope upon his determination and pledge to "throw away the bottle." Even his wife, vacillating as is her attitude toward him, while inclined to criticize him, yet expresses sympathy and a maternal feeling for him.

How the alcoholic achieves the limelight as a consequence of drinking is illustrated in all the attention which he subsequently receives. Family conferences are held; plans are worked out to help him resist the temptation to drink; new inducements are offered him; and in general he occupies the center of the stage. Thus, for example, a program is worked out by the family requiring him to report each day to a sister, or a wife may meet him at the close of the day's work and thus protect him from the influence of drinking companions. The consequences are that the subsequent exemplary behavior under this regimen convinces those concerned that a cure has been effected. The moment the scheme is abandoned, however, the alcoholic relapses into drinking. Obviously, the cause of the relapse is not that new crises have arisen or that his former drinking companions have reasserted their influence, but that he no longer receives the attention which he got under the regimen of supervision. Observing the collapse of his attention-consuming role, he again reinstates it through another drinking debauch.

How deceptive may be the immediate circumstances surrounding drinking may be illustrated by the following incidents. In one case, the alcoholic became drunk instead of appearing at the funeral of his brother. In another, he failed to go with his children to the hospital to see his wife, becoming drunk instead. At first sight, it would appear that drunkenness in each instance represented an avoidance of the sorrow and pain involved in these circumstances. More thorough analysis, however, revealed that the first person's relationship with his brother had not been such as to call out any deep sorrow and that the second quarreled recurrently with his wife, accusing her of infidelity, as a projection of his own sexual impotency. The more plausible interpretation of both instances is that each was a rebellion against the attention given to another member of the family. The subsequent attention which each received as an aftermath of his drunkenness confirms this interpretation.

Thus it becomes clear that the behavior of the alcoholic cannot be understood except with reference to the basic pattern of personality developed in earlier familial interaction. Alcoholism provides a way of recapturing at least temporarily the attention-receiving role of the early familial group. This recapturing of the childhood role, however, is much more the aftermath of drinking, than something which is obtained exclusively under the influence of liquor.

The consequence is, that in order to understand the alcoholic, it is necessary to keep in mind this basic pattern of personality. The moment segments of behavior are detached from the total configuration, the picture becomes distorted. In this distortion, single factors are considered causes of alcoholism with little realization upon the part of the researcher that these factors may have a wider application than the alcoholic, or if not, that they are but part of a larger causal complex. Methodologically, therefore, the paramount need in the study of the alcoholic is to see his drinking behavior as a part of the larger pattern of personality disorganization.

Like other forms of personality disorganization, therefore, alcoholism can only be understood as it performs a function in the attempts at social adjustment of the individual. That the consequences of excessive drinking are such as to be only temporarily satisfying, and therefore represent what from an objective viewpoint is inadequate, is of no importance in the understanding of the behavior. What is of importance is the fact that for the moment at least this type of response is within the range of possibilities set by a pattern of personality for the achievement of what to him seem to be essential goals. So long as alcoholism works, he uses it, and when it breaks down, he is likely to abandon it for other devices within this range, or else becomes enmeshed in an ever-increasing drive to make it work until the personality becomes wholly disintegrated.

This does not mean, however, that there are no questions which remain unanswered regarding the character of the alcoholic personality. Of paramount importance in the clearer differentiation and understanding of the alcoholic is the need for comparing more thoroughly this type of personality with other significant types of unadjusted personalities. In any case, the present analysis provides a frame of reference within which comparisons can be made from the psychocultural point of view.

23. PERSONALITY AND SOCIAL FACTORS IN INTOXICATION AND ADDICTION

by Donald L. Gerard *

What are the personality characteristics of men who compulsively use alcoholic beverages or opiates so that these drugs become the dominant or one of the predominant themes of their existence? Why do some individuals use alcohol excessively? Why do others use opiates? In view of the remarkable differences and in some ways antithetical effects of these drugs upon the human organism, it would be gratifying if we could describe equally remarkable differences in the personality characteristics or dynamic needs of the alcoholic and the opiate addict. Clinical experience, however, does not support neat analogies between the psychopharmacology of alcohol and the opiates, or between the psychopathology and dynamics of alcoholism and opiate addiction. There are a number of aspects in which the alcoholic and the opiate addict are substantially alike, some others in which they are different. One valid generalization would be that alcoholics and opiate addicts are remarkably similar with regard to at least five areas of their life and relationships. Each of them has been written about extensively elsewhere; they will be summarized here briefly.

The first is the area of regressive, infantile or oral needs. Both the alcoholic and the opiate addict are occupied unconsciously, and sometimes consciously, with achieving autistic experiences of satiation and contentment, with associated fantasies of omnipotence. For both the alcoholic and the opiate addict there is a pseudosocial aspect to their ingestion of the pharmacological sources of these experiences. In the case of the opiate addict the social aspect is in terms of the setting of the obtaining and using of drugs; but the asocial nature of the enjoyment of an individual who is "high" in a group is immediately evident both to the user and to the outside observer. There is a social aspect in the early stages of drinking for some alcoholics, just as there is for the nonproblem drinker; the asocial element may be less evident particularly in the borderline alcoholic. For the confirmed alcoholic, however, the goal of drinking is akin to the goal of opiate intoxication. In the final scene of a binge, where the setting is a lonely hotel room or an alley, the actor barely awake, resolving the discomfort he experiences with the return of consciousness by taking another pull at

* From "Intoxication and Addiction," *Quarterly Journal of Studies on Alcohol, 16* (1955), 689–97.

the bottle, a phenomenon is evident which differs in pharmacological detail but not in psychological essence from the addict's "high" or the "junky's paradise." The alcoholic who makes use of alcohol to enter a semi-stuporous condition, as the opiate addict who seeks to attain a condition of detached satiation, manifests a need for regression to an isolated, infantile state of diminution of bodily tension.

Wikler [1] has offered the hypothesis that an important function of opiates for the opiate addict is to diminish "primary" drives, such as those of hunger, thirst, awareness of pain, and sexual tension. This appears to be an extremely significant concept in both a symbolic and a pharmacological context. To attain a diminished awareness of "primary" drives or of tension within the body is analogous to attaining the quiet satisfaction of an infant who has been well fed, well changed and well put to bed. The term "orality" has relevance for this diminution of bodily tension and "primary" drives in that the addict and the alcoholic both interpret and perceive their pharmacological satisfaction through ideas, associations and dreams in which the mouth and the stomach, incorporation and ingestion, are explicit or readily inferred.

The addict can attain diminution of bodily tension fairly easily; the alcoholic can attain similar satisfaction with difficulty and only by going through the entire sequence of events related to acute intoxication as described above. The addict, in short, attains his regressive contentment rapidly, neatly, predictably and almost at once. The alcoholic attains a similar regressive state gradually, progressively, messily and at the cost of losing consciousness. The fact that alcoholics not infrequently become opiate addicts, but that opiate addicts rarely become alcoholics (except in a conscious attempt to accept the sanctions against opiate use), attests to the idea that the regular use of opiates provides a better solution than does chronic alcohol intoxication for a similar complex of urges and problems, and not a different solution for a different set of problems.

The second common characteristic of the chronic alcoholic and the opiate addict is that they are very isolated individuals who readily accept the possibility of narcissistic self-gratification and deeply question the likelihood, at least for themselves, of mutually rewarding adult relationships. One of the values of their pharmacological satisfaction is that they are able to give to themselves what they themselves want. They have a magic way to attain satisfaction which is interpersonally separate from, or in a neutral relationship with, other individuals. They are gratified to learn that they can put something into themselves which will wipe out tension, discomfort and awareness of reality, and afford the regressive satisfaction discussed above.[2] This self-administration has a double significance—one regressive

1. A. Wikler, "A Psychodynamic Study of a Patient during Experimental Self-regulated Re-addiction to Morphine," *Psychiatric Quarterly,* 26 (1952), 270–93.

2. I must accentuate here that these statements do not pertain to the drug but to

in the sense outlined above, and the other, in a sense, sexual. In Rado's terms, the use of alcohol for pleasure and elation initiates "an artificial sexual organization which is autoerotic"; pharmacogenic pleasure replaces genital pleasure.[3] The attachment of the alcoholic to his bottle while on a binge is an explicit substitute for any attachment to living human beings. The alcoholic need not give up biological sexuality but he does give up sexuality in the sense of a mature, mutually considered relationship with a human being of the opposite sex. In place of the world of people the alcoholic takes for his "object" a self-administered source of pleasure and satisfaction.

In the opiate addict the replacement of sexuality by the drug is evident in three ways. First it diminishes or replaces genital urges or needs. Second, it leads to orgastic impotence or extreme orgastic delay. Third, following intravenous administration of an opiate, especially heroin, there is a non-genital experience which is perceived by addicts as analogous to masculine sexual orgasm. This consists of a sudden intense feeling of "impact" in the abdomen followed by relaxation and nodding. However, the genital orgastic impotence of the male addict does not necessarily lead to giving up biological sexuality.

The third area in which alcoholics and opiate addicts are similar is in their sexual organization and life. Both alcoholics and opiate addicts are individuals whose psychosexual development is arrested at a pregenital level and in whom a variety of psychosexual pathology is grossly evident. Latent homosexuality—an unconsciously motivated, consciously unacceptable orientation toward homosexual relationships—is commonly referred to as a significant dynamic force in both alcoholism and opiate addiction. This appears to be an approximation to a more valid generalization. By itself, it seems erroneous; there are, for example, many overt homosexuals who are alcoholics and opiate addicts. This suggests that suppression of a latent homosexual conflict is not a necessary factor for either of these syndromes. A more accurate generalization may be that the alcoholic and the opiate addict both are persons who have failed in varying degree to develop a definite sexual role or identification. Among the special cases of this indefiniteness of role and identification is an orientation toward homosexual closeness which, because it is unacceptable for the adult male in our culture, is often perceived with great anxiousness. Another common exemplification of immaturity in sexual role and identification is a compensatory sexual athleticism. Though this is well known among alcoholics, it is also a frequent occurrence among opiate addicts who, despite or perhaps because of their

the meaning or effect of the drug on the individuals who are alcoholics or opiate addicts. I doubt that social drinking or, in certain settings, social opiate use, has the same significance as alcoholism or opiate addiction in our society.

3. S. Rado, "Psychoanalysis of Pharmacothymia," *Psychoanalytical Quarterly, 2* (1933), 1–23.

orgastic impotence, become involved in male prostitution or gigolo relationships in which they are "successful" through their absent or delayed orgasm,
which permits them to maintain erection for an extraordinarily long time.
Bisexuality and perverse infantile sexuality—with special preference for
oral genital contacts—are also commonly noted among alcoholics and
opiate addicts.

The fourth common characteristic is marked conflict in the area of poorly
sublimated dependency wishes. Consciously, the alcoholic and the opiate
addict experience difficulty in caring for themselves as independent, competent mature adults, while unconsciously they often desire and fear a
passive relationship with a stronger person who will care for them. One of
the common clinical manifestations of the problem is the alcoholic who
marries a maternal woman but who cannot bear to be with her, nor bear to
be without her. Both alcoholics and opiate addicts often take "flights into
custody" where they can be, in large measure, dependent, immersed in an
institutional routine and regime, against which they can vigorously "protest." In the institution they are cared for and dependent, yet can rationalize
this dependent state as one which is imposed upon them. One of the difficulties in the treatment of both alcoholics and opiate addicts lies in their
extreme sensitivity to the dependency aspects of therapeutic relationships,
so that they may run away from treatment in order to impede awareness
of dependent wishes directed toward the therapist.

The fifth common characteristic is masochism. Both the alcoholic and
the opiate addict pay too high a price for their regressive pleasures. They
pay with insult, injury, loss of social status, depression, social rejection.
They pay with delirium tremens and the withdrawal syndrome, not once
but many times. They return to alcohol or to opiates against their "better
judgment." However, in harming themselves with the drug or with its
social interpersonal consequences, they harm not only themselves but intro-
jected parental figures whom they wish to punish severely for real or
fantasied infantile or childhood domination, seduction or frustration. The
younger addicts or alcoholics not infrequently declare that they intend to
give up using alcohol or opiates because they now recognize that the pattern of living associated with their addiction hurts their mother, and they
cannot bear to do this. This particular statement is an excellent predictor
of relapse.

Choice of Drug

Why do some individuals become opiate addicts and others alcoholics?
One of the first points which seem important is that there is no free market
in intoxicants in this country. Thus the use of alcoholic beverages rather
than opiates is not analogous to using tea in preference to coffee. Opiates
are obtainable only with fairly considerable difficulty in this country, although not so much difficulty as the law-enforcement agencies wish for.

Opiate drugs have an oriental, esoteric, illegal flavor, and only in certain subcommunities, in the Bohemias, slums, criminal or delinquency-ridden areas of the city, is their use at all prevalent. There is a widely held prejudice against opiates and their use. Alcohol, on the other hand, is presently available to almost any person. If the individual lives in a "dry" area he need drive only a few miles to a place where alcoholic beverages are for sale. Drinking is condoned. People drink for a variety of reasons, of which the reasons of an incipient alcoholic are only one special case. When one buys a fifth of whisky one may join the select company of certain men of distinction. When one buys a sixteenth (of an ounce) of heroin, one is regarded as a "junky." Hence the odds are heavily weighted in our society in the direction of sedative intoxication with alcohol rather than with one of the opiates.

Thus the social situation, in which a variety of cultural-historical factors play a significant part, is extremely important in determining whether a person with the personality characteristics described above will experiment with opiates, alcohol, neither or both. If the individual is a Negro or Puerto Rican youth living in an East Harlem slum in New York City, there is a substantially good chance that he may use alcohol but also will try heroin or morphine.[4] If he is a white middle-class resident of a middle western town, it is quite unlikely that he will become involved with one of the opiate drugs but there is a good likelihood that he will try alcoholic beverages. I have never seen a Jewish alcoholic in a clinic or hospital. I am sure they exist, yet I am confident they are rare. On the other hand, I have seen not many but a very evident group of Jews who were opiate addicts. Although alcoholism is reputedly common among urban metropolitan men of Irish descent, I also see an evident minority of Irish opiate addicts. There may be well-structured cultural forces which diminish the use of alcohol for intoxication among Jews, and cultural forces which enhance the use of alcoholic beverages for intoxication among the Irish.[5] It may be that the limited cultural experience with opiate drugs of both the Jewish and the Irish urban cultural groups results in a lack of sanctions surrounding opiate use, so that factors pertaining to social structure and individual personality are more relevant for opiate addiction within these groups than any cultural factors. Consequently the cultural factor in the choice of alcoholism or opiate addiction is by no means necessarily simple or dichotomous, so that a person of a particular social group can become either an alcoholic or an opiate addict. In this connection, male nonwhites, according to the Federal Vital Statistics, have the highest incidence of psychosis associated with alcoholism,

4. I. Chein, et al., *Studies on Narcotics Use among Juveniles,* Report No. 1, Research Center for Human Relations, New York University. Presented before the Committee on Drug Addiction and Narcotics of the National Academy of Sciences and the National Research Council, September 30, 1955.

5. See Part IV, Chapter 20, pp. 263–77.

but they probably also have the highest incidence of opiate addiction as well. As indicated above, alcoholics not infrequently become opiate addicts. The question of the social factors in opiate addiction, alcoholism, or drug use of any sort, is a large and complex one. Not only do such factors play a role in determining the choice of drug but they also color and modify the types of behavior experienced by the user. For example, the cannabis (marijuana, hashish, bhang) user in jazz circles in New York City or Chicago will become boisterous, talkative, silly, argumentative and provocative, seeking sexual adventure, and the like. In jazz circles the cannabis habitué will not use alcohol concurrently.[6] In North Africa, on the other hand, cannabis and alcohol are used simultaneously.[7] In the United States some individuals will use alcohol under one set of circumstances and under another, cannabis. In India, on the other hand, certain individuals use cannabis in order to attain a state of religious detachment, exultation and contemplation, while the use of alcohol at any time is entirely rejected by them. Thus the problem of the choice and meaning of the sedative-intoxicant drug in relation to the social, cultural, and historical situation becomes extremely complex.

It is of interest to note that some rather minor aspects of personality may play a remarkably important role in deciding whether alcohol or opiate addiction will occur. Some people are disgusted by the idea of sticking a needle into themselves. Others are equally revolted by the taste or odor of alcoholic beverages. Still others are motivated to the use of alcohol rather than opiates because of single aspects of the effects of the drug. Alcohol seemingly makes many people loud-mouthed; more accurately, many people become loud-mouthed when they drink alcoholic beverages. This can be very distressing to a fastidious, gentlemanly adolescent who feels that boorishness is a crime, or to a youth for whom keeping cool, controlled, distinguished, is a major albeit transitory adolescent need. Similarly, a colleague described a young homosexual alcoholic who sought treatment for his alcoholism because he was told he was "nasty" when intoxicated, and it genuinely and deeply distressed him to feel that he could be nasty at any time or under any circumstances.

It may be that physiological or biochemical individual differences play an important role in the choice of drug, especially for those living in a milieu where both alcoholic beverages and opiate drugs are available. It may be that for some individuals alcohol has a more evident effect of dissolving inhibitions than it has for others, in whom it acts in a more directly sedative fashion. The person who becomes sleepy after a few cocktails is not likely to regard alcoholic beverages as a "stimulant," as a way of getting "high."

6. H. S. Becker, "Becoming a Marijuana User," *American Journal of Sociology, 59* (1953), 235–42.

7. G. M. Carstairs, "Daru and Bhang. Cultural Factors in the Choice of Intoxicant," *Quarterly Journal of Studies on Alcohol, 15* (1954), 220–37.

With opiates, there may be some individuals who find their deep-seated tensions alleviated while they can remain awake to enjoy the regressed state with its relaxation and calm detachment, whereas others may get little more from the experience than neutral restfulness or sleep.

Some authors have suggested that there ought to be notable differences in the personality structure or dynamic characteristics of opiate addicts and alcoholics because alcohol causes a "release of inhibitions" while opiates dampen the inhibited impulses themselves. This hypothesis suggests that because alcohol causes "release of inhibitions" people who seek release drink alcohol; similarly, opiates cause dampening of impulses, therefore people who want to deal with deep conflicts through dampening their impulses use opiates. Although this question of release versus suppression of impulses may play a role in the socially condoned drinking or socially condoned opiate use of nonaddicted individuals in certain populations, it seems to be irrelevant to the question of alcoholism or opiate addiction in this country. The motivations for social drinking are not the motivations for alcoholism. Alcoholics do not drink as they do in order to attain "release of inhibitions." They drink, just as the opiate addicts take drugs, to get deep, regressive, infantile satisfactions, and to reestablish within themselves a state of psychic well-being. One of the reasons for the dissatisfactions of the alcoholic is that alcohol does not do this very well. One of the reasons for the satisfaction of the opiate addict is that opiates accomplish these goals very well indeed.

In my opinion, alcoholism and opiate addiction are different paths to the same goal. A clinical observation that supports this statement is that opiate addicts become involved in all the acting out behaviors observed among alcoholics. For example, they break their ties with their families, become involved in overtly hostile relationships with parents and siblings, lose jobs, have downward occupational mobility, become derelicts, ruin their careers, and so forth. Both alcoholics and opiate addicts become involved with prostitutes and homosexuals. Both alcoholics and opiate addicts get involved in fights, accidents and arson, causing others or themselves to suffer loss of life or limb. However, there is a difference in the timing of these events. The alcoholic acts out while beginning or progressing in the extent of his intoxication. The opiate addict, on the other hand, becomes involved in acting out usually while he is not maximally intoxicated but rather when he is returning from intoxication to his sober state. The alcoholic blames his acting out on his malcoordination and loss of judgment. His rationalization for his behavior is that he is intoxicated, poisoned, and therefore not really responsible. The addict, on the other hand, if he rationalizes his acting out at all,[8] will refer to a need to prevent symptoms of withdrawal. In both

---

8. The opiate addict does not have as strong a need to rationalize his compulsive use of drugs as the alcoholic has to rationalize his compulsive drinking. The special subculture of opiate addicts in our society, with its own argot, mores and traditions,

opiate addiction and alcoholism there are extraordinary individual differences in the extent and type of the acting out behavior, despite controllable similarities in the extent, duration or severity of the compulsive use of alcohol or opiates, emphasizing that the behaviors elicited are related to the individual and the needs of his personality and not to the intoxication itself. For example, it seems likely that the nonalcoholic individual when intoxicated will behave very differently, in the laboratory or in the community, from the alcoholic at the same level of alcohol in the blood.

gives support to the individual opiate addict and perceives the nonaddict as a "square"; within this subculture opiate addiction is seen as the norm and abstinence as the deviant state.

24. ALCOHOLISM: THE ROLE
OF SOCIAL AMBIVALENCE

by Abraham Myerson *

To the curious student of his fellow man, one of the most extraordinary phenomena in the strange history of mankind has been the rise of
asceticism. Hedonism or the worship and seeking of pleasure and satisfaction can easily be understood. Appetite in whatever direction, whether for
the ingestion of foods or for the sexual act, is biological, related to survival
and reproduction, in line with instinct, and gives a native pleasure which
once experienced becomes consciously sought for. It is really easy to understand phallic worship and it is not difficult to understand the gourmand since
these are extensions into exaggeration and social hypertrophy of normal
trends found throughout the animal kingdom.

The case is different with asceticism. Here is a trend which, at least on
the surface, runs counter to desire and satisfaction, which is a denial of
pleasure and its validity, and which carried to its logical ending is against
reproduction and even personal survival. It declares through its relative in
thought and attitude, obscenity, that certain parts of the body are vile and
certain acts unworthy unless sanctified in some manner. It is the opponent
of hedonism. Pleasure in and of itself is stigmatized as unworthy except for
the pleasure of renunciation and self-denial.

These two trends—hedonism and asceticism—create an ambivalence of
human attitude and opinion of extraordinary importance for the social
historian and the social psychologist and are particularly relevant to the
understanding of the controversies that range around sex and alcohol. This
ambivalence is extraordinarily marked concerning sex. On the one hand,
man extols the sexual situations. He builds up cultures which worship the
organs. Even where this does not take place, he uses song, story, clothing,
perfume to increase sexual desire and to give sex a wide-spreading, ramify-
ing importance. Music, the arts, literature become great instruments for
the evolution and building up of the sexual life. A cult of beauty appears
which ramifies into the economic life and shows itself in dollars and cents
in the economic importance of beauty shops, cosmetics, scents, and style
which have no relevant relationship to warmth and covering and are largely
decoration. Mystery is added to the grosser visceral relationships of sex, so
that men and women are seen in an amorous and seductive glow rather than

* From "Alcohol: A Study of Social Ambivalence," *Quarterly Journal of Studies
on Alcohol, 1* (1940), 13–20.

PLATE XI

Drink and Love. Painting by Rembrandt. (Self-portrait with his wife, Saskia.)
Courtesy of the Gemäldegalerie, Dresden.

PLATE XII

Drink and Music. Painting by Gérard Honthorst. Courtesy of the Rijksmuseum, Amsterdam.

in the stark colors of their sex. The bed itself, which is the civilized symbol of the sexual act, is an instrument for the luxurious development of the sexual relationships. These are social aphrodisiac forces, hedonistic in trend, building up and developing the sexual life so that man has become the most sensual of the animals.

On the other hand, sex is fiercely denounced and the organs of generation declared obscene and the symbols of obscenity. Reproduction becomes carnal. Man is born into sin. He becomes a third excretion born between urine and feces. Ascetic cults in which punishment of the body by the ingestion of just enough food to keep its functions together in that form called life and in which every effort is made to destroy all pleasure taking, all comfort, all luxury, spring up everywhere. The East is their main source. The Hindus, the Essenes of the Jews, large groups of early Christians, the primitive Buddhists, and leaders of Puritanism—all these religious groups and individuals denounce the flesh and strive to immolate it in order to reach Heaven or Nirvana. In fact, the classical example is finally the revolt against all desire, expressed in Buddhism, so that the ultimate goal becomes the extinction of appetite and the disappearance of the individual in a nondesiring and nondesirous infinity.

The result is that each individual in the Western culture, with which we are concerned, is bombarded by at least two sets of forces: one which extols and stimulates his sexuality; the other which inhibits and represses it and is socially anaphrodisiac in its nature. Conflicts of all kinds arise and human sexual conduct represents all types of intermediate stages between full sensuality, uninhibited and hyperdeveloped, and the negation of sexuality as expressed in complete continence and in an extolled virginity. Underground sexuality appears and since the human being is both male and female in varying degrees and since his own body may furnish by its own acts sensual pleasure, homosexuality, heterosexuality, and autoeroticism become expressed in various acts, open or surreptitious. Social hypocrisy becomes an enormous factor because the endocrines know no morality, and yet the individual in whom they lodge and whose acts they influence is social and must conform outwardly at least. One need not invoke any unconsciousness to trace in human activity all kinds of diverted, perverted, and converted sexual activities.

What has been said above of the ambivalence of man concerning the sexual relations also applies to the use of alcohol. It has been extolled in song and incorporated in the customs of man as the basis of good fellowship. To drink in common is to declare formal social amity and unity. It is a symbol of peaceful dealings as well as that of common action. In the Jewish religion the glass of wine shared by bride and groom is the prelude to the formal declaration of marriage by which the two individuals become one. In the Christian church the wine becomes the symbol of the unity between God and man and the implied unity of the congregation of all Christians.

The drinking song chants the theme that "all good fellows get together" over the various types of bottles, cups, and wassails. "Have a drink" and "Be a good fellow" have become synonymous. To refuse the drink is in many cases equivalent to the declaration that one is not a fellow to the other man. For many the barroom or its equivalent is the place where men get together in more intimate fashion and in more complete fellowship than anywhere else. Omar Khayyam becomes the representative in the most glorified form of all the literature which says that the *vintner* sells something for which he gets no equivalent in money; that repentance, sorrow, frustration, and all the mental ills of badgered man are drowned in wine or its equivalent. It would be gilding the lily to cite examples of this widely prevailing social attitude. Hospitality and the business deal; the celebration of victory, of the entrance into marriage, of the birth of the new individual, of all future success and desired achievement, use the medium of alcohol. As it is the chief chemical solvent in the laboratory, it is extolled as the chief social solvent of everyday life.

Ranged against this hedonistic attitude is the completely opposite one. A man drinks and puts that in his belly to steal his brains away. It is the source, or at least one of the sources, of all immorality. Scientifically stated, inhibition disappears and the individual plunges himself into debauchery. He loses self-control and with it coordinated purpose and so is plunged into poverty, becomes the drunken beggar, or in our American slang the "bum."

Moreover, the very pleasure which alcohol gives is a snare and a delusion, a trap to imprison the unwary in the grim habit of alcoholism. The scientists come along and show that the tapping reflex becomes lessened with a drink and so those antihedonists to whom efficiency rather than pleasure becomes the goal of life point this out as showing the destruction of personal achievement and dignity which even any indulgence in alcohol may bring. In the main, the people who most fiercely denounce alcohol are puritanical, using this term in one of its meanings, in all their relationships. They believe in duty, religion, work, and the sober activities. While at the present time they do not explicitly denounce pleasure, this tends to be implicit in their total reactions. They are the descendants of the ascetic. They find scientific substance for their opinions and propaganda, just as now all groups appeal to science as one, at least, of the final courts of appeal.

Science itself, in so far at least as this is represented by psychiatry, tends to find reasons for alcoholism in mental aberration or disturbance of one type or another. There appears to be a particular relation between alcoholism and the neuroses, the depressive psychoses, and certain psychopathic states, of which the term "psychopathic personality" which includes all kinds of diverse conduct not accepted in the community, is a vague description.

"The chronic alcoholic is what he is" because he seeks to *escape* from his neurosis, from his depression, his frustrations, his dissatisfactions with life, and all the socially unacceptable and personally distasteful trends in his own character. There is even a relationship to heredity postulated by some workers, so that if there is mental disease in the family and alcoholism as well, the two are related biologically and alcoholism becomes a substitutive psychosis or neurosis. All this sounds very well and has enough background in the very nature of alcohol and its effect on the human being to sound credible. Alcohol does create a euphoria. It also creates anesthesia. It falsifies the social situation of the individual so that men in trouble and in desperate situations often drink to excess. To get drunk so as to forget it all may be very common in life and certainly is very common wherever life is represented in striking color, such as the movie, the stage, and the book.

But when one compares this solution of the problem with the statistical facts concerning alcoholism, a great discrepancy appears which I have pointed out elsewhere; namely, that there are at least two groups in the population in whom neuroses, psychoses, and psychopathic personality appear up to statistical expectation, who have trouble enough of all kinds, and yet who remain relatively free from alcoholism. It is to be emphasized we are now differentiating between drinking and alcoholism. I refer the reader to the original paper on this subject,[1] but summarizing it at this point one may state as follows:

A certain racial and cultural group, called the Jewish people, have, practically speaking, no alcoholism, whether this is gauged by arrests for alcoholic excess or confinement in an institution for mental disease because of alcoholic psychoses. When one studies the Jews on the basis of the appearance of acute and chronic alcoholism, alcoholic psychoses, and the various neuritides as well as the alcoholic brain damage, one finds a group relatively and conspicuously free of such disorders. Yet no one can deny that the Jew has his full share of neuroses, psychoses of the depressive type, and in a broader and more poignant sense he has plenty of social trouble with frustration, insecurity, and anxiety as psychological reactions. It is, therefore, not sufficient to have a difficult situation in life, to be neurotic or depressively psychotic, to drink to that excess which is labeled alcoholism.

Moreover, this is definitely further shown by the case of one-half of the human species, the females of the race. Here alcoholism is definitely more common than amongst the Jews, but for every one female alcoholic there are seven or eight male alcoholics. Statistics from hospitals of all types, whether psychiatric or general, confirm this completely. Yet there is no doubt in the mind of any man experienced in psychiatry or in the world that women have their full share of trouble; that they have neuroses and depressive psychoses to the full extent of their mates or their brothers and

1. Abraham Myerson, "The Social Psychology of Alcoholism," *Diseases of the Nervous System, 1* (1940), 43–50.

fathers; that they are frustrated sexually, economically, and socially; that within them boil all kinds of diverse conflicts; and that if escape were the chief reason for alcoholism there would be one female alcoholic for every male of the same genre. Since this is not the case and since only one female alcoholic exists for seven or eight males, there must be some other factor at work to account for the discrepancies in statistical involvement.

My answer in the paper which I cite is that social tradition and social pressure are all-important factors in the genesis of alcoholism, in addition to whatever personal difficulty or personal disability harasses the individual. On the Jew there rests an age-old tradition, possibly brought about by the fact that the Jews have always lived in a state of constant seige in which the alcoholism of any member was dangerous to the group and they have, therefore, built up a tradition which is sternly against the use of alcohol in excess. I stress the words *in excess* because there are few temperance societies amongst the Jews, and social drinking is present as well as drinking for the sake of health, such as the "schnapps" before meals. Ceremonial drinking is at all times present amongst the Jews. But there has been organized a bitter, uncompromising attitude toward alcoholism, so that no matter what other qualities a man may possess, the fact that he is a drunkard or drinks heavily debars him from social advancement in his group, from marriage with a "nice" girl, from partnership in a business, and from that friendly interplay and cooperation by which an individual advances in life.

Similarly with the women of the race. Although they have been gradually emancipated from many of the inhibitory influences which for many centuries weighed upon them, nevertheless there still obtains the tradition that woman must be nicer than man in her conduct, at least in so far as the major part of women are concerned. I have cited this as the example: If a dozen young Harvard men were to go out on a "tear" and became drunk and created social disturbance, they would not be fiercely condemned. Indeed, most men would say, "I was young myself once." A general attitude of protection and of excuse, nay, even a sort of implicit or explicit praise for being a lusty and gusty young fellow would appear. But suppose a dozen of their Radcliffe girl contemporaries were to carry on a similar social exploit, a great social hullabaloo would be raised. Preachers would pound pulpits and find a new proof of the degeneracy of the people of the times. Editorial writers would wet their pencils with social vitriol and everywhere there would be horror and social condemnation. The girls in the case would be exposed to a social wrath and social punishment infinitely greater than that accorded to their brothers and sweethearts. This would be the case even today, for in spite of the cocktail bar and the drinking that women do, women live under a different social pressure and in a certain sense in a different world than do their mates. Since men and women in general fear social punishment in its forms of disapproval and ostracism, the women are exposed to severer pressure in these directions. It is the thesis of this paper that it is this social attitude which in large measure accounts for the lesser amount of alcoholism amongst women.

It may be, as the Jew becomes Americanized or as the social tradition concerning woman relaxes and the social expectation and punishment become changed, that Jews and women will drink in the same measure as other races and as the other sex. But traditions do not disappear overnight. They remain, even if they are not voiced as much; they are incorporated in the tie that binds a child to his parents and a group to their ancestors. A new attitude must have a long time to operate before it becomes completely effective, and while new attitudes are appearing, they need time to change the essential social reactions expressed against alcoholism. One may summarize the above by saying: sobriety is not expected so much of the Gentile as of the Jew; sobriety is not expected so much of the man as of the woman; and punishment for inebriety is not meted out in equal measure to the Gentile as to the Jew, to the man as to the woman.

Therefore, it is not true, in my opinion, that excessive drinking springs mainly from neurosis, psychosis, or conflict. One of my colleagues, Leo Alexander, has coined a phrase, "exuberant drinking"; and this, I think, is an apt description of a great deal of drinking. Men drink in celebration as well as for relief. They drink to lend ceremony, color, and fellowship to life, just as surely as to banish anxiety, dread, and frustration. They drink out of recklessness and abandon which is not at all necessarily a compensation for an inherent caution and fatigue of spirit. They drink, too, because the inhibitions of life seem at times ridiculous and often alcohol represents not an *escape* but a *revolt* against the overstressed, perhaps necessary caution, decorum, and orderliness of existence.

A chemical which enhances even for a time social communion and good fellowship, which wipes out social distinction and difference, which has become the symbol of good fellowship, must have very solid reasons for existence in a world in which these trends of the human being have difficulty in expressing themselves. I do not believe we should throw the baby out with the dirty water. The problem of alcoholism is a serious one. No drug addiction that we know of is as important in Western civilization. The amount of social damage done by alcoholism is enormous and if drinking is used as a way of escape, it is a futile one and overcostly. But even these facts, however widely they may be spread and to what extent they may be elaborated statistically, do not alter the fact that the alcoholic beverages serve useful functions in society, and that the moderate drinker shows no inferiority in any respect whatever to the total abstainer and in general he is probably a more personable fellow, easier to get along with, and having a better time out of life.

What we, who are interested in alcoholism, must do, it seems to me, is to take note of the battle between asceticism and hedonism and to build up the third leg of the Hegelian trinity. There is the thesis of hedonism which becomes excessive and disastrous. There is the reaction, the antithesis of asceticism which goes too far in the opposite direction. We may establish as logical synthesis the temperate use of alcohol. We may properly desire that relaxation of inhibition and of tension which is valuable no matter whether the tapping reflex is diminished or not. There are times when, and places where, that chemical psychological compound known as man needs chemicals to alter his reactions. Alcohol is a sort of chemotherapy for undue stress, for the overdeveloped purpose, for the effect of those social organizing forces which become too onerous. It releases exuberance, good fellowship, and friendliness, all of which are exceedingly valuable to man. The synthesis of temperance, of the wise use of alcoholic beverages, is a necessary part, I think, of the battle against alcoholism. Against unwise hedonism, against extravagant asceticism, we need to build up the code of temperate hedonism and successful self-control.

This does not mean a lessening of social control of the use of alcohol. It means taking into account human nature and human needs. It means that we must not minimize the pleasure principle and its importance in human life. It also means that we must guard against chemical overaddiction and that we must keep the sale and the use of alcoholic beverages away from the unrestricted play of the profit principle by legislation. The main road to the prevention of alcoholism is a personal temperate attitude brought about by the development of a new and wise social tradition, which may appropriately be labeled "enlightened hedonism."

25. SKID ROW

Frequent mention is made of the difficulty of understanding the role of drinking in our complex society with its numerous groups and subgroups. By contrast, studies of primitive societies are able to point up the function of alcohol use because of the uncomplicated structure of the group. There is a subgroup in present-day life, inhabiting the metropolitan jungles called Skid Row or Skid Road, in which alcohol plays a major role. Recent studies have attempted to measure the significance of social controls within this group, particularly as related to the use of alcohol.

For many people Skid Row *is* the problem of alcohol—submarginal standards of living, erratic job performance, more or less persistent and conspicuous drunkenness, panhandling, arrests and jail sentences, and other behavior patterns operating outside the limits of ordinary social life.

There is some evidence that drinking is a secondary aspect of Skid Row and that the investigator seeking to understand the problem must look behind the surface picture of drinking and drunkenness. The extract below, from the study of Jackson and Connor, illustrates an attempt to analyze the structure of Skid Row as it appears in one city and to evaluate the significance of group sanctions in support of drinking as a factor in perpetuating Skid Row on the one hand and thwarting rehabilitation of its members on the other.

THE SKID ROAD ALCOHOLIC

*by Joan K. Jackson
and Ralph Connor* *

It is common knowledge that the Skid Road of any major American city has a large population of alcoholics. Yet few articles which take cognizance of this concentration are to be found in the literature on alcoholism. What articles there are deal with the drinking patterns of homeless men rather than with the reasons why this area attracts the alcoholic, how residence in it affects personality, and the significance it has for the treatment and prognosis of this type of alcoholic.

In view of the widely held stereotypes concerning this section of American cities, it is not surprising that the pertinence of Skid Road for the study

* From *Quarterly Journal of Studies on Alcohol, 14* (1953), 468–86.

of alcoholism has been overlooked. The Skid Road is regarded as the area of the homeless man, of the "bum" and the "drunk," considered to be synonymous terms. The residents are held to be down and out, to have lost ambition, self-respect and other important values of our society, and to have drifted to the Skid Road as the last place where they could survive. There is little expectation that anything can be done to make these men members of the "respectable" community again. The missions, the police and the occasional nonreligious charity organization have been left to do any "reforming" they can, and their small success is thought to confirm the impression that these men are hopeless. In this, as in other stereotypes, there is just enough truth to make the whole stereotype appear convincing.

The high concentration of alcoholics suggests that a study of the Skid Road way of life should provide insights into the persistence of alcoholism in this group and into ways in which this type of alcoholic can be treated. A similar approach has yielded vital clues for planned social action in the areas of juvenile delinquency and criminology, where it has been demonstrated that continued association with an antisocial way of life and the consequent lack of response to socially approved patterns of behavior result in the persistence of antisocial tendencies. In addition, many studies of religious colonies have shown that residence in an area which possesses a way of life markedly different from that of American society ill equips the average person for participation in the society beyond his own group.

*   *   *

Social Segments

The Skid Road population in Seattle can be divided into several segments for the purpose of analysis. Although there is some interaction between them it tends to occur mainly within the segment.

(*1*) *The Nonalcoholics.* (*a*) The permanent residents who have pensions or other sources of income and are not alcoholics. These men stick together in permanent cliques which exclude the transients from membership. (*b*) Transients, many of whom drink heavily but are not alcoholics. These men may buy drinks for the alcoholic and provide him with aid and companionship from time to time but do not tend to become part of the alcoholic's group.

(*2*) *The Alcoholics.* (*a*) The older alcoholics, who tend to live in one place over a long period of time and who stick together or are isolates. Frequently these men have pensions. Their landlord often takes charge of them, cashing their checks, doling out money, caring for them in illness, and generally meeting their needs. (*b*) The "bums," men who do not adhere to Skid Road group standards. They are avoided by other alcoholics and by each other as much as possible. (*c*) The "characters," men who behave erratically or in a bizarre fashion. These men, too, are avoided and avoid each other, as they are likely to be "picked up" (arrested) by the police. (d) The "winos," individuals who habitually drink wine and also have a run-down appearance, a fetid smell, "wine sores," and a tendency to unpredictable behavior. These characteristics, according to the Skid Road folklore, are caused by wine. "Wino" tends to be a derogatory term and it seems that the wino rarely recognizes himself as such and resents being referred to by this label. These men group together, apparently as a result of being rejected by the "lush" group. (e) The "rubby-dubs," who habitually drink nonbeverage alcohol. These are few in number and tend to be social isolates. (f) The "lushes," the prestige group of alcoholics on Skid Road and the group with which the present paper is primarily concerned. They maintain social distance from the other groups, although the line between them is often difficult to specify with precision. Most of the lushes drink wine frequently and nonbeverage alcohol when desperate. They tend to be in better physical and mental health than the winos and the characters, while their adherence to the mores of Skid Road society differentiates them from the bums.

The lush segment tends to be composed of temporary residents of Skid Road. Some spend most of their time there and only occasionally return to sobriety, jobs and participation in the usual American way of life. Others spend most of their time off Skid Road. The factors which determine the proportion of time on Skid Road are not known. The evidence suggests that the length of the drinking history is only one of many variables involved.

The temporary character of their residence, along with the extent and type of social interaction which takes place among the lushes, suggests that they have not yet become assimilated into the Skid Road culture. In sociological terms, they are "marginal men," midway between two different cultures, who are pulled by both and unable to make a satisfactory permanent adjustment in either.

The lush segment of the Skid Road population consists of a large number of small groups, some of which stay together over a long period while others are in a state of flux most of the time. Between these latter groups there is a somewhat fluid border, members drifting away from one group and into another continually.

When the alcoholic arrives on Skid Road he is placed as soon as possible into his appropriate status category, on the basis of which interaction with him occurs. For example, if he is a character he will be avoided as much as possible. If he is assigned to the lush group, only the nonalcoholics will exclude him.

The Functions of the Lush Groups

The lush groups provide for mutual survival and emotional support. To reap the benefits of membership in such a group, the alcoholic must adhere to group standards and accept obligations imposed upon him. Violation of group standards means not only rejection from a particular group but also isolation from the lush segment as a whole.

As members of a group, all are assured of a steady supply of alcohol, the ability to acquire alcohol being one of the criteria for membership. Members of some groups take turns begging and working while the rest of the group drinks. In other groups all the members are active in their search for money at the same time. In still others begging is not tolerated. As long as one member has the price of a bottle, the whole group drinks. In addition to drinks, "flops" (sleeping accommodations) and clothing are shared.

The group usually tries to protect its members from the police. When the rumor circulates that a squad car has entered the area, efforts are made to remove incapacitated members from view. There are variations in the degree to which personal risk will be taken to protect fellow members from arrest, but it is a rare group that will make no effort.

If a member becomes physically ill, help is given. The members of some groups will stay sober to nurse the ill member. Most will forego their own drinks to supply him if the illness is defined as being due to a lack of alcohol. Most groups will make sure that a seriously ill member is picked up by the police; some will take him to a hospital. A few are indifferent and desert the sick member after robbing him.

There is a common definition among the alcoholics that Skid Road is a refuge, that is, that it meets their emotional needs. From his group, the alcoholic receives unquestioning acceptance, and only those demands are made upon him which he is willing and able to meet. The informants felt that these demands were less than those the larger society made on them, although to the investigators they seemed to be different not in degree but in type.

The group's unqualified acceptance, as compared to acceptance in a non-Skid Road group, and its function in enabling the alcoholic to escape feelings of inadequacy for a time, are recognized by some alcoholics. The informants agreed that Skid Road drew them because there they could still act as "big shots" when they could no longer do so elsewhere. As their drinking progressed they became less and less accepted as "big shots" in their own class groups. Stories of self-importance came to be challenged in the face of a paucity of deeds to support the claims. Unable to accept themselves as "ordinary," they descended a notch on the social scale to find a new group which would be impressed both by their stories and by their higher social status. Gradually this group, too, rejected them, and they moved down again. Ultimately they reached Skid Road. Here no one asked questions or demanded performance to back their claims. Their boastful tales were no longer subject to the restraints of listener skepticism, and they were elaborated upon considerably.

The informants commented that after a time they came to believe their stories to be fact and could no longer differentiate between fact and fiction. While these tales are accepted without question on Skid Road, no prestige is derived from them. If the individual feels more adequate by indulging himself in this manner, the group members will keep their disbelief to themselves. (It is of interest that members of other groups will manipulate such a person for their own ends at times by being extremely deferential to him and by publicly praising his past "exploits," especially if he has money to buy them a drink.)

When the alcoholic who has been off Skid Road for a time returns he feels a relaxation of tension and a sense of leaving his worries behind him. If members of his last group are still on Skid Road and he rejoins them, no one asks where he has been or what he has done. He can volunteer the information if he wishes, but there is no necessity to do so. No member of the Skid Road groups inquires about his family, his job, his marital status, or any other area of his life. On Skid Road his failures, his successes, and the other criteria for acceptance in the larger society become irrelevant. This lack of emphasis on the past and a taboo on telling one's troubles make rationalizations unnecessary for the time being, as there is no stimulation of feelings of guilt, remorse or inadequacy. He is able to drift for a time while the group provides for him and makes his decisions. The informants claimed that once on Skid Road they "stopped thinking." What they apparently meant was that worry and mental conflict diminished.

Hitting the Skid Road

When the alcoholic first arrives on Skid Road, he has usually been geographically and socially mobile for some time. In both respects the approach to Skid Road has been gradual, and enroute he has learned many of the techniques for getting along with the type of people who inhabit this area as well as some of their attitudes and their esoteric language, both of which are shared with transient groups throughout the United States.

It is not difficult to contact a potential group on "hitting the Skid Road." The newcomer casually gets into conversation with a resident. He says he has just arrived in town and may tell a bit about where he was before this. He then gleans from his new acquaintance what vital information he can, such as the attitudes of the law enforcement agents in the area, the location and the price of flops, and so forth. If it happens that both have been to the same places, worked for the same company, or known the same people, he will be asked whether he can go in on a bottle. If this is not proposed to him, the newcomer will suggest that he has a certain amount to put toward such a purpose. (Usually he admits to having less money than he actually possesses in order to protect himself against being "rolled"—robbed while drunk—at a later time.) At this point the resident suggests that they find others to make up the whole price, and the alcoholic is now a member of a group.

The man who has been on Skid Road before chooses his first contact with caution. He knows the attributes of certain "undesirables." He would not approach an unshaven man because such a person is more likely to be picked up by the police. He can recognize a wino, and unless he has defined himself as such (which is rare, as "wino" tends to be a derogatory term applied to others), he will not choose a person of this description.

The alcoholic who arrives on Skid Road for the first time and is not sophisticated in its ways must learn by experience. However, if he makes a bad choice another resident may "tip him off" that his new acquaintance is a bum or "jail bait." He will then extricate himself and seek a more reliable entrée to a group.

The group which finally buys the bottle may be permanent or temporary. If the new man finds it uncongenial, he moves off. Whether he stays or leaves, no questions are asked as long as he abides by group standards.

In the group, conversation progresses much as elsewhere and covers a variety of subjects, with two major exceptions: there is no inquiry into the individual's past and he is not permitted to discuss his troubles. Telling trouble is permitted only if he has bought the bottle or has contributed the major share toward its purchase; then others are obligated to listen.

A newcomer to Skid Road is welcome to the group. He may have news of old acquaintances and he probably still has money, clothes, and luggage which can be pawned or shared. In addition, he may be dressed well enough to be able to panhandle (beg) in the "uptown" areas without being jailed. He is less likely to be picked up by the police and, being in better health than the rest of the group, he can play an active part in seeing that the rest are off the streets at the time of a raid.

While the groups supply many satisfactions for the alcoholic, the type of relationship is peculiar, judged by the standards of the outside society. In many ways these seem to be primary groups but they are not characterized by intimacy or mutual trust and identification. Few alcoholics trust other group members and many stay with groups in which there is no one they like as a person. Several of the informants stayed with groups because they felt superior to them, others, because the group was necessary to survival. But all felt that the unquestioning acceptance of the group was vitally important.

Being part of a group, even temporarily, entails certain obligations. If an alcoholic who has left one group for another gets some money, he feels compelled to go back to his original group and buy them a bottle if he has benefited from them without contributing his share. Not only is this a felt obligation but the first group claims a right to have part of the money spent in this way. If he is caught treating the second group without having repaid the first, it is legitimate to accost him.

There seems to be little leadership in the group. Action may be initiated by almost any member. Whether or not the rest of the group follows him depends largely on their mood of the moment. No one ever tells the others to do anything. One individual will say what he is going to do and the others decide as individuals whether or not to join him.

In some groups there seems to be some division of labor. Two of the patients had belonged to groups which used the same individual (who was only tolerated by the group) as the "runner" (the one who went to buy the bottle). Another patient had belonged to a group where the new member, who happened to be in better health and had a better appearance, was sent to do the panhandling in an area where he would have been arrested had he been less well dressed. They also used him to get clothing from charitable and religious organizations to which he was not yet known. The members of Alcoholics Anonymous, however, felt that there was little division of labor of any permanent type.

Through the informal discussion of experiences, Skid Road events, and people, the alcoholic learns group definitions of behavior and means of manipulating social situations to his benefit. He learns that certain behavior is required in order to remain in a group. The member must hold up his end in terms of financing bottles. He must never, unless invited, break into the "pitch" of another alcoholic who is speaking with a "live one" (an individual likely to buy him a drink). Both these behaviors are in the realm of group mores and hence compulsory. He must not discuss his troubles. In certain groups he cannot panhandle (in the sense of begging for money rather than a drink), while in others it is permissible as long as he contributes to the general fund. In some groups he must keep reasonably clean and well shaven, as he is less likely then to be picked up by the police; in other groups this is not a necessity. Ideally, he should follow a ritual in terms of drinking up a bottle. If he has contributed to it, he should drink in turn, his turn being dictated by the size of his donation, and he should take only one gulp each round of the bottle.

Gradually the newcomer picks up the group definitions. The mission comes to be regarded as an agency which exploits the residents of Skid Road and the outside society. Tales are numerous of missions being "rackets." A few missions are exempted. As a result of this definition the alcoholic has no qualms about exploiting the mission if he can, although the majority consider it not worth the effort, as it entails too many "ear bangings" (sermons) and "nose dives" (prayers). The group defines as "mission stiffs" those who continuously exploit the missions at this price. The individual accepts this definition and feels slightly superior that he has not stooped to this. The homosexual is defined as immoral; hence some groups consider it permissible to rob him whenever possible. The Roman Catholic clergy and certain lay individuals who work for missions are defined as "easy touches," but in terms of respect. The bartender is defined usually as completely untrustworthy and as being out to get as much as possible for himself.

The newcomer becomes adept at judging the right type of approach to a "live one" in order to get a drink from him. He learns methods of evading the police and he learns how to get benefits from the missions without being exposed to the religious service. He learns the appropriate behavior in jail if he should be unfortunate enough to land there, and he learns that he should stay out of jail, if at all possible, on Saturdays.

He is well informed about the personalities and idiosyncrasies of the judges and has the benefit of the experiences of his group to draw on in his efforts to avoid being sentenced. However, should he wish to stay in jail to regain his health, he knows how to manipulate the judge so that the probability of receiving a sentence is high. There is evidence from the patients, also, that they learn ways of reacting to hospitals and hospital personnel. For example, one patient discussed with another, in the hearing of one of the investigators, what he had been told about the inadvisability of telling the psychiatrist about certain attitudes and events. He listed several criteria which, he had been told, would ensure commitment to a mental hospital.

The Skid Road groups aid one another also in their efforts toward survival, often across status lines. For example, the grapevine makes it known when police are in the area and the individual groups try to ensure that all their members are off the streets. Similarly, the grapevine keeps track of erstwhile Skid Road members. As one alcoholic stated it, "The grapevine knows you are in jail or hospital before you sober up and find it out yourself." In the same way news will circulate about possible job opportunities from time to time.

The esoteric language of Skid Road also cross-cuts status lines. A knowledge of it indicates membership in the Skid Road social organization and facilitates the identification of in-group members. The individual who possesses the language feels at home with others using it and feels as one of them. As the language appears to be similar across the country, a knowledge of it makes for ready acceptance when the individual moves from place to place.

All the informants felt that residence on Skid Road was only a temporary arrangement and planned to leave and "make good." Being a Skid Road resident is not incorporated easily into the self-conception of the alcoholic. As our informants were off Skid Road when we spoke to them, in some cases apparently permanently, it is possible that lack of self-definition in terms of Skid Road membership is a sign of being amenable to treatment. The Alcoholics Anonymous members seemed to agree that they stopped drinking at the point where sobriety was the only alternative to accepting such a self-definition, when they had reached a point where they could no longer ignore the permanent hold that Skid Road had on them.

Once the decision has been made to leave Skid Road, the alcoholic is faced with a number of very difficult barriers to hurdle. Usually he has no money or clothes and is in extremely poor physical condition. Thus, he must get a job which pays by the day or find some means of getting work clothes, food, and a place to sleep until payday. A very small number are in a position to take a job which pays at the end of a week or two. The vast majority are forced to search for the few one-day jobs available. In either case, however, they are not able to leave Skid Road immediately.

All the informants agreed that to be able to maintain sobriety it was absolutely essential to leave one's group. If the man who wishes to stop drinking gets off Skid Road, there are fewer difficulties involved. His group will make no effort to keep him, nor will they regard his leaving them as desertion. There is an unspoken expectation that he will be back. If he does return later, there is no prying; it is just as if he had been to the Skid Road of another town for a time. If he stays on Skid Road and has a job which pays by the day, it is difficult for him to retain enough of his pay to handle his own needs. He has strong feelings of obligation toward those who have helped him in the past. He knows the terrors of being without a drink and it is difficult to resist aiding others going through that stage. If his payday is only weekly or biweekly and he remains on Skid Road during that time, drinks and friends are always available. In his state of health the strain of a job is not to be minimized. Inevitably during the week there will be periods of discouragement, and this is more likely if he lacks food and a place to sleep. When he feels low in spirits his friends are nearby to give him a drink.

The alcoholic who wishes to stop drinking may ship out on a "gandy crew" (railroad gang) as a first step in this direction. [1] This type of work gets him off Skid Road, provides him with room and board until he is paid. Even here, however, he is still with a group which is or was drinking heavily, and the temptations to drink on payday are tremendous. For those who feel a need to be a "big shot," the temptation to return to Skid Road and play Santa Claus to their erstwhile friends until their funds are gone is strong.

Our informants felt that a large number of men postponed leaving Skid Road because of such difficulties until they were arrested or hospitalized, or met some other crisis. Members of Alcoholics Anonymous report a high degree of success among men who have spent time at the Seattle Police Farm and Rehabilitation Center and have formed Alcoholics Anonymous contacts to help them during the transition period. In such cases the break with the Skid Road group was already made and they had food under their belts as well as clean clothing. Going back to Skid Road compelled the man to accept the fact that he had been lying to himself about wanting to leave it. This constitutes a crisis for the individual. This is the time when he is

1. "Gandy crews" are more commonly resorted to by alcoholics as a means of gaining money for another spree and as a respite. However, the man who wishes to leave his excessive drinking and Skid Road permanently can also make use of them.

forced to choose whether to sink or swim, the time referred to by Alcoholics Anonymous as "reaching bottom." It is significant that the action toward stopping drinking is initiated in a situation in which the alcoholic has been exposed to the majority group's standards and at a time when he is separated from his Skid Road group.

"Reaching bottom" is defined as a state of mind rather than in terms of a series of events. Sometimes an event, such as the loss of the family group, will coincide with the psychological crisis. As stated above, the crisis seems to occur at that point where the alcoholic can no longer regard Skid Road as temporary but must face the fact that he belongs there. The crisis is intensified, for those who have continued to think of themselves as superior to other Skid Road inhabitants, when they are forced to define themselves as being on the same level as other members of their group.

The Problem of Rehabilitation

The Skid Road alcoholics, like other types of deviants, have tended to seek out social relationships with others who share their particular pattern of deviant behavior. On Skid Road they find a congenial atmosphere where the condemnation of their behavior by the larger society is missing, and a group which enables them to survive. Once they have become members of such groups they become isolated from the larger society; the new group reinforces their deviant tendencies and all those characteristics which are useful to the group. Socially approved motivations and patterns of behavior which are not useful go unrewarded or are actively discouraged. As the individual becomes more and more incorporated into the deviant way of life and as group sanctions become effective and group definitions accepted, the chances for behavior in a socially approved manner steadily diminish. Rehabilitation involves redefining situations, behavior, and motivations in a socially approved manner.

The difficulties of bringing about a redefinition are great. The individual has been isolated for varying periods of time from the usual ways of interacting with others. Even before his Skid Road days he may not have been secure in the company of others or adequately motivated toward conformity. He may have had little experience with the rewards to be gained from the give and take of approved social groupings. On Skid Road, however, he has been comfortable in his interpersonal relationships. After he has stopped drinking, if he comes to a time of stress he knows that the group is there and that he can return to it. He still has a choice, and his group will always be in active competition with those who seek to retain him in the larger society.

The strains he will experience, at least during the initial period of sobriety, are intensified by his past Skid Road group membership in other ways. The lack of incentive and rewards for steady and efficient work on Skid Road have allowed whatever skills and persistence he possessed earlier to become rusty through disuse. The jobs he has held have been of a type held by other Skid Road residents and he is probably no longer acquainted with other job possibilities and has lost the skills for applying for them.

The inactive alcoholic—the alcoholic who has stopped drinking—has pressure put on him by friends, relatives, and often the physician and social workers, to start out from the status position he occupied before he began to drink heavily. The man himself may feel that his self-respect can be regained in no other way. When the attempt is made to participate again at the former status level, however, the inactive alcoholic often finds the experience frustrating. He no longer knows how to act with this group of people and the techniques of social interaction learned on Skid Road stand in the way of ready acceptance. It is no longer possible to avoid the emotional give and take of group life and, perhaps for the first time in his life, he must learn to manage this. Nor does he share the meanings and goals of the new group immediately. The greater his acceptance in the new group the easier it will be for him to do so.

Unfortunately, however, the ways in which acceptance is gained on Skid Road and off it are markedly different. If it is known that he has been an alcoholic his acceptance in the larger society will be of a probationary character. This is anxiety-provoking and gives rise to an idealization of the unquestioning acceptance by the Skid Road group. In the larger society he is accepted on the condition that he forego drinking. His new group may seem to be on the alert for evidence of failure; and any evidence, circumstantial or real, poses a threat to any gains he has made.

When the alcoholic comes off Skid Road for treatment and rehabilitation he is in a position analogous to that of the immigrant. However, he has less respectability and a past which, unlike that of the immigrant, cannot offer rewards in terms of idealization or be communicated. The strains he suffers are similar to those of the immigrant in other ways in that he must acquire new patterns of behavior, new definitions of situations, and new motivations.

There is rarely a recognition of these difficulties on the part of treatment agencies. The main objective of treatment, it is assumed, is to make the man stop drinking. Other benefits, if considered at all, are thought to follow almost automatically. To rehabilitate the Skid Road alcoholic, however, more seems to be necessary. If his Skid Road group is not to exercise drawing power upon him, some other type of rewarding group must incorporate him so that he can take over socially approved motivations and behavior. If the individual is treated in isolation from any group ties it is doubtful that these can be engendered.

26. ALCOHOL AND MORALITY

The colonists who established the foundations of this country in the 17th century were motivated to make new homes where they could worship according to the dictates of conscience. Freedom of worship is one of our great traditions. Today in the United States, instead of one or two churches which exert marked influence on public opinion and government, as is the case in some European countries, we have numerous religious bodies varying in membership and influence. These churches have played an important part in the attempt to resolve questions about the use of alcohol, but their objectives and the theological principles on which they base their conclusions have caused serious differences of opinion. These differences have constituted a barrier to reasoned consideration of some of the issues which must be resolved before progress can be expected.

A basic issue which arose about 1850 concerned the morality of the use of alcohol in any form. Biblical interpretation by certain theologians established to the satisfaction of some of the clergy that the wine referred to favorably in the Bible was unfermented grape juice. This justified a belief that the drinking of any beverage containing alcohol was inconsistent with the teachings and example of Christ.

Not all church leaders accepted this interpretation and a split developed even among churchmen who had worked for temperance. Those who accepted the new interpretation considered that a moral obligation was imposed on them to eliminate from society as far as possible the manufacture and use of beverages containing alcohol. The historical development of this controversy and the resulting division among churches is reviewed in the paper presented below by the Reverend O. T. Binkley.

A second issue followed logically from the first—the morality of alcoholism. Because no distinction was made between drunkenness and alcoholism, rejection of one as sinful behavior implied rejection of the other. Although many individual churchmen attempted to help the alcoholic, failure was attributed to perverseness of the drinker rather than to the nature of his illness. In the effort to condemn the sin, the church was led to condemn the sinner—and all who contributed to his condition. Not every church adhered to this philosophy. The Salvation Army, the Volunteers of America, and the few bodies maintaining missions for the homeless offered a religious approach to rehabilitation. However, as a result of the activity of Alcoholics Anonymous and the opening of tax-supported treatment facilities in many states and provinces the attitudes of the churches are undergoing modification. Dr. H. J. Clinebell's paper, *The Ethics of Alcoholism*, summarizes these changes and the factors which have contributed to the change. The organized Dry movement in the United States has been identified with certain churches for more than a century. Some other churches, while condemning drunkenness, have been lukewarm, even indifferent, to legal prohibition. Finally, there has emerged a strong anti-prohibition group led by the organized alcoholic-beverage industry but drawing considerable support from the public. Unlike the divisions in public sentiment which frequently arise over national issues—for example, the question of Federal aid to education, or labor-management problems such as the closed shop—the alcohol issue is deeply rooted in our historical past, is advanced with intense emotionalism supported by convictions of morality, and admits of no compromise. The tragedy of the Wet and Dry fight, from the point of view of public policy, lies in the withdrawal from the contest of those humanitarian agencies and civic leaders who might bring to the controversy some semblance of objectivity and critical analysis of the basic issues. The editorial by Dr. Howard W. Haggard, written more than a decade ago, presents the position of the average citizen, The Forgotten Man, who is caught between the barbs of two powerful adversaries. There is little evidence that the situation has changed significantly since 1945.

ATTITUDES OF THE CHURCHES

by Olin T. Binkley *

The churches in the United States have an opportunity to participate affirmatively in a constructive approach to the problems of alcohol. In addition to clarifying the moral issues involved in the alcohol problem, the churches can cooperate with educational, medical, psychological, and legal agencies in a program of research, rehabilitation, and public education.

Social scientists, who are aware of the complexity and the magnitude of the alcohol problem in American society, think that cooperative community effort is needed to provide facts about alcohol, to help alcoholics and their families, and to lay the foundation of a more effective social control of alcoholic beverages. In this endeavor community cooperation is a dynamic social process, but it is more than a social process. It is a spiritual experience to which the contribution of the churches and of adequately trained pastors is crucial.

* From "The Churches and the Problems of Alcohol," a paper presented at the First Annual Summer Studies on Facts about Alcohol, sponsored by the North Carolina Alcoholic Rehabilitation Program, June 1952.

In view of these considerations, let us examine the attitude of the churches toward the problems of alcohol in history and in modern American society.

The attitude of the churches and of church leaders has been influenced by the Bible. The starting point, therefore, for one who would understand the teaching of the churches concerning alcoholic beverages is an honest and thorough study of the ethics of Judaism in the Old Testament and of the ethics of early Christianity in the New Testament.

An inductive study of biblical ethics discloses not a legalistic set of absolute rules to govern drinking habits for all time but an articulation of guiding principles and a religious perspective. In spite of inconsistencies and contradictions in the interpretation and applications of biblical principles regarding alcoholic beverages, three facts are clear and incontrovertible.

In the Bible a moderate use of wine as a beverage, and as a medicine, is recognized as an acceptable practice. It must be admitted, I think, that there is ambiguity in the biblical views of wine and its uses. For example, one writer says that wine "maketh glad the heart of man" (Ps. 104:15), and another declares that "wine is a mocker, strong drink a brawler" (Proverbs 20:1). The biblical writers are aware of the hazards involved in the use of alcoholic beverage, but the Old Testament indicates that the use of wine as a beverage was an approved custom in Hebrew culture and the New Testament contains the injunction to Timothy, "Be no longer a drinker of water, but use a little wine for thy stomach's sake and thine often infirmities" (1 Tim. 5:23). In this connection, I shall quote a few sentences and a story from a lecture delivered by a Methodist theologian in the South:

> Undoubtedly Christians in their fight against alcohol have been convinced that they were doing the work of Christ. The ruin which the business spreads in our society is a challenge to everyone who would think with the mind of Christ. But the interesting thing is that Jesus never said a word against it, and habitually used wine himself . . . This reminds me of a sermon which a brother preacher heard in the moonshine section of the eastern mountains several years ago. The preacher, reflecting his own social environment as all of us are apt to do, was denouncing the whole crusade against alcohol. After citing uses of wine in the Old Testament, he went to the New, and said that Jesus had started his ministry at a wine supper, the marriage feast at Cana, and had ended it with a wine supper in the upper room; and in a moving peroration he declared that he had read his Bible through from Genesis to Revelation, and that there was but one man in it who asked for water—and he was in hell where he ought to be!

On the pages of the Bible one finds stern warnings against indulgence in alcoholic beverage and unqualified condemnation of drunkenness. Noah and Lot are reproved for their excesses, the prophets of Israel utter searing criticism of drinking and pronounce woe "unto them that rise up early in the morning that they may follow strong drink; that tarry late into the night, till wine inflame them" (Isaiah 5:11), and the author of the Book of Proverbs presents a classical exposure of the hazards of strong drink: "Look not thou upon the wine when it is red, when it sparkleth in the cup, when it goeth down smoothly: at the last it biteth like a serpent, and stingeth like an adder" (Proverbs 23:31–32). In the New Testament drunken stewards are reproved (Matt. 24:49), drunkards are excluded from the kingdom of God (1 Cor. 6:10), and all who desire to be known as the followers of Jesus Christ are instructed to be "not drunken with wine, wherein is riot, but be filled with the Spirit" (Ephesians 5:18).

There are anticipations of the doctrine of voluntary abstinence in the Bible. In the Old Testament two groups of total abstainers are mentioned: (1) the Nazirites, who abstained for a limited period from cutting their hair and from drinking wine (Num. 6:3–4; Amos 2:12), and (2) the Rechabites, who refused to drink wine or to participate in the enjoyments of city life (Jer. 35:1–11). In the New Testament Paul applies the principle of consideration for the weaker brother and writes, "It is good not to eat flesh, nor to drink wine, nor to do anything whereby thy brother stumbleth" (Rom. 14:21).

These convictions—that drunkenness is a sin, that there are hazards in the use of alcoholic beverages, and that voluntary abstinence is a commendable action—profoundly influenced the thought and practice of the churches from the beginning of the Christian movement. The Catholic Church teaches that temperance is one of the four cardinal virtues and that drunkenness is "intrinsically wrong." Neither Martin Luther nor John Calvin was a teetotaler, but among Protestants there is a marked tendency toward a rigoristic ethic of abstinence.

There is in essential Christianity a revolutionary passion for social justice. This impulse to social reform has been strong in American Protestantism, and it provided the dynamic and the underlying philosophy of the modern temperance movement.

In the early days in America, church people did not object to the use of alcoholic beverages and even Puritan ministers sometimes took too much. However, in the years following the Revolutionary War, there came a strong reaction against alcoholic intemperance and a firm determination to do something about it.

The Quakers and the Methodists were the pioneers of the temperance crusade and they injected a deep moral earnestness into the movement. In 1785, a Quaker physician of Philadelphia, Dr. Benjamin Rush, published a tract entitled *An Inquiry into the Effects of Ardent Spirits upon the Human Body and Mind.* He had witnessed the harmful effects of alcohol upon the health and homes of heavy drinkers and he maintained that alcohol is not necessary to heat the body in cold weather or to strengthen it in hot weather. He closed with a powerful plea for all the churches to join in a crusade against intemperance.

The first strategy used by the churches and the temperance organizations was a plea for voluntary abstinence. Preachers and physicians spoke against the use of distilled liquors. The American Temperance Society was organized in Boston in 1826. It was founded largely by clergymen and it pledged its members to abstinence from strong spirits. Before 1800 all the religious denominations in North Carolina took action against drunkenness, and between 1825 and 1850 most of the Quakers in America discontinued the use of alcoholic beverages on their tables and on social occasions.

The second phase of the temperance crusade was the attempt to prohibit the manufacture, sale, and use of alcoholic beverage by state and federal legislation. After the Civil War the alcohol problem was intensified and it became a major interest of most of the churches. Two organizations, drawing their leadership and much of their financial support from the churches, became effective agencies for securing state and national prohibition. They were the Woman's Christian Temperance Union and the Anti-Saloon League. By 1916, 19 states had forbidden the sale of liquor and 26 others had local option. In 1919 the prohibition amendment was ratified and it went into effect on January 16, 1920. According to Dr. K. S. Latourette, "It was primarily the Christian, and especially the Protestant forces of the country which had brought about this consummation."

It is true that many church people were indifferent to the crusade. The Catholics, Lutherans, and Episcopalians were reluctant to commit themselves without reservation to total abstinence, and many of them were immune to the contagious emotionalism of the dry forces. On the whole, the Episcopal Church was opposed to the prohibition movement. However, when the Eighteenth Amendment became the law of the land, most of the leaders of the Episcopal Church took the view that good citizens should observe it and the General Convention expressed disapproval of its violation.

We have drifted far in the direction of secularism, and American society is less Christian in its basic presuppositions and motivations than the numerical strength of the churches might suggest. Indeed, the increase in church membership during recent decades was accompanied by a decline in moral discipline, and the social consciousness of the churches is unquestionably low.

Within the churches, however, there are responsible and articulate persons who know that there is an alcohol problem in American society. What are their attitudes toward the problem?

The churches are not of one mind on the use of alcoholic beverage, but a large number of church people think that voluntary total abstinence as a norm for church members, and as a guiding principle for youth, is consonant with the spirit of the Christian ethic. They base their criticism of moderation, and their plea for abstinence, upon three considerations: (1) moderate drinking makes men careless of their social responsibilities and engenders hazards in our complex culture, (2) popular consumption of alcoholic beverages is a factor in producing the disease of alcoholism, and (3) moderate drinking increases the social pressure toward drink upon youth and has a detrimental influence on spiritual development and religious achievement.

The churches have not relaxed their critical attitude toward the liquor traffic, but they have shifted their emphasis from legislative control to educational methods of counteracting the destructive effects of alcoholic beverages. This shift in emphasis is reflected in the official resolutions and policies adopted by the churches.

*   *   *

The churches are awakening to their responsibility to assist in the rehabilitation of alcoholics. Concentration upon the goal of eliminating alcoholic beverages from the community has sometimes obscured the opportunity of church leaders to minister to problem drinkers, but increasingly churches and pastors are demonstrating a genuine concern for excessive drinkers and for their families. This new attitude toward persons hurt by alcohol is clearly stated in a resolution adopted by the 158th General Assembly of the Presbyterian Church in the U. S. A. :

We begin with pastoral and social concern for alcoholics and excessive drinkers and for their families. Alcoholics, as well as their families, need the full ministry of the Church. We recognize that once drinking has passed a certain point alcoholism is a disease; that is, the drinking cannot be stopped by a mere resolution on the part of the drinker. He needs treatment, not punishment; understanding, not condemnation.

Under no conditions will pastors permit drinking behavior to produce a withdrawal of pastoral concern for drinkers. We shall encourage the establishment of clinics and other facilities, when properly conducted, for the diagnosis, referral, and treatment of alcoholics.

Foresight is one of the highest manifestations of intellectual power, and it is difficult to predict the attitudes of organized religion toward the alcohol problem in the days ahead. There are, however, two hopeful possibilities.

The first is that competent and devoted pastors will seek to understand the dynamics of a drinking culture, to bring alcoholic beverages under a more effective social control, and to participate as members of a healing team in the diagnosis and treatment of alcoholics.

The second is that the churches, under the guidance of discerning and ethically sensitive leaders, will advocate a nonalcoholic way of life, translate the findings of research on alcohol into a program of education, interpret and strengthen community agencies established to aid alcoholics, and demonstrate the relevance of the Christian gospel, and of the social ethic which issues out of it, to the complex problems related to alcoholic beverages in a technological civilization.

THE ETHICS OF ALCOHOLISM

by Howard J. Clinebell, Jr.*

Inebriety has been a simple moral problem to the layman for so long that the underlying problems are only now receiving attention from physicians. A Minneapolis newspaper recently printed a story about "John Bones" who was sentenced to the workhouse for the 107th time. The tone of the article was one of whimsical despair at the unalterable depravity of "Mr. Bones" who has willfully spent some 18 of the past 20 years as a guest of the city.—*Charles C. Hewitt*

One question concerning alcoholism in which most religious leaders are keenly interested is this: What is the ethical problem in alcoholism? It is obvious to them that alcoholism is not a simple moral problem, and yet they are aware of the fact that there must be ethical implications involved. It seems probable that failure on the part of many ministers to find adequate answers to this question is one important reason why organized religion has not made a larger contribution to the solution of the problem.

One of the leading Roman Catholic authorities in the field of alcoholism is John C. Ford, professor of moral and pastoral theology, Weston College, Weston, Massachusetts. At the annual meeting of the National Committee on Alcoholism on March 18, 1955, Father Ford made a statement that should be an axiom in the clergyman's approach to alcoholics. He said, "One must never approach an alcoholic on the basis of what is usually called 'morality.' " Anyone who has been afforded an insight into the mentality of even one alcoholic can vouch for the validity of this statement. From a practical standpoint, to moralize with an alcoholic is the ultimate in counseling futility.

However, it is essential that a minister be clear in his own mind as to what the ethical problems are in alcoholism. This is not simply an exercise in the theory of ethics, but has definite practical implications. For whether an individual is aware of it or not, his relationship with alcoholics will be influenced by what he believes in his heart concerning this basic question. To the person concerned with the ethical dimension of living it is not satisfying simply to say that alcoholism is a sickness, implying that the ethical issue has thereby been eliminated. To him every personal and social

* From *Understanding and Counseling the Alcoholic* (Nashville, Abingdon Press, 1956), Chapter 7. Copyright 1956 by Abingdon Press.

problem is also an ethical problem. From the 146 questionnaires returned by the ministers who attended the first seven years of the Yale Summer School of Alcohol Studies, it is apparent that there exists not only a considerable variety of opinion but also some confusion regarding the nature of the ethical problems in alcoholism. This is not surprising in the light of the fact that the answer involves one's entire orientation concerning morality and human behavior in general.

Sin and Alcoholism

Does alcoholism involve sin and, if so, in what sense or senses? In what way is the sin involved related to the sickness involved? These are difficult questions to which there are no facile or complete answers. It is important to recognize at the outset that the word "sin" has been used in a variety of ways in the literature on ethics. Most of these uses or definitions have been applied to alcoholism. Here is an evaluative summary of some of the more frequent conceptions:

1. Alcoholism is a sin and not a sickness from start to finish. Only a very small minority of the Yale ministers (about 5 per cent) held to this position. This was the view which we encountered previously in the study of the rescue mission. According to this conception, alcoholism begins as the sin of drinking and ends as a sinful habit. It is entirely a matter of immoral behavior. At no point can it be called a genuine sickness, except perhaps a "sin-sickness."

The inadequacy of this view will be obvious to anyone who is acquainted with the scientific evidence concerning alcoholism. Whatever the disagreement among different scientific schools of thought regarding the causes of the problem, there is wide agreement that in its advanced stages alcoholism is both a psychological and a physiological disease. The "all-sin" view errs in oversimplifying the causation of alcoholism, ignoring the psychological, social, cultural, philosophical, and perhaps physiological factors which play significant roles in its etiology.

2. Alcoholism begins as a personal sin and ends as a sickness. This would seem from the questionnaires to be one of the most common views held by clergymen. Earlier we saw it as the predominant view of the Salvation Army approach. Briefly put, this is the view: Drinking alcohol is, per se, a sin, for a variety of reasons. One who drinks exposes himself to the danger of becoming an alcoholic. Once the drinking has passed a certain point and is out of volitional control, it becomes a sickness. Although the person is no longer responsible for drinking—since he now drinks compulsively, i.e. beyond the control of his will—he is responsible for having caught the compulsion or illness.

This view is more adequate than the first. It is more apt to result in effective therapy since it recognizes that in its advanced stages alcoholism is a sickness. This view, like the first, has the limitation of oversimplifying the causation of alcoholism, ignoring or de-emphasizing a complex array of factors . . . It is not within the scope of this study to attempt to adjudicate the disagreement among sincere Christians as to whether drinking per se is a sin. However, if one chooses to regard it as a sin, it is well to remember that even the early drinking of the alcoholic is part of a total behavioral pattern which is strongly influenced by his damaged personality as well as by cultural pressures. He is not a completely free agent. The alcoholic is a compulsive person even before he becomes a compulsive drinker. If personal sin implies personal freedom of choice, then the sin involved in the early stages of alcoholism is limited to the degree that the person's freedom is limited. Here we are in the middle of the key problem of ethics —responsibility—which we shall discuss subsequently.

3. Alcoholism is a sickness which involves the sin of abuse. This view holds that it is the abuse and not the use of alcohol which constitutes the sin in alcoholism. This is the Roman Catholic point of view. The sin is the sin of excess involved in becoming and remaining an alcoholic. The Catholic Church recognizes that a neurotic compulsion is involved in at least some alcoholics' behavior and holds that "culpability is reduced according to the strength of his neurosis."

This position, together with position 2, has the practical difficulty of making it necessary to establish a degree of responsibility or to find a line of demarcation beyond which a person is not responsible. In a concrete case this is utterly impossible.

4. Alcoholism is a sickness which is caused by a combination of factors involving both sin and sickness. This is a fair statement of the view of those ministers who regard drinking as wrong but who also recognize the existence of various etiological factors which are beyond the control of the individual. From an entirely different standpoint, it also expresses the view of Alcoholics Anonymous. As has been said, A.A., although it takes no sides in the matter, does not regard drinking as morally wrong. It emphasizes its conviction that the alcoholic has an "allergy" to alcohol. It goes on, however, to express its belief that one is driven to drink by selfishness —the word "sin" is not used—and its symptoms. One is responsible for these factors which produce the "mental obsession" to drink, even though one is not responsible for having an atypical physical response to alcohol. We will evaluate this A.A. conception of responsibility subsequently.

5. Alcoholism involves sin in the sense that it has destructive consequences. This is the first of three nonjudgmental conceptions of sin as applied to alcoholism. One of the Yale ministers wrote: "Alcoholism is a sin in that it hinders the person from abundant living and true happiness. It is not a sin insofar as morals are concerned." Another wrote: "It is a sin in the sense that it detracts from his relationship with God, his family, and his community." These are descriptions of the consequences of alcoholism rather than judgments as to the responsibility involved. If sin is

defined as anything which harms personality, then alcoholism is most certainly a sin. If one accepts this definition of sin as a legitimate one, there can be no quarrel with the application.

6. Alcoholism is a social sin. One of the Yale ministers stated this point of view very well when he said: "Alcoholism is a sin only in the sense that it is a sin attributed to society, especially a Christian society—that we have been unable to bring about a world free from the tensions and conflicts of the present day. I do not consider it a personal sin."

Another put it this way: "It may be a sin, but it is more a symptom or an evidence of a sinful condition in some parts of our society—more sinful for Christian and civilized people to not only allow but promote the conditions that cause it."

Whatever one's view of the personal responsibility involved on the part of the alcoholic, one can certainly accept the fact that "society greases the slope down which he slides." The chaos and psychological insecurity of our world, the confusion and conflict of values regarding drinking and drunkenness, the traumatic circumstances to which many children are subjected—these are a part of the sickness of our society of which the sickness of alcoholism is one manifestation. In discussing the ethical aspects of alcoholism E. M. Jellinek said in effect at the Yale Summer School of 1949: "Alcoholism certainly is a moral problem. If six out of every hundred persons who went swimming at a certain beach contracted a disease that had all sorts of destructive effects, it would certainly be regarded as a question of public morals and safety." Society is involved in the causation of alcoholism; it therefore has a responsibility for its treatment and prevention.

7. Alcoholism involves original sin. In presenting this point of view I am not discussing the untenable position of biblical literalism which holds that man's nature is corrupted by the sin of a generic ancestor, Adam. Instead I am attempting to describe the dynamic meaning which is implied in the conception of "original sin" (a meaning which has been reaffirmed by the findings of modern depth psychology), the only sense in which the conception is intelligible.

It is a fact of experience that, as someone has said, "Every man is born with a pack on his back." This is to say that each person must take into account the "given" in his own particular situation—the hereditary and environmental factors, the historical situation into which he happens to have been born, the elements of powerful childhood conditioning which occurred before he was in a position to exercise power of choice, and the inherent limitations of his finitude which are involved in his existential or ultimate anxiety. Further, a realistic analysis of human experience leads one to the conclusion that all evil cannot be explained as the result of ignorance, as the Socratic tradition has claimed. There seems to be a certain recalcitrance at the very center of man's nature which inhibits him in doing that which he knows to be good. This has been referred to, in traditional language, as the "bondage of the will." Even in his best acts, man seems to have an inescapable self-centeredness—a condition which causes him to deify his institutions, the things he has made, and even himself. The alienation from God which results from this idolatry is at the very root of man's aloneness and anxiety. By making himself the center of the universe, man cuts himself off from his own fulfillment—a fulfillment which can take place only as he establishes a genuine relatedness to the rest of creation and to the Creator.

This tendency toward self-deification, which is close to the heart of the concept "original sin" as the term is used by many contemporary theologians, is quite evident in the alcoholic. The selfishness of the alcoholic is, as we have seen, to a large extent a symptom of inner conflict and insecurity; but his selfishness is also to some degree an expression of the unredeemed nature of man. As we have seen in the discussion of the etiological factors in the introductory chapters, the alcoholic is an illuminating example of the influence of the "given" on human behavior. Whether or not one uses the term "original sin"—and its usefulness has certainly been limited by the manner in which it has been employed by the literalists—the facts of experience which men were trying to verbalize when they coined the term must be taken into account in understanding the alcoholic and his situation.

In deciding where one stands in the matter of the ethical problems involved in alcoholism, one may well combine several of the conceptions mentioned. An adequate view must certainly include recognition of the factors mentioned under sections 5, 6, and 7. The conception expressed in section 4 will undoubtedly prove satisfying to many ministers, though the difficulties involved should certainly be faced. At this point, the truth of the statement made earlier in this chapter—that there is no facile or complete answer to the question—should be apparent. The following discussion should make it more so.

The Problem of Responsibility

A more systematic examination of the problem of responsibility in the light of depth psychology as it is related to alcoholism is now in order. Before pushing ahead it is well to heed the reminder of David E. Roberts:[1]

> The concept of responsibility has been a source of endless difficulties in psychology, philosophy and theology. Any one who has pondered the problems of freedom and determinism will probably sympathize with the sentiment which prompted Milton to assign discussion of this topic to some little devils in Satan's legions who liked to bandy it about during moments of relaxation—without getting anywhere.

Depth psychology has demonstrated that much of man's behavior which had formerly been attributed to free will, inherent badness, or chance, is

1. In *Psychotherapy and a Christian View of Life.* New York, Scribners, 1950.

actually caused by unconscious forces over which one has no control. It does not follow that the personality is a sort of robot whose behavior is completely determined by external or internal forces. What is implied is that all behavior is *caused*—that it does not simply happen by *chance*— that the realm of the psyche is orderly and law-abiding. All behavior is caused and, equally important, the self is one of the causes, to a greater or lesser degree. The goal of spiritual or psychological health is the enhancement of self-determinism—the growth in the capacity of a self to achieve responsibility for itself. To the extent that a person is driven by inner compulsions, he is not self-determining and therefore not able to be responsible. The relatively self-determining self is able to handle the factors in the "given" and mold them in a creative fashion. The compulsive person is the victim of the "given." He is driven and determined by it. In other words, there are many factors—heredity, environment, historical circumstances, childhood conditioning, unconscious drives—which impinge on the person as he makes a decision. The manner in which the self relates or arranges these factors is the creative element. The more compulsive a person is, the less creative he can be about the use of these factors and the more machine-like are his reactions.

There must be some degree of self-determination in any person who is not completely detached from reality, but in many persons it is greatly limited. The evidence we have concerning the early life and adjustment of alcoholics points, in many cases, to a serious limitation of their capacity for self-determination. Everything we know points to the appropriateness of a nonjudgmental attitude toward the alcoholic.

Christian theology has held that all men are sinners, in the sense that they tend to abuse the degree of freedom which they possess. Alcoholics, of course, share in this attribute of humanity. The important thing to remember is this—the factors which separate alcoholic sinners from other sinners (that is, the factors which make alcoholics alcoholics) are factors over which there is little self-determination. Real understanding of the alcoholic and the etiology of his sickness leads one directly to the feeling expressed by the familiar words used as a motto in A.A., "There, but for the Grace of God, go I." This is not sentimentalism, but the essence of psychological insight and the basis for real Christian charity. When one reaches this point in his feeling toward alcoholics—a point which involves considerable self-understanding—he is no longer interested in trying to pin sin on the alcoholic. His only interest is in helping him to grow in his capacity for self-determination. He can now approach the alcoholic without condescension and is therefore in a position to help him.

Objections to the "Sickness" Conception of Alcoholism

One objection to the sickness conception of alcoholism is that it provides an excuse for the alcoholic and thus keeps him from feeling responsible for his sorry condition. This objection has its counterpart in the traditional

Augustinian-Pelagian controversy. David E. Roberts wrote: "Pelagius was an earnest, practically minded moralist who was convinced that men could promote good ends if they tried hard enough; therefore, he sought to close off the 'excuse' that they are compelled to do evil by sinful predispositions."

Instead of attempting to settle the matter on theoretical grounds, I would like to turn directly to the practical question, How does growth in the capacity for self-determination and responsibility occur? Psychotherapy and A.A. have given us our clearest answers. Psychotherapy has shown that one does not cure irresponsibility or egocentricity by a direct attack upon them, nor does one produce real self-determination by increasing the individual's guilt-load. The assumption of traditional moralism is that by emphasizing the individual's personal culpability, one would make him more responsible and more moral. Psychotherapy has demonstrated the basic fallacy of this assumption. By increasing the guilt-load one makes the individual more driven by compulsion, less self-determining, and therefore less responsible. Direct attacks on irresponsibility and egocentricity only increase defensiveness and inaccessibility to help. The moralistic approach may change surface behavior through psychological pressure, so that it seems that the individual is behaving more "morally" because he may be more compliant to the ethical code of a particular subculture. But if a real morality involves self-determination, the individual is actually behaving less morally rather than more so. His concern will be with compliance to a code and not with basic human values.

Psychotherapy has shown that growth in the capacity for self-determination comes as the person feels less guilty and more able to accept himself. When the individual begins to realize that many of the things about his life for which he has been blaming himself, consciously or subconsciously, are actually the result of early experiences over which he had no control, he becomes better able to accept responsibility for making constructive changes. By proceeding on the assumption that people are what they are to a large degree because of their basic character structure, a structure which was formed in the very early years of life, psychotherapy has been able to release many from the vicious cycle of guilt and compulsion which has made self-determination impossible. It is well to remember that this can happen in psychotherapy because the individual feels accepted by the therapist and can therefore lower his defenses and face the truth. Equally important the therapist can accept the person because he has resolved his own conflicts to a large degree and can accept himself. Here is a basic problem of all counseling, including the counseling of alcoholics.

A.A. teaches the same lesson with one important modification. Almost every alcoholic has a terrific guilt-load. The counselor whose orientation is moralistic overlooks this because the fact does not fit the moralistic formula that guilt is the means of producing moral responsibility. He overlooks it, too, because the alcoholic usually hides his real feelings behind a wall of indifference. This wall is his defense. A direct attack only increases his need to defend himself. A.A., in contrast, immediately reduces the alcoholic's guilt-load by providing him with two things: group acceptance and the sickness conception of alcoholism. It says, in effect, "You are not responsible for the fact that you have an allergy to alcohol." Then, within the web of meaningful interpersonal relations, A.A. proceeds to utilize the alcoholic's growing capacity for self-acceptance and responsibility by saying in effect, "But you can become responsible for changing your personality pattern so that you won't be driven to drink." Note that A.A. waits until the person is sober and feels accepted in the group before encouraging him to face up to the necessity of personality change. The timing is crucial.

We have seen that the Emmanuel approach, in contrast to A.A., recognized that selfishness in adults is a symptom of childhood emotional deprivation and inner conflict, and saw the importance of unconscious motivation and childhood conditioning. Theoretically the Emmanuel approach was closer to depth psychology and superior to A.A. in its handling of responsibility. From a practical standpoint, however, A.A. has two advantages. First, in our culture, with its tradition of voluntaristic moralism, it is difficult for people to accept the idea that an individual is not personally responsible for having a neurosis and yet is responsible to society for getting help, i.e., for becoming more responsible. Second, in our present cultural setting the A.A. emphasis on a physical component in alcoholism is probably more effective than the concept of psychological causation in reducing the guilt-fear load and facilitating therapeutic change.

Another thing demonstrated by A.A. is the importance of waiting until the alcoholic is able to accept at least minimal responsibility for himself before attempting to help him. It also shows the importance of utilizing this minimal capacity for self-determination when it emerges. A.A. insists that the individual must be willing to be helped before A.A. can help him. An alcoholic is often literally unable to accept help until he reaches a certain point psychologically, his "bottom." He is incapable until then of accepting responsibility for accepting help. Any counselor will save himself a lot of frustration if he remembers this, rather than assuming that the alcoholic could accept help if he really wanted to. Once the minimal capacity for self-determination has emerged, it is crucial that it be utilized in the counseling process. Only as this capacity is respected and employed will it grow. . . .

If it were true that emphasizing the sickness conception of alcoholism tends to deter the alcoholic from getting help because he now has an excuse for his trouble, a case could be made against the use of the conception. Actually, the opposite is true. So long as an alcoholic thinks of his trouble as primarily a matter of will power and morality, he will tend to go on struggling futilely to reform himself. This is what cultural patterns of thought have taught him to do. On the other hand, if he thinks of his trouble as primarily a sickness, he will tend to seek the help he must have if he is to recover. There are strong pressures in our society for sick people to get treatment.

THE WETS AND DRYS

by Howard W. Haggard *

The late great sociologist William Graham Sumner held archaic views on alcoholism, but he developed an idea and coined a term—"The Forgotten Man"—which are pertinent to present controversies on alcohol, and particularly to the influence of these controversies on the humanitarian and scientific solution of the problems of alcohol.

The Forgotten Man is the average citizen who, although numerically predominant, is lost to sight and hearing because of the attention engaged by noisy minorities. He is only the spectator who casts the ballot.

The same division often extends to minorities. There are minorities within minorities. The minority-minority may give the plumage to the whole minority.

The groups called the drys and the wets are both minorities. The characters which they display to the public are determined largely by their own vociferous minority-minorities.

The majority of those who at present see abstinence as the solution to the problems of alcohol are honest, sincere ladies and gentlemen. They hold personal convictions, but they do not quiver with emotion and call names when these convictions are not accepted by others. They seek and respect the truth and would follow sound leadership toward any sensible solution of the problems of alcohol if such leadership were developed. As a group, however, they are stigmatized by the leadership imposed by an aggressive minority which has the peculiar unscrupulousness of the self-virtuous and narrow. This minority-minority is constituted by the persistent, emotional advocate of prohibition seeking political power.

The same situation exists among the men associated in various ways with the beverage-alcohol industry—the wets to the drys. The majority are respectable normal-minded citizens who are honestly trying to carry out —in a tradition in which they take a pride—a business which is legal. They are concerned about the abuses of their product, but it is a concern which perhaps may be compared to that which the manufacturers and salesmen of automobiles might have about the injuries and deaths on the highways. They, too, want and respect truth and decency. They have started con-

* From "The 'Wets' and 'Drys' Join Against Science," editorial, Quarterly Journal of Studies on Alcohol, 6 (1945), 131–4.

structive measures which are intended to ameliorate some of the ills associated with their trade; notable among these are the self-regulatory and policing principle of the brewing industry and the pleas for moderation in the publicity of some distilleries. But again they are disproportionally influenced and stigmatized by a minority—a "powerful faction"—which in its anxiety displays almost paranoid symptoms. Members of this minority are exact counterparts in ethics, principles, and political maneuvers of the aggressive prohibitionists. They fight continually—with violence and with any tactics—against dry propaganda which they discover in the mention of the fact that some men get drunk. To them constructive efforts to alleviate the evils of excessive use of alcohol are construed as admissions of guilt and as steps toward defeat.

Both minority-minorities underestimate the good sense of the public and feel so insecure that they fear the public will not be impressed unless facts and figures are of astronomical proportions. The illogic and the exaggeration lead to such absurdities as the following: A dry organization, deploring the money wasted on liquor, put the annual bar bill for the United States—and the bill included all collaterals such as loss of employment, accidents and sickness—at 20 billion dollars. This figure was decried as an exaggeration by the wets—and it is. But the wets in publicity intended to show the unfairness of illicit sales stated that in addition to the 7 billion dollars spent on legitimate liquor in 1945 the American public would spend some 35 billion dollars on black market liquor. That is a bar bill alone of 42 billion dollars—double the one of the drys (including collaterals) which was vehemently denied.

So irrational have been the thinking, sayings, and doings of both minorities that, paradoxically, each side is in danger of achieving the goals of the other. The wets in thumping out their defense against wet baiting by the drys often provide fine dry ammunition. Many a prohibitionist has been created by the deliberate blindness to fact and the offensive defense of the wets, and many a prohibitionist has been lost through the intransigent, emotional pamphleteering of the drys.

The importance of the conflict between the wet and dry minorities in its influence on public opinion is not in merits but in magnitude. The shoutings, the dust kicked up, the emotional rantings, magnify the conflict out of proper proportions. It appears to assume such magnitude that sides must be taken: one is either a wet or a dry. The unfortunate consequence is that the neutral grounds of humanitarian aid and of scientific study are invaded. The humanitarian who wants to aid the alcoholic and the scientist who wishes to study the problems of alcohol find that they are viewed as outsiders forcing their way into a private fight. Both minority-minorities regard them with suspicion and in their insecurity even go to the length of joining together against the intruders.

A particularly pathetic but natural example of this attitude is the way in which some militant wets and drys view the humanitarian efforts of recovered alcoholics to rehabilitate other alcoholics. There are in the United States many thousands of respectable and productive citizens who formerly were alcoholics. Many of them have banded together in the effort to help the less fortunate alcoholics. From their deep insight they view the alcohol problem not as coming out of a bottle but as originating in the man. They believe that some men show psychological and physiological peculiarities which render them incapable of being moderate drinkers, but only abstainers or excessive drinkers. They do not assume that they should be protected in their own peculiarity by depriving all citizens of the moderate use of alcohol of which they are incapable. They are not prohibitionists; they are personally dry. Their sin in the eyes of the narrowest wets and the drys is that their efforts have attracted public attention and aroused public sympathy. Their view as to the seat of the alcohol problem in individual peculiarities is foreign to, and therefore suspicious to, both wets and drys who struggle to keep the problem in a battle.

The scientist who wishes to work dispassionately on the problems of alcohol finds that he is in the same bed with the rehabilitated alcoholic— viewed with suspicion and stigmatized by both wet and dry factions. The scientist has attempted—and with growing success—to popularize the humane belief that alcoholism is an illness and that the alcoholic deserves not moral degradation, not jail sentences, but the dignity of the medical care which is the right of every man who is ill. The scientist has advocated clinics and other institutions for the cure and rehabilitation of alcoholics. He has demonstrated that rehabilitation is possible.

But the conception of alcoholism as an illness and the founding of clinics for rehabilitation are taken as subtle anti-wet and equally subtle anti-dry propaganda. It appears that they simultaneously focus attention on the alcohol problem and hide it. Here, the narrow wets and the drys are in perfect agreement with the subordination of humanitarian views to vested interests and to abstract principles.

The scientist has drawn the fire of the wet because in the publicity on his views he has broken a taboo. The taboo is of word magic, according to which, by never pronouncing such harmful words as "drunk," "drunkenness," and "alcoholic," it is believed that the phenomena designated by these words are made nonexistent. The assumption is made further that anyone who breaks the taboo is a dry. Thus a news letter—which gives the liquor trade what it may like to read but not what it should read—says: "If you analyze it, if you break down the reams and reams of articles about 'alcoholics are sick and must be forgiven, etc.,' if you piecemeal the phrases and sentences cleverly placed in the articles, you will realize that they are undermining public opinion against liquor."

The scientist cannot grasp the logic of this argument. To him it appears as the always unpleasant sight of vested interest attempting to subordinate broad humanitarian interest.

He can, however, comprehend the attitude of the extreme drys toward rehabilitation of the alcoholic and can see equally clearly the always unpleasant sight when the proponents of an abstract principle attempt to subordinate humanitarian interests to a preconception.

With only a few notable exceptions prohibition organizations now oppose the rehabilitation of the alcoholic. To take him off the street and hide him from public eye in clinics, to rehabilitate him would be—so it is held—entirely to the benefit of the liquor trade. The "drunk" is the prohibitionist's best advocate; without him there would be—for most of the public—no alcohol problem. This attitude makes sense but it does not make humanitarianism.

Legitimate scientific research and scientifically oriented clinical and educational work on alcohol have suffered greatly through public mistrust generated by the conflict of the wets and drys. Research needs public support—not necessarily financial support, but moral support. Such support can be gained only with great difficulty when the assumption of partisanship is made and forced upon the scientist. The scientist does not take sides. He is interested only in the truth and in its humanitarian application. And the truth appears to be the one issue that both wet and dry minorities fear most.

The obstruction to the solution of the problems of alcohol has lasted too long. In spite of obstacles the growing numbers of scientists interested in the problem and the growing numbers of rehabilitated alcoholics, in close cooperation, will—in spite of opposition—gain the needed public support. The Forgotten Man will make himself heard, and the way will be opened to realistic solutions of an important social and medical problem.

SUPPLEMENTARY READINGS FOR PART IV

1. J. C. Ford, *Man Takes a Drink*. New York, P. J. Kenedy, 1955.
2. A. R. King, *Basic Information on Alcohol*. Mount Vernon, Iowa, Cornell College Press, 1953.
3. H. J. Clinebell, Jr., *Understanding and Counseling the Alcoholic*. Nashville, Abingdon Press, 1956.
4. H. D. Kruse, ed. *Alcoholism as a Medical Problem*. New York, P. Hoeber, 1956.
5. H. Levy, *Drink; an Economic and Social Study*. London, Routledge & Kegan Paul, 1951.
6. Report of the Manitoba Liquor Enquiry Commission, Winnipeg, 1955, esp. pp. 118–206. Includes a general summary of regulatory laws in England, Canada, the United States, India, and Pakistan, in addition to comments by E. M. Jellinek regarding the current use and control of alcoholic drinks in countries of Europe, the Near East, Australia, and South America.
7. C. R. Snyder, *Alcohol and the Jews. A Cultural Study of Drinking and Sobriety*. New Haven, Publications Division, Yale Center of Alcohol Studies; and Glencoe, Illinois, The Free Press; 1958.
8. E. M. Lemert, "Alcoholism and the Sociocultural Situation," *Quarterly Journal of Studies on Alcohol, 17* (1956), 291–324.
9. S. Harris, *Skid Row, U.S.A.* New York, Doubleday, 1956.
10. D. J. Pittman and C. W. Gordon, *Revolving Door: A Study of the Chronic Police Case Inebriate*. New Haven, Publications Division, Yale Center of Alcohol Studies; and Glencoe, Illinois, The Free Press; 1958.
11. R. Fox, *Alcoholism, Its Scope, Cause and Treatment*. New York, Random House, 1955.
12. *Alcoholics Anonymous*. Revised. New York, Alcoholics Anonymous Publishing, Inc., 1955.
13. M. Mann, *Primer on Alcoholism*. New York, Rinehart, 1950.
14. L. Syme, "Personality Characteristics and the Alcoholic. A Critique of Current Studies," *Quarterly Journal of Studies on Alcohol, 18* (1957), 288–302.
15. State and provincial alcoholism treatment agencies publish pamphlet material and research studies.

PLATE XIII

A (left). Kiddush cup, silver gilded, Germany, 18th century. Engraved around the rim in Hebrew is: "Remember the Sabbath Day to keep it holy. Remember it [with the benediction] over wine." (Photograph by F. J. Darmstaedter.) Courtesy of the Jewish Museum, New York.

B (center). Greek wine cup (cantharus), pottery, 4th century B.C., typical of vessels often depicted in drinking scenes in ancient Greek art. Courtesy of the Yale University Art Gallery, New Haven.

C (right). Dutch drinking glass, 17th century. Courtesy of the Victoria and Albert Museum, London.

A. Punch bowl, showing coopers at work. Bone porcelain, England, 18th century. Courtesy of the Victoria and Albert Museum, London.

B. Spirits kegs. George III Lambeth stoneware, England, ca. 1815. Courtesy of Parke-Bernet Galleries, Inc., New York.

PART V

CONTROLS

INTRODUCTION

During World War I, the increased demand for alcohol in the production of explosives and the need to conserve cereal grains for food resulted in the establishment of wartime prohibition of the manufacture and sale of alcoholic beverages in many countries of Western Europe, in the provinces of Canada, and in the United States. This brief experience with legal controls on a broad basis furnished a stimulus in many countries for an extension of the system into the years following the end of the war in 1918.

Prohibition of the manufacture and sale of alcoholic drinks has been advocated for decades as the solution to problems associated with drinking. In some countries the prohibition movement has been highly organized. However, there has also been marked resistance to the principle. Although the resistance before enactment of legislation has often been relatively unorganized, it is possible to distinguish certain groups who oppose the elimination of alcoholic beverages. One group comprises people directly concerned with the beverage industry. Another challenges the power of government to invade an area of individual rights, i.e., the right to purchase and consume alcoholic beverages, a right which has sometimes been equated with freedom of worship. Others who are individually concerned with the consumption of alcohol protest any interference with their recreational pursuits on emotional rather than logical grounds. In most countries there have been individuals relatively indifferent to the issue; others have expressed concern at the increased cost of government if revenue derived from the sale of alcoholic beverages should be eliminated.

Apparently attitudes fluctuate at different times among a substantial number of people, so that group sentiment sufficient to insure the passage of prohibition legislation may be aroused at one point, and at another, provides the balance of voting power to modify or repeal existing legislation. The history of prohibition in several countries reveals definite cycles in terms of alternating public support and rejection of the legislation.

Generalizations regarding the effectiveness or ineffectiveness of legal prohibition in those countries where it has been tried are misleading. Variables operate in each country. Among these variables are geographic area, size and composition of population, degree of industrialization, the ratio of urban to rural areas, cultural attitudes toward drinking, homogeneity of ethnic background, and church membership. Of major significance is the system of government which has been followed and the degree to which individual citizens participate in and support the democratic process.

Three countries have been selected to illustrate attempts at control of drinking through legislative action. Sweden has had a modified system of control for nearly a century, and the Swedish system has been singled out as being remarkably effective. During the present century, Finland has experimented both with total prohibition and with modified controls. The population in these two countries is relatively homogeneous and problems arising from the control of alcoholic beverages in urban as well as in rural sections are illustrated. Sweden and Finland have had a long period of temperance activity with support for the temperance movement coming both from government and from the church. In each country, recent developments have produced changes in legislation which are of interest to students of alcohol problems.

In the United States, National Prohibition was in effect from January 1920 to December 1933. This experiment followed more than 50 years of alternating acceptance and rejection of prohibition at various government levels in many of the states. The intensity of feeling generated by the events of the Prohibition Era and by Repeal has not subsided with the passing of the years. The emergence of the two loosely defined categories of "Wets" and "Drys" and the continuous conflict between them in state legislatures and in the Congress has had the effect of obscuring in popular thinking many of the social issues surrounding drinking practices in this country.

Drinking customs have undergone change in the last decade or two and presumably attitudes toward prohibition have similarly been modified. The papers reproduced in this section suggest the nature and direction of these changes since 1930.

27. SWEDEN AND FINLAND

THE LIQUOR CONTROL SYSTEM IN SWEDEN

by M. Marcus *

In order properly to understand the Swedish temperance question, it is necessary to bear two things in mind from the very beginning. The first is that Sweden produces neither wine nor hops, but that the country, which is anything but fertile in many places, grows plenty of potatoes, and that it is therefore potato spirit, which has an extremely high alcohol content, that constitutes the greater proportion of the alcohol consumed by the Swede.

The second fact to be remembered is that, down to the middle of the last century, the consumption of potato spirit was very general amongst all classes of society, and moreover that such large quantities of it were consumed that it was really possible to speak of a general abuse. It is not necessary to dwell here on the causes of this regrettable circumstance, which are chiefly to be sought, on the one hand, in the coldness of the climate in the greater part of the country, with a long and dark winter, and, on the other hand, in the fact that potato spirit was extremely cheap and within easy reach of everybody. The fact was that a large part of the peasant population distilled their own spirits, just as they produced the corn for their own bread.

It is clear that this state of things was bound gradually to lead to attempts to bring about a reform. A strong temperance movement was initiated during the first half of the 19th century and about the middle of the century succeeded in bringing about legislation which led to the disappearance of the small distilleries—that is to say, chiefly the distilleries for household requirements.

It may be said that the legislation referred to, which came into force in 1855, forms the basis on which the present restrictive system in Sweden has since been developed. In principle it was a matter of legislation based on the granting of licenses—that is to say, the right to manufacture and sell spirits was made dependent on permission granted by an administrative authority. The right of manufacture was not circumscribed by any specially burdensome regulations, except in respect of taxation.

On the other hand, the right to sell potato spirit was limited by special detailed regulations; and even at this early stage there appears the division of the trade into the wholesale trade, the retail trade, and sales for con-

* From *The Liquor Control System in Sweden*. Stockholm, P. A. Norstedt & Söner, 1946.

sumption on the premises, which has since remained one of the most distinctive characteristics of the Swedish system. Above all, however, this legislation concentrated itself on a rational organization of the retail trade; and an attempt was made to restrict the retail trade, especially in the provinces, where it was to be limited mainly to the towns, and placed in the hands of special companies enjoying the exclusive right of sale in their districts. The fundamental principle governing the activities of these companies was to be the elimination of all private financial interest in the trade, an object which it was sought to attain by preventing the company from drawing anything more than a small interest on the capital employed, and by devoting all the remaining profits to public purposes.

The most famous of the companies formed on the basis of this legislation was founded in 1865, in Gothenburg; as a result of this the whole system came to be called the Gothenburg system. The company superseded a large number of the dram shops or saloons in the town and turned them into restaurants for the working classes, where warm food was served at moderate prices. The results of this system soon showed themselves in the decrease in crimes and misdemeanors traceable to drink. The accruing profits were employed for public purposes. The promising beginning of the Gothenburg system soon led to the formation of other companies of the same kind in most of the towns in Sweden.

Nevertheless it was soon to prove that the capacity of the Gothenburg system to promote temperance was severely restricted. The movement was concerned only with the sale of potato spirit, while such strong drinks as cognac, whisky, punch, etc., for which there now began to be a demand in Sweden, and also all kinds of wine, were sold by private dealers. All restaurants and eating houses, other than those which were directly owned by the company, lay entirely outside its control. Moreover, as most of the surplus profits on the operations of the company were to fall to the local authorities, they later became so dependent financially on these profits that their zeal in keeping the sales within reasonable limits was relaxed. In order to remedy these drawbacks in some measure, a regulation was put in force in 1913, prescribing that the profits of the spirit companies should be transferred to the state; and the government was to be allowed to devote only restricted amounts to general state purposes.

It was at this period that the plan which was destined to triumph later under the name of the Bratt system was first put forward for public discussion. In 1909 Sweden was exposed to a general strike, during which the authorities found themselves compelled entirely to prohibit the sale of spirits; and this prohibition, which was in force for six weeks, led to extremely favorable results throughout the country from the point of view of sobriety.

Encouraged by these results, the temperance societies succeeded in 1909 in organizing a great independent plebiscite on the question of prohibition.

The result was 1,900,000 votes for, and only 17,000 against. The total population of the country in that year was about 5,500,000.

Dr. Ivan Bratt, who at this period was a physician in Stockholm and took an active interest in the drink question, did not believe in the possibility of carrying through prohibition, although he had been able to observe how successful it was for a few weeks. The success he attributed solely to the fact that all the adverse forces—private distilling, smuggling, and all kinds of illicit trading—had not had time to make themselves felt. The solution which Dr. Bratt sought was not total prohibition, but restrictions imposed on the individual, a control of individual consumption. The possibility for individuals to obtain alcohol was not to be removed by law, but was to be limited by control; and this control was to be exercised by the companies. On the basis of a provision in the existing law to the effect that the companies were to work in such a way that the sales of alcohol should lead to the least possible social harm, and bearing in mind the fact that most of the alcohol consumed was obtained through the retail trade and not at cafés, restaurants, etc., Dr. Bratt worked out a system under which anybody who desired to buy a bottle of spirits for private consumption must have a permit from the company in his district, which, within the maximum limits fixed by the law, decided on the quantity which each person was allowed to buy. The companies were to exercise constant and strict supervision of the purchases of their customers, and to revoke the permits of those who abused them.

At first Dr. Bratt's proposals encountered resistance in various quarters, but in other quarters they were welcomed as a serious attempt to promote temperance. They were first put into practice by Dr. Bratt himself in 1913, when he became the managing director of the company in Stockholm, which was then reorganized under the name of the Stockholm system. Later, when the whole legislation was revised on the initiative of the government, Dr. Bratt himself being invited to cooperate, it received the impress of his ideas, and, in the form introduced in 1917, the Bratt system was incorporated into Swedish legislation.

During the years that have passed since 1917, the Bratt system has taken still deeper root, both under the influence of the experience gained from its application, and, above all, owing to the fact that the wholesale trade also has been brought under the system.

In accordance with the provision of the law of 1917, private retailing of wines or spirits has been forbidden since 1919, when the whole retail trade became the monopoly of the system companies. In principle, the law was not opposed to the wholesale trade being carried on, as up to that time, by private persons. Nonetheless it soon became evident that the monopoly of the companies in the retail trade called for a monopolization of the wholesale trade to complete and supplement the organization and general aims of the companies. For this purpose it was absolutely necessary to deprive the wholesale trade of any kind of private financial interest. In this manner all interest of that kind was to be eliminated from the two principal branches of the liquor trade, and the profits were to be at the disposal of the public authorities. Another important desideratum was to organize the wholesale trade in such a way that the goods handled should be exactly branded, and all risk of adulteration be removed. Experience showed that these desiderata would be best realized within the scope of a compact wholesale commercial enterprise, in which private financial interests had no place. Furthermore, apart from decided advantages accruing to the consumers, there was the advantage that there would be fewer causes of conflict with the wine-producing countries—conflicts which might otherwise be anticipated as a result of the Swedish policy of restriction.

Influenced by these considerations, in 1917 Dr. Bratt and his friends founded an enterprise under the name of Aktiebolaget Vin- & Spritcentralen. At its start this undertaking bought up most of the Swedish spirit rectifying plants and thus became the largest purveyor of the chief article of consumption. Later on, in 1917–18, Spritcentralen acquired all the private firms in the country dealing in wines and spirits and all the rectifying plants which, up to that time, had not become its property, and thus, at the beginning of 1919, the company possessed in fact the monopoly of both the manufacture and wholesale distribution of Swedish-made spirits and of the wholesale trade in all other spirits, beer being excluded. By its constitution the company was bound to distribute only a small dividend to its shareholders and to place all surplus earnings at the disposal of the state.

In this way the program for the organization of the wholesale trade was realized, and the final aim of the system, initiated privately, was formally confirmed by the law of 1923, by which Spritcentralen and its subsidiary companies obtained from the government the monopoly of the wholesale trade in the Kingdom.

Later on the legislation in this sphere was revised, but the leading principles are still the same. The new laws were put into force in 1938.

The working of the Swedish system will be clearer if you imagine for a moment that you are a member of the Swedish community, and that you desire, as is but natural, to satisfy your requirements of intoxicating liquors.

If it is merely a question of beer, the matter is quite simple. Beer is the principal table drink of the Swedes, and it is consumed in considerable quantities: in 1939 the consumption amounted to about 300,000,000 liters, or about 47 liters per inhabitant. You can obtain almost as much beer as you desire, whether for domestic consumption or at cafés or restaurants, but it does not contain much alcohol—at most 3.2 per cent by weight. Stronger beers may not be either imported or brewed in Sweden, except for medicinal and technical use. Moreover about 40 per cent of the Swedish beer is so weak that it does not contain more than 1.8 per cent by weight of alcohol. Restrictive legislation in this field passed through many stages before the present position was reached. But the very small alcohol content of the beer that we have today also explains how it has been thought possible, without any great risk, to exclude it from the system of restrictions imposed for spirits.

If you desire other beverages—that is to say wine, cognac, whisky, liqueurs, or potato spirit—the matter is not so simple, and you immediately come into contact with the Bratt system. If you live in Stockholm, for instance, and wish to buy wine or spirits for home consumption, you must first of all apply to the Company which holds the monopoly of the retail trade in spirits, and which is called the Stockholm system. You must state in writing your name and occupation, the amount you pay in taxes (in order to give an idea of your social position), and you must state the quantity of spirits that you believe you ordinarily require. The Company then makes inquiries in order to verify your statements. If it proves that you have not yet attained your twenty-first year, or that you have been found guilty of drunkenness or of certain crimes or misdemeanors more than once during the last few years, it is impossible for you to become a customer of the Company. If, on the other hand, the results of the inquiries are favorable, the Company issues to you a copy of the famous *motbok* (permit book)— which is said to have been published in a larger edition than any other book. At the present moment (1946) more than 1.7 million Swedish subjects possess it. The book is very much like a check book, one form from which is employed for each purchase. When you receive this book you are informed how many liters of spirits you have a right to buy each month. In 1939 the legal maximum was 4 liters per mensem (during the war reduced to 3 liters), but this quantity was not in fact granted to more than one-fifth of the holders of permit books. As a rule a book is issued to only one member of each household. But few men under 25 receive these books, and particular care is exercised as regards their issue to women.

Almost without exception this maximum applies only to spirituous liquors. No limits are prescribed for the purchase of wine; but all purchases made, and thus those of wine also, are recorded and continuously checked by the Company, and if the Company finds that they exceed the limit which is considered reasonable for the holder of the book and the requirements of his household, this may lead to restrictions. Otherwise the book is yours for life, if you do not abuse alcohol. It makes you a customer of that one of the Company's shops which is nearest to your home. Before the war, which has of course greatly restricted the supply of all kinds of spirits and wines, you were able to find an extremely good assortment in the shops, and your taste, however fastidious it might be, would undoubtedly have been satisfied. You would certainly have found also that the prices were very moderate, making due allowance for the heavy state taxes on all spirits (and since the end of 1939 on all wines too).

The book covers only domestic consumption, and it has nothing to do with consumption away from home, in restaurants and cafés. But it is characteristic of the alcohol consumption in Sweden that only one-tenth of the stronger spirits, and only one-fifth of the wine, is consumed away from the home. Hence the quantities bought on the book are very considerable.

But the consumption of spirits at restaurants and cafés is by no means unrestricted. It was so, it is true, during the early years of the Bratt system; but it was quickly recognized that those who were not satisfied with the ration allowed by the book found their way to the restaurant or café and there drank alcohol in far too large quantities. It was necessary to regulate this consumption, and this was done by limiting the allowance of spirits at the restaurants and by making this allowance contingent on the ordering of cooked food. Thus, when you are at a restaurant in our country, you can drink as much light wine as you please at your meal, but for port, sherry, and madeira the maximum is a quarter of a bottle per person. With regard to spirits, such as brandy, cognac, whisky or liqueur, you are not allowed, at one and the same visit to the restaurant, to drink more than 15 centiliters after 3 P.M., and only 7.5 centiliters before that hour.

The restaurant keeper is bound to observe these regulations. By contract he purchases all his spirits from the Company; and moreover his financial interest in selling unlimited quantities has been removed by depriving him of the profits on sales in excess of a certain maximum, fixed by the Company for each restaurant. This maximum is gradually decreasing during a period of 25 years, after the end of which the restaurant keeper no longer has any profit on sales of spirits.

The system companies which are thus the sole legitimate sources of supply, both for private customers and for restaurants and cafés, number 41 at present. Their field of activity is for the most part in the towns, and the rural population have to go to the nearest town for their supplies of spirits. In 1939 the total sales of the companies (direct and to restaurants) amounted to 35 million liters of strong liquors, and to 6.3 million liters of wine, of the selling values of 231 and 39 million crowns respectively. These figures include heavy duties to the state, amounting in 1939 to something like 185 million crowns, or 70 per cent of the whole sum.

The boards of the system companies comprise, in each case, one member elected by the shareholders and two members elected by municipal authorities, while the fourth and fifth members, the chairman and the vice chairman, are appointed by a state authority, the Board of Control, the principal function of which is the supervision of all the companies and the general enforcement of the law.

The whole of the retail trade here described is supplied by the similarly monopolized wholesale organization, that is to say Aktiebolaget Vin- & Spritcentralen. Half the members of the board of Spritcentralen (including the chairman) are chosen by the government, which also appoints a controlling auditor. The share capital amounts to 15,000,000 Kr., of which

14,600,000 Kr. is in the form of 5 per cent preference shares, and 400,-000 Kr. is in the form of ordinary shares, the dividend on which is limited to 5½ per cent, and which represents the majority of votes at the shareholder's meetings. The preference shares are owned by a State Fund, the ordinary shares by a syndicate of ten persons, approved by the government, pledged to sell their shares at par to the state on demand. Hence these shares are indirectly controlled by the government. All the profits of the Company, after the distribution of the dividend and a restricted transfer to certain funds, fall to the state. Spritcentralen owns all the rectifying plants of Swedish spirits in Sweden. The Company is the sole importer of wines and spirits. Spritcentralen makes every effort to obtain every brand at the place of production. In order to give satisfaction to consumers, and also to the exporting countries, the Company deals with a constantly growing number of firms, especially in the case of wines. The Company only provides the wines with labels indicating exactly the source and the quality of the goods, and never blends Swedish alcohol or other substances with imported spirits without indicating it distinctly on the label.

The prices charged by Spritcentralen are fixed—as are those of any other merchant—in relation to the cost price, the state of the market, and the customers' purchasing power. There is no great fear of the Company's attempting to abuse its monopoly by raising its prices and thus making excessive profits, since the profits of the shareholders are limited, and the surplus falls to the state. The directors, like all the employees, receive fixed salaries, and there is no sort of commission. The state authorities have also expressed the wish that the wholesale company should strive, above all things, to obtain goods of satisfactory quality, and that the question of profits should be of secondary importance.

The Swedish restrictive system does not strive in the first place to cut down the total consumption, but to eliminate the social evils resultant on the abuse of alcohol. These depend at least as much upon the manner of consumption as on the total amount consumed. Still the system can also exercise a considerable influence in the direction of decreasing consumption.

From 1913 to 1939 the consumption of spirits has been reduced from 39 to 30 million liters per annum. These figures mean 69 deciliters per head of population in 1913 and 48 deciliters in 1939, or a reduction of about 30 per cent.

Convictions for drunkenness are not a reliable indication of the part played by alcohol in the matter of social evils. They do not even afford an exact measure of the extent to which acute alcoholism exists in a community, since only such cases of drunkenness are recorded as are brought before a court by the police. In spite of that, the increase or the decrease of the convictions for drunkenness during a succession of years in one and the same country, or at one and the same place, gives a fairly good idea of the changes in sobriety during the same years, provided that police action has not been changed to any considerable degree owing to alterations in the law or other circumstances.

As regards Sweden, all the evidence seems to indicate that, in respect of police action during the last 15 or 20 years, the situation has developed in the direction of greater severity in dealing with intoxicated persons. Therefore, even if convictions for drunkenness were as numerous now as at the beginning of that period, we might nevertheless be justified in assuming that conditions have improved.

As a matter of fact the number of convictions for drunkenness has fallen considerably from 1913/15—the years immediately before the restrictive system was put into operation. For the whole country the decrease is from 93 to 51 per 10,000 inhabitants or about 45 per cent. This favorable development has in all probability been the result of several cooperating factors. Partly it is to be attributed to the activities of the system companies, partly it is due to the fact that successful attempts have been made to check the production of homemade spirits, which flourished during the war of 1914–18 (as a consequence of the severe restrictions necessitated by the shortage of foodstuffs) and partly it is due to the activities of the temperance movement.

In the history of the Bratt system and its repercussions on public opinion it is possible to distinguish two main periods, the boundary line between which lies about 1922. The first period, the successful establishment of the system in Stockholm, is characterized by a rapid succession of reforms in the spirit of the Bratt ideas, which encountered more or less strong opposition. During the second period one can speak of a stabilization and leveling out of the restrictions, unaccompanied by the forced expansion of the first period. The general public accustomed themselves to the restrictions and increasingly admitted their justification.

In the years when Dr. Bratt was engaged in a long struggle for his ideas, he divided the Swedish people into two classes on the basis of their attitude to the question of temperance: those who called for total prohibition, and those who, advocating status quo, opposed any kind of reform. The Bratt system took a middle course. In the first place it attacked abuse and left the moderate drinker in peace as far as possible. These ideas have been in a great measure realized. Sobriety has improved considerably, and it cannot be denied that the activities of the system have contributed to this satisfactory result, though there are different opinions as to its importance in relation to other nonlegislative factors. During its life the system has had to weather many storms, and at times it was near foundering. But it was borne up by ideas which have proved their lasting vitality, and its principal features have never been shaken.

The creator of the system has himself repeatedly said that it is in the light of experience that its value must be judged, and he has also declared that more depends on the manner of its actual application than on the paragraphs of the law which establishes it. To what extent it can be applied to other countries naturally cannot be foreseen; and its originator never dreamed of regarding it as an export article.

On the other hand, it ought to be observed that the opposition raised in prohibitionist quarters, which has never ceased during the activity of the system, recently succeeded in getting Parliament to agree to holding an inquiry into the whole question of alcoholic liquors in Sweden, and a government commission began an inquiry.

SWEDEN: SEQUEL

by Arne Skutin *

On October 1, 1955, the major provisions of the Bratt system were substantially modified by act of the Swedish Parliament. This action was in accordance with recommendations of a commission appointed by the government to reappraise the entire liquor control plan. Individual permits to purchase liquor are no longer required. Limitations on the quantity of drinks to be purchased in a restaurant have been removed although distilled spirits and a new strong beer, 4.5 per cent by weight of alcohol, can be served only with food. A central distribution system, Nya Systemaktiebolaget, under government supervision replaces the several regional or local systems for distribution and sale. Under the old system, the major emphasis was given to legal control. The new legislation places emphasis on freedom for the individual with regard to his drinking habits but also requires greater responsibility. It also provides for systematic activity in the fields of education, study of social problems related to drinking, leisuretime activities among teen-agers and the construction of a research hospital with approximately 60 beds for patients with alcohol problems.

Under the Bratt system, machinery for controlling drinking abuses was established at the local level through Temperance Boards. These committees or boards have authority to intervene and institute remedial procedures for individuals who are abusing the use of alcohol. Established first in 1913, the Boards operate in nearly every community. Welfare agencies carry the same responsibility in areas where a Board does not exist.

The Stockholm Board employs approximately 150 people under the supervision of an executive director. Services include 14 district offices staffed by a corps of inspectors and 3 social workers; a medical center; a driving license bureau to which violators of drinking and driving laws are referred; an information center, opened in 1955; 2 outpatient clinics; and 2 hostels, e.g., residential units for homeless alcoholics. In accordance with the new legislation wider powers are assigned to the Temperance

* This information regarding revision of the Swedish control system since 1955 was furnished by Mr. Arne Skutin, executive secretary, Stockholm Temperance Board.

Boards enabling them to interfere at an earlier stage with abuse of alcohol and making it possible to offer remedial measures before a serious case develops. In order to encourage the local Temperance Boards to increase their activities, the state in 1954 increased support to the extent of 60 per cent of operating expenses.

One of the consequences of the new policy concerning sales of alcoholic beverages was an increased consumption of spirits. In comparison with the period October 1, 1954–September 30, 1955, 33 per cent more hard liquor was sold in the period October 1, 1955–September 30, 1956. Sales of wines, on the other hand, decreased by 19 per cent during the same period. The new strong beer has not proved successful in changing the drinking habits from hard liquors to milder alcoholic beverages.

Increased consumption and an upsurge of convictions for drunkenness was more or less expected during a period of transfer from the one system to the other. The fact that no reduction in consumption figures can be noticed and that the caseload of treatment agencies and outpatient clinics steadily increased led to great concern among the authorities. On November 1, 1956, the price of the most commonly used distilled drink, the potato spirit, was raised by about 20 per cent. As a result of this action a diminishing demand for this spirit occurred, whereas consumption of wine increased.

In order to further eliminate the unfavorable development of the unrestricted liquor policy, the authorities on July 1, 1957, introduced a system of control regarding purchase of liquor. In accordance with this system the Temperance Boards are authorized to list persons known for excessive drinking and bar them from purchasing liquor. The control is exercised by the liquor shops and anybody would be required to identify himself on demand.

As an additional effort to improve the situation, in 1957 the state raised its subsidies to the Temperance Boards to the level of 75 per cent of their expenses. Along with this program of giving support to treatment and rehabilitation in the communities goes an intensified action of making more inpatient facilities available at clinics, convalescent homes, hostels, and farms.

PROHIBITION IN FINLAND

by Sakari Sariola *

Background

The home distillation of spirits was prohibited in Finland in 1866 and the production of alcohol was shifted to an industrial basis. This measure

* From "Prohibition in Finland, 1919–1932: Its Background and Consequences," *Quarterly Journal of Studies on Alcohol,* 15 (1954), 477–90.

had two main purposes: to offer the authorities ways and means of reducing drunkenness; and to make possible the levying of taxes on liquor sales. Heavy taxation of alcoholic drinks was thought to discourage their excessive use. Further alcohol policy measures were introduced in the last century which were exclusively legislative and restrictive and thus reflected the social philosophy of the era, which placed the main emphasis on legislative compulsion rather than on the education of the individual. Since very little understanding of individual treatment existed at that time, attitudes toward excessive drinking were formulated along the consideration of "sin" and morality.

The Finnish legislation was first concerned with production and sales of distilled spirits only, but in 1883 and 1895, respectively, regulations were imposed also on malted beverages and wines.

Finnish society showed the first tokens of an industrialization process in the last decades of the 19th century, affecting especially the wood and textile industry; farming was being gradually mechanized and farming techniques improved. Large numbers of farm workers were detached from farm work and lost the security derived from their traditional source of livelihood. The price of land went up; mass migration toward the cities and industrial centers took place. This formed in the cities a new social category of unskilled industrial labor whose members, in the change to cash payment, soon obtained economic capacities somewhat higher than their cultural standards. Drunkenness appeared to a great extent among these groups and became one of the key problems which Finnish society had to tackle. In accord with the legislative restrictions, a strong absolutist (total abstinence) movement was founded holding a close alliance with Lutheran religious thinking which it has since then maintained. Only in recent years, since World War II, has the absolutist movement shown active interest in finding a scientific basis for its policies which for a long period prior to 1932 included total prohibition. Today the interest of the movement in the sphere of alcohol policy is concentrated on holding the total of liquor sales as low as possible by making legal access to alcohol as difficult as possible.

Thus, since the last decades of the 19th century, legislative measures on liquor were determined by the strong influence of the absolutist pressure groups and a high regard for restrictive legislative measures as the preventive method par excellence in problems of drunkenness. Around the beginning of the present century legislation was extended to cover some aspects of the consumption of alcohol besides its distillation and sale. Total prohibition was applied in certain limited areas and times, such as at fairs and on market days, national holidays, and so forth. However, these amendments were not codified into any systematic or comprehensive body of liquor laws. In 1904, therefore, the Government appointed a committee to rework the alcohol legislation of Finland. The committee proposed local option, and a definition of beverages concerned in liquor legislation, and pointed to the need of systematizing the prevailing restrictions in production, sales and consumption of alcohol.

In the papers of this committee, the goal of alcohol legislation is expressed as a policy "to diminish the consumption of alcohol, to prevent its abuse and to check its consequent injurious effects." This is still the leading principle on which Finnish alcohol legislation is based. The wording of the legislative principle has been a cause of disagreement in more recent discussions of alcohol policies in this country; for some claim that the legislative principle intends an arrangement of *liquor sales* that will maintain them at the minimum, while others argue that the wording of the above legislative principle has an accent on the *prevention of abuse and its ill effects*. The latter opinion maintains that the abuse of alcohol is affected strongly by other factors than the availability of alcohol, and that these are of a social economic and social pathological nature, that prohibition has other undesirable byproducts, and that the alcohol problem will be satisfactorily faced only when the people having access to alcohol assume individual responsibility, "drinking mores," and a relatively higher cultural level.

The work of the committee on alcohol legislation of 1904, when terminated, was nevertheless not handed over to the Parliament for discussion. There had been almost simultaneously—in 1906—a drastic parliamentary reform in Finland, granting a considerably wider representation in Parliament to the workers class [1] and to the middle class than they had had in the earlier Finnish Parliament, which had been established on the antiquated principle of "estates" (Nobility, Clergy, Bourgeois and Landowners). Also, for the first time in Finland (and incidentally among the first in the world) women were given the right to vote. Workers unions, established in Finland before and around the turn of the century, had traditionally been inclined to prohibitionist thinking. Women were also traditionally in favor of total prohibition. Very soon it became evident that the new Parliament would not treat the "liberal" program as proposed by the committee of 1904 as favorably as the old estates assembly might have done. The issue of alcohol policies has since then been greatly exploited in party politics and a "prohibitionist" line became one of the principal assets in party politics.

As a result, instead of taking up for discussion the suggestions of the committee on alcohol legislation of 1904, the newly constituted Parliament passed a bill, in 1907, designed to introduce total prohibition in Finland. This first bill was not enforced, and a similar law, passed by Parliament in

1. The workers party consisted mostly of Socialists, with notable Marxist influence, who were at that time mainly concerned with cooperatives, workers education, social security, etc. However, a more radical wing among the Socialists grew in strength later, especially during the years of World War I, 1914–17.

1909, was also delayed by the Government throughout the period that Finland remained an autonomous Grand Duchy of the Russian Empire. Only the first Parliament in independent Finland of 1917 had sufficient influence over the Government to have the prohibition bill enforced.

Labor and Prohibition

Since pressure from politically organized Finnish Labor has played a most important role in the development of liquor policies in this country, it may be of interest to review Labor attitudes toward liquor legislation in particular detail.

Labor policies toward the end of the last century were marked by the influence of philanthropic leaders, with goals perhaps somewhat separated from the level of practicality. Under the influence of a well-known absolutist writer, the Labor leaders in 1898 adopted a policy of the "drinking strike," referring to the voluntary refusal of workers to consume alcohol in any form. This movement had a strong temporary appeal. Historians of the era report of many "notorious drunkards" subscribing to the idea and advocating it among industrial workers. In one industrial city, violent measures were taken by laborers to close the local liquor store. Workers Absolutist Associations were founded. The movement gained in strength to a membership of about 70,000 workers.

Although the "drinking strike" gradually quieted down, it had important political consequences. "Drinking strike" was connected with the cause of prohibition. After this episode, Finnish Labor was officially for total prohibition. Local labor unions, one by one, signed petitions demanding prohibition. In 1900, Parliament was officially asked by a petition carrying more than 140,000 signed names to promote immediate prohibition laws.

In these efforts the absolutist movement outside Labor readily joined. Labor realized that the absolutist program had been a rewarding asset; many members in the unions were only vaguely aware of the political goals of the labor movement but rallied to the ideals of the fight against drunkenness. This was especially the case with women.

In the election for the newly organized Parliament of 1906 the issue of liquor policies played an important role. Not only Labor but other parties as well had already realized the effectiveness of an absolutist program in their campaign. It became apparent that no party felt inclined to support openly the previous policies of mere restrictions in production and sales and partial restrictions of consumption. Instead, most parties included in their official program the proposal for prohibition. In 1907, Parliament proposed by four-fifths of the cast votes that the Government prepare the outline for a law of prohibition.

After this resolution the question of prohibition became more and more a political weapon. In the minority, some rightist members of Parliament initiated a cautious campaign for their cause. Their main argument was the unfeasibility of total prohibition. The Socialist press criticized the double standards of these writers, claimed that a small section of Parliament was intentionally trying to delay prohibition even though it had been accepted by Parliament. In this complex situation the Government did not readily start working on a prohibition program. Certain proposals of the Government to Parliament in 1908 concerning liquor taxes showed that, instead, the Government's policies were designed either to postpone prohibition or to propose a system of local option.

In the year 1908 the Religious Workers Party made an official inquiry about the delay apparent in the promulgation of prohibition. The answer given by the Government was not exhaustive; "This matter will be taken up in due course," it was said.

The rightist press made occasional definite statements that the prohibition law as proposed by Parliament was illegal, since "it was merely a propagandist trick." Another argument ran in the direction that it had already been settled that alcohol policies were to be shaped along the lines suggested by the committee of 1904, and that no contradictory proposals should be discussed before the Government had laid out its program based on the committee's work. Another argument which was occasionally raised was the need of the State and the communities for alcohol tax revenue. Experience with the previously tried measures of restricting consumption, it was further argued, had been discouraging. The French Government had made it known that in case Finland would adopt prohibition, they were "disinclined to continue discussions on a loan of 50 million markkas to Finland." Some opinions appealed to the responsibility for national security; "Without a secure basis in our national economy we will be defenseless in case of political attacks."

The delay of prohibition started mass demonstrations in various parts of the country, organized by Labor with the sympathy of the absolutist movement. When Parliament convened in 1909 the first issue to be discussed was the demand of the Socialists about the status of this affair, but this question to the Government was not answered before the Czar adjourned Parliament on the grounds of an arrogant opening speech by the chairman. The Labor press went on to claim that this speech was intentionally so formulated as to save the Government from the looming vote of no confidence.

After a new Parliament was elected in 1909, the Government made it clear that it was not ready to work out the laws of prohibition. The attitude of the Government was immediately labeled by the Socialist press as "cowardly and against parliamentary principles." A new proposal for prohibition was made by the Socialists and was adopted in Parliament by the same four-fifths majority as before, after long debates mainly on the fiscal consequences of the proposal.

Demonstrations for prohibition were newly organized by Labor around

1911 in key localities. In repeated explanations on the matter by the Government it became evident that the Government was determinedly against the promulgation of such a law. It was the first time under the new parliamentary system, wherein Parliament and the Government had clearly opposite and uncompromising views on an issue. It was thus a test question concerned with a vital principle of Finnish democracy, that the Government should be subject to the mandate of the confidence of the elected Parliament.

The absolutist movement, since 1880, had considered local option mainly as a step toward total prohibition. The rapidly awakening enthusiasm and idealism in matters of temperance of the newly organized Labor movement, however, caused great sections of the absolutists to believe that total prohibition could be achieved directly. A change in the absolutist programs was made corresponding to Labor's proposals. The alliance between the absolutist movement and organized Labor proved beneficial for both, and other parties soon realized that campaigning with total prohibition as the official goal was a political necessity. The attitude of Labor can perhaps be best understood in relation to its newly discovered self-confidence, the realization of its new social role, and its definite belief in Labor's strength in the pursuit of idealistic goals as contrasted to what it considered antiquated liberal and nonidealistic conservative thinking.

After prohibition became one of the decisive political issues, Labor sponsored the idea of prohibition more persistently than ever, and most discussions during the years from 1909 to the beginning of World War I were framed in reference to political interests rather than to empirical social considerations. Labor strongly felt that drunkenness was one of the greatest social evils within its ranks and instinctively chose the most extreme methods to fight this evil. Not only Labor but a great section of the Finnish nationalist movement was attracted by the ideals of absolutism in its idealistic belief in Finnish national strength and in the moral characteristics of the Finns. These people were likely to contrast the patriotic cause and absolutist principles to the "foreign" liberal ideals represented by the Russian administration and by the Swedish party of Czarist Finland.

Prohibition

During World War I, liquor trade in Finland was made virtually illegal through temporary wartime administrative legislation and not through the usual parliamentary process. Only highly taxed mild beverages were allowed to be served in selected restaurants.

With the attainment of national independence in 1917 the parliamentary request for prohibition was speeded. The Government until 1917 had been strongly under the influence of the Russian administrators and of the Swedish-speaking people in Finland whose party consistently had been the only one not to include prohibition in its program. The Government which came to power in 1917 was mainly composed of nationally oriented elements who wanted to pay full respect to the opinion of the country's highest legislative body. Among the first parliamentary deeds was the approval of prohibition, ratified to be enforced as of July 1, 1919.

The prohibition law forbade the production, import, sale, transport and storage of alcohol except for medical, technical and scientific purposes. The State assumed the monopoly of producing alcohol for legal purposes. The prohibition legislation was subsequently amended in regard to the details of action in cases of violation of the law.

With the start of prohibition, general attention became focused on a more practical level of consideration. The law soon necessitated a network of officials, inspectors and boards in charge of alcohol crimes. Among other agencies, the police force was heavily burdened with cases of home distillation and smuggling. In the first year of prohibition, coastal guards seized 8,000 liters of smuggled spirits; this item rose rapidly to 110,000 in 1920, and 520,000 in 1924. Thus very soon after the beginning of prohibition it became apparent that in the years to come the Finnish Government would not be able to overcome smuggling from Estonia, Germany and other countries. In 1925 a leading advocate of prohibition, Vaino Voionmaa, wrote: "Experience has shown that smuggling cannot be abolished in the Nordic countries with merely local measures in the various countries. Smuggling of spirits is internationally organized, functioning systematically in sea areas. . . . International smuggling requires international counteraction."

Many other consequences of the prohibition law now became apparent. Drinking went on under cover. The law was ridiculed by the degree to which it was violated in the broad layers of society. Drinking habits were influenced unfavorably. Crimes of violence increased rapidly. Even those who had been used to moderate drinking were dissatisfied by the state of affairs, and many people who earlier had been indifferent about the goals of Drys and Wets began to get interested in the liquor question and generally tended to take sides with the Wets.

The abolishment of prohibition was also to be primarily a matter of political exploitation. As early as in 1924 some rightist newspapers had polled their readership and found a contrast between the general opinion and the opinion prevailing in the legislature. The Liberal party was the first to suggest, in 1926, the use of a referendum in the matter. The principal aim of this initiative was not to abolish prohibition but to have accurate information on the stand of the people. Local option was, however, offered as the alternative to total prohibition.

The two biggest parties in Parliament, the Agrarian and the Social Democratic, were the only ones to give unfailing official support to prohibition. They regarded the suggestion of a referendum as a bold attempt to overthrow prohibition. Since the Government was inclined toward a referendum, however, these parties did not offer great resistance. The

Social Democratic Party, especially, had placed referendum high among the democratic institutions, so that little open resistance was to be expected from this side.

In 1931 the Government appointed a research committee to carry out an inquiry about the drinking situation during prohibition and to make recommendations. The committee almost unanimously recommended that some liquors should be allowed, that wine up to 11 per cent (by volume) and beer up to 3.2 per cent should be free.

With the onset of the depression years the State budget suffered severe losses of revenue and the unemployment situation faced the Government with a deficit of 150–400 million markkas for the fiscal year 1932. In locating new taxation targets, the question of alcoholic-beverage sales received serious attention.

A committee of cabinet members in 1931 recommended a referendum, and it was decided to hold it at the end of the year 1931. The question put to referendum gave the possibility of endorsing one of three propositions: (a) maintenance of prohibition, (b) free production and sale of mild drinks, or (c) free production and sale of all spirits. The latter alternatives included a system of controls of sales and taxation.

Only 28 per cent of the votes cast gave their support to the first proposition. The second received the least support, only 1.4 per cent of the votes. The third was supported by a majority of 70.6 per cent. It was interesting to note that women voters were stronger for total prohibition than men voters. Whereas one-third of the women were in favor of prohibition, less than one-fourth of the men wanted it. Only 44.4 per cent of the citizens of voting age cast a ballot.

Although in the analysis of the reaction against prohibition all the factors cannot readily be identified, it is apparent that there was a general resentment of the excessive interference in private matters by the officials in charge of alcohol inspection. Furthermore, unemployment appeared to have made people realize that economic necessities might sometimes prove some ideas impractical. Also, a strong patriotic movement had arisen in reaction to Communist propaganda work during the depression years. This movement opposed strongly the "political hypocrisy" displayed in parliamentary discussions on prohibition.

New Alcohol Legislation

In January 1932 the present alcohol legislation was drawn by Parliament. In a vital paragraph it provides that "The liquor trade shall be arranged in a manner to check illegal trade in alcohol, to reduce the consumption of alcohol to the minimum, and to prevent drunkenness and its injurious effects."

It had been the aim of the legislators to take only one step away from prohibition. Since alcohol could not be entirely abolished, its consumption should be kept to a minimum. The restriction of consumption would have one important criterion: that the restrictions should not be so severe that illegal trade would appear. On this base the State Alcohol Monopoly (Oy Alkoholiliike Ab) was established, in 1932, to manage the production, distribution and sale of alcoholic drinks.

It is the ambiguity between the restrictive principle of sales and between the principle of checking the ill effects of drunkenness that has been the cause of most disputes in the area of alcohol policies since 1932. The Monopoly at present maintains liquor stores in cities and industrial centers only; there are no retail stores in the Finnish countryside. The Monopoly has instituted, besides, an individual inspection system of the buyers. Each person wanting to buy alcoholic drinks in a store must apply for a passbook in which a record of his purchases is kept. An individual found to be using alcohol in excess, or so as to cause economic burden to his family, public annoyance, or danger in his locality, is denied the right to buy liquor by withdrawal of his personal license. There are no quotas prescribed as to the maximum of liquor that may be purchased, but each individual case of misuse is judged separately by inspectors employed by the Monopoly. The usual procedure is for these inspectors to issue "official warnings" before the right to use the passbook is withdrawn from an individual. The decision on withdrawal of passbook is made by a committee to which the community and the Monopoly appoint the members.

Among more recent alcohol policy measures has been an attempt, since 1951, to favor mild drinks in price and relatively open access to their purchase, as compared with spirits. . . .

The Finnish liquor monopoly is thus not only a commercial concern in charge of the production and retailing of liquors but also the agency which is now directly responsible for matters of alcohol policy. However, in many details a relatively narrow range has been left by the liquor legislation, and the Monopoly is restricted to the framework of this legislation. Certain legislative reforms backed by the Monopoly are at present awaiting parliamentary approval. These include, for example, permission to send liquor by mail and to make beer available in food stores, including the countryside where there are now no liquor stores.

Local communities, under the present legislation, have the right of veto on the establishment of liquor stores in their area. Every community with a liquor store must appoint a communal inspector in charge of reporting on the temperance status in the area, and of drawing the attention of officials to crimes against the liquor laws, drunkenness, and so forth.

Present Tendencies

The consumption of alcohol in Finland is lower than in most European countries (1.8 liters of absolute alcohol per capita of the total population in 1951). The Finnish pattern of drinking, however, tends to cause many undesirable effects. It has been calculated that the per capita rate of arrests for drunkenness is about seven times higher in Finland than it is in Sweden. The rate of homicides is high. The Finns drink at irregular intervals—very often it is on Saturdays—and they tend to use great quantities of alcohol at a time.

The absolutist movement in Finland is still quite strong. The absolutists are not officially in favor of further attempts along the lines of prohibition but are in opposition to any form of expanding the liquor trade from its present scope. The absolutist movement evidently gains in weight through the fact that it has the official support of the Government in the form of considerable grants used for promoting absolutist ideals. Since the Alcohol Monopoly is also a State enterprise, a unique situation has been created in that the State which is running the official liquor trade is also concretely supporting the absolutist actions which, lately, have concentrated much of their effort on attacking the policies of the Monopoly.

Recognition of the alcohol question as a field of scientific research has only recently received serious attention and backing by the Monopoly. The recognition of this aspect was marked by the establishment, in 1951, of a Department for Social Research in the Monopoly to study the characteristics of Finnish society in relation to alcohol questions, and, also in 1951, of a foundation for the study of alcohol problems. There is close collaboration between these two agencies: The head of the Research Department also functions as the secretary-general of the Foundation.

The Foundation is organized so as to gather scientific basis for the orientation of future liquor policies in the country. It is administratively and financially dependent partly on the Finnish Alcohol Monopoly but independent in terms of its research scope and operations. These are decided upon by the Administrative Committee of the Foundation, which is drafted to represent the interests of the men in charge of the official alcohol policy measures as well as those of outside scientific experts. The Foundation has given various grants to outside scientists, physicians, sociologists and psychologists, every year since its establishment, to encourage individual research related to alcohol problems. The main effect of these grants has probably been a growing interest in the alcohol problem as a scientific research topic. However, in order to promote more systematic research, the Foundation has itself initiated a series of research projects of a sociological and psychological nature. Among these studies there has been a sociological survey on drinking habits in Finnish Lapland. This area was selected for research not only because the people in Lapland have strongly shown their dissatisfaction about the degree of smuggling and black marketing of liquors, and about the economic burden of getting alcohol legally, but also because the difficulty of access to liquor in the area has resulted in conditions where local prohibition still practically prevails in a relatively underdeveloped social and economic setting.

The study on Lapland produced, among others, the following findings: A persistent extensive black market of liquors has developed in the area.

The use of technical alcohol-containing medicaments, ointments and other fluids, with acute health risks, was widespread, especially among the youth.

The great majority of males in the area (78 per cent) was in favor of the opening of liquor stores in the rural centers.

In order to buy legal drinks an average of one working day per month per person using alcohol was spent in travel to the nearest liquor store.

Frequency of consuming alcoholic beverages was somewhat increased with higher socioeconomic status of the individual, but the quantities used at a time were slightly decreased.

One of the main ideological resistances to drinking seemed to be the control exerted by religion. Secularized absolutist thinking seemed to have little influence, or it was even widely deprecated or discredited.

Important social correlates to drinking were found: e.g., social control exerted by intimate environment and alleviated by the situation of the nearest liquor store in another town. Heaviest drinking usually occurred during trips to fetch liquor from town.

Other social factors associated with excessive drinking were marital status, education, and occupational stability. There were grounds for assuming that an unskilled, socially and occupationally unstable worker experiences a more definite risk of becoming an alcoholic than a worker with a steady job and family ties.

* * *

Conclusion

The Finnish experiment with prohibition has reflected mainly the necessity of having the level of discussion on the matter raised to an objective, scientific level. As long as political considerations are the main criteria, there is no guarantee that opinions are formulated in the responsible manner that the importance of this social problem deserves.

A second consideration is the necessity of understanding the nature of alcoholism. Laymen are still widely inclined to think that alcoholism is a form of "bad manners," that it can be corrected by legislative measures. The superficiality of this view should be made clear to people. The necessity of combined medical, psychiatric and social therapy should be appreciated.

At best, changes in drinking habits can be effected only gradually. Changes in legislation to correspond gradually to the present state of knowledge on alcoholism should be made, and the different steps taken in a new direction should be subjected to experimental research.

As has been the case with both somatic and mental diseases, alcoholism and drunkenness should be made a topic of wider scientific interest. Only by this means can the hazards inherent in making a political or religious issue of this psychosomatic pathological disturbance be avoided.

A more permissive attitude toward control of sales of alcoholic beverages has developed since the preceding paper was prepared. No permit is now required to buy beer or wine having a low alcohol content. The practice of denying the right to purchase alcoholic drinks to individuals whose consumption appears to be excessive is followed less consistently than formerly. The Finnish Foundation for Alcohol Studies is now conducting research in the field of physiology as well as in psychological and sociological areas.

28. THE UNITED STATES

The chain of circumstances which culminated in National Prohibition in the United States was tremendously complex. The late 19th century was characterized by a rapid increase in population including an influx of hundreds of thousands of immigrants from the countries of Europe. Dramatic changes took place as a result of improved modes of transportation, growing industrialization, and rising standards of living. As the nation matured, interest in humanitarian reforms arose. Many of the unfavorable conditions of work and family life which characterized urban unskilled and semiskilled workmen were attributed to the use of alcohol. Leaders of certain churches acknowledged a moral obligation to do something for the "working classes" and the elimination of sales of alcoholic beverages and the saloon appeared as logical objectives. Humanitarian zeal combined with a spiritual motive provided the driving force that set the philosophy of legal prohibition in motion on a national scale not only in this country but also in many parts of the world.

The prohibition movement produced an enormous literature. Much of this material is buried in libraries and is of little significance today. Yet the issue is still alive and the principles underlying the movement are being advanced although the tactics employed by leaders of the temperance organizations have undergone considerable change since enactment of the Twenty-first Amendment.

The material reproduced here is in no way intended as a comprehensive presentation of the historical arguments for and against legal prohibition. The papers selected reflect the attitudes of some significant segments of the American public in the fight for national prohibition and later for repeal. It is reasonably clear that the key to any solution in the United States to questions about drinking and intoxication resides in the possibility of constructive changes in attitudes toward drinking and the acceptance of social responsibility for the problems associated with intoxication.

PROHIBITION AND REPEAL

*by Raymond G. McCarthy
and Edgar M. Douglass* *

Before 1840, legislative action concerned with the alcoholic-beverage industry in the United States was purely regulatory in character. It was not intended to be repressive. The decline of the philosophy of moral suasion, however, was followed by the development in temperance circles of a sentiment for legal prohibition. This was the stage at which the temperance movement became identified with prohibition and the word temperance acquired a new definition. The philosophy of social reform by political action became crystallized in the Maine Law of 1851.

Temperance Fraternal Orders

The years between 1840 and 1860 saw the emergence of temperance societies which originated as social and fraternal organizations. While some of these organizations were of local interest only, a number of them grew to nationwide scope and influence. Typical of the latter was the Sons of Temperance, organized in New York City in 1842. The members declared they were joined together for self-protection by total abstinence. They agreed to provide mutual assistance to one another in time of illness and to encourage self-culture by the elevation of character and the development of qualifications for the duties of American citizenship. They sought to provide an active social life which was nonsectarian and nonpartisan. Among their declared aims was the suppression of the liquor traffic. The Sons of Temperance developed rapidly. Limited membership was allowed women and provision was made for associated activities for children. In 1844 a national division was organized with 6,000 members, which by 1850 had increased to 230,000. Lodges soon existed in all the New England states, in many of the middle and southern states east of the Mississippi River, in Iowa, Arkansas, California and Mississippi, in four Canadian provinces, and in England. They established their own publishing house and developed an active social organization which had its core in the temperance pledge and in a positive program intended to bring about prohibition. In 1920 they reported a membership of 600,000.

A temperance society which ultimately wielded international influence was the Independent Order of Good Templars, established in New York State in 1850. By 1855 the Templars were numerous enough to organize a grand or national lodge on the principle of individual total abstinence,

* From *Alcohol and Social Responsibility* (New York, Thomas Y. Crowell Co. and Yale Plan Clinic, 1949), pp. 25–41.

with a program of no-license and prohibition. This was the first such organization to admit women to full membership. By 1858 they had extended their influence to Canada. Although their ranks were divided during the War between the States over the question of the membership of Negroes, they boasted 400,000 members at that time. In a decade they had established lodges in Great Britain and Ireland, and an international organization became effective. In 1902, with lodges functioning in most of the countries of Europe and in North Africa, Australia and New Zealand, the name was changed to the International Order of Good Templars. There were juvenile temples for children and junior lodges for young people. The Good Templars are credited with having established a form of organization which was later to influence the Woman's Christian Temperance Union and give direction to the Anti-Saloon League. In 1869 the Templars took the initiative in calling a conference which culminated in the organization of the National Prohibition Party.

Unlike the temperance associations of the first half of the nineteenth century, the new organizations provided an active social life for thousands of people. Just as the National Grange movement which was taking form at this time offered social and practical advantages to farmers, so the temperance organizations, established on the principle of abstinence and with a program of action pointing toward prohibition, gave their members fraternal associations and mutual support. This produced legislation-minded and aggressive temperance groups from which potential support for prohibition was to be developed in the period from 1880 to 1900. The societies, however, were independent and frequently competitive.

Early State Prohibition Laws

The Maine Law is often referred to as a milestone on the road to national prohibition. Although the Oregon Territory was organized in 1844 with a dry clause in its constitution, this Territory was remote from the center of population and from national activity. Maine, however, commanded much prestige, and the prohibition forces greeted with enthusiasm the successful drive which culminated in state action in 1851. Between 1851 and 1855 state prohibition of the manufacture, distribution and sale of alcoholic beverages became effective in all the New England states and in Minnesota, Michigan, Indiana, Delaware, Iowa, Nebraska and New York. This represented more than a third of the thirty-one states in the union.

These early experiments with state prohibition were short-lived. By 1863 eight of the thirteen had repealed the legislation and four others had modified the law significantly. Only in Maine was the original legislation maintained. All reform legislation was undoubtedly affected by the war and pre-war conditions of the period; popular interest was almost completely attracted to the problems of slavery and secession. In view of the later arguments of wets and drys about the effect of war conditions between 1915 and 1920 on voting for or against prohibition, the 1855–63 experience presents an interesting contrast.

Two events of significance to the alcoholic-beverage industry occurred in 1861. Because of the need for additional revenue to finance the war, the Internal Revenue Act of 1862 levied a heavy tax on alcohol, making it a significant source of government revenue. Partly as a result of this action and partly because it was already on its way from being an insignificant part to becoming the major part of the alcoholic-beverage industry, there originated in the same year the United States Brewers Association. This group was aggressive, legislation-minded, organized on a national basis and adequately financed—the characteristics of the temperance groups half a century later.

Reconstruction and national economic and political issues in the years immediately following the war obscured the prohibition question temporarily. Beginning in 1880 there was a second wave of activity for legislative control of the sale and distribution of alcoholic beverages. Eight states passed prohibitory laws. Again the experiment was short-lived. Most of these states had repealed the legislation by 1904.

During the decade preceding the first World War a third wave of prohibitory legislative action developed, this time showing its greatest strength in the South and West. When the United States entered the war in 1917, twenty-five states had some kind of prohibition laws. By 1919, when the Eighteenth Amendment became effective, the number had increased to thirty-three. These states comprised 80 per cent of the land area of the United States and more than 50 per cent of its population. If the local option areas in the other states are included, the manufacture and sale of intoxicating beverages had been declared illegal in 95 per cent of the land area of the country, containing 68 per cent of the population. It should be noted, however, that the legislation was often less stringent than the Eighteenth Amendment. Furthermore, although the area and population of the United States were by political measurement becoming more and more dry, by measurement of the consumption of alcohol no parallel trend was to be observed.

The National Prohibition Party

Before 1870 the prohibition question had been of relatively minor importance as a national political issue. Most of the activity had been centered in local, county or state elections. Representations had been made to the Republican and Democratic Parties to take a definite stand on the issue, but without success. In 1872, as the result of the initiative taken by the Order of Good Templars, the first country-wide ticket of the National Prohibition Party appeared. The leaders in the temperance movement had become convinced that their goal must be the complete suppression of the trade in intoxicating liquors.

The Prohibition Party never attained either numerical or political strength. Its greatest direct success at the ballot box was in 1892, when it polled 270,000 votes. Although the National Prohibition Party made its appeal on the basis of a great moral issue, few even of the supporters of prohibition were willing to desert the older parties with their broader bases of interest. The National Prohibition Party was in effect superseded on the political scene by the advent of the Anti-Saloon League in 1895. The party still exists, however, and polled more than 90,000 votes in the 1948 election.

The Woman's Christian Temperance Union

The second half of the 19th century was an era of social reform, marked by the beginnings in this country of widespread interest in problems of human relations. The War between the States settled the question of slavery, and the rights of the Negro to citizenship and suffrage were written into the Constitution. The legal position of women was becoming a political issue. A few states made a start in granting them limited legal rights, but suffrage—except in local affairs—was withheld until the first states granted it in the 1890's. Colleges and universities were opening their doors to women who soon began to gain admission to the professions. The ability of women successfully to organize, administer, and promote a program of social reform was demonstrated in their efforts in support of temperance education and for the correction of the evils associated with the licensing system of that day.

By 1870 the women of several states had banded together to exert influence, by prayer and mass meetings, on saloonkeepers and license boards. Their program was essentially one of persuasion and they achieved remarkable success, particularly in Illinois, Michigan, and Ohio. Although their work at first had little organization, it grew into state temperance leagues which served to focus attention on temperance and on the potential power of women's organizations. An outcome of this activity was the organization in 1874, at Cleveland, of the Woman's Christian Temperance Union. The first meeting was attended by delegations from seventeen states; in 1875, at the first annual convention, representatives from twenty-two states were present. Women of intelligence and ability were attracted to the movement and gained positions of leadership. The program of the Woman's Christian Temperance Union was comprehensive enough to enable it to expand into an international organization.

The founders of the W.C.T.U. outlined a many-sided approach to the problem of the reform of drinking customs. The scope of the program is indicated in a pledge agreed upon at the first convention:

We therefore formulate and for ourselves adopt the following pledge: "I hereby solemnly promise, God helping me, to abstain from all distilled, fermented and malt liquors including wine, beer, and cider, and to employ all proper means to discourage the use of and traffic in the same."

To confirm and enforce the rationale of this pledge, we declare our purpose to educate the young; to form a better public sentiment; to reform so far as possible, by religious, ethical and scientific means, the drinking classes; to seek the transforming power of divine grace for ourselves and for all for whom we work.[1]

Under the leadership of Miss Frances Willard from 1879 until her death in 1898, the W.C.T.U. set up a variety of specific departments of work, including prevention, education and legislation. Emphasis was laid on temperance mass meetings, medal contests, concerts, posters, exhibits and the circulation of quantities of literature. An official journal, The Union Signal, was established and has continued in publication to the present time. Active programs for young people, temperance teaching in the public schools and Sunday schools, and petitions to medical societies were inaugurated. The Loyal Temperance Legion for children was established to teach abstinence and to train for Christian citizenship and moral leadership. There was also a program for young adults.

The W.C.T.U. envisioned the teaching of the subject of physiology and hygiene, particularly in a light favorable to the practice of total abstinence, to all children. Temperance lessons were prepared for use in school textbooks, and leaflets for Sunday schools. Its Scientific Temperance Bureau headquarters in Boston developed an extensive library. As a result of these activities, instruction about the harmful effects of alcohol and narcotics first became obligatory in schools under Federal jurisdiction by act of Congress. Later, state legislatures were persuaded to pass similar legislation, until at present every state in the nation requires instruction about alcohol and narcotics in its public schools.

In 1883, through the influence of Miss Willard, the World Woman's Christian Temperance Union was established and the work introduced into forty-three countries. The scope of the program visualized by the framers of this association was expressed as follows:

The World W.C.T.U. was the first organization of Christian Women to make an international appeal for the establishment of total abstinence, scientific temperance training in the schools, courts of international arbitration, the promotion of equal moral standards, the enfranchisement of women, and the abolition of the manufacture and sale of beverage alcohol. The badge of the society is a bow of white ribbon and its motto is: "For God and home and every land."[2]

At the first world convention, held at Boston in 1891, delegates from more than forty countries attended. There was a membership of more than

1. Cited from the *Standard Encyclopedia of the Alcohol Problem*, Vol. 6.
2. Cited from *ibid.*, Vol. 1.

200,000. In 1929 fifty-one countries, with a total paid membership of more than 600,000 were represented.

The W.C.T.U. developed the most comprehensive educational program for abstinence and prohibition in the United States. Acting through state branches, the organization sought to influence legislative, social and religious activities. Its methods were flexible and emphasis could be shifted to meet particular situations in different areas. This organization has to its credit the promotion of a major share of the educational activities concerning alcohol in the public and church schools of this country.

On the political front the W.C.T.U. cooperated with other temperance organizations in supporting local option movements. In 1913 a committee of one thousand women was named by the W.C.T.U. to join with the Anti-Saloon League in support of the Hobson Resolution for a constitutional amendment on prohibition. The organization carried on a sustained and consistent drive to bring about a modification of social attitudes which would culminate in prohibition, based on the viewpoint that the only problem is alcohol and the only solution, prohibition.

The Anti-Saloon League

The most highly organized and influential body striving for prohibition was the Anti-Saloon League of America. The League grew out of the realization by temperance leaders of the inefficiency of more than a hundred temperance organizations working separately. It was an outcome also of the realization of the potentialities in well-organized state legislative programs, which had been demonstrated in Ohio. The Oberlin, Ohio, Temperance Alliance, organized in March 1870, developed a program which culminated first in local option laws in the college towns of Ohio and later in an attempt to launch a state-wide movement for township local option. At about the same time as the Temperance Alliance became the Ohio Anti-Saloon League, in 1893, a similar league was getting under way in Washington, D.C. In December 1895 the Washington Anti-Saloon League took the initiative in calling a convention for the organization of what was to become the Anti-Saloon League of America. The league, describing itself as "the church in action against the saloon," inaugurated a program of publicity and pledges for financial support, and a consistent plan of opposition to wet candidates and support of dry candidates in all states on a nonpartisan and interdenominational basis. On a county, state and national scale the organization operated with the slogan: "Education, legislation and law enforcement."

Through the Lincoln-Lee Legion of young people the League became active in Sunday schools and church organizations, distributing literature and sponsoring pledge-signing programs. It sought the cooperation of industrial leaders to secure the nomination and election of public officials pledged to support anti-liquor legislation. It brought pressure on Congress and on state legislatures to approve local option on prohibition. The effectiveness of the League's program was aided by the publications of the American Issue Publishing Co. of Westerville, Ohio, which became the official publishing house. Campaign literature of the state Anti-Saloon Leagues, pamphlets, leaflets and broadsides were printed in large quantities. The official organ, The American Issue, was distributed widely. Research, publicity, exhibits and press and lecture bureaus were fostered. The League also supported the activities of the Scientific Temperance Federation of Boston and the research department of the W.C.T.U.

Guided by able leadership and backed by adequate finances, the League was a powerful influence in the progressive stages leading to the adoption of the Eighteenth Amendment. On the national scene the League was largely responsible for the exclusion of alcoholic beverages from Army posts; prohibition of their sale in Federal buildings; prohibition of their transportation through the United States mails; prohibition of their sale to Indians; the Webb-Kenyon Act which made it illegal to ship liquor into dry states; prohibition bills for Alaska and Hawaii; exclusion of advertisements of liquor from the United States mails; and wartime prohibition in World War I.

The success of the Anti-Saloon League in obtaining prohibitory legislation has been attributed to the skillful direction of the state programs through a national board of directors, combined with an adequate financial system. Voluntary contributions were secured from wealthy citizens and a system of financial pledges through subscriptions was instituted in many of the churches. Because the League was nonpartisan it was able to enter a local political campaign either for the candidate who showed sympathy with the League's point of view or against individuals alleged to sympathize with the alcoholic-beverage industry. The enactment of the Eighteenth Amendment has been generally credited to the leadership and strategy of the Anti-Saloon League.

In 1918 the national officers of the League decided to cooperate with representatives of the temperance organizations of foreign countries. At a conference held in 1919 in Toronto and in Washington, D.C., representatives from fifty different countries established the World League Against Alcoholism. The League declared its intention to achieve, by education and by legislation, ". . . total suppression throughout the world of alcoholism which is the poisoning of the body, germ plasm, mind, conduct and society, produced by the consumption of alcoholic beverages."

Passage of the Eighteenth Amendment

In viewing the rise of national legislation to control alcoholic beverages, it must be remembered that such a development was in no way unique during the first two decades of the twentieth century. Rather was the opposite the case. This was the era of the trust-busters and the muck-rakers.

This was the period of legislation for reform in the field of conservation of natural resources and in the field of human rights, especially of children and of labor. This was the 20-year period which saw legislation such as the Pure Food Law, The Clayton Act, the Inter-State Commerce Act, the establishment of the Federal Trade Commission, the passage of an amendment allowing a federal income tax, the adoption of provisions of initiative, referendum and recall, and many other laws in the area labeled social progress and reform.

Some of the social reforms incorporated into law during this period were relatively new, especially insofar as legislation was concerned. The concept of prohibition of the alcoholic-beverage industry by legislative action was not new. It had been publicized for half a century and adopted in many sections of the country. Local option conditions, however, and even state-wide prohibition, were unsatisfactory to the temperance forces, who saw that any who wanted liquor could get it. The leaders of the organized prohibition movement believed that the abolition of alcoholic beverages could be achieved only by incorporating the prohibition philosophy into the basic law of the land. They recognized the difficulties involved in a drive to bring about a constitutional amendment, but they were confident that the long-term results would justify the effort.

The issue of prohibiting alcoholic beverages involved a series of complex social problems. It appears certain that for many thousands of persons the logical merits of the specific issue were secondary to such matters as their affiliation with a particular economic or religious or other group, or secondary to their feeling that something, unspecified, should be done. This is true of political action on many issues; it is mentioned here because of the long drawn-out controversy on both the passage and repeal of National Prohibition in which the opponents regularly argued about the ideas of the mass of the public, intimating or stating that the mass acted with clear-cut conceptions about the logical merits of either program. In retrospect it seems clear that the great majority of the public was neither wet nor dry despite the claims of the leaders of various groups. If anything, the great majority would seem to have been dissatisfied with the situation concerning the distribution and use of alcoholic beverages before, during and after Prohibition.

Prior to the first World War, however, there had developed an organized logic and a varying scale of individual attitudes in support of some form of prohibition. The active majority of temperance advocates joined in supporting the movement for a prohibition amendment. There were some temperance advocates who still favored moral suasion over legislative action, but they had little organized power. There were many persons, not associated with the temperance movement, who were sympathetic toward a program which held out the promise of eliminating the social and individual distress resulting from excessive drinking, although some of these were

opposed to placing sumptuary law in the Constitution; this category, however, was unorganized and had no positive program to offer as an alternative. No organized group equipped with a systematic logic was present
to lead an opposition, with the possible exception of components of the
alcoholic-beverage industry. Not only were they in a poor position to lead
any national movement but they were split among themselves and lacking
in any positive program for meeting the undeniable problems associated
with drinking and with the business.

As early as 1876 a bill was introduced in Congress which proposed to
prohibit—beginning in the next century the manufacture and sale of
distilled intoxicating liquors. Similar bills were introduced in many subsequent years in the Senate and House. The result of joint action by committees of the Anti-Saloon League and the Woman's Christian Temperance
Union was the Hobson Joint Resolution, calling for a constitutional prohibition amendment, which was introduced in the House of Representatives
and rejected in December 1915. In December 1917 it was passed by the
House and the Senate. The Eighteenth Amendment to the Constitution was
ratified by thirty-six state legislatures by January 16, 1919, and became
effective one year later.

The theory of nationwide prohibition was not without precedent in other
countries. Russia, during the war period of 1916–17, eliminated the sale
of beverages containing more than one and one-half per cent alcohol. Finland, after gaining independence from Russia, continued the prohibition
law until 1918. In Iceland, as early as 1908, a plebiscite approved prohibition, which became effective in January 1915. It was repealed after
seven years.

Administration of the Eighteenth Amendment

Establishment of nationwide prohibition in the United States, a country
with a heterogeneous population of 120,000,000, an extensive land area
and coastline, and a federal system of forty-eight state governments,
presented problems radically different from those of smaller centralized
countries. While it is customary to think of the United States as comprising
a common people under a united government, it must not be overlooked
that there are sharp differences between our rural and our highly industrialized urban areas, sectional divisions with distinct economic and political
characteristics, and wide variations in the social and religious attitudes
which predominate in different regions and among different groups. As
an administrative problem, the enforcement of the Prohibition Amendment
turned out to be an undertaking of stupendous magnitude, never successfully carried out.

Machinery for administering and enforcing the Eighteenth Amendment
was provided by the Volstead Act, passed by Congress over President
Wilson's veto in October 1919. This was the Act which defined an intoxi-

cating beverage, prohibited under the Eighteenth Amendment, as one that contained one-half of one per cent (or more) alcohol. The Volstead Act was necessarily an involved piece of legislation. It contained more than sixty provisions, some of which ultimately required construal by the courts. Successive Prohibition Administrators urged Congress to make various changes but no action was taken before 1929. By that time the forces seeking to discredit prohibition were well organized, public sentiment had apparently undergone considerable change, and there was widespread criticism of any effort at enforcement.

Proponents of National Prohibition have leveled many criticisms at the administration of the law, implying that were it not for the administrative shortcomings this type of attempt to control the problems of intemperance would have been effective. Many of the criticisms are undoubtedly justified although the implication drawn is open to serious question. Among these administrative or executive blunders were the following: (1) The function of enforcing the law was placed in the Treasury Department rather than in the Justice Department. (2) To allow production of alcohol for scientific, industrial, medicinal and sacramental purposes, a most complicated license and permit system was developed, a system almost incapable of adequate supervision. (3) At no time during Prohibition was there adequate personnel for enforcement of the law. (4) The personnel was not subject to Civil Service until 1927 and was never paid on a basis sufficient to attract effective or, often, honest workers.

There was practically no precedent on which the government could base a comprehensive program of enforcement of the Volstead Act. Moreover, the situation throughout the country was anything but static. As the supplies of legal liquor existing in 1920 dried up, an increasing flow of illicit liquor began to take its place and changes in enforcement policy became frequently necessary. The difficulties of securing convictions and the indifference and even resistance toward enforcement displayed by many state and local officials as well as large sections of the public began to render the law ineffective.

The smuggling of liquors into the country and the resulting spectacular clashes between Prohibition agents and lawbreakers made lurid headlines and news stories. But a more important source of illegal alcohol existed within the country. In spite of an elaborate permit system, illegal liquor moved from bonded warehouses to bootleggers. Supplies of alcohol released for industrial purposes found their way to unlicensed warehouses and were converted into varieties of gin and whisky. Many denaturing plants were established to meet a demand for commercial alcohol—a demand which had increased vastly during Prohibition. Unlicensed distilleries were numerous. Apparently there was no lack of consumers for the illegal beverages.

The purchase and use of intoxicating beverages was not forbidden under the law. Theoretically, possession for other than personal and family use constituted a violation. Practically, possession without evidence of offering for sale could rarely be prosecuted successfully. The courts were naturally reluctant to issue warrants for the search of private premises without evidence of sales. A still could long be operated with impunity, or a building be used for the storage of illegal liquor, by installing a family in the premises and thus giving it the color of a domicile immune to search. In other situations it was necessary for agents to pose as purchasers and drink with customers to secure evidence. Such tactics, sometimes on the part of drunken agents, were challenged by foes of Prohibition as violating American traditions of fair play.

Ardent prohibitionists insisted that the major weakness of the Volstead Act resided in its failure to make the purchaser as well as the vendor of the illegal liquor guilty of crime. There is serious doubt that a law could have been passed which incorporated such a provision. It is obvious, however, that the enforcement of Prohibition was handicapped in a situation in which one party to a transaction was a criminal and the other party—without whom the transaction could not have been consummated—was blameless.

Many explanations have been made of the failure of Prohibition, including inadequate enforcement, and corruption in public office. It cannot be doubted that one ingredient which would be essential for the successful enforcement of a prohibition law was ultimately lacking—popular support. However much public sentiment the advocates of Prohibition had mustered in favor of the experiment before the Eighteenth Amendment was passed, sufficient popular support for its enforcement was not in evidence in the succeeding years. This is not to state that the experiment was a failure to the same extent or in one fashion throughout the land. As a national program, however, the 1919–33 attempt fell short of its goals.

The Repeal Movement

Organized opposition to the enforcement of the Eighteenth Amendment began even before the law became operative. The Association Against the Prohibition Amendment was established in April 1919. Its announced aims were to prevent the country from going dry under wartime prohibition on July 1, 1919, and to prevent the Eighteenth Amendment from becoming operative on January 16, 1920. The Association, which at this time drew its membership chiefly from the brewers, planned to challenge the constitutionality of Prohibition on the ground that it was a Federal encroachment on states rights. A fund was established for the support of a lobby against state enforcement acts. In 1923, in part as a result of activity by the Association, the New York State legislature repealed its enforcement law.

After 1926, direction of the Association Against the Prohibition Amendment was assumed by industrial and financial leaders of national status.

An efficient propaganda machine was created and provided with adequate funds. The goal of the Association became outright repeal of the Eighteenth Amendment. It worked to develop a strong anti-prohibition sentiment in the country and to oppose Congressional appropriation of funds to maintain the Bureau of Prohibition. It took the position that Prohibition was a failure and was generating disrespect for law, and that the Eighteenth Amendment was unenforceable and therefore should be repealed. Money was made available in different states for the support of wet candidates in opposition to dry. In 1929 the enforcement laws of Wisconsin, Montana and Nevada were repealed, and Illinois followed suit in 1931.

The Association Against the Prohibition Amendment developed a group of supporting organizations which included the Woman's Organization for Repeal of National Prohibition, the Voluntary Committee of Lawyers, the Authors and Artists Committee, and the Crusaders, made up of young members of well-known American families. These organizations sponsored a sustained program of criticism of prohibition enforcement activities. Quantities of literature, pamphlets and newspaper articles appeared throughout the country. During the depression period of 1931 and 1932 the argument that repeal would put men back to work, not only in the brewing, wine-making and distilling industries but in all other related businesses, was not without appeal to the masses of unemployed workers as well as small businessmen and home owners.

Prohibition advocates have been bitterly critical of the A.A.P.A. They accuse the Association leaders of favoring repeal for the purpose of gaining reductions in personal and corporate income taxes through increased government revenue from liquor taxes. There is no doubt that not only the wealthy but millions of other citizens believed that since liquor was being sold, it should be taxed.[3] In any prolonged depression public dissatisfaction with existing conditions develops rapidly on an emotional level and a change of any kind appears to hold promise of relief. Nor can it be doubted that there was widespread disappointment with results of Prohibition.

Leaders in the Prohibition movement who had been critical of President Coolidge and Secretary of the Treasury Mellon for their seeming indifference toward more adequate enforcement greeted the election of Herbert Hoover in 1928 with considerable satisfaction. Presidential candidate Alfred E. Smith had openly stated his position as an avowed wet in contrast to Mr. Hoover's dry position. After his election, however, Mr. Hoover did not develop an aggressive policy in support of the Prohibition law. In 1929 he appointed the Wickersham Commission to investigate crime in the nation. A committee of eleven outstanding citizens, after many months of study, expressed the view that the Eighteenth Amendment should

3. One of the most widely used slogans in the campaign to repeal state prohibition in Kansas in 1948 was, "You've got it—Why not make it legal?"

be enforced. There were dissenting opinions, however, and one member submitted an individual report recommending drastic changes in the entire Prohibition program. Newspaper publicity about the Wickersham Report was conflicting. Members of the Commission were in agreement that conditions under the Volstead Law were unsatisfactory. Many journalists, after studying the Report, declared that in its conclusions it justified referring the question of Prohibition back to the people.

The high point of sentiment for repeal developed during 1931 and was reflected in the attitude of the two major parties in the preparation of platforms adopted at the national presidential conventions of 1932. Mr. Hoover was the Republican party candidate for reelection on a platform which could be considered dry. When he agreed that the country should have an opportunity to pass on an amendment which would allow the individual states to deal with the problems, he and his party were actually parting company with the thousands of prohibitionists who had first supported his election. The Democratic party platform and Franklin D. Roosevelt, the Democratic candidate, declared bluntly for repeal of the Eighteenth Amendment and for the submission of a repeal amendment to conventions in the states. Moreover, immediate modification of the Volstead Act was recommended to legalize beer and wine of low alcohol content.

The presidential candidate of the Prohibition party in 1932 polled only a few thousand votes. Mr. Roosevelt was not elected solely because he spoke unequivocally for allowing beer immediately and for prompt repeal of the Eighteenth Amendment. Economic and social distress and uncertainty provided a great deal of the motivation for a political upheaval which swept the Democratic party into office. But the proposal to relegalize alcoholic beverages was manifestly popular. Nine days after his inauguration President Roosevelt called on Congress to modify the Volstead Act so as to legalize beverages containing not more than 3.2 per cent alcohol by weight. A measure to this effect was passed by Congress and signed by the President on March 22, 1933. The Twenty-first Amendment, after being passed by Congress and approved by conventions elected for that purpose in three-fourths of the states, was proclaimed the fundamental law of the land on December 5, 1933. Thus the Prohibition era was ended.

Actually it was the close of the third Prohibition era. The attempt to control the problems of intemperance by political prohibition of the manufacture and sale of alcoholic beverages had again failed. The failure was far greater than most people realized. Perhaps the outstanding product of the experiment was the fact that public concern about the problems of intemperance was forgotten in the dramatic fight about Prohibition. Attacking or defending the concept Prohibition achieved the center of the stage and succeeded in pushing all other matters into a position of obscurity. The word *temperance*, for example, had come to mean *Prohibition*. In 1934 there was no program for the alleviation or prevention of alcoholism, nor was there a group prepared to meet this problem. Since the passage of the Eighteenth Amendment a new and vexatious problem related to intemperance had risen—drunken driving of automobiles. There was no program and no group to cope with this problem. Between 1918 and 1934 the customs of drinking and the segments of the population using these customs had changed rather dramatically. There was no program of education to meet this change. Furthermore, attempts to do anything along any of these lines were handicapped because they were popularly interpreted as movements for or against Prohibition.

It is possible that repeal of the Eighteenth Amendment solved some of the problems of the Eighteenth Amendment. It is certain that it solved few of the problems of intemperance. It is probable that the same comment could be made of the repeal of the earlier prohibitory laws. In the long years of attempts to control the problems of intemperance in the United States by moral suasion and by political prohibition of the manufacture and sale of alcoholic beverages, one fact remains clear. The problems are still with us. Only two states now have a partial statewide prohibition. All the states have the problems of intemperance.

Contemporary novels and motion pictures set in the prohibition era typify acts of violence, corruption in law enforcement, rum running, and speakeasies controlled by criminal syndicates. Certainly the late years of Prohibition presented a spectacle of irresponsibility and disrespect for law in many metropolitan areas. Vituperation and recrimination were not uncommon in the public press and from the speaker's platform. Yet it is often overlooked that many responsible citizens were seeking a solution to the problems which had arisen and were acting in a rational and controlled manner.

The following paper is an attempt at rational analysis of the issues. But in 1930 the arguments it advanced were entirely outside the range of people who were reacting emotionally against the Eighteenth Amendment. Mr. Kirby was reaching the individuals already convinced of the soundness of his arguments.

The exchange of letters between Professor Irving Fisher and some of the leaders of the burgeoning automobile industry indicates the gap which existed between conservative wets and drys.

The widespread belief in 1930 that the increasing availability of radio programs, motion pictures, and moderately priced automobiles would ultimately displace drinking as a recreational activity for the average man is of interest in view of the current expansion of all types of recreational resources paralleled by an extension of drinking customs.

THE LOGIC OF PROHIBITION

by Byron C. Kirby *

A decade or so ago the American people, after intensive thought, study and deliberation, decided that they wanted prohibition. They wanted it for social reasons, for economic reasons, for political reasons, for moral reasons; they wanted it in order to reduce poverty, in order to minimize the squandering of incomes, in order to eliminate at least one of the causes of the birth of weak, sickly, handicapped children. Finally, they desired it in order to banish the saloon, the most efficient agency for the breeding of sin, vice, political corruption, infamy, and moral turpitude extant. In short, the people demanded prohibition as an initial step toward cleansing and purifying the national environment; as an essential factor in rendering America a safe place in which to rear children and to foster families. Consequently, the Eighteenth Amendment was adopted.

The enactment of this law created a problem of greater subtlety than the Emancipation Proclamation of 1863 produced. Thousands of people, because of their tastes and their lack of proper training, knew of no leisure except the drinking of liquor and the pursuit of multiform, contaminating ramifications that go with it; thousands, at a stroke of the pen, were rendered social orphans. Their only type of amusement had been taken from them. For this reason it is logical to expect enforcement to be difficult. It will be difficult for many years to come; it will be arduous until the type of citizen who is stimulated by primeval modes of amusement gives way to people who are motivated by a different standard of training, ideals, morals, and culture. Nevertheless, the movement is progressing.

An analysis of the political discussions, as well as of the results of the last election shows, among other things, that even the suggestion of the return of pre-prohibition days creates within the minds of the majority of the American people a feeling of repugnance. Liquor is gradually going the way of the pillory, the sweat shop, the political boss, and slavery. However, because of propaganda of various types in the press, on the stage, in the movies, on the platform, in certain kinds of universities, etc., the exit is destined to be slow, tedious, and painful.

The agencies cited above advance the following arguments in opposition to Prohibition: (1) Prohibition robs the people of their pleasures; (2) Prohibition enforcement causes many innocent people to be shot by dry agents; (3) Prohibition is an infringement upon the rights of the individual; (4) Prohibition is moral legislation; and (5) Prohibition cannot be enforced.

* From *Scientific Temperance Journal, 39* (1930), 1–5.

(1) In regard to the first argument, it is a serious criticism of the culture, of the refinement, of the education, of the intellectual acumen of the American people to say that they cannot find any pleasure in life unless they are under the influence of liquor. Such a statement is an insult to the decent, respectable, law-abiding majority who have learned to substitute the love of beauty, of art, of literature, of music, of sports, of contests, of travel, of intellectual competition, and of cultural pursuits for intoxication of one degree or another, for fighting, for gambling, and for major immorality. The rank and file of the American people enjoy themselves on a higher plane today than they did fifty years ago; they have progressed beyond the status of the pithecanthropus erectus. What is more, they will continue to advance with the years.

(2) Several people have been killed by enforcement agents. Nevertheless, we do not fully know the circumstances under which they met with their misfortune. Perhaps they were in questionable company; perhaps they closely resembled someone for whom the officers were watching and, when they were told to halt, disregarded the command. It is surprising the extent to which people are being taught, both systematically and incidentally, to scoff at authority. In any event, however, it is too bad these accidents occurred; it is better to let many criminals escape than to kill one innocent man. Dry agents must be men of intellectual power, reserve, and self-control as well as of firm purpose.

There is another side to this question, however. The opponents of Prohibition seem to be unmindful of the fact that many innocent mothers, many innocent men, and many innocent children are killed by people who are intoxicated. This fact does not condone the other. Nevertheless, it is significant that many more people are killed by individuals who are intoxicated than by dry agents. Furthermore, a drunken man can never be trained so as to react in any fashion other than that which is essentially inimical to the welfare of the group, while enforcement officials can be so selected and so educated that the lives of innocent people will never, of necessity, be endangered.

(3) It is argued that Prohibition is an infringement upon the rights of the individual. This is the old argument based upon personal liberty and individualism. It is a childish, animalistic argument, since selfishness and individualism are characteristics of the child under ten years of age and of the animal. As the child becomes older, he learns to think, if he be properly educated, along altruistic lines, along social lines, and in terms of the welfare of the group.

If a man lives alone on an island a thousand miles from civilization, he is perfectly free to poison the water supply, to dump his garbage in front of his house, to cut off a leg, to cut off his head, to roam at large even though he may have the leprosy or smallpox, to spend his total time with his wine kegs, etc. But when this man becomes a member of society, he must learn to think in terms of others; he must realize that the exercise of his selfish rights may interfere with the rights of his fellows; that the basis of effective social intercourse is the surrender, upon the part of each individual, of non-essential, conflicting barbarisms for cultural, harmonious, constructive ends which tend to preserve the best there is in everyone. That is growth; that is the proper type of unfoldment; that is true fruition. The difference between the Heidelberg man and the man of today lies in the fact that, throughout the development, bad, non-essential characteristics have been sacrificed for good, essential, altruistic, social attitudes.

The effect of all law which emanates from popular demand is not to destroy the sane, logical, social, constructive rights of anyone, but rather to guarantee these essential privileges to all. No one has any basic privilege, in society, to become intoxicated or semi-intoxicated since, by so doing, he places himself in a mental condition conducive to stealing, to destroying property, to insulting respectable citizens, to disgracing his family, or to killing someone. The case records of criminals show that there is a high degree of correlation between intoxication and misdemeanor. Furthermore, both the movies and the stage emphasize the potency of alcohol as an incentive to crime in that each often portrays the villain as drinking a certain amount of distilled liquor before going to commit his misdeed.

(4) Another of the arguments advanced against prohibition is that it involves moral legislation. This contention carries with it the connotation that it is wrong to attempt to legislate morality into the behavioristic mechanism of the individual; that law is primarily concerned with political relationship. This idea is fundamentally wrong. The ultimate end of all legislation is the preservation of the essential rights of all people—the welfare of mankind. The purpose of the law is to guarantee freedom to the individual insofar as he is capable of enjoying freedom; to foster education and culture; to protect each citizen from murder, from theft, from indecency, from violence; and, in general, to create an environment conducive to the development of the best that there is in each inhabitant. As a matter of fact, the foregoing principles constitute the basic philosophy effectuated in the Federal Constitution, and in the various state enactments, as is evidenced by the following provisions: habeas corpus acts; the fostering of education; freedom of worship; trial by jury; the abolition of slavery and of involuntary servitude; the right to vote; Prohibition act; laws against murder, theft, etc. Reduced to its last analysis, the motivating principle underlying all legislation is the constructive modification of the environment as a basic factor in human welfare. Any type of control aimed at shaping this force is basically moral and social. What is more, it is logical. Consequently, the argument opposed to the Prohibition law upon the ground that it is moral legislation is beside the point.

(5) It is contended that since the Eighteenth Amendment cannot be enforced, it should be repealed. No law can be enforced absolutely. There

is slander, thievery, adultery and murder today in spite of legislation opposed to these types of conduct. Yet, no one holds that, for this reason, laws relating to the above kinds of behavior should be stricken from the statutes. In the case of Prohibition, even though it cannot be enforced absolutely, still, through systematic, scientific, logical, concentrated effort, it can be administered with such effect that the evil results of the liquor traffic will be rendered negligible in exactly the same way that the far-reaching effects of robbery are nullified. In this latter case, the desired ends are accomplished in spite of the fact that many teach that stealing is proper under certain conditions.

In order to function, the organization for enforcement must be more fundamental, more systematic, more rigid; it must recognize the importance of three agencies which are basic to the attainment of desired ends; namely (1) uplifting, intelligent, constructive suggestions in the movies, on the stage, on the platform and in the press; (2) a type of formal education that tends to instill the proper ideals, attitudes, standards and likes; and (3) universal participation in elections.

(1) A prerequisite to the effective administration of the Prohibition law is a feeling, a knowledge, a conviction upon the part of the people that the liquor traffic is inimical to the welfare of society. The great majority of the citizens today have that feeling. The difficulty in enforcement arises in connection with the minority of 15 or 20 per cent, whether they be rich or poor, who, because of unhappy experiences, unfortunate environmental background or ineffective educational procedure, have not been rendered capable of enjoying life on a plane consistent with social progress. The problem arising has two phases; (a) it is necessary to help the majority maintain its present view; and (b) every effort should be made to lead the minority to see the logic in the new order of things. The press, the stage, the movies, periodicals, etc., should portray definitely the fact that alcohol is essential neither to fame, wealth, success, happiness, nor salvation. The movies, instead of suggesting that the success of every social gathering depends upon the amount of wine consumed, should portray the fact that people can be just as happy without intoxicants; college officials, faculty members, etc., instead of construing the Constitution, religion and the Bible to be synonymous with alcohol and with selfishness should be of such caliber as to be able to progress with American cultural tendencies. The character and the personality of the college student are not yet formed. He needs constantly to come in contact with the proper philosophy, the proper attitudes, ideals, and standards. In all too many cases the university has as bad an effect upon the student as the saloon of pre-Prohibition days. Society needs more men like Ford and Edison—real men of affairs, men of ideas, men of accomplishments, who can give a banquet, and enjoy it, without craving something that they should not have; men who are not only content to conform to law, but who are glad to advocate the principle

that true happiness is a product of a cultivated mind rather than of a sordid stomach.

(2) Children should be taught systematically in every grade in school, the physical, social, economic, and moral evils connected with the use of alcoholic drinks. Furthermore, through the agency of an enriched curriculum, they should be trained effectively in various cultural appreciations. Music appreciation, art appreciation, literature appreciation, public speaking, dramatics, the love of active participation in sports, etc., should be taught each child systematically and scientifically throughout his total school experience so that, in after life, they will tend to become automatic reflexes in his nature, leading him to spend his leisure time in such a way as to render him, each morning, better physically, mentally and morally than he was the previous day. The love for alcohol, for gambling, for immorality and for the coarse and vulgar must be superseded by a love for things that are more ennobling, more uplifting, more substantial and, at the same time, more economical. Education functions to the degree in which it effectuates this end.

(3) Proper enforcement is contingent upon sympathetic, efficient administrative agencies. It is useless to expect the wet element to do much toward making a community dry, although in many cities this work is left entirely to it. One of the steps essential in remedying this situation is securing 100 per cent participation in elections.

Generally, most of the voting is done by a small minority who are urged by one kind of propaganda or another. The great majority do not participate. Such a course is inimical to the welfare of democracy. The broadminded, the far-seeing, the honorable, intelligent citizen must vote in order to nullify the influence of the intriguer; in order to keep the ship of state at even keel. The problem now arises of inducing everybody to cast his ballot. The solution lies, to a great degree, (a) in making voting easy and (b) in making it a strictly private affair. Practically every individual would vote if he could do so leisurely in his own residence, and then mail the ballot to the proper central agency. As it is, voting is a burdensome duty; people do not care to take time to go to the polls; they do not like to run the gauntlet of election officials; and they dislike to vote hurriedly because of the danger of losing their ballots. Some will argue that it is impossible to devise a workable scheme whereby each individual can vote at home; but it is not. A systematic, reliable, up-to-date record of the name, age, address, race, sex, place of employment, signature, etc., of every inhabitant of the political unit should be kept on file. This would render voting by mail as sound and safe a policy as that of conducting business upon a credit basis or, through the agency of checking accounts.

Such a plan, scientifically evolved and skillfully administered, would be a basic step toward reforming our whole political system. It would bring a different type of officials to the fore.

In conclusion, (1) alcoholism has a bad effect, mentally, physically, and morally upon the individual; (2) this results, logically, in undesirable, disintegrating social, economic and political influences; (3) because of (1) and (2), the drinking of alcoholic beverages is not an inalienable right any more than is the use of cocaine or morphine; (4) the use of intoxicants is not essential to happiness; and (5) the Prohibition amendment is in perfect accord with the letter and spirit of the Constitution. Consequently, the nation, the states and the local units should adopt intelligent, systematic, far-reaching, stringent, cooperative measures to enforce it.

INDUSTRIALISTS' OPINIONS ON PROHIBITION

by Irving Fisher *

If the motor-car and high-powered enterprise are symbols of the forces that have displaced the saloon, how do automobile manufacturers and captains of industry regard Prohibition? How far do their views find scientific and legal confirmation?

Wet View

In correspondence with Pierre S. duPont, Chairman of the General Motors Corporation, Chairman of the Board of E. I. duPont de Nemours Company, and Chairman of the Executive Committee of the Association Against the Prohibition Amendment, Irving Fisher wrote Mr. duPont:

May I make query on your very candid letter of 27th July, 1928, in which you state: "Clearly in any country that has not been reduced to a condition of absolute slavery of one man to another, the choice of conduct on the question of drink, in moderation, should be left open. I need hardly warn you that I do not grant this choice to those whose indulgence is such as to deprive others of their equally sacred rights."

It was reported concerning the duPont de Nemours Company, in a hearing before the United States Senate Subcommittee of the Judiciary and as part of a confidential file submitted in evidence Nov. 20, 1918, belonging to Hugh F. Fox, Secretary of the U. S. Brewers' Association, that the Advertising Manager of the company "explained how for years past the duPonts have absolutely prohibited the use of intoxicants by their employees, and now with the rush of war orders, the prohibition ban has been drawn even closer." Camillus Kessler, employed by Mr. Fox, reported to him: "After calling on several of the men in the offices in Wilmington, I took the ferry and went across the river to Penn's Grove, where one of the largest of the duPont factories is located. There I talked

* From *The "Noble Experiment"* (New York, Alcohol Information Committee, 1930), Chapter 2.

with the Chief of Police, some of the men who work in the high explosives department, and one of the guards. They all assured me that there was not a drink to be had in Penn's Grove. The only bar in the town had been closed by the duPonts and if any workman wanted a drink of any kind he would have to go to Wilmington, or some other neighboring town.

"It is reported if a guard is seen taking a drink off duty, he is immediately discharged. If a workman comes to work with the slightest indication of liquor on his breath, he is not allowed to work. From all that I could see, Prohibition could not be more effectively enforced than it is in Penn's Grove. I was informed by the officials and by men who had worked in the other factories of the company that the same conditions exist in all the duPont Company factories."

May I ask whether the same Prohibition rule is in force in the factories of E. I. duPont de Nemours & Company under your Chairmanship of its Board of Directors? If so, is it not because, as you say in your letter to me, you "do not grant this choice to those whose indulgence is such as to deprive others of their equally sacred rights"?

If you would prohibit moderate drinking in the duPont de Nemours plant, would you also prohibit moderate drinking in all shops where accidents might occur through the use of modern high-powered machinery?

Would you prohibit moderate drinking by the drivers of motor cars?

Do you agree with Henry Ford in his statement that in this fast-driving and high-powered age even the moderate use of intoxicants has no proper place?

Or would you prohibit the use of intoxicants to the workingmen of this country and allow it to their employers?

These questions are asked in no spirit of unfriendliness, but to elicit your view as a responsible employer of labor and one who has had much to do with the placing of millions of motor cars on the highways of this country, of how indulgence in alcoholic liquors can be made compatible with the sacred rights of those who lives may be endangered by the man who, as you phrase it in your letter to me, is "willing to submit" to "ills for the sake of some advantage, real or fancied, that will result from his drink."

Mr. duPont replied:

I believe there is some confusion in regard to Prohibition by law and Prohibition by an employer. If certain work involving danger to life and property requires absolute sobriety, I cannot find fault with the employer refusing to employ a man who shows any sign of contact with alcohol when he reports for work, and, in fact, where the employer may be held liable for the action of the man employed, he may, if he choose, properly decline to employ a man who uses intoxicants at any time. This is no different from refusing to employ a man whose sight or hearing is in any way defective, for jobs requiring great keenness in those senses. It is purely a matter of choice of the man most suitable for the job. I do not know any rule of the duPont Company which requires total abstinence of any employee. I am quite certain that men are not permitted to go to work after having indulged in alcoholic drinks in a manner to be detected by ordinary inspection, but I feel equally confident that there is no rule about drinking after work is done.

It is quite possible that there was an exception to the above statement during the war when strenuous efforts were being made in every direction to get the best out of the men, whether they were willing or not. I shall look this up and let you know, but I do not consider the point of great moment.

There are many jobs open to-day to the man who drinks in moderation, especially those who confine their drinking to the hours of relaxation after work. I know a number of men who are very much in favor of Prohibition (for the workingman) who drink nothing themselves during business hours, but who are pretty heavy consumers of alcoholic liquors after the day's work is done. I am quite confident that they do themselves no physical harm nor do they impair their mentality; but I do not admire their inconsistency.

I employ about 150 to 300 men on my personal payroll. I have no rule whatever as to drinking and know of very few cases where the question has come up in any way. If a man should appear for work under the influence of liquor, or even smelling of it, I should call his attention to the fact that I had noticed the occurrence and request that there should be no recurrence. I am sure that many of the employees have liquor in their homes which they use in proper moderation; in fact, a questionnaire sent out to them recently developed a reply of "No" from many in answer to the question: "Do you totally abstain from the use of alcoholic liquors, including wine and beer?"

Lest you should have failed to notice it, the result of this questionnaire sent to 300 employees and their wives brought forth about 80 per cent replies within two weeks. The majority of them agreed that conditions under Prohibition were undesirable and advocated a change. A similar questionnaire sent to the voters of the State of Delaware brought forth replies from about half of those sent out, of which 40 per cent of the total, or 90 per cent, replied "Yes" to the following questions:

"1. Do you believe that much harm results from abuse of drink under the Prohibition laws that are in force in this country?

"2. Do you believe that alcoholic liquors, such as beer, wine, whisky, and gin, may now be bought, illegally but freely, by those who wish to buy?

"3. Do you believe that the general disregard of Prohibition laws is leading to other lawlessness?

"4. Do you think that change in existing Prohibition laws is needed?"

As to your question of whether I should prohibit in the duPont Company plants if it were my business to decide, I should not prohibit drinking, but I should not employ men who come to the plant under the influence of liquor, unless it were possible, as it frequently is with employees directly controlled, to encourage the man to confine his drinking to after working hours.

I employ a number of men for driving cars, as I do myself, and there is no prohibition on any of us to refrain from drinking. But I should not take a drink before driving a motor car on a public road, and, to be exact, I should think it well to allow a couple of hours to elapse after taking a drink before driving, lest in case of accident I should be held accountable for something not my fault.

If safety on the road is a thing to be further safeguarded, it is much more necessary to examine people strictly for their capacity and ability to drive than to issue a Prohibition order against drinking. Many drivers are more dangerous sober than others are when drunk. The prohibition against drinking does not stop the drinking, but a refusal of license for those unfitted for driving, because of physical or mental disqualifications, would be very helpful in avoiding accidents.

To me it seems that many of these questions concerning drink fail to realize that there is a great difference between drinking in a way that interferes with a man's capacity to steer a normal course and drinking, the result of which is not apparent by an ordinary test. The greater part of drinking must occur after working hours and when people are in a position where they are not called upon to execute their utmost endeavors. Drinking furnishes to many the same kind of relaxation that all expect to have in the evenings, playing games, reading light literature, attending theatrical performances, the movies, etc. During those hours we cease our effort toward constructive work. We are in a state of relaxation where we can drop off to sleep or do many other things that are exceedingly dangerous were we on an active and important job. I repeat that it is during these hours that many take a drink which helps their relaxation. I confess that it has no such effect upon me.

Those who oppose Prohibition have no objection whatever to strict disciplining of those who injure or jeopardize others by their excesses. Prohibitionists would find probably 90 per cent of the population ready to assist in this matter of protection, but they are unwilling to assist in a rule that condemns the innocent along with the guilty.

It is one of the ridiculous phases of the Prohibition movement that there is no attempt to prohibit a man's drinking alcoholic beverages. If any wrong is done it is the drinker who does it, yet to-day he is the man who escapes. The man who makes, the man who sells, the man who transports, and at all times the man who possesses liquor, are all guilty under the law; but, the man who drinks, the very one that is at fault, is allowed to go scot-free, unless his delinquencies actually jeopardize somebody. Is this not the most monumental inconsistency?

Mr. duPont replied to a further suggestion from Irving Fisher, as follows:

This is in reply to your letter of September 1 (1928), suggesting the difficulty or impossibility of discriminating between the temperate and the intemperate, therefore recommending a blanket prohibition which takes care of the latter and "does not really harm the former." In these few quoted words is summed up the history of bad government from time immemorial. The Romans undoubtedly thought that it did not harm Christians to try to make them Pagans. The early Catholics had the same opinion concerning the conversion of Protestants to Catholicism. Doubtless King George III and his parliament thought that the American Taxes did not really harm the people of the colonies. The slaveholders thought that the slaves were not only unharmed but were better off as slaves than as free men. Some of them still think so. Thousands of instances might be cited. The whole principle of good government is to devise laws that do good, not those that simply avoid doing harm in the opinion of the dictator. The whole Prohibition question comes from the wrong point of view on this one point.

Irénée duPont, President of the duPont Company, stands shoulder to shoulder with his brother in opposition to the Eighteenth Amendment and its supporting laws. John J. Raskob, Vice President and Chairman of the Finance Committee of the same company and a director of General Motors, resigned as Chairman of the Finance Committee of General Motors in order to manage the campaign for the Presidency of Governor Alfred E. Smith of New York. Mr. Raskob, like the brothers duPont, bases his opposition to the Eighteenth Amendment on the plea of personal liberty. He says:

I am not a drinking man (this does not mean I never take a drink), am a director in corporations employing over three hundred thousand workmen, and have a family of twelve children ranging in ages from five to twenty-one years. The thing that is giving me the greatest concern in connection with the rearing of these children and the future of our country is the fact that our citizens seem to be developing a thorough lack of respect for our laws and institutions, and there seems to be a growing feeling that nothing is wrong in life except getting caught. . . .

A large number of people feel that a majority in this country have no more right to curtail their freedom with respect to drinking beer, wines or even spirits than they have to deny religious worship. These people feel they do no wrong in the eyes of God when they buy and consume beer, wines and liquors in spite of the law. They feel that those who have the money to pay for such beverages and have them analyzed can drink without risk of health, while those who cannot do so must either do without or take great risks of being poisoned. It is for this reason that the great mass of our workmen and poor people feel that Prohibition does not prohibit but is a scheme to deny them something which their more fortunate brothers with money can have almost at will. Is it any wonder they should rebel?

My experience is that children like to be with older folks, are quick, alert and particularly keen on listening to what their elders say and do. What impressions are registering on the minds of my sons and daughters when they see thoroughly reputable and successful men and women drinking, talking about their bootleggers, the good "stuff" they get, expressing contempt for the Volstead law, etc? At our home we can and do teach temperance in all things; none of our children drink intoxicants, but what ideas are forming in their young and fertile brains with respect to law and order? They observe people in every walk of life merrily violating foolish blue laws, foolish speed laws, etc., that every sensible citizen knows are made to be broken and not enforced. The farmers in Connecticut and Delaware legislatures were strong enough to have laws passed prohibiting Daylight Saving Time in those States. They would not tolerate the desire of city folks to have an hour more of daylight in which to play in the summertime. The result is that Yale University in Connecticut and the people of the city of Wilmington in Delaware rebel, pay no attention whatever to the law, and merely all agree to set their watches back an hour at 2:00 A.M. on a certain Sunday in April and return to Standard Time in October. This is another illustration of the failure of Prohibition born of intolerance and lack of respect for liberty and freedom.

The attitude of Messrs. Raskob and duPont is typical of that assumed by industrial leaders who oppose Prohibition.

Dry View

In yet another communication to Pierre S. duPont, Irving Fisher summed up the Dry comment on the attitude of the maker of automobiles and high explosives, as follows:

Speaking with the responsibility of a large employer and of one whose business it is to encourage the driving of automobiles on crowded highways, are you quite sure you have scientific backing when you say, "To be exact, I should think it well to allow a couple of hours to elapse after taking a drink before driving, lest in case of accident I should be held accountable for something not my fault"?

These words are quite different from those used by Dr. Francis G. Benedict, after most exhaustive tests of the effects of alcohol in the Nutrition Laboratory of the Carnegie Institution of Washington. Dr. Benedict remarks: "Inflexible science says: Moderate user, keep off! For at least four hours after a dose of alcohol formerly considered permissible, you, as a motor vehicle operator, may well be considered a menace to society."

When it is pleaded that the greater part of drinking must occur after working hours, it must be noted, also, that the greater part of driving for pleasure occurs after working hours. In view of the fact that there are between twenty-three and twenty-four million motor cars on our highways is not the case, then, as regards the public policy of Prohibition, on all fours with the private policy of Prohibition in the duPont and other plants of the country, which forbids the use of intoxicants by men who are engaged in dangerous occupations?

What other public policy than that of Prohibition, at least of the traffic in intoxicants, is practicable in circumstances where a "moderate" drink during four hours after it has been taken may result in a fatal collision?

The argument on the score of personal liberty implies, it is true, personal liberty to drink. You point out the seeming inconsistency of the Eighteenth Amendment and its supporting laws in not depriving drinkers of this liberty while they do prohibit the manufacture and traffic in liquors. Personally I should have favored the prohibition only of the public traffic, reserving the privilege of citizens to brew and drink intoxicants privately in their homes, if they so elect. But I think you will agree with me that the Federal Supreme Court speaks with better authority than either of us can claim when it says, in the case of Samuel v. McCurdy (267 U.S. 188, 197): "The ultimate legislative object of Prohibition is to prevent the drinking of intoxicating liquor by any one because of the demoralizing effect of drunkenness upon society. The State has the power to subject those members of society who might indulge in the use of such liquor without injury to themselves to a deprivation of access to liquor in order to remove temptation from those whom its use would demoralize, and to avoid the abuses which follow in its train."

It will be difficult for most readers to follow you when you say that such statements, made by the most profound interpreters of our democratic government, "sum up the history of bad government from time immemorial." In Duncan Townsite Company v. Lane (245 U.S. 307), the United States Supreme Court also says: "It must now be regarded as settled that, on account of their well-known noxious qualities and the extraordinary evils shown by experience commonly to be consequent upon their use, a State had power absolutely to prohibit manufacture, gift, purchase, sale or transportation of intoxicating liquors within its borders without violating the guarantee of the Fourteenth Amendment . . . And considering the notorious difficulties always attendant upon efforts to suppress traffic in liquors, we are unable to say that the challenged inhibition of their possession was arbitrary and unreasonable or without proper relations to the legitimate legislative purpose."

As to the practicability of enforcing Prohibition against the drinker, who, as you justly observe, is the very one at fault, Mr. Ernest H. Cherrington states the case as follows: "Many States had and still have laws which forbid drinking intoxicating liquor in public places. Laws forbidding such drinking in private places might face constitutional obstacles, unless such offenses were made felonies. It would have been possible to forbid all drinking by law, as also to legalize confiscation of all liquor in this country, when the Eighteenth Amendment went into effect, but since the enemies of this national policy have shown themselves prepared to combat it by invoking every possible technicality and law's delay, it seemed unnecessary to take this step inasmuch as, according to the decisions of the Supreme Court, as well as of many lesser courts, the end sought—the abolition of the drinking of intoxicants—could more readily be obtained by the methods that were taken."

In the face of this reasoning the seeming inconsistency of the National Prohibition Laws tends to disappear. And Mr. Cherrington speaks with the scientific and legal backing which opponents of Prohibition notably lack when he adds: "Neither behind the wheel of the chauffeur, at the throttle of the locomotive, the stick of the aviator or the lathe of the machinist, nor anywhere else in our crowded American life, is there a place for the man whose nerves are shaken by any indulgence in alcoholic drinks. The Eighteenth Amendment was intended to outlaw absolutely all such beverages."

The plea of personal liberty to drink acknowledges in terms this intent when it opposes the law. It clashes with the private prohibition of drinking imposed by employers of labor, and it clashes with the policy of National Prohibition which is imposed by the public for identical reasons. It is this identity of public and private policy that leads me to wonder why you, who believe in the strict disciplining of those whose acts injure or jeopardize the safety of others, assent to such disciplining by means of private prohibition in the industries of the country, and dissent from it when applied, among other cogent reasons, for the sake of public safety on the public highways.

Motor Car Heads Support Prohibition

Many heads of the automobile industry, differing with Messrs. duPont and Raskob, confirm by their testimony the views expressed above. Henry Ford, for example, said in an interview at Sudbury, Mass., during August 1928:

> If the law were changed, we'd have to shut down our plants. Everything in the United States is keyed up to a new pace which started with Prohibition. The speed at which we run our motor cars, operate our intricate machinery, and generally live, would be impossible with liquor. No, there is no chance even of modification.

In like vein, R. H. Scott, President of the Reo Motor Car Company, declares his conviction that "the return of public drinking-places would make the motor car a menace on the highways and would stop the sale, to a large extent, of the cheaper cars, as the money would be spent over the bar."

Alfred P. Sloan, Jr., President of the General Motors Corporation, expressed his dissent from the views of Messrs. duPont and Raskob when he announced September 3, 1928, his support of Herbert Hoover for President, concluding his reasons as follows:

> Having been intimately connected with industrial problems for many years, I am thoroughly convinced that Prohibition has increased our national efficiency, has added to the purchasing power of the people and given us an advantage in our competition for foreign trade.
>
> At the same time, I recognize that conditions respecting the observance of the law are far from satisfactory and time may prove the necessity for some adjustments. If so, I am for having those adjustments brought about by an executive in sympathy with the economic benefits that the closest possible adherence to the Prohibition idea is sure to bring about.

Following Mr. Sloan's statement, W. C. Durant, President of Durant Motors, Inc., cabled from Europe his offer of a prize of $25,000 for the best and most practicable plan to make the Eighteenth Amendment effective, saying:

> Big business leaders who have the largest stake in law observance publicly and privately violate this law and countenance its violation by others. Instead of using their wealth and influence to create public opinion demanding law enforcement, our business men of character and position are the chief support of the master criminal class, the bootlegger.
>
> It is not surprising that the flagrant example of lawlessness on the part of the men highest in their communities has undermined respect for law in their children, their servants, their employees, and all classes of citizens, including public officials and judges.

No doubt Mr. Raskob and the brothers duPont represent a minority of sentiment against Prohibition among heads of American business. This is certainly the case in the great industry in which they rank among the leaders. After exhaustive inquiry, Professor Herman Feldman of Dartmouth College testifies in his book:

> In the automobile trade itself, the saloon is regarded as a competitor of the car. Some automobile manufacturers seem to be opposed to its return on that score alone. While some do not credit Prohibition with being a factor in its expansion, the industry as a whole does; and the makers of the more moderate priced cars are particularly strong on this issue.
>
> The antagonism of the Ford Motor Company to a return of the saloon is, of course, known. The sales department of the Willys-Overland Company believes that the abolition of the saloons has resulted in an increased market for passenger cars. Another concern which prefers that we do not use its name, makes a strong argument of the same point and ends with the succinct assertion that: "Gasoline and booze don't mix." The Distribution Manager of the Franklin Automobile Company explains: "The sale of a car like the Franklin is influenced by the demand for used cars. In other words, the bigger the market for used Franklins, the bigger the market for new Franklins. In this respect also Prohibition has, we believe, helped to provide the funds with which the purchases are made." And so on it goes among most of the makes widely sold.

Among the other means of public diversion that have supplanted the saloon, Professor Feldman quotes the Association of Motion Picture Producers and Distributers of America, the organization of the largest concerns, as stating:

> Since the abolition of saloons the moving picture theatre has become the social center and to a surprising extent the recreation of those who before frequented drinking establishments.

Dr. Feldman also speaks of considerable testimony from industrial insurance agents, employers, and the radio industry itself. He continues:

The latter regards the abolition of the saloon as a factor in bringing the radio into homes where it might not have come so soon otherwise. One manufacturer explains: "In my own experience, various chauffeurs whom I have employed have shown an eagerness to go to their homes to listen in to some particular program which was to be on that evening; whereas, heretofore, it appeared to me that they have considered their homes more or less places to get food and shelter."

Moderate-drinking Driver Menaces Safety

It is manifest, therefore, that the rapid changes that have taken place in the means of relaxation in the life of the masses in America have effectually disposed of the argument that they must stupefy themselves with alcohol in order to gain a respite from their workaday cares. Furthermore, the fact that the whole population has become mobile, multiplying and making constant the dangers of the highways, has made literally true the saying that a man who has drunk a glass of beer is one glass of beer drunk. A committee of the British Medical Association reports:

The word "drunk" should always be taken to mean that the person concerned is so much under the influence of alcohol as to have lost control of his faculties to such an extent as to render him unable to execute safely the occupation in which he is engaged at the material time.

The Nutrition Laboratory of the Carnegie Institution of Washington has spoken on this point with respect to a moderate-drinking motor car driver during the four hours following his drinks. In a letter to Irving Fisher, Robbins Stoeckel, Commissioner of Motor Vehicles of Connecticut, speaks from his experience:

A really drunken driver is usually not dangerous, because he is so easily and quickly detected, or incapacitated, as being found asleep in his car at the curb. The really dangerous driver is the man who has had one or two drinks only, who still thinks he is in possession of his faculties, but whose driving judgment has been impaired. On the public highways moderate drinking is more dangerous than immoderate, and on this account the authorities in order to protect the public safety must reckon with the effects of moderate drinking.

On the side of constitutional right, therefore, as decided by the highest tribunal in America, on the side of scientific investigation of the effects of moderate drinking on the average human individual, and on the side of experience in promoting safety from accidents on the highways and in the factories of the nation, the weight of evidence is altogether in favor of Prohibition.

29. THE WOMAN'S CHRISTIAN TEMPERANCE UNION

For three-quarters of a century the Woman's Christian Temperance Union provided leadership in the drive to eliminate alcohol. During many years before passage of the Eighteenth Amendment, the WCTU held a position of considerable status nationally. Since Repeal, its influence has been less significant. Interpretation of the changes which have produced this reduction in prestige and leadership appear in the study by J. R. Gusfield. The shifts which have occurred within the organization reflect to a considerable degree the changes in attitudes toward drinking and control of drunkenness which have developed in this country in the last three decades.

SOCIAL STRUCTURE AND MORAL REFORM: A STUDY OF THE WCTU

by Joseph R. Gusfield *

Social changes affect the fortunes of organizations and movements no less than they do the fate of individuals. Movements which try to alter the manners, tastes, and daily habits of large numbers of people are peculiarly vulnerable to shifts in the culture of the population. Few social movements in American history have achieved as many successes and witnessed as many disappointments as the temperance movement. In the one hundred and fifty years during which the organized movement has been a significant part of American life, it has gone through a process of "boom and bust," from activity and success to quiescence and failure. The last seventy-five years have been particularly beset with steep rise and equally steep fall. The high point of the movement was reached in the passage of the Eighteenth Amendment and the nadir in Repeal and the period following.

This paper examines the Woman's Christian Temperance Union, one important segment of the temperance movement, during the last eighty years. We have tried to discover the way in which the movement has changed and some of the reasons which help explain that change.

* From *The American Journal of Sociology, 61* (1955), 221–32.

The Problem

Previous studies of social movements have dealt largely with organizations that have increased in numbers and influence. Such studies have indicated a gradual modification in the structure and ideology of the movement. As the movement grows, it tends to adapt itself to its society and to power and prestige for its original goals. This process has been described in the now familiar theory of the "institutionalization of social movements."

Recently, Messinger has shown how the adaptive process has affected a declining social movement, the Townsend Movement. Here the adaptation to loss of influence and adherents was in terms of the loss of the movement's actual mission and the emphasis on the preservation of the organization as such. New activities of the Townsend clubs are understandable only as devices to perpetuate the organization's membership, income, and power.

The WCTU cannot be called a "successful" movement. Its fundamental goal, the changing of American drinking habits, is less realizable today than in earlier periods. Neither is it analogous to the movement in decline. Membership figures indicate that the size of the organization, while less than before Repeal, is still above 200,000 and actually growing now in membership (Table 1).

TABLE 1.—*WCTU Membership, by Decades*

Year	Membership	Year	Membership
1881	22,800	1921	344,892
1891	138,377	1931	372,355
1901	158,477	1941	216,843
1911	245,299	1951	257,548

While the WCTU is far from decline or death, temperance norms have lost a great deal of their power in American culture. Their political power, as pressure groups, is far less than before and during Prohibition. The percentage of dry communities in the United States is far less than in the period before the passage of Prohibition, and fewer Americans are abstainers today.

The change in American drinking habits and the increased permissiveness of drinking norms have presented the WCTU with an environment more hostile to the doctrine of total abstinence than was true in the years of the organization's formation and development. The reaction of the WCTU to this changed situation forms the subject of this paper. We want to know whether the change in environment has led to changes in the goals and doctrine of the movement. We further seek to explain changes, or lack of change, in the organization.

Several possible modes of reaction suggest themselves to us. Faced with a now more hostile environment, the WCTU might change to achieve greater acceptance within the new norms. This would entail giving up much of the earlier mission for the sake of organizational values, which is the adaptation suggested by the Townsend Movement cited above. Second, it is conceivable that we may find little change in the face of changed conditions. Third, it is also conceivable that we may find changes which increase the gap between the public and the organization.

The Pre-Prohibition Period: Temperance as Social Welfare

Moral Reform and Social Welfare. The American temperance movement during the nineteenth century was a part of a general effort toward the improvement of the worth of the human being through improved morality as well as economic conditions. The mixture of the religious, the equalitarian, and the humanitarian was an outstanding facet of the moral reformism of many movements. Temperance supporters formed a large segment of movements such as sabbatarianism, abolition, woman's rights, agrarianism, and humanitarian attempts to improve the lot of the poor.

In these efforts there is evident a satisfaction with the basic outlines of the economic and social system. What is attempted is the extension of the system to include the underprivileged. The reforms proposed attempt to alleviate suffering through humanitarian actions by those in advantageous positions or to reform the habits of the suffering as a way to the improvement of both their character and their material situation. There was clearly a relationship between the two. Moral reformism of this type suggests the approach of a dominant class toward those less favorably situated in the economic and social structure. Barnes has pointed out that many of the social movements of the nineteenth century were composed of people bent on reforming others rather than themselves. Abolitionists were rarely former slaveowners. Except for one short episode in the 1840's, the temperance movement has drawn to it people of little or no experience with drinking.[1]

The goals and doctrine of the WCTU were part of this humanitarian moral reform movement in the period before Prohibition. This is most evident in the late nineteenth century but remained a strong aspect of WCTU activities well into the Prohibition period.

In its auxiliary interests the WCTU revealed a great concern for the improvement of the welfare of the lower classes. It was active in campaigns to secure penal reform, to shorten working hours and raise wages for workers, and to abolish child labor and in a number of other humanitarian and equalitarian activities. In the 1880's the WCTU worked to bring about

1. The Washingtonian Movement was the response of former drunkards, who made an organized attempt to reform drunkards. The rest of the temperance movement would not unite with them. Cf. John Krout, *The Origins of Prohibition* (New York, Columbia University Press, 1928), pp. 182–222.

legislation for the protection of working girls against exploitation by men. During the late nineteenth century several committees were active among lower-class groups, among them the Department of Work with Miners, the Department of Work with Lumberers, and the Department of Work among Railroadmen, which directed their efforts toward converting the worker to Christianity, bringing him material comforts, and spreading the gospel of temperance.

The activities of the WCTU in the pre-Prohibition era appear to be the actions of a socially dominant group, essentially satisfied with the major outlines of the social structure. The social welfare efforts can be viewed as attempts to raise the lower classes to a level of behavior held out to them by the dominant middle-class citizen. This view is supported by the paternalistic character of much of WCTU social welfare activity during this period. For example, in 1882 the WCTU established a Kitchen Gardens Department to train "uneducated and untrained girls" in the arts of cooking and household management. The aim of this activity was explicitly stated as the preparation of housemaids, and it was hoped that occupational training would protect the girl from the temptations of city life. The same training and the same rationale are found in the WCTU industrial schools established to aid "fallen women."

The WCTU played an important role in the leadership of the woman's movement in the late nineteenth century, but this was not the only concern of the organization with questions of social justice. The labor movement had strong support from the WCTU. The Knights of Labor aided the temperance activities of the WCTU. The WCTU supported the struggle for the 8-hour day and the 6-day week and many of the strikes of the 1890's, though it balked at the use of violence. Its support of the labor cause is illustrated in the report of the Committee on the Relations between Temperance and Labor for 1894. Employers were urged to refrain from "kindling the spirit of animosity among those already struggling under the iron heel of oppression" and thus provoking violence.

These are illustrations of the interest of the WCTU during the nineteenth century in economic and social reform. It is difficult to find activities in which moral reform is clearly distinct from economic or social reform. Prison reform, for example, was stressed as a way to rehabilitate character, to convert men to Christianity, and to prevent the suffering of prisoners.

After 1900 this humanitarian interest appears less frequently, although it is still an important aspect of WCTU activities. Two things become evident. First, the humanitarianism and the equalitarian concern for the poor have greatly decreased. The Committee on the Relation of Temperance and Labor, for example, has shifted its major concern from labor issues to the propagation of the temperance cause among workers. The reports of this committee after 1900 show an interest in the morals and character of the worker. Thus in 1909 the report of this committee stated:

"Urge working men and women who work for wages to cultivate a sense of responsibility in the thoroughness of their work and to consider their employer's welfare as well as their own."

The second point is that humanitarian concerns are not ignored, although decreased in emphasis, prison reform and child welfare receiving considerable attention. Between 1900 and 1920 the WCTU allotted one of the largest segments of its budget for its center at Ellis Island devoted to aiding incoming immigrants. In 1919 a huge Americanization project was begun, reminiscent of the paternalistic pattern described above. It set aside $40,000 for the purpose, the second largest single appropriation in its history.

After 1900, however, the moral reformism of the WCTU is more frequently separated from a concern with the underprivileged. With the development of the Anti-Saloon League after 1900, temperance aims become important in the campaign for legal sanctions against the sale of alcoholic beverages. Yet the emphasis on the lower classes as the object of WCTU reform is still present.

Temperance as Reform of the Underprivileged. An effort to improve the lot of the poor and the underprivileged was not only displayed in the WCTU's auxiliary concerns. The very doctrine of temperance can be seen as directed toward changing the habits of the lower classes. The materials usually depict the drunkard as a worker. Temperance is frequently presented as the solution to economic problems, the route to success, whereas drinking is seen as the path to economic and social ruin. The WCTU did make some efforts to promote temperance sentiment among socially elite groups through a Department of Drawing Room Conversion. These proved unsuccessful and were abandoned.

A popular slogan of the temperance movement, in the nineteenth century, was that "drink is the curse of the working classes." Total abstinence was viewed as the solution to the problem of poverty. A story in the *Union Signal* entitled "The Strike at Dennis Moriarity's" illustrates how the WCTU saw temperance as the answer to the worker's problems. Dennis, son of a workman on strike, refuses to fetch beer for the strikers, insisting that they could pay their bills, even while on strike, if they didn't drink. The strikers are impressed by his reasoning. One says, "It's the saloon that hurts and keeps us poor. I've been wondering all this while why Debs and the rest of the leaders didn't see it."

In the above story the immigrant as well as the laborer is the central character. Irish and German immigrants were often depicted in the fiction of the WCTU as drunkards or shown in the process of reformation. Often it was the son or daughter of the immigrant who effected the reformation through his or her experiences with the WCTU. This type of story again presents the idea that acceptance of temperance is a mode of assimilation into middle-class life.

That temperance is a key to class position is seen in the fates of the middle-class man who violates the temperance norms and the lower-class immigrant who accepts such norms. Lapses are punished by the loss of economic and social position. The WCTU was active, both before and after the turn of the century, in spreading the idea that "lips that have touched liquor shall never touch mine." Through its young girls' groups it tried to make sobriety in the male a prerequisite for marriage. The following story from a WCTU journal illustrates the awful consequences of drink for the middle-class male:

> Ned has applied for a job, but he is not chosen. He finds that the potential employer has judged him to be like his Uncle Jack. Jack is a kindly man but he spends his money on drink and cigarettes. Ned has also been seen drinking and smoking. The employer thinks that Ned lacks the necessary traits of industriousness which he associates with abstinence and self-control.

The implications of the above story seem clear. The man who wants to succeed must have the requisite character. He must appear to possess the characteristics of sobriety which indicate the other virtues of thrift, industry, and self-control. Temperance is thus a way not only to conform to morality but to achieve social and economic welfare. The WCTU was acting as a vehicle of progress and improvement of the poor and underprivileged.

Analysis of Committee Reports. We have classified the various committee reports found in the *Annual Reports* of the WCTU. The treatment of issues in these reports demonstrates the existence of the humanitarian reformist orientation in earlier periods. As Prohibition struggles became fiercer, the WCTU decreased its humanitarian interest. Moral conformity appeared apart from a concern with the welfare of the downtrodden. For example, the Department of Rescue Work had been interested in the improvement of the working girls' morality, wages, and living conditions as one consistent goal. By 1916 this department was chiefly concerned with efforts to limit fashion changes in the name of morality. The social welfare interest had disappeared. The interest in temperance more frequently appears unrelated to other welfare considerations. It is not until after Repeal, however, that the reports indicate unalloyed moral reform and temperance interests more frequently than humanitarian reform unalloyed or mixed with other interests (Table 2).

Humanitarian Reform and Social Dominance. The great concern of the WCTU with the lower classes was a dominant feature of its aims during the period from its formation in 1874 to the passage of Prohibition. It is not drinking per se that is emphasized but the drinking problems of the poor and the working classes. Even where drinking in upper classes is berated, a prime concern is the impact of upper-class drinking patterns on the lower classes.

TABLE 2.—*Classification of WCTU Committee Reports, by Period and by Interests* *

	Humanitarian Reform (%)	Moral Reform (Unalloyed) (%)	Temperance (Unalloyed) (%)	Other (%)	N †
1879–1903	78.6	23.5	26.5	15.3	98
1904–1928	45.7	30.7	33.1	18.0	127
1929–1949	25.8	37.0	48.2	1.2	81

* Source: Sample of every fifth *Annual Report* of the WCTU.
† Percentages total more than 100 due to several interests in some committee reports.

In its temperance doctrine as well as in its alliances with social movements of a reformist nature, the WCTU attempted to cope with the problems posed for urban America by the advent of urbanism, immigration, and industry in the late nineteenth century. The large industrial working class with its alien culture clashed with the rural image of virtue. A social group whose own position was relatively secure could best react to this threat by ameliorative reforms.

The doctrine of temperance appears to function in this fashion in the pre-Prohibition period. Implicit in the logic of the activities and the doctrine of the WCTU was a basic satisfaction with the social order. The problems of the underprivileged can be solved in two ways. In one, greater kindness and humanitarianism can be extended to those who have not been fortunate. This is the motif in activities such as prison reform, work with "fallen women," better labor conditions, and other reform measures described. The demand for greater equality for women is an attack on the system of male superiority, but this is not generalized into an attack on other parts of the social and economic system.

Second, the doctrine of temperance itself suggests a solution consonant with the dominance of the group and the concern with injustice and suffering. If the lower classes and the immigrants will acquire the habits and social codes of the native middle classes, their problems will be solved. In short, assimilation into middle-class, Protestant culture is the reformist solution the WCTU offered in the pre-Prohibitionist period.

It is noteworthy that, prior to the 1920's, we find no condemnation of the American middle classes in WCTU literature. The good, churchgoing people of American Protestantism are seldom depicted as drinking. It is to this class that the WCTU looks for support of its aims. In defending the canons of sobriety, the WCTU could act as a representative of this class. An article in the *Union Signal* in 1889 put this as follows: "The class least touched by the evil thus far is that which here, as elsewhere in the land, forms its bone and sinew—the self-respecting and self-supporting class whose chief pleasures in life center in and about the home."

PLATE XV

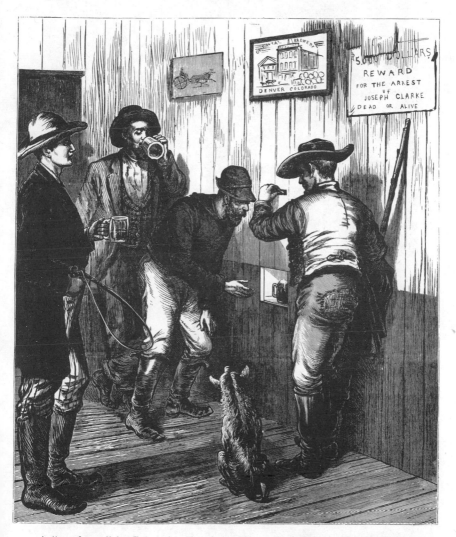

A "speakeasy" in Colorado. Sketch by Harry Ogden. From *Frank Leslie's Illustrated Newspaper*, July 7, 1877.

PLATE XVI

A. A saloon in Montreal. Sketch by E. R. Morse. From *Frank Leslie's Illustrated Newspaper*, Feb. 6, 1875.

B. Women against liquor. Singing hymns in front of a saloon in Ohio. Sketch by S. B. Morton. From *Frank Leslie's Illustrated Newspaper*, Feb. 21, 1874.

The "Moralizer-in-Retreat"

The political strength of the temperance movement in America has been greatest in those states with large proportions of Protestant and rural populations. With the decline in supremacy of the rural culture, both in city and in country, the norms of temperance have become less respectable. The advocates of temperance now face a more hostile environment in which they cannot enunciate a moral code and assume large segments of population in agreement with them. In the phrase of David Riesman, they are "moralizers-in-retreat."

With the repeal of the Eighteenth Amendment, the WCTU found itself in a radically new situation. It could no longer assume that the norms of abstinence were really supported by the dominant middle-class elements in American life. The total abstainer became a figure of disapproval and ridicule rather than a figure of power and respect.

WCTU leaders interviewed generally felt that the total abstainer no longer had a position of respect in the community. They saw this as a change which has affected the churchgoing middle classes as well as the secularized groups. The same theme is evident in the journals and in the speeches and reports from convention proceedings. The following interview excerpts are fairly typical:

> There has been a breakdown in the middle classes. The upper classes have always used liquor. The lower classes have always used liquor. Now the middle class has taken it over. The thing is slopping over from both sides.

> You know that today church people drink. That's the reason for the poor showing of the WCTU. It's been that way since Prohibition. There are many that believe but won't sign the pledge. They are afraid that they might want to take a drink.

The WCTU was seen, by the leaders interviewed, as lower in prestige today than in an earlier period when temperance norms held a stronger position in the American society. Leaders contrasted the prestigeful social composition of earlier periods with the present composition. Examples such as the following appear frequently in the interviews:

> When this union was first organized, we had many of the most influential ladies of the city. But now they have got the idea that we ladies who are against taking a cocktail are a little queer. We have an undertaker's wife and a minister's wife, but the lawyer's and the doctor's wives shun us. They don't want to be thought queer.

> I remember when the X's lived in the house that is now the Hotel W. They were the finest people in the town, and they were temperance people.

> When I joined, women of prominence and social prestige were in it. They were the backbone of the churches and the schools.

The WCTU is recognized by its membership as having retreated from a past position of greater influence, power, and prestige. To be a member of the WCTU is therefore harmful to social acceptability in many groups. It opens her to ridicule from people whose opinion is important to her. This is frankly realized by the WCTU. The literature of the organization does not hide the fact. For example, a membership drive pamphlet contained the following description of one type of WCTU member, Mrs. I-Would-if-I-Could: "She wouldn't think of asking for money or inviting anyone to join. She knows the organization is not especially popular in some groups. . . . There are times when she prefers not to mention her membership."

Local leaders also described the low esteem of the WCTU in their communities:

> People don't like us. Some of the churches don't respect us.
> Well, as you have probably learned, this isn't the organization it used to be. It isn't popular, you know. The public thinks of us—let's face it— as a bunch of old women, as frowzy fanatics. I've been viewed as queer, as an old fogy, for belonging to the WCTU. . . . This attitude was not true thirty years ago.

The WCTU is acutely aware of what it has been and of what it has become. The present position of unpopularity might lead to several different types of reaction. One possible position would be a reversal of past doctrine and the embracing of a doctrine of moderate drinking. This would be the acceptance of the new standard of the middle classes. Another possibility might be a de-emphasis of temperance aims and a substitution of other aims, such as those of a social welfare nature or an attack on "popular" enemies, such as drug addiction or juvenile delinquency.

The alternatives considered above all imply the importance of maintaining the popularity and acceptance of the organization in middle-class circles. If the organization should attempt to maintain its old doctrines, it could no longer be representative of prestigeful segments of American life. With the social base of dominance undermined, can the WCTU continue a reformist attitude toward lower classes, or must it become a sectarian critic of the class it once represented?

Moral Indignation: Censure of the New Middle Class

The characteristic doctrine of the WCTU is no longer humanitarian reform of the underprivileged. Instead it is an indignation directed against the middle-class moderate drinker. Total abstinence is presented as behavior morally demanded, apart from social welfare considerations. The new standards of the middle class are seen as defections from the traditional morality of abstinence.

"Moral indignation" as used here is not equivalent to the use of the term by Ranulf. We are not concerned with the "disinterested tendency to inflict punishment" but rather with the quality of anger generated by the failure of others to recognize standards of morality which the actor recognizes. The definition of "indignation" given by *Webster's New Collegiate Dictionary* accurately conveys our meaning. It is "righteous wrath" and "anger excited by that which is unworthy, base, or disgraceful." In understanding this emotion in the WCTU, we must keep in mind the fact that abstinence was once a respectable middle-class doctrine. The middle-class drinking habits are not only in conflict with WCTU norms; they are defections from past standards.

A fiction story in the *Union Signal* illustrates this sense of moral indignation toward the new doctrine of temperance. The story is entitled "Today's Daughter." Ruth, sixteen, is taken to a party at the home of a new boy who has just moved into the neighborhood. The boy has told Ruth's family that he is glad the new house has a game room in the basement. Aunt Liz is suspicious. She knows that many of the houses in the neighborhood now have bars in the basement game rooms. Ruth's mother tries to still these suspicions: "We're not living in the Victorian period. . . . I'm sure the Barrets are alright [*sic*]. They joined the church last Sunday." Aunt Liz's reply greatly unnerves Ruth's mother: "As if that meant respectability *these days!* Many's the church member who drinks and smokes and thinks nothing of it."

This episode contains the significant parts of the current position of the WCTU. Here are people of moderate incomes, in the same neighborhood and members of the same church as the WCTU adherent, yet the indexes of social class, religion, and ethnicity are no longer good assurances of abstinence.

Conflict between the doctrine of the total abstainer and a new "middle-class psychology" is evident. The following story is an apt illustration in which the new middle class is criticized for defection from the Protestant norms which supported and sustained the temperance doctrine. The story is entitled "When Yesterday Returned." Jane, the heroine, reveres her "old-fashioned, Christian grandmother" who taught her the temperance pledge. Jane's mother ridicules temperance as prudishness and says that it hinders her social position. The struggle between the two groups, the newer and more prestigeful moderate drinkers and the old-fashioned abstainers, is epitomized after Jane scolds a visitor who asked for whisky before dinner.

> When the guest had gone her mother informed her in no uncertain tones that "such plebian mannerisms" were rude. And furthermore if there were to be any more such old-fashioned, prudish notions exploited before such persons as Mr. Forsythe, the family's opportunities for social prestige would be lost forever and Jane's visits to her grandmother curtailed.

The figures of the underprivileged poor and the laborer no longer appear as the center of WCTU interest. In their place is the middle-class, churchgoing, moderate drinker. Toward him the WCTU displays resentment rather than reformist concern. Typical remarks of interviewees stress the moderate drinker:

> We fear moderation more than anything. Drinking has become so much a part of everything even in our church life and our colleges.
> Since Repeal, people are drinking who wouldn't have before. They are held in great regard. The social drinker has a greater effect on children than the drunkards.

In past decades moderate drinking might have subjected the drinker to fear of loss of reputation or damaged career. Some writers have lately maintained that career routes more and more demand the skills of fellowship, personal attachments, and the ability to be the "good fellow." This means that the culture may place great value on tolerance of others, in drinking as well as in other behavior. This makes the moral reformer even more reprehensible in the life of the new middle-class culture.

In reaction to this, the WCTU has poured out wrath against the defector from standards of abstinence who talks of taking an "objective" stand toward the problem. One interviewee complained of the Yale School of Alcohol Studies:

> You as a teacher must take a stand against smoking and drinking. Do you know of the Yale center? Well, I went down there one night. When they were through, you didn't know whether they were for it or against it. They didn't want to commit themselves. What can they expect students to do?

This attitude has made it difficult for the WCTU to co-operate with organizations which viewed drinking from a social welfare interest in curing or preventing alcoholism. Insistence on the vital importance of legal restriction of the sale of drink has continued. The president of the WCTU took an "unbending" position when she said: "Between right and wrong only one ground is possible and that is a battleground." [2]

The fact that "good people" are drinking is a chronic complaint among interviewees and in the pages of WCTU literature. One membership pamphlet voices this lament as follows:

> The greatest difficulty to be found today among youth, in anti-alcohol education, is the fact that "good people" are using liquor. Beautifully gowned women sipping their cocktails in lavish cocktail

---

2. *Annual Report of the WCTU* (1952), p. 87. Recently, with the retirement of the past president, there has been a "softer" attitude toward the Prohibition question and toward co-operation with non-Prohibitionist antialcohol groups. The general condemnation of the middle-class drinker still remains the focus of WCTU doctrine, however.

lounges give the impression that it is an extremely cultured thing to do.
. . . Even within some of the best homes, the bar is set up.

The social position of the moderate drinker in the concern of the WCTU
is not that of the poverty-stricken, the socially elite, or the nonchurchgoer.
It is rather the class from which the WCTU formerly drew its power and
which formed the base for a doctrine of social reformism. Interviewees
stressed the change in the churchgoer as the cause for the new respectability
of drinking:

> The churches aren't helping, some of them. We went to the home of a
> professor for a church meeting, and she [his wife] served sherry. The
> football coach's wife makes no bones about it. She serves liquor.
> It creeps into the official church boards. They keep it in their ice-
> boxes. . . . The minister here thinks that the church has gone too far,
> that they are doing too much to help the temperance cause. He's afraid
> that he'll stub some influential toes.
> The churches aren't doing enough. . . . Many nominally take a
> stand, but many don't follow it locally. There was one churchman in L.
> who had beer at his daughter's wedding. Another churchman in H. had
> wine at a wedding that really flowed. And this was the Church of the
> Brethren!

The WCTU has not attempted to reformulate its previous temperance
doctrine in the direction of popular acceptance, despite the changed milieu
in which it must operate. Rather it has swung in the direction of a greater
sectarianism which carries it strongly into conflict with previous sources
of adherence. How can we explain this? Why has it not accommodated to
the new situation? Some light may be shed on this question by the analysis
of the social composition of the movement between the years 1885 and
1949.

Increasing Class Distance. We have studied the social composition of
local leaders in the WCTU through the use of directories of officers
published in annual state WCTU reports. These list the local officers and
their addresses for each city, town, and village in which there is a unit.
With these lists, we then utilized city business directories, which gave us the
occupation of the husband of the officer. We were limited in choice of
cities by availability of state reports for each of the four years chosen—
1885, 1910, 1925, 1950—and by the availability of city directories for
each of the cities and years. However, we were able to compile comparative
data for thirty-eight cities in five states (Table 3).

The results of this study indicate that the socioeconomic status of the
local leadership has diminished during the period 1885–1950. There has
been a relatively steady decrease in the percentage of professional people,
proprietors, managers, and officials and a relatively steady increase in
the skilled and unskilled groups. More and more, the social base of the

WCTU appears to be lower middle class and lower class rather than the earlier picture of upper middle and lower middle classes.

TABLE 3.—*WCTU Local Leaders in Five States (Connecticut, Michigan, Illinois, Minnesota, Maryland) Classified by Husband's Occupation (in Per Cent)*

	1885 (N = 193)	1910 (N = 348)	1925 (N = 392)	1950 (N = 408)
Professional and semi-professional	22.6	15.1	12.0	12.4
Proprietors, managers, and officials	30.4	22.0	21.2	16.3
Clerical and sales	26.1	21.8	21.0	20.3
Skilled labor	22.1	26.6	25.3	28.2
Unskilled and semi-skilled	6.5	12.3	19.6	22.8
Farm	2.3	2.2	0.9	0.9

This suggests an answer to the question posed above. The present social composition of the movement cannot duplicate the pretense to social dominance from which a reformist position is possible. Further, the very class structure of the movement accentuates the split between the upper and the lower middle classes which appears in the interviews and documentary materials. A uniform middle-class culture is less of a reality than it was in earlier periods.

One would anticipate that the groups most susceptible to norms encouraging drinking are precisely those upper-middle-class groups making up the world of the professional, business executive, and salesman—the new middle classes whose religion is less evangelical and whose norms emphasize fellowship, toleration, and leisure. These seem to be the groups who have left the WCTU. Their higher socioeconomic status would have afforded them leadership had they remained.

The data suggest that temperance norms have filtered down to lower socioeconomic groups. The moral indignation of the movement is explainable by the resentment engendered by the defection of the upper middle class. These are no longer available as models with which the religiously oriented in America can identify. The quality of "moralizing" has ceased to be respectable. The adherents of rural nineteenth-century values epitomized in the doctrine of total abstinence do not have available tangible models of success and prestige in social levels above them. Nevertheless, they nourish expectation that the values on which they have been raised will be the values of groups above them in status. Their resentment is understandable as a response to the realization that their expectations are no longer true.

Conclusion

This study has demonstrated a shift in the doctrine and social composition of a moral reform movement. The earlier stages of the WCTU were shown to have been characterized by an attitude of moral reform directed toward the lower classes. In this stage, social composition data indicate that the WCTU represented a socially dominant class.

Today the WCTU is an organization in retreat. Contrary to the expectations and theories of institutionalization, the movement has not acted to preserve organizational values at the expense of past doctrine. In adhering to less popular positions it has played the role of the sect and widened the gap between WCTU membership and middle-class respectability. Analysis of social composition in this stage indicates that the movement is today less upper middle class in composition than in earlier periods and more lower middle and lower class in composition. In this respect, as well as in the changed drinking norms of the upper middle classes, the split within American Protestant middle classes has been widened.

The moral indignation of the WCTU today is a very different approach to temperance and to the American scene from the reformism and progressivism of the late nineteenth and early twentieth centuries. The plight of the "moralizer-in-retreat" is the plight of the once powerful but now rejected suitor. The symbols at his command no longer ring true in the halls where once they were heard with great respect. He cannot identify easily with those above him in status, because they now repudiate his morality. It is the sense of the historical shift, fully as much as the absolute clash in values, that has soured his reformism and generated his resentment.

30. THE NEW PROHIBITION DRIVE

by Alfred McClung Lee *

The waves of prohibitionist and anti-prohibitionist agitation that have swept the United States during the past century and more furnish significant case materials on aspects of cultural change, cultural lag, and social control. These materials are illuminating, in my estimation, in connection with such general subjects as these: (1) the nature of reformist movements, in their societal, social psychological, and psychological aspects; (2) the relationships between moralistic-emotional and scientific opinions in dry and wet propagandas and strategies; and (3) the probable consequences of educational and legalistic efforts at social change, such as the drys and wets have promoted, in terms of anticipated and unanticipated goals and consequences.

Within the necessary limits of a paper, it is hoped to touch upon some conclusions reached along such lines during a detailed survey of dry and wet agitational work, with especial reference to the new prohibition drive. Naturally only samples and brief summaries of data may be given here, but it is hoped that the quotations and summaries capture and transmit pertinent characteristics of the originals. . . .

For the sake of brevity, this paper sketches and seeks to analyze these factors bearing upon the new prohibition drive: (1) major strategies, (2) the drives for the Eighteenth and the Twenty-first Amendments compared with the present prohibition drive, (3) the groups involved in the present struggle, the anatomy of agitation, (4) their philosophies, and (5) their tactics. Adequate treatments of the historical perspectives into which the present drive should be fitted, of the characteristics of the specific pressure groups involved in the struggle, of the propaganda theories and techniques used by these groups, and of other pertinent matters cannot be treated within the limits of an article, but it is thought that the discussion of the aspects chosen permits certain generalizations concerning techniques of social agitation that might be suggestive in the study of other pressure programs.

1. *Major Strategies.* Dr. Purley A. Baker, General Superintendent of the Anti-Saloon League of America at the time, outlined the whole sequence of steps in dry major strategy at the League's Victory Convention in Washington in 1919 as follows:

* From "Techniques of Social Reform: an Analysis of the New Prohibition Drive," *American Sociological Review*, 9 (1944), 65–77.

When we had township option we could do little with wet townships about us:

When we had municipal local option we could do little with wet cities about us:

When we had county option we could do but little with wet counties around us:

When we had state option we could do little with wet states around us:

And now, what does it mean to have wet countries around us with the system of transportation now in the world?

For a hundred miles down in Texas and Louisiana and all those border states rum would rule in pandemonium as it comes across the border. Mexico must be cared for. South America must be cared for. The nations of the earth must be helped.

This outline of the steps in dry strategy naturally oversimplifies the whole program. It leaves out of consideration the role of the manufacture of bootleg liquor and many of the consequences of the greater ease with which "high-powered rot-gut" can be transported secretly than the more bulky wines and beers. But it gives the steps taken in the thinking and action of the drys as they drove on for the Eighteenth Amendment in the years before 1919 and also since repeal as they have begun to seek the restoration of nationwide prohibition.

The major strategy of the anti-prohibitionist forces is not so programmatic. It consisted before 1919 and it still consists chiefly of fighting the efforts of the drys to extend the prohibition areas and the scope of restrictive legislation, of precipitating efforts to repeal local-option prohibition laws and ordinances, and of generally discrediting prohibition as a technique for the promotion of temperance or abstinence.

In the light of such high strategies by the protagonists in the struggles, let us attempt to sum up the influence of ten major factors in bringing success first to the drys, then to the wets, and to examine the operation of these ten factors today in the new prohibition drive:

2. *The Drives for the Eighteenth (Prohibition) and the Twenty-first (Repeal) Amendments Compared with the Present Prohibition Drive.* Here are ten factors that apparently contributed powerfully to the success of dry strategy in the drive culminating in the ratification of the Eighteenth Amendment January 16, 1919:

a. *Drink and religion are competitors.* As William James has pointed out, the "sway of alcohol over mankind is unquestionably due to its power to stimulate the mystical faculties of human nature, usually crushed to earth by the cold facts and dry criticisms of the sober hour . . . The drunken consciousness is one bit of the mystic consciousness, and our total opinion of it must find its place in our opinion of that larger whole." In other words, religious mysticism and alcoholic mysticism can only be understood psychologically as phases of mystical experiences generally.

Thus, as Clark Washburton points out, "liquor dealers, religious organizations, and the moving picture exhibitors are natural competitors for patronage." And it has taken a long time for all three to come to some recognition of this competitive situation and for some workable adjustments between them to appear. The first adjustment attempted by the ministers was to eliminate what they regarded as an unnecessary and vile competitor to their search for souls to convert to Christianity, with the Saloon representing most directly the Devil.

b. *The farmers and villagers wanted to maintain the influence of their ideals over the country.* The first prohibition drive was also a part of an attempt by rural and village people to regain something of their waning influence in the United States and to impose their way of life upon urban dwellers. What seems to objective observers to have been a quixotic waste of Protestant reforming energy upon the subduing of a windmill, looked to the country folk as a way of preventing American cities—to which their children were being drawn—from going the course of Sodom and Gomorrah and taking the whole country with them.

c. *Evangelical Protestants raised the cry of "Rum, Romanism, and Rebellion."* With the Roman Catholics not showing in general any enthusiasm for prohibition and with many Irish and other Roman Catholics identified with the Saloon, the evangelical Protestants turned to the old nativist appeal with the cry of "Rum, Romanism, and Rebellion" and its equivalents, especially in the extremely rural and Protestant districts. The fact that the Protestant Episcopalians also did not show any enthusiasm for prohibition was discounted on the grounds that they are "tissue-paper Catholics" and tend to identify themselves with the Anglican Catholics of the Church of England. The anti-Roman-Catholic enthusiasm of the old Protestant nativist movements that went into the Ku Klux Klan during the period immediately following World War I was thus canalized into the prohibition movement before and during that war.

d. *Prohibition gained greatly from votes against the excesses and political power of specific saloon keepers.* Every sizable community contained at least one "bad saloon" that came to typify in the minds of the citizenry the evils of the Saloon System and the Whisky Trust. As William Allen White wrote in the Chicago Tribune of March 10, 1908, "It is not a prohibition wave but an anti-saloon wave, a protest against the product of the liquor business as it has developed in this country." And Peter H. Odegard points out, "Moderate drinkers and total abstainers, who balked at the idea of absolute prohibition, were willing to admit that the American saloon had become a noisome thing." In other words, there is general agreement that a large share of the vote against Liquor in the first prohibition drive was a vote against the excesses and political power of specific "poor men's clubs," certain especially obnoxious saloons.

e. *Business interests looked upon drinking as bad for their employees.*

Drinking employees, they thought, were both inefficient and dangerous. They looked upon them as improper workers in a machine civilization and also as probable agitators and strikers. Representatives of management believed before 1919 that saloons in working-class districts were hotbeds of agitation for shorter hours, improved conditions, and higher wages. They therefore believed that prohibition would help to "civilize" their employees. Representatives of other business interests, such as the vendors of non-alcoholic beverages, also looked upon prohibition as a means of diverting funds from Liquor to "more useful" outlets. And so did some who were interested in savings, home-construction, food, automobiles, etc.

f. *Prohibition appealed to southerners as a way of keeping the Negro "in his place."* This was especially true in the urban districts where Negroes had a tendency to "get ideas" and to "get out of hand." As Clark Washburton notes:

"In the first prohibition wave, when the Negroes were under the complete domination of plantation owners, and in the second, when they still resided chiefly in the rural areas and the domination of white landlords was almost as complete as under slavery, the south was virtually untouched by the movement. But with the migration of the Negroes to urban areas, drunkenness and crime associated therewith became serious Negro problems. The third wave of statewide prohibition began in the south and by 1917 the entire section was legally dry. Throughout the south state laws and national prohibition have been enforced more stringently among the Negroes than among the white population."

Suppressed and frustrated Negroes, members of a submerged caste, with some release given them through drink, sometimes threatened to forget to "stay in their place," and the whites handled the situation in the same fashion as they had handled the problem of Negro voting: with laws that applied to Negroes, not to whites.

g. *Professional evangelists, reformers, and other demagogs found in the dry drive an attractive and profitable outlet for their talents,* especially under the auspices of the W.C.T.U. and the Anti-Saloon League. They therefore flocked to it and gave it power and direction.

h. *Large contributors to political movements and campaigns found that the drys offered a more attractive issue than did those who stressed issues more fundamental to the control of our economic and political institutions.* The "era of muckrakers" of about 1901 to 1912, so labeled by Theodore Roosevelt, struck many business leaders in particular as having an unsettling tendency. The Prohibitionists merely attacked Booze, the Saloon, the Whisky Trust, and the Brewers, but Lincoln Steffens, Ray Stannard Baker, Upton Sinclair, and others went after the political bosses, the public utilities, patent medicines, advertising, and even capitalism itself. Let the reformers have Booze and the Saloon! Let that keep them busy!

i. *The identification of beer with German immigrants to this country and of those immigrants with pro-Germanism in World War I reacted to the discredit of Booze and the Saloon.* Many breweries were owned by Americans of German birth or ancestry, and the group was represented in part by the National German-American Alliance, which carried on propaganda against prohibition. As a result, Congressional investigations (then as now a prime way to provide a sounding board for propaganda) firmly identified in the minds of many the breweries with the enemy, by derivation all Liquor with pro-Teutonic influences.

j. *Liquor became a wartime sacrifice.* In World War I, as in World War II, Americans deprived themselves of many things to defeat "the Kaiser" in a great upsurge of courageous and puritanical self-sacrifice, and Liquor was one of these sacrifices. As Harry Elmer Barnes has it, "Prohibition was sneaked over under the cover of the prevalent hysterical tendency of the people of the United States to save and sacrifice to defeat the Kaiser. Prohibition was part and parcel of war idealism, as much as the freeing of repressed peoples, the sanctity of treaties, the battle for democracy, and the like."

And so wartime prohibition came, and then as Prohibitionist Irving Fisher of Yale University admitted in 1926, Constitutional "National Prohibition came prematurely, before a proper try-out of wartime prohibition had sufficiently prepared the population of the large cities for Constitutional Prohibition." A more objective student of the subject, John Allen Krout, observes that Federal Prohibition through the Eighteenth Amendment came to many Americans in 1920 "with something of a shock. Though they were aware of the political power possessed by the enemies of the liquor traffic, they had not realized that the reformers were so near the goal." Naturally the super-pressure tactics of the Anti-Saloon League, the Woman's Christian Temperance Union, et al. had much to do with the surprise factor in this victory, the immediate growth of anti-Prohibition agitation.

Let us review now the operation of these same ten factors in the counter-drive for the Twenty-first Amendment. Here is a summary:

a. *Drink and religion are competitors.* They continued to be competitors, but ministers and especially laymen were learning that the age-old problems of Liquor cannot be solved by outright and immediate suppression. In a democracy, laws resemble rather closely the mores or they do not "work," and the mores are patterns of behavior and not of idealization.

b. *The farmers and villages wanted to maintain the influence of their ideals over the country.* During World War I, the world of our villagers and farmers had expanded, and the automobile and radio made it expand even more during the 1920's and early 1930's. What had been thought of as the "urban type of mind" became less bound by geography, more a psychological factor that might and did appear throughout the country.

c. *"Rum, Romanism, and Rebellion."* The Ku Klux Klan reached a peak possibly in 1924 with what may have been as many as 6,000,000 members. It had a resurgence in the 1928 campaign to "Keep the Pope Out of the White House," the contest between Alfred E. Smith and Herbert Hoover (in which Hoover won). But such organizations as the National Conference of Christians and Jews, formed in 1928, were pointing the way toward more sensible relations between our religious and cultural minorities, emphasizing among other things that we all belong to minorities. Organized Protestantism as a whole had set its course strongly against intolerant movements that capitalized upon such differences, and the wave of new ecstatic Protestant groups that began to blossom in World War II had not gained much prominence as yet.

d. *Prohibition had gained greatly from votes against the excesses and political power of specific saloon keepers.* But the Liquor Gangster, the Beer Baron, and the Speakeasy Mobster now loomed as more horrible persons to dread than the dimming vision of the old-time Saloon Keeper and the Whisky Trust. On the sound propaganda theory that people would vote against a specific menace under their noses but not necessarily against a vague "system," the wets did exactly what the drys had done in the previous drive: they dramatized the excesses and political power of specific speakeasy operators.

e. *Business interests had looked upon drinking as bad for their employees.* Now business representatives had come to at least four conclusions, or their actions and statements suggested that they suspected these conclusions:

(1) that their workers could organize effective unions and strikes without a saloon to help them;

(2) that so-called "private prohibition" enforced upon the employees of a given industry for reasons of efficiency and safety worked as well or better than National Prohibition and the need for such prohibition was not eliminated by National Prohibition;

(3) that the allegation that Prohibition would make workers a better market for consumers' goods did not appear to be as substantial an argument in depression as were the more direct contributions repeal promised to make to the offsetting of technological unemployment and to aiding with the mounting tax burden; and

(4) that bootlegging subsidized a power outside of the business community with which it was quite difficult to deal on satisfactory terms.

f. *Prohibition appealed to southerners as a way of keeping the Negro "in his place."* And it still worked that way, especially in the cities. But the southerners preferred to have a Democrat for President, even with repeal as the cost, and they knew that they would find "ways and means" to keep "the niggers in their place," as they put it.

g. *Professional evangelists, reformers, and other demagogs* found themselves up against new competition for adherents and subsidies. The decay of fundamentalist religious beliefs, the rise of the motion picture as a substitute for the sawdust trail, the development of national personalities through the radio as personal leaders for greater masses of people, all these things undermined the followings of the old-time gospel performers who did so much to stir up popular support for the Eighteenth Amendment drive. The modern counterparts of the old-time religious demagogs, too, such as Father Charles E. Coughlin of Royal Oak, Michigan, built up some followings, but they failed as yet to "deliver the vote."

h. *Large contributors to political movements and campaigns* continued to believe that the drys offered an attractive issue with which to distract attention from issues more fundamental to the control of our economic and political institutions, but to keep prohibition alive as such an issue, repeal also had to be an issue and a live one. Prohibition as an accepted and accomplished goal, if such could have been possible, would have eliminated a valuable issue entirely.

i. *The identification of brewers with pro-Germanism* disappeared as a matter of any significance in the general postwar revulsion against what had become known, with sarcasm, as the "Crusade to make the World Safe for Democracy." With *Fortune* magazine and congressional committees branding wars as the products of the munitions makers, with the American Legion and other patriotic bodies attempting to take the "profits out of war," pro-Germanism temporarily ceased to serve as a term of rebuke.

j. *Liquor as a wartime sacrifice* naturally was also a thing of the past. World War I was long ago. Few dreamt in those days of the possibility of World War II.

In the early years of the depression, economists were making estimates that repeal would yield revenues of $2,500,000,000 to $3,000,000,000 a year, by analogy with the British tax rate and excise system and barring a return of the saloon. These figures looked inviting to many. As Barnes put it in 1932, "The one possible source of pressure which may achieve repeal or revision of Prohibition lies in the current depression. This, together with the deficit in the Federal budget, may suffice to offset the dry lobby and give legislators courage to vote as they think and drink." Fletcher Dobyns had a slightly different emphasis, and he explained it seven years after repeal in his book, *The Amazing Story of Repeal* (1940). This lawyer attributed repeal to the machinations of a small group of wealthy men who believed that liquor taxes would relieve them of part of their tax loads. In their enthusiasm over Dobyns' analysis, the drys chose to forget that it was a dry, James A. White of Ohio, who invented the slogan, "No money is tainted if the Anti-Saloon League can get its hands on it," a principle that had been very useful in financing Prohibitionists in their drive for the Eighteenth Amendment.

That both National Prohibition and repeal should have come because people with personal axes to grind interested themselves in these projects is no surprise to a social scientist. A careful student of the subject estimates that "the Eighteenth Amendment, which Wayne B. Wheeler once estimated cost sixty-five million dollars to secure, was repealed at a cost of but twenty million dollars." If such pressure tactics had not taken place, the social scientist would have cause for surprise. Motive power for such dynamic promotion must come from somewhere.

So much for a summary of the operation of the ten factors during the drives for the Eighteenth and Twenty-first Amendments. Let us examine their status in the present drive for the extension of prohibition.

a. *Drink and religion are competitors.* But organized religion is giving more and more evidence, particularly through pronouncements of the Federal Council of the Churches of Christ in America and of certain denominational spokesmen, that approaches to the liquor problem other than immediate prohibition grow in favor. Alcoholics Anonymous, for example, is a cooperative movement of alcoholics who seek to aid themselves with the help of a "Power greater than ourselves." It has gained wide institutional support (Roman Catholic, Protestant, Jewish, and other). It points to one of several different religious approaches to alcoholism and the alcohol problem. The members of Alcoholics Anonymous, incidentally, even though they are seeking to be total abstainers, are as a whole bitterly resentful of the prohibitionists. As Jack Alexander states in The Saturday Evening Post of March 1, 1941, "I met and talked with scores of A.A.'s, as they call themselves, and found them to be unusually calm, tolerant people."

b. *The farmers and villagers* still numbered many who wanted to restore the influence of their ideals over the country. Through the demands of Army, Navy, and factory employment in World War II, however, they continued to become more the members of an urbanized country and less the exponents of a narrow morality that they wished to enforce upon their fellow countrymen.

c. *"Rum, Romanism, and Rebellion"* or perhaps some tie-up between prohibition and Jew-baiting or Negro-beating may become a factor again in the promotion of prohibition. Such comments as the following from *Progress: Publication of the International Reform Federation* in 1943 are not unusual:

> The wets are waking up to the power of protest and are sending in petitions against the Bryson Bill evidently obtained in the saloons from the character of the foreign names attached as well as the sender.

The "character of the foreign names" is a native-American catch-phrase. But such excesses, such divisive tendencies, have had a "lid clamped on them" during World War II. They represent, however, a real danger for the postwar period not only to those fearful of prohibition and its consequences but also to those who dread authoritarianism born of such hysterical scapegoat-beatings. Such events as the Detroit race riots of the week of June 20, 1943, and other racial clashes and frictions may issue forth in a new nativist movement after World War II, similar to the Ku Klux Klan after World War I. Demagogs are now available—Father Charles E. Coughlin, Rev. Gerald L. K. Smith, and Rev. J. Frank Norris, all of the Detroit area, for examples. But then demagogs always arise when the opportunities for their work are present. They can smell societal decay afar, and they swarm to it.

d. *Prohibition had gained greatly from votes against the excesses and political power of specific saloon keepers.* Repeal had also gained greatly from votes against the excesses and power of similar speakeasy operators. Until the distillers and brewers so far forget this point as to think that America has come to like the saloon whether or no, so long as the distillers and brewers put up a reasonably accurate and convincing facsimile of self-regulation, they will keep this irritant within manageable limits.

e. *Business interests* on the whole, as the preceding list (e) indicates, have learned their lesson so far as prohibition is concerned in connection with their employees.

f. *Prohibition still appeals to southerners as a way of keeping the Negro —especially in the cities—"in his place."* With race riots and other evidences of friction flaring in northern cities, the role that anti-Negro feeling may play in future dry agitation—as point (c) above brings out —is uncertain and menacing.

g. *Professional evangelists, reformers, and other demagogs* are likely to find "softer pickings" in movements more strictly economic and political in character than were the old-time dry revival meetings, the tremendous money-raising orgies of the Anti-Saloon League and its affiliates and competitors, and the W.C.T.U.

h. *Large contributors to political movements and campaigns* may once more find prohibition an enticing political issue, but to be workable such an issue would probably have to come riding back in as a part of the ideology for an authoritarian drive, the kind of abstinence Adolf Hitler and his Nazi Party advocated for the "Master Race."

i. *The identification of brewers with pro-Germanism* did not materialize again during World War II. On the contrary, the inept leadership of the drys permitted the prohibitionist lobby to get itself identified with an obviously labeled pro-fascist, "Capt." Edward Page Gaston, United States Director of World Prohibition Foundation and organizer of the New Vigilantes of America in 1932 and of its successor, the Patriotic Guard of America. Pro-Germans also seized upon such foolish and unpatriotic dry canards as the Pearl-Harbor-drunkenness story and used them for subversive purposes. This embarrassed many a sincerely convinced prohibitionist who was also a patriotic American.

j. *Liquor as a wartime sacrifice* is one of the factors that most nearly approximates its World War I characteristics. If it were not for the bitter experiences of National Prohibition and if it were not for the sizable and vocal anti-prohibitionist sympathies of the Army and Navy, more progress might have been made toward wartime prohibition. As the war goes on, however, indications increase that liquor, wine, and possibly also beer will dry up more and more, and then what? Wartime expedients have a way of staying on and on.

These comparative analyses of the Eighteenth and Twenty-first Amendments and present drives in the light of ten major factors emphasize the roles of life-conditions and events in the success of agitations for changes in law and custom. This material also furnishes background for the other three points to be discussed, beginning with what was referred to above as "an anatomy of agitation":

3. *The Groups Involved in the Present Prohibition Struggle.* The most obvious differentiation between the dry and wet movements in the present prohibition struggle is that the drys, like so many reformist groups, are led by people who are motivated by a kind of fanaticism; the wets, like so many conservative groups, are led by professionals who are motivated less by burning zeal and more by finite considerations. Since both movements have some social types in common, it will be useful to characterize first the types to be found in the more complex one, the dry movement, and then to identify those also found among the wets.

In such an attempt to sum up observations on the "sorts of people" active in the dry movement, it is helpful at the outset to discuss what is meant by fanaticism, defined briefly as a "frenzied partisanship or blind zeal in any cause, whether religious, social or political." Fanaticism has been further described in "its authentic occurrence" as "the effect of three passional components," as follows: (*1*) "extreme narrowness and rigidity of temper," (*2*) "unyielding determination to make the fixed idea triumph over men," and (*3*) "callousness to pain . . . uncommonly insensitive to human suffering, often to the point of cruelty." In short, as Isaac Taylor puts it in his old book on Fanaticism (1834), it is "Enthusiasm inflamed by Hatred."

It is not contended that all drys are out and out fanatics, specimens of the "authentic occurrence" of fanaticism. The contention is that fanaticism is a variable part of the make-up of drys, as it is of the mentalities of those dedicated to other Causes of the sort: anti-tobacco, anti-swearing, Sunday observance, anti-card-playing. Rather extreme fanaticism can be illustrated with Frances E. Willard, long-time leader of the National W.C.T.U., who tells in her *Glimpses of Fifty Years* how she decided to side up with the Prohibition Party, as follows:

It was a solemn and exalted hour in which my brain teemed with the sweet reasonableness of such a course, and my conscience rejoiced in its triumph over considerations of expediency. Nothing has ever disturbed the tranquil assurance that I was then helped to make a logical and wise decision inspired from Heaven.

Without dealing further in specific personalities, one can summarize observations on the kinds of personalities drawn into their movement by the drys by saying that they attract: (*1*) agitators, (*2*) professional promoters, (*3*) bureaucrats, (*4*) "heelers," (*5*) "just members," (*6*) "fronts," and (*7*) "fellow travelers." These are not mutually exclusive categories. They are rough types. Some agitators are somewhat professional in their grasp of promotional techniques. Some professional promoters exhibit a degree of fanaticism beyond that expected and sometimes beyond that desirable in such a technician. Bureaucrats constitute a special class of "heelers," one might say, and the lines between "heelers" and "just members" and between "just members" and "fellow travelers" have no distinctness. As the term suggests, "fronts" are "fellow travelers" who are sufficiently prominent and unlabeled to give a function broader respectability. In addition, the basis of motivation of a given person may change as time goes on; the agitator may work out a new basis of adjustment for his personality problems and thus develop into a professional promoter and then, as more time passes, he may ripen or disintegrate (as you view it) into a bureaucrat. Others are bureaucrats from the outset, and still others may go through transitional stages from agitator to "fellow traveler."

The agitators, the real fanatics, both paid and volunteer, furnish the emotional drive, the unflinching zeal, the really dogmatic and uncompromising fanaticism that serves as the spearhead of drives and programs. Professional promoters differ from agitators chiefly in being motivated primarily by "professional" (monetary, service, artistic, security-giving, status) considerations rather than by The Cause (a fanatical drive to attain a "necessary" goal). Professional promoters have the talents of public speakers, publicity agents, writers, lobbyists, as do agitators, but the professional promoters also include among them experts in the broader field of public relations, a perspective on society that requires somewhat more objectivity and technical competence than an agitator is likely to accumulate. As a matter of fact, truly professional promoters contribute most importantly an objectivity unmixed with emotionalism that helps to stabilize and direct a movement.

Trailing behind the agitators and professional promoters in any movement come those of small talents and narrow aspirations, the bureaucrats, those who see opportunities for jobs as such and little more, the people who know the arts of memo-passing, protective-coloration, and self-preservation and who care for little else than the comparative security thus provided.

The "heelers" and "just members" of any movement are the great rank-and-file, those who for many reasons need the kinds of psychological and social satisfactions a pressure group or Cause organization can offer them. "Heelers" are the more or less faithful foot soldiers of the army; "just members" are the casual contributors, the members of the audiences, the people who "think it's a good thing" and "want to be identified with it." Prohibition and the Anti-Saloon League or W.C.T.U. give the heelers focal points to which they orient themselves and through which they can get a greater feeling of security in an unsatisfactory, vaguely shifting world. For that matter, both agitators and heelers get something of the same satisfaction out of the prohibition movement that others get out of other forms of religious mysticism or out of alcoholic beverages.

Through visits from traveling leaders and experts on The Cause and through the publications of city, state, and national dry organizations, their principal media of communication, the propaganda "line" is not only kept constantly before the rank-and-file of the movement, but the "line" is kept fresh in its applications, through constantly relating dry philosophy to new situations and personalities as they arise. The circulation of *The National Prohibitionist,* the National W.C.T.U. *Union Signal,* and the like is not impressive, but the various types of dry organization members absorb their contents and pass the propaganda along to the much larger body of "fellow travelers." The way in which dry propaganda filters, for example, into the elementary and secondary school textbooks of the country has been surveyed by Anne Roe, and this penetration has been tremendous.

The wets number in their movement chiefly: (*1*) professional promoters, (*2*) bureaucrats, (*3*) "just members," (*4*) "fronts," and (*5*) "fellow travelers." During the Prohibition period, the wets numbered some agitators and heelers, but the maintenance of the status quo in any field has little attraction for the fanatic and for those entranced by the romance of The Cause. The wets do not promise human salvation through the achievement of a clearly defined goal; their goals, as they see them, involve merely the promotion of a tolerant society, the provision of a pleasant diversion, the continuance of an ancient industry that pays excessive taxes and provides many jobs.

How do such social types, drawn into the two opposing camps, compete with each other for the support of the vast and indifferent majority? How do they hold their adherents, get new ones, and extend their grasp over the minds and actions of fellow travelers? Their philosophies, stressing the appeal of such philosophies to adherents, will help to develop this picture.

4. *Their Philosophies.* The play *Ten Nights in a Bar-Room,* a propaganda piece that ranks with Uncle Tom's Cabin, may be said to epitomize the philosophy of Prohibitionists and the substance of their popular propaganda efforts even today. In it, Liquor and the Saloon lead Frank Slade irrevocably from the ways of Decency to those of Murder and Damnation. There is no compromise, no effort to see the good in the evil person's mind,

the evil in the mind of the saint, the brotherhood under the skin of "all God's chillun"; all is Good or Evil. The first sip of beer, even the first cigarette, can thus lead only to the criminal's dock, the gallows, and a forgotten grave.

Dry philosophy succeeds—when it does—because of the hold that one or more powerful appeals in it can secure over the minds of old and new adherents. The following list outlines briefly seven of the chief of such appeals inherent in dry philosophy.

a. It provides a religiously-sanctioned scapegoat into which frustrations may be projected and upon which pent up aggressions may be vented.

b. It furnishes religiously-sanctioned child-substitutes into which drys can project their idealizations, as compensations for their own inadequacies, which sometimes include the lack of children or of the "right kind" of children. In short, having exaggerated or frustrated needs for such satisfactions, the drys can thus find a channel through which they can express those needs in the attempted management of others.

c. It caters to exaggerated needs for Perfection, the sort of thing the late Justice Oliver Wendell Holmes summed up in an essay on "Natural Law," published in his *Collected Legal Papers,* when he said, "It is not enough for the knight of romance that you agree that his lady is a very nice girl— if you do not admit that she is the best that God ever made or will make, you must fight." He calls this demand for the superlative the factor that drives some men to drink and points out "that this demand is at the bottom of the philosopher's effort to prove that truth is absolute and of the jurist's search for criteria of universal validity which he collects under the head of natural law."

d. It offers a formula for simplification, a simple and all-explaining ideology, that orients drys to the world's complexities.

e. It gives a pattern for regression. Individuals frustrated by their daily contacts with unpleasant reality frequently feel a compulsion to go back in their imaginations and behavior to periods at which they fancy they were more content and especially more secure, usually at some period in their childhood. Dry philosophy permits some to take that way of experiencing again some of the joys associated with a sternly disciplined home.

f. It supplies, more generally speaking, a way to flee from reality into its mysticism, a flight from the woes of this wicked work-a-day world to a "finer plane of understanding." This mysticism is part of the sort of thing adherents enjoy in secret societies. It derives in the case of dry philosophy from certain religious conceptions, theological theorizings, and psychological needs, and it has as one of its symptoms and characteristics a special language, somewhat different in meaning and detail from that defined in the ordinary dictionary.

g. It encourages, through common goals, mystical conceptions, and special language, the identification of adherents with the movement and with one another in a manner that assures at least some of them of a higher degree of psychological security than they might otherwise find.

As the brief descriptions of these seven psychological appeals indicate, they are not sharply separable conceptions but rather aspects of the whole appeal made by dry ideology to old and new adherents. The mind cannot be categorized, and these seven appeals are labeled and described merely to indicate seven aspects of certain people's interrelated personalities which —to a greater or less degree—find in dry philosophy the fulfillment of needs and other satisfactions.

From the foregoing analysis, those acquainted with the psychology of alcoholics can appreciate the statement that the mystical appeals of alcohol and of dry philosophy have much in common. The devotees of alcohol also find in it elements that cater to their exaggerated needs for perfection, simplification, and identification.

The appeals of the philosophies of the wet propagandists are more difficult to analyze because there is no one wet philosophy, no finely wrought wet ideology. The anti-prohibition position appeals for reasons ranging from a well-developed thirst for alcoholic beverages to a dread of the societal consequences of prohibition legislation and enforcement, from the psychotic or neurotic or merely emotional to the "normal" and logical. This lack of a well-worked-out set of rationalizations, aside from the intellectual ones provided by tolerant liberalism and the commercial ones supplied by industrial apologists, reflects the conservative character of the wet position and the rear-guard type of fight the wets tend to carry on, a kind of combat common among conservative groups when not too hard pressed.

5. *Their tactics.* The (1) major strategies, (2) events and climates of opinion, (3) groups involved, and (4) philosophies converge upon programs of implementation. And both the wets and the drys forward their efforts through the common tactics of (a) publicity, (b) political pressuring, and (c) "boring from within," to borrow another term from those used to describe left-wing political tactics. These means of promotion naturally overlap somewhat, but they provide rough headings under which to sum up very briefly this dynamic aspect of the subject.

a. *Publicity.* Lacking currently as sympathetic treatment in the general-circulation press as they would like to have, the drys depend chiefly for publicity upon such media as their own periodicals, country and smalltown weeklies, their own organizations, public speakers, special holidays, handbills, posters, etc. The wets, chiefly represented by the manufacturers and distributors of liquors, wines, and beers and their trade associations, distribute their messages through newspaper and magazine advertising, radio, posters, and special devices placed in bars and liquor stores.

Despite the volume and persistence of the efforts of both wets and drys, however, the effectiveness of all such publicity projects depends upon the extent to which they can and do make plausible explanations of facts, experiences, needs, events, desires felt by their audiences. When the "climate of sentiment" is unfavorable, the drys or the wets beat the winds; when a particularly irritating saloon or other sore-spot helps to change that "climate," the drys make strides in a given area; when a dry orator or organization is discredited, the wets benefit.

b. *Political pressuring* is the term commonly given to all the ways Americans have devised for forcing politicians to translate their glittering doubletalk into behavior representative of special interests, the interests of the pressuring group. The partly accurate popular conception is that Booze and Bribery account for the bulk of such pressuring, but the Anti-Saloon League demonstrated from its earliest days the virtues of bludgeoning representatives with petitions, letters, telegrams, and delegations. External pressures brought to bear upon governmental functionaries from Washington to the smallest governmental unit, cleverly organized, plus "horse-trading" and the "right kind" of contacts and friendships have tremendous power in "aiding legislators to decide what the people want and need."

c. *Boring from within* can include practically everything not grouped under the preceding. No "simon pure" pressure group can obtain a very large audience in terms of its own membership. As a purist sect, its demands upon its membership attract the fanatical minority and repel the tolerant or indifferent majority. Similarly no commercial pressure group can hope to obtain a very large audience in one industry in terms of those directly connected with the business in question. Both seek, therefore, to spread the "message" as widely as possible through "fellow travelers" and "neutral" publicity media, to achieve segments of their programs piecemeal through compromises and deals, and to establish as many "common fronts" as possible with other organizations, and these are the chief "boring from within" tactics. And the public, parochial, and private school systems of the United States are always the first goals for any extensive boring efforts of the sort. As Frances E. Willard liked to say, "We must go among the children with our temperance work. Mighty weapons will be hurled against them when they emerge from the sheltering fortress of home—they ought not to go forth unarmed."

Anne Roe, in her *Survey of Alcohol Education in Elementary and High Schools in the United States* (1943), tells how the drys effected the change, repeal, and re-enactment of state laws dealing with alcohol education until now all the states have mandatory legislation in this area. In the materials used recently, the "horror-provoking illustrations of diseased livers, and many sweeping statements, have been discarded along with the purely moralistic orientation." In other words, Dr. Roe says that the public-school program is now alleged to be " 'scientific, unemotional, pedagogical,' and great emphasis is laid on these descriptive terms. But in spite of the recognition of the desirability of a scientific approach, the motivation remains essentially moralistic, as is apparent from a scanning of the newer publications." The Roman Catholic parochial schools, Dr. Roe concludes, identify "temperance" with "moderation," not "teetotalism," and she says it appears that their "general position [is] that alcohol is one of God's creations and is therefore not inherently evil, but can be abused." Dr. Roe credits Miss Bertha Rachel Palmer's *Syllabus in Alcohol Education* (published by the National W.C.T.U., sixth edition 1941) with having great influence upon the courses of study throughout the country despite its distortions of scientific fact and other inaccuracies.

While the wets do not have ecclesiastical machinery for sanctioning their boring tactics and can only offer non-emotional scientific and commercial arguments, they try to offset the activities of the drys in "neutral" territories and to do what boring they can on their own behalf.

Within the limits of this brief paper, the foregoing attempts to set forth a sketch of some of the things that may be learned from studying such a reform movement as that currently agitated by the prohibitionists. Naturally this is only one case, even though comparative materials are brought to bear upon it from other cases, directly and by inference, and from more general studies. Also space has prevented adequate treatments of the historical perspectives into which the present drive should be fitted, of the characteristics of the specific pressure groups involved in the struggle, of the propaganda theories and techniques used by these groups, and of other pertinent matters.

Among other things, this type of social-psychological and historical synthesis and analysis has the merit of bringing the sociologist closer to what might be called clinical societal materials than more individualistic and more generalized (including many statistical) approaches. Such a clinical approach, bringing one into contact with vibrant societal struggles and other processes, can perhaps eventually furnish significant data for useful societal guidance in such areas.

As to the relation of such positions as those of the drys and wets to coping with the roles of alcohol in modern society, one is immediately impressed by the fact that more energy is expended upon the promotion of pat propaganda theories than upon attempts to work out sensible and workable programs. An outstanding student of social dynamics and of alcohol has pointed out that "the public must understand its kinship with the problem drinker before it will be possible for many to accept his difficulties as their own." He believes that this adjustment could be effected through the reiteration of "these four kinetic ideas":

1. That the problem drinker is a sick man, exceptionally reactive to alcohol.
2. That he can be helped.
3. That he is worth helping.

4. That the problem is therefore a responsibility of the healing professions, as well as of the established health authorities and the public generally.

The next step that might be taken in this thinking would be to the societal maladjustments of which alcoholics and many other types of neurotics and psychotics are by-products and to an attempt to cope with these maladjustments. In pursuing such lines of thought, however, one quickly leaves the prohibitionist and the business-as-usual wet far behind.

31. PATTERNS AND ATTITUDES

SYSTEMS OF LEGAL CONTROL

by Raymond G. McCarthy
and Edgar M. Douglass *

After the ratification of the Twenty-first Amendment in 1933 administrative systems providing for the control of the manufacture, distribution and sale of alcoholic beverages were set up in the several states. The legislators sought to frame laws which would (*a*) correspond with the expressed will of the people in each state for the regulated sale of alcoholic beverages; (*b*) avoid the return of the evils of social irresponsibility which had been attributed to the alcoholic-beverage industry under pre-Prohibition systems and (*c*) ensure an adequate tax revenue to units of government. The second article of the Twenty-first Amendment prohibited the transportation, importation or possession of intoxicating liquors for delivery or use in violation of any state law. The purpose of this section of the Amendment was to guarantee Federal protection for any state in which prohibition statutes would remain in force or be enacted.

Since 1933, state legislatures in setting up liquor control systems have adopted either the monopoly plan or the license system. States following the monopoly plan function through a board or commission which usually maintains a monopoly on the wholesale distribution and package retailing of distilled spirits. The board may purchase spirits in quantity and sell them through official stores. The sale of beer and wine in privately owned outlets, stores, restaurants and taverns is ordinarily allowed under license. Many monopoly states permit the sale of distilled liquor by the glass in selected outlets.

Proponents of the monopoly system believe that reducing the opportunities for private profit in the sale of distilled spirits will eliminate competition and reduce the sale of beverages of high alcohol content. A state board engaged in the purchase and distribution of spirits is assumed to be in a position to exercise closer supervision over the liquor business within the state than a purely administrative commission. The plan in operation does not always exhibit the advantages anticipated by its supporters. It has been successful in many states as a revenue-producing system, and this aspect has sometimes received the sole emphasis, or only limited effort has been directed toward educating the public concerning the possibilities and dan-

* From *Alcohol and Social Responsibility* (New York, Thomas Y. Crowell Co. and Yale Plan Clinic, 1949), pp. 63–9.

gers of abuse of alcoholic beverages and for the prevention of excessive drinking. In all fairness it must be stated that public information programs about alcohol emanating from appointive commissions or boards are a recent development for which there is little precedent. Several states are making commendable efforts in this direction and others are beginning to show an interest in the problem.

The following 17 states have adopted some form of monopoly plan:

Alabama	New Hampshire	Vermont
Idaho	North Carolina	Washington
Iowa	Ohio	Virginia
Maine	Oregon	West Virginia
Michigan	Pennsylvania	Wyoming
Montana	Utah	

North Carolina is classified by some writers as a license state. Actually a modified monopoly plan is operated in which 26 county dispensaries function under state supervision.

In the license states the granting of different types of licenses to private citizens for the sale of alcoholic beverages is usually under the supervision of a state commission appointed for this purpose. In a few instances the responsibility is assigned to other state officials. The following 29 states have adopted the license system:

Arizona	Kansas	New Mexico
Arkansas	Kentucky	New York
California	Louisiana	North Dakota
Colorado	Maryland	Rhode Island
Connecticut	Massachusetts	South Carolina
Delaware	Minnesota	South Dakota
Florida	Missouri	Tennessee
Georgia	Nebraska	Texas
Illinois	Nevada	Wisconsin
Indiana	New Jersey	

The District of Columbia, under Congressional administration, has a license system. Oklahoma permits state and county licensing for the sale of beer containing not over 3.2 per cent alcohol by volume. Both Oklahoma and Mississippi allow the sale of beverages having not over 4 per cent alcohol by volume. Both Oklahoma and Mississippi have state prohibition of beverages containing more alcohol than the above-mentioned amounts. In November 1948 Kansas repealed a constitutional amendment, originally passed in 1880, which prohibited the sale of alcoholic beverages except beer, and is now operating under the license system.

The powers and duties of state control boards vary widely. All states prohibit sales to intoxicated persons and to minors, although the legal definition of a minor and conditions for the legal sale of beer or wine differ among states. A consistent effort has been made to dissociate the alcoholic-beverage business from corrupt political practices and to prevent irresponsible people from engaging in the trade.

Whether one system of legal controls has distinct advantages for society in comparison with another is not readily apparent. Per capita consumption of absolute alcohol has been lower in monopoly states than in license areas although an upward trend which began in 1940 was somewhat more noticeable in the monopoly than in the license states. Consumption rates ordinarily are higher in urban than in rural sections and the monopoly states generally are more rural. The indications are, however, that the social forces which prevail among groups are of most significance in determining rates of consumption of alcoholic beverages. Contrasting rates of chronic alcoholism in monopoly and license states, Dr. E. M. Jellinek concludes:

> There is no evidence that the monopoly system as a whole had any definite effect on the rate of inebriety. It must be remembered, however, that the label "monopoly state" does not denote essential common elements of the 16 states so designated.[1] There are extraordinarily great differences in the administration of the monopoly system among these 16 states. In fairness, it must be said that a true monopoly system has not been tried.[2]

The latter statement, of course, applies to conditions within the United States.

Classifying state liquor control plans under either the monopoly or the license system is convenient. There are, however, differences in individual state regulations under each category. For example, Connecticut and Delaware have exclusive state administration in the issuance of licenses: Massachusetts and Florida, state and county participation. In Maryland, a license state, seven counties operate liquor dispensaries having a monopoly of the sale of beverages with an alcohol content above a fixed percentage, and one county has an absolute monopoly of the wholesale distribution of all alcoholic beverages within the county. In Minnesota, local governing bodies—counties, cities, towns, boroughs—license the retail sale of all alcoholic beverages, except by druggists and public carriers. Municipalities may also own and operate exclusive liquor stores.

Among monopoly systems comparable differences are to be observed. West Virginia and Washington have exclusive state administration. In Wyoming, there is state monopoly of wholesale sales, but counties and municipalities may license for retail distribution. Virginia maintains a state monopoly but counties and municipalities may require that local licenses be obtained by state beer and wine licensees. Idaho licenses for onpremises

1. Jellinek does not classify North Carolina as a monopoly state.
2. E. M. Jellinek, "Recent Trends in Alcoholism and in Alcohol Consumption," *Quarterly Journal of Studies on Alcohol, 8* (1947), 1–42.

consumption with state, county and municipal participation. In Maine, hotel licensees may sell in the original package to registered room guests.

Several states make a distinction in the administration of regulations governing the sale of beer compared with beverages of higher alcohol content. Idaho, Iowa and Louisiana have boards or commissions specifically for control of the licensing of beer or other beverages having an alcohol content below a given strength, which varies from 4 per cent by weight in Iowa to 6 per cent by volume in Louisiana. The West Virginia Non-Intoxicating Beer Commission administers regulations governing beer having an alcohol content of not over 3.2 per cent.

Local option is the right of the citizens of a local governing unit, county, city or town, to vote to permit or prohibit the sale of different kinds of alcoholic beverages within the area of the unit. Local option laws in some form are in effect in thirty-six states, while twelve states and the District of Columbia have no such provision. Thirty-two states permit a direct vote on the sale of beer. However, seven states do not provide for option on the sale of beer of 3.2 per cent alcohol by volume or less, and two states on beverages containing 5 per cent alcohol by weight or less. Local option only on the sale of spirits by the drink is permitted in three states.

The local option laws of most states require that elections be held on special dates by petition of a specified number of voters. In Illinois, Pennsylvania and Ohio, the election, called by petition, must coincide with a common election date which occurs once every two years. In Maine, New Hampshire and Massachusetts, local option questions on the sale of alcoholic beverages appear automatically on the ballot every two years, and in Vermont, each town must vote annually on the issues. It was estimated at the close of 1948 that approximately 27 million people, or 19 per cent of the population reported in the 1940 census, reside in legally "dry" areas.

* * *

In some states all of the revenues go into the general fund; in others a part is allocated to counties or municipalities. License fees frequently revert to the municipality where the outlets are located. South Carolina earmarks 65 per cent of the revenue to the general fund for public school use. State welfare, aid to dependent children, old age assistance, and debt retirement accounts are recipients of allocated amounts deposited in the general funds by various state Alcohol Control Boards. Massachusetts levies a special excise tax to pay bonuses to World War II veterans. In Connecticut 9 per cent of the license fees are allocated to the state Commission on Alcoholism for the treatment and rehabilitation of alcoholics and for educational activities designed to prevent the development of alcoholism.

As the cost of maintaining government services has increased, state legislatures have investigated new or additional sources of revenue. Gasoline and cigarettes have been taxed progressively, and the sales tax has been resorted to with increasing frequency. The alcoholic-beverage industry has become a common object of increased levies in many states. There develops from time to time organized opposition to state income taxes, or increased gasoline and sales taxes. Relatively little consumer resistance to increased taxes on alcoholic drinks arises. Lobbyists for the industry are active in state capitols when legislation to increase the tax load is introduced. Yet, eventually, the tax is paid by the consumer and there is only limited evidence to suggest that increased taxes result in lower consumption in this country. Individuals and organizations opposed to the sale of alcoholic beverages are likely to support an act to "soak" the industry and the drinker. State agencies in general are concerned primarily with meeting rising budgets by whatever legal measures are at hand. The result has been a one-sided emphasis on taxing alcoholic beverages to produce revenue with only a minimum of effort directed toward legislation designed to control, that is, to provide information for the consumer, regulation for the industry and prevention and correction of the problems of alcohol and of alcoholism.

THE PRESENT SITUATION

Since the end of World War II the organized dry forces have concentrated their legislative efforts in support of local option drives with less emphasis on national prohibition. There has been only limited activity in one or two areas designed to bring about statewide prohibition. Major attention has been given to measures which will eliminate interstate advertising of alcoholic beverages. Publicity has been generated regarding traffic accidents and fatalities related to driving under the influence of alcohol. Drinking as a factor in crime, divorce, juvenile delinquency and other social problems is attacked. Both at the state and local levels, the drys consistently support restrictive legislation affecting the liquor industry—for example, reduction in the number of outlets in a community, limitation in hours of sale, and liability of retailers for sales to minors. A development on the positive side is reflected in renewed interest in education about alcohol in the public classroom, in short summer courses and among community groups.

To a considerable extent, leadership of the movement has been taken over by young men who have not been conditioned by the techniques which dominated the dry movement in the years of Prohibition and repeal. There is evidence that the leaders are seeking to incorporate in their philosophy and in their publications some of the scientific findings with respect to the action of alcohol in the body. Acceptance is growing of alcoholism as a kind of illness which is related to but not primarily caused by alcohol. The need for treatment resources for the alcoholic is recognized. However, while the situation varies in different parts of the country, the lines of communication for the dry organizations, e.g., through their publications, have not expanded significantly. They are still supported chiefly by those individuals who traditionally are in sympathy with the dry philosophy. There is little evidence of new popular support for the movement.

The alcoholic-beverage industry today is following more or less the same public relations program in effect since 1934, which is essentially a denial of accusations made by the drys. While the techniques of the United States Brewers Foundation differ somewhat from those of the public relations group representing the distillers, the goals are substantially the same. Where local option movements develop, the industry provides support to those opposing the efforts to vote an area dry. Through the various advertising media, the industry house organs, and the identification of social drinking with men and women of status, a drive for consumer acceptance in a competitive market is maintained. Acceptance of alcoholism as a major concern has been at a superficial level although funds for physiological research and some social research have been made available by the distilled beverage interests. The brewing industry takes the position that beer is not a factor in the development of alcoholism, but has contributed some funds for research on effects of alcohol.

Considering the long history of controversy over alcohol and the organized effort and funds expended by wets and drys during the last two generations, it would appear that little has been accomplished. In 1937 Professor Albert Coates, Director of the Institute of Government at the University of North Carolina, commented: "If prohibition laws have not solved the liquor problem, neither has the absence of prohibition laws. The records of the centuries give the wets and the drys little cause for arrogance and much cause for humility. The problem of liquor still calls for all the understanding of statesmanship all citizens can summon." [3] It might be added that the problem also calls for investigation by social scientists who will be concerned with social attitudes, cultural patterns with respect to drinking, and changing social institutions in our society. The problems are sufficiently extensive to warrant critical investigation at the research level. At the present time, while there is some increased interest on the part of graduate students, and while understanding of alcoholism and its treatment has expanded remarkably, comparatively little systematic attention is being given to the role of social drinking in our society, and the relationship of such drinking to the problems of intoxication and to alcoholism.

3. A. Coates, "Liquor and the Law in North Carolina, 1795–1937," *Popular Government, 4* (1937), 1.

SUPPLEMENTARY READINGS FOR PART V

1. *Standard Encyclopedia of the Alcohol Problem,* Ernest H. Cherrington, editor-in-chief, Westerville, Ohio.
2. J. A. Krout, *The Origins of Prohibition.* New York, Knopf, 1925. An important reference source on the social and economic aspects of drinking customs from colonial times to the passage of the Maine Law in 1851.
3. I. Fisher, *The "Noble Experiment."* New York, The Alcohol Information Committee, 1930.
4. E. Gordon, *The Wrecking of the Eighteenth Amendment.* Francestown, N. H., The Alcohol Information Press, 1943.
5. H. Asbury, *The Great Illusion. An Informal History of Prohibition.* New York, Doubleday & Co., 1950.
6. R. Fosdick and A. Scott, *Toward Liquor Control.* New York, Harper & Bros., 1933. A review of liquor control systems in Europe and the United States before 1920 with recommendations for a system of control under repeal.
7. *The Annals of the American Academy of Political and Social Sciences, 109* (1923) is devoted to a discussion by several authorities of the effectiveness or lack of effectiveness of Prohibition.
8. G. Nelker, "Svensk kronika" ("Swedish Chronicle"), *Tirfing 41* (1947), 49–64.
9. Report of the Manitoba Liquor Enquiry Commission (Winnipeg, 1955), esp. pp. 118–70, 170–206. Includes a general summary of regulatory laws in England, Canada, the United States, India, and Pakistan, in addition to comments by E. M. Jellinek regarding the current use and control of alcoholic drinks in countries of Europe, the Near East, Australia, and South America.
10. "Temperance Welfare," in *Social Sweden. A Government Survey* (Stockholm, Social Welfare Board, 1952), pp. 263–84.

32. CONCLUSION

The record of history indicates that the use of some form of fermented or distilled beverage has characterized almost every society in every part of the world. Intoxication in varying degrees has often accompanied drinking practices. Yet, the function of alcohol and the symbolism of the drinking act and of intoxication have had different meanings among the numerous societies.

Alcoholic drinks have been used for their food value, to quench thirst, and for medicinal purposes. For many people, the sharing of small amounts of an alcoholic beverage has been an accepted social act which improves group interaction and solidarity. Among others, the ability to consume large quantities has been a prestige symbol. Severe and prolonged intoxication in some primitive tribes was sanctioned as a form of spiritual experience which facilitates communion with the supernatural.

In some groups, intoxication produced a release of inhibitions characterized by a wide range of behavior extending from boisterousness and quarreling to extreme aggression and violation of every level of ordinary group norms of conduct. In primitive societies, individual drunkenness outside the ritual occasions did not appear. In others, drinking behavior not dissimilar from that which is today called alcoholism—behavior accompanied by physical ailments and psychological disorganization—was not uncommon.

It may be assumed that the action of alcohol in the human system was no different two thousand years ago than it is today. While it is probable that nutritional standards have varied considerably and the substitution of alcohol calories for other nutrients produced a greater incidence of polyneuropathy and other deficiency diseases in the past, the neurological response to different concentrations of alcohol has not changed perceptibly throughout the centuries.

Further evidence for this supposition can be found in the comments in the early literature regarding the severe effects of hangover. Complaints can be found that certain varieties of wine are more likely to produce acute headache than others. Apparently those who wished to consume large amounts of alcohol centuries ago could expect to pay a price in physical discomfort and suffering. Various remedies for relief of hangover have been handed down from one generation to another, but the hangover techniques were no better in 50 B.C. than they are today. Although the quality of the alcoholic beverages sold in modern times has been considerably improved, the human body protests when it is chemically abused.

A few societies were able to develop reasonably effective control over intoxication. The Spartans, a people with a strong military tradition who emphasized physical efficiency, issued a daily ration of wine to soldiers, but drunkenness was comparatively unknown. The early Romans and the Ethiopians were abstemious people. On the other hand, the Chinese and the Jews historically consumed substantial amounts of beverages containing alcohol, and intoxication must have occurred because of the warnings that were issued against it. Yet at no time did it become a serious threat to either of the groups. Indeed, the Chinese today regularly drink all types of alcoholic beverages, yet public drunkenness in New York's Chinatown is a comparative rarity, according to Barnett, and in no way a problem for the police. There are warnings against drunkenness in both the Old and New Testaments but there are parallel recommendations of the moderate use of wine. With the exception of a few rigoristic groups the concept of total abstinence is almost entirely absent in the early Hebraic and Christian tradition.

The Chopras, in their report on drinking customs in India, observe that nations long exposed to the effects of alcohol appear to have a relatively low rate of alcoholism. They refer particularly to the people of southern Europe along the Mediterranean Sea where alcohol addiction is considerably less frequent than in northern European countries. Certainly alcoholic excesses were common among the Greeks and Romans at one period of history although rates of alcoholism are low among Italians and Greeks today. But this interesting observation is contradicted by the evidence concerning the use of alcohol among the Chinese and the Jews—no newcomers to heavy drinking—and yet social control of inebriety has operated among them from the earliest times.

Exposure to the effects of alcohol unquestionably is a factor in the development of intoxication and extreme drinking behavior. But this is not sufficient to explain the kinds of controls that have emerged among some cultures and the failure of such controls to function in other countries, for example in the United States. Where there is a relatively close-knit homogeneous society with stable, well-integrated institutional patterns, the use of alcohol is incorporated in the institutional life and tends to reinforce social values and patterned behaviors. Conversely, as societies undergo change and become more diversified, values change and new norms of behavior emerge. These are often in conflict with the old. When drinking practices and intoxicated behavior are accepted by some groups within the society, they intensify the division. Because it is in conflict with the old patterns, the act of drinking acquires values which are reinforced by persistent drinking and defense of intoxication. When this challenge to traditional norms becomes identified also with systematic violation of the traditional moral standards, it emerges as a formalized pattern of behavior in its own right.

As drinking excesses begin to constitute a threat to social or ethical values an anti-drinking movement arises. Where those opposed to drinking are numerous and have sufficient status in the society, sanctions against drinking and against intoxication emerge and conformity may be enforced. This is characteristic of a simple society in which it is almost impossible to live without conforming. However, where the society is complex and where the anti-drinking group is loosely organized or in the minority, the sanctions against drinking they propose will not necessarily be effective among other groups within the society.

References to drinking and not drinking are misleading. Anacharsis, a Greek, is reported to have made the comment that the vine bears three kinds of grapes. The first is for pleasure, the next for intoxication, the third for disgust. There are certainly those individuals in every contemporary society who use small amounts of alcohol for pleasure. There are others for whom intoxication is the goal, and these and the alcoholics present problems associated with uncontrolled drinking. From another point of view it might be said that for some people the use of alcohol is always immoral. A second group drinks within a moral framework and rejects the principle advanced by the first group. A third group—some excessive drinkers and others who are not—drink outside a frame of moral principle; for them the act of drinking is amoral. Given these multiple facets surrounding drinking customs in a society such as ours, it is understandable that there has been difficulty in developing a constructive approach to some of the problems of alcohol.

In every age there have been men to speak out against the excesses of drunkenness. Plutarch did not hesitate to characterize himself as a water drinker. Socrates declared that one should not expect to find good friends in men addicted to the wine cup. Plato advocated moderation when he observed that hard drinking reveals the goodness of the good man and the rascality of the wicked. He believed that drinking teaches moderation by experience with excess and by purging the soul. So concerned was he about drunkenness among his countrymen that he was prepared to become a prohibitionist unless the state should make an orderly use of the institution of drinking bouts, taking it seriously and practicing it with a view to temperance.

Seneca expressed a wish for a war to jolt his countrymen out of their sensuality, contrasting a sober life with that of the drunken mob. He wrote of men who by reason of the almost numberless measures of wine they had drunk were nothing but wine strainers. Horace contented himself with a small portion of wine each day, but criticized his servant who complained that in the country he was denied the pleasures of the wine shop which he had sought in the city.

Students in every age have been characterized by an exuberance of spirits both emotional and alcoholic. Criticism of their behavior comes down even to the present day. But in our society, as Myerson pointed out, the criticism is mixed with a kind of tolerance among many observers. "Boys will be boys. It is well for them to sow their wild oats as early as possible and then to get down to business as adults." This tolerance, however, does not extend to women students.

Control of intoxication through prohibitory legislation has been tried in different societies since ancient times. In an effort to reduce the consumption of rice from which wines and beers were brewed, prohibition was decreed in China. However, the enforcement was not widely carried out. Indeed, the use of wine was not entirely prohibited, but only drinking parties of three or more persons. At a later period when the emperor became alarmed at the people's indulgence, he ordered a pamphlet printed and a form of education about alcohol was introduced to teach the ethics of wine drinking.

Many societies have experimented with legal control at one time or another. Where there has been a relatively homogeneous group, the degree of effectiveness of control has been greater than in more complex populations. Local option in sections of Finland and in some of the rural areas in this country has appeared to operate reasonably well. Those who advocate the policy insist that it is very effective and should be applied in other areas. Those in opposition assert that where local option prevails, bootlegging increases, the cost of liquor to the consumer rises, and low-quality, even toxic, beverages are consumed.

The constitutionality of prohibition on a state or national level has been challenged in the past on the ground that it invades the basic rights of the individual. But court decisions have established that there is no violation of constitutional rights.

The drys assert that where prohibition has been attempted on a broad scale there has never been adequate enforcement. Those who oppose legal controls insist that enforcement will always be impractical where a substantial segment of the population is opposed to such a law. Certainly the fluctuation of popular sentiment in support of, and later against, the elimination of alcoholic beverages by law has been such that serious doubt arises about the appropriateness of this approach to control of intoxication in a complex society.

A century of effort by the organized dry forces to turn the American public away from the use of alcoholic beverages has apparently produced a stalemate. It is difficult to determine to what degree the publicity and public relations activity of the liquor industry have contributed to this result. There is contradictory evidence on both sides. Certain gains are made from time to time in winning dry acceptance in local option elections, but this occurs chiefly in rural sections or in counties with a history of dry sentiment. The urban areas remain consistently wet. A Gallup Poll released April 1, 1957, indicated that 69 per cent of persons interviewed said they would oppose a law prohibiting the sale of alcoholic beverages nationally, 26 per cent would favor such a law, and 5 per cent were undecided. This indicates little change from 1933–34, when 70 per cent voted for repeal of the Eighteenth Amendment.

The drys have waged an active campaign to curtail liquor advertising, but consumption rates have been lower in the last decade, when advertising expenditures for beer, wine, and distilled spirits reached proportions never previously recorded. Per capita consumption of beer, which has been widely publicized on television during the last five or six years, has not shown a significant rise. High pressure advertising programs may reflect intense competition to maintain brand names in a stable market.

Those who oppose alcohol publicize statistics on arrests for drunkenness, accidents and fatalities connected with driving under the influence of liquor, divorce, crime, welfare and hospital costs attributed to intoxication. They contrast annual expenditures for alcoholic beverages with the much smaller amounts spent for maintenance of public schools and churches. These statistics are impressive and attention-getting. Some are valid; others are almost meaningless because drinking or drunkenness may be only one of several variables involved in a specific situation.

The average social drinker for whom drinking holds only minor importance sees little relationship between himself and those drinkers whose behavior is responsible for the social disturbances underlying the statistics. He is unable to accept the assertion made by the drys that he shares responsibility because he accepts the custom of drinking. When he is pressed, he rejects both the drys and the excessive drinker and leaves the resolution of the situation to others. Unfortunately there is no one to assume the responsibility.

The issues in our society posed by repeated intoxicated behavior are real. At the moment, no one is able to say just how extensive they are. Alcohol and drunkenness may be primary factors or only circumstantial. Divorce, crime, unemployment, indigency, or antisocial conduct in any form are multiphasic. Drinking may precipitate an episode in some cases, but it may provide only a rationalization for behavior in others.

Drinking to intoxication is sanctioned by some groups in our society, and this is not limited to the lower socioeconomic levels. Generally speaking, there has been no attempt to distinguish alcoholism from voluntary intoxication. The latter can be influenced by social pressure, even by legislative enactments (e.g., driving under the influence), but social attitudes and punitive action have had little constructive effect on the alcoholic.

Since 1945, 34 states have established facilities for the specialized treatment of alcoholism. Knowledge about causation of the disorder and technical skills in treatment are progressing. But there is little evidence of increasing understanding of means for preventing the illness in its early stages. This is primarily a matter of a change in group attitudes toward intoxication, a change that will attach disapproval rather than prestige to the consumption of substantial amounts of alcohol over extended periods of time and the associated behaviors.

The late Dr. Abraham Myerson declared that we need a new social tradition in which intoxication will be frowned upon. He stressed the importance of this tradition particularly for young people. But social traditions emerge slowly. An attitude of rejection of intoxication in one or more subgroups might contribute to reduction of at least some of the excesses which are presently associated with drunkenness. Obviously there can be no universally accepted pattern in our complex culture but the tradition might well operate with varying degrees of effectiveness at different social levels. To the extent that it operates reasonably well at one or more levels, it may become possible to localize those areas in which intoxication-caused social disturbances are most prevalent and as a consequence devise new techniques for reducing their severity.

It is difficult to visualize how such a social tradition can be generated in our society. The economic costs associated with drunkenness, the individual and social disorganization which occur, these and other elements have limited appeal to the majority of users of alcoholic beverages. Progress will not emerge merely on an economic level. Indeed, the charges and countercharges at this level are responsible for the stalemate which has occurred. The major problem which exists centers on the fact that we have not defined problems of alcohol and intoxication. We have talked about them as though they have been defined, we have introduced resolutions to correct some of the conditions without always recognizing that these are surface elements in an extremely complicated social pattern.

According to Thorner,[1] at the root of the prohibition drive is a moral philosophy based on asceticism, although the focus and activity in recent years have been on the social disorders resulting from excessive drinking. Thorner refers to the prohibition leadership of the ascetic Protestant churches in this country as follows:

1. Isidor Thorner, "Ascetic Protestantism and Alcoholism," *Psychiatry, 16* (1953), 169–70.

The pharmacological effects of alcohol, when viewed in relation to the psychological structures and personality ideals of ascetic Protestants in general and Christian Scientists in particular, suggest an explanation for the attitudes of these groups toward alcohol. Alcohol is a central nervous system depressant. Among the induced psychic changes are an increase of confidence, blunting of memory, removal of inhibitions, and a tendency to impulsive action. There is no good reason why ascetic Protestants should object either to an increase of confidence or to a blunting of memories if they are unpleasant. But there is reason indeed for anxiety feelings about the removal of inhibitions and the tendency toward impulsive action. This is true to the degree that the ideal-typical personality is based upon inhibition, distrust of impulse, and deliberate control of the affective life in behalf of a rational organization of action oriented toward some kind of achievement. The incautious use of alcohol tends to interfere with achievement, especially when close coordination is required. More importantly, however, alcohol is feared because release from rational control of life, the freeing of impulse, and the venting of inhibition and repressed aggressions are tempting in the degree that they are strenuously avoided. Because the temptations are so dangerous and the consequences so devastating in terms of the personality ideal, the ascetic Protestant tends to take an uncompromising position against the use of alcohol. . . .

It is because of the profound importance of emotional control that ascetic Protestants manifest moral and emotional intensity in their roles as prohibitionists. They experience misgivings over breaches in discipline, and interpret submission to the "appetites" as a sign of moral weakness. Tobacco and liquor are felt to be chinks in the armor of impulse control, faults that open the gate to delinquency and hinder social and moral improvement, impediments to the creation of the City of God on earth. The backbone of the temperance movement is made up of the more fundamentalist ascetic Protestant sects. While the financial, economic, social, and moral costs of alcoholism figure prominently in the temperance campaign, the psychological appeal is primarily to the basic value-attitude which holds emotional discipline to be a great good in itself and to the anxiety aroused by threats of impairment to this discipline. In addition, there may well be some element of hidden envy of those who do relax their discipline.

Thorner's interpretation of the prohibition movement leaves the fundamental issue one of morality. The drinker and the drunkard, the manufacturer and the seller of liquor, and all who participate or profit in any manner constitute a threat to the moral life with which there can be no compromise. This takes on the characteristics of a crusade and because of the moral element, an individual must either join or be considered an opponent.

Obviously these rigid lines do not operate generally. Although prohibition is a form of Protestant energy,

It is [according to Thorner] a form of energy not of *all* Protestants but only of *ascetic* Protestants, not of Lutherans, Episcopalians, and Anglicans. If the Episcopalians do not show much enthusiasm for prohibition (like the Roman Catholics and the Jews, for that matter) and are called "tissue-paper Catholics," it is in part because prohibition does not have for them the same psychological and moral significance. Again, prohibition is frequent among rural and village people; yet this is not a characteristic of the less urban areas as such, but appears because ascetic Protestantism is stronger in those areas. Nor can economic and political factors satisfactorily explain the motivation of prohibitionists.

There exists a gradient in morals with respect to drinking among the several churches which generally subscribe to a code of absolute morality. A conflict as fundamental as this appears to offer minimal prospect of compromise. Those who are psychologically and morally moved to challenge drinking customs and the alcoholic-beverage industry find little formal support among their religious confreres who see drinking as a matter of individual judgment and conscience—not an issue of social morality.

This results in the anomaly of a set of social problems for which there is no acceptable spokesman. A century and a half ago, Dr. Benjamin Rush and later Reverend Lyman Beecher raised their voices in protest against drunkenness. Neither would be listened to today by temperance leaders because they denounced drunkenness, not drinking.

It is true that the temperance forces sought to improve conditions in the early 19th century by moral suasion and appeal to the dignity of the individual. This approach was ineffective in a young, mobile nation in which social, political, and religious changes were taking place rapidly. But the emergence of the American pledge of total abstinence based on the interpretation of unfermented Biblical wines introduced an entirely new element in the temperance drive which culminated in legislative pressure to eliminate all drinking. The ineffectiveness of this approach has been demonstrated in the history of the last half-century.

Notwithstanding all of the publicity regarding the problems of alcohol, we have not yet defined what we mean. Obviously, there are different meanings for different people, but these are impressionistic, oversimplified, or specific to a local situation or area. In reality, we know little about social drinking or its relation to problems of intoxication. The act of drinking is a learned experience but we have only certain assumptions about the process. What are the dynamics underlying the total abstinence position today? What is the nature of the defensive hostility expressed on the one hand by some drinkers toward abstainers, and on the other by temperance followers toward users of alcohol? We have opinions about the surface patterns. We need understanding of the underlying motivations.

There exists at the present time no agency equipped to explore these questions. The state alcoholic-beverage control authorities serve chiefly as regulatory and revenue collection bodies. State and municipal health officers conduct programs of prevention and treatment for certain types of chronic diseases, including, to some extent, the treatment of alcoholism. But intoxication among excessive drinkers who are not alcoholics is not an illness, and the health agencies leave responsibility for dealing with such cases to the police and correctional officers.

The problem of intoxication has many ramifications which complicate any approach to it. In Sweden and Finland, government supported research centers are studying alcoholism and also problems of drinking and intoxication. The objective is control, not prohibition. Not one of the state-supported alcoholism treatment agencies in this country has a responsibility for intoxication-produced problems. Many are organizing programs of education, but the emphasis is on education for the prevention of alcoholism. Perhaps this marks the extent of responsibility for a government agency. But the wider responsibility still is present—and as yet has not been assumed.

Some systematized and controlled approach to understanding of attitudes toward drinking and intoxication is imperative before any real improvement can be expected. Research techniques for evaluating patterns of attitudes at the community level have been devised by social scientists. A multidiscipline research team, adequately financed and operating independently of any special interest group, should be assembled with responsibility for developing and testing a series of hypotheses regarding drinking practices and attitudes in several communities or sections of communities. The origin, strength, patterns, reinforcing agents, and sanctions for intoxication should be explored. At the same time, techniques for modifying attitudes which might lead to some degree of control of intoxication can be investigated.

The recruiting of staff, determination and testing of methodology, and development of suitable research instruments will be a long-range process. Moreover, the climate in which the project will operate may be one of suspicion on the part of participants directed toward the research team. But this is the essential material to be studied—the resistances, hostilities, defensiveness, and misunderstandings concerning drinking habits and attitudes. Unless such research is conducted and rational concepts are tested and applied, little change can be expected. This would mean that only organizations and individuals with vested interests will be active, with a continuation of the stalemate that has existed for years.

Social attitudes change slowly, but they do change. The history of

the tuberculosis movement illustrates this. Fifty years ago, it was considered a disgrace to contract the disease, and patients and their families concealed the condition as long as possible. Today mass X-ray surveys are conducted in schools, industrial plants, and even on street corners. Prevention and diagnosis in the early stages are the watchword. Public attitudes have changed and public cooperation is excellent.

Restrictive legislation, authoritarian fiat, appeals to intelligence or to spiritual motive, increased retail prices for various beverages, arrests and sentences for drunkenness, revocation of license for driving under the influence, increased taxation on the beverage industry—these and countless other maneuvers have been attempted. This is a piecemeal approach to a complex problem in a complex social structure. As yet, no one has defined the total problem which essentially is interwoven with the culture patterns of our society. Control of intoxication will emerge only after acceptance of responsibility by the society in which the condition originates. The development of a system of social controls is a job of social engineering. It will not be achieved by well-meaning pressure groups.

INDEX

A.A. *See* Alcoholics Anonymous

Abolition, 400

Abstinence, 221, 267–8, 327; stressed by Buddha, 124. *See also* Prohibition, Temperance

Addict, drug. *See* Drug addiction; Intoxication, by opiates

Adolescents, drinking by. *See* College; High school

Africa, Africans, 107

Age, of drinkers, 161–2, 174, 179, 182, 198, 205–30, 234, 242–3

Aguardiente, 74, 94–5

Alcohol: addiction-producing or habit-forming, 26; and aggression, 255–9, 264; as analgesic, narcotic, and hypnotic, 26; as anesthetic, 1, 12, 17, 26, 309; consumption statistics, 152, 170, 172–3, (Canada) 171, 173, (France) 152, (U.S.) 180–1; and culture, 260–2; derivation of the word, 42; education about, 168–9; as food, 109; industry, 154; Japanese myth of origin, 125; kinds of beverages, 7–8 (*see also* Beverages, varieties); knowledge about effects of, 201–2; as medicine, 16–7, 42–3, 90, 108–9, 154–5, 267; motivation for use of, 2 (*see also* Motivation); as sedative, 1, 26, 253–5; use in primitive societies, 254–5. *See also* Physiological action of alcohol; Psychological action of alcohol

Alcoholics, 30–4: among Chinese, 131; cultural milieu, 292, 294–6; compared with drug users, 28 ff.; economic adjustment, 292; female, 287; among Jews, 273 n., 302, 309–11; marital adjustment, 294; motivation for drinking, 295; personality characteristics, 288 ff., 298–305; personality pattern, 296–7; pseudoadjustment to life, 1; psychocultural analysis of, 287–97; psychogenetic factors, 290–7; in Santiago, 101 ff.; sexual factor, 292–4; on Skid Row, 313–23 (*see also* Skid Row); social factors, 298–305; symbols of

status, 293–4; types, 27. *See also* Alcoholism

Alcoholics Anonymous, 129, 203–4, 332, 335–7

Alcoholism, 91, 231: ambivalence of hedonism and asceticism as explanation of, 306–12; attitudes affecting rates of, 267–77; in Canada, 171–3; in Chamula, 81 ff., 278–86; in Central America, 73 ff.; cultural differences in rates of, 263–77; disease concept, antagonism to, 335–8; and drug addiction, 276, 298–305; in England, 160–1; and escapism, 310; and ethics, 330–8; ethnography, 278–86; etiology, 287–8, 298–9; factors facilitating (in Russia), 146–7; in France, 153–8; and homosexuality, 287–8, 293; in India, 111–3; among Indians of Chamula, 81 ff., 278–86; among the Irish, 265, 276; among Jews, 273 n., 302, 309–11; knowledge about, 202–4; legal responsibility, 334–5; and occupation, 276; prevention and control, 312; rates in various countries, 172–3; relief of anxiety as factor, 263–4; in Russia, 140 ff.; in Santiago, 99–105; sex ratio, 105, 309–11; and sin, 331–4; social pressure in development of, 310; and inner tensions, 267; utilitarian attitude toward drinking, 275. *See also* Alcoholics

Algaroba beer, 87–8

Algeria, wine from, 149

Alvarado, R., 99–105

Antabuse, action of, 9

Anti-Saloon League, 370, 374–5, 377

Arabs, wine poetry of, 67–8

Argentina, 87

Armagnac, 150

Association Against the Prohibition Amendment, 379–80

Assyria, royalty drinking wine in, *facing* 68

Athens. *See* Greece

Atole, 76, 81

447

Attitudes, 206–7, 215, 252 ff.: about abstinence, 268; alcohol and good fellowship, 307–8; alcohol and immorality, 308; of churches and churchmen, 324–41; toward drinking (England), 167–8; toward drunkenness, 199; effect on rates of alcoholism, 267–77; ritualistic, 269–70; utilitarian, 273–6. *See also* Motivation; Prohibition
Australia, 107
Authors and Artists Committee, 380
Aztecs: drinking and religious worship, 73–4; secular drinking, 74

Bacon, S. D., 208, 219–30
Balearic Islanders, abstinence of, 64
Bales, R. F., 263–77
Bali, Balinese, 273, 276, *facing* 69
Barnett, M. L., 123–4
Bastide, H., 158–9
Baur, E. J., 211–8
Bayeux Cathedral tapestry, *facing* 160
Beer, 179, 350: as gruel, 112
Belgium, compared with other countries, 172–3
Beverages, alcoholic, 8, 42: Assyrian royalty drinking wine, *facing* 68; ceremonial use of, 123–5, 127–8, 267 (*see also under names of countries*); comparison of drinkers by type of, 179–80, 183, 193, 212; consumption statistics, 151–2, 161, 170–2; Egypt, beer brewing, *facing* 38; Egypt, grape harvesting, *facing* 39; in France, 149–51; Japanese myth of origin, 125; employment as medicine, 16–7, 42–3, 154–5; processes of preparation, 88–9; religious use, 342, *facing* 114, 115, 248, 249; in Russia, 130 ff.; substances used in making Chinese wine, 113; types used by New York City Cantonese, 123; used by South American Indians, 86–91; use of beer in "Ultima Thule," 63–4; wine making in Egypt, *facing* 39; wine watered by Greeks, 48–9 n.
Beverages, varieties: aguardiente, 74, 94, 95; algaroba beer, 87–8; Armagnac, 150; atole, 76, 81; beer, 179, 350, as gruel, 112; brandy, 43; Calvados, 150–1; Canadian whisky, 123; chi, 258; chicha, 76, 94–5; cider, 149; cognac, 123, 150; distilled spirits, 43; gouri,

106; Jagla, 106; kashiri, 86; kawim, 86; kawin, 86; Khola, 106; kirsch, 150; koumiss (kumys), 42, 137; kvas, 130; laopani, 112; madur, 106; madya, 106; massato, 86; mead, 42, 88; pachwai, 111–2; paishti, 106; paiwari, 86; palm wine, 87, 107; potato spirit, 347; rum, 151; sake, 106, 124; sansankudo, 127; Scotch whisky, 123; shamshu, 106; shaoshing, 115; shirozake, 127; soma, 106; sura, 106; tari, 40, 111; toso, 127; tsieu, 113–4; vodka, 134 ff.; whisky, 43, 123; wine, 42; zu, 109
Bible, attitudes toward drinking in, 68–9, 326–7
Binkley, O. T., 325–30
Bloch, H. A., 2
Bolivia, 87
Bootlegging, 136, 140
Brahmins, 276
Brandy, 43
Bratt system (Sweden), 348 ff.
Brazil, 87
British Temperance League, 169
Bunzel, R., 73–86, 278–86
Byzantium, 51

Calvados, 150-1
Canada, Canadians, 170–5: alcoholism, 171–3; changes in drinking tastes, 170; drinking in, compared with other countries, 170–4
Canadian whisky, 123
Carpenter, J. A., 23
Carthage, Carthaginians: hard drinking of, 64; limited drinking by soldiers, 39
Catholics, 174
Central America, 73–86, 278–86
Chaldeans, restrictions on selling wine, 67
Chamula, Mexico, 278–86: drinking at fiestas, 82; drinking a social act, 82–3; drunkenness in, 81–4; stages of intoxication, 83–4
Chappell, M., 208
Chi, 258
Chicha, 76, 94–5
Chichicastenango (Guatemala), 75–81, 282 ff.: drinking ceremonies of the fiestas, 76, of the zarabandas, 76–9; drinking confined to market days and festivals, 75–6; results of drunkenness, 78–81

Chile, 87, 89, 99–105
China, Chinese, 113–24: alcoholics, 121; alcoholism and drug addiction compared, 122 n.; ceremonial wine ladle, *facing* 115; ceremonial wine vessel, *facing* 114; drinking by New York City Cantonese, 123–4; early regulation of drinking in, 39–40; food, 120–1; intoxication, 113; prohibition, 118–9; temperance, 113, 117–8; wine-drinking customs, 114–20; wine games, 119–20; wine-making, 113–4
Chopra, G. S., 106–13
Chopra, I. C., 106–13
Chopra, R. N., 106–13
Churches, and drinking, 174, 325–30
Cider, 149
Clark, C. D., 211–8
Clinebell, H. J., Jr., 330–8
Cognac, 123, 150
College, drinking and drinkers in, 219–30: abstainers, 221–4; administrative policy, 224–6; advice to students, 221–2; age, 221; attitudes, 225; frequency and incidence, 219, 222; motivation, 222–4, 226–9; parental influence, 221, 222; religious affiliation, 220, 223–4, 230; socioeconomic factors, 219, 224
Colombia, 86–7
Conger, J. J., 22–3
Connor, R., 313–23
Control of drinking, legal and social, 345–435: in Finland, 356–67; the new prohibition drive, 412–28; in Russia, 134 ff.; supplementary readings, 435; in Sweden, 347–56; systems, 429–34; in the United States, 369–97; Woman's Christian Temperance Union, 398–411. *See also* Prohibition; Temperance
Cooper, J. M., 86–91
Costa Rica, 88
Crimes, related to drinking, 142–4, 146–7
Crusaders (repeal group), 380
Customs and practices, drinking, 39–178: supplementary readings, 175, 246. *See also* Drinking customs, ancient; Drinking customs, modern

Dacia, 70
Denmark, 172–3
Dionysos, *facing* 248
Distilled spirits, 43

Distillery, medieval, *facing* 161
Douglass, E. M., 205, 369–82, 429–34
Drinking: ages of drinkers, 161–2, 174, 179, 182, 198, 205–30, 234, 242–3; and aggression, 255–9; American habits, 2; by Andean Indians, 91–9; Assyrian royalty, *facing* 68; attitudes, 167–8, 252, 263, 307–8; in Bible, 68–9, 326–7; before breakfast, 102–3; in Canada, 170–5; by Cantonese of New York City, 123–4; Catholic doctrine, 327; by Central American Indians, 73–86; ceremonial, 283; by Chinese, 113–24; Chinese wine games, 119–20; climatic factor (in India), 107; in college, 219–30 (*see also* College); cultural factors, 249 ff., 294–6 (supplementary readings, 342); as custom, 1, 13, 251 ff.; and delinquency and crime (in Russia), 141–4; and driving, 397; and education, 174, 243; in England, 160–9; ethical factors, 249 ff. (supplementary readings, 342); ethnic factor, 268 ff.; ethnological factors (in India), 106–7; European habits, 2; in Finland, 356–67; in France, 149–59; frequency, 107–12, 235, (in England) 161; frequency by size of community, 185, 188, 196; frequency of individual imbibing, 75, 81–3, 95–6, 101–5; heritage of, 42–3; in high school, 205–18 (*see also* High school); Hollanders in Bali, *facing* 69; in India, 106–7; Indian ruler, *facing* 69; inhabitants of Mediterranean Basin, 71; by Irish, 265–6; Japanese customs, 124–5, 127–9; and morality, 324–41; motivation, 108–11, (in Russia) 148; motivational patterns, 231–8, 252–62; nativity background, 174; ancient Nordic attitude, 72; and occupation, 276, (in India) 108; practices, 39–178 (*see also* Drinking customs, ancient; Drinking customs, modern); parental influence, 207, 209, 213, 216, 221, 241–5; Protestant attitudes, 327–9; and race, 106–7; religious factors, 174, 249 ff., 267–8 (supplementary readings, 342); religious and social factors (in India), 107–8; in Russia, 130–48 (*see also* Russia); and sexual activity, 77, 97–8; size of community, 174; social differences (U.S. and Canada), 174; and socioeconomic groups,

Drinking (continued)
174; statistics (see names of countries);
substitute means of adjustment, 276–7;
in Sweden, 347–56 (see also Sweden);
and temperance, 107; in the United
States, 179–246 (see also United
States); urban vs. rural background,
244; in Washington State, 190–204; by
women (see Women, drinking by).
See also Alcoholics; Alcoholism; Control of drinking; Drunkenness; Intoxication; Motivation; Prohibition
"Drinking age population," 179
Drinking customs, ancient: Africa, 64–6;
Arabia, 67–8; Assyria, 67; Babylonia,
67; Carthaginians, 64; Dacia, 70;
Egypt, 65–6; Ethiopia, 65; Gaul, 62–
3; Goths and Vandals, 70–1; Greece,
44–53; Hittites, 67; Huns, 71; Jews of
the Bible, 68–9; Liguria, 63; Mesopotamia, 67; Numidia, 64; Persia, 69–70;
Portugal, 63; Rome, 53–61; Scythia,
70; Semites, 67; Spain, 63; "Ultima
Thule," 63
Drinking customs, modern: Canada,
170–4; Central and South America,
73–105; China, Chinese, 113–24; Eng-
land, 160–9; France, 149–59; India,
106–13; Japan, 124–9; Russia, 130–48;
United States, 179–245
Drug addiction, 26 ff., 276, 298 ff.: compared with alcoholism, 30 ff.
Drunkenness, 269: arrests for, 365; con-
victions for, 353–4, 356. See also
Alcoholics; Alcoholism; Drinking; In-
toxication; Skid Row
Drys. See Wets vs. drys
DuPont, I., 392
DuPont, P. S., 388–92, 393–5
Durant, W. C., 396

Ebers Papyrus (1500 B.C.), references to
beer and wine in, 1
Ecuador, 86
Education, 243: as factor in drinking,
174, 185–6, 188, 197–8, 205–18, 219–
30. See also College; High school
Efron, V., 130–41
Egypt, ancient, 39: beer brewing, facing
38; drinking, 65–6; drinking by women,
65; grape harvesting, facing 39;
Hathor, the wine goddess, 65; Osiris
the god of the vine and wine, 42;

student drinking, 66; wine making,
facing 39
Eighteenth amendment, 207, 371, 375,
380 ff., 385, 405: administration, 377–
9; passage, 375–7. See also Prohibition
England, 107, 160–9: attitudes toward
drinking, 167–8; bars, 164–5; convictions for drunkenness, 160; drinking
habits, 160–2; education about alcohol,
168–9; frequency of drinking, 161;
licensed premises, 163; public houses,
165–7; registered clubs, 162–3
Enriquez, W., 99–105
Eskimos, 107
Ethiopia, temperance in, 39, 65

Far East, 106–29: China, 113–22; India,
106–12; Japan, 124–9
Feldman, H., 396–7
Field, M. G., 141–8
Finland, 377: arrests for drunkenness,
365; compared with other countries,
172; consumption per capita, 364–5;
government alcohol monopoly, 364;
labor and prohibition, 359–61; new
alcohol legislation, 363–4; present tendencies, 364–5; background of prohibition, 356–9; consequences of prohibition, 362
Finnish Foundation for Alcohol Studies,
365, 367
Fisher, I., 388–97
Ford, H., 395
Ford, J. C., 330
Foreign-born drinkers, in the U.S., 195
France, 107, 149–59: alcoholism, 153–8;
brandies, 150; Calvados consumption,
151; cider in Normandy, 149–50; compared with other countries, 172–3; consumption per capita, 152, 158–9; drinking problems, 156–7; Government
Alcohol Agency, 151–2; liquor expenditures, 152; prevalence of drinking,
154; public houses, 152–3; public
opinion on drinking, 158–9; smuggling
brandy, 150; overproduction of wine,
149

Gaul, Gauls: penalties of intemperance,
63; restrictions on planting vineyards,
40; effect of wine on, 39; introduction
of wine, 62–3
Gerard, D. L., 26–34, 298–305

Germans, ancient: fondness for alcoholic drinks, 70–1; law against importation of wine, 71

Gilchrist, D. R., 210

Gothenburg system (Sweden), 348 ff.

Goths, 71

Gouri, 106

Greece, 107: Attic states, 44–51; Bacchus, 42; comparison of city-states in respect to drinking, 50; extent of drinking, 44 ff.; non-Attic states, 51–3; Spartan abstemiousness, 49–50; symposia, 39, 48–9; composition of wines, 42; wine in religion, *facing* 248, 342

Greenberg, L. A., 7–13

Group influence, 239–45

Grüss, J., 71

Guatemala, 73–81

Guianas, 87–8, 90

Gusfield, J. R., 398–411

Haer, J. L., 239–45

Haggard, H. W., 338–41

Hallowell, A. I., 264

High school, drinking and drinkers, 205–18: ages, 205, 208–10, 213–4, 218; attitudes, 206–7, 215; behavior patterns, 215–8; cultural differences, 215–6; frequency and incidence, 205 ff.; at home and away, 213; Kansas study, 208 ff.; kinds of beverages, 212; Nassau County study, 208 ff.; parental influence, 209, 213; Racine County study, 208 ff.; religious groups, 207, 214, 216; size of community, 213; social controls, 217–8; "socialization," 216–7; socioeconomic factors, 214; Utah study, 207–8; Washington, D.C., study, 205–7

Hittites, fondness for wine, 67

Holland, drinking glass from, *facing* 342

Honduras, 86–7, 89

Horton, D., 1, 251–62, 265–6

Huns, 71

Iberians, abstinence of, 64

Iceland, 377

Incas, 94

Independent Order of Good Templars, 369

India, 40, 106–13: aboriginal races, 107; alcohol as a euphoric, 110; alcoholic beverages of, 106; climate and drinking, 107; drinking for food value, 109; ethnological factors, 106–7; medicinal use of alcohol, 108–9; motivation for drinking, 110–1; occupational factor, 108; religious and social factors, 107–8; ruler feasting and drinking, *facing* 69; use of tari and pachwai, 111–2

Indians, of Central and South America. *See* Chamula; Chichicastenango; Chile; Peru

Indians, Mexican, 278–86

Indians, North American, 107, 254, 258–60, 264, 270, 277

Inebriety. *See* Intoxication, alcohol

Intemperance, of Greeks, 44 ff.

International Order of Good Templars, 370

Intoxication, alcohol, 273: Andean Indians, 93–4; attitudes toward, 199–200; Canada, 171–3; Chamula, 81–6; Chichicastenango, 78–81; Chinese, 113, 117; convictions (Canada), 171–2; England, 160 ff.; events leading to, 27–8; India, 111–3; Northeastern American Indians, 264; South American Indians, 89–90; Irish, 265; comparison with opiate intoxication, 30 ff.; Rome, 1; early Russia, 131; Santiago, 99 ff.; World Health Organization report, 26. *See also* Alcoholics; Alcoholism; Drinking; Drunkenness; Intemperance

Intoxication, by opiates: effects of chronic opiate use, 32–3; stages of, 28

Ireland, Irish, 265, 274–6, 402: compared with other countries, 172

Italy, 107: compared with other countries, 172–3

Jackson, J. K., 313–23

Jagla, 106

Japan, 124–9: Confucian teaching about drinking, 124; custom of drinking toso, 127; historical review of drinking, 126–7; modern drinking customs, 128–9; myth of origin of alcoholic beverages, 125; prohibition in, 125 ff.; sake, 124–5, 127–8; temperance in, 126 ff.

Japanese National W.C.T.U., 129

Japan Temperance Union, 129

Jellinek, E. M., 18, 21, 103–4, 333, 431

Jews, 68–9, 107, 174, 269–73, 302, 309 ff., *facing*, 249, 342

Johns, C. H. W., 67
Juvenile delinquency, in Russia, 141–2

Kashiri, 86
Kawim, 86
Kawin, 86
Keller, M. 13–7, 105
Khola, 106
Kirby, B. C., 383–8
Kirsch, 150
Knight, R. P., 27
Koumiss (Kumys), 42
Kvas, 130

La Barre, W. 120–2
Laopani, 112
Lapland, 366
Lavers, G. R., 160–9
Lee, A. M., 412–28
Lepchas, of India, 257
Lifshitz, M., 231–8
Ligurians, abstinence of, 64
Lisansky, E. S., 18–25

McCarthy, R. G., 18–25, 205–11, 369–82, 429–34
McCluggage, M. M., 211–8
Macedonia, 51–3
McFarland, R. A., 18, 21
McKinlay, A. P., 44–72
Madur, 106
Madya, 106
Mangin, W., 91–9
Marchesse, I., 99–105
Marconi, J., 99–105
Marcus, M., 347–55
Marden, C. F., 182–9, 231–8
Massato, 86
Masserman, J. H., 22
Maxwell, M. A., 190–204
Mead, 42, 88
Mesopotamia, drinking, 67
Mexico, 278–86
Moore, M., 114–20
Moors, abstemiousness of, 64
Morality and alcohol: attitudes of the churches, 325–30; alcoholism, 330–8
Moslems, 268, 276
Motivation, 200–1, 215, 226–9, 231–8: of abstainers, 201, 215, 220–4; age as fac-

tor, 234–5, 242–3; aggressive impulses, 255–9, 264; anxiety, 252–5, 263–4; of alcoholics, 295; business courtesy, 232; celebrations, 232–3; convivial drinking, 273–4, 307–8; education as factor, 243; euphoric effect, 232 ff.; influence of family and friends, 239–45; and frequency of drinking, 235; liking for taste, effect, etc., 232–3; parental influence, 207, 213, 216, 221; relaxation, 234; ritual, 267, 269–73; sex, 234–6, 241–2; sociability, 232–3, 236; social ritual, 267; social vs. individual reasons, 232 ff., 267; stimulating appetite or digestion, 232–3; taboos against drinking, 267, 273, 275; thirst, 232–3; urban vs. rural background as factor, 244; utilitarian purposes, 267, 273–4; in wet and dry areas, 237
Mouchot, G., 40, 149–59
Mowrer, H. R., 287–97
Muller, M., 106
Myerson, A., 306–12

National Committee for Education on Alcoholism, 238
National Prohibition Party, 371–2
Netherlands, compared with other countries, 172
Nicaragua, 86
Norway, compared with other countries, 172
Numidia, temperance in, 64

Oberlin Temperance Alliance, 374
Occupation, as factor in drinking, 195
Ohio Anti-Saloon League, 374
Opiates, use of, by Chinese, 122 n. See also Drug addiction; Intoxication, by opiates
Order of Good Templars, 371

Pachwai, 111–2
Paishti, 106
Paiwari, 86
Palm wine, 87, 107
Panama, 90
Paraguay, 87
Parental influence on children's drinking, 207, 209, 213, 216, 221, 241–5

Patterns of drinking, 182 ff.
Persia, 39, 69–70
Peru, 86, 91–9
Physiological action of alcohol, 7–17: blood, 9; brain, 11–2; chemistry of alcohol in the body, 9; energy from alcohol, 15; as food, 10–1; glands, 13–4; heart and circulation, 15; individual tolerance, 12–3; kidneys, 13; length of life, 15–6; lethal concentration, 12; liver, 12; nervous system, 11–2; rate of oxidation, 9; stomach, 8, 10; supplementary readings, 35; tissues, 10
Popham, R. E., 170–5
Portugal, ancient, 39, 107
Potato spirit, 347
Poznanski, A., 42–3
Prohibition, 181, 268, 340, 346, 354: in China, 118; in Finland, 356–67, 377; in Iceland, 377; in early Japan, 125, 127; in modern Japan, 129; in Russia, 377; in the United States (criticisms of) 378–9, 383–6, (early state laws) 370–1, (failure of) 379, (history of) 369–82, (industrialists' opinions on) 388–97, (logic of) 383–8, (new drive toward) 412–28, (repeal movement) 379–81, (requisites for success) 386–7. See also Eighteenth amendment; Temperance
Prohibition drive, "new" compared with earlier drives, 413–21: groups involved, 421–3; philosophies of the groups, 423–5; major strategies, 412–3; tactics, 425–7
Protestants, 174
Pryzhov, I. G., 130 ff.
Psychological action of alcohol, 18–25: auditory discrimination, 19; emotional behavior, 22–5; non-emotional behavior, 18–22; higher-order intellectual functioning, 21–2; impairment of judgment, 21; muscular strength, 20; speculative conclusions, 24–5; tactile sensation, 19–20; typing, 20–1; word association, 21; supplementary readings, 35

Races, temperate, 107
Rado, S., 29
Raskob, J. J., 392–3

Reasons for drinking. See Motivation
Religions, and drinking, 174. See also names of religions
Riley, J. W., Jr., 182–9, 231–8
Robinson, C. E., 44
Roe, A., 22
Rome: abstemiousness, 53–4; attitude toward drinking by women, 58–61; attitude toward excessive drinking, 1; Bacchus, 42; debauchery, 54–8
Rosenblat, E., 99–105
Rowntree, B., 160–9
Rum, 151
Rural vs. urban drinkers, 179, 185, 188, 216
Russia, 107, 130–48: crime and delinquency, 141–4; cultural importance of alcoholic beverages, 130; current drinking, 141–8; drinking by farmers, 144–5; drinking houses, 132 ff.; drunkenness, 131, 138; historical outline of drinking, 131–41; prohibition in, 377; Pryzhov source of information, 130; proposed remedies for drinking problems, 147–8; saloons, 134–40; Soviet explanation for alcoholism, 145–6; temperance organizations, 141

Sake, 106, 124
Saloons: in Montreal, facing 405; in Russia, 130 ff.
Sansankudo, 127
Santiago, Chile, 99–105
Saracens, abstemiousness of, 65
Sariola, S., 356–67
Scandinavia, 107
Scientific Temperance Federation of Boston, 375
Scotch whisky, 123
Scott, R. H., 395
Scythia, 70
Sex, of drinkers. See Women, drinking by
Seymour, T. D., 44, 50
Shamshu, 106
Shaoshing, 115
Shirozake, 127
Sin, and alcoholism, 331–4
Skid Road. See Skid Row
Skid Row, 313–23: "hitting" the Road, 317–22; functions of the lush groups,

Skid Row (continued)
315–7; rehabilitation, 322–3; social segments, 314–5
Skutin, A., 355–6
Slater, A. D., 207–8
Sloan, A. P., Jr., 395
Socioeconomic factors, 185–6, 188, 199, 207, 214, 216, 219
Solari, G., 99–105
Soma, 106
Sons of Temperance, 369
South America, 86–105: drinking in, 89–90; reasons for Indian drinking, 90–1
Spain, 39, 107: abstinence in, 64
Sparta. See Greece
Speakeasy, in Colorado, facing 404
Spirits. See Alcohol; Beverages, alcoholic; Beverages, varieties; Potato spirits
Stockholm system (Sweden), 351
Stoeckel, R., 397
Straus, R., 208, 219–30
Sumeria, libation ewer from, facing 114
Sura, 106
Sweden, Swedish, 347–56: beer, 350–1; Bratt system, 348 ff.; compared with other countries, 172–3; controls on restaurant drinking, 352; convictions for drunkenness, 353–4, 356; drinking horn, facing 115; Gothenburg system, 348 ff.; liquor control system, 347–55; permit books, 351; prices of spirits, 351; Stockholm system, 351; system companies, 352; Temperance Boards, 355–6; wholesale liquor company, 352–3
Switzerland, compared with other countries, 172–3

Tari, 40, 111
Tartars, 42
Tasmania, method for making fermented liquor in, 42
Temperance, 327–8, 354: attitudes, 167, 169; Chinese, 113, 117–8; Confucius, 124; definitions, 381; fraternal orders, 369–70; in Japan, 126–7, 129; organizations in Russia, 141; in Sweden, 347 ff. See also Abstinence; Prohibition; Woman's Christian Temperance Union
Tierra del Fuego, 86
Toso, 127

Tsieu, 113–4
Twenty-first amendment, 429
Tyrrhenians, hard drinking of, 64

United Kingdom, compared with other countries, 170, 172–3. See also England
United States, drinking and drinkers in, 179–245: abstainers, 179, 188, 215, 219; age of drinkers, 179, 182, 198, 205–30, 242; attitudes toward drinking, 199–200, 206–7, 215, toward drunkenness, 199; beverages used, 179–80, 183, 193, 212; college, 219–30 (see also College); compared with other countries, 170, 172–4, 179–82, 188, 191; consumption statistics, 170, 172–4, 179–82, 188, 191; "drinking-age" population, 179; drinking patterns, 182 ff., 240–4; economic factors, 186, 188, 207, 214, 219; education as factor, 185–6, 188, 197–8, 205–30 (see also College; High school); frequency, 183, 188, 191–2, 205 ff.; by size of community, 185, 188, 196; geographical areas, 179, 188; group influences, 239–45; high school, 205–18 (see also High school); incidence of drinking, 179 ff., 191; knowledge about alcohol and related problems, 201–4; motivation of abstainers, 201, 215, 220–4; motivation of drinkers, 200–1, 215, 226–9; motivational patterns, 231–8; native and foreign-born drinkers, 195; occupations, 195; influence of parents on children, 207, 213, 216, 221; places for drinking, 194; prohibition, 369–82; new prohibition drive, 412–28; races, 186, 188, 412–28; religious differences, 186–9, 197, 207, 214, 216, 220–1, 223–4; socioeconomic differences, 185–6, 188, 199, 207, 216, 219; state monopoly plans for sale of alcoholic beverages, 430; state license systems for sale of alcoholic beverages, 430; urban and rural differences, 179, 185, 188, 216; Washington State, 190–204; Woman's Christian Temperance Union, 398–411; women, 179, 183–5, 188, 191–3, 197, 207, 209, 213 ff., 241
United States Brewers Association, 371

Varela, A., 99–105
Venezuela, 87–8

Vodka, 134 ff.
Volstead Act, 377–8, 381
Voluntary Committee of Lawyers, 380

Warriner, C. K., 211–8
Washington State, drinking and drinkers in: age, 198; amounts drunk, 193–4; attitudes, 199–200; drinking frequency and education, 197–8; drinking frequency and sex, 197; drinking frequency and size of community, 196–7; frequency and incidence of drinking, 191–2; two generations compared, 192–3; income, 199; knowledge about alcohol, 201–4; motivation, for drinking, 200–1, for abstaining, 201; native and foreign-born, 195; occupation, 195; places for drinking, 194; religious affiliation, 197; type of beverage, 193; veterans and nonveterans, 198
Washington Anti-Saloon League, 374
W.C.T.U. See Woman's Christian Temperance Union
Webb–Kenyon Act, 375
West Virginia Non-intoxicating Beer Commission, 432
Wets vs. drys, 237, 325, 338–41, 346, 362, 380, 381, 388–97, 412 ff.; Chinese, 115–6, 118–9
Whisky, 43
WHO. See World Health Organization
Wickersham Report, 380–1
Wine, 42

Wine market, facing 161
Woman's Christian Temperance Union, 370, 372–4, 377, 398–411: committee reports, 403; conclusions, 410–1; humanitarian reform, 404; moral indignation, 406–9; moral reform and social welfare, 400–2; the "moralizer-in-retreat," 405–6; pre prohibition period, 400–4; social dominance, 404; socioeconomic changes, 409–11; temperance as reform of the underprivileged, 402–3
Woman's Organization for Repeal of National Prohibition, 380
Women, drinking by, attitudes, customs, and habits: Andean region, 95–6; Athens, 48; Canada, 173–4; Chaco, South America, 90; Egypt, 65; England, 161–2; Guatemala, 76–7; Mexico, 81; Rome, 55–61; Santiago, 101–3, 105; Sweden, 351; United States, 179, 183–5, 188, 191–3, 197, 207 ff., 227 ff., 234–6, 241–2, 252, 259, 287, 309–11
World Health Organization, 26, 129
World League against Alcoholism, 375
World Woman's Christian Temperance Union, 373

Yale Center of Alcohol Studies, 12, 22
Yale Summer School of Alcohol Studies, 331, 333
Yamamuro, B., 124–9

Zu, 109, 112

3